Internet
Starter
Kit

for
Macintosh
3rd Edition

Internet Starter Kit for Macintosh

3rd Edition

Adam C. Engst

Hayden
Books

Internet Starter Kit for Macintosh, 3rd Edition

©1995 Hayden Books, a division of Macmillan Computer Publishing

Library of Congress Catalog Number: 95-60415
ISBN: 1-56830-197-9

97 96 95   4 3 2

Interpretation of the printing code: the rightmost double-digit number is the year of the book's printing; the rightmost single-digit number is the number of the book's printing. For example, a printing code of 95-1 shows that the first printing of the book occurred in 1995.

The Hayden Books Team

Publisher

David Rogelberg

Aquisitions Manager

Karen Whitehouse

Manager of Product Development

Patrick Gibbons

Development Editor

Brad Miser

Copy/Production Editors

Meshell Dinn
Steve Mulder

Marketing Manager

Andy Roth

Publishing Coordinator

Rosemary Lewis

Interior Designers

Fred Bower
Barbara Kordesh
Kevin Spear

Illustrator

Kevin Spear

Cover Designer

Jay Corpus

Production

Gary Adair, Angela Calvert,
Dan Caparo, Laurie Casey,
Kim Cofer, David Garratt,
Aleata Howard, Shawn MacDonald,
Joe Millay, Erika Millen, Beth Rago,
Gina Rexrode, Erich J. Richter,
Christine Tyner, Karen Walsh,
Robert Wolf

Indexer

Chris Cleveland

Composed in Palatino and Futura

License Information

To Our Readers

Dear Friend,

Thank you on behalf of everyone at Hayden Books for choosing *Internet Starter Kit for Macintosh* to enable you to explore the Internet. The Internet is the fastest growing, and most exciting, aspect of our modern society. Without the right guide, participating on the Internet can be difficult. We have carefully crafted this book and disk to enable you to both learn about the Internet and actually get on it. We wish you the best in your explorations and hopefully, we'll meet you there soon!

What you think of this book is important to our ability to better serve you in the future. If you have any comments, no matter how great or small, we'd appreciate you taking the time to send us email or a note by snail mail. Of course, we'd love to hear your book ideas.

Sincerely yours,

David Rogelberg
Publisher, Hayden Books and Adobe Press

You can reach Hayden Books at the following:

Hayden Books
201 West 103rd Street
Indianapolis, IN 46290
(800) 428-5331 voice
(800) 448-3804 fax

Email addresses:

America Online: Hayden Bks
AppleLink: hayden.books
CompuServe: 76350,3014
Internet: bradm@hayden.com

Dedication

To my lovely and talented wife, Tonya, without whose patience and writing skills I would certainly have gone stark raving mad long ago.

About the Author

Adam C. Engst

Adam C. Engst is the editor and publisher of *TidBITS*, a free electronic newsletter distributed weekly on the worldwide computer networks to over 150,000 readers. After graduating from Cornell University with a double-major in Hypertextual Fiction and Classics, he worked as an independent consultant in Ithaca, New York, where he started *TidBITS* in April of 1990. He now lives in Western Washington with his wife, Tonya, and cats, Tasha and Cubbins, but seems to spend most of his time corresponding via electronic mail with friends and associates around the globe.

After writing the first edition of *Internet Starter Kit for Macintosh* (released in September of 1993), he was somehow rooked into coauthoring *Internet Explorer Kit for Macintosh* with Bill Dickson, and the first edition of *Internet Starter Kit for Windows* with Cory Low and Mike Simon. These titles were published in April of 1994, and the second edition of *Internet Starter Kit for Macintosh* came out in August of 1994. In March of 1995, the second edition of *Internet Starter Kit for Windows* was published, again in collaboration with Cory and Mike.

Like anyone who attempts to condense the immensity of the Internet into a single book, he is certifiably crazy. His favorite quote (which reportedly comes from Alan Kay, an Apple Fellow and Xerox PARC alumnus) is: "The best way to predict the future is to invent it."

Acknowledgments

Thanks

Many people have helped me throughout the writing of this edition, and with previous editions of the book. I especially want to thank my wife Tonya, who not only helped out but put up with me during the final few weeks of each edition, which is not a task for the faint of heart. I must also thank my editor, Brad Miser of Hayden Books, who went out of his way to help make the book a success.

Thanks as well to my mother, who now runs her own Web server on a Power Mac 8100/80, and my father, who has become quite the late night Internet denizen. I'd also like to thank all the readers of *TidBITS* because they have kept me going these last five years. Finally, thanks to the many readers and supporters of the previous editions of *Internet Starter Kit for Macintosh*. Word of mouth goes a long way, and the book wouldn't have lasted nearly this long without such support from so many individuals in the Internet community.

If I've forgotten anyone, my sincere apologies. Please accept my absent-minded thanks.

Surrogate Editors

Thanks are due to the many people who helped edit portions of this and previous editions of the book and those who either provided me with information or helped test the ISKM Installer. I wish only that I had room to give everyone the full credit they deserve.

Alan Oppenheimer, Alwin Li, Amanda Walker, Amir Rosenblatt, Andrew Green, Barbara Maxwell, Bill Cockayne, Bill Dickson, Bill Gram-Reefer, Bill Lipa, Brian Hall, Brian Lichorowic, Cary Lu, Chad Magendanz, Chuck Shotton, Chuq Von Rospach, Cory Low, Dave Winer, David Thompson, Draper Kauffman, Drummond Reed, Erik Speckman, Franklin Davis, Geoff Duncan, Glenn Fleishman, Gordon Watts, Guy Kawasaki, Guy Stevens, Harry Morris, Herb Effron, Ian Brown, Igor Livshits, James Skee, Jeff Needleman, Jeff Steele, Jim Matthews, Jim O'Dell, John Baxter, John Hardin, John Mah, John Norstad, John Werner, Jonathan Lundell, Jud Spencer, Katie Hudson, Kee Nethery, Ken Landau, Ken Stuart, Larry Blunk, Laurent Humbert, Len MacDonell, Leonard Rosenthol, Mark H. Anbinder, Mark McCahill and the Gopher Team, Mark

Verber, Mark Williamson, Meshell Dinn, Michael Tardiff, Michael Wellman, Mikael Hansen, Mike Goode, Mike Simon, Paul Celestin, Pete Resnick, Peter Broadribb, Peter Fraterdeus, Peter Lewis, Quinn, Richard Ford, Rick Watson, Roger Brown, Roger Jacobs, Ross Scott Rubin, Roy Wood, Roz Ault, Rusty Tucker, Sandro Menzel, Scott Gruby, Sky Dayton, Steve Dagley, Steve Dorner, Steve Michel, Steve Mulder, Steve Worona, Werner Uhrig, and Will Mayall.

Software Thanks To...

Although I don't have room to individually acknowledge the programmers of all the software I mention in the book, I do want to thank those who graciously allowed me to include their programs on the disk, including the following:

Leonard Rosenthol, and all the folks at Aladdin Systems, for StuffIt InstallerMaker and StuffIt Expander

Garry Hornbuckle and the MacTCP team at Apple Computer, for MacTCP

Larry Blunk and Merit Network, for MacPPP

Amanda Walker and InterCon Systems, for InterSLIP

Peter Lewis, for Anarchie

Peter Lewis, again, and Quinn "The Eskimo!", for Internet Config

Steve Dorner and Qualcomm, for Eudora

John Hardin of MCC's EINet group, for MacWeb

Other Invaluable Aid Provided By...

Liam Breck, for helping set up the Info-Mac Archive mirror software at `ftp.tidbits.com`

Paul Celestin, for creating and maintaining the Providers of Commercial Internet Access list

Ed Morin, Ralph Sims, Michael Tardiff, and Scott Anderson of Northwest Nexus for technical assistance above and beyond the call of duty and for providing my Internet connections

Charles Cooper of OneWorld, for hosting the Web pages over the last year

Geoff Duncan, once again, for creating the *Internet Starter Kit for Macintosh* Web page

And finally, Tonya Engst, for writing chapter 26, "Create Your Web Page," editing chapter 29, "Step-by-Step Internet," and for just generally being wonderful

Contents at a Glance

Table of Contents

Introduction

Before anything else, please believe me when I say that this book is not a manual to be ignored after you've ripped the disk from the back cover and stuffed it in your Macintosh. Using the Internet is not like using a word processor. There are some quirks and confusions that I explain, but they may frustrate you to no end if you don't bother to read the sections about using the different programs. Also, if you don't bother to read the instructions provided for, say, connecting to an Internet provider, and then you call the provider for help, you cannot expect them to be happy about explaining over the phone what I've already explained in the book.

That said, I want to tell you a little about how I designed *Internet Starter Kit for Macintosh*, because I think it will help you make the most of the book in the limited time that we all have. As with any broad subject, some parts of the Internet won't interest you in the slightest, and that's fine. However, I feel that it's important to cover many of these topics even if they won't interest all of my readers. So, let's look quickly at each of the five parts that make up this book, and I'll tell you what to expect.

Part I: Introduction and History

This part stays fairly general, introducing you to the book and to the Internet, and trying to offer a way of looking at the world through Internet-colored glasses. Chapter 1, "Welcome," serves as the introduction. Chapter 2 seeks to answer the question, "Why is the Internet Neat?" The third chapter, "What is the Internet?," tackles a more difficult issue and attempts to explain just what the Internet is. Next, Chapter 4, "The Internet Beanstalk," traces a line down the history of the Internet, branching off to look briefly at other topics of potential interest. If you're new to the Internet, you should definitely read the first three chapters, and if you're at all interested in a historical perspective, read the fourth.

The fifth chapter, "Exploring the Internet," is excerpted from *Internet Explorer Kit for Macintosh*. I wanted to provide a sense of what life is like on the Internet, so I talked my co-author on that book, Bill Dickson, into putting together this chapter with me. If you like Chapter 5, you may want to pick up a copy of *Internet Explorer Kit* in a bookstore—it contains lots of great stuff we couldn't fit into the excerpt.

Part II: Internet Foundations

Part II is required reading for novices because it covers network foundations in terms of basic usage and social customs. It's important because it provides much of the Internet's community knowledge. If you want to know how email is constructed, for example, or when you should avoid using FTP, you should read this part. Community knowledge can be difficult to pick up without spending a lot of time on the Internet, so these chapters can save you a lot of time and trouble.

Chapter 6, "Addressing & URLs" covers the basics of addressing and focuses tightly on Uniform Resources Locators, or URLs, which are used to provide a coherent method of identifying Internet resources such as Web pages and files available via FTP. Chapter 7, "Email Basics," looks at email usage and mailing lists, and Chapter 8, "Usenet News Basics," is devoted exclusively to Usenet news. Chapter 9 describes "TCP/IP Internet Services," those being services that require a full Internet connection, such as Telnet, FTP, WAIS, Gopher, and the World Wide Web. Finally, Chapter 10, "File Formats," discusses the many file formats you find on the Internet.

Part III: Partial Internet Access

The five chapters in Part III discuss choosing an Internet connection along with examining four different methods of accessing the Internet. Chapter 11, "Choosing a Connection," addresses how you go about choosing a provider when faced with the myriad choices awaiting you. Chapter 12, "Commercial Services," starts off the rest of the section by looking at what can be the easiest (although limited) method of Internet access—using a commercial online service such as CompuServe or America Online. Chapter 13, "Bulletin Board Systems," takes a quick look at some popular types of bulletin board software that can both provide access to the Internet and can be accessible through the Internet. Chapter 14, "Shell Account Enhancements," tells you about different programs that you can use to obtain a graphical interface on the ugly Unix command-line interface of the shell account. Chapter 15, "UUCP Access," explores an older, but still useful, method of access that provides only electronic mail and news—the UUCP connection.

I include Part III in *Internet Starter Kit for Macintosh* because I feel that you should have as much information about the different ways of connecting to the Internet as possible. If you don't plan on using any of these methods of connecting to the Internet, feel free to ignore chapters 13 through 15 entirely. I won't be offended, but please do read Chapter 11, "Choosing a Connection," because it will help you learn what questions to ask of a potential Internet provider, and that's important.

Part IV: Full Internet Access

Chapters 16 through 29 of Part IV look in depth at the most powerful and flexible method of connection to the Internet—the MacTCP connection. Although the other methods of connection are important and useful (and often more cost-effective), nothing compares with the range and quality of software available for Macs connected to the Internet and running MacTCP. I felt so strongly about helping readers get a full MacTCP connection to the Internet that Hayden Books licensed MacTCP from Apple and included it on the disk that comes with this book. Other programs that you need to immediately start using a MacTCP connection via your modem are also included. Speaking of the disk, chapter 16 tells what's on it and how the installer works.

Chapters 17, "MacTCP," 18, "PPP," 19, "SLIP," and 20, "Troubleshooting Your Connection," take you through the sometimes pesky details of configuring your Macintosh to connect to the Internet. This may seem like more information than is necessary, and it is, assuming everything works perfectly. But, as we all know, there's no way to guarantee perfection in this world, so all the information in these chapters, especially Chapter 20, "Troubleshooting Your Connection," tips the scales in your favor against the entropy of the universe. At least, that's how I like to look at it.

Although chapters 17 through 20 will get you on the Internet with a MacTCP connection, nothing happens until you run a MacTCP-based program. That's what I cover in chapters 21 through 28, starting with "Email" and "Usenet News," and continuing on to "FTP," "Gopher," and "World Wide Web." Bringing up the end are chapters on "Utilities & Miscellany" and "Integrated Programs."

Chapter 26, "Creating Your Web Page," rather than talking about MacTCP-based software specifically, instead takes you through the process of creating your own home page for the World Wide Web. In the process I look at the various HTML editors and other related programs.

Finally, Chapter 29, "Step-by-Step Internet," takes a bare bones approach to teaching you how to use the most popular MacTCP-based programs, some of which are included on the disk. If you're uncertain how to perform basic tasks with these programs, this chapter is for you.

Again, there's probably quite a bit more information here than you absolutely have to know. That's why I've opted for describing in detail only the most important programs, and providing capsule reviews of the remaining applications. After you finish reading these chapters, you should have a good idea of what's out there; even if you don't use these programs right away, you can always come back to this section to read up on a program that you've just downloaded.

Part V: Appendices

The fifth part of this book is a collection of appendices for browsing and skimming.

Appendix A, "Internet Starter Kit Providers," lists providers that have agreed to offer a special deal to Internet Starter Kit for Macintosh readers. I've also included custom configurations for these providers on the ISKM disk so that you can use the ISKM Installer to configure your Macintosh to work with any of them. This is by far the easiest method of configuring MacTCP and MacPPP for a specific provider!

Appendix B, "Providers of Commercial Internet Access," comes from the Celestin Company; it is a large list of Internet providers around the world—complete with telephone and email contact information. If none of the providers listed in Appendix A, "Internet Starter Kit Providers," are appropriate for you, browse through this list (it's sorted by area code and country) to find another provider that may better meet your needs.

Appendix C lists the HTML tags covered in chapter 26, "Creating Your Web Page."

Appendix D, "Glossary," briefly explains some of the common terms and acronyms that you're guaranteed to run into on the Internet.

Last, but not least, comes the ever-popular index and an online information sheet that you might find useful for recording various details about your Internet connection.

Welcome to *Internet Starter Kit for Macintosh*, welcome to the Internet, and please, make yourself at home.

ADAM C. ENGST

May, 1995

I

Introduction and History

In this part of *Internet Starter Kit for Macintosh*, I introduce myself and give you a look at what the Internet is, why it's so neat, and where it came from. I also give you a glimpse of what life on the net is like. These five chapters convey the proper mindset for thinking about the Internet, a mindset without which you may find the Internet an overwhelming place.

Chapter 1, "Welcome," starts out slowly to allow us to introduce ourselves to one another. It also lays out the basic requirements for using the Internet. Chapter 2, "Why is the Internet Neat?," talks about what makes the Internet a special place, and chapter 3, "What is the Internet?," supports that by attempting to define the Internet. Chapter 4, "The Internet Beanstalk," provides a brief look at the past and future of the Internet, although if you don't like reading about history, feel free to skip it. If you find yourself condemned to repeat history at some later time, though, don't blame me, since chapter 4 provides the background that you need to understand why the Internet is the way it is and how it works politically. Finally, chapter 5, "Exploring the Internet," gives you a feel for what life on the net is really like. It's an excerpt from my book *Internet Explorer Kit for Macintosh* (Hayden Books, 1994), co-authored with Bill Dickson.

Welcome

Welcome to the *Internet Starter Kit for Macintosh, 3rd Edition*. I have two goals for this book, at least one of which hopefully applies to you as either its prospective buyer or proud new owner. First, I want to tell you about the Internet—what it is and why it's so wonderful (and I mean that in all senses of the word, especially the bit about becoming filled with wonderment)—and introduce you to a number of the services and resources that make it one of humankind's greatest achievements. Second, I want to show you how to gain access to the Internet and how to use many of the Macintosh tools available for working with it. I've even included some of these tools on the disk that comes with this book so that you can get started right away. For those tools that I didn't have room for on the disk, I tell you where on the Internet to go to get them. But before I start, let's skip the small talk and introduce ourselves.

Who Are You?

I haven't the foggiest idea who you are. That's not true, actually; I can make a couple of guesses. You probably are a Macintosh user, because if you aren't, only about half of this book will hold your interest. You probably are also interested in the Internet; otherwise, only about two percent of the book is worth your time. Given those minor prerequisites, this book should provide hours of educational entertainment, just like Uncle Milton's Ant Farm. The major difference is that the Internet Ant Farm is worlds bigger than Uncle

Milton's, and if you go away on vacation, all the Internet ants won't keel over—although you may be tempted to do so when you get back and see how much you have to catch up on. The Internet never stops.

I've written this book for the individual, the person behind that most personal of personal computers, the Macintosh. In the process, I undoubtedly will disappoint the die-hard Unix system administrators and network gurus who talk about X.400 and TCP/IP in their sleep (which doesn't come often because of the amount of Jolt cola they consume). I'm aiming this book at students and staff at universities, which often have wonderful connections to the Internet, but seldom provide any guidance about what's out there. And I'm aiming at user groups, who can teach their members about the Internet with the aid of a good book and disk resource. I'm also aiming at ordinary people who have a Mac, a modem, and the desire to start using the Internet. And, yes, I'm even aiming at those Unix system administrators because what better way to get those annoying Macintosh users off your back than by giving them this book?

I should note that this book will not particularly help you learn how to become a provider of information, a publisher if you will, on the Internet. That's an entirely separate topic that deserves its own book, which I may someday write. This particular book is for Internet consumers, not publishers.

What Do You Need?

This book, of course—why do you think I wrote it? But beyond that…

First, you need a Macintosh. That's not absolutely true, because you can use any sort of computer to access the Internet, but to get the most out of this book you should use a Macintosh. (For those of you who use Windows, check out *Internet Starter Kit for Windows*.) You don't need a fast Macintosh, although it would be nice. When I wrote the first edition of this book, I used an elderly SE/30, and although I've since moved up to a Centris 660AV, most things I do on the Internet haven't changed much with the faster Mac.

Second, you need some type of physical connection to the Internet. This connection may take the form of a local area network at work or, more likely, a modem. A 2,400 bps modem works, though only barely, and the faster the better, with a 28,800 bps modem being the best. If you start out with a 2,400 bps modem, be prepared to buy a new one soon. That speed will become intolerable quickly, and why make something as fascinating as the Internet intolerable?

Third, I recommend that you use System 7 or later, if only because I haven't used System 6 in over four years and have no idea whether the software included on the disk works under System 6. That's not entirely true—some of the basic programs will work—but many others, including the best ones, now require System 7. All of my instructions assume that you are using System 7. If you need to upgrade, talk to your dealer.

Fourth, you need an account on a host machine somewhere. In Chapter 11, "Choosing a Provider," I cover how to find an appropriate account for your needs.

Fifth, you need a certain level of computer experience. This stuff simply is not for the Macintosh novice. If you don't know the difference between a menu and a window, or haven't figured out how to tell applications and documents apart, I recommend that you visit your local user group and ask a lot of questions. A number of excellent books also are available. My favorite is *The Little Mac Book,* by Robin Williams. You can also read your manuals, but frankly, as good as Apple's documentation is, Robin does a better job.

Finally, you may need to adjust your expectations. The Internet is not a commercial service like America Online or CompuServe. Customer service representatives are not available via a toll-free call 24 hours a day. The majority of people on the Internet have taught themselves enough to get on or have been shown just enough by friends to connect to the Internet. The Internet is very much a learning experience; even with as much information and guidance as I provide in this book, there's simply no way to anticipate every question that might come up through those first few days. The Internet is what you make it—so don't be shy. No one greets you on your first dip in, but at the same time, people on the Internet are some of the most helpful I've ever had the pleasure to know. If you are struggling, just ask and someone almost always comes to your aid. I wish that were true outside of the Internet as well.

Who Am I?

"Who am I?" is a question that I often ask myself. In the interests of leaving my autobiography for later, I must limit the answer to the parts that are relevant to this book. My name, as you probably figured out from the cover, is Adam Engst. I started using computers in grade school and had my first experience with a mainframe and a network while playing Adventure over a 300 baud acoustic modem (you know, where you dial the number and stuff the receiver into the modem's rubber ears) on a computer that my uncle used in New York City. I used microcomputers throughout high school, but upon entering Cornell University I learned to use their mainframes. In my sophomore year, I finally found the gateway to BITNET (the "Because It's Time" Network) in some information another user had left behind in a public computer room. Finding that initial bit of gateway information was like finding a clue in Adventure—but don't worry, it's not that difficult any more. From BITNET I graduated to using a computer connected to Usenet (the User's Network, generally synonymous with "news"), and around the same time I learned about the vast Internet, on whose fringes I'd been playing.

After graduating from Cornell in 1989, I set up my own Internet access using QuickMail for Macintosh. QuickMail was overkill for a single person because it's designed to be a network electronic mail program, so I eventually switched to a more appropriate program called UUCP/Connect. Several years ago, my wife and I moved from Ithaca, New York (where we had grown up and where Cornell is located) to the Seattle, Washington area. In the process, I learned more about finding public-access Internet hosts in a place where you know no one in person. In many ways, the Internet kept me sane those first few months. My Internet access changed over time, and although I kept using UUCP for email, I switched first to a SLIP account with Northwest Nexus before writing the first edition of the book and then, for the second edition, to a PPP account. Several months after the second edition of this book came out, I finally broke down and got a direct connection to the Internet. My Macs are permanently on the Internet now.

Throughout this Internet odyssey of the last nine years, I've used the nets for fun, socializing, and general elucidation. In the last five years, I've also written and edited a free, weekly, electronic newsletter called *TidBITS*. It focuses on two of my favorite subjects: the Macintosh and electronic communications. *TidBITS* is both a product and a citizen of the Internet. It has grown from a 300-person mailing list that once crashed a Navy computer running old mail software, to an electronic behemoth that lives on every network I can find—boasting an estimated 125,000 readers in over 55 countries.

So that is the reason I'm writing this book (well, there are those incriminating photographs of publishing industry VIPs that I have digitized and poised to distribute to the net at large). Any questions? I hope so, but hold off until you've finished the book. And for those of you already marking things up with those nasty yellow highlighters, don't; I promise there is no quiz awaiting you.

Changes

Keep in mind that the Internet changes quickly and constantly; trying to capture it in a snapshot requires high-speed film. I've got that film, so the image of the Internet that I present here isn't blurry or out of focus, but it's impossible to cover, or even discover, everything that deserves to be in *Internet Starter Kit for Macintosh*. Thus, if you want to keep up with the changes, it's partly up to you to get out on the Internet and see what's happening. I can help a bit, and I do, with some World Wide Web pages that track the latest Macintosh Internet programs and other events of importance, but in the end, you have to decide the extent to which you want to stay up to date.

This book has itself evolved and grown along with the Internet, and it is now in its third edition. I've left in place the best parts of the first and second editions, inserted some new ways of explaining the Internet, updated the software discussions to cover the latest releases, and added in some great new programs that have appeared since the second edition hit the shelves. I've also reevaluated the utility of some sections, particularly the appendices, and have taken the bold step of actually removing information that I feel is no longer useful or appropriate. I've shrunk discussions of many software programs to capsule reviews to make the book easier to browse. And in general, my editor and I have tried to tighten up the book. It's too easy for a book to grow uncontrollably, much like a Microsoft application, and I refuse to submit to the nefarious disease of creeping featuritis.

The first two editions of *Internet Starter Kit for Macintosh* distinctly changed my life, for the better. I've been asked to speak at conferences, interviewed via email and on the radio, filmed for TV, and fed food that was pre-chewed for my convenience by weasels on interminable cross-country airplane flights. But the reason I put up with all the hassle is that I truly love the Internet and believe that it's worth preserving, protecting, building, and explaining. If I can infect others with my enthusiasm for the Internet via this book, I think the world becomes a better place. And that's the goal in the end.

Why Is the Internet Neat?

Unless you've just idly picked up this book based on its bright cover while waiting for your spouse to choose the right gift for Aunt Millie's birthday, you probably have some sense that you should be interested in the Internet. Given the Clinton administration's emphasis on a national data highway system, many a poor reporter has written or broadcast a story on this Internet thing.

Those stories almost always make those of us who live and breathe the Internet cringe because they almost always miss the point. The stories either crow about the technological achievement and vast worldwide coverage of the Internet (while failing to explain that it is definitely not a commercial service staffed by friendly nerds in white coats, and ignoring its human dimension), or they provide a gratuitous human interest story about how two people met on the Internet and got married eleven days later because typing to each other was such a moving experience. Sure, this stuff happens, but such gee-whiz stories never touch on the commonplace parts of the Internet: the discussion groups, information databases, and selfless volunteer work that keeps the whole thing running. That's a shame, and I vow to avoid that slippery slope.

But I should be talking about why you should be interested in the Internet, instead of ragging on the mediocre descriptions from people who apparently aren't. Keep in mind that I may miss your favorite reason to use the Internet—

one woman's Brownian motion generator is another man's cup of tea. In addition, remember that technology is seldom used for its intended purpose. The Internet started as a method of linking defense researchers around the country; it has grown beyond that use in ways its creators never could have imagined.

Electronic Mail

For many people, electronic mail (or email) is the primary reason to get on the Internet; they simply want to be able to send mail to someone else on the Internet. Once you're on, though, you're likely to strike up many new friendships and end up with a long list of electronic correspondents. Because it's quick and easy, email is an excellent way to stay in touch, even with people whom you regularly talk to on the phone. Even though I talk to my parents often, I also send them email because it's more appropriate for quick notes. Email messages are even better than an answering machine for conveying simple information. At one point, for example, the local Macintosh user group held steering committee meetings at my house. I could have called all the steering committee members before each meeting to remind them about it, but because all I wanted to say was, "Don't forget the meeting tomorrow night," contacting them was easiest via email.

Email sometimes gains the least likely converts. One friend of mine is best described as a telephobe—he hates talking on the telephone and only has one at his house, out of necessity. He had been equally disparaging of computers and email until he was forced to try it, after which he became an instant email proponent. He discovered that with email, he no longer had to play telephone tag with coworkers or try to arrange meetings to talk about simple topics. Email enabled him to work more flexible hours because he didn't care when his coworkers were present, and their email was waiting whenever he wanted to read it.

Discussion Groups

A large number of people read and participate in the thirty or so discussion groups, also called *newsgroups*, about the Macintosh, and far more people contribute to thousands of other non-technical discussions. Several years ago, when I went away on a bike trip, my Macintosh started sounding the Chords of Death and displaying the sad Mac face along with an error code. My wife couldn't contact me to tell me about it, but she posted a help message on one of the Macintosh discussion groups. Within a few days she had received answers from Macintosh experts around the world, all telling her that code meant we had a bad memory card. (Luckily, the card turned out to be only badly seated.)

Similarly, when we were in the process of buying a car, I started reading appropriate messages on one of the discussion groups dedicated to talking about cars. The messages were of some help, but I wish I had known then that there was an entire discussion group devoted to Hondas, the make we were looking at most.

Software

For many Macintosh users, some of the most immediately useful and interesting things about the Internet are the *file sites*. File sites are computers on the Internet that are accessible to everyone (more or less) and store thousands of the latest and greatest *freeware* and *shareware* (where you pay the author if you use the program) programs for the Macintosh. An equal or greater number of file sites exist for other platforms, most notably for the omnipresent PCs from IBM, Compaq, Dell, and the other 17 million clone makers. Finding specific numbers is difficult, but I think it's safe to say that thousands of people download files every day from the most popular *archive sites* (just another name for file site).

Part I Why Is the Internet Neat? 2

Information at Your Electronic Fingertips

The popularity of email and newsgroups notwithstanding, the massive databases of information impress some people the most. A couple of years ago, a friend came over to look at a QuickTime movie of the Knowledge Navigator film clip. The Knowledge Navigator is ex-Apple CEO John Sculley's idea of what information access will be like in the future—an anthropomorphic "talking head" that acts as an *information agent*, searching through massive databases of information on the user's command. The Knowledge Navigator film portrays a professor preparing for a class discussion about deforestation in the Amazon rain forest by looking at data retrieved by his electronic agent.

The film is fairly neat, but after watching it, I remembered that I also wanted to show my friend Wide Area Information Server (WAIS). Using the Macintosh WAIS software, we connected to WAIS and typed in our query, "Tell me about deforestation in the Amazon rainforest." After about 10 seconds, WAIS returned a list of 15 articles from various sources that dealt with just that topic, sorted by relevance. Talk about knocking someone's socks off—my friend was staring, mouth open, tongue lolling, and completely barefoot, so to speak. Although WAIS doesn't have an infinite number of databases, it does have over 700 (including *TidBITS*), and more appear all the time.

Although I have no numbers to back this up, I get the impression that the largest quantity of raw information is available via FTP (File Transfer Protocol). Even if that's not true, more data is still transferred via FTP than any other method on the Internet, although the World Wide Web is catching up fast. The freeware and shareware programs for the Mac that I mentioned above are available via FTP, as are electronic editions of books, newsletters such as *TidBITS*, fiction magazines such as *InterText*, and huge numbers of other files.

Gopher, another method of transferring information over the Internet, is also quite popular. It's easy to set up a Gopher server—so anyone who has good information and a dedicated Internet connection can do it. WAIS databases require high-powered computers, whereas a ten dollar shareware program from an Australian programmer named Peter Lewis enables someone to set up a Gopher server on a Macintosh (I've done it for some friends here in Seattle—it took about an hour). More than 2,300 Gopher servers exist today, and the information available on them includes things like Macintosh price lists at major universities (they often contain Apple's prices as well, making them useful for comparison even if you don't attend a university), Internet statistics, tech support information from Apple, and press releases from the U.S. government.

Finally, a vast amount of information appears on a daily basis on the World Wide Web, a service created by CERN, the high-energy physics research lab in Switzerland. Other methods of providing information over the Internet have been pretty much restricted to text until the data is downloaded to a Mac or PC. But the World Wide Web supports text with fonts, sizes, and styles, graphics within the text, sounds, animations, and movies; and all of it is interconnected with hypertext links. For many folks with information to provide to the Internet, the World Wide Web is the way to go. For instance, I've seen Web pages ranging from a beautiful collection of fractals (some even animated), to a wonderful museum-style paleontology exhibit at the University of California at Berkeley, to an extensive set of pages from a group called INFACT Online devoted to a campaign to stop tobacco companies from marketing cigarettes to children.

The Lemming Factor

Aside from the personal communications, the discussions on every imaginable subject (and many you'd never imagine), and the databases of information, the Internet is neat for yet another reason: It's what I sometimes call the "lemming factor." That is, if so many people from so many cultures and walks of life are connecting to the Internet, something has got to be there. Don't scoff; no one makes all these people log on every day and spend time reading discussion lists and sending email. People aren't forced to increase Internet traffic at a whopping rate of 20 percent per month. They use the Internet because they want to, and few people are happy when they lose Internet access for any reason. And as much as "lemming factor" may imply people are getting on Internet because their friends are, they aren't doing it from peer pressure (well, okay, so I hassled my parents into getting connected, but they love it now). People connect to the Internet because it is becoming more than just an elite club of technoweenies—it has become a virtual community in and of itself.

The allure of the Internet sets it apart from other communities such as religious, charitable, or humanitarian groups. No implied theological punishment exists for avoiding the Internet, and although its attraction somewhat resembles that of volunteer groups such as the Red Cross, those organizations often depend on people's belief systems. The Internet continues to thrive because of the volunteer labor pumped into it; but also important is the fact that it provides as much information as an individual can handle, and in this day and age, information is power.

The Internet is What You Make of It

Whatever advantage you want to take of the Internet, remember two things. First, the information available on the Internet has generally avoided the processing introduced by the mass media (although more of the mass media arrives on the Internet constantly as well). If you want some unfiltered opinions on both sides of any issue ranging from the death penalty to abortion to local taxes, people usually are discussing the issue at length somewhere on the net. Because of the lack of filtering, you may read a bit more about any one subject than you do in the mass media.

Second, you get only the information you want. For about a year, my wife and I followed a weekly routine with the Sunday *Seattle Times.* First, we'd compete for the comics and then for the *Pacific Magazine,* which has in-depth articles. Then we'd settle down: I'd read the Sports section and the Business section, and my wife proceeded to the Home & Garden section. Good little stereotypes, weren't we? The point is that I was completely uninterested in reading at least three-quarters of the two-inch thick stack of paper, and so was my wife. So why were we paying for the entire thing only to bring it home and recycle half? A good question, and one that newspaper publishers should get their duffs in gear and answer.

Tonya and I answered it by ceasing to bother with the Sunday paper. Not only was it a waste of paper resources, especially considering that we didn't read most of it, but it was a waste of time to flip through much of the parts that we did read. Instead, I've started getting the news I want on the Internet, through a combination of mailing lists, newsgroups, and Web pages that cover my interests closely. I can't get all the comics that I'd like to read yet, but *Dilbert* from Scott Adams, an Internet-only cartoon called *Dr. Fun,* and some of the *Slugs!* cartoons that my friend Dominic White drew for *Internet Explorer Kit for Macintosh* have all appeared in recent months.

The same overkill problem applies to junk mail. I instantly throw out about 90 percent of the *snail mail* (the Internet term for paper mail) I get, whereas almost all email I get is at least worth reading.

On the Internet, when all is said and done, I get only what I ask for. Periodically, my interests change, so I switch things around, but I don't have to read, or even deal with, topics that either bore or irritate me—such as anything unpleasant happening in Northern Ireland or Beirut. Try avoiding such topics in the mass media. It's just not possible.

Now that I think of it, there's a third point I want to make about information on the Internet. Most of it, as I said, is free of media processing. That's because most of the information comes from individuals and small groups rather than large publishing conglomerates that own hundreds of newspapers and magazines around the world. Even though I'm not going to tell you anything about how to set up an Internet machine to provide information over the Internet, be aware that you as an individual don't necessarily need your own machine. You could run a small mailing list from a Mac, and you could easily post a newsletter or report of some sort to discussion lists without a dedicated machine. And, if what you want to do requires an FTP site or mainframe that can run mailing list software, ask around; someone may be willing to provide that sort of access to you. This is how I've published *TidBITS* for the last five years. As long as you're providing useful information for free, you'd be surprised how many people may step forward to help you.

Champing at the Bit

I know you're all excited about the Internet now that you know why it is so neat. But, you're probably saying to yourself, "Self, it sure sounds like I can do lots of cool things on the Internet, but just what the heck is this Internet thing, anyway?" Glad you asked yourself that question because that's precisely what we will talk about next.

What Is the Internet?

What is the Internet? That question is tremendously difficult to answer because the Internet is so many things to so many different people. Nonetheless, you need a short answer to give your mother when she asks, so here goes:

> *The Internet consists of a mind-bogglingly huge number of participants, connected machines, software programs, and a massive quantity of information, spread all around the world.*

Now, let's see if I can put those various parts into some kind of meaningful context.

Size

To say the Internet is big—in terms of people, machines, information, and geographic area included—is to put it mildly. How big is it? Let's take a look and see.

People

The Seattle Kingdome seats approximately 60,000 people for a sellout Mariners baseball game (a once-in-a-lifetime experience for the hapless Mariners). That's about the same number of people who read a single, mildly popular newsgroup on the Internet. If all of the estimated 30 million people on the Internet (according to some sources; others estimate much lower numbers) were to get together, they'd need 500 stadiums each the size of the Kingdome to have a party. I could calculate how many times that number of people would reach to the moon and back if we stacked them one on top of another, but I think I've made my point.

Machines

In the infancy of the computer industry, IBM once decided that it did not need to get into the computer business because the entire world needed only six computers. Talk about a miscalculation! Many millions of computers of all sizes, shapes, and colors have been sold in the decades since IBM's incorrect assumption. An estimated 4.9 million of these (4,852,000 as of January 1995, for those of you who like the digits) are currently connected to the Internet. I keep having trouble with these numbers because they change so frequently. In the first edition, I used 1.7 million computers as the basic number. I had to change it to that at the last minute because the manuscript I'd originally sent to Hayden Books used 1.3 million, the number from a few months before. When we published *Internet Starter Kit for Macintosh, Second Edition* in August of 1994, I updated the number to 2.3 million, and here I am, not even a year later, updating to 4.9 million. See Table 3.1, which lays out the data collected by Network Wizards over a number of years. You can find the latest version of this data via the Web at:

```
http://www.nw.com/
```

Table 3.1
Internet Host Growth

Date	Number of Hosts
January 95	4,852,000
October 94	3,864,000
July 94	3,212,000
January 94	2,217,000
October 93	2,056,000

Date	Number of Hosts
July 93	1,776,000
April 93	1,486,000
January 93	1,313,000

Information

I can't pretend that the Internet offers more pieces of useful information than a good university library system, but that's only because a university has, in theory, a paid staff and funding for acquisitions and development. Information on the Internet is indeed vast, but finding your way around proves a daunting task. However, neither could I pretend that finding a given piece of information in a large research library would be any easier without the help of a skilled reference librarian.

Information on the Internet also changes and seems to appear more quickly than in a physical library, so you never know what's arrived since you last visited. Also, keep in mind that Internet information is more personal and fluid than the sort of information in a library. Although you may not be able to look up something in a reference work on the Internet, you can get ten personal responses (some useful, some not) to almost any query you pose.

Geographic Size

Explaining how large the Internet is geographically is difficult because, in many ways, messages traveling over the network connections don't give a hoot where they are going physically. Almost every industrialized nation has at least one machine on the Internet, and more countries come online all the time. But geographical distance means little on the net. For example, I mail issues of *TidBITS* to our mailing list on Monday night. People down the road from me find it in their mailboxes on Tuesday morning, as do subscribers in New Zealand and Norway.

Note

Although I don't know if this is still true, several years ago Norway had the highest per-capita density of Internet machines.

A friend described the Internet as ranging from Antarctica to the space shuttles, from submarines to battle tanks, from a guy riding a bicycle around the globe to others crossing oceans in a yacht, from kids in kindergarten to the most eclectic gathering of brains.... Well, you get the idea.

Perhaps the best way of wrapping your mind around the Internet is to recall the old joke about blind men all giving their impression of an elephant based on what they can feel. Like that elephant, the Internet is too large to understand in one mental gulp (see figure 3.1).

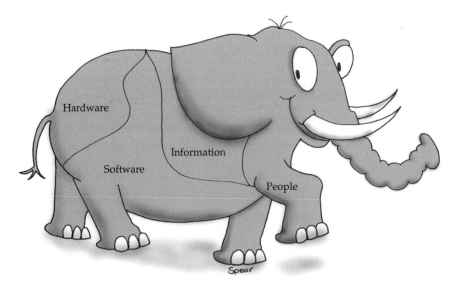

Figure 3.1   *The Internet Elephant* — Elephantidae internetus.

Some people may think of the Internet in terms of the people that are on the net (this is my favorite way of looking at it). Technical people may insist that the machines and the networks that comprise the physical Internet are the crux of the matter. Software programmers may chime in that none of it works without software. Others may feel that the essence of the Internet lies in the information present on it.

In fact, all of these people are equally right, although as I said, I personally prefer to think of the Internet as millions of people constantly communicating about every topic under the sun. The amount and type of information, the hardware and software will all change, but the simple fact of people communicating will always exist on the Internet.

People—Doing What They Do Best

The most important part of the Internet is the collection of many millions of people, *homo sapiens*, all doing what people do best. No, I don't mean reproducing, I mean communicating.

Communication is central to the human psyche; we are always reaching out to other people, trying to understand them and trying to get them to understand us. As a species, we can't shut up. But that's good! Only by communicating can we ever hope to solve the problems that face the world today. The United Nations can bring together one or two representatives of each nation and sit them down with simultaneous translations. But via the wire and satellite transmissions of the Internet, anyone can talk to anyone else on the Internet at any time—no matter where they live.

I regularly correspond with friends (most of whom I've never met) in England, Ireland, France, Italy, Sweden, Denmark, Turkey, Russia, Japan, New Zealand, Australia, Singapore, Taiwan, Canada, and a guy who lives about 15 miles from my house. (Actually, my wife and I finally broke down and went to visit the guy up the road, and he's since become one of our best friends in Seattle and the managing editor of *TidBITS*.) I've worked on text formatting issues over the networks with my friend in Sweden, helped design and test a freely distributable program written by my friend in Turkey, and co-written software reviews with a friend in New Zealand, who had been one of my Classics professors back at Cornell. On the net, where everything comes down to the least common denominator of *ASCII* text, you don't worry about where your correspondents live. Although people use many languages on the net, English is the *de facto* language of the computer industry, and far more people in the world know English than English speakers know other languages.

During the Gulf War, while people in the U.S. were glued to their television sets watching the devastation, people in Israel were sending reports to the net. Some of these described the terror of air raid sirens and worrying about SCUD missiles launched from Iraq. No television shot of a family getting into their gas masks with an obligatory sound bite can compare with the lengthy and tortured accounts of daily life that came from the Israeli net community.

The Internet also helped disseminate information about the attempted coup in the former Soviet Union that led to its breakup. One Internet friend of mine, Vladimir Butenko, spent the nights during the events near the Parliament. When everything seemed to be clear, he went to his office, wrote a message about what he'd seen, and sent it to the Internet. His message was widely distributed at the time and even partially reprinted in the *San Jose Mercury News*.

Although people on the Internet are sometimes argumentative and contentious, is that entirely bad? Let's face it, not all the events in the world are nice, and people often disagree, sometimes violently. In the real world, people may repress their feelings to avoid conflict, and repression isn't good. Or people may end up at the other extreme where the disagreement results in physical violence. On the Internet, no matter what the argument (be it about religion, racism, abortion, the death penalty, the role of police in society, or whatever else), there are only three ways for it to end. First, and mostly likely, all parties involved may simply stop arguing through exhaustion. Second, both sides may agree to disagree (although this usually only happens in arguments where both sides are being rational about the issues at hand). Third, one person may actually convince another that he is wrong; though I doubt this happens all that often since people hate to admit they're wrong. But notice, in none of these possibilities is someone punched, knifed, or shot. As vitriolic as many of these arguments, or flame wars, can be, there's simply no way to compare them to the suffering that happens when people are unable to settle their differences without resorting to violence.

Most of the time on the net, an incredible sense of community and sharing transcends all physical and geopolitical boundaries. How can we attempt to understand events in other parts of the world when we, as regular citizens, have absolutely no clue what the regular citizens in those other countries think or feel? And what about the simple facts of life such as taxes and government services? Sure, the newspapers print those info-graphics comparing our country's tax burden to that in other countries. But this information doesn't have the same effect as listening to someone work out how much some object, say a Macintosh, costs in France once you take into account the exchange rate and add an 18 percent VAT (value-added tax), which of course comes on top of France's already high income taxes. It makes you think.

If nothing else, that's the tag line I want to convey about the Internet. It makes you think.

Maybe with a little thought and communication, we can avoid some of the violent and destructive conflicts that have marked world affairs. Many of the Internet resources stand as testament to the fact that people *can* work together with no reward other than the satisfaction of making something good and useful. If we can translate more of that sense of volunteerism and community spirit back into the real world, we stand a much better chance of surviving ourselves.

Hardware

Getting down to the technical data, more than 4.9 million computers of all sizes, shapes, and colors make up the hardware part of the Internet. In addition to the computers are various types of network links, ranging from super-fast *T-1* and *T-3* lines all the way down to slow 2,400 bps modems. T-3 was also the code name for Microsoft Word 6.0— but I digress. That often happens when I'm talking about relatively boring things like networks, because what's important is that the Internet works. Just as with your telephone, you rarely notice its technical side unless something goes wrong.

Computers

The computers that form the Internet range from the most powerful supercomputers from Cray and IBM all the way down to your friendly local Macintosh and garden-variety PC clones. You can split these machines into two basic types: *host* computers and *client* computers. Host computers are generally the more powerful of the two, and they usually have more disk space and faster connections. Although, I don't want to imply that host machines must be fancy, expensive computers; Apple's popular FTP site at one point ran on an aging Mac II (however, it did use Apple's implementation of Unix, called A/UX).

Similarly, client machines also can be large, powerful workstations from companies like Sun and Hewlett-Packard. Because their task of sending and receiving information for a single person (as opposed to many people) is more limited, clients generally require less processor power and storage space than host machines. Basically, it can be a waste to use a $10,000 Unix workstation as an Internet client (although they can make great client machines, if you have the money to throw around). In my opinion, microcomputers— Macs in particular—make the best clients. Why spend lots of money and a large amount of configuration time when an inexpensive, simple-to-set-up Macintosh does the job as well or better?

Part I What Is the Internet?

For the most part, I look only at client hardware and software in this book. The gritty details of setting up an Internet host and the many programs that run it aren't all that interesting to most people, not to mention the fact that I haven't the foggiest idea of how to configure a Unix workstation to be an Internet host. I'll leave those tasks to the wonderful people who are already doing them. (First rule of the Internet: Be extremely nice to your system administrator.) If you want to get into the administration end of things, O'Reilly & Associates publishes a long line of books on Unix and network administration, including one called *Managing Internet Information Services* that is a must read for anyone who wants to run Internet servers on a Unix machine.

Note

> *You don't need to use Unix on an Internet host, and in fact, you can run an FTP, Gopher, or World Wide Web server on a Mac with no trouble. But this setup requires a fast and constant connection to the Internet, and again, I'm aiming this book more at users of Internet information, not information provider wanna-bes. Maybe the next book.*

Networks

In basic terms, two computers attached together form a *local area network*, and as that network grows, it may become connected to other independent local area networks. That configuration is called an *internet*, with a small *i*. The Internet, with a capital *I*, is the largest possible collection of inter-connected networks. I could spill the gory details of what networks are connected to the Internet and whether they are true parts of the Internet (as defined by using a set of *protocols* called *TCP/IP*, or Transmission Control Protocol/Internet Protocol, the language that Internet machines speak), but that information wouldn't be very useful to you.

An Internet old-timer once commented that "Internet" technically only applies to machines using TCP/IP protocols. He said the term once proposed for the collection of all the interconnected networks, no matter what protocols they used, was "WorldNet." That term seems to have faded into obscurity—unfortunately, since it's rather apt. Common usage now includes "Internet" (the safest term, though it's technically inaccurate), "the net" (sometimes capitalized), and "cyberspace" (a heavily overused term from William Gibson's science-fiction novel Neuromancer, *which, ironically enough, he wrote on a manual typewriter with images of video games, not the Internet, in his head). Lately, the term "information superhighway" (an unfortunate term that has spawned imagery of toll booths, speed bumps, on-ramps, and road kill, but which means almost nothing in the context in which it's generally used) is in vogue.*

Worrying about the specific network protocol details is generally pointless these days because many machines speak multiple languages and exist on multiple networks. For instance, my host machine speaks both TCP/IP as an Internet client and *UUCP* (Unix to Unix CoPy) as a UUCP host. My old machine at Cornell existed in both the Internet and in the BITNET worlds. The distinctions are technical and relatively meaningless to the end user.

Modems and Phone Lines

For most people using a microcomputer such as a Macintosh, a *modem* generally makes the necessary link to the Internet. Modem stands for modulator-demodulator (glad you asked?), and it enables your computer to monopolize your phone, much like a teenager. You may not need a modem if you study or work at an institution that has its local area networks attached to the Internet. If you are at one such site, count yourself lucky and ignore the parts of this book that talk about finding connections and using the modem. But remember those sections exist; one day you may leave those connections behind, and nothing is more pitiful than someone pleading on the nets for information on how to stay connected after graduation or other significant life changes.

Certain new types of connections, including high-speed ISDN (Integrated Services Digital Network) may be the death of the modem as we know it. However, even ISDN connections require a box called a terminal adapter to enable the computer to appropriately pass data over the ISDN lines. In addition, even for folks with normal telephone line connections to the Internet, the modem itself may fade into the background—or rather, into the innards of the computer. It's already possible to almost completely emulate a modem in software on Apple's Macintosh 660AV, 840AV, and Power Macintosh computers. Eventually, wireless modems may become common, so the details of making a connection may fade away entirely. Or at least that's what I hope happens.

Note *In an exaggerated show of acronym making, normal phone service is known as POTS, or Plain Old Telephone Service. Don't the people who came up with this have anything better to do with their time?*

It's beyond the scope of this book to tell you what sort of modem to buy, but most reputable modem manufacturers make fine modems with long or lifetime warranties. Some companies sell extremely cheap modems, which often work fine in most cases, but you may also get what you pay for.

Part I   What Is the Internet?

Note *I don't want to bash specific manufacturers, but many Macintosh users have had good luck with modems from Supra and Global Village, and I personally have owned modems from these two companies along with modems from Telebit and Practical Peripherals. Apple's Express Modem can be a bit flaky at times, but it's one of only two choices for the PowerBook Duos. (Global Village makes the more expensive PowerPort/Mercury Duo.)*

Suffice it to say that you want the fastest standard modem you can lay your hands on, and as of this writing, the fastest standard means that you want a modem with the magic word *v.34* stamped prominently on its box. That word, which says that the modem supports a certain standard method of transmitting information, ensures that your modem talks to most other modems at a high rate of speed, generally 28,000 bits per second (bps). (This speed, although fast for a modem, doesn't even approach that of a local area network [the standard LocalTalk networking built into every Macintosh runs at 230,000 bps]).

Note *Although v.32bis, the protocol used for 14,000 bps modems, is probably still more common, I recommend that you buy a 28,000 bps modem, given the choice.*

Modem manufacturers often make claims about maximum throughput being 57,600 bps or higher, but real speeds vary based on several variables such as phone line quality and the load on the host. Except in laboratory situations and near black holes, modems never reach the promised maximum speed. The main point to keep in mind is that it takes two to tango; the modem on either end of a connection drop to the slowest common speed (usually 2,400 bps) if they don't speak the same protocols. Just think of this situation as my trying to dance with Ginger Rogers—there's no way she and I could move as quickly as she and Fred Astaire did.

You may see such terms as v.fast and v.terbo (or v.turbo), but remember what I said about needing two to tango. If your provider doesn't use modems that also support these non-standards, there's no point in worrying about anything other than v.32bis or v.34 for right now.

Actually, there are more caveats to the modem question than I'd like to admit. Modems work by converting digital bits into analog waves that can travel over normal phone lines, and—on the other end—translating those waves back into bits. Translation of anything is an inherently error-prone process, as you know if you've ever managed to make a fool of yourself by trying to speak in a foreign language.

A large percentage of the problems that I've seen people have since the first edition of this book were related to their modems. Modem troubles are exacerbated by the fact that modem manuals are, without a doubt, the worst excuse for technical writing that I've ever seen. They're confusing, poorly written, poorly organized, and usually concentrate on the commands that the modem understands without providing any information as to what might go wrong. So, as much as I'd like to pretend that modems are all compatible, and that setting one up to communicate with an Internet host is a simple process, it may not work right away. If you encounter problems after first checking all the settings to make sure you've done everything right, you should then check your settings against those in your modem manual. It's also worth asking your Internet provider for suggestions on settings for your modem.

I can't tell you how unhappy I am to have written that last paragraph, but it's just how the world is. You probably didn't get a driver's license without passing a written test, practicing with an adult, taking Driver's Ed, and finally passing a practical test. Perhaps more apt, you probably weren't able to find anything in a school library until one of the teachers or librarians showed you around. If your modem works on the first try, great! If not, don't get depressed—not everything in this life is as easy as it should be. If it were, we'd have world peace.

Anyway, modems connect to phone lines, of course, and residential phone lines are generally self-explanatory, although at some point you may want to get a second line for your modem. Otherwise, those long sessions reading news or downloading the latest and greatest shareware can irritate loved ones who want to speak with you. (Of course, those sessions also keep telemarketers and loquacious acquaintances off your phone.) I also thoroughly enjoy being able to search the Internet for a file, download it, and send it to a friend who needs it, all while talking to him on the phone.

Not all telephone lines are created equal, and you may find that yours suffers from *line noise*, which is static on the line caused by any number of things. Modems employ error correction schemes to help work around line noise, but if it's especially bad, you may notice your modem slowing down as it attempts to compensate for all the static. When it's really bad, or when someone induces line noise by picking up an extension phone, your modem may just throw up its little modem hands and hang up on you. You can complain to the phone company about line noise; as I understand it, telephone lines must conform to a certain level of quality for voice transmissions. Unfortunately, that level may not be quite good enough for modems, especially in outlying rural areas, but if you're persnickety enough, you can usually get the phone company to clean up the lines sufficiently.

Note

If you connect from home and order a second line from your phone company, don't be too forthcoming about why you want the second line. Although they provide no additional quality or service, business rates are higher than residential rates. Some phone companies are sticky about using modems for non-business purposes, which is why this point is worth mentioning. If you connect to the Internet from your office, there's no way around this situation.

Software

As for the software, the programs that probably come to your mind first are the freeware and shareware files stored on the Internet for downloading—things such as games, utilities, and full-fledged applications. I'll let you discover those files for yourself though, and I'll concentrate on the software available for connecting to the Internet, much of which is free. Other programs are shareware or commercial, although most don't cost much. I'll talk about pretty much every piece of software I know about for working on the Internet in Part IV of this book. Although there's no way for the book's discussion to keep up with the rate at which new and updated programs appear, I provide the latest versions of all the freeware and shareware programs on my file site, `ftp.tidbits.com`. Don't worry about the details now—I'll get to them later in the book.

For the time being though, I want to hammer home a few key points to help you understand, on a more gut level, how this setup all works. First, the Internet machines run software programs all the time. When you use electronic mail or Telnet or most anything else, you are actually using a software program, even if it doesn't seem like it. That point is important because as much as you don't need to know the details, I don't want to mystify the situation unnecessarily. The Internet, despite appearances, is not magic.

Second, because it takes two to tango on the Internet (speaking in terms of host and client machines), a software program is always running on both sides of the connection. Remember the client and host distinctions for machines? That's actually more true of the software, where you generally change the term *host* to the term *server*, which gives the broader term *client/server computing*. So, when you run a program on the Mac, say something like Fetch (an FTP client that retrieves files), it must talk to the FTP server program that is running continually on the remote machine. The same is true no matter what sort of connection you have. If you're using a Unix command-line account and you run a program called Lynx to browse the World Wide Web, Lynx is a client program that communicates with one or more World Wide Web servers on other machines.

Think of a fancy restaurant where they bring around a dessert cart filled with luscious pastries at the end of your meal. You're not allowed to get your grubby hands on the food itself, so the restaurant provides a pair of dessert tongs that you must use to retrieve your choice of desserts. That's exactly how client/server computing works. The dessert cart is the server—it makes the information, the desserts in this example, available to you, but only via the client program—the dessert tongs. Hungry yet?

Client application (Mac Web, Eudora, and so on)

This is you (use your imagination, will you?)

Your Internet Provider

Server (a Web server for example)

Third, FTP and Fetch are the high-level programs that you interact with, but low-level software also handles the communications between Fetch and an FTP server. This communication at multiple levels is how the Internet makes functions understandable to humans and still efficient for the machines, two goals that seldom otherwise overlap.

So, if you can cram the idea into your head that software makes the Internet work on both a high level that you see and a low level that you don't, you'll be much better off. Some people never manage to understand that level of abstraction, and as a result, they never understand anything beyond how to type the magic incantations they have memorized. Seeing the world as a series of magic incantations is a problem because people who do that are unable to modify their behavior when anything changes, and on the Internet, things change every day.

Information

More so than any other human endeavor, the Internet is an incredible, happy accident. Unlike the library at Alexandria (the one that burned down) or the Library of Congress, the Internet's information resources follow no master plan (although the Library of Congress, as do many other large university and public libraries, has its catalog and some of its contents on the Internet). No one works as the Internet librarian, and any free information resources that appear can just as easily disappear if the machine or the staff goes away. And yet, resources stick around; they refuse to die—in part because when the original provider or machine steps down, someone else generally feels that the resource is important enough to step in and take over.

> **Note**
>
> *Interestingly, much of the Library of Congress Gopher site was built on volunteer time by government employees. They created and still maintain the site in addition to their regular duties on their own time, because they believe in the principle of the widest possible dissemination of government (and other non-copyrighted) information to the taxpayer.*

Andy Williams at Dartmouth, for instance, runs a mailing list devoted to talking about scripting on the Macintosh, specifically about AppleScript and Frontier (an Apple event-based scripting program from UserLand Software that is now starting to become an especially interesting tool in controlling some Internet programs like Eudora and Netscape). Andy also originally made sample scripts and other files pertaining to Frontier available, but he was not able to keep up with the files and still do his real job (a common problem). Luckily, Fred Terry at the University of Kansas quickly stepped in and offered to provide a Frontier file site because he was already storing files related to two other Macintosh programs, QuicKeys and Nisus. (Fred also rescued the Nisus mailing list when Brad Hedstrom, the list creator and administrator, had to bow out, and Fred's probably a sucker for stray dogs too.) Fred felt that keeping the information available on the Internet was important and that the sacrifice was sufficiently small.

Just to fill in more of the story, Fred was actually running a list about AppleScript on his site, along with lists about QuicKeys and Nisus. When it became clear that discussions about scripting on the Macintosh overlapped both the AppleScript and the Frontier list, Fred and Andy got together and created a single list at Dartmouth—today's MacScripting list—and they've continued to collaborate, with Dartmouth picking up both the Nisus and QuicKeys lists as well.

Andy's something of a sucker for resources in need of a home, as well. When a man named Bill Murphy came up with a method of translating our issues of *TidBITS* into a form suitable for display on the World Wide Web, he ran into the problem of not having a sufficiently capable machine to provide that information to the Internet community. Who should step in but Andy, who offered the use of a World Wide Web server that he runs at

Dartmouth. Between Bill's and Andy's selfless volunteer efforts, the Internet had yet another information resource for anyone to use.

These are just a few examples of the way information can appear on the Internet. Damming the Internet's flow of information would be harder than damming the Amazon with toothpicks. In fact, some of the Internet's resiliency is due to the way the networks themselves were constructed, but we'll get into that later. Next, let's look at the main ways information is provided on the Internet.

The Internet Post Office

You can think of an Internet host machine as a post office, a large post office in a large metropolitan area. In that post office, huge quantities of information are dispensed every day, but it doesn't just gush out the front door. No, you have to go inside, sometimes wait in line, and then go to the appropriate window to talk to the proper clerk to get the information that you want. You don't necessarily pick up mail that's been held for you at the same window as you purchase a money order. Internet information works in much the same way. But on an Internet host, instead of windows, information flows through virtual ports (they're more like two-way television channels than physical SCSI ports or serial ports). A port number is, as I said, like a window in the post office—you must go to the right window to buy a money order, and similarly, you must connect to the right port number to run an Internet application. Luckily, almost all of this happens behind the scenes, so you seldom have to think about it. See Table 3.2 for a list of some common port numbers.

Table 3.2
A Few Common Port Numbers

Port Number	Description
20, 21	File Transfer Protocol (data on 20, control on 21)
23	Telnet
25	Simple Mail Transfer Protocol
53	Domain Name Server
70	Gopher
79	Finger
80	World Wide Web
110	Post Office Protocol - Version 3
119	Network News Transfer Protocol
123	Network Time Protocol
194	Internet Relay Chat Protocol

Part I   What Is the Internet?   **3**

> **N o t e**
>
> *I found this information in RFC (Request for Comment) 1340 via the Web or Gopher at* `is.internic.net`. *All of the RFCs that define Internet standards are stored there should you want more technical information about how parts of the Internet work at their lowest levels.*

So, in our hypothetical Internet post office, there are seven main windows that people use on a regular basis. There are of course hundreds of other windows, usually used by administrative programs or other things that people don't touch much, but we won't worry about them. The main parts to worry about are email, Usenet news, Telnet, FTP, WAIS, Gopher, and the World Wide Web. Each provides access to different sorts of information, and most people use one or more to obtain the information they need.

Now that I've said how they're all similar, in the sense of all working through connections to the proper ports, there are some distinctions we must make between the various Internet services.

Email and Usenet news (along with MUDs and Internet Relay Chat) are forms of inter-personal communication—there is always a sender and a recipient. Depending on the type of email message or news posting, you can use different analogies relating to the paper world, and I'll get to those in a moment.

All of the information made available through other main parts of the Internet, such as Telnet, FTP, WAIS, Gopher, and the World Wide Web, is more like information in libraries than inter-personal communication, in the sense that you must visit the library specifically, and once there, browse or search through the resources to find a specific piece of information. These services have much more in common with traditional publishing than email and news.

> **N o t e**
>
> *I should note that, in my eyes, the difference between browsing and searching is merely that when you're browsing, you're not looking for a specific piece of information. Perhaps you only want some background, or simply want to see what's out there. When you're searching, you usually have a particular question that you want answered.*

No matter what you use, there is still some sort of communication of information going on. With email and news, it's generally informal and between individuals, whereas with the rest of the Internet services, the information is usually more distilled—that is, someone has selected and presented it in a specific format and in a specific context. None of these distinctions are hard and fast. Much informal information is available via Gopher, for instance, and it's certainly easy enough to find distilled information via email. I'll try to give you a sense of what each service is good for when talking about them later on.

Electronic Mail

Email is used by the largest number of people on the Internet, although in terms of traffic, the heaviest volumes lie elsewhere. Almost everyone who considers herself connected to the Internet in some way can send and receive email.

As I said previously, most personal exchanges happen in email because email is inherently an inter-personal form of communication. All of your email comes into your electronic mailbox, and unless you let them, no one else can easily read your mail. When you get a message from a friend via email, it's not particularly different than getting that same message, printed out and stuffed in an envelope, via snail mail. Sure, it's faster and may have been easier to send, but in essence personal email is just like personal snail mail.

Because it's trivial to send the same piece of email to multiple people at once, you also can use email much as you would use snail mail in conjunction with a photocopy machine. If you write up a little personal newsletter about what's happening in your life and send it to all your relatives at Christmas, that's the same concept as writing a single email message and addressing it to multiple people. It's still personal mail, but just a bit closer to a form letter.

The third type of email is carried on *mailing lists*. Sending a submission to a mailing list is much like writing for a user group or alumni newsletter. You may not know all of the people who will read your message, but it is a finite (and usually relatively small) group of people who share your interests. Mailing list messages aren't usually aimed at a specific person on the list, but they are more intended to discuss a topic of interest to most of the people who have joined that list. However, I don't want to imply that posting to a mailing list is like writing an article for publication because the content of most mailing lists more resembles the editorial page of a newsletter than anything else. You'll see opinions, rebuttals, diatribes, questions, comments, and even a few answers. Everyone on the list sees every posting that comes through, and the discussions often become quite spirited.

The fourth type of email most resembles those "bingo cards" that you find in the back of many magazines. Punch out the proper holes or fill in the appropriate numbered circle, return the card to the magazine, and several weeks later you'll receive the advertising information that you requested. For instance, I've set up my Macintosh to send an informational file about *TidBITS* automatically to anyone in the world who sends email to a certain address (**info@tidbits.com**, if you're impatient and want to try something right away). A number of similar systems exist on the Internet, dispensing information on a variety of subjects to anyone who can send them email. A variant of these auto-reply systems is the *mailserver*, which generally looks at the Subject line in the letter or at the body of the letter and returns the requested file. Mailservers enable people with email-only access to retrieve files that otherwise are available only via FTP.

Usenet News

Like email-based discussion lists, Usenet news is interpersonal information—it comes from individuals and is aimed at thousands of people around the world. Unlike email, even unlike mailing lists, you cannot find out who makes up your audience. Because of this unknown audience, posting a message to Usenet is more like writing a letter to the editor of a magazine or major metropolitan newspaper with hundreds of thousands of readers. We have ways of estimating how many people reach each of the thousands of Usenet groups, but the estimates are nothing more than statistical constructs (though hopefully accurate ones).

Almost everything on Usenet is a discussion of some sort, although a few groups are devoted to regular information postings, with no discussion allowed. The primary difference between Usenet news and mailing lists is that news is more efficient because each machine receives only one copy of every message. If two users on the same machine (generally multi-user mainframes or workstations at this point) read the same discussion list via email, getting the same information in news is twice as efficient. If you have a large mainframe with 100 people all reading the same group, news suddenly becomes 100 times as efficient because the machine stores only the single copy of each message, rather than each individual receiving her own copy.

In many ways, Usenet is the kitchen table of the Internet—the common ground where no subject is taboo and you must discuss everything before implementing it. In great part because of the speed at which Usenet moves (messages appear quickly and constantly, and most machines don't keep old messages for more than a week due to lack of disk space), finding information there can be difficult. Think of Usenet as a river, and you must dip in to see what's available at a specific point in time because that information may disappear downstream within a few days.

> **N o t e**
>
> *The speed at which messages disappear from Usenet varies by group and by the machine you use. Each administrator sets how long messages in a group will last before being expired or deleted from the system. Messages in newsgroups with many postings per day may expire after a day or two; messages in groups with only a few postings per week may last a month. Since complete Usenet traffic is about 200 MB of information each day, you can see why the short expiration times are essential.*

You can, of course, always ask your own question, and you usually get an answer (though it may be one you don't like), even if it's the sort of question everyone asks. Common questions are called Frequently Asked Questions, or *FAQs*, and are collected into lists and posted regularly for newcomers. Luckily, the cost of disk storage is decreasing sufficiently so that some people and organizations are starting to archive Usenet discussions. These enable you to use search engines like WAIS to go back and search for information that flowed past in a mailing list or newsgroup a long time ago.

Telnet

Telnet is tough to describe. The best analogy I can think of is that Telnet is like an Internet modem. As with a standard modem, Telnet enables your computer to communicate with another computer somewhere else. Where you give your modem a phone number to dial, you give Telnet an Internet address to connect to. And just like a modem, you don't really do anything within Telnet itself other than make the connection—in the vernacular, you telnet to that remote computer. Once that connection is made, you're using the remote computer over the Internet just as though it were sitting next to you. This process is cool because it enables me to telnet to the mainframes at Cornell University, for example, and use them just as I did when I was actually in Ithaca, and not 3,000 miles away in Seattle.

> **N o t e**
>
> Telnet, FTP, and Gopher ca*n all work as both nouns describing the service or the protocols, and as verbs describing the actions you perform with them. If Telnet or Gopher is capitalized in this book, it's a noun describing the service; if it's in lowercase, it's a verb describing the action. (FTP is always capitalized in the book, because it's an acronym.) Unfortunately, others on the Internet aren't as consistent (and they don't have editors checking on their text), so this isn't a universal convention.*

I realize that I'm supposed to talk about information in this section, but Telnet is such a low-level protocol that it's impossible to separate the information that's available via Telnet from the protocol itself.

Most people don't have personal accounts on machines around the world (and I never use the Cornell mainframes any more either), but a number of organizations have written special programs providing useful information that anyone can run over the Internet via Telnet.

Say I want to search for a book that's not in my local library system. I can connect via Telnet to a machine that automatically runs the card catalog program for me. I can then search for the book I want, find out which university library has it, and then go back to my local library and ask for an inter-library loan.

Or, for a more generically useful example, if you telnet to `downwind.sprl.umich.edu 3000`, you reach the University of Michigan's Weather Underground server, with gobs of data about the weather around the entire country.

> **N o t e**
>
> *Sure you could telnet to the Weather Underground. Or, if you have a MacTCP connection to the Internet, you could download the fascinating Blue Skies application and get a graphical interface that makes the weather a lot more interesting. See the chapter in the MacTCP-based software section entitled "Utilities & Miscellany" for more about Blue Skies.*

File Transfer Protocol (FTP)

FTP feels like it's related to Telnet, but in fact that's an illusion—the two are basic protocols on the Internet, but are otherwise unrelated. While Telnet simply enables you to connect to another remote computer and run a program there, FTP enables you to connect to a remote computer and copy files back and forth. It's really that simple.

More data is transferred via plain old FTP than by any other method on the Internet, and it's not surprising because it's a least-common denominator that almost every machine on the Internet supports. Like Telnet, you must be directly connected to the Internet while using FTP, although there are a few special FTP-by-mail services that enable you to retrieve files stored on FTP sites by sending specially formatted email messages to an FTP-by-mail server.

There are probably millions of files available via FTP on the Internet, although you may discover that many of them are duplicates because people tend to want to give users more than one way to retrieve a file. If a major file site goes down for a few days, it's nice to have a *mirror site* that has exactly the same files and can take up the slack.

Note

Mirror sites are important because as the Internet grows, individual machines become overloaded and refuse to accept new connections. As with anything that's busy (like the phone lines on Mother's Day, the checkout lines at 5:00 P.M. on Friday afternoons at the grocery store, and so on) it always seems that you're the one who gets bumped or who has to try over and over again to get through. Don't feel special—hundreds of other people suffer exactly the same fate all the time. Mirror sites help spread the load.

In the Macintosh world, several sites with lots of disk space (several gigabytes, actually) store a tremendous number of freeware and shareware programs along with commercial demos and other types of Macintosh information. If you think your local BBS has many files, wait until you see the two main file sites for the Mac, `mac.archive.umich.edu` and the Info-Mac Archive site currently at `sumex-aim.stanford.edu`. I would estimate that between 20 and 100 new files appear in the Info-Mac Archive archive every week—certainly enough to keep you busy if you enjoy exploring freeware and shareware software for the Macintosh.

The vastness of the number of files stored on FTP sites may stun you, but you have access to a tool that helps bring FTP under control. Archie takes the grunt work out of searching numerous FTP sites for a specific file. You ask Archie to find files with a specific keyword in their names, and Archie searches its database of many FTP sites for matches. Archie then returns a listing to you, providing the full file names and all the address information you need to retrieve the file via FTP.

N
o
t
e

If you have MacTCP access to the Internet, you can use a program I included on the disk called Anarchie, which is an FTP and Archie client program for the Mac. Just ask Archie to find a file, and when the results come back, double-click on the file to retrieve it. And people complain about how hard the Internet is!

WAIS

I mentioned using WAIS to search for information about deforestation in the Amazon rainforest in the preceding chapter, but that's only the tip of the iceberg. WAIS originated from a company called Thinking Machines, but has now split off into its own company, WAIS, Inc. Using the tremendous processing power of Thinking Machines' Connection Machine supercomputer or another powerful computer, WAIS can quickly (usually under a minute) return a number of articles to English-language queries, sorted by the likelihood that they are relevant to your question. WAIS is limited only by the information that people feed into it.

Last I counted, there were over 700 sources available for searching within topics as diverse as Buddhism, cookbooks, song lyrics, Supreme Court decisions, science fiction book reviews, and President Clinton's speeches. For all the sources on non-technical topics, I'm sure an equal number exist about technical topics in many fields.

N
o
t
e

People talking about WAIS (pronounced "ways," I hear) tend to use the terms "source," "server," and "database" interchangeably, and so do I.

Perhaps the hardest part about WAIS is learning how to ask it questions. Even though you can use natural English queries, it takes your question quite literally, and only applies it to the selected sources. So, if you asked about deforestation in the Amazon rainforest while searching in the Buddhism source, I'd be surprised if you found anything.

Since the rise of the World Wide Web's popularity, WAIS seems to have faded into the background a bit. It's not that WAIS servers aren't still being used heavily, but they're being used as search engines behind the scenes, usually through a Web page interface.

Gopher

Gopher, which originated with the Golden Gophers of the University of Minnesota, is an information browser along the same lines as FTP, but with significant enhancements for ease of use and flexibility. Numerous sites—over 2,300 at last count—on the Internet run the host Gopher software, placing information in what are colloquially called *gopher holes*. When you connect to a Gopher site, you can search databases, read text files, transfer files, and generally navigate around the collection of gopher holes, which is itself called *Gopherspace*.

Gopher can be quite useful in terms of actually making information available that you need to answer specific questions. Part of the reason for this opinion is *Veronica*, and to a lesser extent *Jughead*, which enable you to search through Gopherspace as Archie enables you to search for files on anonymous FTP servers.

> **Note**
>
> Veronica *and* Jughead *were both named to match* Archie *(from the* Archie *comics), but Veronica's creators at the University of Nevada did come up with an acronym as well—Very Easy Rodent-Oriented Net-wide Index to Computerized Archives. Jughead stands for Jonzy's Universal Gopher Hierarchy Excavation And Display. Glad you asked?*

Veronica searches through all of Gopherspace, which is useful, although badly phrased searches (Veronica doesn't use natural English, as WAIS does) can result in hundreds of results. Jughead searches a subset of Gopherspace and can thus be more accurate, though less comprehensive.

One of the special features of Gopher is that it provides access to FTP (and Archie) and WAIS, and can even run a Telnet program to provide access to resources only available via Telnet. Gopher also can work with other programs to provide access to special data types, such as pictures and sounds. When you double-click on a picture listing in Gopher, it downloads the file and then runs another program to display the picture. This sort of integration doesn't generally work all that well if all you have is Unix command-line access to the Internet.

World Wide Web

When I wrote the first edition of this book in mid-1993, the World Wide Web existed, but lacked a good client program on the Macintosh. I managed to write a paragraph or two back then about NCSA Mosaic, the Web browser that was officially released a few months after I finished the book, but there simply wasn't much on the Web at that point. Now there are at least four well-known Web browsers for the Macintosh alone, and I'm sure more are on the way. Everything about the Web has changed since that first edition. It's become much, much larger, and the resources available on it have become incredibly diverse and far more useful.

> **Note**
>
> *You may see the World Wide Web referred to as simply "the Web," "W3," or sometimes as "WWW."*

The Web brings a couple of very important features to the Internet. First, unlike Gopher or anything else, it provides access to full fonts, sizes, and styles for text, and can include images onscreen with no special treatment. Sounds and movies are also possible, though often too large for many people to download and view. Second, the Web provides true hypertextual links between documents anywhere on the Web, not just on a single machine. For those unfamiliar with *hypertext*, it's a powerful concept that enables you to navigate flexibly through linked pieces of information. If you read a paragraph with a link promising more information about the topic, say results from the last Olympic Games, simply click on the link, and you'll see the results. It really is that simple, and the World Wide Web enjoys the highest profile of any of the Internet services.

There are more machines whose names start with **www** than anything else now, and the Web is in second place and rapidly catching up with FTP in terms of the amount of data transferred. Nothing touches it in terms of pure sexiness, although many Web servers that you see suffer from the same problem that many publications did after the Macintosh made desktop publishing popular: they're designed by amateurs and are ugly as sin.

Summing Up

I've tried to answer one of the harder questions around, "What is the Internet?" The simple answer is that the Internet is a massive collection of people, machines, software programs, and data, spread all around the world and constantly interacting. That definition, and the explication I've provided about the various parts of the Internet elephant, should serve you well as we look next at the history of this fascinating beast.

The Internet Beanstalk

Unlike the Greek goddess Athena, the Internet did not spring from the head of some Zeusian computer scientist. It was formed by a process of relatively rapid accretion and fusion (but keep in mind that this industry is one in which computer power doubles every few years). In 1980, there were 200 machines on the Internet—that number is now about 4.9 million. The grain of sand that formed the heart of this giant electronic pearl came from the U.S. Department of Defense (DoD) in 1969. I'm pleased to be older than the Internet, having been born in 1967, but I'm not enough older to talk authoritatively about world conditions at that time. So, please bear with my second-hand retelling.

Cold War Network

In the 1950s, the Russian Sputnik program humiliated the United States. To better compete in the space race, the U.S. space program (at the time under the auspices of the military) received major government funding. That funding came from the DoD under its Advanced Research Projects Agency (ARPA). In the early 1960s, the space program left the military to become NASA, but ARPA remained, and as with many government programs that have seemingly lost their reason to exist, so did its funding. What to do with the money?

The DoD was, at that time, the world's largest user of computers, so J.C.R. Licklider and others proposed that ARPA support large-scale basic research in computer science. ARPA didn't originally require that the research it supported be either classified or directly related to military applications, which left the door open for far-reaching research in many fields. In 1963, ARPA devoted a measly $5 to $8 million to its computer research, the Information Processing Technologies Office (IPTO), first under Licklider, and then subsequently under the 26-year-old Ivan Sutherland, who had developed an early (perhaps the earliest) graphics program at MIT. After Sutherland, a 32-year-old named Robert Taylor headed IPTO. Taylor managed to double IPTO's budget at a time when ARPA's overall budget was decreasing, and even admitted to diverting funds from military-specific projects to pure computer science.

Around this time, the ARPAnet (Advanced Research Projects Agency Network) began connecting various computers around the country at sites performing research for ARPA. Computers were expensive, and sharing them was the only way to distribute the resources appropriately. Distribution of cost via networks proved to be an important force in the development of the Internet later on as well. Proponents like Taylor ensured the early survival of the fledgling ARPAnet when it was all too vulnerable to governmental whimsy.

In 1969, Congress got wind of what ARPA was up to in terms of funding basic research with money from the defense budget. Three senators, including the still-active Edward Kennedy, pushed through legislation requiring that ARPA show that its programs were directly applicable to the military. In the process, ARPA's name changed to reflect its new nature; it became the Defense Advanced Research Projects Agency, or DARPA. (Years later, the name changed back to ARPA again, just to confuse the issue.) Bob Taylor became entangled in some unpleasant business reworking military computers in Saigon during the Vietnam War and left DARPA shortly thereafter. He was succeeded by Larry Roberts, who played a major role in getting the then two-year-old ARPAnet up and running. Stewart Brand, founder of *The Whole Earth Catalog*, wrote at the time:

> *At present some 20 major computer centers are linked on the two-year-old ARPAnet. Traffic on the Net has been very slow, due to delays and difficulties of translation between different computers and divergent projects. Use has recently begun to increase as researchers travel from center to center and want to keep in touch with home base, and as more tantalizing sharable resources come available. How Net usage will evolve is uncertain. There's a curious mix of theoretical fascination and operational resistance around the scheme. The resistance may have something to do with reluctance about equipping a future Big Brother and his Central Computer. The fascination resides in the thorough rightness of computers as communication instruments, which implies some revolutions. (Stewart Brand, in* II Cybernetic Frontiers, *Random House, 1974)*

So if DARPA had to justify the military applications of its research, what survived? Well, the ARPAnet did, and here's why: As leaders of the free world (pardon the rhetoric), we needed the latest and greatest methods of killing as many other people as possible. Along with *offensive* research must perforce come *defensive* research; even the DoD isn't so foolish as to assume we could wage a major war entirely on foreign soil. For this reason, the tremendous U.S. interstate highway system served double duty as a distribution medium for tanks and other military hardware. Similarly, the Internet's precursor was both a utilitarian and experimental network. ARPAnet connected both military research sites (hardware was expensive and had to be shared) and was an experiment in resilient networks that could withstand a catastrophe—including, in the imaginations of the DoD planners of the day, an atomic bomb.

Interestingly, the resiliency of the ARPAnet design, as carried down to the Internet, has led some to note that the Internet routes around censorship as it would route around physical damage. It's a fascinating thought, especially in regard to Stewart Brand's earlier comment about Big Brother. If anything, the Internet actually has served to reduce the threat of a Big Brother, because it makes communication between people so fluid and unrestricted. But, I anticipate myself.

Gateways

As a result of the machinations described previously, the Internet Protocol, or IP (the second half of TCP/IP) was created. Essentially, the point behind IP systems is that each computer knows of, or can determine, the existence of all the others, and thus route packets of information to its destination via the quickest route. While doing this, they are able to take into account any section of the network that's been bombed out or has merely been cut by an over-enthusiastic telephone repairperson. This design turns out to work well; more importantly, it makes for an extremely flexible network. If your computer can get a properly addressed packet of information to a machine on the Internet, that machine will worry about how to deliver it, translating as necessary. That's the essence of a *gateway*—it connects two dissimilar networks, translating information so that it can pass transparently from one to the other.

In the early 1980s, the military began to rely more and more heavily on the ARPAnet for communication, but because the ARPAnet still connected a haphazard mix of research institutions, businesses doing defense work, and military sites, the military wanted their own network. And so the ARPAnet split in half, becoming the ARPAnet and the Milnet (Military Network). The ARPAnet continued to carry traffic for research sites, and even though the military now had its own Milnet, traffic passed between the ARPAnet and the Milnet by going through gateways.

The concept of gateways proved important in the history of the Internet. Alongside the development of the Internet came the development of a number of other, generally smaller, networks that used protocols other than IP, such as BITNET, JANET, and various others. These also included some like Usenet and CSNET that didn't care what protocols were used. These networks were regional or dedicated to serving certain types of machines or users.

Perhaps the largest driving force behind the Internet is that of the need to connect with other people and other networks. The grass is always greener on the other side of the fence, and gradually gateway sites sprung up so that email could pass among the different networks with ease.

Usenet

I'm going to take a brief break from the Internet itself, because at approximately the same time the ARPAnet split, a host of other networks came into being, probably the most interesting of which was Usenet, the User's Network.

Usenet started in 1979, when some graduate students decided to link several Unix computers together in an attempt to better communicate with the rest of the Unix community. The system they created included software to read news, post news, and transport news among machines. To this day, that simple model continues, but whereas once two machines were on Usenet, today there are hundreds of thousands. The software that transports and displays Usenet news now runs on not just Unix machines, but on almost every type of computer in use on the networks. The topics of discussion have blossomed from Unix into almost any conceivable subject—and many inconceivable ones. Like all the other network entities, Usenet quickly grew to be international in scope and size.

Unlike many of the other networks, Usenet truly grew from the bottom up, rather than from the top down. Usenet was created by and for users, and no organization—commercial, federal, or otherwise—had a hand in it originally. In many ways, Usenet has provided much of the attitude of sharing that exists on the Internet today. In the past, you usually got a Usenet *feed* (that is, had another machine send news traffic to your machine) free of charge (other than your telephone charges) as long as you were willing to pass the feed on to someone else free of charge. Due to commercial pressures, the days of the free feeds are essentially no more, but the spirit of cooperation they engendered remains in much of what happens on the Internet.

I don't want to imply that Usenet is this happy, carefree network where everything is free and easy, because in many cases it's a noisy, unpleasant network that exists because of the utility of some of the information that it carries. Despite the attitude toward sharing, the survival of Usenet is due in large part to the resourcefulness of network administrators at major sites. Faced with mounting telephone charges for long distance calls between Usenet hosts, these administrators found a way to carry Usenet news over the TCP/IP-based Internet rather than just the previous modem-based UUCP connections. Thus, they prevented the costs of carrying Usenet from coming to the attention of the bean counters poised to strike unnecessary expenses from their budgets. The TCP/IP connections of the ARPAnet, and then the Internet, were already paid for. So, by figuring out how to carry Usenet over those lines, the network administrators managed to cut their costs, keep users happy, and save Usenet from itself in the process. In other words, Usenet may be an anarchy, but it wouldn't stand a chance without some occasional help from high places.

BITNET

Shortly after Usenet took its first faltering networked steps, Ira Fuchs of City University of New York and Greydon Freeman of Yale University decided to network their universities using IBM's then-new NJE communications protocol. Although this protocol later expanded to support Digital Equipment's Vaxen running VMS and even some implementations of Unix, the vast majority of machines on BITNET (the "Because It's Time" network) have always been IBM mainframes. Fuchs and Freeman made their connection in the spring of 1981. BITNET grew rapidly, encompassing over 100 organizations on 225 machines by 1984, and by 1994 reaching the level of 1,400 organizations in 49 countries around the world. Most BITNET sites are at universities, colleges, and other research institutions.

BITNET has always been a cooperative network; members pass traffic bound for other sites free of charge, and software developed by one has been made available to all. Unlike Usenet, however, BITNET developed an organizational structure in 1984. This took the form of an Executive Committee, made up of representatives of all the major nodes on the network. Also in 1984, IBM presented a large grant that provided initial funding for centralized network support services. This grant, coupled with the fact that most of the machines on BITNET were IBM mainframes, gave rise to the erroneous rumor that BITNET was an IBM network. In 1987, BITNET became a nonprofit corporation. In 1989, it changed its corporate name to CREN, the Corporation for Research and Educational Networking, when it merged its administrative organization with another of the parallel educational networks, CSNET (the Computer+Science Network). Today, BITNET is in something of a decline, due in large part to the nonstandard NJE protocol in an increasingly IP world.

NSFNET

The next big event in the history of the Internet was the creation of the high-speed NSFNET (National Science Foundation Network) in 1986. NSFNET was developed to connect supercomputer sites around the country. Because supercomputers are terribly expensive, the NSF could afford to fund only five (and even then they received some major financial help from companies like IBM). With this limited number, it made sense to network the supercomputers so that researchers everywhere could use them without traveling great distances. At first, the NSF tried to use the ARPAnet, but that attempt quickly became bogged down in bureaucracy and red tape.

The NSF therefore decided to build its own network. Merely connecting the five supercomputer sites wasn't going to help the vast majority of researchers, of course, so the NSF created (or used existing) regional networks that connected schools and research sites in the same area. Then those networks were connected to the NSFNET.

To quote from W.P. Kinsella's *Shoeless Joe*, "If you build it, they will come." Perhaps not surprisingly, once all of these networks were able to communicate with one another, the supercomputer usage faded into the background. Other uses, most notably email, became preeminent. One of the important features of the NSFNET was that the NSF encouraged universities to provide wide access to students and staff, so the population of and traffic on the net increased dramatically.

In 1987, the NSF awarded a contract to a group of companies to manage and upgrade the NSFNET. This group was made up of IBM, MCI, and Merit Network, which ran the educational network in Michigan. The group dealt with the massive increase in traffic by replacing the old lines with much faster connections.

Eventually the NSFNET had entirely supplanted the ARPAnet, and in March of 1990, the ARPAnet was taken down for good, having played the starring role for 21 years. Similarly, another national network, CSNET, which had connected computer science researchers around the country, closed its electronic doors a year later, all of its traffic having moved to the faster NSFNET.

NREN

The NSFNET is all fine and nice, but in many ways it discriminated against "lower" education—two-year colleges, community colleges, and the much-maligned K–12 schools. To save the day, then-Senator Al Gore sponsored a bill, passed in December of 1991, called the "High-Performance Computing Act of 1991." Gore's legislation created a new network on top of (and initially using) the NSFNET. This new network is called the NREN, for National Research and Education Network. Along with providing even faster speeds, the NREN specifically targets grade schools, high schools, public libraries, and two- and four-year colleges. In working with the thousands of people who subscribe to *TidBITS*, I see a lot of email addresses, and it's clear to me that these educational institutions are joining the Internet in droves. A day rarely passes when I don't see something from someone whose address clearly labels him or her as a teacher at a grade school or even a student in a high school.

Alert readers probably have noticed that NREN looks a lot like CREN, and in fact, the acronyms are similar—with reason. CREN recognizes the need for an integrated National Research and Education Network. In fact, as the IBM-created NJE protocol gradually disappears in favor of the more powerful and popular IP, CREN has said it will disband, merge with NREN, or cooperate with it as appropriate—though only when NREN exists with access rules, funding, and usage policies that allow a clean transition. Currently, CREN feels that the NREN does not provide consistent policies regarding these issues.

Who Pays?

More and more of the Internet is being created and run by commercial organizations. All a commercial provider has to do is to pay for its part of the network, just as universities pay for their connections and government departments pay for theirs. The difference is that unlike universities or government organizations, commercial providers want to make money, or at least break even, so they in turn sell access to their machines or networks to other providers or to end users.

The gut reaction to the commercialization of the Internet from the old-timers (who remember when you could get a Usenet feed merely by asking) is often negative, but most people believe that the Internet must accept commercial traffic. In part, this response is true because the only alternative to accepting commercial traffic is actively rejecting it, and no one wants to sit around censoring the Internet, were that even possible. In many ways, the question has already been decided because there are now more **com** addresses than **edu** addresses, the previous champ.

Commercialization also allows small organizations to create the equivalent of wide-area networks that previously only large businesses could afford. A company such as Microsoft can spend the money to install an international company network, but few companies are so large or so wealthy. Many may not need such an international network, but they may need enhanced communications. Email can be a powerful medium for business communication, just as it is for personal communication. And, if transferring a file via FTP or email can save a few uses of an overnight courier, the connection can pay for itself in no time.

In addition, whereas in the past you had to work at a large business or university to gain Internet access, it has become far easier for an individual to get access without any such affiliation, although the costs are, of course, more obvious. Easier independent access couldn't have happened without increased participation by commercial interests.

The commercialization issue has another side. The U.S. government still controls the NREN, which is a large portion of the Internet and connects many of the major educational sites. As more commercial providers get into the business, the government is gradually relying more and more on them rather than duplicating their effort. This move has much support because the commercial providers can then make money, which is what they want to do, and the government can save money, which is what many people want the government to do.

The concern is, of course, that these commercial providers will want to make too much money and will raise rates significantly or start charging usage-based fees rather than the flat-rate fees that have been more common for this type of service. I don't worry too much about this concern, mostly because the competition is heavy in the Internet field, and prices are seldom high in extremely competitive fields. In addition, it's not as though the federal funding was necessarily a significant part of the Internet budgets at many institutions.

When these issues started to come to a head in 1994, M. Stuart Lynn, then the head of Cornell Information Technologies, noted that the Internet is a global network, and some countries, such as New Zealand, already have usage-based pricing. So even if the NREN moved to usage-based pricing, most of the global Internet wouldn't be affected. Stuart Lynn also commented that the federal subsidy is trivial to many institutions, and at Cornell it is equivalent to two cans of beer per student per year. In other words, even if Cornell had to rely on a completely commercial network (which may or may not be usage-based), its costs would not change noticeably.

Note *It's worth noting that people like flat-rate fees for most things (telephone service and cable service come to mind), and in the past most personal Internet accounts from commercial providers have been usage-based, with a recent trend toward flat-rate service in the past few years. I believe the increasing number of flat-rate SLIP and PPP accounts from various commercial providers was helped in part by the first edition of this book, with its flat-rate offer for SLIP access from Northwest Nexus. I'm unaware of any other widely available flat-rate accounts that predate the offer from Northwest Nexus. Of course, I could be wrong, but I like to think I had a positive influence.*

The trick is to remember that someone always pays for the Internet. If you have a free Internet account thanks to your school, remember that the institution is paying for that connection and funding it in part from your tuition. If your workplace offers Internet access and doesn't limit your use of it, consider that a benefit of working there, along with retirement and health benefits. And an increasingly large number of people, like me, pay directly, usually somewhere between $5 and $30 per month. Sure beats cable television.

Remember how I previously said that the NSFNET was created to carry supercomputer traffic but soon found itself being used for all sorts of tasks? That's another basic principle to keep in mind about how the Internet is funded. The network links were created for a specific reason (supercomputer access), and because of that reason, the money necessary to create and maintain those links was allocated in various budgets. Thus, when traffic unrelated to the supercomputer access travels on the same network, it's piggy-backing on the lines that have already been paid for out of existing budgets. So it seems free, and as long as the ancillary traffic doesn't impinge on the supercomputer access, no one is likely to complain. It's much like using your friend's Mac's processing power to generate processor-intensive pictures when he's not using his Mac. As long as your use doesn't slow down the things he wants to do, he probably won't mind, especially if it helps you finish your work sooner. But, if your use prevents him from doing his own work, he'll probably become less generous about it.

So, when the NREN moves completely from governmental to private control, most people won't see the difference because their organizations would continue to foot the bill, especially if the costs didn't change. To poorly funded organizations such as grade schools and public libraries, which may only be able to afford their Internet connections with help from the government, the danger is there. Oh, and where do you think the government gets the money? Taxes, of course. So you end up paying one way or another.

Politics

After all of this discussion, you're probably confused as to who runs what on the Internet. Good, that's the way it should be, because no one person or organization runs the Internet as such. I think of the Internet as a collection of fiefdoms that must cooperate to survive. The fiefdoms are often inclusive as well, so one group may control an entire network, but another group controls a specific machine in that network. As a user, you must abide by what both of them say, or find another host.

I don't mean to say that there aren't some guiding forces. The NSF exercised a certain influence over much of the Internet because it controlled a large part of it in the NSFNET. Thus, the NSF's Acceptable Use Policies (which state that the NSFNET may not be used for "commercial activities") became important rules to follow, or at least keep in mind, and I'll bet that many commercial providers used them as a starting point for creating their own less restrictive, acceptable use policies.

Several other important groups exist, all of which are volunteer-based (as is most everything on the Internet). The Internet Architecture Board, or IAB, sets the standards for the Internet. Without standards, the Internet wouldn't be possible because so many types of hardware and software exist on it. Although you must be invited to be on the IAB, anyone can attend the regular meetings of the Internet Engineering Task Force, or IETF. The IETF's meetings serve as a forum to discuss and address the immediate issues that face the Internet as a whole. Serious problems, or rather problems that interest a sufficient number of volunteers, result in working groups that report back to the IETF with a recommendation for solving the problem. This system seems haphazard, but frankly, it works, which is more than you can say for certain other organizations we could probably name.

Other networks undoubtedly have their controlling boards as well, but the most interesting is Usenet, which has even less organization than the Internet as a whole. Due to its roots in the user community, Usenet is run primarily by the community, as strange as that may sound. Every network administrator controls what news can come into her machine, but she can't control what goes around her machine. The converse applies as well—if a sufficient number of network administrators don't approve of something, say a newsgroup creation, then it simply doesn't happen. Major events on Usenet must have sufficient support from a sufficient number of people.

Of course, some people's votes count more than others. These people are sometimes called *net heavies* because they often administer major sites or run important mailing lists. The net heavies consider it their job (who knows how they manage to keep real jobs with all the work they do here) to keep the nets running smoothly. Even though they often work behind the scenes, they do an excellent job. Shortly after I started *TidBITS*, for instance, I was searching for the best ways to distribute it. I wasn't able to run a mailing list from my account at Cornell, and *TidBITS* was too big to post to a general Usenet group every week. After I spoke with several of the net heavies, they allowed me to post to a moderated newsgroup, `comp.sys.mac.digest`, that had up to that point been used only for distributing the Info-Mac Digest to Usenet.

If you want to get involved with what organization there is on the Internet, I suggest that you participate and contribute to discussions about the future of the nets. Gradually, you'll learn how the system works and find yourself in a position where you can help the net continue to thrive.

You should keep one thing in mind about the Internet and its loose controlling structure: It works, and it works far better than do most other organizations. By bringing control down to almost the individual level but by requiring cooperation to exist, the Internet works without the strong central government that most countries use and claim is necessary to avoid lawlessness and anarchy. Hmm...

The Internet makes you think, and that's good.

Oh, and remember Bob Taylor, one of the early heads of ARPA's IPTO? Several years later he helped found Xerox PARC, which employed luminaries such as Douglas Engelbart (inventor of the mouse), Alan Kay (a current Apple Fellow), Bob Metcalfe (inventor of Ethernet), and Larry Tesler (who was, and may still be, head of Apple's Advanced Technology Group). And, of course, Xerox PARC was where Steve Jobs saw the Xerox Alto workstation and its graphical interface, and at that moment, in many respects, the Macintosh was born.

The Future

I hope this chapter has provided a coherent view of where the Internet has come from, along with some of the people and networks that were instrumental in its growth. After any history lesson, the immediate question concerns the future. Where can we expect the Internet to go from here?

I'm an optimist. I'm sure you can find someone more than happy to tell you all the horrible problems—technical, political, and social—facing the Internet. I don't hold with such attitudes, though, because something that affects so many people around the world didn't appear so quickly for no reason. In one way or another, I think most people understand on a visceral level that the Internet is good, the Internet is here to stay, and if they want to be someone, they would do well to get access today and contribute in a positive fashion. Of course, books like this one only encourage such utopian attitudes.

In any event, I predict that the Internet will continue growing at an incredible rate. You might make an argument for the rate of growth slowing from its 15 percent per month rate based on the fact that it's silly to assume that anything can continue to grow at such a breakneck speed. A naysayer also might point at the massive influx of novices as endangering the Internet, or point at the increased level of commercialization as a major problem. I feel that such growth is self-propelling and that bringing more people and resources onto the Internet only further fuels the expansion. I think that growth is good—the more people, the more resources, the more opinions, the better off we all are.

I also expect to see the Internet continue to standardize, both officially and informally. At lower levels, more computers will start to use IP instead of BITNET's NJE or the aging UUCP protocols. It's merely a matter of keeping up with the Joneses, and the Joneses are running IP. At a higher level, I think that using various network resources will become easier as they start migrating toward similar interfaces. Just as it's easy to use multiple applications on a Mac because you always know how to open, close, save, and quit, so it will be easier to use new and enhanced services on the Internet because they will resemble each other more and more. Even now, people rely heavily on network conventions such as prefixing site names to indicate what services they provide, like `ftp.tidbits.com` for FTP, `gopher.tidbits.com` for Gopher, and `www.tidbits.com` for the World Wide Web.

And yes, I fully expect to see the Internet become increasingly commercial, both in terms of where the service comes from and in terms of the traffic the Internet carries. However, we must remember the old attitudes about commercial use of the Internet. In the past, commercial use was often acceptable if it wasn't blatant, was appropriately directed, and was of significant value to the readers. In other words, I'll be as angry as the next person if I start receiving automatically generated junk email every day, just as I receive junk mail via snail mail. If such things start happening, the course of action will be the same as it always has been: politely ask the originator to stop once, and then, if that doesn't work, flame away—that is, send back an outrageously nasty message.

Even though I'm optimistic, I know that problems will occur. For example, consider the so-called Green Card debacle. In the spring of 1994, the husband and wife law firm of Canter & Siegel posted a blatantly commercial message advertising a green card lottery and immigration services. That wasn't the problem. The problem was that they posted it to 5,000 Usenet newsgroups, an act called *spamming*. Discussions about Celtic culture, Macintosh communications (where I first saw it), and Washington state politics were all interrupted, along with thousands of others completely apathetic about anything to do with immigration. Or at least they were apathetic until they were bludgeoned repeatedly with Canter & Siegel's post. All of a sudden, everyone cared a great deal about immigration, and sent 30,000 flame messages (more than 100 megabytes of text) to the offenders. That many messages was far more than Canter & Siegel's provider, Internet Direct, could handle, and their machine went down like a boxer on the wrong end of a knock-out punch.

Part I   The Internet Beanstalk 4

The aftershocks keep coming, with Internet Direct suing Canter & Siegel for violating acceptable use policies (it seems that Canter & Siegel never signed the terms and conditions form) and for the detrimental effect the post had on business. In return Canter & Siegel counter-sued for loss of business, claiming some ludicrous percentage of the messages were requests for more information (though they refuse to provide any verifiable data). Needless to say, Internet Direct disabled their account immediately, and details about Canter & Siegel's history began to surface. They'd been kicked off of other providers for similar smaller-scale posts in the past, they'd been suspended from the bar in Florida in 1987 for conduct the Supreme Court of Florida deemed "contrary to honest," and so on. Canter & Siegel garnered a huge amount of press (most of it negative, but as the saying goes, "I don't care what you say about me as long as you spell my name right."). They even announced in a newspaper interview that they were setting up a company to provide services to other companies who wanted to flood Usenet with advertising, and they wrote a book (which has received awful reviews) about how to advertise on the Internet. That's a bit like Bonnie and Clyde writing a book about bank security.

The Canter & Siegel fiasco raises the question of how the Internet should be policed. In the past, and the present, any transgression has been dealt with much as it might have been in the perhaps-fictional view of the American Old West. Everyone takes justice into his own hands, and if a few innocents are hurt in the process, well, it was for the greater good. When Canter & Siegel spammed Usenet, thousands of people spammed them back.

This process is more commonly known as *mail bombing*. Mail bombs are generally small Unix programs (before you ask, I don't know of any for the Mac and don't condone their use in general) that simply send a user-configured number of messages (using a specified file as the message body) to a given address, potentially ensuring that none of the mail bomb messages come from real addresses. A better solution came from a Norwegian programmer, who created a spambot (his term, not mine) program that somehow figures out which newsgroups Canter & Siegel spammed (yes, it has happened again, although on a smaller scale each time) and bounces the spamming message back to them, along with a short note daring them to sue him, since he's in Norway.

Frontier justice sounds like great fun, especially when slimy lawyers are on the other end, but it raises some interesting issues. Mail bombing a machine doesn't affect just that machine—it affects many of the machines nearby on the Internet. In the case of a public machine like Internet Direct's **indirect.com**, it also hurts an innocent business and hundreds of innocent users who also use that machine. And, although the Internet as a whole can deal with the occasional mail bomb attack, if such things happened every day, they would seriously impair Internet communications. Such possibilities raise the specter of regulation, something that most Internet users disapprove of (though certain usage regulations are built into the service agreements of almost every Internet provider for liability reasons). So, will the government get involved and lay down the law about inappropriate Internet use? Probably not. The people who must do the regulation are the providers themselves—there's no way to prevent everyone from retaliating from such spam attacks as Canter and Siegel's, so the best place to stop them is at the level of the providers. They can simply refuse to give problem users an account or remove accounts when abuse occurs. But the government itself? I certainly hope not.

I don't believe that the Internet will ever be governed to a much greater extent than it now is (at least in the U.S.), simply because I don't believe it's feasible. How can you govern something that spans the globe or police something that carries gigabytes of data every day? The U.S. government could easily ban pornographic postings, say, but how does that affect someone from a different country? Or how does that affect U.S. users retrieving the pornographic images from another country? Remember, the Internet can just route around censorship. It's all very confusing, and it will be some time (if ever) before the government understands all of the issues surrounding the Internet sufficiently to produce reasonable legislation. Of course, that begs the question of unreasonable legislation, but that's always a fear.

The way the government as a whole currently views the Internet reminds me a bit of the joke about how to tell if you have an elephant in your fridge. The answer is by the footprints in the peanut butter—it's the middle of the night, and the government is standing at the open door, yawning and blinking at those massive footprints. Luckily, different parts of the government are starting to wake up, which should help dispel the dangerous ignorance that has marked certain past government Internet actions.

For example, there was the Steve Jackson case, in which the Secret Service completely inappropriately confiscated the computer systems of a popular publisher of role-playing games. The damage award from that case enabled Steve Jackson Games to create an Internet provider called Illuminati Online (`io.com`). Perhaps the greater problem now with the government's view of the Internet is that it seems more concerned with regulating occasional outrageous behavior than with using the power of the Internet to further the public good. Personally, I prefer my government to be more interested in helping than in regulating. Of course, then there are the people who would prefer that the government just stayed out of the way, but somehow I doubt that will happen any time soon.

Past and Future—Next, the Present

I've tried to give a glimpse of the history of the Internet, from its first stumbling steps as the military- and research-based ARPAnet to the swift NSFNET and NREN, along with the commercial providers of today. If nothing else, it's worth noting that those who ignore history are condemned to repeat it, and by paying attention to the mistakes of the past, perhaps we can avoid making them again. The future will also bring new problems and new opportunities, but for the moment we can only speculate as to what those may be. But put all that out of your mind, because the next chapter takes you on a tour of the Internet of today.

Exploring the Internet

Before I dive into the "hows" of the Internet, I'd like to take a chapter to discuss the "whys." I spend most of the rest of this book talking about how to do things—how to use Anarchie to retrieve a file, how to use Eudora, how to use NewsWatcher, what's neat about MacWeb, and so forth. But, it makes sense to spend a little time first talking about why you would want to use email, read news, talk to people via IRC (Internet Relay Chat) or browse the World Wide Web.

The problem with attempting to give you a sense of why you would want to do these things is that for most readers, I don't know you personally. Any specific example I give may or may not interest you, so I instead talk about the things that I do on the Internet and the ways I use the Internet in my daily life. Although you and I are undoubtedly interested in different subjects, if you just sit back in a comfortable chair and read through this chapter, I hope you'll get a better sense of what life on the Internet is really like.

Don't sweat the details in this chapter. It's not meant to be technical at all and you've got the rest of the book to answer any niggling details. If you don't recognize a program name or an Internet service, don't worry about it—just mentally note it for later and come back after you've read the later chapters. As odd as it may sound, consider this chapter a work of fiction. It's not that the subject matter is contrived, but instead that you must suspend disbelief and just flow with the text. After all, you don't worry about how Ian Fleming enabled his fictional master spy, James Bond, to drive a car that could metamorphose into a submarine, right?

After you've read the rest of the book and have gotten on the Internet, you might come back to this chapter and see if you can perhaps duplicate some of the examples that follow. You never know what you might find when you retrace the steps of a fictional, or not so fictional, character.

Actually, I've already written an entire book, called *Internet Explorer Kit for Macintosh*, devoted to this less-technical subject matter. My co-author on that book, Bill Dickson, has graciously agreed to join me for a chapter to go over some of the material we cover in *Internet Explorer Kit for Macintosh*. Hi, Bill!

`Bill: Hi, Adam! Hello, Readers!`

Adam: You'll notice that we've just switched over to a dialog format. In keeping with the more informal nature of this setting, we'll present this chapter as a sort of extended conversation. It worked well in *Internet Explorer Kit for Macintosh*, as we were able to draw on each other's experience with different aspects of the Internet, and interject with questions where appropriate.

`Bill: Think of it as a quick spin around the Internet in the back seat of a Macintosh convertible, with Adam and I sitting up front and taking turns driving. Kick back and relax, and we'll see if we can show you something interesting.`

Adam: And I suppose the first thing we'll do is what most people do when they get their first car—we'll go visit some friends.

People

Adam: News stories about the Internet love to quote big numbers, since big numbers impress people. I suspect that's mostly because few people have ever sat down and counted to a million, or even much past a hundred. Today's youth probably consider it sufficient to watch that many digits flash by on the computer screen, muttering that if Zeus had intended us to count to a million, he would have given us a million toes—and wouldn't that have made "This little piggy" difficult?

So, you hear a lot about how there are millions of computers on the Internet and how the growth rate increases at some 15 percent per month. It's equally *chic* to talk about the hardware and software and the myriad of protocols, each with an acronym like FTP or HTTP, all of which mean little to the average person, even to the average Internet user.

Let's face it, a vast number of people drive cars in the world, and I'm willing to bet that almost none of them know how powerful their cars' engines are in terms of horsepower. Here's the important fact about the Internet: people.

The Internet is about people. The actual number is unknown, and relatively unimportant, other than the number of zeros, since estimates place the population of the Internet between 20 and 50 million people worldwide. That's a large pool, and there's a pretty good chance that someone you know, or even many people you know, have access to the Internet.

```
Bill: The first thing many of us do when we arrive on the Internet is
look for our friends. It's only natural; it's harder to make new friends
than to stick with old ones. So, we sit down at our computers, try to
imagine who we know, anywhere in the world, who might be able to receive
email over the Internet, and we start hunting around for them.

This can be a great deal harder than it sounds. Paradoxically, the
Internet—one of the greatest tools for the exchange of information de-
vised since Gutenberg started mashing ink onto paper with wooden blocks—
can't keep track of who is using it. Or rather, it could, but nobody's
ever bothered to tell it how. So, silly as it may sound, there is no
comprehensive directory of Internet users. Not even close. Some sites
maintain their own directories, but the information can be pretty dated,
and you've still got to know where to look.
```

Adam: To illustrate this fact, we're going to look around for Bill. Now, you may think this is strange, even pointless, as Bill is obviously pretty close by or he wouldn't be able to raid my fridge for beer while writing this chapter.

```
Bill: Hey! It's my beer, bucko!
```

Adam: What dark secrets does the Internet hold? Perhaps the Whois server can provide some details on one William R. Dickson, possibly exposing his sordid past as the illegitimate son of a third world dictator. Let's find out.

First, we'll try a little Unix program called Whois. It turns up a William E. Dickson, but no William R. Dickson. Even if it had found him, all that Whois provides is an address, phone number, and email address, which aren't enough to suspect illegitimacy (see figure 5.1).

```
╔═══════════ dickson@rs.internic.net (198.41.0.5):Whois ═══════════╗
║ Dickson, David G. (DGD10)     (614) 223-3134                    ║
║ Dickson, David G. (DGD11)     (614) 223-3134                    ║
║ Dickson, Mike (MD61)  dp_mkd@tourism.tdoc.texas.gov (512) 320-9445 ║
║ Dickson, Scott (SD153)  SCOTT@ONTEK.COM   (714) 768-0301         ║
║ Dickson, William E. (WED)  BILL@WCIU.EDU    (818) 398-2357       ║
║                                                                  ║
║ The InterNIC Registration Services Host ONLY contains Internet Information ║
║ (Networks, ASN's, Domains, and POC's).                          ║
║ Please use the whois server at nic.ddn.mil for MILNET Information. ║
╚══════════════════════════════════════════════════════════════════╝
```

Figure 5.1   *Probably not the illegitimate son of a third world dictator; also, not our man.*

You must be careful when finding people in this manner since some names are relatively common. You might be embarrassed if you send an intensely personal letter to an old flame you located on the Internet, only to find out that you'd found somebody else's old flame.

But I don't give up easily, and I do want to see if I can turn something up on Bill. I like to use Gopher, which is a program created by the University of Minnesota to provide access to all sorts of information on the Internet. Gopher knows a number of ways to search for people, so first I'm going to try something called Netfind (see figure 5.2).

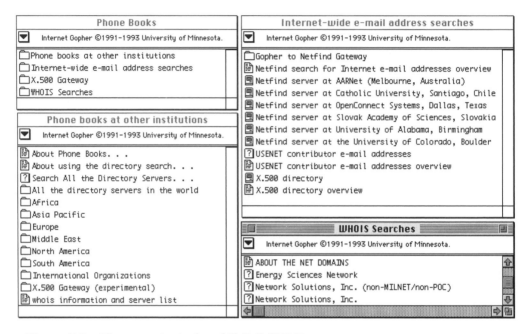

Figure 5.2   The many tentacles of G.O.P.H.E.R.

Netfind only works if your target works at a large business or university, and Bill's workplace—a Popular Copy Shop—isn't included. Strike two (Whois was strike one). Next up is something called X.500, which sounds like a robot but turns out to be a large white pages database maintained by some organization in England. It wants tons of information, including department and organization, that Bill doesn't have, so that's a strike as well. Ah, but now I see something that searches Usenet contributor email addresses, and I know that Bill occasionally posts to the Usenet newsgroups—maybe that will find him. Blast it, Gopher reports, "Could not connect," which means that the machine that runs that service or the network to that machine is down—maybe it's frozen. Strike four. Internet machines go down fairly frequently, but don't worry about it—they usually come back up in a few hours or the next day, so there's no need to panic and ask if the site has gone away. Just try again later.

I'm beginning to worry that I can't find Bill at all on the Internet. I know he exists, since he raids my fridge, but is it possible that he has erased all trace of his existence from the nets, in an attempt to cover up his horrible past? Hm, I just found an item called something like "Search all the directory servers in the world." Unfortunately, it doesn't know of any Dicksons. Hey, wait a minute, it doesn't know about any Smiths, either. I wonder what world it's on? Strike five.

Next up is a service called Veronica which knows how to search through all Gopher databases in the world (or at least, a lot of them) to find files matching the search term. I start a Veronica search on "Dickson" and am immediately rewarded with lots of... information that I don't want, including reviews of Gordon Dickson's books and a report (co-authored by a professor I knew) about computers in a dorm at Cornell University, Clara Dickson Hall. It's a small world, but, sigh, strike six (see figure 5.3).

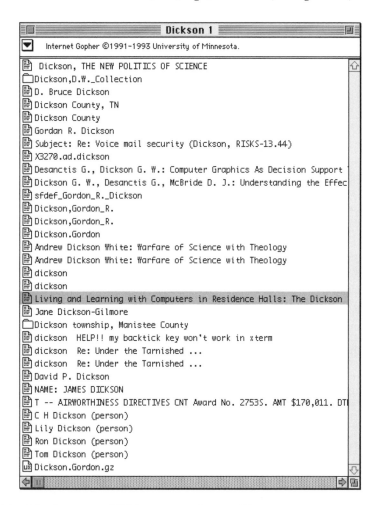

Figure 5.3   *No shortage of Dicksons out there, still not our man.*

This is beginning to annoy me. Two outs later, and my reputation as an Internet guru is at stake. I have one last trick to find some record of Bill on the Internet. I know he uses a Macintosh, and thus very well may read and contribute to the Info-Mac Digest, which is a discussion list about all things Macintosh. I also happen to know that the entire list is archived and indexed in WAIS, which stands for *Wide Area Information Servers*, and contains many massive databases of information on all sorts of topics. Last I checked, there were over 700 databases in WAIS, so I'm going to search in a database that collects Macintosh information for some sign of Bill (see figure 5.4).

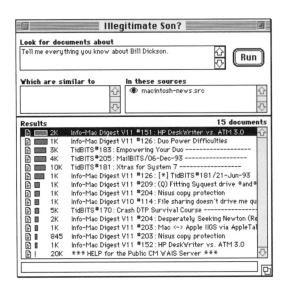

Figure 5.4   *Captured at last—the elusive Bill Dickson.*

Adam: You readers can't see this because I didn't want to embarrass Bill by showing his posting in public, but take my word for it, the selected posting and some of the others in figure 5.4 are from Bill, and it comes complete with his email address.

```
Bill: Argh! Found me!
```

Adam: I assure you that it isn't always this hard. On the other hand, it isn't always this easy, either. Sometimes finding people works immediately and at other times it's almost futile. Don't worry, just don't rely on these methods. I certainly don't. The telephone is almost always the most reliable method of finding someone's email address—just call and ask them.

Net Alter Egos

Adam: Superman, Batman, the Black Cat, Spiderman, Phoenix—all of these comic book heroes and heroines shared one feature other than great bodies and skintight uniforms that showed every curve. They all had alter egos who could mix in normal society without anyone else's realizing their true identities. One minute, mild mannered reporter Clark Kent was being brow-beaten by Lois Lane the next minute (and a phone booth later), Superman was saving the world from the latest crazed supervillain. Bruce Wayne and Batman, Peter Parker and Spiderman… Can anyone who has read comic books not have wanted an alter ego at some point? Our alter egos could do what we didn't want to, and would be stronger, smarter, and always ready with a clever comeback to any insult from dastardly villains of every ilk.

The Internet doesn't change your physical appearance or abilities, but because of the lack of visual interaction, it enables you to portray yourself in any manner you so choose. Some people might become crusaders for truth and justice, albeit in a single discussion list, whereas others might turn into psychotic lunatics in a subconscious rebellion against abusive parents or whatever. I doubt that most people change all that radically in their net personas, but keep in mind that you can never know what any given net citizen is like in person, without a face-to-face meeting.

There is another phenomenon that relates to this concept of net alter egos—that of amplification. Because the Internet enables any single person to send a message to tens of thousands of other people around the world and to maintain intellectual discussions with numerous people on a number of different topics, the Internet *amplifies* the individual, or enables her to do far more than any single person could do outside of the Internet.

The Internet thus enables the individual to become more important and more influential than would otherwise be possible in real life. Of course, the extent to which this happens is directly related to the level of interest and utility of your postings. Those who do good stuff are respected, whereas those who merely clog the Internet with garbage are universally reviled. Well-known, yes, but infamous.

Bill: There's something about the Internet that makes some people cut loose a little bit. Not everybody; Adam's email, for instance, conveys his real personality fairly accurately.

Adam: I'm not sure if he's flattering me or being subtly underhanded. Must be his background as the illegitimate son of a third world dictator.

Bill: We'll never know, will we? But, many people have an "electronic personality" that is distinctly different from their "real" personality.

It bothers me when people put quotation marks around words that don't need them, so let me assure you that I mean it in this case. The question that arises here is, given that the pressure of face-to-face interaction (and the possibility of embarrassment that goes along with it) are largely absent on the Internet, do people behave more or less naturally when they communicate this way?

Well, the answer, of course, is both. There, that clears it right up, doesn't it?

Let's take as an example one form of human interaction that's in abundant supply on the Internet: flirtation. People love to flirt electronically! Since it's so unlikely that you'll ever actually meet the target of your wiles, there's no fear of rejection; since you're judged entirely by your words (and skillful use of smileys), you don't need to worry about your weight or your hair. So, what you'll find is that people who couldn't possibly force themselves to buy somebody, anybody, a drink in your typical cocktail bar become remarkably fluent in the language of romance when you put them behind a keyboard and monitor. Which is the real person? Hard to say. Obviously, the talent for personal interaction is there, but that talent seems to take a vacation when there's another person around to actually interact with.

Likewise, you'll find people on the Internet telling total strangers things they'd never say to many of their friends if they had to say them face-to-face. Incredibly personal information will find its way into your email from surprising sources. People are willing to bare their souls, revealing aspects of themselves you'd never see in person.

There also are people who would be polite in person, but who may, since they need not worry about getting punched in the mouth, sound off in an abrasive manner about anything that bothers them—which frequently turns out to be rather a lot.

This stuff is all very interesting and could probably be the subject of many studies involving mazes and cheese and spilled ink. But there's another sort of alter ego you'll encounter on the Internet, and that's the deliberate role of an actor. People actually construct a part for themselves to play, and present that character as their network personality. Some do so as a disguise, playing the role as if it were a real person. Others make no secret of the fact that they are playing a part. The role may be played for the network at large, in discussion groups and correspondence, or only for a specific group of people in some corner of the Internet where such role-playing is the norm.

This is one of the most fascinating things about the Internet for me, and I've wholeheartedly participated from time-to-time. I currently play several roles, including a six-foot anthropomorphized pickle in a virtual community called FurryMUCK, a nigh-omnipotent (but highly irresponsible) Author in the Author's Altiverse of Superguy Digest, and a Supreme Court Justice on the Politics list. It may sound weird to you, but it all makes perfect sense to each of those three groups of people.

Adam: Bill?

Bill: Yes?

Adam: You're really strange.

Bill: Yes. But lovably so. Net personalities can manifest in some unusual ways, even if you don't turn into a giant walking pickle. Sometimes it takes the form of an affected quirk: there are three people on the Politics list who refuse to use capital letters. One of them explained her reasons to me; she is a relatively shy person, and feels that lowercase conveys her personality more accurately by implying a small, quiet speaking voice.

Adam: Although most people are extremely pleasant in email because they know that email lacks the body language and intonations of normal speech, there are exceptions. I suspect that most of these occur simply as a matter of limited time to answer email messages, or perhaps as a subconscious response to the frustration of being asked the same question over and over again. I once received over a hundred copies of the same message from different *TidBITS* readers, all of whom forwarded it to me because it raised some serious questions about an article I had written. I had actually seen the message before publishing the article, but failed to mention that fact within the article itself, so I shouldn't have been the slightest bit upset with any of the individuals who tried to warn me about a potentially bad situation. Nonetheless, I was a bit peeved at having to deal with over a hundred of these messages, so I decided to write a single reply that was sufficiently generic, and then to send it back to each person. That allowed me to stay pleasant, whereas if I had had to reply to each message individually, by the end I would undoubtedly have been writing "You're wrong—and probably stupid. -Adam." That's not a particularly nice way to respond to someone who was just trying to help, and it seldom helps to be testy.

Bill: I've got a specific example. Norman is a long-standing member of the Politics discussion list, to which I've belonged on-and-off since, oh, 1988 or 1989. Norman's politics are almost always diametrically op- posed to mine, and he's extraordinarily outspoken about them—sometimes to the point of offending many list members. He can be abrasive, and more than a few people have called him obnoxious.

Adam: He sounds like real winner.

Bill: Well, early in my career on Politics, he and I got into a nice little row over something I can't even remember anymore. It was extraordinarily heated online, flames going back and forth like there was no tomorrow. Neither of us was especially civil. So you can imagine my surprise when the phone rang one day, and there at the other end of the line was Norman.

We talked some, and he was surprisingly pleasant. We talked about the car I was about to buy, life in general, a bit of political stuff, things like that. Although I still disagreed with him strongly, I found it hard to dislike him after that.

Basically (as later correspondence with him suggested), I think he just likes to argue. The volatile arguments on the Politics list are fun for him. Not that he doesn't believe what he's saying, he does; but he gets a blast out of intense argument, and writes accordingly. It's his Internet personality.

Adam: Of course, these examples prove nothing, since it's equally common for people to interact better remotely than they do in person. There have been a number of occasions on which I've conversed quite happily with someone via email, and then, when the time came to meet them, found that I wasn't all that fond of them. Usually, the meeting also dampened later email conversations, since it's difficult to communicate with someone you've met without recalling your impressions of that meeting.

In one respect, I like this facet of Internet communication more than any other, because it says that when we communicate purely on a conscious, intellectual level, we can often do so far better than when we're staring into each other's faces. I see the Internet as important not because of the information available on it, but because of the ways it opens channels of communication between people who would never otherwise talk due to barriers of language, geography, religion, or even philosophy.

It's interesting, because people can find almost any excuse to avoid talking to one another in person, whereas online you can't pry them apart with an electronic crowbar. Although I won't pretend that talking on the Internet could solve the world's problems, the model of communication where anyone can say anything and is allotted attention commensurate with the coherence and interest of the message, is one I would love to see more of in the world.

Bill: Net personalities are part of life on the Internet, and you get used to them. Eventually, you begin to learn where you can expect to find certain kinds of personalities, much in the way that you learn which bars to visit on a Saturday night to find your kind of crowd.

The personalities you'll encounter will be many and varied. People can be pretty much anything they want to be on the Net. Superheroes are favorites, along with many other fictional characters. Some people even choose the names of real, more famous people. This, of course, raises a little question. If you're chatting on the Fly Fishing channel on IRC, and suddenly "Madonna" signs on, how do you know it's not… well, it couldn't really be… Nah.

Could it?

Celebrities

Adam: I once watched a multi-part PBS television series called "Fame in the Twentieth Century." It used fabulous old photographs, newspapers, and newsreel footage to make the point that although initially an event might give someone fleeting fame, only the mass media could provide lasting fame. In the process of working its way through each decade of the twentieth century, the show examined the lives of people like Al Capone, who was addicted to his media-reflected fame, Charles Lindbergh, who tried to escape it, only to become all the more famous for attempting to avoid the spotlight, and even Madonna, whose fame is the result of being one of the most skilled self-promoters in the world today.

How does this all apply to the Internet? I'm not completely certain, except to note that the concept of fame seems to translate directly to the Internet as another medium of information exchange. The icons of popular culture are starting to appear in various ways on the Internet, which is an interesting process to note in its own right, since that which makes one popular in *People* very well may turn you into a laughingstock on the Internet. This is not to imply that the Internet rejects all the heroes of popular culture, or that there are no home-grown Internet legends. Both traditional celebrities and Internet celebrities exist on the nets, but the Internet being what it is, you can never quite predict how people will react to the arrival of a celebrity.

```
Bill: There's no telling how many celebrities are lurking on the
Internet. Some say Harry Anderson of Night Court fame is out there some-
where on the Internet, possibly reading rec.arts.magic. Rush Limbaugh is
on CompuServe, and Tom Clancy supposedly is connected through America
Online. Of course, if Harry Anderson has an America Online account, does
that mean he uses the Internet, or is even aware that he can send mail to
it? Not necessarily.
```

```
It's sort of interesting, seeing who chooses to make him- or herself
known. You generally won't find big-name mass-appeal celebrities, but you
can find many, many people who would be considered celebrities in certain
circles. Game designers and writers can often be found getting feedback
on the Internet by mingling with the people who buy and play their games.
I wouldn't know them if I tripped over them, but they're well known in
the gaming community. On the Mac newsgroups, asking a question about a
program will often bring you an answer from its author.
```

Adam: While some people have brought their fame to the Internet, there are a number of people whose fame has yet to spread beyond the Internet. In the Macintosh world of the nets, one of the most famous net denizens, John Norstad, hails from Northwestern University. Although he no longer works on it except when events require him to, John is best known for his free anti-virus program called Disinfectant. John created Disinfectant in response to early Macintosh viruses (evil little programs designed to reproduce them-selves within other files on your computer, making you feel unclean, and sometimes causing damage in the process) and continued to improve it over the years. It has become a commercial-quality piece of software, and being free, is something that I recommend that every Macintosh user have and use periodically.

More recently, John turned his attention to his current project, a Macintosh program called NewsWatcher that enables Macintosh users with full Internet access to read and reply to messages on Usenet, which is home to the many thousands of newsgroups, or discussion lists, on almost every imaginable topic. NewsWatcher had actually been started, and then dropped, by Steve Falkenburg, a programmer from Apple. John picked up the program from Steve and enhanced it significantly, turning it into what I feel is the best of the Internet newsreaders on the Macintosh. Once again, NewsWatcher remains completely free to users everywhere, and although he retains final control over what goes in, John has had help from numerous people on the nets. In essence, then, NewsWatcher has become a community project, something to which any programmer can contribute and which any Macintosh user connected to the Internet can use and enjoy.

In real life, John works at Northwestern University, so I asked him via email just why he works on projects like Disinfectant and NewsWatcher and if he minds being an Internet celebrity. I'll let him answer those questions in his own words.

John Norstad: That's a hard question, and I get asked it a lot. I'll try to give a serious answer, at the risk of being pretentious.

I am passionate about free software. For me, developing free software in my spare time is more than just a hobby. I'm also passionate about the Mac. It's so incredibly clear to me that the Mac is the very best computer anywhere, period. I don't understand why there's any controversy at all about this. I'm also passionate about the revolutionary potential of the Internet, and the Mac's role on the Internet. It has certainly changed my life, and with the right software and services and access, it can change other people's lives, too.

The best kind of programming is an act of artistic creation. Truly great programs are works of art. They have beauty and elegance and truth and purity. They are much, much more than just a random collection of features. Writing this kind of program is much, much more than just "software engineering."

For me, the only way to even attempt to create this kind of software is to have total freedom and complete control over the entire development process. My best programs are the ones I've written on my own time, not as official projects as part of my job.

I've discovered over the 30 years I've been a programmer that as soon as money is involved in any way with the software I write, I in some way lose some significant amount of control over the software. By developing free software, I retain complete control. I don't have to respond to market pressures, or to often-misguided customer complaints and requests, or to lawyers or marketing people, or to bosses, or to magazine reviewers, or to shipping deadlines, or to financial pressures, or to anyone or anything else. If you don't like one of my free programs, tough. I'll give you double your money back.

There's no question that the extent to which my programs are good and even begin to approach being in any sense the works of art I want them to be is because of this freedom.

In short, "free" software = "freedom" for the software creator. For me, this freedom is what it's all about. Sure, I'd like to be rich, but I've got enough money to support my family well, and it's more important to have the freedom.

Programming as an act of creation is an addiction. The only reason I write Mac programs is because of this urge to create. I don't do it because my bosses tell me to do it, or for money, or as a public service, or for fame. I do it to feed the monkey on my back.

This is nothing new or startling or unique. Any good programmer who really cares about his or her work will tell you much the same thing.

I'm very fortunate to find myself in a working environment that makes this all possible. I have a good job with good pay, and Northwestern gives me a very large amount of control over my work and encourages and supports my independent projects like Disinfectant and NewsWatcher. Few people are so lucky.

Adam: And as far as being a celebrity?

John Norstad: It's very much a mixed blessing.

I get way too much mail and way too many phone calls. Way too many people want me to do way too many things. Email is sometimes like a Chinese water torture. I have to keep up with it every day, or I get hopelessly behind. If I leave town for three days or a week, when I get back it takes a whole day or two just to get caught up. I sometimes have to be ruthless and quite rude when I reject requests for help or requests to speak or requests for interviews or requests for whatever. This is unpleasant, because I don't like being nasty to people.

But overall, becoming a minor "celebrity" in the Mac world (a somewhat larger than average fish in a rather small pond) has been very pleasant. The very best thing that has happened is that it has given me the opportunity to become friends and colleagues with some of the best Mac programmers in the world. It's also very pleasant to have people recognize and appreciate my work. I really enjoy getting simple thank you notes via email and postcards from all over the world and having strangers come up to me and thank me at conferences and all that sort of thing.

Awards are nice, too. I went to San Francisco to receive the MacUser Editors' Choice John J. Anderson Distinguished Achievement award. It was a very fancy black tie affair. I got to give a short speech, and I brought home an incredibly large and beautiful Eddy statue. This was definitely the thrill of a lifetime.

Finally, I have to admit that my "celebrity" status is pretty cheap, and is entirely due to being lucky enough to have written Disinfectant in the late 1980s, just when the virus problem was becoming more serious and seriously over-hyped by the press. Sure, it's a very good program, and I'm a very good programmer, and viruses are a serious problem, and my program is a serious and successful attempt to deal with the problem, but it's still just one program, and I'm still just one programmer. There are many, many developers in the Mac world who have done much more work and much better work and much more significant work and are much smarter than I am, but who haven't gotten anywhere near the same recognition as I have.

Finding Your Niche

Adam: The first task that faces any Internet newcomer, or *newbie*, in Internet parlance, is finding the group of people with whom you want to hang out. This of course assumes that you're not an antisocial hermit who doesn't want to have anything to do with other people. Don't become discouraged if it takes you some time to find just the right place. If you were anything like me, it took years during adolescence to do the same thing in real life, and I can guarantee that it won't take that long on the Internet.

As with anything on the Internet (and in real life, for that matter), many ways of finding your future group of friends exist. They range from extremely low-tech methods, such as asking someone in person or looking in a book, to the high-tech methods of running complicated searches in WAIS databases.

```
Bill: One of my main social groups on the Internet is the Politics list,
a group devoted to the discussion of current events, political theory,
and all those other government-related topics that make you unpopular at
parties.
```

Adam: If the conversation turns to education reform in Nicaragua, you know it's not going to be one of those parties where people balance spoons on their noses.

```
Bill: Well… don't be too sure. I wound up as part of the Politics crowd
through a rather complicated series of events. Around this time in my
college career, I had signed up for a Political Science minor, and I was
quite fascinated with much of what I was learning. It's been so long now
that I don't remember the exact details, but one of the various people who
I'd met through entirely different channels on the Internet told me about
the Politics list. He wasn't subscribed to it, but he thought it might
interest me, and pointed me in the right direction. I signed up, and I've
been there every since. In fact, I am now a Supreme Court Justice.
```

Adam: You are not. You're lying.

```
Bill: Am too! Within the context of the Politics list, anyway. There are
three Supreme Court Justices, and I'm one of them.
```

Adam: Okay, say I wanted a cabinet position. How would I find the Politics list?

```
Bill: Well, I can't be sure you'd be offered one, but let's say you are
interested in Politics anyway, and you decide to look around for it. If
you don't know where to look—or even what you're looking for—how can
you hope to find it in the vast sea of Internet resources?
```

```
Well fortunately, the LISTSERV programs that run many of the mailing lists
themselves are pretty helpful. They maintain a complete list of lists,
called (not surprisingly) LISTSERV Lists. You can retrieve this list fairly
easily from any LISTSERV, such as listserv@ricevm1.rice.edu, by sending
email to it with the words "LIST GLOBAL" in the body of your message.
```

Adam: If you don't want to keep your own copy of the list of mailing lists, but do want to be able to get at it when you need it, you can find it in numerous places online. Beware that it's a lot of data, so the files are large and sometimes unwieldy. One place that I like to look for this sort of thing is in the newsgroup, **news.lists**, which contains periodically updated lists of lots of useful information, along with some utter trivia such as the most prolific Usenet poster of the month (see figure 5.5).

```
┌────────────────────────── news.lists ──────────────────────────┐
│ ▤                                                            ▣   │
│ -   Changes to List of Active Newsgroups, Part I            ▲   │
│ -   Changes to List of Active Newsgroups, Part II              │
│ -   Changes to Mailing Lists Available in Usenet              │
│ -   Changes to Alternative Newsgroup Hierarchies, Part I      │
│ -   Changes to Alternative Newsgroup Hierarchies, Part II     │
│ -   Changes to How to Construct the Mailpaths File            │
│ -   Changes to List of Moderators for Usenet                 │
│ -   Publicly Accessible Mailing Lists, Part 4/6              │
│ -   List of Periodic Informational Postings, Part 1/7        │
│ -   List of Periodic Informational Postings, Part 2/7        │
│ -   List of Periodic Informational Postings, Part 6/7        │
│ -   List of Periodic Informational Postings, Part 7/7        │
│ -   Changes to List of Periodic Informational Postings       │
│ -   List of Periodic Informational Postings, Part 3/7        │
│ -   List of Periodic Informational Postings, Part 4/7        │
│ -   List of Periodic Informational Postings, Part 5/7        │
│ -   Known Geographic Distributions                           │
│ -   Public Organizational & Logical Network Distributions    │
│ -   News Administration Macros for Geographic Distributions  │
│ -   Known University Distributions                           │
│ -   Publicly Accessible Mailing Lists, Part 1/8             │
│ -   Publicly Accessible Mailing Lists, Part 2/8             │
│ -   Publicly Accessible Mailing Lists, Part 3/8             │
│ -   Publicly Accessible Mailing Lists, Part 4/8             │
│ -   Publicly Accessible Mailing Lists, Part 5/8             │
│ -   Publicly Accessible Mailing Lists, Part 6/8             │
│ -   Publicly Accessible Mailing Lists, Part 7/8             │
│ -   Publicly Accessible Mailing Lists, Part 8/8             │
│ -   Sites honoring invalid newsgroups (by site)             │
│ -   Sites honoring invalid newsgroups (by group)            │
│ -   Articles rejected at news.uu.net during the past week   │
│ -   Top 25 News Submitters by User by Kbytes for the last 2 weeks │
│ -   Top 25 News Submitters by User by number of articles for the last 2 weeks │
│ -   Top 25 News Submitters by Site by Kbytes for the last 2 weeks │
│ -   Top 25 News Submitters by Site by number of articles for the last 2 weeks │
│ -   Top 25 News Groups for the last 2 weeks                 ▼   │
│ -   Total traffic through uunet for the last 2 weeks        ▣   │
└─────────────────────────────────────────────────────────────────┘
```

Figure 5.5   *Lists, lists, lists; we've got lists.*

Adam: As you can see, there are a number of postings for the "Publicly Accessible Mailing Lists." That's because the entire list is too large to put in a single message. Just download all of the messages if you want to keep your own copy for searching, but remember that the details change frequently. I also like searching the entire list of groups via the Web, at this site:

```
http://alpha.acast.nova.edu/listserv.html
```

Lurking

Adam: The next trick, once you've found a group that interests you, is learning how to assimilate without seriously offending your new-found acquaintances. The first thing most people do, or at least should do, is lurk. Don't worry, we're not suggesting that you spend your spare time in dark alleyways, frightening passersby. On the Internet, lurking is an innocuous occupation practiced by the vast majority of Internet users. It simply means that you read and observe the goings-on without actually contributing to the group. Think of the old adage about how children should be seen and not heard. On the Internet, no one even sees the lurkers, and there's nothing to hear from a lurker, either.

Bill: Let's take a newsgroup on which I lurk as an example. The group **comp.sys.powerpc** is devoted to discussion of the PowerPC machines from IBM and Apple. People talk about everything from the number of transis-tors on the chip to the speeds we can expect from it in the next year to the reasons it may or may not wipe the floor with its Intel competition. Much of this information and conversation is extremely technical, far more technical than I am. I can understand much of it, but I sure don't know enough to contribute intelligently to the conversation. So I just sit there and read and soak it in—the possibilities offered by these new machines interest me, but I don't know enough about them to post con-structively.

Adam: I do much the same thing that Bill does, with a list called Newton-L that comes from **listserv@dartmouth.edu**. I think some of the Newton technology represents the future of computing in terms of intelligent assistance, so I like to stay up to date on what people say about the MessagePad.

Introducing Yourself

Adam: Once you do decide to participate in the discussions (and we strongly recommend that you do so when you feel you have something useful to add), be careful at first, since people are often judged on first impressions on the Internet. If you act as though you're Zeus' gift to the nets, people will quite correctly consider you to be a serious jerk. I suppose that if "serious jerk" describes you well, you might want to stick with that tone in your posts, but if you want anyone to listen to you and respond in a thoughtful and intelligent manner, you should pick up a little humility at the 7-Eleven.

Bill: And some beef jerky while you're at it.

Adam: Bill, you're a vegetarian.

Bill: I'm not positive that beef jerky contains animal products.

Adam: Good point—do vegetarians eat petrochemicals? In general, discussion lists are little worlds all to themselves, so what you've done or said in one group generally won't be known in another. This can be both good and bad—if you were a major contributor to one group and move to another, your reputation probably will neither precede, nor follow you. You must prove yourself all over again, although I'd hope that you would know how to go about it more quickly the second time. However, if you managed to become known as a major drip on one list, you can move to another and enjoy a clean slate.

One of the Gang

Adam: We've talked about the processes of finding the group of people with whom you want to hang out, how not to offend them immediately—by lurking and watching what goes on, and some basics about introducing yourself to the list. But what about the majority of the time you spend on the list? How do you assimilate into the day-to-day conversations that ebb and flow across the wires? How do you become one of the gang, and how do you ascend to a chair on the front porch from which you can sit and spit while trading tall tales? Hopefully, it's mostly a matter of being your normal friendly self, but here are a few other things to consider.

```
Bill:  The means of becoming accepted in your group varies quite a bit. I
believe my acceptance into a social group called the Pink Iguana Tavern
began the day I started a pie fight. It began simply enough—I chose a
safe target, the woman who had introduced me to the group in the first
place. I knew that planting a virtual pie in her face wouldn't upset her
greatly, so she was my target. Of course, she had other friends present
on Relay (the precursor to Internet Relay Chat, the interactive chatting
part of the Internet) that night, and one of them, Frank, I think, sprang
to her defense by informing me that I had just received a banana cream
pie pressed firmly against my face. Somebody else who had probably been
just looking for an excuse to get Frank leapt to my defense, and soon the
proprietor had wheeled in the virtual dessert cart. The rest is history.
```

Adam: Sounds virtually messy.

```
Bill: Yes, but virtually tasty too. Of course, not every group will ac-
cept you on the basis of your written slapstick skills.
```

Adam: Since many of the discussion lists and Internet groups exchange useful—at least to the participants—information, making yourself useful always speeds the assimilation process. The more I learn about the business world, the more I realize it's not so much what you know, it's who you know. On the Internet, however, that doesn't fly. No one gives a hoot who you know, but if your knowledge is valuable to the members of the group, they appreciate it.

```
Bill: It is usually best to let others decide whether your knowledge is
valuable to the members of the group, rather than deciding yourself, if
you truly want to get along with them.
```

Adam: You must still dole out your knowledge with the online equivalent of a smile, since no one likes a know-it-all in the real world or on the Internet, even if you do. Know it all, that is.

I've tried to practice what I'm preaching here on the main groups in which I participate currently, the Info-Mac Digest and the **comp.sys.mac.comm** newsgroup. The Info-Mac Digest carries general Macintosh discussions, and since I know that there are plenty of knowledgeable and helpful folks on the list, I don't attempt to answer every question to which I happen to know the answer. However, if a question comes up in one of my fields of expertise, such as MacTCP connections to the Internet, Nisus (the word processor I use), recent events in the industry, or certain PowerBook issues, I try to jump in and help out. Much of the research I do for articles in *TidBITS* aids me in this process, so even if I decide not to write an article about something, I often share the knowledge I picked up on Info-Mac. As I see it, if I know an answer that no one else on the group is likely to know, it's my duty to my friends to pass on that bit of information.

Signal-to-Noise

Adam: One of the reasons for the proliferation of Usenet newsgroups is that they tend to split into much smaller groups to bring the signal-to-noise ratio back into line.

Bill: Whack! Two minute penalty for jargon.

Adam: Humph. Let me explain, will you? *Signal-to-noise* is a phrase that probably comes from a field like electrical engineering or something, but it's quite simple with regard to information on the Internet. *Signal* is information that interests you, and *noise* is information that you would prefer never darkened your monitor. The concept applies well to many fields—for instance, in terms of music, for me, Leonard Cohen is signal, whereas Kate Bush is noise.

Bill: Hey!

Adam: Knew that would get a rise out of you. Note that I didn't say that signal was information that was generally interesting, since it's not. Signal is information that interests you, and possibly no one else. What interests Bill may bore me stiff, and vice versa. That's why we participate in different groups on the Internet. But, in fact, any group talks about a large number of different topics, and as an individual, you may find yourself utterly uninterested in most of them. That's fine—there's no one checking up on you to see if you read all the messages in a group.

Of course, if you have a technical bent, you'll consider any socializing to be noise, since it doesn't convey useful information for you. And, for the socialites (or is it socialists?), the socializing might be all you want from life.

Bill: The concept of signal-to-noise doesn't apply everywhere, of course. You need a focus of some kind in order for noise to interfere with it. The Pink Iguana Tavern, for instance, was entirely a social group—everything we talked about could be considered signal. Or noise, if you prefer. But nothing was outside the intended topic of discussion, since there wasn't one.

Interactive Internet

Adam: OK, here comes a fun section.

Bill: Yes, this one should really irritate our production folks. That's great fun. "Wow," I'll say, "how can we ever make something like this look good?" "Don't worry about it," Adam will respond. "That's why Hayden has production people!" Then we attempt to laugh in a sinister manner, like the late Mr. Vincent Price would.

Adam: Most people communicate on the Internet through email or Usenet postings. These are roughly analogous to letters and telegrams—the sender sends when she's ready, and the recipient collects the mail when he's ready. Eventually, the process reverses and then repeats itself, and thus is a conversation born.

Bill: If you're better about writing your mail than I am, anyway. But there are other ways to communicate and interact on the Internet that involve live, real-time conversations. This is analogous to the telephone or, to be more specific, the party line. You actual carry on your conversations with people as you sit at your terminal, typing what you want to send as you read what other people are saying to you. If it sounds confusing, just wait a few paragraphs and all should become clear.

Adam: First, we plan to visit an area—called a "channel"—on IRC, which stands for *Internet Relay Chat*. We're not going to settle for attempting to tell you about IRC; we'll let the people who hang out there tell you themselves.

Bill: And then we'll pay a quick visit to FurryMUCK, an example of a multi-user role-playing environment where everyone pretends to be anthropomorphized animals. Except me, of course. I'm a six-foot tall anthropomorphic pickle.

Adam: Sigh, leave it to me to find the one guy who can't even act weird in synch with everyone else.

Bill: Damn straight.

Adam: Bear in mind that we've edited *very* heavily. There was far too much material to include here; we've only taken excerpts, and even those were edited for content and appearance.

Bill: But in some sense, our editing better retains the proper flavor of the discussions than the original transcripts do. After you've spent some time on IRC or on a MUD, your brain filters out much of the extraneous garbage that we've filtered for you here, and starts putting together fragments of conversation into a coherent whole.

Adam: Let's get started with our first stop on IRC, the #superguy channel.

IRC—#superguy

Bill: I suppose that in this section, since I actually know everyone who participates, I should provide a cheat sheet, so our readers know which person matches to which nickname.

Adam: Yeah, I could have used that to begin with.

Bill: Okay, **Rubicon** is Eric Burns, **Superuser** is Bill Paul (commonly known as the Man with Two First Names), and **the_Swede** is Gary Olson. You'll see us refer to each other by all these names and by others in this conversation.

Adam: Keep in mind, folks, that Bill knows these people pretty well. As a result, a lot of the silliness is the product of years of practice.

Bill: And beer.

Adam: I guess. First, let's take a picture so you can see what's happening.

```
*** Server:    AdamEngst has joined channel #superguy

*** Server:    BillDcksn has joined channel #superguy

<BillDcksn>    All right, everybody, Adam's going to switch into
               greyscale and take a snapshot.

<AdamEngst>    Smile for the snapshot...

<the_Swede>    heh...

<Superuser>    Won't that hurt?

<the_Swede>    my, i feel so... grey...

  <Rubicon>    Cheese!!!!!!!!!! <Bill's, that is>

<the_Swede>    beeeer!

<Superuser>    Prozac!!!
```

Bill: In the ensuing pandemonium, we did manage to take a snapshot. Notice the nice interface in Homer, and the fact that you can even see pictures for some of us (see figure 5.6).

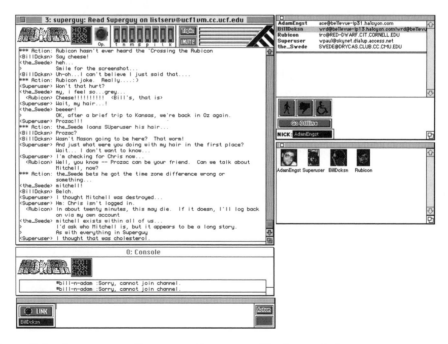

Figure 5.6   *Superguy authors; yes, they are really that weird.*

```
<AdamEngst>    OK, after a brief trip to Kansas, we're back in Oz
               again.
<Superuser>    Wait, my hair...!
*** Action:    the_Swede loans Superuser his hair...
<Superuser>    And just what were you doing with my hair in the first
               place? Wait... I don't want to know...
  <Rubicon>    Well, you know — Prozac can be your friend.
<Superuser>    I thought that was cholesterol.
<BillDcksn>    So didn't we have some interview questions or something?
<AdamEngst>    OK, first question - perhaps stupid. Do you get anything
               "productive" done on IRC? Or is email more useful?
               Obviously it depends on your definition of productive.
<the_Swede>    what... this isn't productive?
<Superuser>    Well, we collaborate a lot on Superguy writing, and it's
               easier to discuss things live than via mail.
  <Rubicon>    Productive... well, as a co-writer of Superguy, I'd have
               to say yes. It's a place where I can contact other of my
               Superguy authors and discuss upcoming events and the
               like.
<the_Swede>    the only time i recall ever doing something productive
               here is while the bills and i were working on a
               storyline back in december...
<Superuser>    In case you haven't guessed, we don't use IRC for work
               purposes.
<the_Swede>    i don't have net access at work, as they expect me to do
               actual work or something...
<Superuser>    The fiends.
<BillDcksn>    Well, unless we can turn Superguy into a meal ticket...
<Superuser>    I just had a meal, thank you...
  <Rubicon>    Well — I can list some 'practical' applications.
<Superuser>    Go ahead: I dare you.
  <Rubicon>    In my guise as a mild-mannered English Lit type person,
               I have had actual scholarly discourse on here — and
               therefore I have found productive use of IRC. Nah nah
               nah
```

Bill: Eric's comment touched off a massive dose of silliness that has
been edited out for brevity. However, you can find much more of its kind
in *Internet Explorer Kit for Macintosh*, where this very conversation is
reproduced in all of its glory.

Adam: Well, most of its glory, anyway. We next tried to get back onto an interview question...

      `<BillDcksn>`   `Okay, guys, this is for Adam's benefit. And don't try to lie, because I know the answer:`

      `<the_Swede>`   `awww... telling the truth's no fun...`

      `<Superuser>`   `No, you can't borrow any money.`

      `<Rubicon>`   `So what's the next question, o Writer-types? :)`

      `<BillDcksn>`   `Would you say your electronic persona, in an environment like IRC, is different from your real-life persona?`

      `<Superuser>`   `What real-life persona...`

      `<BillDcksn>`   `Oooooo, good answer :)`

      `<Superuser>`   `Hell™, I barely have a real-life, let alone a persona...`

Adam: Is Hell trademarked?

Bill: `In the Superguy universe, Hell™ is actually a corporation, and yes, the name is trademarked. The main offices are in Fong's Enchilada Emporium, a Mexican restaurant staffed by the souls of the damned.`

Adam: Why is it that every time I ask you a question about Superguy, I wish I hadn't?

      `<the_Swede>`   `in IRC? not really... i'm not on often enough for that... on the muck, yes...`

      `<Rubicon>`   `Ooo... tough question...`

      `<Superuser>`   `Dowh!`

      `<the_Swede>`   `okey dokey...:)`

      `<Rubicon>`   `I would say my electronic persona is very like my real persona — my friends who I have met online and then met in life say I'm a lot like who I say I am on the net :)`

      `<Superuser>`   `Except that in real-life, Eric looks like a hot-dog vendor. :)`

      `<BillDcksn>`   `Two points!`

      `<the_Swede>`   `or, without his beard, like one of the super mario brothers...`

      `<Rubicon>`   `Hey, Bill — they know what I look like. I'm on their screen, remember?`

      `<BillDcksn>`   `Adopts an interviewer persona. "So then, would you say that people sign onto IRC to insult each other?"`

```
<Superuser>    %^&^#&*(%*(O^*!

<the_Swede>    *^(&*^%%$#%&*(%*&%^&^$&#^!

<AdamEngst>    Seems the answer is yes.

<the_Swede>    umm... well, actually, not really...

<Superuser>    Hmm... you are going to edit all this before putting it
               into the book, yes?

<AdamEngst>    Maybe. They're going to like the insulting parts of the
               book, Bill.

<Superuser>    I thought we were the insulting parts of the book.

<the_Swede>    hey, readers! your mothers dress you funny!
```

Adam: Hmm, on that note, let's move on to another form of live inter-personal interaction on the Internet.

MUCKing with the Furries

Bill: Adam and I are now going to enter a different sort of interactive setting, known as a MU*.

Adam: A what?

Bill: A MU*. The asterisk is a wildcard, allowing the term to stand for MUD, MUCK, MUSH, or whatever the latest variety is. MUDs were the first of this set of programs, and the term stands for Multi-User Dungeon or Multi-User Dimension, depending on who you're talking to and perhaps on the MUD in question.

Adam: This sounds like a different type of IRC. Similar idea, correct?

Bill: Well, on a basic level, yes. It's a program that enables numerous people on the Internet all to interact with each other in real time. But MUDs and their ilk open up a whole new realm of possibilities.

Adam: I've heard that MUDs are an environment of sorts, in which you can move about and role-play, much like a game.

Bill: Yes, but in many of them the role-playing is much more like theatre than like a game of Acuras & Attorneys.

Adam: Is that a real game?

Bill: Good lord, no.

Adam: Phew!

Bill: A MUD has another important feature—it is user-modifiable. If you join a MUD and create a character, and the owners of the MUD permit it, you can build your own home and describe it. Other characters (and, by proxy, their players) can then visit and explore your home, experiencing it as you have defined it. There is a very real sense of space on a MUD.

Adam: That's difficult to wrap the mind around. What do you mean by the character's home? The character is just an artificial construct, right?

Bill: Not if you're a good enough actor. But I realize this can be confusing to talk about, so I'm not going to try to explain it further. It would be far better simply to show you.

We'll visit a MUCK known as FurryMUCK. The concept is a bit interesting: the characters are all anthropomorphized animals, creatures known as "furries."

Adam: Oh, great... you're going to introduce me to something I don't understand, using as an example, something else I don't understand.

Bill: Yup! Brace yourself... we're going to jump right into an interesting bit of the conversation we had while we were visiting, in which our hosts discussed the differences they see between MUDs and IRC.

```
          ____  '                  _ _ _   _     _  _   ,
         /   '              ' ) ) ) ' ) / / )  ) ' ) /
     ,-/-, . . __  __ __  , / / /  / / /     / -<
    (_/   (_/_/ (_/ (_/ (_/ / ' (_  (_/ (_/  /   )
                        /
                        '
```

AdamEngst says, "We've just spent some time on IRC - how do you
                think the socializing here is different? Do you
                use IRC at all?"

Mer'rark walks in from Sable Street.

Mer'rark says, "Slice was telling me there's some guys writing a
                book about this place?"

FoxTrot yaps, "Here it is a little different then IRC because
                people have characters they use to express
                themselves."

Triggur whickers, "This environment is much richer than IRC. Less
                artificial."

ErmaFelna says, "There's more of a sense of *place* here... you
                can move around, have a distinct concept of
                rooms and objects... this is much more of a game
                as well."

Dekhyr says, "Never been on IRC. Or any 'social MUD' for that
                matter, except this one. And this one only two
                weeks ago. Used to play hack-n-slash MUDs. Got
                bored of it. Socializing this way for some

> reason seems to be better than the pot-luck I
> tend to get in RL."

FoxTrot yaps, "Also, IRC is highly topic oriented, here, you can
go somewhere and the topic will change a lot."

Kimiko nods at FoxTrot.

ErmaFelna says, "This place is much more flexible than IRC; it's
a lot easier for the players to modify the
general environment. Anyone can add new commands
for people to use, or reprogram portions of the
setup. I've written programs to do anything from
making a lock that only lets the people inside
choose who can come in, to creating an object
that can be used as a container."

Dekhyr says, "Probably the thing I like about Furry most of all
is that you *need* a kind of extroverted imagination to even play a furry in the first place."

Adam: As it happens, we visited FurryMUCK very shortly after a rather unflattering
description of the place appeared in *Wired* magazine. Our hosts took the opportunity,
while talking to us, to rebut the article, fairly convincingly. A little bit of that conversation:

AdamEngst says, "What do furries generally think about the outside view of MUDs and this MUCK in specific? Is
that view unrealistic or off-base?"

Triggur whickers, "Uhhhh... 'too kyoot' is a common reaction :)
lots of outsiders think this place is too sticky
sweet, especially from a MUD standpoint."

FoxTrot yaps, "They are quite often biased towards one activity,
as WIRED illustrates."

Dekhyr says, "I think everyone latches on to the erotic sector of
MUCK. Too emotionally charged."

Dekhyr says, "Some people couldn't imagine playing a MUD. They
feel it's a waste of time."

Lynx purrs, "Dunno, you tell me, what's the outside view of MUDs
and MUCKs?"

AdamEngst says, "Well, the addictive nature of MUDs is certainly
mentioned a lot."

Kimiko nods, they ARE addictive... worlds can be created here...

Lynx nods. This is true. Stay away, AdamEngst, you'll find your
free time slipping away...

ErmaFelna says, "This particular MUCK has a very general theme,
which means that things tend to be extremely
free-form. What big events do happen tend to be

```
                        very fast versions of co-operative story-tell-
                        ing, with a lot of the same difficulties: one
                        person can Deus Ex Machina the plotline and ruin
                        it for everyone else."
Pickle declares, "Erma, is there a set of rules to guide things
                        like that?"
ErmaFelna says, "Rules? Not really... just politesse and some
                        general guidelines."
Triggur whickers, "thank GOD there's no rules :)"
Kratsminsch says, "I've also used the MUCK to contact experts in
                        certain fields, when I got lost trying to fix
                        something RL."
Kimiko does that too! (have a computer Q? @shout for an answer!)
Bill: And lastly, in one of my favorite moments, we got to see
that old-timers like to berate the newcomers on MUDs, just like
in real life:
Pickle declares, "How long has Furry been around?"
ErmaFelna says, "It's been around a little over three years, now.
                        Of course, some of us have been MUDding since
                        before Furry existed."  She nods over to Lynx.
Lynx mumbles something about how when HE was a kit, we had to
                        telnet 12 miles uphill through thick snow and
                        line noise to get to a MUD, and then we
                        telnetted 12 miles back the other way, also
                        uphill, to get a response back, and we LYKED yt.
Bill: And on that note, I think it's time to move on.
```

Browsing the Second-Hand Bookstore of the Internet

Adam: The Internet is many things to many people, but when we were trying to think about how to express the range of information available on the Internet, all we could think of was a second-hand bookstore.

```
Bill: That's because in a second-hand bookstore, you're likely to wander
around, gazing aimlessly at the books until something catches your eye,
at which point you'll pick it up and browse through it.
```

Adam: And even if you're looking for something about cooking, say, you don't go to a second-hand bookstore with a specific idea of what you want to buy. You go thinking,

"Maybe I'll buy a cookbook today." If you want Julia Child's *The Way to Cook* specifically, you'll go to a fancy new bookstore.

```
Bill: We're going to wander aimlessly on the Internet for a while, seeing
what we may see.
```

Adam: And then we'll look for some general categories of information, just so you can see approximately the sorts of things that are out there. Once again, don't worry about the technical details of what we do here. Just file them away in the back of your mind, and once you've played with some of the Macintosh programs yourself, perhaps read this section again to get a feel for how people actually use the Internet.

Aimless Wandering

```
Bill: Some days you get up and realize you want to do something, but
you're not at all certain exactly what. I do, anyway. This is the sort of
day that often leads me into one of the more active parts of town, window
shopping and hanging out in bookstores, thumbing through anything that
catches my eye, or in music stores, flipping through all the compact
discs from A to Z.
```

```
While I'm looking around, I often find one or two items of interest that
I want to take home with me. I find many other things that have an inter-
esting cover or a nice store display, but which completely fail to live
up to the initial intrigue. But I never feel I've wasted my time, because
of the unexpected finds.
```

```
We're now going to take a semi-random drive through some of the informa-
tion that you can find on the Internet. At first, we're going to use a
program called Mosaic that simplifies browsing on the World Wide Web.
```

Adam: Let me explain a little bit about this World Wide Web that we're traveling on before I go much further. The World Wide Web is made up of many documents that include text, graphics, sounds, and even movies, but most importantly, these documents contain links to other documents scattered around the world. As I write this, there is no way to see a list of everything that exists on the Web.

Not only can you not see a list of all the documents on the Web, you can't even see a list of all the machines that are part of the Web. Because of this fact, numerous sites have created sets of links that collect and categorize various different types of information. You might think of these sites as live encyclopedias—as new resources appear, the people who run these encyclopedia sites check out the new resources and add them to the encyclopedia.

There are two basic groupings that I've seen in encyclopedic sites—chronological and topical. The NCSA What's New page is an example of a chronological listing—the only way you can find resources in it is to browse through them. And, if the resource you're looking for appeared before the current month, you have to switch to a different What's New page for the month in which that resource appeared. It's great for browsing and lousy for searching.

Bill: We're going to take a quick spin around the Web now, with Adam driving. Let's see if he can take us somewhere fun, shall we?

Adam: I'm starting my trip at the National Center for Supercomputing Applications, mostly because that's where their NCSA Mosaic program takes you first, by default.

Bill: Just to clarify—Mosaic is what we call a *client program*. The World Wide Web isn't a program, *per se*, though there are programs that make it perform different functions. These are called *server programs*, and their job is to offer up the Web's information using standard procedures. A client program familiar with these procedures is required in order for you, the user, to obtain and make use of the information.

Remember the description used earlier? You might think of the server software as being a dessert cart; you're not allowed to put your filthy paws on the pastries, so you need a client, a set of tongs, perhaps, to obtain that tasty éclair. Mosaic is our set of tongs. There are other tongs now available, such as MacWeb and Netscape Navigator.

Adam: Nice simile, Bill, but now I'm getting hungry. All right, I'm going to act on whim now and use a link on the NCSA Home Page to go back in time and look at the old What's New page from November. I remember some good stuff from back then.

Hmm, here's something that sounds interesting. What do you suppose the Fractal Microscope is, Bill?

Bill: No idea. How would they get a fractal onto the slide? Do you need a cover slip? If you cut a fractal in half, will both halves regenerate?

Adam: Ahem. It seems to be in some way related to a program, written by NCSA for schools, with which students can explore fractals, and thus, the art and science of mathematics. I think it runs on a supercomputer, which means that it's really fast. But for the life of me, I can't find anything that lets us play with it. That's why I wasn't a biology major at Cornell—they wouldn't let me play with the electron microscope freshman year. And now I appear to be too old to play with the Fractal Microscope.

Bill: Salescritters often use fractal programs to show off the graphics capabilities of a computer. There must be some out there for the Mac—want to find one?

Adam: Sure—we'll use WAIS for this one. I'm going to search through all of the Info-Mac

Bill: Pretty cool. Can we actually see any of these images on the Internet?

Adam: It appears so—at the Fractal Microscope server I see a link to a gallery of fractal images located in France. Going there we first see a link to the image of the guy who maintains this server. The server also claims to have animations as well as static images, but let's stick with the pictures, since animations are often quite large and will take a long time to download so we can view them (see figure 5.8).

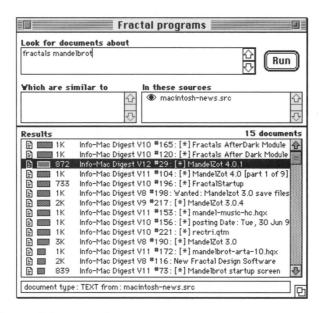

Figure 5.7   *Plenty of them out there.*

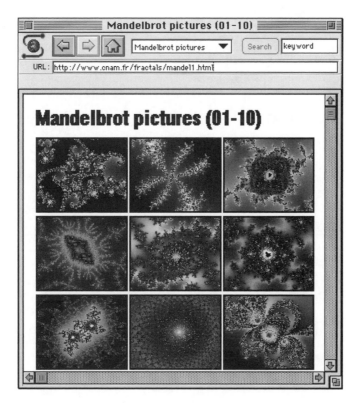

Figure 5.8   *The tenth image removed for symmetry's sake.*

Adam: Time to switch back to the What's New page and browse some more. Here's something for the online activists to get their teeth into—a server called INFACT Online.

Bill: What's that stand for?

Adam: I don't know—they don't seem to say. It appears to have something to do with an anti-tobacco campaign. Let's go there and read more about it. Yes, it is indeed true Internet activism, and their specific mission is to store information relating to the campaign to force tobacco companies to stop marketing cigarettes to children (see figure 5.9).

Figure 5.9   *Smoke. Look cool, smell bad.*

Poking around some more on this server turns up an open letter to the Internet so you can learn more about what they're trying to do and why. Also located here are some form letters that you can download, fill in, and mail to the chief executive officers of various tobacco companies. I like the logos (see figure 5.10).

Figure 5.10   *Say it ain't so, Joe.*

Bill: This server seems to be quite a bit better-organized than most. Who set this thing up?

Adam: Judging from the home page, it's maintained by a man named Tom Boutell. He's even provided a link to his own home page.

Bill: Let's go there. I'm jealous—I've always wanted my own home page.

Adam: It includes a picture of him and even a sound that says "I live in Seattle. I telecommute to New York. It's a hell of a drive."

Bill: Hey, another Seattlelite. Where does he live?

Adam: Wait a minute—here's a pointer called "Where I live." Clicking on that takes us to, hmm, looks like a site run by Xerox PARC (Palo Alto Research Center), home of many Very Smart Folks who have come up with ideas like the graphical interface for computers, which has evolved into the Macintosh and Windows interfaces.

The Xerox PARC site shows a map of the Northwest with Seattle roughly in the center, but it's not particularly detailed (see figure 5.11).

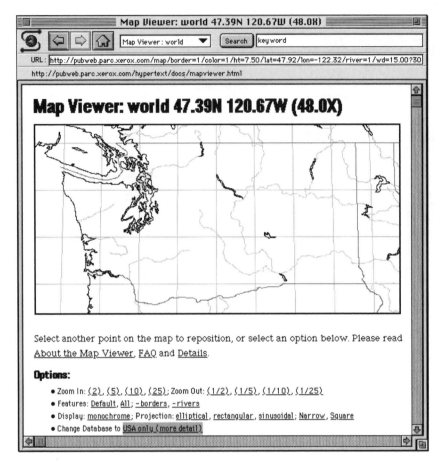

Figure 5.11   Our little corner of the world.

There seem to be various different controls for zooming in—Awk! The host machine at Xerox just went down. Blast it, just as it was getting interesting. Humph, we'll have to come back later when the machine is back up. That sort of thing happens on the Internet, and you never know whose fault it is. Thus, it's best to just assume that not everything is perfect and avoid stressing out over machines that you can't connect to.

`Bill: Such is life.`

Adam: Let's try another link from the What's New Page. I've always been a sucker for dinosaur exhibits in museums, so let's take a peek at the University of California at Berkeley Paleontology Exhibit—I've heard other people say that it's well done.

It has a nice entry page that I can't show you because the picture was too large to fit into a reasonable figure. Those of you who can, just go there yourself and browse around. Instead, let's check out the About page (see figure 5.12).

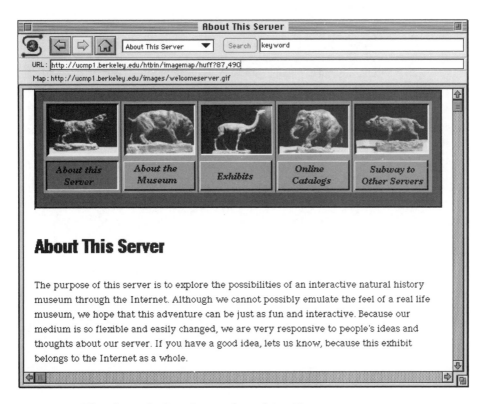

Figure 5.12 *They have the best icons of anything I've seen yet.*

Adam: In this case, they have all sorts of statistics about how many people have stopped in for a look around. In January 1994, the UC Berkeley Paleontology exhibit served 1,242,427,149 bytes of information contained in 98,401 files. That's over 1.2 gigabytes of information, and when you average it out, it comes to 3,514 files of 44,372,398 bytes (44M) per day.

Bill: That's a lot of information to send around the world on the Internet.

Adam: And it's growing all the time. In the first nine days of February 1994, the site averaged over 62 megabytes of data each day. I've heard statistics that say the traffic on the World Wide Web increases at over 300 percent per month. We're probably boring our nice readers with all these numbers, so let's go check out the exhibits (see figure 5.13).

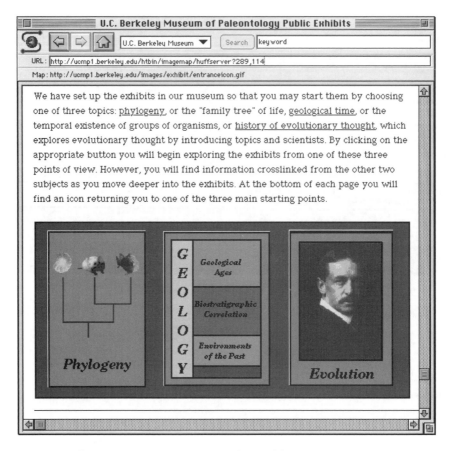

Figure 5.13   *Where to start, that's always the problem.*

Bill: Ooo, good stuff.

Adam: I see that I can quite easily spend the rest of my afternoon here, browsing through the exhibits, and all without hurting my feet. So let's stop wandering and see if we can find something specific.

I Wonder If

Adam: Although the World Wide Web is the best place for aimless wandering and for finding information on a given topic, there are other tools. In order to find out what information is available on some general topic, I sometimes turn to WAIS databases and Gopherspace.

Bill: What about Archie?

Adam: Archie also is a good tool for answering a nagging curiosity, although Archie's information generally seems to be less useful to me than what I find via WAIS and Gopher, mostly because all that Archie finds is files, and then you must transfer them to your Mac before you can find out whether there's anything useful inside. Anyway, let's start with penguins.

Bill: Penguins? You're going to use the most powerful information tool in history to search for flightless waterfowl?

Adam: Smile when you say that. Just to placate you, I'll start with an Archie search via Anarchie. It finds a good number of files (see figure 5.14) with the word "penguin" in the title, although there are number of duplicates, and most of the rest appear to be graphics files, including a scan of the cover from Berke Breathed's *Penguin Dreams and Stranger Things*.

Name	Size	Date	Zone	Host	Path
penguin-dreams.jpg	155k	10/14/93	5	ftp.sunet.se	/pub/pictures/comics/Bloom.County/penguin-dreams.jpg
penguin-dreams.txt	1k	10/14/93	5	ftp.sunet.se	/pub/pictures/comics/Bloom.County/penguin-dreams.txt
penguin-registration-nums.hqx	23k	9/18/91	1	wuarchive.wustl.edu	/systems/mac/info-mac/Old/card/penguin-registration-nums.hqx
penguin-serial-numbers.hqx	34k	6/29/91	1	wuarchive.wustl.edu	/systems/mac/info-mac/Old/card/penguin-serial-numbers.hqx
penguin-utilities.hqx	116k	6/29/91	1	wuarchive.wustl.edu	/systems/mac/info-mac/Old/card/penguin-utilities.hqx
penguin.bitmap	6k	6/3/92	1	sumex-aim.stanford.edu	/pub/exp/images/penguin.bitmap
penguin.icon	2k	7/29/88	1	emx.cc.utexas.edu	/pub/mnt/images/icons/SunView/penguin.icon
penguin.pcx	4k	4/16/92	1	hpcsos.col.hp.com	/mirrors/.hpib0/hp951x/pcx/penguin.pcx
penguin.tar.Z	591k	10/6/93	2	ftp.opsc.ucalgary.ca	/pub/blob/papers/penguin.tar.Z
penguin.txt	4k	2/20/93	1	ftp.nevada.edu	/pub/ccsd/ANTARCTICA1/penguin.txt
penguin.uss.tek.com	-	8/11/93	1	ftp.uu.net	/published/usenix/faces/penguin.uss.tek.com
penguin.uss.tek.com	-	8/21/93	1	ftp.cs.umn.edu	/pub/doc/published/usenix/faces/penguin.uss.tek.com
penguin.Z	1k	1/21/94	1	csd4.csd.uwm.edu	/pub/optimus/Graphics/animals/penguin.Z
penguin1.jpg	170k	7/30/92	5	sauna.cs.hut.fi	/pub/store/jpg/Misc/penguin1.jpg
penguin2.jpg	177k	7/30/92	5	sauna.cs.hut.fi	/pub/store/jpg/Misc/penguin2.jpg
penguins	-	4/10/93	1	ftp.luth.se	/pub/misc/lyrics/p/penguins
penguins	-	11/5/93	1	ftp.uwp.edu	/pub/music/artists/p/penguins
penguins.msa	284k	11/10/92	1	wuarchive.wustl.edu	/systems/atari/umich.edu/Games/penguins.msa
rsp-penguin.icon.Z	1k	4/17/88	5	huon.itd.adelaide.edu.au	/pub/sun-icons/rsp-penguin.icon.Z
rsp_penguin.gif	1k	1/5/93	1	ee.lbl.gov	/poskbitmaps/sun_icons/rsp_penguin.gif

Figure 5.14   *Penguin files on the Internet.*

Bill: What's that one that lives in a "lyrics" folder?

Adam: I suspect it's the lyrics to a song done by a group called The Penguins. Let's retrieve the file and take a look. Whee—it seems to be the lyrics to "Earth Angel." We'll spare you.

Bill: Kate Bush it's not.

Adam: Enough of these files, and I'm not sure that I want to delve any further in that group's lyrics. Next up is a swing through Gopherspace, using TurboGopher and searching via Veronica. Although it often makes a difference how you search for things in Veronica, in this case I think "penguin" will probably find most everything we could want. The range of penguin items in Gopherspace is much broader than the range of files that merely have the word "penguin" in their names (see figure 5.15).

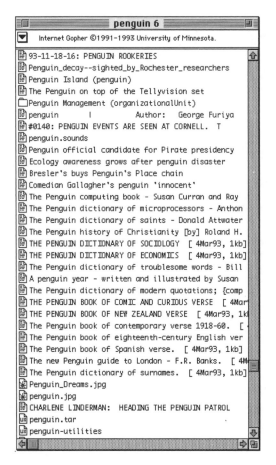

Figure 5.15   *Penguins in Gopherspace.*

Adam: Look at all those books written for penguins. You never realized that penguins were such literary birds, did you Bill?

Bill: Those are books from the publishing house called Penguin Books.

Adam: Oh. Are you sure?

Bill: Positive. But what's that bit about penguin events at Cornell?

Adam: A friend told me about that a while back. It's some thoroughly obscure physics thing where the Feynman diagram of it looks vaguely like a penguin.

Bill: Oh, come now. You're making that up.

Adam: No I'm not. Take a look at figure 5.16.

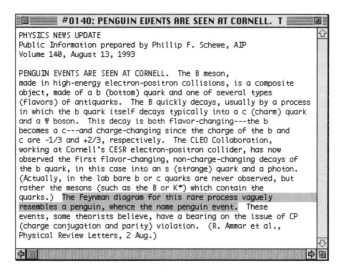

Figure 5.16   *Penguins infiltrate high-energy physics.*

Bill: Say, what have we got out there on movies? I need some information for my Lambada film festival.

Adam: First, Bill, that's a terrible idea. Second, you should save it for later, when we find specific things. Third, umm, what's a Lambada?

Bill: True, that's a bit more specific than we want right now. The Lambada is a type of dance, Brazilian I believe, in which the partners get extraordinarily close. It makes for terrible movies. How about just general movie information?

Adam: That, we've got (see figure 5.17).

Bill: Well, I think that's an adequate warm-up. We've browsed and searched on general topics just to see if they're out there — I think now it's time we work on something a bit more practical.

Adam: Yes. Lest our readers begin to think that the Internet is useful only to browsing bookworms with time on their hands, let's see if it can answer some specific questions for us. Will we be able to find what we're looking for? Will any good information exist? Will our editor tell us we're blathering too much? Is there any other way I can create some suspense?

Bill: Only way to find out is to try it. Let's go dig for some answers.

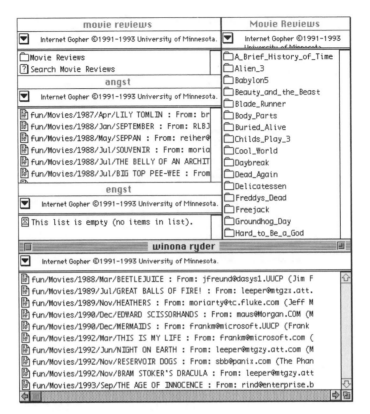

Figure 5.17 *The electronic Siskel and Ebert.*

Looking for Files in All the Wrong Places

Bill: We've separated the things we're going to look for into two groups
that we're going to call "files" and "facts." A file is any given thing
that you want to obtain—a program for your computer, for instance, or a
back issue of an electronic journal that you can obtain over the
Internet, such as *InterText* or *Møøse Droppings*. You also may find the
lyrics to that song that's been driving you crazy for the past 36 hours,
such as the theme to "Gilligan's Island."

Adam: Whatever you do, folks, don't think about it! Just drive the millionaire and his wife straight from your mind. Don't let it take hold! Don't think about the theme to "Gilligan's Island"! Just relax, and sit right back, and you'll hear a tale, a tale of a fateful trip…

Bill: Adam, that was a terrible thing to do! Folks, I apologize. After we've gone out onto the Internet and located some files, we'll start looking for facts. A *fact* is any piece of information that you can locate on the Internet—the answer to a riddle, help on a specific problem you may be having, or perhaps a concert date.

Let's get started; maybe we can distract you so you don't think about the theme to "Gilligan's Island" too much. We're going to be downloading a few things, so I'll want to make some room. Hold on while I clean up my desktop a bit here...

Adam: Wait, how did you do that?

Bill: Do what?

Adam: You dragged that icon into your menu. The Mac doesn't normally allow that.

Bill: Oh, that's MenuDropper, by David Winterburn! I couldn't live without it, and as freeware, you can't beat the price.

Adam: Well, let's go get it. This is a case where a direct approach could work well: I know MenuDropper's name, and I know where Macintosh utilities are stored. I could probably find it relatively quickly by browsing through the directories on **sumex-aim.stanford.edu**.

Bill: But you can never get into that site these days. It's become extremely popular, and tends to be completely filled with as many users as it can support, all the time. So we're probably going to have to find another source.

Adam: True, and that's a good use for Archie, since we can ask Anarchie to search for the file and tell us where it lives. A double-click later and it will be on my hard disk.

Bill: I should note once again that Archie is the name of the program that runs on the Internet machine, whereas Anarchie (pronounced like "anarchy," not "an archie") is a Macintosh client that talks to the remote Archie server.

Adam: I'm going to take advantage of a small piece of information I happen to know from having been around for a while. There are two main sites that archive Macintosh files, and they have slightly different naming schemes. The Info-Mac folks like putting dashes between words, whereas the administrators of the site at **mac.archive.umich.edu** don't use any separator at all. Since we're searching for a file called MenuDropper, I suspect that it will be called either "menu-dropper" or "menudropper" so I'll search on both of those words.

Bill: And the winner is...?

Adam: Anarchie was able to find a number of sites that carry the same file. In this instance, I'm afraid we're going to have be rude and request a file from overseas, since I know for a fact that the U.S. sites that we've found are down (see figure 5.18).

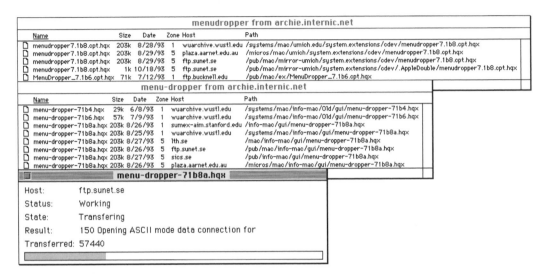

Figure 5.18   The Scandinavian version of MenuDropper.

Adam: Luckily, it's early evening here in Seattle, which means that it should be the middle of the night in Sweden, where the file we're snagging lives. If you must use a site on the other side of the ocean, please try to do so in the middle of the night there, when you aren't likely to interrupt people trying to do real work.

Bill: I've heard of a game called Bolo that can supposedly be played over the Internet. You can locate ongoing games and join in, teaming up with and fighting against people you've never met. Could be fun.

Adam: Sounds like you've been watching too much violence on television again. But sure, let's see if we can find it.

Bill: Shall we do an Anarchie search? We know what we're after, and it's a program, so we know it'll be stored at an FTP site. This kind of search is what Archie was made for, and Anarchie will make it easy to retrieve the file once we've found it.

Adam: In many cases, you'd be right about a situation like this. But Bolo's extremely popular, and there has been an awful lot of Bolo-oriented stuff produced. I suspect you may be disappointed by Archie on this one.

Bill: Good lord, you're right. Anarchie was set to tell us about the first 100 items it found with "bolo" in their names, and it did that

```
admirably—unfortunately, the actual game itself didn't turn up in the
list! We'd have to boost that 100-item limit way up to find the program,
I bet.
```

Adam: I can't quite say why, but this feels like a job for Veronica. Since it's just as easy to retrieve files via TurboGopher as with Anarchie, there's no real reason not to search with Veronica and, if it finds anything, download directly in TurboGopher. The only thing I don't like about downloading files in TurboGopher is that it doesn't tell you how large the file is, so you don't know how long it will take, or how far along you are at any given time. Nevertheless, there are a ton of Bolo folders and one of them contains Bolo 0.99.2 (see figure 5.19).

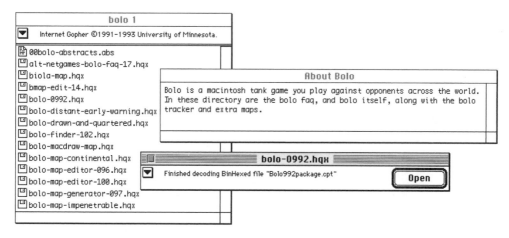

Figure 5.19   *More than one way to skin a tank game.*

Adam: For our last "thing" search, let's find a weather map. I'm pretty sure some of those exist on the Internet, and it would be nice to see what sort of weather we're having right now.

```
Bill: Why don't you look out the window?
```

Adam: Because it's dark.

```
Bill: Oh, right, you live in the 'burbs. There aren't many streetlights
outside of the city.
```

Adam: Okay, let's see if we can figure out what sort of weather system is over the East coast, hammering on our parents.

```
Bill: For the reader at home, it's hard to tell, but this is taking a
while. If you like, I could entertain you with my rendition of various
pirate songs from Peter Pan while we wait.
```

Adam: No, wait! I've found a weather map. It wasn't as easy as I thought it should have been, though. I did a Veronica search on "weather map" but every one of the folders of weather maps that it found turned out to be a bum steer.

Bill: Interesting mental picture on that phrase. So that's what was happening when you were downloading that file for twenty minutes. I thought you were downloading Willard Scott himself for a while there.

Adam: Yeah, I didn't time it, but the file was almost two megabytes large and was a gorgeous satellite picture of the planet, complete with white parts that might have been clouds.

Bill: Oh, yeah, I see it. It's pretty, why don't we use that figure?

Adam: Because you can't tell from the picture what part of the planet you're even looking at.

Bill: Hmm. True. In fact, you can't even tell which planet it is. How do weatherbeings interpret this stuff? You might as well hand them a Picasso.

Adam: No kidding. But I did eventually figure out how to find a better map of the United States. I remember seeing something about weather once in a list of Internet resources maintained by Scott Yanoff. You can get a copy of this list from Scott's machine, and you can find out what machine that is by using Finger on Scott's address. I've done this before so my copy of Finger remembered it.

Bill: Lucky.

Adam: I prefer to think of it as foresight. Anyway, once I retrieved the entire Special Internet Services list, I found a site mentioned as having weather information, so I went there with TurboGopher, found the maps, and downloaded one (see figure 5.20).

Adam: Moving on to less concrete problems, here's a question that has always bothered me.

Bill: What's that?

Adam: What are the risks of buying gas at a gas station with a credit card from one of those automated pumps? I like using them since they're a lot faster than dealing with the cashier, particularly if they make you pay first and go back for change. But, at the same time, I've seen a bunch of receipts just lying around, which says to me that people don't particularly protect their credit card numbers.

There's a fabulous mailing list called Risks Digest that focuses on the risks of technology, and I'll bet this is the sort of thing that they've talked about at some point. I've noticed postings from that group come up when I search the Connection Machine Server via WAIS, so let's see if there is anything (see figure 5.21).

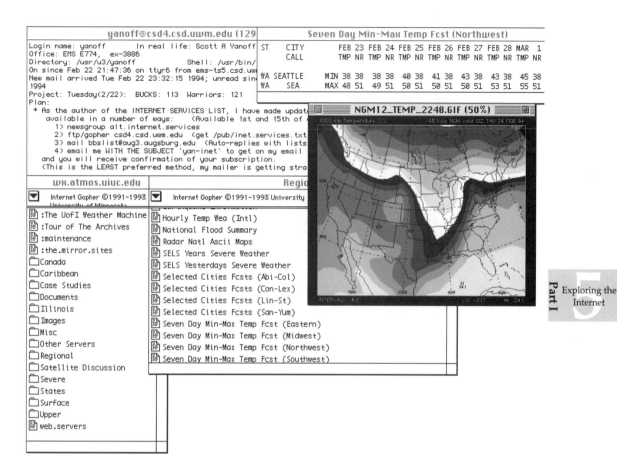

Figure 5.20   *Fifty percent chance of something in your area tonight.*

Bill: That's one thing I like about WAIS, the ability to use real English sentences as you did there, "Tell me about using a gas pump and a credit card." But I've never seen anything in that "Which are similar to" box before. What's that for?

Adam: Glad you asked. That box provides a truly interesting part of WAIS called "relevance feedback." *Relevance feedback* is a phrase that basically means: "Show me more like this one." So, in the example above, I first searched for the search phrase alone and found a few articles that matched what I wanted, but there were also some that were far from the subject. By asking WAIS to find more like the article, I dropped in the relevance feedback box, I narrowed the search and found more articles that were on the topic I wanted. You can do that with either an entire article, as I did above, or with just a part of an article.

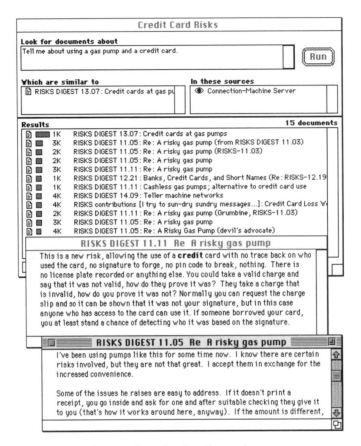

Figure 5.21   *Name, number, and expiration date, please.*

```
Bill: Clever. That would allow you to narrow the search, as you did, or
broaden it by loosening the original parameters while allowing the rel-
evance feedback to keep the answers on track.
```

Adam: Relevance feedback requires a good WAIS program on the Mac or PC, though, and although you can search through a WAIS database from within Gopher or the World Wide Web, clients for those two generally don't support WAIS's fancier features, like relevance feedback, quite as well. That's why I generally prefer to use MacWAIS whenever I'm searching in WAIS. The same principle applies elsewhere, so, for instance, although you can retrieve files stored on an FTP site with TurboGopher, it's not as good at doing so as Anarchie or Fetch from Dartmouth College. Similarly, even though the World Wide Web servers can show you the contents of Gopher sites, Mosaic isn't nearly as slick as TurboGopher when it comes to navigating through Gopherspace. There's always a right tool for the job.

Owning an Internet Press

Adam: Since the beginning of time, or at least since Gutenberg first stamped out his Bible, people have wanted to publish. After all, someone clever said that freedom of the press goes to those who have a press. The obstacles to becoming a publisher are vast, but generally boil down to money, as so much does these days. To publish a simple newsletter today you must pay for design and production and printing and distribution, and you probably even must buy a mailing list from some guy wearing a trench coat in a dark alley.

Bill: But on the Internet, many of these problems disappear, or are at least made far more manageable. Newsletters, magazines, fiction and the like abound, all published by people who probably couldn't dream of being able to publish their work in the standard way.

Adam: As this is a topic that is near and dear to my heart, we'll start by talking about newsletters, and my very own *TidBITS*.

Newsletters

Adam: I'm not quite sure of the technical difference between a newsletter and a magazine, but it seems to be related primarily to length. Newsletters are generally under twenty pages or so, and magazines usually seem to check in closer to one hundred or more pages. The small size of newsletters makes them easy to distribute through email and Usenet news, which is a big plus. This is the route Tonya and I took with *TidBITS*.

Bill: Of course, even if you paid for nothing else to put out your news-letter, there's still the question of your own time. Do you make any money on *TidBITS* to compensate for the time you spend on it?

Adam: We do, although it was hard to decide how to go about it. After much thought, we settled on a Public Broadcasting-style sponsorship program for *TidBITS*. We set it up so that our sponsors can distribute more information directly to interested readers via email—those who are interested send an email message to a specific address mentioned in the issue, and the information comes back automatically.

Bill: Pretty neat setup. Why don't you tell us more about *TidBITS* itself? I'd like to show our readers what these publications are like, not just the logistics of publishing them over the Internet.

Adam: Okay. In *TidBITS* we cover all sorts of news related to the world of the Macintosh, although the actual mission statement is to report on anything computer-related that interests me, which often includes information on the Internet and electronic communications.

Bill: Egotist.

Adam: Realist. If it doesn't interest me, I won't write about it well. I also have a short attention span and become interested in lots of different topics. Every now and then I worry that no one is interested in what I'm writing, but the readership continues to grow and provide positive feedback, so I guess that's not a major problem.

At first, being personally interested in every topic was especially important, since I wrote 90 percent of the articles in the first year, and although I continue to write a large number, many other people help out. We encourage other people to submit articles.

Bill: As a matter of fact, even I've contributed an article or two. You didn't pay me anything, though—does anyone earn anything from writing for *TidBITS*?

Adam: Not directly, since we don't earn anything from the direct distribution of each issue either—the sponsorships are for the act of publishing *TidBITS* so they pay for the hardware, software, and connection expenses that we incur, not to mention the long hours I put in each week researching articles, writing articles, editing articles, and generally putting the entire issue together. Tonya contributes articles occasionally, and edits each issue, which makes the issues much better than they would be otherwise.

However, if you've ever tried to submit an article to *MacUser* or *Macworld*, you know how hard that is. I'm not nearly as picky as they are because I don't have a staff that's paid to write. I also don't pretend to be an expert on every topic, so although I'll happily write about Internet topics, say, I try to get other people to write about high-end desktop publishing or databases, about which I know little. So, writing for *TidBITS* is a way to practice writing, assuming you have some valuable knowledge to share, of course, a way to see how your writing might be edited, and a way to become published.

Bill: Speaking from the point of view of somebody who's just breaking into this professional writing stuff, is an article for *TidBITS* going to look as good on a resume as an article for *Macworld*?

Adam: That I don't know, since I'm not the sort who particularly cares about where someone has been published before. If you're an expert about something and you write well, I couldn't care less if you've been published somewhere. I think it's generally a matter of someone who's paying for an article wanting to know that some other publication took a risk on paying you for a different article. I hope that some of the people who write for *TidBITS* get to use us as proof that they're good writers. Hey, it worked for you.

Bill: Oh. Did it?

Adam: Sure, it's not as though I ever read your newsletter, *Møøse Droppings*, or *Superguy Digest*—I knew you could write your way out of a paper bag because of the stuff you did for *TidBITS*. And the email we've exchanged, of course, but that's slightly different.

Bill: Oh. I'll consider myself flattered. How else is *TidBITS* different from a normal newsletter?

Adam: The part that I both love and hate is that it's really easy for most of our readers to reply to articles that they read in *TidBITS*. I enjoy this immensely when they pass on information I didn't know, or make insightful comments, or even just write to say that they appreciate *TidBITS*. It's good for the psyche.

```
Bill: And the bad part?
```

Adam: Do you know how hard it is to reply to over 150 personal messages each day? Some days I spend so much time replying to email that I have no time to even think about writing new articles for the next issue, much less working on these books. I also don't like it when time constraints force me to be more terse than I'd like. I prefer to explain fully when answering a question, but it's gotten so that it takes too long.

The other reason for keeping *TidBITS* relatively small is that I'm sure most of our readers are busy people, too, and they probably allot a certain amount of time to read *TidBITS* each week. If I doubled the size one week, they'd have to spend twice as much time reading. It's easier to stick with the formula that has worked for so many years, streamlining and enhancing when appropriate, but not for the sake of change alone.

```
Bill: The small size also helps in distribution, of course.
```

Adam: Definitely. At 30K per week, *TidBITS* fits in email relatively well and also traverses Usenet in the `comp.sys.mac.digest` group. If it were a couple of hundred kilobytes large, I wouldn't be able to use the newsgroup for distribution as easily, and people would dislike receiving it in email as well. *TidBITS* is also available on the World Wide Web and Gopher servers.

Magazines and Books

Adam: There are an increasing number of paper magazines that have in some way expanded to the Internet. They don't usually publish the full text of their articles on the Internet, and none attempt to recreate the entire look of the magazine online. That may change, although I expect that the reluctance is entirely due to the fact that they cannot easily charge for the magazines on the Internet.

```
Bill: There are also some technical problems, of course. Some new soft-
ware would permit easy electronic transmission of magazines while retain-
ing the original look of the publication, but those programs aren't free
and are far from widespread.
```

Adam: And besides, people aren't accustomed to paying for Internet services and most likely would decide that there are plenty of other good things to check out instead of the commercial resource.

```
Bill: That makes sense. I wouldn't pay for most things on the Internet,
not because they aren't good, but, as you say, because there are plenty
that are good and free. Many of these are magazines and journals that
exist solely on the Internet, with no paper counterpart.
```

Adam: *Wired* magazine, one that does cross over between the Internet and standard print media, appeared about a year ago and has grown quickly in popularity, being as someone in IRC said, "the tabloid of the electronic geek set." Another friend said something to the effect of *Wired's* motto being "The world is ending, but you can buy cool stuff." Apparently, *Wired's* editor didn't think this was particularly funny, which may indicate the existence of a grain of sand from which can grow a pearl of truth.

Bill: Pithy. A tortuous metaphor, but pithy.

Adam: Thanks. I think. I like reading the magazine though, since more so than most of the ones I get, there are actual honest to goodness ideas in *Wired*. At this point in my life, I have a voracious appetite for ideas, and even if I don't always agree with *Wired's* articles, I find them interesting. That FurryMUCK article was pretty one-sided, though, and with the headline, "MUDS: Sex with the FurryMUCKers" on the cover, rather unfair, I thought.

Bill: It certainly distressed enough people—er, furries on FurryMUCK itself, as we could plainly see when we visited.

Adam: *Wired* has done quite well, nonetheless, at putting its Internet access where its mouth is, so to speak.

Bill: I suppose it does sound rather hypocritical to wax lyrical about the coolness of the Internet but not provide any Internet resources.

Adam: Precisely. *Wired* has set up a rather well-designed World Wide Web server for anyone to use, and they have released the full text of articles in back issues of the magazine. Good thing, since two of mine were lost in the mail at some point while moving last year (see figure 5.22).

Bill: Magazines and other periodicals are one thing, but what about those of us who prefer to read novels? Are there any actual books available on the Internet?

Adam: Absolutely. One of the most fascinating and ambitious projects on the Internet must be Project Gutenberg, conceived of and ably directed by Michael Hart. Project Gutenberg's goal is to give away one trillion electronic texts by December 31, 2001.

Bill: That's a lot of electronic books!

Adam: Yup, but Project Gutenberg only anticipates distributing 10,000 separate titles—their one trillion number comes from the one hundred million people they anticipate will read their texts by that time. I don't believe they have any way of tracking how many readers they get.

Bill: Even still, 10,000 is a lot. How are they managing it?

Adam: It's quite clever, actually. Project Gutenberg started in the early 70s. They work on a doubling scheme, so in 1993 they released four books each month, and in 1994, they hope to release eight books each month. It's like that game on a checkerboard, where you put down a penny on the first square, two pennies on the second square, four pennies on the third square, and so on. It adds up to a huge amount of money, and similarly Project Gutenberg will end up with a huge number of electronic texts.

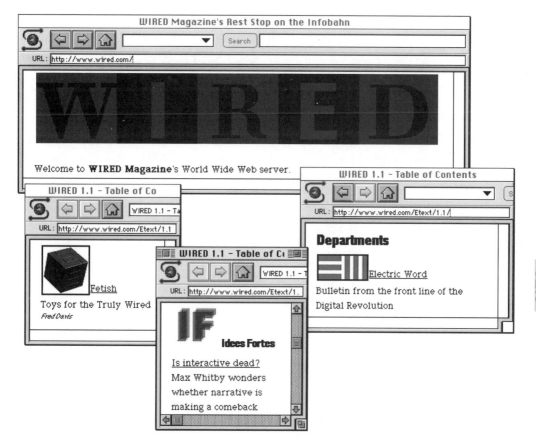

Figure 5.22 *Better graphics than most Web sites.*

Bill: Where do they get their material? Electronic texts don't grow on directory trees, you know.

Adam: Perhaps the most impressive part of the entire project is that it's done entirely with volunteer labor by hundreds of people around the world. For instance, you could type a book into the computer, proofread it, and submit it to Project Gutenberg, assuming of course, that it was out of copyright or that it was done with permission. I suspect that most people use scanners to capture the pages of the book and then use optical character recognition software to turn it into editable text.

Bill: Working in a Popular Copy Shop has taught me that copyright can be a very tricky business. How do they handle it, making sure that a book is indeed in the public domain?

Adam: There are some basic rules, although I gather that copyright searches make up a large portion of the work for Project Gutenberg volunteers now. Needless to say, such a loose organization cannot afford to be sued by a large publisher for copyright infringement. The rule they use most often states that works first published before January 1, 1978 usually enter the public domain 75 years from the date copyright was first secured, which usually means 75 years from the date of first publication. There are a number of other variations on this, and in other countries the general rule is the life of the author plus 50 years, but exceptions exist, and even today, the electronic version of *Peter Pan* comes with a note that says it may not be downloaded outside of the United States due to some strange copyright deal.

Bill: That raises the question of foreign language texts. Do they work with them at all? And how do they feel about some of the alternative distribution methods we talked about above?

Adam: They only concern themselves with English language texts, and prefer to use straight text since it's universal. However, when you're in the position of Project Gutenberg, if someone wants to give you a copy of an electronic text in, say, Acrobat format, you're not going to turn it down. And although they primarily make their works available in text format, I imagine that's primarily a limitation of volunteer labor—they would love to be able to make versions available on the World Wide Web and in Acrobat format, and so on.

Bill: Project Gutenberg is extremely impressive, and highly ambitious. It sounds like a huge amount of work. What keeps them going?

Adam: It's hard to say for sure, since I'm sure everyone does it for a slightly different reason. I don't know if they will reach their goals, but I do know that they have provided a storehouse of useful and interesting information for today's Internet. Also, the volunteers who make Project Gutenberg happen stand as a shining example of what normal people can do on the Internet if they want to. Perhaps that's what impresses me the most about many of these publishing projects—it's amazing what the human mind can do if it merely wants to and is given the freedom to express itself widely via the Internet.

Moving On

Adam: Now that we've had a quick little jaunt around the Internet, let's move on to discussing some of the nuts and bolts of how the Internet actually works. Keep what you've seen here in mind; when I explain specific tools to you later on, think about how they can help you explore the Internet and find your own way through the maze of information.

Bill: And hey, if you liked this chapter, check out our other book! That will help me eat something besides microwave burritos from time to time!

Adam: That may be the most blatant plug I've ever seen, Bill.

Bill: True. I have no shame. 'Bye, folks, and enjoy the rest of the book!

Adam: Thanks for the help, Bill!

II

Internet Foundations

So far, we've looked at the Internet in the abstract only, and it's important that you have an overview of the world you are entering. Like all things electronic, however, the Internet is terribly picky about the details; you must know exactly what to type and where to click. Moreover, unlike on your friendly local Macintosh, on the Internet real people see what you type, so I also talk about the social customs of the Internet, the manners and mores that everyone eventually learns. And, because I hope the Internet becomes something about which you talk with friends, I try to pass on some of the jargon and modes of speech.

Chapter 6 covers the basics of "Addressing & URLs" so you can figure out how email addresses and machine names are formed. In it, I also talk about Uniform Resources Locators, or URLs, which are used on the Internet to provide a coherent method of identifying Internet resources such as Web pages and files available via FTP. Chapter 7, "Email Basics," focuses on email usage and mailing lists, and chapter 8, "Usenet News Basics," is devoted exclusively to Usenet news. Chapter 9 describes "TCP/IP Internet Services," those being services that require a full Internet connection, such as Telnet, FTP, WAIS, Gopher, and the World Wide Web (although I do pass on a few tricks for using Usenet, FTP, Archie, and even the Web through email in chapter 7). Finally, chapter 10, "File Formats," discusses the many file formats you find on the Internet.

Keep in mind that this information is all background—I don't tell you the specific details of how to deal with programs on the Internet or anything like that, until Part III and IV. Nevertheless, I feel that this is important background, so unless you've spent a fair amount of time on the Internet already, I recommend that you read through these chapters.

Text Styles

As a convention, I write all network addresses, whether they are machine names, full email addresses, or URLs, in this `monospaced font`. Note also that any punctuation following the address is not part of the address itself; instead, it's required by my seventh grade English teacher, who was adamant about ending clauses with commas and sentences with periods. Every now and then, I leave off a period when it confuses an address that ends a sentence, but the thought of her beet-red face (I'm sure she was very nice, but she reminded me of a lobster) looming over always makes me add that period. So remember that addresses *never* have any punctuation at the end.

Commands that you type exactly as written **look like this**; when there is a variable that you have to fill in, it *looks like this*. So, **TYPE** *this* means to type the word **TYPE**, followed by whatever is appropriate for *this*: your name, a file name, a directory name, a machine name, or whatever.

Finally, any text that shows up as though it scrolled by on a terminal window appears in its own monospaced font, line-by-line, much like the following lines.

```
To: The Reader <reader@iskm.book.net>
Subject: Style conventions
From: Adam C. Engst <ace@tidbits.com>

I hope these conventions don't seem too onerous - it can be hard in a
book to show precisely what the user sees, as opposed to what was or
should be typed.

cheers ... -Adam
```

Addressing & URLs

Before I can tell you about email, retrieving files via FTP, browsing the Web, or much of anything else, I must discuss how email addresses and machine names are formed, where they come from, and that sort of thing. Along with these details about email addresses and machine names, you must learn about URLs, or Uniform Resource Locators. URLs provide a coherent method of uniquely identifying resources on the Internet, ranging from Web pages to files available via FTP to WAIS sources. But let's start at the beginning…

Addressing

A rose may be a rose by any other name, but the same is not true of an Internet computer. All Internet computers think of each other in terms of numbers (not surprisingly), and all people think of them in terms of names (also not surprisingly). The Internet uses the *domain name system* to make sense of the millions of machines that make up the Internet. In terms of the numbers, each machine's address is composed of four numbers, each less than 256. People are generally bad about remembering more than the seven digits of a phone number, so the folks working in this field came up with a program called a *domain name server*. Domain name servers translate between the numeric addresses and the names; real people can remember and use the names while real computers can continue to refer to each other by number. That way, *everyone* is happy.

Domain name servers, although generally part of the background technology that enables the Internet to work seamlessly, are tremendously important. Without them, very little on the Internet works these days.

Despite the fact that all Internet numeric addresses are sets of four numbers, the corresponding name can have between two and five sets of words. After five, it gets out of hand, so although it's possible, it's not generally done. For instance, one of the machines I use now is called **king.tidbits.com** (three words), and the machine I used at Cornell was called **cornella.cit.cornell.edu** (four words). The domain style addresses may look daunting, but in fact they are quite easy to work with, especially when you consider the numeric equivalents, such as **204.57.157.13** for **king.tidbits.com**. Each item in those addresses, separated by the periods, is called a *domain*, and in the following sections, you are going to look at them backward, or in terms of the largest domain to the smallest.

A random aside for those of you who are students of classical rhetoric: The process of introducing topics A, B, and C, and then discussing them in the order C, B, and A is called chiasmus. *This little known fact is entirely unrelated to the Internet, except that after the first edition of this book I took a lot of good-natured ribbing on the Internet about my classical education, so I figured I should at least pretend to know something about the topic.*

Top-level Domains

In any machine name, the final word after the last dot is the *top-level domain*, and a limited number of them exist. Originally, and this shows the Internet's early Americo-centric view, six top-level domains indicated to what type of organization the machine belonged. Thus, we ended up with the following list:

- **com** = commercial
- **edu** = educational
- **org** = organization, usually nonprofit
- **mil** = military
- **net** = network
- **gov** = government

That setup was all fine and dandy for starters, but as the number of machines on the Internet began to grow at an amazing rate, a more all-encompassing solution became necessary. The new top-level domains are based on countries, so each country has its own two-letter domain. Thus, the United Kingdom's top-level domain is **uk**, Sweden's is **se**, Japan's is **jp**, Australia's is **au**, and so on. Every now and then another country comes on the Internet, and I see a domain code that totally throws me, as Iceland's **is** code did the first time.

Note

If you'd like to see the complete list of country codes, check out this URL:

```
http://www.nw.com/zone/iso-country-codes
```

The United States has this system, too; so, for example, The Well, a popular commercial service with links to the Internet, is **well.sf.ca.us**. Unfortunately, because so many sites already existed with the old domain names, it made no sense to change them. Thus, we have both types of top-level domain names here in the U.S., and you just have to live with it.

You may see a couple of other top-level domains on occasion, **bitnet** and **uucp**, such as in **listserv@bitnic.bitnet** or **ace@tidbits.uucp**. In both of these cases, the top-level domain indicates that the machine is on one of the alternative networks and may not exist directly on the Internet (otherwise, it would have a normal top-level domain such as **com** or **uk**). This setup isn't a big deal these days because so many machines exist on two networks that your email gets through just fine in most cases. In the past, though, few connections existed between the Internet and BITNET or Usenet, so getting mail through one of the existing gateways was more difficult. Keep in mind that because a machine whose name ends with **bitnet** or **uucp** is not usually on the Internet, you cannot use Telnet or FTP with it.

Many machine names are as simple as it gets: a machine name and a top-level domain. Others are more complex because of additional domains in the middle. Think of an address such as **cornella.cit.cornell.edu** as one of those nested Russian dolls (see figure 6.1). The outermost doll is the top-level domain, the next few dolls are the mid-level domains, and, if you go all the way in, the final doll is the userid (which I'll explain soon enough).

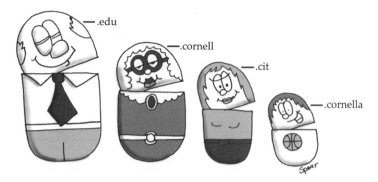

Figure 6.1   *The Russian doll approach to Internet addresses.*

Mid-level Domains

What do these mid-level domains represent? It's hard to say precisely, because the answer can vary a bit. The machine I used at Cornell, known as cornella.cit.cornell.edu, represents one way the mid-level domains have been handled. The machine name is **cornella**, and the top-level domain is **edu**, because Cornell claims all those undergraduates are there to get an education. The **cit** after **cornella** is the department, Cornell Information Technologies, that runs the machine known as **cornella**. The next part, **cornell**, is obvious; it's the name of the overall organization to which CIT belongs. So, for this machine anyway, the hierarchy of dolls is, in order, machine name, department name, organization name, and organization type.

This is similar to how my system is set up now, since I control the **tidbits.com** domain, and each of my Macs has a name within that domain. So, for instance, my desktop Mac is called **penguin.tidbits.com**, and my server is **king.tidbits.com**.

In the machine name for The Well, **well.sf.ca.us**, you see a geographic use of mid-level domains. In this case, **well** is the machine name, **sf** is the city name (San Francisco), **ca** is the state name (California), and **us** is the country code for the United States.

Mid-level domains spread the work around. Obviously, the Internet can't have machines with the same name; otherwise, chaos would erupt. But because the domain name system allows for mid-level domains, the administrators for those mid-level domains must make sure that everyone below them stays unique. In other words, I could actually name my machine **cornella.tidbits.com** because that name is completely different from **cornella.cit.cornell.edu** (though why I'd want to, I don't know). And, if they wanted, the administrators at CIT could put a new machine on the net and call it **tidbits.cit.cornell.edu** without any trouble, for the same reason. More importantly, the administrators don't need to bother anyone else if they want to make that change. They control the **cit** domain, and as long as all the machines within that domain have unique names, there aren't any problems. Of course, someone has to watch the top-level domains because it's all too likely that two people may want **tidbits.com** as a domain (but I've already got it, so they can't have it). That task is handled by the Internet Network Information Center, or InterNIC. As a user, you shouldn't have to worry about naming problems, because everyone should have a system administrator who knows who to talk to, and you need the cooperation of your provider anyway—you can't set up a domain on your own.

There is yet another way to handle the mid-level domains, this time in terms of inter-mediate computers. Before I got my current address, I had a connection from a machine called **halcyon**, whose full name was **halcyon.com**. My machine name was **tidbits.halcyon.com**. In this case, **tidbits** was my machine name, **halcyon** was the machine through which all of my mail was routed, and **com** indicated that the connection was through a commercial organization. I realize that this example is a bit confusing, but I mention it because it's one way that you can pretend to have an Internet address when you really have only a UUCP connection (a different sort of connection that transfers only email and news). All my mail and news came in via UUCP through **halcyon**, so by including **halcyon** in my address, I created an Internet-style address.

The other way of pretending that a UUCP connection is a real Internet connection for address purposes, is to have your host set up an *MX record* (where MX stands for Mail Exchange). An MX record is a pointer on several true Internet machines to your site.

Machine Name

The next part in the full domain name is the machine itself; for example, in the name **penguin.tidbits.com**, **penguin.** is the name of my machine. In my case, the machine is a Macintosh 660AV, but people use all sorts of machines, and because the system adminis-trators often are a punchy, overworked lot, they tend to give machines silly names. Large organizations with more centralized control lean more toward thoroughly boring names, like the machine at Cornell, which was called **cornella** (as opposed to **cornellc** and **cornelld** and **cornellf**).

Note

*For those who are wondering, the naming scheme I use is based on the names of species of penguins. Also, if you're wondering why you can send email to **ace@tidbits.com** if my machine is really called **penguin.tidbits.com**, it's because of the magic of the domain name system. Since most people like shorter addresses, it's common to map the shorter domain name, **tidbits.com**, to point to the server that handles mail specifically, **king.tidbits.com** in my case. Then, I set Eudora to look for mail on **king.tidbits.com** and everything works swimmingly. These are the sort of machinations that Internet providers continually deal with. Luckily, you as the user can usually ignore them.*

One of the reasons for boring names is that in the early days, machines on BITNET had to have names with between six and eight characters. Coming up with a meaningful unique name within that restriction became increasingly difficult. Usenet doesn't put a limit on the length of names, but it requires that the first six characters be unique. Currently, the Internet allows the second level domain to be up to 24 characters, and the third level domain can be up to 72 characters. In no case can the full domain name go over 256 characters, however.

If you remember that machines often exist on the Internet as well as on one of these other networks, thereby blurring the distinctions, you'll see the problem. The limitations of Internet machine names are less rigid, so alternative connections dictate what names are acceptable.

Often, special services keep their names even when they move to different machines or even different organizations. Because of this situation, a machine that runs a service may have two names, one that goes with the machine normally and one that points solely at that service. For instance, the anonymous FTP site that I use to store all the software I talk about in this book is called `ftp.tidbits.com`. But in fact, it runs on a machine called `ftp.halcyon.com`, and I could move it to any other machine while still retaining the `ftp.tidbits.com` name. This situation is not a big deal one way or another.

To summarize, you can have multiple domains in a machine name, and the further you go to the right, the more general they become, often ending in the country code. Conversely, the further you go to the left, the more specific the domains become, ending in the machine name because it's the most specific.

But what about email addresses, which have userids? They're even more specific than machine names, because you can have many userids on a single machine.

Userid

Now that you've looked at the machine name, you can move on to the *userid* or *username*, which identifies a specific user on a machine. Both terms are equally correct (with two exceptions—the commercial online service GEnie and the FirstClass BBS software both treat userids and usernames separately) and commonly used. If you set up your own machine, or work with a sufficiently flexible provider, you can choose your own username. Choosing your own name is good because then your correspondents can more easily remember your address, assuming of course that you choose a userid that makes sense and is easy to type. If I made my address `ferdinand-the-bull@tidbits.com`, people who typed the address slightly wrong and had their mail bounced back to them would become irritated at me.

Unlike Macintosh filenames (and America Online and eWorld userids), Internet userids cannot have spaces in them, so convention dictates that you replace any potential spaces with underscores, dashes, or dots, or omit them entirely. Other reasonable userids that I could use (but don't) include **adam_engst@tidbits.com** or **adam-engst@tidbits.com** or **adam.engst@tidbits.com** or **adamengst@tidbits.com**. However, all of these names are more difficult to type than **ace@tidbits.com**, and because I have good initials, I stick with them.

Unfortunately, there are a limited number of possible userids, especially at a large site. So Cornell, for instance, with its thousands of students and staff, has opted for a system of using initials plus one or more digits (because initials aren't all that unique, either—in fact, I once asked for my initials as a userid on one of Cornell's mainframes and was told that ACE was a reserved word in that machine's operating system, though no one could tell me what it was reserved for).

Microsoft uses yet a different scheme: first name and last initial (using more than one initial to keep the userids unique). As Microsoft has grown, common names such as David have been used up, so the company has started other schemes such as first initial and last name. Why am I telling you this? Because knowing an organization's scheme can prove useful at times if you're trying to figure out how to send mail to someone at that organization, and so that I can note a societal quirk. At places like Microsoft where people use email so heavily, many folks refer to each other by email names exclusively. When my wife, Tonya, worked at Microsoft, she had a problem with her username, **tonyae** (first name and last initial) because it looked more like TonyAe than TonyaE to most people.

The real problem with assigned userids comes when the scheme is ludicrously random. Some universities work student ID numbers into the userid, for instance, and Compu-Serve userids are mere strings of digits like 72511,306. I believe the scheme has something to do with octal numbers or some such technoweenie hoo-hah. I don't speak octal or septal, or any such nonsense, and as a result, I can never remember CompuServe userids.

Remember that email addresses point at an individual, but when you're using services such as Telnet or FTP, no individual is involved. You simply want to connect to that machine, and you have to connect *sans* userid. This restriction may seem obvious, but it often trips people up until they get used to it. For example, it seems that you could just FTP to **anonymous@space.alien.com**. The system doesn't work that way, though, and you FTP to **space.alien.com**, and once there, log in as **anonymous**. More about FTP in later chapters.

Punctuation

Enough about userids. What about all this punctuation? Better known as Shift-2 (on U.S. keyboards anyway), the **@** symbol came into use, I imagine, because it's a single character that generally means "at" in traditional usage. The **@** symbol is generally universal for Internet email, but not all types of networks have always used it. For instance, some BITNET machines once required you to spell out the word, as in the command **TELL LISTSERV AT BITNIC HELP**. Luckily, almost everything uses the **@** symbol with no spaces these days, which reduces four characters to one, and probably has saved untold person-hours worth of typing over the years.

On some European keyboards there is no @ key, but you can still type the character by pressing ⌘-Option-1.

As long as you're learning about special characters, look at the dot. It is, of course, the period character on the keyboard, and it serves to separate the domains in the address. For various reasons unknown to me, the periods have become universally known as dots in the context of addresses. When you tell someone your email address over the phone, you say (or rather I'd say because it's my address), "My email address is ace at tidbits dot com." The other person must know that "at" equals the @ symbol and that "dot" equals the period. If he's unsure, explain yourself.

Alternative Addresses

You may see two other styles of addressing mail on the Internet, both of which work for sites that aren't actually on the Internet itself. The first, and older, of the two is called *bang* addressing. It was born in the early days when there were relatively few machines using UUCP. Not every machine knew how to reach every other machine, so the trick was to get the mail out to a machine that knew about a machine that knew about a machine that knew about your machine. Talk about a friend of a friend! So, you could once have sent email to an address that looked like **uunet!nwnexus!caladan!tidbits!ace**. This address would have sent the mail from **uunet** to **nwnexus** to **caladan** to **tidbits** and finally to my userid on **tidbits**. This approach assumes that your machine knows about the machine **uunet** (run by the commercial provider UUNET) and that all of the machines in the middle are up and running. All the exclamation points are called "bangs," appropriately enough, I suppose. On the whole, this style of addressing is slow and unreliable these days, but if you use a machine that speaks UUCP, you can occasionally use it to your advantage. For instance, every now and then, I try to send email to a machine that my UUCP host, **nwnexus.wa.com**, for some reason can't reach. By bang-routing the mail appropriately, I can make another Internet machine try to send the mail out, sometimes with greater success.

The other sort of special addressing is another way to get around the fact that your machine, or even your network, isn't connected to the Internet as such. In this case, you must provide two addresses: one to get to the machine that feeds your machine, and one to get to your machine. The problem here is that Internet addresses cannot have more than one @ symbol in them. You can replace the first @ symbol with a % symbol, and the mailers then try to translate the address properly. My old address, **ace@tidbits.halcyon.com**, also could have been **ace%tidbits.uucp@halcyon.com**. These tricks are ugly and awkward, but sometimes necessary. Luckily, as the Internet grows and standardizes, you need fewer and fewer of these addressing tricks.

Enough on machine names and email addresses, then. If you keep the previous discussions in mind when you're using the Internet, you shouldn't be confused by any address you see. And if you are confused, perhaps that address is seriously malformed. I've seen it happen before.

URLs

Before I talk about any of the various TCP/IP-based Internet services, I want to explain *URLs*, or Uniform Resource Locators. These constitute the most common and efficient method of telling people about resources available via FTP, the World Wide Web, and other Internet services. URLs have become so popular that the Library of Congress has even added a subfield for them when it catalogs electronic resources.

> **Note**
>
> *URL generally stands for Uniform Resource Locator, although some people switch "uniform" for "universal." Despite what I've heard from one source, I have never heard anyone pronounce URL as "earl;" instead, everyone I've talked to, including one person from CERN who helped develop the World Wide Web, spells out the letters.*

What are URLs?

A URL uniquely specifies the location of something on the Internet, using three main bits of information that you need in order to access any given object. First is the URL scheme, or the type of server making the object available, be it an FTP, Gopher, or World Wide Web server. Second, comes the address of the resource. Third and finally, there's the full pathname or identifier for the object, if necessary.

> **Note**
>
> *Don't worry if I talk about Internet services that you haven't read about in detail yet. That's what the next few chapters are for, but I wanted to explain the way that people (including me in this book) provide pointers to specific resources available via the various services like FTP, Gopher, and the World Wide Web.*

This description is slightly oversimplified, but the point I want to make is that URLs are an attempt to provide a consistent way to reference objects on the Internet. I say "objects" because you can specify URLs not only for files and Web pages, but also for stranger things, such as email addresses, Telnet sessions, and Usenet news postings.

Table 6.1 shows the main URL schemes that you're likely to see.

Part II

Addressing & URLs

6

Table 6.1
Common URL Schemes

Scheme	Internet Protocol	Sample Client
ftp	File Transfer Protocol	Anarchie
gopher	Gopher protocol	TurboGopher
http	HyperText Transfer Protocol	MacWeb
mailto	Simple Mail Transport Protocol	Eudora
news	Net News Transport Protocol	NewsWatcher
wais	Wide Area Information Servers	MacWAIS

URL Construction

If you see a URL that starts with **ftp**, you know that the file specified in the rest of the URL is available via FTP, which means that you could use FTP under Unix, FTP via email, or a MacTCP-based FTP client such as Anarchie to retrieve it. If the URL starts with **gopher**, use TurboGopher or another Gopher client. If it starts with **http**, use MacWeb, NCSA Mosaic, or Netscape or some other Web browser. And, finally, if a URL starts with **wais**, you can use MacWAIS or another WAIS client.

> *You can use a Web browser to access most of the URL schemes in Table 6.1, although Web browsers are not necessarily ideal for anything but information on the World Wide Web itself. Web browsers work pretty well for accessing files on Gopher servers and via gateways to WAIS databases, but FTP via a Web browser is clumsy (and may fail entirely with certain types of files, such as self-extracting archives). Similarly, although it's handy to use mailto URLs to send mail, I dislike doing so because then I don't have a record of my outgoing mail, as I do when I send mail from Eudora. And, no Web browser stands up to NewsWatcher in terms of news capabilities.*

After the URL scheme comes a colon (**:**), which delimits the scheme from what comes next. If two slashes (**//**) come next, they indicate that a machine name in the format of an IP address will follow, such as with **http://www.apple.com/** or **ftp://ftp.info.apple.com/**. However, if the URL points at an address in some other format, such as an email address like **mailto:president@whitehouse.gov**, the slashes aren't appropriate and don't appear.

N o t e

In some rare circumstances, you may need to use a username and password in an FTP URL as well. A URL with a username and password might look like this:

```
ftp://username:password@domain.name/pub/
```

The last part of the URL is the specific information that you're looking for, be it an email address or more commonly, the path to the directory of the file that you desire. Directory names are separated from the machine name by a slash (/). You may not have to specify the path with some URLs if you're only connecting to the top level of the site.

So, for instance, let's dissect a URL that points at the Product Support page on Apple's Web server:

```
http://www.apple.com/documents/productsupport.html
```

First off, the **http** part tells us that we should use a Web browser to access this URL. Then, **www.apple.com** is the name of the host machine that's running the Web server. The next part, **/documents/productsupport.html**, is the full path to the file the Web browser shows us, so **/documents** is a directory, and **productsupport.html** is the actual file inside the **/documents** directory.

If an FTP or Gopher URL ends with a slash, that always means it points at a directory and not a file. If it doesn't end with a slash, it may or may not point at a directory. If it's not obvious from the last part of the path, there's no good way of telling until you go there. Thus, this URL points at a directory and will return the directory listing of the files there:

```
ftp://ftp.tidbits.com/pub/tidbits/
```

However, this URL points directly at a file:

```
ftp://ftp.tidbits.com/pub/tidbits/issues/1990/TidBITS#001_16-Apr-90.etx
```

Because most Web servers enable the creation of a default file that serves in the absence of a specific file in the URL, it's usually less important for Web users to realize whether or not they're specifying a file or a directory. In other words,

```
http://www.tidbits.com/tidbits/index.html
```

points at a file, but the Web server running on that machine will display the same file (because it's the default), if you simply used this URL:

```
http://www.tidbits.com/tidbits/
```

Part II   Addressing & URLs   *6*

Using URLs

All of these details aside, how do you use URLs? Your mileage may vary, but I use them in three basic ways. First, if I see them in email or in a Usenet posting, I often copy and paste the host part into Anarchie (if they are FTP URLs), or I paste the whole thing into MacWeb or Netscape (if any other scheme). That's the easiest way to retrieve a file or connect to a site if you have a MacTCP-based Internet connection.

> **Note**
>
> *Actually, thanks to some slick programming, all I'd really do is Command-click on the URL in NewsWatcher, say, and it would automatically transfer that URL to the appropriate client program, Anarchie, TurboGopher, MacWeb, or whatever.*

Second, if for some reason I don't want to use MacWeb or Netscape (I far prefer Anarchie for FTP, for instance), sometimes I manually dissect the URL, as we did with the Product Support page on the Apple Web server, to figure out which program to use and where to go. This method takes more work, but sometimes pays off in the end. (You *can* put a screw in the wall with a hammer, but it's not the best tool for the job.)

Third and finally, whenever I want to point people to a specific Internet resource or file available for anonymous FTP, I give them a URL. URLs are unambiguous, and although a bit ugly in running text, easier to use than attempting to spell out what they mean. Consider the example below:

```
ftp://ftp.tidbits.com/pub/tidbits/issues/1995/TidBITS#261_30-Jan-95.etx
```

To verbally explain the same information contained in that URL, I would have to say something like: "Using an FTP client program, connect to the anonymous FTP site **ftp.tidbits.com**. Change directories into the **/pub/tidbits/issues/1995/** directory, and once you're there, retrieve the file **TidBITS#261/30-Jan-95.etx**." A single URL enables me to avoid such convoluted (and boring) language; and frankly, URLs are in such common use on the Internet, you may as well get used to seeing them right now.

> **Note**
>
> *URLs sometimes have to break between two lines in publications. If you see a two-line URL that doesn't look quite right, stick the two lines back together when you're typing or pasting it into a Web browser, perhaps without a hyphen that might have been introduced in the production process.*

So, from now on, whenever I mention a file available via FTP or a Web site, I'll use a URL. If you try to retrieve a file or connect to a Web site and are unsuccessful, chances are either you've typed the URL slightly wrong, or the file or server no longer exists. It's *extremely* likely that many of the files I give URLs for will have been updated by the time you read this, so the file name at the end of the URL may have changed.

So if a URL doesn't work, and this is a general piece of good advice, try removing the file name from the last part of the URL and look in the directory that the original file lived in for the updated file. If all else fails, you can remove everything after the machine name and work your way down to the file you are after.

If, after all this, you'd like to learn more about the technical details behind the URL specifications, check out:

```
http://info.cern.ch/hypertext/WWW/Addressing/URL/Overview.html
```

Weird Characters

There is one rather messy part to URLs that you don't usually have to deal with, but that comes up on occasion, most commonly in relation to Gopher URLs. There are certain characters which cannot appear in certain parts of a URL, including spaces. And if one of those characters would appear, it's replaced with what's called an *escape code*, consisting of a percent symbol and the hexadecimal number corresponding to that character.

The reason this comes up most often in relation to Gopher URLs is that Gopher allows extremely long titles for files and directories, and allows pretty much any character within them, including spaces, slashes, question marks, and so on. So a Gopher URL may look a bit like this:

```
gopher://gopher.tc.umn.edu/11/Information%20About%20Gopher
```

Notice all the %20 escape codes that stand in for what are spaces on the real Gopher menu title.

For the most part, you don't have to worry about the way the spaces and other characters (see Table 6.2 for a list of some common ones that will show up in a URL as escape codes) are translated—I just wanted to show you that this sort of thing happens so you won't be confused the first time you see a URL with all sorts of what seem like garbage characters in it.

Table 6.2
Some Reserved Characters in URLs

Character	Escape code replacement
=	%3D
;	%3B

continues

Part II   Addressing & URLs

Table 6.2
continued

Character	Escape code replacement
/	%2F
#	%23
?	%3F
:	%3A
space	%20
~	%7E

A Self-Addressed Internet...

I believe that I promised early on in this book that there would be no quiz, but if I were going to break my promise, this is probably the chapter I'd do it in. You cannot get around on the Internet unless you understand how machine names and email addresses are put together. And, as the World Wide Web continues on its steamroller path to become the most popular of Internet services, a working knowledge of URLs, no matter how ugly they may seem to you now, is absolutely essential if you're to understand where you're going and what you're seeing.

Email Basics

Electronic mail is the most pervasive application on the Internet, and for good reason. What better way to communicate with so many people so quickly? But to use and understand email properly, I must show you how it's constructed, the relevant social mores and pitfalls, and how you can use it.

Email Construction

What makes up an email message? Most messages have two important parts, with a third part that doesn't have to appear. The first two parts are the *header* and the *body* of the message, and the third, non-essential part, is the *signature*. For simplicity's sake, let's work backward.

Signature

Signatures are just about what you'd expect—some text that goes at the bottom of every message you send; many email programs, including Eudora, which I've included on the ISKM disk, provide a facility for creating signatures. Most people include their names (real or pretend) in their signatures; it's considered good form to include your preferred email address in your signature as well, just in case the address in the header isn't useful for some reason or another. After you get past the basics of name and email address, however, you can put anything you like in your signature. Many people lean toward clever quotations or manage to express some sporting partisanship of their favorite team, usually with an erudite "Go Weasels '95" or some such. (It's hard to grunt in ASCII.) I prefer clever quotations, especially so if changed once per day—not that I have time or energy to think them up or type them in every day. Here is a signature that must have taken some time to create, because all the lines and dashes had to be typed in the right place:

```
/ =======================================================================\
 | |                                                                   | |
 | |   _                                                               | |
 | |  *  \          Sorry, a signature error has occurred.             | |
 | |   _!_                                                             | |
 | |  /  !_  \        /===========\          /==========\              | |
 | | !      !        !   Resume   !          !  Restart !              | |
 | |  \ __ /         \ — — — — — /          \ — !\ — — /               | |
 | |                                          !  \                     | |
 | \===================================================!   _\================/
                                                      ! /\ \
                                                       \_\
```

Courtesy of A. Marsh Gardiner, **gardin@harvarda.harvard.edu**

Many people also use signatures to disclaim their messages. The signature acts as a disclaimer, usually stating that the opinions and facts stated in the preceding message have no relationship to the organization paying for the account or employing the individual. Disclaimers are important online because readers have no context in which to take postings. If Ferdinand the Bull posts a glowing review of specific species of cork tree, for example, he should also note at the bottom of his review that he is a paid consultant of Corking Good Times International, and is therefore biased. More common are glowing reviews from users who "have no relationship with Corking Good Times International, other than as a satisfied customer." Disclaimers also serve to ensure that no one takes the words of a single employee as the policy of the entire organization. Marketing departments hate that. "But Joe said online that Apple was going to give free Macs to everyone whose birthday falls on the second Tuesday of odd months this year." "Yeah, sure buddy."

One warning, though. Mailing lists that are published as *digests*—that is, lists in which a moderator collects the day's messages and concatenates them into a single file—frown on or even reject postings with multiple line signatures. This suggestion makes sense, if you think about it. A large digest file can have 50 messages in it, and if every person has a four-line signature, the digest suddenly becomes 200 lines longer than necessary. But enough about signatures, let's look at the meat of the message.

Body

What you put in the body of your letter is your business. I can recommend several practices, however. First, get in the habit of pressing the Return key twice between paragraphs to insert a blank line between them; that additional white space makes email messages much easier to read. Nothing is harder to read than page after page of unbroken text.

Actually, something *is* worse than unbroken text, and that's page after page of unbroken text in capital letters. DON'T USE ALL CAPS BECAUSE IT LOOKS LIKE YOU'RE SHOUTING! No one uses all capital letters for long because everyone hates reading it and will tell you, nicely the first time, to stop.

I suppose now is a good time to talk about manners in terms of the sorts of things you should consider when writing email. Email differs from normal mail in many ways. Think of the difference between a short note to your mother, a memo at work, and a formal business letter. Most email falls somewhere between the short note and the memo, and seldom do you ever see an email message with the formality and rigidity of a business letter. Although I'm giving this information in the context of email, it applies equally as well to postings on Usenet; so if you like, reread this section, substituting posting for email everywhere.

How do you start these messages? In many ways, email acts as the great equalizer. Most of the time, you know someone's name and email address when you send email to him, nothing more. **joeschmoe@alien.com** could be a janitor, a summer intern, or the president of a Fortune 500 firm. Similarly, any address ending in **edu** can link to a student, some member of the staff, a world-renowned professor of underwater basket weaving, or the president of the university. You have no way of knowing, unless that fact somehow comes up in conversation.

Most people react to this lack of context by treating everyone with the same level of polite, but informal, respect. Seldom do people use their titles, so equally seldom do correspondents use those titles in email. Everyone is on a first-name basis. I once took a class with the astronomer and science advocate Carl Sagan while I was at Cornell, and the first day of class, an awed undergraduate (but braver than the rest of us) asked, "How should we address you, Dr. Sagan?" He replied, "You can call me Mr. Sagan, Professor Sagan, Dr. Sagan, or Herr Doktor Professor Sagan," he paused, "or you can call me Carl." Carl it was then, and the class benefited greatly from that level of informality, just as the Internet does.

In light of this knowledge, when I started using email I thought about the differences between email and paper mail (hereafter called by its true name in the Internet community, snail mail). The standard salutation of "Dear" sounds inappropriately formal and stilted to my ears (apologies to Miss Manners). Since email more closely resembles spoken communication than written, I opted for the less formal and more colloquial "Hi," which has served me well. Some people forego the salutation completely, relying solely on the first name, but that approach feels abrupt to me, as if someone called me on the phone and stated my name without a "Hello" or so much as a questioning tone. Do what you like, though; no one has laid down rules on this matter.

What you say in the letter itself deserves more thought, however. Because email is so quick and it's so easy to respond without thinking, many people often reply hastily and less politely than they would had they taken a moment to consider. Remember, you want to achieve a certain effect with an email message, just as you do with any form of communication. If you simply whack your first thoughts into a message, it probably won't properly convey your true feelings. If you want information from someone, phrasing your request politely only increases your chances of getting that information, and if you wish to comment on someone else's words, doing so in a reasoned and level-headed manner ensures that that person won't immediately consider you a serious jerk.

You also must remember that informal though email may be, it lacks most of the nonverbal parts of communication that we seldom consider in normal speech. All inflection, body language, and facial expressions disappear, and it doesn't help one whit if you make them while composing the letter. Email is ASCII text only, and only two ways exist to convey inflections such as sarcasm or irony that would be obvious in spoken conversation. First, polish your writing skills. There is no substitute for clear and coherent writing. Many people find writing difficult, but I recommend that you don't think of composing email as writing, but as speaking to someone who sees your words but cannot see or hear you. Most people who claim they can't write have little trouble making themselves understood when speaking.

Second, utilize *smileys*, or as they are sometimes known, *emoticons*. Smileys are strings of punctuation characters meant to be viewed by tilting your head (which is usually easier than tilting your monitor) to the side. (If they still look wrong, try tilting your head to the *other* side.) People have come up with literally hundreds of different smileys, and you can find lists containing them on the Internet. Seth Godin has even compiled many of them into a book, *The Smiley Dictionary*, published by Peachpit Press (and there is at least one other book, published by O'Reilly & Associates, on the same somewhat silly topic). I take the view that only two, or maybe three, smileys are at all useful in normal email. The first is the happy face **:-)**, which implies that what you just said was meant as humor or at least shouldn't be taken too seriously. I often use it to imply that I would have said that bit with a smile. A variant of the happy face uses the semicolon instead of the colon **;-)** and (because of the wink) implies that the preceding sentence was somewhat sarcastic or ironic. Finally, the frowning face **:-(** implies that you aren't happy about whatever you just said.

I use smileys relatively heavily in email, where I don't have time to craft each letter as carefully as I would like. I miss not being able to use them (I could, but no one would understand) in snail mail occasionally, and I actively try to avoid using them in *TidBITS*, favoring instead words that convey my feelings without the smiley crutch. When in doubt, use smileys. If I say in email, "Well, that was a stupid thing to do," the message is much more offensive than if I say, "Well, that was a stupid thing to do. **: -)**" Believe me, it is.

I may have given the impression that the Internet is this utopia where everyone always behaves nicely and ne'er is heard a discouraging word. Unfortunately, that's not so, and in reality you see plenty of *flaming* on the nets. Flaming happens when, in a PC discussion list, you innocently mention that you like your Macintosh, and 17 people immediately jump on you in email and pummel you within an inch of your electronic life for saying something so obviously stupid and incorrect when everyone knows that only weenies, wimps, and little wusses use those toy Macintosh computers, which are good only for paperweights—and expensive paperweights at that, because you can buy three completely configured, top-of-the-line Pentium-based PCs for the same price as a used Macintosh Classic—without a hard drive. And by the way, did I mention that your mother wears combat boots and your father wears ballet slippers? **: -)**

The preceding paragraph is flaming (except for the smiley, which I threw in to indicate that I was kidding about your parents' footwear), and if you must respond to an inflammatory message, which I don't recommend, do it in email. No one else wants to read your flames. Think before you lower yourself to flaming; it never solves anything. I have found in almost every case that replying calmly and clearly embarrasses anyone (assuming that person is normal and rational, which is not always a good assumption) so thoroughly that she immediately apologizes for being such a jerk. And yes, I know how hard it is not to just tee off on someone. Restrain yourself and rest assured that everyone who sees your restraint will think more highly of you for it.

Note

My favorite method of responding to long and vitriolic flames is to send back a single-line message reading, "You may be right. -Engst." I heard about this technique in an interview with Tom Brokaw, I think, and it works extremely well, confusing the recipient to no end and generally putting a stop to the flaming.

Often, people flame companies or large organizations that are doing stupid things. Various governments are favorite, though slow-moving and not very challenging, targets. This sort of flaming is more acceptable, although you may start a *flame war* if other people don't share your opinions on some major topic, such as whether the Mac is better than Windows. As a spectator, you may enjoy watching the occasional flame war, as I do, but again, they never solve anything, and they waste a huge amount of *bandwidth* (which is composed of transmission time, people time, and disk storage throughout the world).

Part II   Email Basics   7

Actually, I've decided that in some respects a certain amount of flaming can be positive, because there are only three ways of ending an argument on the Internet. Agree to disagree, win your opponent over to your side, or stop from exhaustion. In no case does anyone get knifed or shot, and if participating in a flame war lets someone blow off some steam, that's better than their going home and abusing their children. Everything is relative.

Keep in mind that no matter what you say, it may not be private. Always assume that gobs of people can and do read every message you send. These people include your coworkers, your system administrator, system administrators on other machines through which your email travels, random pimply-faced fools who like poking around in other people's email, and last, but certainly not least, the government, probably in the form of the CIA, FBI, Secret Service, or National Security Agency. I realize this sounds alarming, and it is most certainly not completely true, but the possibility exists for all of these people to read your email.

In reality, email carries significant privacy, but because you have no guarantee of that privacy, you should stay aware of what you're saying. This suggestion is especially true if you use email at work, where you could lose your job over ill-considered remarks in email. It's always a good idea to check on your employer's policy about email privacy.

There have been a number of court cases regarding ownership of email (Does it belong to you? Does it belong to your employer?) at some large companies like Epson and Borland. Since it may come down to a matter of their lawyers being meaner than your lawyers, don't push it.

This lack of privacy carries over to mailing lists and Usenet news (where you want people to read your messages, but you may not want the government to keep tabs on your postings). In fact, some people have gone so far as to include inflammatory keywords in otherwise innocuous postings, just to trip up the rumored government computers scanning for terrorists, assassins, space aliens, nudists, vegetarians, people who like broccoli, and other possible undesirables.

I almost forgot about *attachments*. Many people like to send each other files in email, and although you can do this by simply encoding the file as BinHex or uucode (I'll talk about these file formats in a few chapters) and pasting it into the body of the message, modern email programs instead enable you to merely attach the file to the message with a specific command.

That's all fine and nice if your recipient also uses an email program that knows how to deal with the attachment, but if not, your friend sees the file, usually encoded in BinHex or uucode, at the end of the message in the body (but before the signature). Large email files can be a pain to deal with unless your email program supports attachments.

Header

Okay, I admit it; I've been avoiding talking about the header so far. I did so because the message header generally looks like a lot of gobbledygook to the novice user, and in fact, it should. The header exists for the computers, not for the users, and you're lucky that you can read it as well as you can. In some programs you can see an abbreviated header, which is good, and in some cases you can ignore the header altogether, which can be a little dangerous because it may not be clear who receives a reply to that message.

As much as the header is technoweenie information that exists primarily for the computers to route mail to you, I recommend that you choose an abbreviated header display if you have one. An abbreviated header shows you information that can be useful, such as who sent the email to you, when it was sent, what the subject of the message is, and to whom it was sent (not always only you—it's easy to send the same piece of email to multiple people).

Take a look at a typical header, culled just now from one of my archived pieces of email (see figure 7.1).

Part II   Email Basics

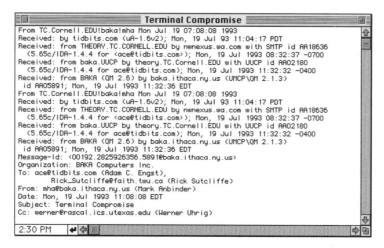

Figure 7.1   *A sample header.*

Let's take a spin through all the different parts of the header, explaining each one along the way and starting with the glop at the top.

```
From TC.Cornell.EDU!baka!mha Mon Jul 19 07:08:08 1993

Received: by tidbits.com (uA-1.6v2); Mon, 19 Jul 93 11:04:17 PDT
Received: from THEORY.TC.CORNELL.EDU by nwnexus.wa.com with SMTP id AA18636
  (5.65c/IDA-1.4.4 for <ace@tidbits.com>); Mon, 19 Jul 1993 08:32:37 -0700
Received: from baka.UUCP by theory.TC.Cornell.EDU with UUCP id AA02180
  (5.65c/IDA-1.4.4 for ace@tidbits.com); Mon, 19 Jul 1993 11:32:32 -0400
Received: from BAKA (QM 2.6) by baka.ithaca.ny.us (UMCP\QM 2.1.3)
  id AA05891; Mon, 19 Jul 1993 11:32:36 EDT
```

The preceding lines are merely routing information that tell you where a message went and when it arrived there. You have to read it backwards to follow the flow, so this message traveled from the QuickMail server at BAKA Computers to the UMCP Bridge (**baka.ithaca.ny.us**), which acts as a gateway for QuickMail messages destined for the Internet. From there it traveled to Cornell's Theory Center, **theory.tc.cornell.edu**, and from the Theory Center, the message bounced almost instantly to **nwnexus.wa.com**, which is my Internet host, and then several hours later to my machine, **tidbits.com**.

You generally can ignore this part of the header, although it can be fun to see where your message went at times. If your message *bounces*—that is, if it fails to go through for some reason and comes back to you—looking at this part in the header helps you determine how far it got and which machine didn't like it. More about how to handle bounces in a bit.

```
Message-Id: <00192.2825926356.5891@baka.ithaca.ny.us>
```

The Message-Id line uniquely identifies each message. It's generally of no use at all, and although it looks like an email address, it's not.

Note   *Only once have I found the Message-Id information useful. For some reason, one of my hosts was duplicating some files that went out, and often the only difference between the messages was that at a certain point they started having different ids. Unfortunately, I never figured out how to solve the problem; I just switched to another host.*

```
Organization: BAKA Computers Inc.
```

The Organization line identifies the organization of the sender, as you may suspect. Individuals often have a good time with this line because they don't have real organizations to put down and can thus include fake organizations like "Our Lady of the Vacant Lot Enterprises."

```
To: ace@tidbits.com (Adam C. Engst),
        Rick_Sutcliffe@faith.twu.ca (Rick Sutcliffe)
```

The To line can have one or more entries, and it specifies, reasonably enough, who the mail was sent to. The recipient may not be you because you might be the person mentioned in the Cc line or even the Bcc line (which you don't see because Bcc stands for Blind Carbon Copy). Most of the time you see a name before or after the email address, but it's not mandatory.

```
From: mha@baka.ithaca.ny.us (Mark Anbinder)
```

Part II   Email Basics

The From line indicates who sent the email and is self-explanatory.

```
Date: Mon, 19 Jul 1993 11:08:08 EDT
```

The Date line lists the date that the email was sent originally, not the time you received it or read it, and should usually indicate the time zone in which the sender lives. Even then I find it difficult to keep track of what time it is in other countries. Do you know the local time in Turkey right now? Some messages use a number, either positive or negative, and the acronym GMT, which stands for Greenwich Mean Time. Unfortunately, this use requires that you know what time it is in Greenwich, England, and that you know how your local daylight savings time is involved. Date lines usually just confuse me.

> *The best way to determine what time it is in another part of the world is to open the Map control panel, click the appropriate spot on the map of the world, and look at the time display. Finding the appropriate spot is up to you. I hope you paid attention in geography class in grade school.*

```
Subject: Terminal Compromise
```

The Subject line should give a clear and concise description of the contents of the email message. In practice, this description often isn't true, especially after a discussion proceeds, changing topics occasionally, with everyone using the reply function to keep the Subject the same. After a while the Subject line bears no resemblance to the contents of the message, at which point it's time to change the line.

```
Cc: werner@rascal.ics.utexas.edu (Werner Uhrig)
```

The Cc line lists all the people who received copies of the message. There is no functional difference from being on the To line or the Cc line, but in theory if you receive only a copy, the message shouldn't concern you as much. In practice I notice little difference.

An abbreviated header probably just shows these five lines and avoids displaying the routing information at the top of the header.

You also may see other lines in the header that identify which program mailed the message, to whom the recipients should reply, the type of data included in the message, how the data is encoded, and that sort of thing. In general, you don't have to worry about anything in the header very much, but it's worth taking a look every now and then to see if you can tell what's going on in there.

Bounces

In a perfect world, all email would get through to its destination quickly and reliably. But just as with snail mail, which can take one to five days to appear, and which sometimes never appears at all, email isn't perfect, and sometimes it will bounce back to you. At times the machine that bounced the mail back to you will give you a hint as to what went wrong, but more often you're on your own.

The most common reason for a bounced message is a typo somewhere in the address. That's one reason that short email addresses are good—they're easier to type and thus less likely to be mistyped. The first thing to do when you get a bounce is to look through the header of the original message (the full headers are usually returned to you) and make sure you typed the address properly. Everyone makes this mistake on occasion.

A common error message in bounced email is "User unknown." This means that the email arrived at the proper machine, which searched through its list of users and decided that it didn't have a user with the name that you used. Again, this is most commonly due to a typo in the userid, although sometimes there are problems on the destination machine that have caused it to forget about a user, possibly temporarily. After checking the address, try resending the message, especially if you've gotten mail through to that address before.

Along with unknown users, you may see error messages complaining about "Host unknown." This is a more serious error that's more difficult to work around if it's not simply a typo. The basic problem is that for some reason one machine, perhaps your host machine or perhaps one further along in the path to the destination, was unable to contact the destination machine. There's not much you can do in this case other than try again a little later, in the hope that the machine you're mailing to has come back up.

One thing to watch out for is that sometimes the header provides an incorrect address to your email program, but the person includes the proper one in their signature. If you have trouble replying to a message, and the address you're replying to is different from an address listed in the signature, try using the signature address instead.

Part II   Email Basics

Note

I find this trick especially useful if the address in the signature is simple, whereas the address from the header is long and convoluted. Simple addresses seem to be more reliable, on the whole, although that's not a hard and fast rule.

Using Email Programs

All email programs share some basic features that you need in order to quickly and efficiently read, reply, and store your email. However, after these basic commonalities, the differences between programs mount quickly, so I concentrate on those differences when I talk about each program later in the book. For the moment, though, let's look at what an email program must do at a minimum.

Reading Email

An email program should enable you to display and scroll through an email message easily. Because you're using the Macintosh, you should be able to do all the standard

Macintosh things to text in a window, such as copying and pasting into a different program, resizing the window to display more text, selecting all the text with a single command, and that sort of thing.

Although you usually can choose the font and size in which you view messages in Macintosh email programs, I recommend that you stick to a monospaced font such as Monaco or Courier. People on the Internet must format tables and graphics with spaces, and monospaced fonts such as Monaco and Courier display these tables and graphics properly. Proportionally spaced fonts such as Times and Helvetica don't work as well because the characters in these fonts can have different widths, with a lowercase *i* being thinner than an uppercase *W*. Few of these features are generally available with a Unix mail program; that's one of the major advantages of using the Mac.

> **N o t e**
>
> *Some email or communications programs come with special monospaced fonts that are supposedly easier to read than the standard Monaco and Courier. If you see fonts like TTYFont, VT100, or Mishawaka, they're designed for displaying Internet email on the screen. I personally prefer Monaco 9 point.*

Navigating and Managing Email

Another important feature of an email program is the manner in which it enables you to move between messages, save messages in different mailboxes, and delete unwanted messages after you've read them. Most email programs display a list of the messages in an In Box area, and some indicate which messages you have already read, replied to, or saved to disk. Opening a message usually opens a new window to display the message, and sometimes closing the window (with or without deleting the current message) opens the next unread message—a nice feature for those who receive a great deal of mail. Being able to sort the list of messages is useful, and you should be able to select multiple messages at once to move them to another mailbox or delete them.

> **N o t e**
>
> *Some of these navigation features may not exist in the email program you use, but with a macro program like CE Software's QuicKeys, you may be able to simulate them.*

Speaking of multiple mailboxes, all email programs should support them, though unfortunately not all do. Most people want to save some of the messages they receive, so a program should allow you to create your own mailboxes for filing away messages on different topics. Of course, if you can create a new mailbox, the email program should enable you to do everything you can do in your In Box to the messages stored in a personal mailbox.

N
o
t
e

Perhaps the worst, and most surprising, offender in the multiple mailbox world is Apple's PowerTalk (released in late 1993), which puts a single mailbox on your Mac's desktop, but loses mail-related information like sender, subject, and date if you copy the messages out of the mailbox to a folder.

While you're managing your email, you will undoubtedly want to delete many of the messages you receive. This area may seem straightforward, but the better email programs follow Apple's lead with the Finder and enable you to trash a file without actually immediately deleting it. The easier it is to delete a message (and it should be very easy since you're likely to eventually want to delete most of the mail you receive), the more likely you will eventually delete something accidentally. If the email program deletes immediately, your message is toast. The other advantage of the two-stage (where a message is put in a trash can before being deleted later) or a delayed delete (where a message is marked as being deleted but isn't actually deleted until you close the mailbox) is that you then don't have to put up with an annoying confirmation dialog box every time you delete a message.

Some of your messages may, in fact, contain programs or other files that you want to save to a normal Macintosh file. A few email programs automatically detect attachments encoded in certain formats (more about file formats later) and decode such messages on their own. But one way or another, you need a simple way to save the message you're looking at without copying and pasting the entire thing into a word processor.

Part II   Email Basics

Replying to Email

Much of the mail you receive requires a reply of some sort, so an email program should make replying extremely easy, either with a command key shortcut or a single click on an icon. An email program also should facilitate *quoting* the original message, or prefixing each line with one or two special characters, usually a greater-than symbol and a space. Using quoting, you can easily include some of the message you're replying to so that the recipient has some context to know what you're talking about. A nice feature is the ability to select just a certain part of the original message and have the email program quote only that selected text in the reply and ignore the rest of the original message (see figure 7.2).

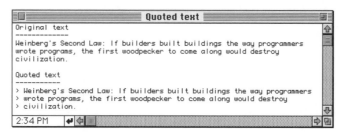

Figure 7.2   Original text and quoted text.

N
o
t
e

Rick Holzgrafe has written a clever little $10 shareware utility called SignatureQuote that enables you to quote messages properly even if your email program doesn't support it. SignatureQuote supports two quoting styles, two signatures that you can paste in, and can join and split text. It's a must-have if you're locked into a lousy email program. It's in:

```
ftp://ftp.tidbits.com/pub/tidbits/tisk/util/
```

Because an email message may have originally been sent to several people, an email program should give you the option of replying only to the sender or to all the people to whom the message was originally sent. At the same time, it ideally should make sure that you see the salient lines in the header. I've spawned a couple of embarrassing scenes by forwarding a message to a friend, and when my friend replied to me, his email program saw that mine had included the original message's address in the Reply-To line in the header. So his reply, instead of going just to me, went back to the sender, which was a mailing list that went to thousands of people. Oops! Luckily, I didn't say anything embarrassing and neither did he, so we were safe, but that's a good example of how two computer professionals who know better could have been thoroughly embarrassed in public. Think of this situation as standing up in a crowded restaurant and shouting loudly that your underwear has holes. You get the idea.

More powerful email programs provide features that can automatically mark or reply to email based on the contents of the header or the body of the incoming message. They often generalize these features so that you can essentially run a *mailserver*, which sends out requested information automatically via email. You also can use this sort of feature to run a simple mailing list, which takes a message to a certain local address and forwards it automatically to a list of subscribers.

N
o
t
e

There are several programs that enable you run your own mailing list from a Macintosh and do things like auto-replies, although they currently require a direct connection to the Internet. Look for MailShare and AutoShare in:

```
ftp://ftp.tidbits.com/pub/tidbits/tisk/tcp/mail/
```

New Email

When replying to email and when creating new mail, an email program should provide all the features that you're used to when you're writing in a Macintosh word processor. In my opinion (which is by no means universal), the standard editors in the character-based Unix world stink (yeah, I know those are fighting words), and I spend so much time writing and editing my email that I couldn't possibly put up with anything other than a decent Macintosh editor. However, because every email program implements text entry and editing on its own, none of them compare to a full-fledged word processor, and a few barely even compete with the free TeachText or its fancier successor, SimpleText. My dream, which isn't all that far off, is to be able to use Nisus Writer, the word processor with which I'm writing this book, for all of my email. With the growing acceptance of Apple events, this change will happen. I just hope it happens sooner rather than later.

I may be odd in this respect, but I think that any email program should make it easy to save a copy of everything you write, preferably automatically. I send more email than most people, often as many as 1,000 messages per month, but I like to be able to go back on occasion and see what I said, forward a message to someone who lost it, or just browse through the thoughts that appeared in my writings at that time. Why bother to keep a diary if you're writing about most of what happens in your life in email to friends?

Finally, whenever you create email, your email program should enable you to send the mail to a *nickname* or *alias*, which is merely another, easier-to-remember form of an email address. So instead of typing `ferdinand-the-bull@cork.tree.com` every time you want to send that person email, you can type the shorter `Bull`. Be careful with nicknames because it's easy to create more than you can easily remember, at which point they don't particularly help any more. Defining nicknames for everyone you might ever send email to is a waste of time; settle for defining a nickname only after you decide that you are likely to send that person email frequently.

> **Note**
>
> *You want to be slightly careful with nicknames, because occasionally the recipient sees the nickname as well as the address. A friend once created a nickname DA BOSS for our supervisor, who thought it was funny when she saw it. I could think of some less humorous situations.*

Part II   Email Basics

Finding People

Now you know how an email program should work and how to read email addresses when you see them littering up this book and the nets in general. But how do you find people to write to? Finding people to write to depends on what you're looking for. Hmm? What does he mean by that?

Assume that there are two types of people—those you already know and those you haven't yet met. The latter group makes up most of the world, and in some respects, they are the easiest to find and talk to because you don't really care who specifically you end up talking to. After all, you don't know any more about one stranger over another, so who you talk to makes no difference.

Friends

When I first started using the networks way back when, few of my friends had accounts, and of them, only my best friend from high school ever managed to send me email more than once. I think I got a total of three messages from him. I tried to convince them, but I just couldn't get my friends to use email. Finally, I decided they all truly hated me (a logical conclusion for a 17-year-old college freshman) and gave up on them. My ego has recovered some since then, because I've found that convincing people to start using email just to talk to me is almost impossible. This argument worked with my parents, after a while, especially after my sister also started using email heavily at Cornell. But otherwise? I can't think of a single person whom I've convinced to use email for my sake, although we recently managed to set my grandmother up with an old Macintosh Classic and an email account. The moral of the story is that you should assume that you can talk only to people who already use email.

Okay, so once past that reality check, how do you find the address of someone who you know uses email? The simplest and most effective method seldom occurs to many net denizens—use the telephone and ask them. This method, low-tech though it may be, has the advantage of being quick, accurate, and easy. Of course, it does ruin the surprise value of that first email note. Such is life. You do need to know your friend's telephone number, or failing that, her address so you can call the all-knowing information computers at the phone company. If you don't even know where your friend lives, she may be trying to hide from you anyway after that ugly incident a while back.

"Aha!" you say, "If the all-knowing phone company computers can give me my friend's telephone number, aren't there all-knowing computers on the Internet that can give me my friend's email address?" Nice try, and good question, but the answer is, unfortunately, maybe. Some computers know what users they support, and you can find some information via services called *Finger*, *Whois*, *X.500*, *Ph*, *Knowbot*, and various others, but that information doesn't help unless you already know what machine to search. Several attempts have been made at linking various directory services on different machines, but I've never found them to be the slightest bit useful. The problem is twofold. First, hooking a local directory of users to an Internet-wide directory requires some effort and certain standards, and inertia being what it is, that effort isn't always made, and the standards don't exist. Second, many organizations shield their users from the outside world for reasons of security and privacy. These shields also make it difficult to determine how many people actually use the Internet because one domain may have two users, like **tidbits.com**, or many thousands of users, like **microsoft.com**.

N o t e

*Frankly, because I find these services so completely useless, I'm not going to bother to discuss them further. That said, if you crave some frustration, go to the University of Minnesota's Gopher server at **gopher.tc.umn.edu** (the Home Gopher server by default, if you use TurboGopher), select Phone Books, and then check out the various different options available* *for searching for Internet email addresses. If you know the organization in question, and they have a Phone Book server, that's the best start—otherwise you're on your own. The main thing you miss via the Gopher route is the Knowbot Information Service. To access it, telnet to* **info.cnri.reston.va.us 185** *and type* **help** *to see the possible commands.*

Acquaintances

As I said earlier in this chapter, finding new friends is easy on the Internet. You don't know people beforehand, so communicating with them in a discussion list via email or news requires nothing in terms of opening lines or trivial small talk about the fallibility of weather forecasters. If you have something to contribute to a discussion, or perhaps if you merely want to make a private comment to one of the people in the discussion, meeting him is as easy as replying to his message. Whether that first contact grows beyond a one-time message depends on many variables, but with so many people, finding correspondents on the net doesn't take long.

As much as meeting people may be easy, finding them again after some time often proves more difficult. You may not remember where a person lives, if you ever knew, and if it's in the United States at all, you probably don't know his telephone number; and frankly, you may not even remember how to spell his name. And yet, all too often I've had long, involved conversations that eventually trail off after several weeks or months, and then I don't hear from that person again. If I haven't saved a message (which contains the all-important email address in the header) or recorded his email address somewhere, I have to hope that my friend has better organizational systems than I do.

I suggest that you figure out some way to keep track of your correspondents' email addresses. Nickname features work well although they may prove unwieldy as a storage mechanism later on. If that's true, I recommend using a standard database or address book program that can handle extra fields for email addresses. This advice may sound obvious, but I can't tell you how many times I've lost an address that I wanted several months later. These days I keep a copy of every piece of email I send, in part so I can search that file, large though it may be, for email addresses that have escaped my short-term memory.

Mailing Lists

There's no accounting for taste, and similarly, there's no accounting for different interests. I may be interested in electronic publishing, tropical fish, and competitive distance running, whereas the next person might favor *The Simpsons*, aviation, and Irish culture. As a result, discussion groups have sprung up around almost every imaginable topic, and if your area of interest isn't represented, it's not too difficult to start your own group. These groups take two forms: mailing lists and Usenet newsgroups. I talk more about Usenet in the next chapter; for now I'll concentrate on mailing lists.

The beauty of mailing lists is that they cover specific topics and they come straight to you, without any extra work on your part. If you find yourself interested in a topic, you can subscribe to the appropriate mailing list, and all the traffic comes directly to your electronic mailbox. This system makes participating in many mailing lists easy, even if you have only email access to the Internet; Usenet access may require more money and effort. Luckily for those of you who cannot get Usenet access, many mailing lists and newsgroups mirror each other.

Mailing lists have several other advantages over Usenet news. Email is ubiquitous on the Internet, whereas access to news is less common (although certainly widespread). Because of the way Usenet news propagates throughout the nets, mailing lists often arrive faster than any given posting in a newsgroup. Because mailing lists arrive in your electronic mailbox, they may seem less intimidating than large newsgroups with many participants. And frankly, many of us who lead busy lives find mailing lists easier to keep up with because we don't have to run another program to read the list, whereas reading news always requires leaving that ubiquitous email program and then running a newsreader.

There are a number of programs that operate mailing lists, the most well-known of which are LISTSERV, ListProcessor (also known as listproc), and Majordomo. They all support similar commands; I'll get into those in a moment. LISTSERV is a commercial program from Eric Thomas of LSoft. It currently requires an IBM mainframe running VM/CMS (although versions for VMS, Unix, and Windows NT are in the works). The Unix-based ListProcessor comes from Anastasios Kotsikonas and is now owned by CREN (remember them from chapter 4?). The Unix-based Majordomo is free as far as I can tell.

There also are many mailing lists that are run through hacks to the Unix mailer software—these generally require some sort of human intervention for subscribing and signing off, although sometimes they use non-standard commands that do the same thing. Have I mentioned yet that I dislike programs that don't work in standard ways? They make life even more confusing than it already is.

Note

You may wonder why LISTSERV doesn't have an E at the end and why it is spelled with all capitals. LISTSERV software has existed for some time on IBM mainframes that run the VM/CMS operating system. This operating system limits userids to eight characters (hence the missing E), and because the operating system itself was originally not case sensitive, all commands and program names have traditionally been typed in uppercase only. The name also may have had something to do with early computer terminals not supporting lowercase, but I can't prove that theory. Just believe me—by convention, LISTSERVs are always addressed in the uppercase, although it doesn't matter any more.

Along with the different mailing list manager programs, you may have to deal with two other variables related to mailing lists—moderation and digests. Each of these possibilities slightly changes how you interact with the list, so let's look at each in turn and then go over the basics of using the list manager software as a subscriber.

Moderated vs. Unmoderated

I suspect many mailing lists started out *unmoderated*, which means that anyone was able to send a message on any topic (whether or not it was appropriate to the group) to the list. The list software then distributed that message to the entire list. You see the problem already—no one wants to read a bunch of messages that have nothing to do with the topic or discussion at hand. Similarly, if a discussion is spinning out of control and turning into a flame war, it's just a waste of time for many people.

Thus was born the concept of the moderated mailing list. To stem inappropriate postings, a moderator reads all the postings before they go out to the group at large and decides which are appropriate. Moderated groups tend to have less traffic, and the messages that go through are guaranteed by the moderator to have some worth. This system is good.

Note

The Info-Mac Digest is a prominent example of a moderated group in the Macintosh world. Although they're usually fairly lenient, moderators Bill Lipa, Gordon Watts, Igor Livshits, and Liam Breck do an excellent job, and their efforts are much appreciated by all. I help out somewhat with Info-Mac, although with the files stored on the Info-Mac Archive, not with the Info-Mac Digest itself.

Part II   Email Basics

On the downside, moderated groups occasionally run into sticky issues of censorship because the moderator may not always represent the views of the majority of the readers. Moderator positions are volunteer only; I've never heard of a mailing list that elected a moderator, although it's certainly possible, particularly among lists that carry traffic associated with a professional organization.

There's a slightly different form of moderation practiced on some other lists that you may be interested in, such as the Apple Internet Users and Apple Internet Providers lists. Run by Chuq von Rospach of Apple, these lists employ a "List Mom" form of moderation, which means that although all postings appear whether or not Chuq approves, he reserves the right to tell people to take off-topic discussions elsewhere. Since I was about to start similar lists when Chuq created the Apple Internet Users and Providers lists, I volunteered to be an Assistant List Mom on Chuq's lists, which means I help steer the discussions so that they stay on track. Needless to say, I recommend both lists highly for discussions about the Mac and the Internet.

N
o
t
e

> *To subscribe to the lists, send email to* **listproc@abs.apple.com** *and in the body of the message (the Subject line can be blank or nonsense), put* **subscribe apple-internet-users Your Full Name** *or* **subscribe apple-internet-providers Your Full Name**.
>
> *Once your subscription has been processed, you will receive an informational file from the list, and then you can start posting questions and helping out with answers that you know. You cannot post to the list until you have subscribed.*

I see no reason to choose to read or not read a mailing list based on its moderation until you've spent a while seeing what goes on in the group. I subscribe to various lists, some moderated, some not, and on the whole, both have their place. Keep in mind, though, that if you post to a moderated list, the moderator may reject your posting. Don't feel bad, but do ask why so that your future submissions stand a better chance of reaching the rest of the group. On the other hand, when posting to an unmoderated group, try to stick to appropriate topics because people hate hearing about how you like your new car in a list devoted to potbellied pigs. Too many misdirected postings to a list may agitate list members to the point of asking for a moderator to limit the discussion.

Individual Messages vs. Digests

When the number of messages in a mailing list increases to a certain level, many lists consider creating a digest version of the list. A digest is simply a single message that contains all the individual messages concatenated in a specific way. Why bother with a digest? Depending on how your email program works, you might find it awkward to receive and read as many as 30 messages a day, especially if your email service, such as AppleLink, charges you a per-message fee to receive email. Just think how many messages you may have waiting after a week of vacation. If the messages are sent in digest form, a mailing list becomes easier to handle for some people because you get one big message instead of lots of little messages.

Unfortunately, digests have problems too. Some email gateways to commercial services (again AppleLink) limit the size of incoming email messages. Thus, digest mailing lists like the Info-Mac Digest, one of the most popular Macintosh mailing lists, can range in size from 30K to over 100K, so very few issues of the digest sneak through the gateways with size limitations. In addition, you may find it easier to read (or skip through) small individual messages, whereas scrolling through a 100K file can take quite a bit of time and can be extremely awkward with some email programs. To add to the complication, certain email programs can break up a digest into its individual messages for easier viewing. I'm talking the email equivalent of digestive enzymes here.

You must decide for yourself whether a digest is easier or harder to work with, but only with some groups do you have any choice. The LISTSERV and ListProcessor software sometimes provide an option that you can set to switch your subscription to a mailing list from individual messages to a single, usually daily, digest. I don't believe you can toggle this option for Majordomo-based lists, but Majordomo list administrators can set up a separate list that sends out a digest—you would simply subscribe to the separate (digest) list instead. These separate digest lists in Majordomo generally have "-digest" appended to the listname.

Mailing List Managers

Mailing list managers sport many sophisticated features for managing large mailing lists, and these features have made the programs popular among the people who start and run mailing lists (you didn't think lists just worked on their own, did you?). For instance, you can easily and automatically subscribe to and sign off from mailing lists run with a mailing list manager without bothering a human (in most cases). This significantly reduces the amount of work that the list administrator has to do. These programs generally also have provisions for tracking the subscribers to a list, and for those who want to remain unknown, concealing certain subscriptions.

Mailing list managers can prevent unauthorized people from sending messages to the list. The *TidBITS* list works this way in theory because only I can send a message, in this case an issue of *TidBITS*, to the list. I say "in theory" because in practice the safeguards have broken down twice, resulting in confusing messages going to the entire list. The LISTSERV that runs the *TidBITS* list also knows to route all replies to postings on the list to me directly, which is normally good, but when these two accidental postings got through the safeguards, I received hundreds of messages from confused readers who didn't know why they had gotten this message. It was a major hassle.

The LISTSERV software knows about other LISTSERVs running on other machines around the world and uses this knowledge to limit network traffic. For instance, I send a single message from my machine to a mainframe at Rice University in Texas that runs the LISTSERV handling the *TidBITS* list. Once the message arrives at Rice, the LISTSERV software checks to make sure it came from me and then sends it out to the many thousands of readers on the *TidBITS* subscription list.

The LISTSERV is smart, however. It doesn't blindly send out thousands of messages, one per user, because that would waste network bandwidth, especially on expensive trans-oceanic links. Instead, the LISTSERV determines how to enlist the help of certain other LISTSERVs running around the world. If it knows of a LISTSERV site in Australia, for instance, it sends a single copy of the message to Australia along with the list of Australian readers to distribute to. If 100 people in Australia subscribe to the *TidBITS* list, only one message crosses the Pacific instead of 100 identical copies of the same message. That's elegant.

I gather that ListProcessor and Majordomo, Unix mail-based mailing list managers, don't have as many features as the LISTSERV software, but that's more from an administrator's point of view. Users generally shouldn't care which they use. Don't worry about it one way or another; you have no choice when picking mailing lists to subscribe to. And despite the added features of the LISTSERV software, the thing that makes the administrative details of a list easy to deal with is the administrator, not the software.

> **Note**
>
> *ListProcessor used to be called Unix-Listserv and was distributed freely (version 6.0c is still free, even now that CREN has bought it and will be selling future versions), but after some unpleasantness regarding the term "Listserv," Anastasios Kotsikonas decided to rename it to avoid confusion. So, if you see references to Unix-Listserv, they're talking about ListProcessor.*

Using LISTSERVs

Most people find dealing with LISTSERVs quite easy; however, you should watch out for a few common pitfalls while working with LISTSERV-based mailing lists. Many of the following commands and pitfalls apply to lists run by the other mailing list managers as well, so it's worth reading through the LISTSERV section even if, for instance, you're dealing with a ListProcessor list.

Every LISTSERV list has two email addresses associated with it: the address for the LISTSERV itself, and the address for the mailing list. Why the dichotomy? Well, the LISTSERV address handles all the commands, things such as subscriptions and requests for lists of subscribers and the like. The mailing list address is where you send submissions to the list, assuming of course that it's that sort of list. Here, I use the *TidBITS* list as an example for my illustrations of the basic tasks you do with a LISTSERV-based mailing list. (The only difference between the *TidBITS* list and many others is that if you send mail to the mailing list address, it doesn't go to everyone else on the list because the *TidBITS* list is dedicated to distributing *TidBITS*, not to discussion, as are most lists. Any mail sent to the mailing list address comes to me, which is fine, because such messages are usually comments on articles.)

If you want to send the LISTSERV that handles the *TidBITS* list a command, such as your subscription request, send it to **listserv@ricevm1.rice.edu**. Notice that nowhere in the address is *TidBITS* mentioned, which is a hint that you have to specify *TidBITS* somewhere else. LISTSERVs ignore the Subject line entirely, so don't worry about filling it in at all. In the body of the message, though, you can put one or more commands, each on its own line.

To subscribe to the *TidBITS* list, you send the preceding address a message with the following command on one line in the body of the message: **SUBSCRIBE TIDBITS** *your full name*, where you replace *your full name* with your real name, not your email address or some cute nickname. If the list administrator has to contact you about a problem, she probably doesn't appreciate having to address you as "Dear Swedish Chef Fan Club Ork Ork Ork." To clarify the preceding command, to subscribe to any LISTSERV mailing list, you send the **SUBSCRIBE** command, a space, the name of the list you want to subscribe to, a space, and then your full name, which must be at least two words (see figure 7.3). I don't know how rock star types like Cher or Prince manage with LISTSERVs, although I did once get mail from someone who really only had one name. I advised him to use "No really, I only have one name" as his last name.

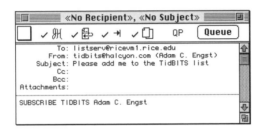

Figure 7.3 *Subscribing to* TidBITS.

> *Prince has legally changed his name to a single character that looks like a little stick figure person. Such characters are called dingbats in the publishing world, so I vote that we simply refer to Prince as Dingbat, or perhaps Prince Dingbat to be unambiguous. Needless to say, there's no way to subscribe to a mailing list using a single non-alphabetic character as your name.*

The LISTSERV always returns a welcome note after you have subscribed successfully. *Keep that note!* It lists various useful commands, such as how to sign off from the list, and it usually provides the address of the list administrator. You can contact the list administrator to handle any problems that the automated program chokes on.

You know what I just said about keeping the welcome message from the LISTSERV. Well, I really mean it! I can't tell you how irritating it is to have someone post the list asking how to signoff when it would have been trivial if they'd just kept that welcome message. Actually, I can tell you how irritating this is, because after the 10th or 100th person does, it's tremendously exasperating! Sorry, I'll quiet down now.

After you have subscribed to a list, you mainly want to read messages (which is easy) and post occasional messages to the rest of the people on the list. Once again, to post a message you send it to the mailing list address, which is always the name of the list at the same machine. If, for example, you want to send mail to the *TidBITS* list (which comes only to me), you send the email to **tidbits@ricevm1.rice.edu**. I realize I've almost beaten this particular horse to death, but I can't emphasize enough the difference between the LISTSERV address and the mailing list address. You send commands to the LISTSERV, and submissions to the mailing list address. Perhaps the most common problem I see on LISTSERV mailing lists is that people forget to send commands to the

LISTSERV address and instead fill up the mailing list with the electronic equivalent of junk mail that no one wants to see. And, of course, sending commands to the mailing list address isn't just annoying and flame-provoking, it's futile because the LISTSERV doesn't respond to them there.

After you've been on a list for some time, the LISTSERV may ask you to confirm your subscription. I set this option with the *TidBITS* list to clean the deadwood from the list every year. Students graduate, employees move on, bulletin boards close up, and those addresses don't always go away, so the LISTSERV wastes network resources sending to a non-existent person. It's much like talking to a politician. After you have received *TidBITS* for a year from the LISTSERV, it sends you a message asking you to confirm that you still want to get the newsletter. If you don't respond within seven days, the LISTSERV removes you from the list, assuming that you don't want to continue receiving email from it. If you respond, you must respond with a command so that you send it to the LISTSERV address, not the mailing list address. The command is simply **CONFIRM TIDBITS** (or the name of whatever list you are asked to confirm).

A portion of the time this confirmation process fails. As I'm sure you noticed in the preceding paragraphs, nowhere do you provide your email address to the LISTSERV, which is supposed to determine it from the header of your message. This idea seems excellent at first because the header should, in theory, have your email address correct, and it doesn't suffer from typos or simple human mistakes that you make if you type it in by hand. However, depending on the routing that your mail takes and how you or your system administrators have your system set up, your address as it appears in the header may change from time to time. Those changes play havoc with the LISTSERV, which is a very literal program. Therefore, when you confirm a subscription, if that confirmation comes from an address the LISTSERV doesn't recognize, poof, it doesn't work. You probably still receive mail to the original address just fine because the address is usually merely a variant on the theme, so many people sit helplessly by as the LISTERV asks for confirmation, rejects it, and then calmly deletes them from the list.

Note

This situation is a perfect example of why computers should never be given direct control over human lives. If you don't properly match for some reason, you're just another file to be deleted.

There is a simple fix. Just resubscribe as soon as the LISTSERV sends either the confirmation rejection or the message saying that it has deleted you from the list. You may get duplicates of everything for a few days, but then the LISTSERV deletes your old address and continues to send to your new one.

If you blow it and misspell your name while subscribing, or perhaps decide to change your name for one reason or another, you can always change your name (only) with the

LISTSERV by sending another **SUBSCRIBE** command. The danger here, as discussed in the preceding paragraphs, is that if your address looks at all different from when you originally subscribed, the LISTSERV happily adds you to the list again, and you receive duplicates of everything. Now is a good time to ask the list administrator for help because the LISTSERV recognizes only your new address, so you can't delete your old address. Bit of a Catch-22 there.

This Catch-22 can apply to trying to sign off from a list normally, as well. Under standard circumstances, if you send the command **SIGNOFF TIDBITS** to the LISTSERV address, it removes you from the list. If your address in the header has changed, however, it doesn't recognize you as a current subscriber and thus doesn't let you sign off. Once again, if you need help beyond what the LISTSERV program can provide, don't hesitate to ask the list administrator, but ask nicely. These people don't get paid to take abuse, and in fact, they don't get paid to administrate a list at all. I'll tell you how to contact a list administrator in a moment.

The reason for this seemingly irritating address feature is that administrators realized early on that it would be way too much fun to sign someone else up for mailing lists if you really don't like him. You could, for example, sign him up for all the special offers in the back of *The National Enquirer*. Some friends of mine once had a war with that game, but one was declared the loser when he received bronzed baby shoes and a free subscription to a white supremacist newsletter, or some such nonsense. I'm sure it would be great fun to sign Bill Gates up for a really far-out mailing list, but it gets old after a while and is generally considered abuse of the networks.

> **N o t e**
>
> *Some LISTSERVs can send you files if you send them proper commands in a message. The LISTSERV at Rice,* `listserv@ricevm1.rice.edu`, *is one of these sites. In fact, it stores Macintosh files that also exist on the popular FTP site* `sumex-aim.stanford.edu`. *You can find site-specific information by sending a HELP command to any LISTSERV, and for the standard LISTSERV information, send INFO REFCARD.*

LISTSERVs support a number of other commands, of which only a few are generally useful. If you want to see a list of all the people who have subscribed to a LISTSERV list, you can use the **REVIEW** command, although many lists no longer return the full list of subscribers to protect against abuses.

The other utility of the **REVIEW** command is that it includes the address of the list administrator at the top, so it's a good way to find out who to ask for help. Using the **REVIEW** command is a good way to see what address the LISTSERV thinks you used to subscribe and then ask the administrator for help. For just the administrator address, you can change the command to **REVIEW SHORT**.

To switch a LISTSERV subscription (you must already be subscribed) from individual messages to a digest format, send the LISTSERV address the command **SET** *listname* **DIGEST**. To switch back to individual messages, send it command **SET** *listname* **MAIL**.

Most of the other commands that LISTSERVs support aren't as interesting, or as much fun to write about, so I'll refrain and let you find them on your own.

Using ListProcessor

Working with a mailing list run by the ListProcessor program is remarkably like working with a mailing list run by the LISTSERV program. The similarity isn't coincidental—ListProcessor started out as a clone of LISTSERV, not in terms of the code, but in terms of the command structure. Thus, the few differences between the two are minimal, especially in the basic functions.

Just as LISTSERVs have a **listserv@domain.name** address, ListProcessors are generally referred to as **listproc@domain.name**, although a number of them may still use the **listserv@domain.name** address left over from when ListProcessor was called Unix-Listserv. And just as the mailing list itself has a different address from the LISTSERV address, something like **listname@domain.name**, so too do ListProcessor lists. In other words, the confusing dichotomy between the ListProcessor address and the list address exists, just as it does with LISTSERV lists. You send commands to the ListProcessor address (in the body of the message—the Subject line doesn't matter) and submissions to the mailing list address. I'm really beginning to feel sorry for this poor horse, since I keep beating it, but I can't tell you how many people fail to understand this basic distinction, and in the process irritate thousands of other people on numerous lists.

To subscribe to a ListProcessor-based mailing list, send **subscribe** *listname your full name* to the ListProcessor address. Just as with the LISTSERV mailing lists, replace *listname* with the name of the list you wish to subscribe to and use your real name in place of *your full name*. ListProcessor figures out your email address from the header of the message.

You leave a ListProcessor-based mailing list by sending the command **unsubscribe** *listname* to the ListProcessor address. The command **signoff** *listname* does exactly the same thing. Just like the LISTSERV lists, if your address has changed, the automated process very well may not work, at which point you must talk to the list administrator.

The command to switch a ListProcessor subscription from individual messages to digest format differs slightly from LISTSERV—send the command **set** *listname* **mail digest** to the ListProcessor address. Frankly, I can't see from the instructions how to switch back to individual messages.

If all else fails, try sending the ListProcessor the **help** command for a simple reference card that explains the options.

Using Majordomo

This is getting kind of boring, but Majordomo works pretty much like the other two mailing list managers. There are two addresses—the Majordomo address to send your commands to (often **majordomo@domain.name**), and the mailing list address to send submissions to (**listname@domain.name**). You also may (if they're running a recent version of Majordomo) be able to send commands to **listname-request@domain.name**.

To subscribe to a Majordomo-based list, send email to the Majordomo address with the command **subscribe** *listname*. Majordomo differs slightly from the other two mailing list managers in that you don't have to specify your full name, and if you like, you can append an email address to the subscription command. This enables you to subscribe someone else to a mailing list, which can be handy—just don't abuse it. The same structure applies to removing yourself or someone else from a list—send **unsubscribe** *listname* to the Majordomo address (**signoff** *listname* works as well).

An easier method of subscribing and unsubscribing to Majordomo-based lists is to send email to **listname-request@domain.name** with either the **subscribe** command or the **unsubscribe** command in the body of the message. Since you've made it clear which list you want to subscribe to with the address, there's no need to include it in the subscription command.

Part II

Email Basics

Finally, you can send Majordomo a **help** command to see what other options are available. I always recommend that you do this, just so you know how and so that you see what's possible.

Neither Rain, Nor Snow…

Since you're likely to use email heavily, I hope you've gotten a sense for how it works, the sorts of things you shouldn't do with it, what an email program should do for you, and what it makes possible in terms of mailing lists. There are thousands of mailing lists available on the Internet, and you can find some wonderful discussions. If you'd like to search for a good one, check out this URL via a Web browser:

```
http://alpha.acast.nova.edu:80/listserv.html
```

But, enough about mailing lists—let's move on to the next sort of discussion lists, the Usenet newsgroups.

8

Usenet News Basics

I've talked generally about the thousands of Usenet newsgroups that hold fast-moving discussions on every imaginable topic. My host machine, for example, carried over 5,000 of them at last count, and that's nowhere near the entire list, which is closing in on 10,000. Hundreds of thousands of people read Usenet every day. It's certainly one of the most interesting, although strange, parts of the Internet.

Note

Prompted by a problem posed by Nicholas Negroponte, head of the MIT Media Lab, Eric Jorgensen of MIT did a survey in early 1994 to determine the average age and gender of Usenet readers. Jorgensen received 4,566 responses to his survey. He figured out that the average age of the Usenet reader is 30.7 years old (with a standard deviation of 9.4). Eighty-six and a half percent of the replies came from men, 13.5% came from women, and 0.1% came from, well, not men or women. Although most newsgroups he surveyed were heavily male-dominated, misc.kids (71% female), rec.arts.tv.soaps (91% female), and rec.food.sourdough (50% female) were notable exceptions. You may be able to find more information about the survey and the full results in:

```
http://www.mit.edu:8001/people/nebosite/home-page.html
```

How is Usenet different from the mailing lists we've just looked at in the last chapter? I see two primary differences, neither of which has to do with the information that flows through them.

First, although mailing lists may be faster to propagate because they go directly to the subscriber, they can be extremely inefficient. If only one person on a machine reads a mailing list, one copy comes in. If, however, 100 people on that machine all read the same mailing list, then 100 identical copies of each posting must come in, eating up disk space and slowing down other tasks. This is bad. In contrast, only one copy of every Usenet message goes to each machine, and any number of people on that machine can read it. So, assuming that both contained an identical posting (which in reality occurs only occasionally), you could greatly reduce your machine's storage load by reading the Usenet news group instead of the mailing list.

Second, many people like mailing lists because they always read their mail but may not always run a separate newsreading program. This situation actually works in favor of news as well. Most email programs are designed for a relatively small number of messages, each completely different and unrelated. In contrast, most newsreaders concern themselves with large numbers of messages, many of which are related, or in a *thread*. So, if you read the news and come across an interesting posting, reading the next posting in that thread is easy (or should be), whether or not the posting is the next one in the list. Following threads in an email program is generally difficult or impossible.

Given those advantages, how does Usenet work, what do the messages on it look like, and how do you generally interact with it?

Usenet Plumbing

For the most part, knowing how Usenet actually works isn't even slightly important to daily life. However, the basic principles may help you to better cope with some of its quirks and limitations.

The entire concept of Usenet is based on one machine transferring postings to another. Scale that up so that any one machine carrying Usenet messages talks to at least one other machine carrying Usenet messages, and you start to see how this simple idea can become an immense and powerful reality. We're talking about thousands of machines and millions of people and hundreds of megabytes of data per day.

If you post a message in a Usenet group, your machine passes the message on to all the machines it talks to, both *upstream* and *downstream*. Upstream loosely refers to the machines that your machine generally gets all of its news from. Downstream loosely refers to the machines that get all of their news from your machine. In either case, those machines continue to propagate your message throughout the network, with the Usenet software that controls the system making sure that your message isn't duplicated *ad infinitum* (Latin for "a hell of a lot of times, which irritates everyone").

The actual process by which your message travels is equally simple, at least in UUCP. The Usenet software creates a batch of messages and compresses the batch to reduce transmission time. When the next machine receives the batch, it unbatches the messages and places the files in directories known by the news-reading software. One testament to the simplicity of this scheme is that not all implementations have to use this technique. (In fact, NNTP, another common method of transferring news, sends only the text of articles that a specific reader requests while reading news.) InterCon's UUCP/Connect on the Macintosh, for example, creates a single file for each newsgroup and appends new messages to that single file (which is much more efficient given the way the Macintosh file system works). However, most Unix machines store the messages as individual files within specific directories, and those directories are directly related to the names of the newsgroups.

Newsgroup Innards

Just as email addresses make sense after you know all the parts, so do the Usenet newsgroup names. Although they resemble email addresses, the basic principles are a bit different.

Note

Although, like email addresses, Usenet newsgroups use periods to separate different parts of the name, people tend not to use them in conversation. If, for example, you were to tell a friend about an interesting discussion on **comp.sys.mac.misc***, you'd say, "Check it out on comp sys mac misc." Part of the problem may be the linguistic clumsiness of saying all those "dots," but I suspect more of the reason is that precision isn't nearly as necessary. Unlike email addresses, you seldom type out newsgroup names. It also may have to do with the fact that newsgroup names are all unique and easily parsed.*

The premise of the Usenet newsgroup naming scheme is that of a hierarchy. The naming scheme makes figuring out how to name new groups easy. More important, it maps over to a hierarchical directory (or folder) structure. On the Unix machines that hold the newsgroups, therefore, you find a directory called **news**. Inside that directory are other directories corresponding to the top-level parts of the hierarchy—**alt**, **comp**, **misc**, **news**, **rec**, **sci**,—and so on. These directories are abbreviations for alternate, computers, miscellaneous, news, recreation, and science, respectively.

Note

I could attempt to create a table listing all the top level hierarchies, but it's a pointless task. There are many local hierarchies that I have no way of finding (just as many other machines probably don't carry the **halcyon** *or* **seattle** *hierarchies that I can see), and I couldn't begin to guess which hierarchies your machine might carry.*

Let's dissect the name of **comp.sys.mac.misc**, a popular newsgroup. If we first look into the **comp** directory, we see more directories corresponding to **lang**, **sys**, and so on. Under **sys** we find many directories, one for each computer system. There are **atari**, **amiga**, **ibm**, **mac**, and gobs of systems that you may never have even heard of. (I certainly haven't heard of all of them.) After we go into the **mac** directory, we find the lowest level directories that correspond to the individual topics about the Mac. These include **advocacy**, **apps**, **databases**, **games**, **hardware**, **misc**, **portables**, **system**, and others. Once inside those directories (feel like you're in a Russian doll again?), you find the files that hold the text of the messages (see figure 8.1).

Figure 8.1   *An abbreviated Usenet hierarchy tree.*

This system may seem a tad clumsy, but remember, as a user you never have to traverse that entire directory structure. It exists to categorize and classify newsgroups, and to provide a storage system that maps onto a Unix directory structure.

> *Historically, this structure was used so that as little C code programming as possible had to be done to store and retrieve Usenet news. A design goal for B-news and C-news, the earliest Unix news servers, was to make as much of it as possible run as Unix shell scripts, precluding any fancy binary database backends. Why was that? Laziness is the mother of some invention.*

Message Construction

On the surface, a Usenet posting looks much like an email message (see figure 8.2).

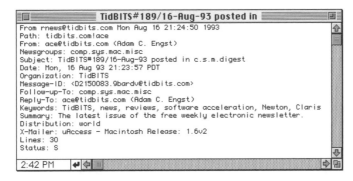

Figure 8.2　*A Usenet header.*

The posting's header holds a From line, a Subject line, and a fair amount of other stuff; next comes the body of the message and a signature.

The header has a few new lines that you may find interesting.

```
Newsgroups: comp.sys.mac.misc
```

First comes the Newsgroups line. It lists, separated by commas, all the newsgroups to which the message is posted. You can post a message to more than one group at a time by putting more than one group in the Newsgroups line. At that point, an article is *cross-posted*. If you must post an article in several groups (which is generally frowned on as a waste of bandwidth), make sure to post via the Newsgroups line and not through individual messages. Individual messages take up more space, because a machine stores only one copy of a cross-posted article along with pointers to it from different groups.

```
Follow-up-To: comp.sys.mac.misc
```

The next Usenet-specific line is the Follow-up-To line, which usually contains the name of the newsgroup in which the article appears. Sometimes, however, you want to post an article in one group, have a discussion, then move back to another group. In this case you put the second group in the Follow-up-To line, because whenever anyone posts a follow-up to your article, the news software makes sure that it ends up in the proper group.

```
Reply-To: ace@tidbits.com (Adam C. Engst)
```

When people reply via email to a newsgroup posting, their newsreaders use the address in the Reply-To line. A Reply-To line makes it easier for people to respond directly rather than cluttering the group with personal messages or those that aren't relevant to the group (especially any flames).

```
Keywords: TidBITS, news, reviews, software acceleration, Newton, Claris

Summary: The latest issue of the free weekly electronic newsletter.
```

Sometimes you see a Keywords and/or Summary line as well. Although they aren't universal or enforced, it's often a good idea to fill in these lines for your article before you post it. That way, people who have set up their newsreaders properly can more effectively filter articles based on keywords. In addition, some newsreaders show only the header and first few lines of an article, and then let the reader decide whether she wants to read the whole thing. A few well-chosen keywords or a concise summary can help make that decision easier.

```
Distribution: world
```

Many articles are only relevant in specific geographic areas. You have two ways to handle this situation. First, if you're selling a car in, say, Seattle, you should post to a specific group that goes only to people in Seattle (more or less, anyway), such as **seattle.forsale**. Many of these site-specific groups exist, even down to the machine. There's a group, **halcyon.slip**, for example, for discussion about issues affecting SLIP and PPP users of the **halcyon.com** machine.

The other way to handle this situation is to use the Distribution line. This enables you to limit the area to which your message is distributed, even if the group encompasses all of Usenet. So, if you want to post a notice about a Seattle British Car Show in **rec.autos**, you should put **seattle**, or possibly **pnw** (for Pacific Northwest), in the Distribution line.

```
Subject: TidBITS#189/16-Aug-93 posted in c.s.m.digest
```

And of course we have the ubiquitous Subject line. Much as it is courteous for you to provide a descriptive Subject line in an email message, it's imperative in a Usenet posting. Most newsreaders these days show the user a list of the messages and their subjects. If you don't provide a good Subject line, far fewer people even notice your message. For example, each week I post an announcement of each issue of *TidBITS* in the **comp.sys.mac.misc** group. Instead of a general Subject line such as "TidBITS posted," I enter "TidBITS#189/16-Aug-93 posted in c.s.m.digest." This tells the reader in precise terms what I posted and where he can find it.

The Newsgroup Stork

Now that you know something about how messages travel from machine to machine and how the naming system works, you may wonder where new newsgroups come from. Whenever I've talked about the range of Usenet groups, I've said something to the effect of "and if there isn't one that matches your interests, you can create one." That is true, but the process is not trivial.

> **N o t e** *Although I summarize the process in this section, if you want to see all the gory details, check out two periodic postings in **news.announce.newusers**. Both "How to Create a New Usenet Newsgroup" and "The Usenet Newsgroup Creation Companion" are required reading for anyone seriously considering creating a new group.*

Remember the first rule in creating new groups: Don't do so unless you are absolutely sure no appropriate group already exists. Usually, you simply haven't found the right group. Once you do, the need to create a group disappears. The Usenet structure lends itself to talking about almost any subject in an existing group. For instance, you can talk about anything Macintosh-related in **comp.sys.mac.misc**. Thus, the second rule of creating a new group: Don't create a group until the traffic in a more general group has grown unmanageable, and stayed that way for some time. As a rule of thumb, wait six months. And, one way or another, make sure you have a Usenet old-timer on your side, to help with the details and steer you clear of any egregious mistakes.

After you are sure the world really does need a group dedicated to discussion of the psychology of smelling flowers from under cork trees, you write a proposal. This *Request for Discussion*, or *RFD*, states what the group is called, what its purpose is, why no existing group serves the need, and so on. Then your job as agitator begins, as you distribute the RFD to groups where interested parties might hang out. Be sure to place the **news.announce.newgroups** group first in the Newsgroups line (so the moderator can correct any problems in the RFD before posting it to **news.announce.newgroups** and the others for you) and to set the Follow-up-To line so that the discussion takes place in **news.groups**. Then you encourage discussion of the topic for 30 days in **news.groups**, all the while collecting responses and modifying the proposal, called a *charter*, accordingly.

After 30 days, if people don't agree on the charter, you must start the RFD process again—with a new and improved proposal, of course. If everyone does agree on the charter, the time has come for a *Call For Votes*, or *CFV*, with clear and unbiased directions on how to vote.

The CFV goes, once again, to all the interested newsgroups, with **news.announce.newgroups** first in the Newsgroups line. It lasts between 21 and 31 days, and you must include the exact end date in the CFV. Once again, your job is to collect and tally the votes via email. (Don't even think of stuffing the electronic ballot box—there's little the Usenet community hates more than a cheat.) You must record each voter's email address along with his Yes or No vote, for later use. You can re-post the CFV during the vote to keep up awareness, but only if you don't change anything from the original CFV.

At the end of the voting period, you post the results—including the total number of votes, and the vote and email address for each—to **news.announce.newgroups** and the other interested newsgroups. Then everyone waits five days, which provides enough time to correct any mistakes or raise serious objections. You need to meet two separate goals to justify a newsgroup. A sufficient number of votes and, within that number, a sufficient number of YES votes. If you have at least 100 more YES votes (for creating the newsgroup) than NO votes, and at least two-thirds of the votes are YES votes, then the group passes the vote.

If, of course, you don't get the required number or percentage of votes, the group doesn't get created. There's no shame in not having your group created. You can even try again in six months if you want; interest may have increased since the original failure. If you fail more than twice, give it up and form your own mailing list. You don't need anyone's cooperation to do that.

If the vote comes out positive, someone (often the moderator of **news.announce.newgroups**) can create the group, sending out the newsgroup control message. Gradually, the group is created at different sites and propagates through much of the network. Why not the entire network? Well, nothing says a machine has to carry every Usenet group in existence. If a system administrator decides that talking about smelling flowers is offensive, she may decide not to carry the group. None of the machines that rely on her machine for news will have the group, either. Nonetheless, groups focusing on technical issues enjoy relatively complete propagation. Even those discussing topics that some people find offensive enjoy wide propagation, and often greater readership, than the technical groups.

Using Usenet

No matter what software you use to access Usenet, you must be aware of some basic concepts, tasks, and features. When I evaluate different newsreaders such as UUCP/Connect, NewsWatcher, and NewsHopper in later chapters, I tell whether the newsreader in question does a good job of handling these tasks and features for you.

Subscribing to Groups

When you first invoke a newsreader, you must subscribe to the groups you want to read. Occasionally, the newsreader automatically subscribes you to a couple of basic groups, such as **news.newusers.questions** and **news.announce.newusers**. For the most part, however, the thousands of available newsgroups are in the unsubscribed category.

> **N o t e**
>
> *Most machines don't carry all of the Usenet groups. If your machine doesn't carry a group you want, you can either ask the system administrator to get it, or go to a machine that lets anyone read news on it. These sites are called public NNTP sites. Be forewarned, however, that few, if any, of these sites still exist, and I know of none. It's a simple problem—whenever a public NNTP site becomes known, so many people try to use it that it immediately stops being public.*

Generally, the first time you start up a newsreader it takes a long time because you have to go through all the groups and figure out which ones to subscribe to. The better newsreaders allow you to sort through the list at different times. In the past, you had to sit for an hour or more just unsubscribing from all the groups that you didn't want to read. It was a major hassle. Even now, allot plenty of time to your first session if you're doing it interactively. (Note: This rule doesn't apply to a UUCP connection, where you request only specific groups.)

Part II

Usenet News
Basics

8

Reading Articles

After you subscribe to a group, it's time to read the articles. Obviously, the first time you read, all the articles are new to you. After that, you want to make sure that you read only previously unread articles. Most newsreaders are extremely good about keeping track of what you've read already. In the Unix world, the **.newsrc** file tracks what you've read. Advanced users can edit that file manually with a text editor, to subscribe or unsubscribe from several groups at once. The Macintosh newsreaders make that task, on the whole, unnecessary.

You've learned what the header for a Usenet article might look like, but many news-readers hide most of the header from you. This is generally helpful, although it can be a pain at times.

Discussions happen in threads, which are groups of related articles, generally with the same or very similar Subject lines. Threads are important because they group both discussions that you want to read and those you don't want to read. Believe me, threads are a very big deal when you have to handle the kind of volume that passes through a popular newsgroup.

When it comes to newsreaders, there are two basic philosophies. The first, which is older, assumes that you want to read 90 percent of the information in a newsgroup. Therefore, the newsreader tries to show you the text of every article unless you explicitly tell it to skip that article or thread. This method may have worked better in the days when Usenet traffic was relatively sparse, but in these modern times, the traffic comes fast and thick. I liken this method to trying to drink from a fire hose.

The second philosophy believes that you want to read only 10 percent of the articles in any given group. With the exception of moderated groups or low-volume groups where every message counts, this assumption is far more realistic. Newsreaders built on this philosophy usually provide a list of the unread messages in a newsgroup, then let you pick and choose which to read. Some newsreaders force you to read each message or thread as you pick it. Others make you pick a whole bunch of them at once and then read them after you've sorted through the entire newsgroup. Both methods have their advan-tages, and a good newsreader lets you work either way.

Note

One of the most frequently asked-for programs in **comp.sys.mac.comm** *is an off-line newsreader, a program that enables you to save articles to disk and then read them when you aren't connected to the Internet. There are a few ways of getting this capability in a newsreader (UUCP is inherently off-line, for instance), and I discuss them later in this book.*

Navigation

After you start reading a set of messages, you need tools for navigating among them. Navigation tools were more important back in the days when character-based Unix newsreaders were all we had. Today, many of the Macintosh newsreaders replace the navigation commands with mouse actions. However, many people (myself included) find the keyboard to be more efficient than the mouse for navigating through news, so perhaps there's still room for some of the old tools.

The most common navigation capability takes you to the next unread message, whether or not it is in the same thread as the message that preceded it. Closely related is the capability to move to the next unread message in the same thread, even if it's not next to the message you were just reading. In a well-designed newsreader, these two capabilities are closely intertwined, so you don't have to know whether or not you're in a thread.

N
o
t
e

Often, these navigation features are encapsulated in a single command linked to the Spacebar, which thus serves as an unusual computer command. Essentially, it says to the newsreader, "Do whatever makes the most sense right here." Computers hate those sort of commands, but the concept works extremely well in a newsreader. The Spacebar scrolls down the page. When you hit the bottom of the article, you probably want to read the next article in the thread, so the Spacebar takes you there. When you finish all the articles in that thread, you probably want to go back up and read the next thread, so the Spacebar takes you back up. Finally, after you read everything in a newsgroup, the Spacebar assumes that you want to read the next newsgroup you subscribe to. By making intelligent guesses, a number of commands can be subsumed under that one key.

You want to group discussions into threads so that you can easily read an entire one, even when it spans a fair amount of real world time. You also want to group discussions so you can ignore them more easily. Despite the fact that people should include descriptive Subject lines in their postings, they don't always. If you see a long thread called "Cool Stuff," you have no idea what it's about. It may pique your curiosity, though, so you start reading, only to find out that it's another "my computer is better than your computer" flame war. Now you need a way to kill the entire thread. Good newsreaders make that effort easy.

An even neater feature is the ability to create a list of Subject lines or topics about which you never want to read. This capability usually applies to anything in the header and sometimes to information in the body of the messages, too. It's extremely useful for customizing your Usenet reading experience. To go even one step further, a few newsreaders provide a feature to only read articles that match certain topics. These are ideal for the truly busy user.

After you read all the messages that interest you, it's generally a good idea to mark the rest of them as read (even though you didn't read them). This way, you don't see them again the next time you read news. Some newsreaders handle this option automatically, whereas others make you mark them manually. Sometimes, especially if you just returned from a vacation, you may want to mark everything as read without even trying to read the waiting messages. Marking everything lets you start with a clean slate and with a manageable number of messages the next day, and is generally referred to as *catching up*. There's no difference between a "catch up" feature and a "mark all as read" feature, but you may see both terms.

Now you know all about navigating around Usenet and reading articles. Many people never move past that point, and are called *lurkers*. The term has no negative connotation, it simply means people who only read and never post.

rot13

I almost forgot. You might occasionally run across articles that are completely unreadable. They may be in a newsgroup specific to a language that you don't understand, but the newsreader can't help with that problem. It can (or should be able to) help you with messages coded in the *rot13* format. Rot13 is a simple coding scheme that assigns a number to each letter of the alphabet, starting with 1 for A, 2 for B, and so on, for every character in a message. It then adds 13 to each number and converts back into letters. The result is an utterly unreadable message, which the poster usually intended because some people might find the message offensive. If you see such a message and are easily offended, don't read it. No one forces you to use the rot13 decoding feature that exists in most newsreaders. If you do, you can't very well complain about the contents. I usually see most rot13 encoded postings in joke newsgroups, protecting the innocent from really sick jokes (see figure 8.3).

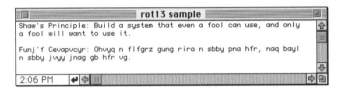

Figure 8.3   *Normal text versus rot13.*

Extracting Binary Files

In the days of yore, when true Internet connections were less common, files were often passed around the world by being posted in special binaries newsgroups, and even today, you'll see groups like **comp.binaries.mac**. Files are still posted to Usenet, although the majority of them seem to be copyright violations of dirty pictures. A good newsreader makes it easy to download binary files posted in Usenet, although I strongly recommend that you use FTP to get files if you have a choice.

FTP works much better than a newsreader for downloading files and saves a ton of bandwidth because the files aren't being transferred to sites where no one will download them. Of course, if you only have a UUCP connection, or for some other reason you can't use FTP, then snagging binary files posted to Usenet may be your only hope.

Replying to Articles

In the course of reading Usenet news, you often see messages that aren't quite clear or that catch your interest for some reason or another. When you see such a message, you may want to send email to the poster. You could, of course, copy down the poster's email address from the header onto a little piece of paper, and when you finished reading news, use your email program to send him a message. However, that process is a pain and wastes lots of little pieces of paper, so most newsreaders support sending mail replies while you're reading news.

Use email replies whenever the rest of the group won't give a hoot about what you have to say. Most of us feel that our words are pearls of wisdom and should be distributed to the widest possible audience. But, try to step back and think about whether your reply is best directed at the individual making the posting or the group as a whole.

People often ask questions on Usenet, saying that you should reply directly to them and that they plan to summarize to the net. Listen to what these people have to say. They only want replies via email, and because they've promised to post a summary of the replies, you don't need to ask for a copy personally (unless perhaps you don't stand a chance of seeing the summary in the newsgroup; even then, ask nicely). If you ever post a question and promise a summary, live up to your promise, even if you get only a couple of responses. No matter how many responses you get, format them nicely with quote characters before each quoted line so that they are easy for readers to understand; messages are often confusing as to who wrote what in a summary. Never re-post entire headers.

As far as what to say when you reply to postings on Usenet, reread what I said about email manners in the last chapter. The same rules apply here. If you must carry out a flame war, do it in email; but if possible, don't do it at all.

Follow-ups

Discussions are the entire point of Usenet, of course, so you eventually gather the courage to post something to a newsgroup. For most people, the easiest way to post a message is to reply to another message, an action called *following up*. A follow-up is easier for the novice because the newsreader fills in most of the lines in the header for you; the lines for Subject, Newsgroups, Distribution, and so on are generally determined by the message you reply to.

Just as in email, you should be given the chance to quote the previous message so that readers can understand the context of your reply. Some newsreaders are picky about the proportion of quoted text to new text, and for good reason. No one wants to read a two-screen quoted letter only to see at the bottom a few words from you: "I agree with all this." Even in newsreaders that don't prevent you from over-quoting, be careful. Try to edit out as much of the quoted text as possible. Remember that most people have already seen that message in its original form, so you're simply jogging their memory. Definitely remove signatures and unnecessary previously quoted text.

Part II　Usenet News Basics

> **Note**　*Using Usenet as a method of getting a message to a specific individual is considered extremely bad form, even if you can't seem to get email to that person. Imagine, everyone's discussing nuclear disarmament, and you suddenly see a message from a college friend. Your note discussing old times at Catatonic University will hold absolutely no interest for the rest of the group. If you find yourself being flamed, suffer and don't do it again.*

Posting an Article

If you really have something new to say, or a new question to ask, don't insert it into an existing thread just because it's easier than posting a new one. Posting a new message should be simple enough in any decent newsreader.

Note

If you cannot post from a newsreader (because you only have an AppleLink account, for instance), you can still send messages to a Usenet newsgroup. Two email posting services exist: **news-group@cs.utexas.edu** *and* **news-group@pws.bull.com**. *Do not send email to* **news-group**, *but to the name of the group to which you want to post, replacing the dots in the group name with dashes. So, for example, to post to* **comp.sys.mac.comm**, *send email to* **comp-sys-mac-comm@cs.utexas.edu**. *Make sure to ask for replies via email.*

In general, you should avoid posting a few things. Avoid copyrighted works such as magazine articles or newspaper stories. Although it's unlikely that anyone could sue the Internet (it would be a bit like boxing with a dense mist), you might be sued for copyright infringement. Besides, posting copyrighted work is not polite. Simply post the complete reference to the article or whatever, along with a summary or selected quote or two if you want to pique some curiosity.

Note

Interestingly, recipes in cookbooks are not copyrighted because they are essentially lists of instructions. However, the instructions for creating the recipe may be protected if they contain anything other than the bare bones instructions, and any preface explaining or describing the recipe is definitely protected. People often post a recipe or two from a cookbook that they particularly like so that others can see whether they like the recipes enough to buy the book.

Perhaps the least obvious but most important works to avoid posting are pictures scanned in from magazines or videos and sounds digitized from TV or videotape. Most of the scanned pictures are varying degrees of erotic images, and unfortunately, most are blatant examples of copyright infringement. The magazines, *Playboy* in particular, don't look kindly on this sort of thing, and legal action might result. Besides, pictures suck up disk space, and the quality of a scanned image doesn't even begin to approach the high-quality photography and printing of most magazines.

In general, you should not post headline events that everyone can read about in the newspaper or possibly in ClariNet (coming up next). I don't mean to imply that you can't talk about these events, but because news travels relatively slowly to all parts of the net, announcing the results of an election or a similar event is just silly. People probably already know about the event, and if they don't, they'll figure it out from the ensuing discussion.

Finally, don't post personal email that you receive unless the sender gives you explicit permission. As with most things on the Internet, posting personal email is a legally murky area, but the etiquette is crystal-clear: It's rude.

ClariNet

Along with all the discussion groups about computers and recreational activities and whatnot, you may see a hierarchy under `clari`. You've found ClariNet. Unlike Usenet, ClariNet doesn't carry any discussions, and in fact, I don't believe that you can post to any ClariNet groups. Instead, ClariNet is dedicated to distributing commercial information, much of it the same stuff that you read in your newspaper or hear on the radio. ClariNet claims over 60,000 daily readers, which isn't too bad in terms of circulation.

Also unlike Usenet, ClariNet isn't free. A site must pay a certain amount to receive the ClariNet news feed, which uses the same transport protocols and newsreaders as Usenet. Sites that receive the ClariNet feed cannot redistribute that feed on to other machines unless those machines pay for it as well. Because of ClariNet's commercial nature, I can't predict whether you even have access to it. It's strictly up to each site.

Much of the ClariNet information comes from press wires like UPI, along with NewsBytes computer articles, and various syndicated columnists such as Miss Manners. A recent arrival is *Dilbert*, the cartoon by Scott Adams (although you have to download each installment and view it in a graphics program, since there isn't a newsreader around that can view graphics internally, although a properly configured Web browser might be able to handle the task). Although you can probably find much of the information in a standard newspaper, ClariNet organizes it extremely well, making reading about a single topic much easier. For instance, some groups carry local news briefs for each state, some carry only news about Apple Computer, and there are groups with tantalizing names like `clari.news.goodnews`, which indeed includes only articles that are good news. (Depressingly, that newsgroup sees very little traffic.)

ClariNet was founded a few years ago by Brad Templeton, who is also well known as the creator of the moderated group `rec.humor.funny`, which accepts only jokes that he thinks are funny (actually, someone else does the selection now). ClariNet is important, because it is specifically commercial traffic flowing via the same methods and pathways as Usenet, perhaps the most rabidly anti-commercial part of the Internet. I don't know the business details of ClariNet, but it has been around long enough that I suspect it's a financial success, and the news that it brings is certainly welcome.

Enough Usenet

Well, that's enough on Usenet. You must experience Usenet to truly understand it, though, so I do recommend that you find a few groups that interest you and lurk for a while once you have your connection set up. You're now ready to learn about the services that require a full connection to the Internet, such as FTP, Telnet, WAIS, Gopher, and the World Wide Web.

TCP/IP Internet Services

I must tread a fine line when talking about Internet services, because the level of connection (and thus the level of service) varies widely. People who can send Internet email, for instance, may not be able to use Gopher or the World Wide Web. The services that I talk about in this chapter (except for FTP and Archie via email) all require a full TCP/IP connection to the Internet. For Mac folks, a full TCP/IP connection to the Internet means that you have MacTCP loaded and properly configured, and either a dedicated Internet connection or a modem connection via PPP or SLIP. If you don't have the proper sort of account and connection, you do not have a full TCP/IP connection to the Internet. To be fair, there are some ways of getting access to these services via America Online, CompuServe, or some of the bulletin board systems, and in those cases you're limited to the software they provide for you.

FTP

Despite the occasionally confusing way people use the term both as a noun and a verb, most people don't have much trouble using FTP. FTP stands for *File Transfer Protocol*, and not surprisingly, it's only good for transferring files between machines. In the past, you could only use an FTP client to access files stored on FTP servers. Today, however, enough other services such as Gopher and the World Wide Web have implemented the FTP protocols that you can often FTP files no matter what service you happen to be using. Heck, you can even FTP files via email. I'll get to the specifics of the different clients in later chapters; for now, here are a few salient facts to keep in mind regarding FTP.

FTP Manners

The Internet does a wonderful job of hiding geographical boundaries. You may never realize that a person with whom you correspond lives on the other side of the globe. When using FTP, however, try to keep the physical location of the remote machine in mind.

First, as with everything on the Internet, someone pays for all this traffic. It's probably not you directly, so try to behave like a good citizen who's being given free access to an amazing resource. Show some consideration by not, for example, using machines in Australia when one in the same area of your country works equally well. Because trans-oceanic traffic is expensive, many machines mirror others; that is, they make sure to transfer the entire contents of one machine to the other, updating the file collection on a regular, often daily basis.

Here's an example. Because the Info-Mac archive site at **sumex-aim.stanford.edu** is popular and kept up-to-date, other sites carrying Macintosh software don't want to duplicate the effort. It's much easier to set up a mirror to **sumex** so that machines in Australia and Scandinavia can have exactly the same contents as **sumex**. Mirroring not only saves work, it also enables users in those countries to access a cheaper, local site for files. Everyone wins, but only if you, the user, utilize local sites whenever possible. You can usually tell where a site is located by looking at the two-letter country domain at the end of the address.

Sometimes, of course, the file you need exists only on a remote site in Finland, for example, so that's where you must go to get it. Another point of etiquette to keep in mind is sensitivity to the time of day at the site from which you retrieve a file. Like most things in life other than universities during exams, more people use the Internet during their daytime hours than at night. Thus, it's generally polite to retrieve files during off hours; otherwise, you're preventing people from doing their work. That's not polite, especially if the file you're retrieving is a massive QuickTime movie or something equally frivolous.

Notice that I said "their daytime hours." Because the Internet spans the globe, it may be 4:00 A.M. where you are, but it's the middle of the day somewhere else. You can figure out the local time by using the Map control panel that comes with your Mac.

FTP Clients

FTP is inherently simple to use, but there's plenty of room for FTP client software to make your life miserable. The following sections, therefore, describe several benefits and features to look for in an FTP client.

Connecting

People usually use an FTP client program to log on to a remote FTP site, find a file or two, download them, and then log off. As such, a disproportionate amount of your time is spent connecting and navigating to the desired files.

A good FTP client enables you to define shortcuts for frequently used FTP sites, along with the userid and password necessary for connecting to them. This benefit is minor but makes a big difference when repeated numerous times. I can't tell you how much I hate typing **sumex-aim.stanford.edu** on a Unix command line when I'm trying to connect to that site with FTP.

Navigating

Once you're on, the FTP client program should make it very easy to move between directories (or folders, in Mac jargon). Some programs do this by emulating the Standard File Dialog used on the Mac to open and save files, which is a good start (although the Standard File Dialog is one of the most confusing parts of the Macintosh interface). It's helpful when the client program remembers the contents of directories. That way, if you go back to one you've already visited, you don't have to wait for it to refresh.

Other programs, Anarchie and Snatcher mostly, take the navigational aspect of FTP one step further, and actually emulate the Finder. Snatcher in particular goes a bit overboard in trying to mimic the Finder, in my opinion.

A useful variant of shortcuts (also known as bookmarks) to FTP site names is the addition of directory information to the site name. Say, for instance, you want to retrieve something from **ftp.tidbits.com**. Not only do you have to enter the host name, userid, and password, but you must also go to the proper directory, which is **/pub/tidbits**.

Listing Style

In Unix, you can choose among several different methods of viewing files. Some show you more information, such as file size and creation date, and others show you less, in order to fit more entries on the screen. Although the Mac doesn't have the problem of trying to fit multiple columns in a list (no Macintosh program uses multiple column lists), not all the FTP clients are good about showing you the entire filename, size, or date. I think this failure is inexcusable, because you need to know how large a file is before you spend an hour retrieving it—especially if you're connecting at a slow speed. Make sure the program you use provides this information. In addition, a truly useful feature is the capability of sorting the listing on date, file size, or whatnot.

Recognizing File Type and Decoding

Much of the time, an FTP client can figure out what sort of file you're retrieving by looking at the extension to the filename. This being the case, the client can make sure it is transferring the file in the proper format. If you're lucky, it even decodes some of the common formats that you see on the Internet.

"Wait a minute," you say. "He didn't mention strange file formats before." Sorry about that. I'll get to file formats in the next chapter, after I've discussed the various different ways that files may appear on your machine. But first, let's look at how you can retrieve files from FTP sites armed only with an email program.

FTP by Email

One of the problems with FTP is that it requires your attention—in fact, pretty much your full attention. In addition, you must have a TCP/IP connection to the Internet. If you're connecting via AppleLink or UUCP, you simply cannot use FTP normally. The one caveat to this TCP/IP requirement is that more and more of the commercial services are starting to support FTP, so you can use FTP on America Online or CompuServe, for instance, without resorting to FTP by email.

> **Note**
>
> *If you're clever and are able to do a little scripting with AppleScript or Frontier, you can script Anarchie to retrieve files automatically.*

There is a solution, although not a terribly good one. You can retrieve files remotely, using only your email program, in two different ways. The most generic way is by using one of the *FTPmail* or *BITFTP* servers. The other way is to use a specific mailserver program that only knows how to serve a specific site, sometimes as part of a mailing list manager such as LISTSERV, ListProcessor, or Majordomo. Let's look at the generic way first.

FTPmail

Using FTPmail or BITFTP isn't particularly difficult, but it can be extremely frustrating. The problem is twofold. First, the main FTPmail server is seriously overloaded. Because it's a free service that someone at DEC runs in their machine's spare time, FTPmail is a low priority. It can take a week for your file to come back. I've even had requests seemingly disappear into the ether. Second, talking to an FTPmail server is like playing 20

Questions—unless you know precisely what you're looking for, where it is, and are able to enter the commands perfectly, you'll get an error message back. And, if that message comes back a week later, you may not even have the original information with which to correct your mistake.

> *When you use email to retrieve files stored on FTP sites, the files often are split into chunks. Usually, you can control the size of the chunks, but manually joining them in a word processor can be difficult. Some email programs, such as Eudora, and various utilities make joining file chunks easier. If you don't use Eudora, check out ChunkJoiner and BinHqx (if the file is a BinHex file). You can find them in:*
>
> ```
> ftp://ftp.tidbits.com/pub/tidbits/tisk/util/
> ```

Talking to an FTPmail or BITFTP server feels much like logging into an FTP site, changing directories, and finally retrieving the file. The only problem is, you must type in the commands all at once. So, to get a file from the main FTPmail server, you would send email to **ftpmail@decwrl.dec.com**, put something in the Subject line (it doesn't care what, but dislikes empty Subject lines), and then, in the body of the message, put a set of commands like this:

```
help

connect ftp.tidbits.com
chdir /pub/tidbits/misc
get easy-view.hqx
quit
```

So, in English, what you're doing is first getting the help file from FTPmail, then connecting to the anonymous FTP site at **ftp.tidbits.com**, then changing into the **/pub/tidbits/misc/** directory, then retrieving the file called **easy-view.hqx**, and finally quitting. If you wanted, you could retrieve more files. And, if you included an **ls** command, FTPmail would return the directory listing to you, enabling you to see what's there before requesting specific files.

Needless to say, there are a number of other commands that FTPmail accepts, and you will probably want to use some of them. They're all explained in the help file that FTPmail returns to you when you send it the help command.

I only know of one other FTPmail server, and it's in Ireland. It uses a somewhat different command set, so I don't recommend using it unless you're in Europe. If you want to find out more about it, send email to **ftpmail@ieunet.ie** and put the single command **help** in the body of the message.

BITFTP

BITFTP stands for BITNET FTP, or something like that. Machines that are only on BITNET cannot use FTP normally, so some enterprising programmers created the BITFTP program to enable BITNET users to retrieve files stored on FTP sites.

I know of only three BITFTP servers. One is in the U.S., another in Germany, and the third in Poland (see Table 9.1). Don't use the ones in Europe unless you too are in Europe—it's a waste of net bandwidth, and probably won't result in particularly good service anyway.

Table 9.1
BITFTP Servers

Server Name	Location
bitftp@pucc.princeton.edu	U.S.
bitftp@vm.gmd.de	Germany
bitftp@plearn.edu.pl	Poland

Retrieving a file from a BITFTP server works similarly to retrieving a file from FTPmail, but the commands are somewhat different. Here's how you retrieve the same file (along with the help file again) that we snagged before. Send email to **bitftp@pucc.princeton.edu** and put these commands in the body of the letter:

```
help

ftp ftp.tidbits.com
user anonymous
cd /pub/tidbits/misc
get easy-view.hqx
quit
```

Enough about BITFTP. You can probably figure out the rest on your own, with the aid of the help file. I wouldn't want to spoil all the fun of figuring some of this stuff out for yourself!

Mailservers

More common than FTPmail or BITFTP programs that serve everyone are mailserver programs that provide email access to FTP archives on a specific site. There are many of these mailservers around, although finding them can be a bit difficult, and I cannot tell which FTP sites that might interest you also have mailservers. I can, however, tell you of a few mailservers that you may find useful. Each has its own command structure.

BART, the mailserver for the massive Macintosh software archives at **mac.archive.umich.edu**, is an extremely useful way to access many Macintosh files, especially since the load on the machine via FTP is often so great that you cannot easily connect.

> **Note**
>
> *BART is short for* Brode's Archive Retrieval Thang. *Glad you asked?*

BART only provides access to the files stored on **mac.archive.umich.edu**. If you want more general access via email, you must use one of the FTPmail or BITFTP servers mentioned previously. Luckily, because BART is so specific, its command structure is relatively simple.

For instance, to retrieve help and StuffIt Expander from BART, you would send email to **mac@mac.archive.umich.edu**, and in the body of the message you would put the following commands:

```
path ace@tidbits.com

help
chunk 1500
send util/compression/stuffitexpander3.52.sea.hqx
```

That's about it. BART limits you to 1,500K and five files per day (the list of files isn't currently considered against your quota), so you can't abuse it. Your quota is cleared every day at midnight (Eastern Daylight Time). Perhaps the main problem with BART is that if there's something wrong with your request, it tends to ignore the request entirely and not send any error messages. So, for instance, if you surpass your quota, BART simply throws out any additional requests and you must send them again after midnight when your quota has been cleared.

Using the chunk command, you should set your chunk size as high as your mailer can handle, because that reduces the load on BART and makes it easier for you to deal with the files on your end.

> **Note**
>
> *You may run into trouble with certain files if you use Eudora to retrieve them via BART. If the submitter also used Eudora or a compatible program to attach the file, here's what will happen: Eudora will start downloading the first chunk from BART, see that it contains an attachment, and then complain when it sees the attachment is too short (since the other parts aren't included). Simply tell Eudora to fetch the attachment again as a normal message, and it will work fine.*

Mailing List Managers

Mailing list manager programs such as LISTSERV, ListProcessor, and Majordomo also often provide access to files, although these files aren't always available via FTP. Most often the files in question are logs of mailing list discussions, but in a few instances, they're more interesting.

The LISTSERV at Rice University that helps distribute the Info-Mac Digest also provides access to all of the files stored in the Info-Mac archives at **sumex-aim.stanford.edu**. Using it is simplicity itself. The LISTSERV doesn't care about directory paths, chunks, or anything like that. You need not specify your email address, or tell the LISTSERV how to encode the files. Instead, all you do is send **listserv@ricevm1.rice.edu** a message with one-line commands that look like any of the following:

```
$MAC HELP

$MAC GET tidbits-267.etx
```

Actually, I'm oversimplifying slightly. There are four commands, all told (see Table 9.2).

Table 9.2
LISTSERV File Retrieval Commands

Command	Function
$MAC IND *ALL*	Gets list of recent or all files
$MAC DIR *directory*	Gets subdirectory contents
$MAC GET *name.type*	Gets Info-Mac archive file
$MAC HELP	Gets help information

The LISTSERV limits you to 250K per day, although if you request a single file larger than that, it won't refuse that single request. Since all new files in the Info-Mac archives are announced in the Info-Mac Digest, you can easily copy the filenames out to a file request message as you're reading, send off the message when you're finished, and have files coming back quite quickly.

Enough about FTP by email. It's like playing Pin the Tail on the Donkey with a donkey the size of... Nah, I'll avoid the easy shot at some sleazy politician. Let's talk next about how you find files via FTP. The answer is Archie.

Archie

Archie is an example of what happens when you apply simple technology to a difficult problem. Here is the problem: How do you find any given file on the nets if you don't already know where it's located? After all, in comparison with finding a single file on several million machines, the proverbial haystack looks tiny, and its cousin, the proverbial needle, sticks out like the sore thumb you get when you find it. In a nutshell, Archie uses normal FTP commands to get directory listings of all the files on hundreds of anonymous FTP sites around the world. It then puts these file listings into a database and provides a simple interface for searching it. That's really all there is to Archie.

Unfortunately, and for reasons I don't fully understand, Archie servers have become less and less useful over time. They're almost impossible to get through to via an Archie client (telnetting to them is the most successful in my recent experience), and much of the time they don't seem to know about certain large FTP sites that I know have the file for which I'm looking. In other words, sometimes Archie simply won't work. Don't worry about it and just try another technique or tool.

Note

Archie was developed in early 1991 by Alan Emtage, Peter Deutsch, and Bill Heelan from the McGill University Computing Center, Canada. Development now takes place at a company founded by Deutsch and Emtage, Bunyip Information Systems. Although the basic Archie client software is distributed freely, Bunyip sells and supports the Archie server software.

You can access Archie via Telnet, email, Gopher, the World Wide Web, and special Macintosh client programs. Some Unix machines may also have Unix Archie clients installed. It seems to me there are two basic goals an Archie client should meet. First, it should be easy to search for files, but when you want to define a more complex search, that should be possible as well. Second, since the entire point of finding files is so that you can retrieve them, an Archie client ideally should make it very easy to retrieve anything that it finds. This second feature appears to be less common than you would expect. On the Mac, only Anarchie can retrieve found files with just a double-click.

Part II — TCP/IP Internet Services

Note

Archie isn't an acronym for anything, although it took me half an hour searching through files about Archie on the Internet to determine that once and for all.

Accessing Archie via email is extremely easy, although the Archie server offers enough options (I'll let you discover them for yourself) to significantly increase the complexity. For a basic search through, merely send email to **archie@archie.internic.net** and put in the body of the message lines like the following:

```
help

find easy-view
find easyview
```

In a short while (or perhaps a long while, depending on the load on the Archie server), the results should come back—the help file that you asked for and the results of your search for "easy-view" and "easyview." The example above uses both terms because I'm not sure of the exact wording of the filename, but experience tells me that one of those two possibilities is likely.

However, if the Archie server you chose is down, or merely being flaky (as is their wont) you may want to try another one. There are plenty. Simply send email to the userid **archie** at any one of the Archie servers from the list in Table 9.3. As usual, it's polite to choose a local server.

Table 9.3
Current Archie Servers

Server Name	Server IP Number	Location
archie.au	139.130.4.6	Australia
archie.edvz.uni-linz.ac.at	140.78.3.8	Austria
archie.univie.ac.at	131.130.1.23	Austria
archie.cs.mcgill.ca	132.206.51.250	Canada
archie.uqam.ca	132.208.250.10	Canada
archie.funet.fi	128.214.6.102	Finland
archie.univ-rennes1.fr	129.20.128.38	France
archie.th-darmstadt.de	130.83.128.118	Germany
archie.ac.il	132.65.16.18	Israel
archie.unipi.it	131.114.21.10	Italy
archie.wide.ad.jp	133.4.3.6	Japan
archie.hana.nm.kr	128.134.1.1	Korea
archie.sogang.ac.kr	163.239.1.11	Korea
archie.uninett.no	128.39.2.20	Norway
archie.rediris.es	130.206.1.2	Spain
archie.luth.se	130.240.12.30	Sweden

Server Name	Server IP Number	Location
archie.switch.ch	130.59.1.40	Switzerland
archie.ncu.edu.tw	192.83.166.12	Taiwan
archie.doc.ic.ac.uk	146.169.11.3	United Kingdom
archie.hensa.ac.uk	129.12.21.25	United Kingdom
archie.unl.edu	129.93.1.14	USA (NE)
archie.internic.net	198.49.45.10	USA (NJ)
archie.rutgers.edu	128.6.18.15	USA (NJ)
archie.ans.net	147.225.1.10	USA (NY)
archie.sura.net	128.167.254.179	USA (MD)

Telnet Usage

Telnet is a bit hard to talk about because using it is just like using a modem to connect to another computer. Telnet simply enables you to connect to a computer somewhere else on the Internet and to do whatever that computer allows you to do. Because Telnet is similar to FTP in the sense that you're logging in to a remote machine, the same rules of etiquette apply (although running a program over Telnet usually places less stress on a machine). As long as you try to avoid bogging down the network when people want to use it for their local work, you shouldn't have to worry about it too much. When you telnet to another machine, you generally telnet into a specific program that provides information you want. The folks making that information available may have specific restrictions on the way you can use their site. Pay attention to these restrictions. The few people who abuse a network service ruin it for everyone else.

What might you want to look for in a Telnet program? That's a good question, I suppose, but not one that I'm all that qualified to answer. For the most part, I avoid Telnet-based command-line interfaces. Thus, in my opinion, you should look for features in a Telnet program that will make using it, and any random program that you may happen to run on the remote machine, easier to use.

It's useful to be able to save connection documents that save you the work of logging into a specific machine (but beware of security issues if they also store your password). Also, any sort of macro capability will come in handy for automating repetitive keystrokes. Depending on what you're doing, you also may want some feature for capturing the text that flows by for future reference. And, you should of course be able to copy and paste out of the Telnet program.

Part II   TCP/IP Internet Services

IRC

IRC, which stands for *Internet Relay Chat*, is a method of communicating with others on the Internet in real time. It was written by Jarkko Oikarinen of Finland in 1988 and has spread to 20 countries. IRC is perhaps better defined as a multi-user chat system, where people gather in groups that are called *channels*, usually devoted to some specific subject. Private conversations also are possible.

> *IRC gained a certain level of fame during the Gulf War, when updates about the fighting flowed into a single channel where a huge number of people had gathered to stay up-to-date on the situation.*

I personally have never messed with IRC much, having had some boring experiences with RELAY, a similar service on BITNET, back in college. I'm not all that fond of IRC, in large part because I find the amount of useful information there almost nonexistent, and I'm uninterested in making small talk with people from around the world. Nevertheless, IRC is one of the most popular Internet services. Thousands of people connect to IRC servers throughout any given day. If you're interested in IRC, refer to the section on it back in chapter 5, the excerpt from *Internet Explorer Kit for Macintosh*. That should give you a sense of what IRC is like. You can find more information in the IRC tutorials posted for anonymous FTP in:

```
ftp://cs-ftp.bu.edu/irc/support/
```

Client programs for many different platforms exist, including two for the Macintosh called ircle and Homer. Much as with Telnet, you're looking for features that make the tedious parts of IRC simpler. I could blather on about all the features you might want, but frankly, if you're using a Macintosh with either a Unix shell account or a MacTCP-based account, just get Homer. It has more features than one would think possible, and can even—in conjunction with Apple's PlainTalk software—speak some or all of the text that flows by.

MUDs

MUD, which stands for *Multi-User Dungeon* or often *Multi-User Dimension*, may be one of the most dangerously addictive services available on the Internet. The basic idea is somewhat like the text adventures of old, where you type in commands like "Go south," "Get knife," and so on. The difference with MUDs is that they can take place in a wide variety of different realities—basically anything someone could dream up. More importantly, the characters in the MUD are actually other people interacting with you in real time. Finally, after you reach a certain level of proficiency, you are often allowed to modify the environment of the MUD.

The allure of the MUDs should be obvious. Suddenly, you can become your favorite alter-ego, describing yourself in any way you want. Your alternate-reality prowess is based on your intellect, and if you rise high enough, you can literally change your world. Particularly for those who may feel powerless or put upon in the real world, the world of the MUD is an attractive escape, despite its text-environment limitations.

After the publication of an article about MUDs, the magazine *Wired* printed a letter from someone who had watched his brother fail out of an engineering degree and was watching his fiancée, a fourth-year astrophysics student, suffer similar academic problems, both due to their addictions to MUDs. But don't take my word for it; read the letter for yourself on *Wired's* Web server:

```
http://www.wired.com/Etext/1.4/departments/rants.html
```

Note

Wired's Web server requires authentication now, which means that you must sign up with them and get a userid and a password before you can get in. It's free, and you can register at:

```
http://www.wired.com/
```

I've seen people close to me fall prey to the addictive lure of MUDs. As an experiment in interactive communications and human online interactions, MUDs are extremely interesting, but be aware of the time they can consume from your real life.

I don't want to imply that MUDs are evil. Like almost anything else, they can be abused. But in other situations, they have been used in fascinating ways, such as to create an online classroom for geographically separated students. There's also a very real question of what constitutes addiction and what constitutes real life. I'd say that someone who is failing out of college or failing to perform acceptably at work because of a MUD has a problem, but if that person is replacing several hours per day of television with MUDing, it's a tougher call. Similarly, is playing hours and hours of golf each week any better than stretching your mind in the imaginative world of a MUD? You decide, but remember: there are certain parts of real life that we cannot and should not blow off in favor of a virtual environment.

Although MUDs are currently text-only, rudimentary graphics will almost certainly appear at some point, followed by more realistic graphics, sound, and video, and perhaps some day even links to the virtual reality systems of tomorrow. I don't even want to speculate on what those changes might mean to society, but you may want to think about what may happen, both positive and negative.

MUDs generally run under Unix, but you could run your own with a Macintosh port of a MUD, called MacMud, and connect to other Unix MUDs with a simple MUD client program, MUDDweller. Even more interesting is the program Meeting Space from a small company called World Benders. Meeting Space is billed as a virtual conference room, and is marketed to large businesses as a money- and time-saving alternative to business trips. However, it's actually a business MUD with a snazzy Macintosh interface and hefty price tag. Meeting Space works over any Macintosh network, including the Internet, and although I don't know of any public Meeting Space servers yet, some were being discussed earlier. For more information about Meeting Space, send email to **wb-info@worldbenders.com** and check out the discussion of it later on in chapter 27, "Utilities & Miscellany."

WAIS

Unlike almost every other resource mentioned in this book, the *WAIS*, or *Wide Area Information Servers*, project had its conception in big business and was designed for big business. The project started in response to a basic problem. Professionals from all walks of life, and corporate executives in particular, need tremendous amounts of information that is usually stored online in vast databases. However, corporate executives are almost always incredibly busy people without the time, inclination, or skills to learn a complex database query language. Of course, corporate executives are not alone in this situation; many people have the same needs and limitations.

In 1991, four large companies—Apple Computer, Dow Jones & Co., Thinking Machines Corporation, and KPMG Peat Marwick—joined together to create a prototype system to address this pressing problem. Apple brought its user interface design expertise; Dow Jones was involved because of its massive databases of information; Thinking Machines provided the programming and expertise in high-end information retrieval engines; and KPMG Peat Marwick provided the information-hungry guinea pigs.

One of the initial concepts was the formation of an organizational memory—the combined set of memos, reports, guidelines, email, and whatnot—that make up the textual history of an organization. Because all of these items are primarily text and completely without structure, stuffing them into a standard relational database is like trying to fill a room with balloons. They don't fit well, they're always escaping, and you can never find anything. WAIS was designed to help with this problem.

So far I haven't said anything about how WAIS became such a useful tool for finding free information. With such corporate parentage, it's in some ways surprising that it did. The important thing about the design of WAIS is that it doesn't discriminate. WAIS can incorporate data from many different sources, distribute them over various types of networks, and record whether the data is free or carries a fee. WAIS is also scalable, so that it can accept an increasing number and complexity of information sources. This is an important feature in today's world of exponentially increasing amounts of information.

The end result of these design features is that WAIS works perfectly well for serving financial reports to harried executives, but equally well for providing science fiction book reviews to curious undergraduates.

In addition, the WAIS protocol is an Internet standard and is freely available, as are some clients and servers. Anyone can set up her own WAIS server for anyone with a WAIS client to access. Eventually, we may see Microsoft, Lotus, and WordPerfect duking it out over who has the best client for accessing WAIS. With the turn the Internet has taken in the past year, however, it's far more likely that we'll see Microsoft, Lotus, and WordPerfect (now a division of Novell) competing with World Wide Web clients. Although WAIS has continued to grow in utility and popularity, it has also faded into the shadow of the snazzier looking Web clients. That's not to say that WAIS isn't being used heavily, just that it tends to work behind the scenes as a search engine for a Web page interface, rather than through a dedicated client program.

At the beginning of this section, I mentioned the problem of most people not knowing how to communicate in complex database query languages. WAIS solves that problem by implementing a sophisticated natural language input system, which is a fancy way of saying that you can talk to it in English. If you want to find more information about deforestation in the Amazon rain forest, you simply formulate your query as: "Tell me about deforestation in the Amazon rain forest." Pretty rough, eh? In its current state, WAIS does not actually examine your question for semantic content; that is, it searches based on the useful words it finds in your question (and ignores, for instance, "in" and "the"). However, nothing prevents advances in language processing from augmenting WAIS so that it has a better idea of what you mean.

In any database, you find only the items that match your search. In a very large database, though, you often find far too many items; so many, in fact, that you are equally at a loss as to what might be useful. WAIS attempts to solve this problem with *ranking* and *relevance feedback*. Ranking is just what it says. WAIS looks at each item that answers the user's question and ranks them based on the proximity of words and other variables. The better the match, the higher up the document appears in your list of found items. Although by no means perfect, this basic method works well in practice.

Relevance feedback, although a fuzzier concept, also helps you refine a search. If you ask a question and WAIS returns 30 documents that match, you may find one or two that are almost exactly what you're looking for. You can then refine the search by telling WAIS, in effect, that those one or two documents are "relevant" and that it should go look for other documents that are "similar" to the relevant ones. Relevance feedback is basically a computer method of pointing at something and saying, "Get me more like this."

The rise of services such as WAIS and Gopher on the Internet will by no means put librarians out of business. Instead, the opposite is true. Librarians are trained in ways of searching and refining searches. We need their experience, both in making sense of the frantic increase in information resources and in setting up the information services of tomorrow. More than ever, we need to eliminate the stereotype of the little old lady among dusty books and replace it with an image of a person who can help us navigate through data in ways we never could ourselves. There will always be a need for human experts.

When you put all this information together, you end up with a true *electronic publishing system*. This definition, pulled from a paper written by Brewster Kahle, then of Thinking Machines and now president of WAIS, Inc., is important for Internet users to keep in mind as the future becomes the present: "Electronic publishing is the distribution of textual information over electronic networks." (Kahle later mentions that the WAIS protocol does not prohibit the transmission of audio or video.) I emphasize that definition because I've been fighting to spread it for some years now because of my role with *TidBITS*.

Note

> *Electronic publishing has little to do with using computer tools to create paper publications. For those of you who know about Adobe Acrobat, Common Ground from No Hands Software, Envoy from Novell, and Replica from Farallon, those programs aren't directly related to electronic publishing because they all work on the metaphor of a printed page. With them, you create a page and then print to a file format that other platforms can read (using special readers), but never edit or reuse in any significant way. We're talking about electronic fax machines. We should enjoy greater flexibility with electronic data.*

So, how can you use WAIS? I see two basic uses. Most of the queries WAIS gets are probably one-time shots where the user has a question and wants to see whether WAIS stores any information that can provide the answer. This use has much in common with the way reference librarians work—someone comes in, asks a question, gets an answer, and leaves.

More interesting for the future of electronic publishing is a second use, that of periodic information requests. As I said earlier in this book, most people read specific sections of the newspaper and, even within those sections, are choosy about what they do and don't read. I, for instance, always read the sports section but I am interested only in baseball, basketball, football to a lesser extent, and hockey only if the Pittsburgh Penguins are mentioned. Even within the sports I follow closely, baseball and basketball, I'm more interested in certain teams and players than others.

Rather than skim through the paper each Sunday to see whether anything interesting happened to the teams or players I follow, I can instead ask a question of a WAIS-based newspaper system (which is conceivable right now, using the UPI news feed that ClariNet sells via Usenet). In fact, I might not ask only one question, but I may gradually come up with a set of questions, some specific, others abstract. Along with "What's happening with Cal Ripken and the Baltimore Orioles?" could be "Tell me about the U.S. economy."

In either case, WAIS would run my requests periodically, every day or two, and indicate which items are new in the list. Ideally, the actual searching would take place at night to minimize the load on the network and to make the search seem faster than the technology permits. Once again, this capability is entirely possible today; all that lacks for common usage is the vast quantities of information necessary to address everyone's varied interests. Although the amount of data available in WAIS is still limited (if you call 700-plus sources limited), serious and important uses are already occurring.

> **N o t e** *There's a project, probably destined to be commercial, in testing now that will provide this sort of an electronic newspaper. I'm not quite sure yet how WAIS is involved in it, but there are some links. Check out this URL for more information:*
>
> `http://www.ensemble.com/`

In large part due to its corporate parentage, the WAIS project has been careful to allow for information to be sold and for owners of the information to control who can access the data and when. Although not foolproof, the fact that WAIS addresses these issues makes it easier to deal with copyright laws and information theft.

Because of the controls WAIS allows, information providers are likely to start making sources of information more widely available. With the proliferation of these information sources, it will become harder for the user to keep track of what's available. To handle that problem, WAIS incorporates a Directory of Servers, which tracks all the available information servers. Posing a question to the Directory of Servers source (WAIS calls sets of information *sources* or *servers*) returns a list of servers that may have information pertaining to your question. You can then easily ask the same question of those servers to reach the actual data.

Most of the data available on WAIS is public and free at the moment, and I don't expect that arrangement to change. I do expect more commercial data to appear in the future, however.

In regard to that issue I want to propose two ideas. First, charges should be very low to allow and encourage access, which means that profit is made on high volume rather than high price. Given the size of the Internet, I think this approach is the way to go, rather than charging exorbitant amounts for a simple search that may not even turn up the answer to your question.

Second, I'd like to see the appearance of more "information handlers," who foot the cost of putting a machine on the Internet and buying WAIS server software and then, for a percentage, allow others to create information sources on their server. WAIS, Inc. already provides this service, but I haven't heard of much competition yet. That service enables a small publisher to make, say, a financial newsletter available to the Internet public for a small fee, but the publisher doesn't have to go to the expense of setting up and maintaining a WAIS server. This arrangement will become more commonplace; the question is when? Of course, as the prices of server machines, server software, and network connections drop, the number of such providers will increase.

WAIS has numerous client interfaces for numerous platforms, but you probably can use either a simple VT100 interface via Telnet or, if you have a MacTCP link to the Internet, a program called MacWAIS. When evaluating WAIS client programs, keep in mind my comments about the two types of questions and the relevance feedback. A WAIS client should make it easy to ask a quick question without screwing around with a weird interface, and it should also enable you to save questions for repeated use (as in the electronic newspaper example). Similarly, with relevance feedback, that act of pointing and saying, "Find me more like this one that I'm pointing at" should be as simple as possible without making you jump through hoops.

Finally, none of the WAIS clients I've seen provide a simple method of keeping track of new sources as they appear, not to mention keeping track of which sources have gone away for good.

Gopher

In direct contrast to WAIS, Gopher originated in academia at the University of Minnesota, where it was intended to help distribute campus information to staff and students. The name is actually a two-way pun (there's probably a word for that) because Gopher was designed to enable you to "go fer" some information. Many people probably picked up on that pun, but the less well-known one is that the University of Minnesota is colloquially known as the home of the Golden Gophers, the school mascot. In addition, one of the Gopher Team members said that there are gophers living outside their office.

Note

Calling yourself the Golden Gophers makes more sense than calling yourself the Trojans, not only considering that the Trojans were one of the most well-known groups in history that lost, but also considering that they lost the Trojan War because they fell for a really dumb trick. "Hey, there's a gigantic wooden horse outside, and all the Greeks have left. Let's bring it inside!" Not a formula for long-term survival. Now, if they had formed a task force to study the Trojan Horse and report back to a committee, everyone wouldn't have been massacred. Who says middle management is useless? Anyway, I digress.

The point of Gopher is to make information available over the network, much in the same way that FTP does. In some respects, Gopher and FTP are competing standards for information retrieval, although they serve somewhat different purposes. Gopher only works for retrieving data; you cannot use it to send data. Also, there's no easy way to give Gopher users usernames and passwords so only they can access a Gopher site.

Gopher has several advantages over FTP. First, it provides direct access to far more types of information resources than FTP. Gopher provides access to online phone books, online library catalogs, the text of the actual files, databases of information stored in WAIS, various email directories, Usenet news, and Archie. Second, Gopher pulls all this information together under one interface and makes it all available from a basic menu system.

> **Note**
>
> *Menu items on a Gopher server are not Macintosh menus, but list items in a Macintosh window under TurboGopher. Keep that in mind, and you'll be fine.*

If you retrieve a file via FTP and the file gives you a reference to another FTP server, you as the user must connect to that site separately to retrieve any more files from there. In contrast, you connect to a single home Gopher server, and from there, wend your way out into the wide world of Gopherspace without ever having to consciously disconnect from one site and connect to another (although that is what happens under the hood). Gopher servers almost always point at each other, so after browsing through one Gopher server in Europe, you may pick a menu item that brings you back to a directory on your home server. Physical location matters little, if at all, in Gopherspace.

Gopher has also become popular because it uses less net bandwidth than standard FTP. When you connect to a Gopher server, the Gopher client software actually connects only long enough to retrieve the menu, and then it disconnects. When you select something from the menu, the client connects again very quickly, so you barely notice that you weren't actually wasting net bandwidth during that time. Administrators like using Gopher for this reason. They don't have to use as much computing power providing files to Internet users.

> **Note**
>
> *There's actually no reason why FTP servers couldn't be rewritten to work this way, as well. Jim Matthews, the author of Fetch, is always going on about how writing an FTP server that used something called lightweight threads would make FTP more efficient. In the meantime, Peter Lewis's Anarchie FTP client for the Mac works much like a Gopher client in that it is continually connecting again and again to your target FTP site, enabling you to perform more than one FTP task at a time.*

Several Gopher clients exist for the Macintosh. The one written by the Gopher programmers themselves is arguably the best Gopher client for any platform. They claim that it's the fastest over slow connections, and although I haven't used clients on other platforms, TurboGopher is certainly fast. You also can access Gopher via Telnet and a VT100 interface. It's nowhere near as nice (it's slower, you can only do one thing at a time, and you cannot view pictures and the like online), but it works if you don't have MacTCP-based access to the Internet.

Veronica

The most important adjunct to Gopher is a service called Veronica, developed by Steve Foster and Fred Barrie at University of Nevada. Basically, Veronica is to Gopher what Archie is to FTP—a searching agent; hence, the name.

N o t e

Veronica stands for Very Easy Rodent-Oriented Net-wide Index to Computerized Archives, *but apparently the acronym followed the name.*

Veronica servers work much like Archie servers. They tunnel through Gopherspace recording the names of available items and adding them to a massive database.

You usually find a Veronica menu within an item called Other Gopher and Information Servers, or occasionally simply World. When you perform a Veronica search, you either look for Gopher directories, which contain files, or you look for everything available via Gopher, which includes the files and things like WAIS sources as well. There are only a few Veronica servers in the world (between four and six, depending on which machines are up), so you may find that the servers are heavily overloaded at times, at which point they'll tell you that there are too many connections and that you should try again later. Although it's not as polite as I'd like, I find that using the European Veronica servers during their night is the least frustrating.

It's definitely worth reading the "Frequently Asked Questions about Veronica" document that lives with the actual Veronica servers. It provides all sorts of useful information about how Veronica works, including the options for limiting your search to only directories or only searchable items. You can use Boolean searches within Veronica, and there are ways of searching for word stems—that is, the beginning of words. So, if you wanted to learn about yachting, you could search for "yacht*." The possibilities aren't endless, but Veronica is utterly indispensable for navigating Gopherspace and for searching on the Internet in general.

Jughead

Getting sick of the Archie Comics puns yet? They just keep coming and, like Veronica, I somehow doubt that this acronym came before the name. *Jughead* stands for *Jonzy's Universal Gopher Hierarchy Excavation And Display*. Jughead does approximately the same thing as Veronica, but if you've ever done a Veronica search on some generic word, you know that Veronica can provide just a few too many responses (insert sarcasm here). Jughead is generally used to limit the range of a search to a certain machine, and to limit it to directory titles. This makes Jughead much more useful than Veronica if you know where you want to search, or if you're only searching on a Gopher server that runs Jughead.

I don't use Jughead all that much, because what I like about the massive number of Veronica results is that they often give me a sense of what information may exist on any given topic. I suppose that if I regularly performed fairly specific searches on the same set of Gopher servers, I'd use Jughead more.

> *The best way to find a generally accessible Jughead server is to do a Veronica search on "jughead -t7." That returns a list of all searchable Jughead servers, rather than all the documents and directories in Gopherspace that contain the word "jughead."*

World Wide Web

The World Wide Web is the most recent and ambitious of the major Internet services. The Web was started at CERN, a high-energy physics research center in Switzerland, as an academic project. It attempts to provide access to the widest range of information by linking not only documents made available via its native *HTTP* (*HyperText Transfer Protocol*), but also additional sources of information via Usenet news, FTP, WAIS, and Gopher. The Web tries to suck in all sorts of data from all sorts of sources, avoiding the problems of incompatibility by allowing a smart server and a smart client program to negotiate the format of the data.

> *CERN doesn't stand for anything any more, but it once was an acronym for a French name.*

In theory, this capability to negotiate formats enables the Web to accept any type of data, including multimedia formats, once the proper translation code is added to the servers and the clients. And, when clients don't understand the type of data that's appearing, such as a QuickTime movie, for instance, they generally just treat the data as a generic file, and ask another program to handle it after downloading.

The theory behind the Web makes possible many things, such as linking into massive databases without the modification of the format in which they're stored, thereby reducing the amount of redundant or outdated information stored on the nets. It also enables the use of intelligent agents for traversing the Web. But what the Web really does for the Internet is take us one step further toward total ease of use. Let's think about this evolution for a minute.

FTP simply transfers a file from one place to another—it's essentially the same thing as copying a file from one disk to another on the Mac. WAIS took the concept of moving information from one place to another, and made it possible for client and server to agree on exactly what information is transferred. When that information is searched or transferred, you get the full text without having to use additional tools to handle the information. Gopher merged both of those concepts, adding in a simple menu-based interface that greatly eased the task of browsing through information. Gopher also pioneered the concept of a virtual space, if you will, where any menu item on a Gopher server can refer to an actual file anywhere on the Internet. Finally, the World Wide Web subsumes all of the previous services and concepts, so it can copy files from one place to another; it can search through and transfer the text present in those files; and it can present the user with a simple interface for browsing through linked information.

But aside from doing everything that was already possible, the World Wide Web introduced four new concepts. The first one I've mentioned already—it's the capability to accept and distribute data from any source, given an appropriately written Web server.

Second, the Web introduced the concept of rich text and multimedia elements in Internet documents. Gopher and WAIS can display the text in a document, but they can't display it with fonts and styles and sizes and sophisticated formatting. You're limited to straight, boring text (not that it was boring when it first appeared, I assure you). With the Web, you can create *HTML* documents that contain special codes that tell a Web browser program to display the text in various different fonts and styles and sizes. *Web pages* (that's what documents on the Web are generally called) also can contain *inline graphics*— that is, graphics that are mixed right in with the text, much as you're used to seeing in books and magazines. And finally, for something you're not used to seeing in books and magazines, a Web page can contain sounds and movies, although sound and movie files are so large that you must follow a link to play each one.

Link? What's a link? Ah, that's the third concept that the Web brought to the Internet. Just as an item in a Gopher menu can point to a file on another Internet machine in a different country, so can Web *links*. The difference is that any Web page can have a large number of links, all pointing to different files on different machines, and those links can be embedded in the text. For instance, if I were to say in a Web page that I have a really great collection of **penguin pictures** stored on another Web page (and if you were reading this on the Web and not in a book), you could simply click on the underlined words to immediately jump to that link. Hypertext arrives on the Internet.

Hmm, I should probably explain hypertext. A term coined by Ted Nelson many years ago, *hypertext* refers to nonlinear text. Whereas you normally read left to right, top to bottom, and beginning to end, in hypertext you follow links that take you to various different places in the document, or even to other related documents, without having to scan through the entire text. Assume, for instance, that you're reading about wine. There's a link to information on the cork trees that produce the corks for wine bottles, so you take that link, only to see another link to the children's story about Ferdinand the Bull, who liked lying under a cork tree and smelling the flowers. That section is in turn linked to a newspaper article about the running of the bulls in Pamplona, Spain. A hypertext jump from there takes you to a biography of Ernest Hemingway, who was a great fan of bull fighting (and of wine, to bring us full circle). This example is somewhat facetious, but hopefully it gives you an idea of the flexibility a hypertext system with sufficient information, such as the World Wide Web, can provide.

Fourth, the final new concept the Web introduced to the Internet is *forms*. Forms are just what you would think, online forms that you can fill in, but on the Internet, forms become tremendously powerful because they make possible all sorts of applications, ranging from surveys to online ordering to reservations to searching agents to who knows what. Forms are extremely useful, and are increasingly heavily used on the Web for gathering information in numerous contexts.

For some time, the Web lacked a searching agent such as Archie or Veronica, a major limitation because the Web is so huge. However, a number of searching agents have appeared, and although they simply don't feel as successful as Veronica yet, I suspect that's merely because I'm less used to them. You can find a page of the Web searching agents at:

```
http://cuiwww.unige.ch/meta-index.html
```

In addition, a number of useful subject catalogs have sprung up; currently my favorite one is called Yahoo, and can be accessed at:

```
http://www.yahoo.com/
```

You can access the Web via a terminal and a VT100 interface, or even via email (which is agonizingly slow), but for proper usage, you must have a special browser.

Note

*To try the Web via email, send email to **listproc@www0.cern.ch** with the command www in the body of the message.*

When you're evaluating Web browsers, there are a number of features to seek. The most important is one that seems obvious: an easy way to traverse links. Because the entire point of a Web browser is to display fonts and styles in text, a Web browser should give you the ability to change the fonts to ones on your Mac that you find easy to read. HTML documents don't actually include references to Times and Helvetica; they encode text in certain styles, much like a word processor or page layout program does. Then, when your Web browser reads the text of a Web page, it decodes the HTML styles and displays them according to the fonts that are available. Sometimes the defaults are ugly, so I recommend playing with them a bit. Many, if not most, Web pages also contain graphics, which is all fine and nice unless you're the impatient sort who dislikes waiting for the graphics to travel over a slow modem. Web browsers should have an option to turn off auto-loading of images or let you move on before the images have finished loading. You should be able to do anything you can do in a normal Mac application, such as copy and paste. You

Part II

TCP/IP
Internet
Services

should be able to save a hotlist, preferably hierarchical, of Web sites that you'd like to visit again. Finally, you should be able to easily go back to previously visited pages without having to reload them over the Internet.

As I said previously, there are a number of ways to access the Web. But frankly, if you use a Mac and don't have access to a MacTCP-based connection, you'll miss out on the best parts, even if you can see the textual data in a VT100 browser such as Lynx.

Wrapping Up

That should do it for the background material about the various TCP/IP Internet services, such as FTP, Telnet, Gopher, WAIS, the World Wide Web, and a few other minor ones like IRC and MUDs. Feel free to flip back here and browse if you're confused about basic usage or what might be important to look for in a client program.

Enough about all the Internet services. But, before we go on and talk about ways you can get Internet access, I should explain about all the different file formats that you run into on the Internet. They're a source of confusion for many new users, so let's move on to chapter 10, "File Formats."

File Formats

On the Macintosh, we're all used to the simple concept of double-clicking on a document icon to open it in the proper application. The Macintosh keeps track of which documents go with which applications by type and creator codes. Thus, we tend not to think about file formats as much as people who use operating systems that lack the Mac's elegance. Nonetheless, every Mac file does have a format, and if you've ever seen the "Application not found" message, you may have wished for an easier way to determine a file's format.

> **Note**
>
> *Various utility programs such as Apple's free ResEdit and PrairieSoft's commercial DiskTop can show you the type and creator codes that the Mac's Finder uses to link documents and applications. You can find ResEdit at:*
>
> ```
> ftp://ftp.info.apple.com/Apple.Support.Area/Apple.Software.Updates/Macintosh/
> Utilities.Software/ResEdit.2.1.3.sea.hqx
> ```

When you start exploring, you quickly discover that most files on the Internet have filename extensions, as is standard in DOS. Unlike DOS, Unix allows long filenames, so you don't have to think of meaningless eight-character names for everything. Extensions are extremely useful on the Internet because they identify what sort of file you're looking at. On the Mac, you see a different icon or you can double-click on the file and see what program launches, but on the Internet, all you get is the filename and extension.

Unlike standard DOS usage, in which every program seems to have at least one or two extensions for its documents (`.wk1`, `.wks`, `.doc`, `.wp`, `.dbf`, `.ndx`, `.idx`, and other thoroughly memorable three-letter combinations), a limited set of extensions is commonly used for files that Mac users care about. These extensions fall into three basic categories: those used to indicate *ASCII* encoding, those used to indicate compression formats, and several others used to mark certain types of text, graphics, sound, and video files.

ASCII Encoding

Programs and other binary data files (files with more than just straight text in them) contain binary codes that most email programs don't understand, because email programs are designed to display only text. Binary data files even include data files, such as word processor files, which contain formatting information or other nonprinting characters. Most programs enable you to save your files in a variety of formats, including text. If you don't explicitly save a file in some kind of text format, then it's probably a binary data file, although there are exceptions.

> **N o t e**
>
> *The main exceptions to this are Apple's TeachText and SimpleText and Nisus Software's Nisus Writer word processor. TeachText and SimpleText can save only text files. Nisus Writer saves its files in such a way that all other programs see them as text files (the formatting lives in the file's resource fork, if you were wondering).*

Computers of different types generally agree on only the first 128 characters in the ASCII character set. (*ASCII* stands for *American Standard Code for Information Interchange.*) The important fact to remember is that after those first 128 characters, which include the letters of the alphabet and numbers and punctuation, a Mac's accented letter may be a DOS machine's smiley face.

Still, people want to transfer files via email and other programs that cannot handle all the possible binary codes in a data file or application. Programmers therefore came up with several different ways of representing 8 bits of binary data in 7 bits of straight text. In other words, these conversion programs can take in a binary file such as the Alarm Clock desk accessory, for instance, and convert it into a long string of numbers, letters, and punctuation marks. Another program can take that string of text and turn it back into a functioning copy of the Alarm Clock desk accessory. I'll leave it to the philosophers to decide whether it is the same program.

Once encoded, that file can travel through almost any email gateway and be displayed in any email program, although it's worthless until you download it to the Mac and decode it. The main drawback to this sort of encoding is that you must always decode the file before you can work with it, although many programs on the Mac decode for you automatically. In addition, because you move from an 8-bit file to a 7-bit file during the encoding process, the encoded file must be larger than the original, sometimes by as much as 35 percent.

Now that you understand why we go through such bother, the Internet uses three main encoding formats (see Table 10.1): *BinHex, uuencode,* and *btoa* (read as "b to a").

Table 10.1
ASCII Encoding Formats

Format	Advantages	Disadvantages
BinHex	Macintosh standard	Least efficient
uuencode	Used by LAN email gateways	Doesn't encode resource fork
btoa	Most efficient	Least common

BinHex

BinHex is by far the most common format you see in the Macintosh world because it originated on the Mac and works best with Macintosh files. In fact, it's basically used only on Macintosh computers. You can identify most BinHex files by the `.hqx` extension they carry. I haven't the foggiest idea why it is `.hqx` instead of `.bhx` or something slightly more reasonable. Keep in mind that BinHex is another one of these computer words that works as a verb, too, so people say that they binhexed a file before sending it to you.

> **N o t e**
>
> *There's another reason for using BinHex when working with Macintosh files. Macintosh files have two forks, a data fork and resource fork. Most other operating systems don't understand different forks, so you need a way to combine the forks into a single file suitable for uploading to a different machine. There are two basic ways to do this, MacBinary and BinHex. MacBinary creates a binary file that combines the two forks, whereas BinHex combines them in a text file. Since text files have other advantages in terms of surviving mail gateways, people use BinHex far more often. MacBinary files must be downloaded in binary mode and usually end with a `.bin` extension. Most programs that can download files understand MacBinary, but if they don't you can get a stand-alone version at:*
>
> `ftp://ftp.tidbits.com/pub/tidbits/tisk/util/`

Part II   File Formats

There are two flavors of BinHex, but they aren't interchangeable. The BinHex 4.0 format was originally created by Yves Lempereur and has been around forever. BinHex 5.0, which also came from Yves, is more recent but unfortunately causes massive confusion because it doesn't turn binary files into ASCII. Ignore BinHex 5.0 entirely, because everyone else does.

Note

BinHex 4.0 is a file format, and numerous programs can encode and decode that format. Yves wrote a program called BinHex 4.0 years ago, but it has some known bugs and should be avoided. I recommend that you use Aladdin's free StuffIt Expander for debinhexing files, especially because it can also expand various compression formats, and because it's on the ISKM disk.

Every BinHex file starts with the phrase **(This file must be converted with BinHex 4.0)** even if another program actually did the creating. Then comes a new line with a colon at the start, followed by many lines of ASCII gibberish. Only the last line can be a different length than the others (each line has a hard return after it), and the last character must be a colon as well (see figure 10.1). Occasionally, something happens to a BinHex file in transit and one line is shortened by a character or two or even deleted. When that happens, the file is toast.

Figure 10.1   *Example of BinHex.*

BinHex suffers from only two real problems other than a confusing name. It is perhaps the least efficient of the three encoding formats, which means that it wastes more space than other formats. Oh well, just because something is the standard doesn't mean it's the best. Its other real problem is that even though tools exist for debinhexing files on other platforms, they aren't common. Use uuencode if you plan to send binary files that have only a data fork (such as Microsoft Word files, for instance) to a user on another platform.

Note

Under Unix, you must use a program called mcvert to debinhex files. If you wish to encode or decode BinHex files on a PC, you can find a PC version of BinHex at:

```
ftp://boombox.micro.umn.edu/pub/binhex/MSDOS/binhex.exe
```

uucode

In the Unix world, uucode (also called uuencode) is the most common format. You can identify a uuencoded file by its **.uu** extension.

Although not in common usage in the Macintosh world, uucode is seen frequently enough that a number of Macintosh programs have sprung up to encode and decode this format. These include StuffIt Deluxe, UULite, and UMCP Tools, among others. You're unlikely to run across uuencoded Macintosh files frequently, mostly because uucode format ignores the resource fork of Macintosh files, making it useful for files that only have a data fork. For example, most programs store their code in the resource fork so uuencoding and then uudecoding a program renders the result totally unusable. You may run across slightly different extensions on occasion; I've also seen **.uud** and **.uue**. They're all the same thing.

> **Note**
>
> *By default, most LAN-based email programs (such as Microsoft Mail) that have Internet gateways encode binary files sent across the Internet in uucode format, since it's the most common.*

Most uuencoded files start with **begin 644**, followed by the filename. From that point on, they look a lot like BinHex files: rows upon rows of ASCII gibberish with each line being the same length. (Actually, these lines may not all look the same length when you're viewing them on the Mac, because Unix machines use the ASCII 10 linefeed character instead of a carriage return, which the Mac uses to end a line.)

> **Note**
>
> *Because the number 644 is related to Unix file permissions (don't ask), other numbers are possible at the top of uuencoded files, although I see them less frequently.*

All uuencoded files end with a linefeed, a space, the word **end**, and another linefeed (see figure 10.2).

Figure 10.2   *Example of uucode.*

btoa

Frankly, I don't know a lot about *btoa*, which stands for *binary to ASCII*. This format (see figure 10.3) is supported by a complementary *atob* convertor, which translates ASCII files back into binary. It is reportedly the most efficient of the three, so a btoa file is slightly smaller than the equivalent uuencode or BinHex file. In addition, btoa retains the multiple forks of Macintosh files, unlike uucode. Despite these seemingly major advantages, btoa doesn't appear nearly as frequently in the Unix world as uuencode, and appears rarely in the Macintosh world. As far as I know, the only program that can decode the btoa format on the Mac is StuffIt Deluxe, through one if its many translators.

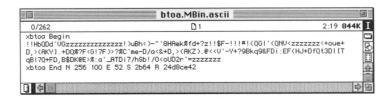

Figure 10.3   *Example of btoa.*

Compression Formats

Along with the various ASCII encoded formats, on the Internet you frequently see a number of file extensions that indicate the files have been compressed in some way. Almost every file available on the Internet is compressed because disk space is at a premium everywhere.

Unfortunately, because the majority of Macintosh files stored on the Internet are binhexed after being compressed, you don't see the full benefit of the compression. Nevertheless, if your original file is 200K and a compression program reduces it to 75K, you're still on the winning side even if binhexing the file increases it back up to 100K.

The folks who run the Internet file sites like two things to be true about a compression format. First, they want it to be as tight as possible, so as to save the most space. Second, they want to be sure that the files stored in that format will be accessible essentially forever. This requires the format of the compressed files to be made public; in theory, any competent programmer can write a program to expand those files should the company go out of business or otherwise disappear.

This second desire has caused some trouble over the years because the compression market is hotly contested. Companies seldom want to put their proprietary compression algorithms (the rules by which a file is compressed) into the public domain, where their competitors can copy them. For a while there was a project on the Internet to create a public format based on some other public compression formats, but it never saw the light of day. As it is, the only compression format widely available in the Macintosh world that is also public domain is that used by StuffIt 1.5.1, an older and less efficient version of the now-proprietary StuffIt 3.0 format.

Most people on the Internet compress Macintosh files in one of three ways: StuffIt, Compact Pro, or as a self-extracting archive. In addition, there are at least three or four other programs that can compress files, but few people ever use them for files posted on the Internet, other than for self-extracting archives.

StuffIt 3.0

Perhaps the most popular Macintosh compression format on the nets today is StuffIt 3.0, which is used by a family of programs—some free (StuffIt Expander), some shareware (StuffIt Lite), and some commercial (StuffIt Deluxe)—from Aladdin Systems. StuffIt files always have the **.sit** extension. The only confusion here is that the StuffIt file format has gone through three main incarnations: 1.5.1, 2.0, and 3.0. The latest versions of all the StuffIt tools can read all of those formats, but not surprisingly, StuffIt 2.0-class tools can read only files created in 2.0 or 1.5.1, and StuffIt 1.5.1 can read only files in its specific format.

Note

Although the StuffIt file format is version 3.0, the latest version of the programs is 3.5—the file format didn't change when Aladdin revised the programs.

This limitation leads to the common problem on the nets whereby people download a file in StuffIt 3.0 format assuming they can expand it with a StuffIt 2.0-class program because of the **.sit** extension. Unfortunately, because all three file formats use the **.sit** extension, the extension provides no useful indication, and StuffIt 2.0 spits up all over a StuffIt 3.0 file. The simple solution to this problem (and most other compression problems) is—and listen carefully—StuffIt Expander.

StuffIt Expander can expand any StuffIt format, it can expand Compact Pro archives, and as an added bonus it can debinhex files as well. It slices, it dices, and… let me just say that no one should be without StuffIt Expander. That's why I put it on the ISKM disk. Thanks are due to Aladdin Systems for making such a useful tool available for free. You can find the latest versions of StuffIt Expander and StuffIt Lite online in the directory:

```
ftp://ftp.tidbits.com/pub/tidbits/tisk/util/
```

There's actually a caveat to StuffIt Expander being free. Aladdin Systems has released a shareware program called DropStuff with Expander Enhancer which, when you pay your shareware fee, gives StuffIt Expander the capability to expand basically all the file formats that the full StuffIt Deluxe can expand through its translators. In addition, you can stuff files quickly by merely dropping them on DropStuff, so it's a doubly useful program. I strongly recommend you register DropStuff with Expander Enhancer if you intend to work with many different file types from the Internet. Another way to get the same functionality is to buy one of Aladdin's commercial programs, such as StuffIt Deluxe or SITcomm.

Part II　File Formats　10

Compact Pro

Compact Pro, a shareware compression utility from Bill Goodman, is almost as popular as the StuffIt family in the Macintosh world. Functionally, StuffIt and Compact Pro do the same thing—create a compressed archive of one or more files. In my experience, both utilities do an admirable job, so personal preference and other features may sway you one way or the other.

Compact Pro files are always identified by their **.cpt** extension. You may see an earlier version of Compact Pro floating around on the nets as well. It's called Compactor and uses the same file format as Compact Pro, so you don't have to worry about which version created a given file. Compactor is just an older version of Compact Pro, but Bill Goodman had to change the name for legal reasons. You can find Compact Pro in:

```
ftp://ftp.tidbits.com/pub/tidbits/tisk/util/
```

Self-Extracting Archives

What if you want to send a compressed file or files to a friend who you know has no compression utilities at all? Then you use a *self-extracting archive*, which is hard to describe further than the name already does. Most compression programs on the market can create self-extracting archives by compressing the file and then attaching a *stub*, or small expansion program, to the compressed file. The self-extracting archive looks like an application to the user, and if you double-click on a self-extracting archive, it launches and expands the file contained within it. Internet file sites prefer not to have many files, particularly small ones, compressed in self-extracting archives because the stubs are a waste of space for most people on the nets, who already have utilities to expand compressed files.

You can always identify self-extracting archives by the **.sea** extension. You can tell by the icon which compression program created any given self-extracting archive, but on the whole it makes no difference. The only exceptions to this naming scheme are self-extracting archives created by Alysis's SuperDisk program, which automatically appends the **.x** to the end of its self-extracting archives. You don't see many, if any, of these.

Unix Compression

Unix has a built-in compression program called, in an uncharacteristically straightforward fashion for Unix, Compress. Compress creates files with the **.Z** extension (note the capital Z—it makes a difference). Although you don't see files with that extension too often in Macintosh file sites, plenty of them exist on the rest of the net. Both StuffIt and a program called MacCompress (available in the URL below) can expand these files, should you need to do so:

```
ftp://ftp.tidbits.com/pub/tidbits/tisk/util/
```

N
o
t
e

Incidentally, MacCompress was written by Lloyd Chambers, who later went on to write DiskDoubler and AutoDoubler, starting the transparent compression market in the Macintosh world.

As far as I know, Compress works only on a single file, but you often want to put more than one file in an archive. All of the Mac compression programs both archive and compress in a single step. Under Unix, however, you need to perform the archiving step before you compress the file (and of course, if you want to mail it to someone, then you need to uuencode it). A program called Tar (which stands for *Tape archive*) archives under Unix; files archived with Tar get a **.tar** extension. If you archive a bunch of files with Tar, then shrink them with Compress, and then uuencode the compressed file to send to someone, the resulting filename may end with **.tar.Z.uue** to indicate what you've done to it and in what order.

Recently, a new format, called *gzip*, has started to take over the Unix world. It's marked by the **.z** or **.gz** extension. Gzip is the free GNU version of ZIP, a popular PC compression format. A Macintosh version, called *MacGzip*, recently appeared to decode these files. You can find it online in:

```
ftp://ftp.tidbits.com/pub/tidbits/tisk/util/
```

N
o
t
e

What's GNU? Not much, what's GNU with you? Sorry, but my editor made me put that in. GNU stands for the paradoxical "GNU's Not Unix" and is a project to create a fully functional version of Unix that you are free to do with as you please.

More Compression Formats

You may run across several other compression formats in your net travels. Not many people use these formats for files distributed to the world, but a few do, so the rest of us have to stay on our toes. DiskDoubler, from Symantec, can create "combined files" that generally have a **.dd** extension. Symantec makes a free DDExpandOnly application available for people who don't own DiskDoubler. Alysis's SuperDisk can create its own **.x** self-extracting archives. Now Compress, from Now Software, can make stand-alone and self-extracting archives. If you run into one of the stand-alone files, look for the free Expand Now application from Now Software in:

```
ftp://ftp.tidbits.com/pub/tidbits/tisk/util/
```

Don't be confused about DiskDoubler's company, because it changed since the first edition of this book. Lloyd Chambers wrote DiskDoubler for his company, Salient Software, which was then purchased by Fifth Generation Systems. Then, Symantec bought Fifth Generation Systems, getting DiskDoubler and the other Salient utilities in the bargain. It's kind of an industry food chain...

If you run across a very old archive, it might have a **.pit** extension, which means that it was created by an old program called PackIt (which I haven't seen in years). Don't bother looking for PackIt, and if you find it, don't create any files with it because it's a dead format. Several of the compression utilities (I don't have a PackIt file to even test this) claim to be able to expand PackIt files, but frankly, no one cares much anymore.

DOS Compression

Unfortunately, at some point you are bound to run into files compressed with DOS programs. In most cases these files are text files that you can easily read on a Mac as long as you can expand them. The most common DOS format is the ZIP format, which uses the **.zip** extension. Several shareware tools, such as ZipIt and UnZip, exist for unzipping these files, and StuffIt Deluxe also includes a translator for unzipping files. You can find these utilities in:

```
ftp://ftp.tidbits.com/pub/tidbits/tisk/util/
```

Almost totally unseen these days is the **.arc** extension, which was a common format several years ago, so there were several DOS programs that created and expanded **.arc** files. Once again, if you see one of these extensions on the Mac, try using StuffIt's translators.

Other File Types

You may want to keep in mind a number of other file type issues, relating both to formatting text files for different systems and to graphics files that you find on the Internet.

Text Files

Text files are universally indicated by the **.txt** extension, and after that, the main thing you have to watch for is the end-of-line character.

Unix expects the end-of-line character to be a linefeed (LF, or ASCII character 10), which usually shows up on the Mac as a little box because it's a nonprinting character in most fonts. The Mac ends its lines with carriage returns (CR, or ASCII character 13), and to further confuse the issue, DOS machines straddle the fence and use a carriage return and linefeed combination (CR/LF).

Because the Internet is nondenominational when it comes to computer religion (that is, the Internet as a whole; almost every individual is rabid about his or her choice of computer platform), most communication programs are good about making sure to put any outgoing text into a format that other platforms can read. Most programs also attempt to read in text and display it correctly no matter what machine originally formatted it. Unfortunately, as hard as these programs may try, they often fail, so you must pay attention to what sort of text you send out and retrieve—via email, FTP, Gopher, or whatnot.

When you're sending files from a Mac, the main thing to remember is to break the lines before 80 characters. "Eighty characters," you say. "How the heck am I supposed to figure out how many characters are on a line without counting them all? After all, the Mac has superior proportionally spaced fonts. Humph!"

Yeah, well, forget about those fonts when you're dealing with the Internet. You can't guarantee that anyone reading what you write even has those fonts, so stick to a monospaced font such as Monaco or Courier. I personally recommend Monaco 9 point if your eyes don't mind. Then, I recommend setting your word processor's ruler (if that's where you're typing the file) to approximately 6.25 inches. That way, you have around 64 characters per line, give or take a few. Finally, if you're using a sophisticated word processor such as Nisus Writer, you can run a macro that replaces spaces at the end of each line with hard returns. If you don't use Nisus Writer, you can probably find an option that enables you to Save As Text, and that inserts returns at the end of each line in the process.

Note

There are also several utilities, including one called Add/Strip, that add returns for you. You can find Add/Strip in the usual place:

```
ftp://ftp.tidbits.com/pub/tidbits/tisk/util/
```

Part II   File Formats   **10**

After your lines have hard returns (carriage returns on the Mac) at the end, you usually can send a file properly, because most communications programs can handle replacing carriage returns with linefeeds or perhaps simply adding linefeeds. If you don't add returns and someone tries to read your text file under DOS or Unix, the file may or may not display correctly. There's no telling, depending on that person's individual circumstances, but you usually hear about it if you screw up. Test with something short if you're unsure whether you can send and receive text files properly.

Often, the Internet client program automatically strips and replaces linefeeds with carriage returns on files coming in from the Internet. If that doesn't happen, you either can use Add/Strip or one of its compatriots, or just run a Find and Replace in your word processor.

If you search for the linefeed (by copying the little box from the document into the Find field in your word processor) and replace it with the carriage return, the file still has hard returns at the end of every line. Instead, try this: Search for two linefeeds; replace them with some special character that doesn't otherwise exist in the document (I usually use Option-8, the bullet); then search for one linefeed and replace it with a space; finally, replace your bullets with carriage returns. As a result, you get nicely wrapped text (assuming of course, that there were blank lines separating paragraphs in the original file).

The other reason to view files from the Internet in a monospaced font with lines delimited by hard returns is that people on the Internet can be incredibly creative with ASCII tables and charts. Using only the standard characters you see on your keyboard, these people manage to create some extremely complex tables and graphics. I can't say they are works of art, but I'm often impressed. If you wrap the lines and view in a proportionally spaced font, those ASCII tables and graphics look like textual garbage.

Setext

One other note on text formatting on the Internet. Ian Feldman, with megabytes of comments from me and several others, has defined a "structure-enhanced text" format specifically for electronic periodicals. Files encoded in *setext* format should have the `.etx` extension. *TidBITS* was the first publication to use setext, but more are switching to it every day. Setext has the advantage of being eminently readable online, where it conforms to the least common denominator of Internet machines (less than 70-character-long lines, only the standard character set, and so on), but special front-end programs enable you to browse a setext file and add structure, navigational capabilities, and enhanced display features such as fonts and styles. The idea is to profit from the best of both worlds, the online text-based platforms and the graphically oriented client machines many of us use.

The trick setext employs to remain so unobtrusive online while retaining a format that special browsers can read is making the code implicit in the text and using accepted online styles when possible (see figure 10.4). The title of a setext file, for instance, is a line of characters followed by another line of the exact same number of equal signs, effectively forming a double underline. Subheads are similar, but they are followed by lines of dashes, forming a single underline. Words that should be bold when decoded are sandwiched by asterisk pairs like `**this**`, and words that should be underlined are sandwiched by underscores like `_this_`.

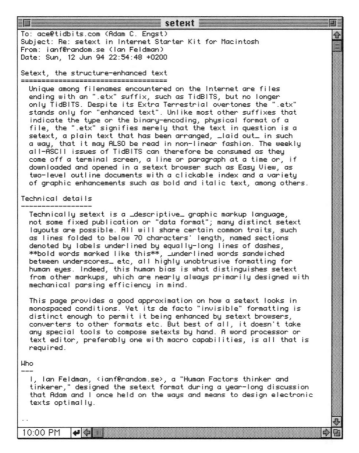

Figure 10.4   *Example of setext.*

It's best to read a setext in a browser such as Akif Eyler's Easy View (primarily a Macintosh browser, although versions are available for Unix and Windows). Easy View can replace the awkward underscores and asterisks with bold and underline styles and can break up a setext into its sections, displaying each subhead separately. But if you can't or don't want to use a program such as Easy View, any program that can display a text file will suffice. You can find the latest version of Easy View in:

```
ftp://ftp.tidbits.com/pub/tidbits/tisk/util/
```

HTML

I don't want to say much about HTML here, because although it's a text file format that you may run into on the Internet, I plan to provide a short tutorial on the basics of HTML so you can create your own Web pages. So, I want to hold off on talking about HTML until chapter 26, "Creating Your Web Page."

Graphics Files

For a long time, graphics files weren't commonly posted on the Internet except for use by users of a specific machine, because Macs were not able to read PC graphic file formats and vice versa. Now, however, you can view some common formats on multiple platforms.

GIF

First among these formats is *GIF,* which stands for *Graphics Interchange Format.* GIF was originally created by CompuServe. GIF files almost always have the extension **.gif**. GIF files are popular on the Internet because the file format is internally compressed, although it can show only 256 colors. When you open a GIF file in a program such as Giffer or GraphicConverter, the program expands the GIF file before displaying it.

> **Note**
>
> *It seems that almost no one can agree on how to pronounce GIF, either with a hard G sound or with a J sound. Take your pick; I won't argue with you either way.*

With the rise of the World Wide Web, two other features of GIF files have become important—interlacing and transparency.

If you save a GIF file in interlaced format (an option in the shareware GIFConverter, for example), some Web browsers can bring in the image gradually rather than all at once. In the current version of MacWeb, the image fades in line by line, with every other line or so being drawn, then the rest of them appearing on subsequent passes. In Netscape, the image appears crude and blocky and gradually becomes more detailed. Interlaced GIFs are useful because the user can stop the image loading or move on if it's a large but uninteresting image. I personally feel that interlaced GIFs should not be used for text-heavy graphics or for what are called image maps on the Web—pictures that have different hot spots for clicking on. The text-heavy images are disconcertingly hard to read as they come in, and the image maps don't work until the entire image has appeared, which can be confusing.

The transparency feature in GIFs also proves useful on the Web. You can't have non-rectangular graphics on the Web, but you can set one color as "transparent," which means that the Web browser will interpret that color as being the same as the color of the browser's background. This enables seemingly nonrectangular graphics and makes using graphics on Web pages more flexible. A little application from Aaron Giles called Transparency enables you to set a transparent color in GIF images. These and other graphics utilities are in:

```
ftp://ftp.tidbits.com/pub/tidbits/tisk/util/
```

JPEG

The second type of file format you may see is *JPEG*, which stands for *Joint Photographic Experts Group*. JPEG files, which are generally marked by the **.jpeg** or **.jpg** extension, use a different form of compression than GIF. JPEG file compression reduces the image size to as much as one-twentieth of the original size, but also reduces the quality slightly because it actually throws out parts of the file that you generally can't see. You can view JPEG files (among other formats) with JPEGView from Aaron Giles, which is available in:

```
ftp://ftp.tidbits.com/pub/tidbits/tisk/util/
```

JPEG files have become more popular on the Internet now that Netscape and the Web browser in TCP/Connect II 2.1.1 can display JPEG images inline, that is, without running a program such as JPEGView.

Why would you want to use one format over the other? JPEG images can have more than 256 colors in them and are thus better for photographic images. GIFs tend to be better for graphics created on the Mac, especially those with only a few colors. And of course, not all Web browsers can display JPEG images inline yet.

Sound and Video Files

With the advent of the World Wide Web, sound and video files have become far more common on the Internet, although they're so large that most people using a modem won't want to spend the hours required to download a short sound or video clip. But if you have either a fast connection or patience, there are several file formats that you should be aware of.

Sound

Sounds come primarily in the *Ulaw* format. Files in this format have the **.au** extension. I know very little about the Ulaw format except that there are two programs on the Mac capable of playing it, UlawPlay and SoundMachine, both written by Rod Kennedy. Both are free and seem to work fine, although SoundMachine has a far more sophisticated interface. It wouldn't take much—UlawPlay merely accepts a file dropped on it, launches, plays the file, and quits. You can find both in:

```
ftp://ftp.tidbits.com/pub/tidbits/tisk/util/
```

Video

There are two video formats that you should know about, *MPEG* and *QuickTime*. MPEG stands for *Motion Picture Experts Group*. It's actually a compression format much like JPEG, although one optimized for compressing video rather than still images. MPEG files generally have the extension **.mpeg** or **.mpg**, as you might expect. The only Macintosh program I know of that can play MPEG files is Maynard Handley's free Sparkle. You can find Sparkle on the Internet at:

```
ftp://ftp.tidbits.com/pub/tidbits/tisk/util/
```

The most common application for playing QuickTime movies is Movie Player (previously called Simple Player), which comes with the QuickTime distribution from Apple. Many other applications, such as Leonard Rosenthol's Popcorn, can play QuickTime movies as well, but Simple Player works sufficiently well for basic QuickTime movies. You can find it, along with the necessary QuickTime extension, at the following URL (sorry for the mega-long URL—that's what happens when Apple uses long directory names and buries things deeply):

```
ftp://ftp.info.apple.com/Apple.Support.Area/Apple.Software.Updates/Macintosh/System.Software/
Other.System.Software/QuickTime.1.6.2.sea.hqx
```

Actually, I lied. There is a third format you may see on occasion, AVI, indicated by the **.avi** extension. It's a Windows video format, and although there are no Mac programs that can play AVI files, there is one that can convert AVI files to QuickTime movies, called, as you might expect, AVI to QuickTime Converter. It's at the URL below.

There is a quirk about QuickTime movies that may trip up budding Web publishers: Because of the two Macintosh file forks, you can't just upload a QuickTime movie to a Web server. Instead, you must first "flatten" the movie using a utility like the freeware flattenMoov. It's in:

```
ftp://ftp.tidbits.com/pub/tidbits/tisk/util/
```

Format's Last Theorem

There you have it, a semiexhaustive (I could have gone into the nitty gritty of each file format, but then you'd have fallen asleep on me) discussion of the major file formats you're likely to run into on the Internet and how to deal with them. I think we've had plenty of background material, so let's move on to figuring out how to choose what sort of Internet access you want and from whom to get it.

III

Partial Internet Access

It's time to talk about how you get Internet access and what it looks like. You have five basic ways to connect to the Internet, each with pros and cons, costs and confusions. I try to explain how you choose between them and how to choose a provider in chapter 11, "Choosing a Connection." Then I discuss Internet access through commercial online services like America Online or CompuServe in chapter 12, "Commercial Services." In chapter 13, "Bulletin Board Systems," I take a brief look at connecting to the Internet via a BBS, or bulletin board system. After that, chapter 14, "Shell Account Enhancements," looks at some utilities that put a pretty face on the hoary Unix shell account. The last chapter, chapter 15, "UUCP Access", in this part is for those who don't want anything other than email and Usenet news. Don't worry about the terms and acronyms just yet; I explain them in the following chapters.

All these methods are in some way limited as to what they provide or what they offer for the future, so Part IV provides all the details related to setting up and using the fifth method of connecting, a full Internet connection based on MacTCP. I should be honest about this—I fully expect that you will want a MacTCP-based connection to the Internet, so that's where I concentrate the most discussion and where the software on the disk helps. If you have a Delphi account or an account on a First Class BBS, for instance, the disk is useless to you.

After chapter 11, "Choosing a Connection," I don't expect you to read all of the chapters in this section. Frankly, if you plan to get a PPP connection as I recommend, there's no reason for you to know about UUCP or enhancements to a Unix shell account. You may still want to read about what the commercial services provide if you're helping a friend with one, or if you also have an account there, but all that depends on your situation.

Now let's look at how you choose between the different types of accounts and how you choose an Internet provider.

11

Choosing a Connection

When the time comes to start thinking about making your first connection to the Internet, the first question you must answer is, "Which Internet access provider should I work with?"

Just so I don't lose anyone, an Internet access provider, also called an Internet service provider or just Internet provider, is a company that you call with a modem to access the Internet. In the same way that you work with your local telephone company to access the world-wide telephone system, so too must you work with an Internet access provider to access the Internet.

Arriving at the proper answer to that question can be either extremely simple or really quite difficult. If you live in a place where there is only one local Internet provider, the answer is quite easy—work with a local provider whenever possible because it's almost always cheaper to make a local phone call than to call long distance. If you're blessed, or cursed, with a multitude of Internet providers, the choice becomes more difficult. Although you may have more to choose from, you also have to spend more time figuring out the differences.

Eliminating Options

However, many people never get to that point, because they're confused by the difference between accessing the Internet through a commercial service like America Online or through a MacTCP-based PPP account with a true Internet provider. Then there are those people who are trying to decide between a Unix shell account and a MacTCP-based SLIP or PPP account. And what about the aging UUCP war-horse? But first, let's talk about what can be the easiest way to get started for many people—the commercial information services.

Commercial Services

In my opinion, there are only a few reasons to choose a commercial online service like America Online, CompuServe, or eWorld over a full Internet connection. First, if your area has a local number for the commercial service, but doesn't yet have a local Internet provider, the costs of accessing the commercial online service can be somewhat lower than calling an Internet provider long distance. You may want to read on to see what I say about how the costs all work out, though, because the commercial online services all charge you by the hour after a certain number of free hours (or if you use certain services, and those costs aren't always as up front as they should be). Nonetheless, it's easy to spend a lot of time on the Internet, and if you've got a local call to America Online, for instance, the $3.50 per hour that they charge after your free hours will probably be less than you would pay for a long-distance call anywhere.

The second reason for considering a commercial online service in favor of a real Internet connection is a bit hard for me to admit, given my obvious Internet biases. Quite frankly, it's often easier to set up an account with eWorld or America Online than it is to configure the necessary software to communicate with an Internet provider. For instance, you can call an 800 number to get a copy of the special software for America Online or eWorld (the numbers are in the next chapter), and they offer tech support for their software. That said, I feel that you pay for that initial ease of use (which isn't guaranteed—I've often had those automated signup processes fail in ways that would confuse a beginner) with software that simply isn't up to snuff in comparison with what you can get for MacTCP-based connections.

For instance, I gave my grandmother a Macintosh Classic for Christmas, and my sister gave her a 2400 bps modem. We got her up on America Online because it was a local call. Both she and my father, who was helping her, have had quite a lot of trouble with the way America Online handles nicknames (my father's used to Eudora), and the first question she sent me after only a few messages was, "How come I can't quote replies like everyone else can?" Well, the answer is quite simply, "America Online's software doesn't do that." I don't quite dare introduce my grandmother to utilities that would enable her to quote replies because they would undoubtedly add to the confusion.

That said, I still feel that America Online was the right choice for her, in large part because she's not really interested in being on the Internet so much as being able to send and receive Internet email. That's perhaps the third reason to use a commercial online service instead of the Internet. If you really aren't all that interested in the Internet and don't plan on spending much time online, you can't beat the commercial services for a combination of inexpensive access (as long as you stick within your free hours each month) and relative ease of use. Since you won't be using the software much, the fact that it may lack (and I speak for all the commercial services here—their software is for the most part mediocre) essential features isn't that important.

Finally, the commercial services all offer a great deal of quality information and files to download. If you have no desire to explore beyond the walls of the commercial service, then by all means, don't bother! You shouldn't get on the Internet just because someone said you had to. You should want to get on, because otherwise you'll probably convince yourself that the Internet is a waste of time. And, you'll be right—for you, the Internet will be a waste of time.

Bulletin Board Systems

The main reason that I'd recommend using a BBS over a full Internet connection is because most BBSs are extremely cheap or free. Increasingly, BBSs provide Internet email and news (often using a UUCP connection, I'll discuss this in a moment), and some are putting in direct Internet connections that enable you to use services like the World Wide Web from within the BBS. I expect more of these services will appear in BBS software in the future.

Because many boards are free, they're also potentially unreliable as well (since the person running the BBS probably isn't watching it 24 hours a day). That can be a serious problem if you rely on your Internet connection for business or important personal communication.

Finding a local BBS can be a daunting task because most communities don't have listings of them in the newspaper or anywhere else for that matter. The best place to start is at your dealer or any local computer store. These people can often point you to someone on the staff who uses bulletin boards, or they may direct you to local user groups, which often operate bulletin boards.

Unix Shell Accounts

Okay, so you've decided that you do want to get on the Internet after all, but you see that one provider is offering a connection for much less than another. Why the difference? Well, in this prefabricated-for-your-convenience example, the first provider only offers a Unix shell account, whereas the second provider offers full SLIP or PPP access so you can use MacTCP-based software. Again, I must bare my biases.

I use a Macintosh because I feel that the Macintosh interface is as good as we've got right now. I won't pretend it's perfect, and I've used plenty of other systems as well. I simply feel, and if you own a Mac you probably agree with me, that I'd rather use a Macintosh than type cryptic commands at a command line.

Well, that's the difference between the Unix shell account and the SLIP or PPP account. If you have a Unix shell account, you'll end up typing at that command line more than you like. If you do end up with a shell account, I strongly recommend that you get a different book because I don't cover how to use Unix at all in this one. I prefer to concentrate on the Macintosh instead, and to cover two operating systems well would be a tremendous amount of work. If you decide to take this route, I recommend Ed Krol's *The Whole Internet User's Guide and Catalog* (O'Reilly & Associates). Ed does a great job of explaining in detail how to work with the Internet on a Unix machine. Besides, Ed's a great guy, and he uses a Macintosh PowerBook Duo and Eudora in real life.

However, there is now some software that I'll talk about in chapter 14, "Shell Account Enhancements," that goes a long way toward giving you SLIP (and soon PPP) access from a Unix shell account. This software, called TIA, or The Internet Adapter, is an impressive feat, but that said, I still don't recommend it for the complete novice. It's Unix software that you must install in your Unix shell account, and there's just enough tricky stuff that it's not easy for the novice. If you've used Unix before and have done some scripting on the Macintosh, you'll probably be fine, though, and a TIA-enhanced shell account may be a great option for you.

Finding a Unix shell account is similar to finding a SLIP or PPP account; although, Phil Eschallier has compiled a list of sites, called the nixpub list, that focuses on Unix shell accounts. To receive the latest copy (this assumes you have an email account somewhere else already, of course), send email to **mail-server@bts.com** and put **get PUB nixpub.long** in the body of the message. The list is approximately 60K.

Also, try calling the help desks at local universities or colleges because some provide limited access to their machines. If you work at a university or large computer-oriented business, of course, you probably simply have to ask the right person, so start with the help desk or the person who takes care of your computers.

UUCP

But what about UUCP? Sure, it's old and slow and limited to email and Usenet news, but UUCP still has some uses. The main one is for an office with a number of people who only want to use email. There's no reason to pay for what is almost always a more-expensive dedicated connection when a cheap UUCP dialup connection will work fine. There are a number of UUCP gateways for the main LAN email packages like QuickMail and Microsoft Mail, and once you've got a UUCP connection set up and working, it doesn't usually require much intervention.

Of course, the real advantage of a UUCP connection via a LAN email package at work is that someone else may have set it up for you. This type of access also is generally free, but the only way to find out about it is to ask the person who takes care of your network. I can't really help you with this type of access because it varies significantly based on how your network is set up and administered.

If you're planning on setting up a UUCP connection, be clear on the fact that a UUCP connection limits you to email and Usenet news, and if you're gatewaying into a LAN email package, possibly not even Usenet news. You will never be able to use FTP, Gopher, or the World Wide Web; it's as simple as that.

Because there are relatively few UUCP connections compared to the number of MacTCP-based connections, you may have a much harder time getting help with any problems on the nets. Of course, that's an advantage of buying a commercial gateway from a company like StarNine (**info@starnine.com**) since they can provide the support.

I guess what I'm trying to say is that UUCP is a good solution for a very specific problem, but it's not really for the faint of heart or for the person who wants full Internet access. Setting up and using a MacTCP-based connection will simply be easier and more rewarding than a UUCP account for most people.

Finding a site that gives you a UUCP feed is more difficult than finding a Unix shell account, although the process is similar, especially in terms of consulting the nixpub list. In my experience, the help desks at universities seldom know about UUCP, even though Unix machines located in the Computer Science or Engineering departments often support it. You might ask around to find out who administrates those computers, then ask nicely whether they provide any UUCP feeds. UUCP is sufficiently efficient that a long-distance call might make financial sense, especially if you don't subscribe to a large newsgroup or receive large programs in email.

MacTCP-based Connections

In the previous sections, I've compared, usually negatively, all of the other methods of connecting to the Internet to a full MacTCP-based connection. I'll be honest—I don't think anything else compares in terms of power, speed, flexibility, and often, expense.

The combination of PPP or SLIP and MacTCP lets you run great Macintosh programs that enable you to do everything on the Internet with a Macintosh interface. Gone are the days of the command line; now you can use programs such as Eudora for email, Anarchie for FTP, NCSA Telnet, NewsWatcher, InterNews, or Nuntius for reading news, and a slew of other wonderful applications such as Netscape, MacWeb, TurboGopher, Finger, and MacWAIS. These programs often work together to provide the most complete Internet solution that you can get. The freeware and shareware programmers in the Macintosh Internet world are always the first to come out with the best programs, giving you an ever-improving interface to the Internet.

Another important fact about MacTCP-based connections is that they offer you choices. Perhaps you prefer Netscape to MacWeb, or Nuntius to NewsWatcher. With a MacTCP-based connection, you can make that choice, whereas a commercial service or BBS limits you to their interface.

Part III

Choosing a
Connection

Finally, now that PPP and SLIP accounts are becoming rather common, the price for moderate to heavy Internet users is often less than you'd pay for a commercial service because many Internet providers offer flat-rate accounts. It's the best of both worlds—great software without a clock ticking in the background.

But enough about the differences between these Internet options. I assume from the fact that you bought this book over one that talks about the commercial services that you are indeed interested in using the Internet to its fullest, and from that, I can assume that you're going to want to find an Internet provider. As I said above, I see two main variables in choosing an Internet provider—cost and service.

Cost

The first and, for most people, most important variable is cost. Unless you have more money than sense, it's not fun to throw money away unnecessarily. However, it can sometimes be difficult to determine the actual cost of your connection, especially if the provider has numerous little charges here and there, and if you have to factor in telephone charges.

Flat-Rate Accounts

The first thing to look for is a flat-rate account, under which you pay a set fee every month, no matter how much time you spend connected. Some accounts aren't technically flat-rate, but have such a high upper limit, like 120 hours each month, that they may as well be flat-rate. If you can get a flat-rate account, do it. They simply can't be beat for most people, and the lack of stress over how large your next bill will be is well worth it, in my opinion.

> **Note**
>
> *Some providers offer discounts if you pay for several months or even a year in advance—it's worth asking them if they have any such discount plans when you sign up.*

Restricted Flat-Rate Accounts

Some flat-rate plans are flat-rate, but come with some reasonable restrictions to prevent people from abusing the service. For instance, Northwest Nexus has a two-hour-on, two-hour-off policy that it can enforce if necessary. Without such a policy, it would be easy for someone to connect and leave the modem connected all day, preventing anyone else from using that modem at the host. Another restriction you may see is a policy of disconnecting connections that haven't had any traffic pass over them in a certain number of minutes. Sometimes this restriction can be a pain because, for instance, I can easily spend longer than ten minutes reading and then responding to a thoughtful message in Usenet news—all the time without sending any traffic. If you have problems with a too-short timeout value, try setting Eudora to check your email every few minutes to force some traffic to go over the connection.

Pseudo Flat-Rate Accounts

A number of providers don't offer straight flat-rate plans, but instead offer flat rates up to a certain number of hours. So, you may pay $30 for 60 hours of use, or something similar. After that hourly limit, the provider usually charges a few dollars per hour. Again, this rate system is designed to make sure that some people don't abuse the system to the detriment of all the other users. If the provider that you're considering uses such a system, you may want to ask if there's any way you can check to see if you're close to the time limit. In addition, I recommend asking what the policy is on isolated incidents in which, say, some emergency happens and you have to leave the computer suddenly while it's still connected, and it's still connected 12 hours later when you can get back. Most good providers will simply credit you with the time if it's a one-time occurrence.

Per-Hour Accounts

I seldom recommend accounts that charge you by the hour because I personally find it very stressful to be continually worrying about the clock ticking off dollars in the background while I'm working. However, per-hour accounts can make sense for people who don't use them often because the overall cost is lower than a flat-rate account's monthly fee. For instance, CompuServe used to use a pricing scheme of $2.50 per month and high hourly fees, and that's the sort of account I still have. Because I don't use CompuServe much, that pricing scheme is actually a lot cheaper for me than its current standard pricing plan, which costs $9.95 per month, even if you don't use it. If you decide to go with a per-hour pricing plan, pay close attention to your bills so that you can tell if it makes sense to switch to a different type of account, assuming that's an option.

Other Fees

The most common additional fee charged by Internet access providers is a startup fee that covers the costs of them adding you to their accounting system and setting up your account and all that. Startup fees also reduce the number of people who join for a month or two and then bail out. Most of the time, startup fees are in the $20 to $50 range. Because you only pay one startup fee, it's not a major way to differentiate between providers.

Although it's less common, some providers charge small amounts for file or email storage, such as $1 per megabyte per month. Since you wouldn't normally store files on the provider's host machine if you use a SLIP or PPP account, the main thing to watch out for is email, which is always stored on the provider's email server until you call in. The catch here is that it's possible to set some email programs to leave copies of the mail on the server, thus wasting space and potentially racking up charges. Only leave mail on the server if you know you need to retrieve it again from another machine.

Another reason that you may be charged for storage space is if your provider allows you to create your own Web page or anonymous FTP directory. If that's true, then you're

Part III

Choosing a
Connection

getting some service for your money, so it should be easy to determine if the service is worth the charge. More on this later, since not all providers offer such services.

Phone Charges

Many people don't think about phone charges properly, which leads to some confusion about how they interact with any fees charged by an Internet provider.

Almost everyone who wants to make an Internet connection using the software with this book along with a Mac and modem has a telephone connection that can make local calls for free (although this is less true in countries other than the U.S.). Thus, a local telephone call won't add to your bill, which is the main reason why I always recommend that people work with an Internet provider that offers a local number.

> **Note**
>
> *I'm assuming that you know the difference between a local call and a long-distance call. Long-distance calls don't have to cover a great distance, but if you can normally make local calls without worrying about per minute charges, any call that has per minute charges is by definition a long-distance call.*

Recently, and this will continue to be even more true in the future, some national Internet providers have sprung up, offering Internet access via existing national or international networks, like the CompuServe Packet Network and SprintNet, both of which have many local numbers around the world. This means that even though you don't pay for the telephone call (a good thing), you usually pay an extra per-hour charge to the Internet provider. The provider then passes this charge on to the company, CompuServe or Sprint, that provides the network. As a result, national providers almost always have some kind of per-hour component to their rate systems. You should make sure that it's a good deal for you before taking it, especially if the per-hour charge is higher than you would pay calling long distance to a provider with a cheaper rate system—of course, the best arrangement is a cheap flat rate with no charge for the phone call. Also, even though you can call a local number to access a national Internet provider, that provider's offices probably aren't anywhere near you, which may make getting support more difficult. I also like to support local businesses.

Many people live where they can't call an Internet provider locally, nor can they call one of the packet-switched networks locally. What to do? Well, there are two basic choices. First, break down and make that long-distance call to an Internet provider that otherwise has good rates and policies. Second, check out Internet providers that offer connections via 800 numbers. Let's look at these two options in detail.

Long Distance

Racking up huge long-distance bills goes against the grain for many of us, myself included, partly because when I was growing up it was long-distance to call just about anyone we knew. However, now that there's plenty of competition in the long-distance market, you can choose a long-distance company that provides the best package for the way you call.

If you just have some basic deal with the long-distance company, it may cost as much as 25¢ per minute, depending on the time of day that you call. However, if you sign up for one of the special calling plans, you can significantly reduce that per-minute charge. For instance, MCI offers a Friends and Family plan that gives a 20 percent discount on calls that you make after 5:00 P.M. and on weekends, or something like that. If the number you're calling also is an MCI customer (many providers set up specific numbers for this purpose), then you get a 40 percent discount. In addition, MCI reportedly has a Best Friends program that gives you a 40 percent discount on any one number. Sprint and AT&T undoubtedly have comparable plans, but because the details vary greatly and since the plans tend to change frequently, you should call to find out what would be best for you. In addition, small long-distance companies have sprung up that offer creative and inexpensive packages. Check your Yellow Pages for a list of the less well-known long-distance providers in your area and compare their prices along with those from the big guys. I've collected some phone numbers in Table 11.1.

Table 11.1
Long-Distance Telephone Company Customer Service Numbers

Company	Customer Service Number
AT&T	800-222-0300
MCI	800-950-5555
Sprint	800-877-4000

In talking with the support people at my provider, Northwest Nexus, I gather that some Northwest Nexus customers have managed to get long-distance telephone rates as low as 7¢ per minute, or $4.20 per hour. It may not be possible for you to get exactly the same rates, so figure out what the best per-minute charge you can get is, and then multiply that by 60 to find the per-hour charge. Keep that charge in mind, because you'll want to compare it to the alternative, calling an 800 number.

Note

One advantage of calling long-distance is that with phone charges more or less the same no matter which Internet provider you choose, you can pick any provider in the country. That enables you to base your decision on variables other than cost, such as support, reliability, and other services.

Part III   Choosing a Connection

800 Numbers

Numbers beginning with the prefix 800 deceive many people because, as we all know, calling an 800 number is free, right? Well, no. When you call an 800 number, any 800 number, the phone company bills the company on the other end just as they would bill you for a long-distance charge. In other words, an 800 number is merely a way of reversing the charges.

If you're calling a tech support number or ordering something from a mail-order company, you probably never see that charge. The company in question merely absorbs it as a cost of doing business and adds it to the overall pricing structure. However, when you call an 800 number to connect to an Internet provider, the Internet provider passes the cost right back to you in the form of a per-hour charge.

There's nothing wrong with this mechanism, but you shouldn't pretend that there's anything different about it compared with a long-distance call. Either way, the telephone company makes money for each minute that you stay online. The only difference is that with a long-distance call, you pay the phone company directly; with an 800 number, you pay the Internet provider, who then pays the phone company.

The problem comes in the rates. It's pretty easy to get discount rates around 10¢ per minute ($6.00 per hour), and as I noted previously, some people have gotten as low as 7¢ per minute ($4.20 per hour). The lowest I've seen an Internet provider go on an 800 number is $5.50 per hour, and frankly, I don't know how that provider, DataBank, Inc. (**info@databank.com**) does it, since everyone else charges between $8 and $12 per hour.

All I'm saying here is that you should assemble as much comparative information as you can before you decide what is or is not the best deal for you. I cannot tell you what's cheapest because I don't know what all the variables are for you—which long-distance company and calling plan you use, whether it's cheaper or more expensive to call long-distance within your state, and so on.

Service

In some ways, making the decision of which provider to use based on cost alone is simple. You figure out the salient numbers, add them all up, and try to determine what your monthly bill will look like. End of story, assuming that one provider stands out over others. But what if cost isn't the deciding factor? What if you discover that there are three providers in your area, and they all charge about the same amount (which wouldn't be surprising, given the demands of local competition in our capitalistic society). That's when you have to choose based on services. As I said above, I'm assuming here that all the providers you've narrowed your choice to support PPP or SLIP so you can use MacTCP-based applications. So what differentiates providers? Reliability (and its cohorts, accessibility and support) and special services such as personal Web pages and custom domain names.

Reliability, Accessibility, and Support

These three topics fit together quite closely and are inherently related to how important a given Internet provider thinks its customers are. If a provider wants to concentrate on doing the best possible job for the customer, none of these three should ever be a problem. But in the real world, trade-offs are made, and in my experience you sometimes get what you pay for in terms of reliability, accessibility, and support.

Just the other day I corresponded with someone who was having all sorts of problems with his account. I couldn't see anything wrong in what he was doing, so I recommended he try another provider that might do things differently. He got an account with the other provider, and everything worked on the first try. I pass on this anecdote because I want to you to realize that you don't have to put up with a lousy provider, for whatever reason. You can always switch to a different one (although of course, then you must go through the decision process of which one to pick again, but hey, you can't have everything!).

Reliability

Reliability is a simple issue, but it's hard to determine before signing up. Do the provider's machines crash often, and if they do crash, does the provider lose email? Can you almost always connect to the outside Internet (sometimes such connection problems aren't your provider's fault, but lie further downstream)? Can you post a message to Usenet news and be sure that it will make it out to the rest of the world?

These are just a few of the questions that you should periodically ask yourself when you're working with a provider. You can't know this information beforehand, except perhaps from talking to an existing customer, and the provider certainly won't tell you if its setup is unreliable. But problems happen, and if they aren't fixed promptly and properly, it's tremendously frustrating. The last thing you want to do is start using a provider in your home-based business, say, and then find out that because of a technical glitch all the email to your account bounced for a week while you were on vacation.

Accessibility

Although it may seem as though I covered accessibility previously, I'm thinking of a more specific issue. This is a simple question. Can you almost always get through to your provider's modems whenever you want to? There's nothing worse than getting a busy signal for hours on end, even with automatic redial. And it's even worse when your provider has bad modems that just ring and ring and ring and…

Busy signals are a fact of life with any provider. The reason is simple. No provider could possibly afford to have one modem and one phone per customer without charging exorbitant rates. Every provider tries to maintain a balance, then, between the number of customers and the number of modems and phone lines. This balance requires that you get busy signals occasionally when you call at the busiest times of night, for instance, after dinner. Otherwise, the provider would be paying for phone lines and modems that would sit unused for the rest of the day—an obvious waste of money.

As providers grow, they must continually add modems and phone lines, and sometimes it can take the phone company a week longer than expected to fill the order for more phone lines. Thus, it's acceptable for a provider to have even bad busy signal problems as long as it's only for a short period of time and those phone lines are on order. If busy signals are a chronic problem, especially at odd times of the day, get a different provider. You can't learn to live on the Internet if you have to spend 30 minutes waiting for a free modem.

Support

Finally, let's face it. The world is not a perfect place, and problems occur. Heck, they occur all the time. But what's important is that the provider will go out of its way to fix the problems promptly, help you when you send email or call, and generally is responsive and responsible.

Technical support is a tremendously hard and stressful job, so not all providers have equally good support staffs, but a provider that wants happy customers will make sure to hire quality support folks.

Another thing to check for is a provider that will inform its customers of known down-time through a mailing list, newsgroup, or login message. It's not nearly as big a deal to not use your account if you know in advance that you can't do so between 12:00 and 1:00 in the afternoon on a specific day.

Finally, if you're using a national provider, you should check on the hours it offers tech support, just in case you happen to be on the opposite coast and can't get support when you may need it. In my experience, local providers generally offer more accessible and better support, perhaps in part because they're not attempting to serve so many people from so many places.

Special Services

It's hard for me to anticipate what sort of special services an Internet provider might offer, but here are a few that I've seen in the past. In my experience, a smaller, local provider is more likely to be flexible enough to offer these sorts of special services than a large national provider (although exceptions certainly exist in both directions).

Custom Domain Names

Many people prefer to have a custom domain name instead of the name of the provider's domain, and some providers can help you get such a name. You can't just pick any name, such as `ibm.com`, because most of the obvious ones have already been taken, but some providers can search for free names from your list and apply for the name for you. Then, unless you get a dedicated connection or move to another provider, that domain name points to your provider's computers.

It's often easier for providers to give out domain names under their domain. So for instance, Northwest Nexus controls the **wa.com** domain, and can provide domain names under that domain (which is merely an alias to another machine) quite easily. My friend Bill got his domain name, **beer.wa.com**, that way. These subdomain names are easier to get because the provider doesn't have to ask the InterNIC for them, but they also aren't portable to another provider.

Personal Web Pages

In this day and age of the World Wide Web, it seems that everyone wants to have his or her own Web page. It's not that hard to create one in HTML (in fact, I'll show you how in chapter 26), but finding a server that will carry it can be a bit difficult. This is another area in which good Internet providers can distinguish themselves. Some may charge a small monthly fee for such a service, but it may be well worth the cost, depending on how badly you want your own Web page.

Personal FTP Directory

As with personal Web pages, it can be handy to have a directory on an anonymous FTP server if you want to put files there for anyone in the world to retrieve. Some providers offer this, and as with the Web pages, some charge extra.

Email Aliases

Although many providers would ask you to get two accounts if you want to let your spouse or children use the Internet on their own, some providers can set up email aliases if you just want to have another email address that comes into the same mailbox as your standard address. So, for instance, you may have your personal account and have a company name email address that is an alias to your personal account.

New Connection Methods

ISDN (Integrated Services Digital Network—a digital phone line) may not be as wide-spread as everyone would like, and in some areas it can be both hard to find and expensive when you do find it. But, if you can get an ISDN connection to your house for a reasonable rate, it would be good if your Internet provider supported it. The same goes for new modem standards, cable modems, and the like. Is your provider going to keep up with new technology so you can connect to the Internet at the fastest possible speed?

Similarly, although this isn't that important right away, if you decide to move up to a dedicated connection via a frame relay 56K line, for instance, can your provider help you? If so, that makes the move much easier than if you have to find a new provider for your dedicated connection.

Part III
Choosing a
Connection

Custom Information

Most Internet providers concentrate on providing access to the Internet rather than providing information on the Internet, but many of them also put together Web pages about events or issues of local interest. I don't consider this a major reason to go with one provider over another, since you can generally get to any such public site, but it may be worth supporting if you find the information truly useful.

Business Services

What if you want to set up a small mailing list or run a Gopher server or something like that, but you don't want to get your own dedicated connection? Some providers offer this sort of service, although always with additional charges. If you're considering using the Internet as a business tool but aren't interested in running your own machine to do so, you might ask around about what sorts of services your provider can give you.

Taking the Plunge

I hope this discussion has given you the information that you need to make an informed choice among the many different Internet service providers out there. Check out appendix A, "Internet Starter Kit Providers," for a list of providers that you can easily use with the custom installation options included on the disk, and appendix B, "Providers of Commercial Internet Access," for a much larger list of providers and their contact information.

The providers listed in appendix A, "Internet Starter Kit Providers," will be easier to work with than the ones listed in appendix B, "Providers of Commercial Internet Access," if only because we've included configuration files on the disk for those listed in appendix A. In addition, they have agreed to give *Internet Starter Kit* readers specials deals on their services.

Even if you've decided to get a full Internet account, many people also have accounts on the commercial services, and that's where I turn my attention in the next chapter.

12

Commercial Services

For many people, the easiest way to access the Internet, although a limited one, is to use a commercial online service, such as CompuServe, America Online, or eWorld. The commercial online services provide their own fee-based services such as email, computer and non-computer related discussions, file libraries, and databases of information. And, just to ward off this question right away, no, you cannot access files or databases on a commercial service via a normal Internet account. If you could, then the commercial service couldn't squeeze any nickels from you, and what fun would that be?

Note

You can access some of the commercial services over the Internet instead of over a modem, but this still requires you to have an account on that service.

Commercial services offer two main advantages over finding a real Internet access provider. First, because they have deals with international commercial network carriers such as SprintNet, finding a local phone number is usually easier. But, you pay for that easier access, usually with the connect-time fee for the commercial service. Second, the commercial services find it easier to offer commercial-quality information, because they can charge users to access that information and then pay the information provider. Hence you find, for example, full-text databases of computer magazines on CompuServe, but you pay extra for any searches in those databases, with the revenue going to the magazine publishers. Remember, to paraphrase the Bard, "All the world's a marketing scheme."

All the commercial services have Internet email gateways, which means that you can use these services to send and receive Internet email. They also have started to add other Internet services, like Usenet news, FTP, Telnet, and Gopher. Some place additional restrictions on email, such as limiting the size of files you can receive, or charging extra for Internet email (as opposed to internal email on that service).

> **N o t e**
>
> *Absolutely none of the commercial online services properly handle quoting for email. When offering quoting at all, they, like AppleLink, append the original letter to your reply, which makes it difficult to refer to different parts of the original in context. If you use any of these services and aren't happy with the lack of decent facilities, try Rick Holzgrafe's SignatureQuote (see capsule review later in the chapter).*

In this chapter, I concentrate on the major commercial services for Macintosh users—America Online, CompuServe, and eWorld—and briefly look at some other, less-commonly used services—AppleLink, BIX, Delphi, GEnie, Outland, and Prodigy. Keep in mind that rates change frequently on these services, to accommodate market pressures and the marketing whim of the day, so the rates I give throughout may not always be accurate.

Having an account on one of the commercial services can be a good way to ease into the Internet because you can send and receive email. Being able to send and receive email enables you to request automated information from the major Internet providers, which makes finding a local connection much easier. In addition, many of the online services provide decent graphical interfaces that are easier to use than character-based interfaces.

Before I get into specifics, take a look at Table 12.1 which summarizes the syntax for sending email between the Internet and many of the commercial online services, including some not mentioned here because they're not used by Mac users or because they're really ugly or expensive.

Table 12.1
Commercial Online Service Addressing*

Service	To the Internet	From the Internet
America Online	`user@internet.com`	`user@aol.com`
AppleLink	`user@internet.com@internet#`	`user@applelink.apple.com`
BIX	`user@internet.com`	`user@bix.com`
CompuServe	`>INTERNET:user@internet.com`	`77777.777@compuserve.com`
Delphi	`user@internet.com`	`user@delphi.com`
eWorld	`user@internet.com`	`user@eworld.com`

Service	To the Internet	From the Internet
GEnie	`user@internet.com@inet#`	`user@genie.geis.com`
MCI Mail	`user@internet.com`	`user@mcimail.com`
Prodigy	`user@internet.com`	`user@prodigy.com`

Note: none of these are real addresses—substitute the username for "user" and the full domain name for "internet.com" as in ace@tidbits.com.

America Online

America Online (see figure 12.1), commonly known as AOL, has been around only since 1989 but has always boasted one of the best graphical interfaces for browsing files and sending email. The way its software handles discussions, however, leaves much to be desired.

Figure 12.1   *America Online Welcome Window, set for TCP Connection.*

In the spring of 1992, AOL opened an Internet gateway, and its popularity grew quickly. In early 1994, AOL added additional Internet services, including access to Usenet newsgroups and limited access to some Gopher and WAIS servers. In the summer of 1994, AOL added TCP/IP connections that enable you to connect to AOL over an Internet

Part III

Commercial Services

connection and run the America Online software at the same time as other MacTCP-based programs. Connecting to AOL via the Internet requires version 2.5.1 or later of the America Online software.

There are rumors afoot as I write this that America Online will be creating some sort of ancillary Internet access service, although no details are available. In late 1994, AOL spent $35 million on a company called ANS (Advanced Network & Services), the company that had managed and operated the NSFnet Backbone Service since 1990. The ANS backbone network is among the largest and fastest public data networks. AOL's acquisition of ANS followed on the heels of two other Internet-related acquisitions, BookLink Technologies and NaviSoft, and AOL may use technology from those two companies to provide Internet client software.

Internet Connections

As I said, you can now connect to America Online over the Internet if you have MacTCP-based Internet access, either through a network or through SLIP or PPP. Of course, this does you no good if you don't already have an AOL account. You can sign up online if you download the AOL software from:

```
ftp://ftp.aol.com/mac/
```

Once you download the archive, you end up with an installer that puts everything in the right places automatically. Then, from the Locality pop-up menu, you choose TCP Connection.

Once you have everything configured correctly, make sure you're properly connected to the Internet (if you use SLIP or PPP), and then click America Online's Sign On button. The login process proceeds normally, but because you've already made the connection to the Internet, it's a bit faster. After you're on, everything works pretty much as normal. Over a 14,400 bps PPP connection, the speed was not significantly different from the normal 9,600 bps modem connection I used to use with AOL. Overall, I found reliability better with the Internet connection, but I've had major communications trouble with AOL, so I may not be a good judge.

I see several advantages to using the Internet access method over the normal modem connection. Many people may only have Internet access at work, so connecting from there is not only possible, but much faster if you have a fast Internet connection. In other cases, Internet access may be cheaper if you must otherwise call AOL long distance (the actual cost of using AOL is the same no matter how you connect). Also, because of the standard way Macintosh Internet programs work, you can use any number of them simultaneously. This simply isn't possible if one application hogs the modem, as is normal with AOL. Finally, Internet access makes it far easier for non-U.S. users to connect.

What are the disadvantages to connecting to AOL over the Internet as opposed to a normal modem connection? There are a lot of access numbers for AOL around the U.S., certainly more than Internet access numbers. If that's true in your area, there may be no reason to bother with the Internet access. But enough about the connection. On to the Internet services that AOL provides.

Internet Services

I may have quibbles with the way they implement things, or how long they take to do so, but AOL deserves major points for providing as much access to the Internet as they do. You can go to the Internet Connection (see figure 12.2) to read more about it from anywhere on AOL by choosing Keyword from the Go To menu. In the Keyword dialog box, type **Internet** and press Return. There's also an Internet Connection button in AOL's Main Menu window.

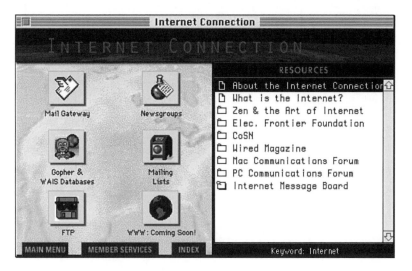

Figure 12.2   *America Online Internet Connection.*

The problem with using AOL for all of your Internet activities is that you're limited by what's available. For instance, until AOL adds support for a Web browser (which should be in the summer of 1995), you won't be able to access anything on the World Wide Web. And, even if AOL does eventually support everything you can do on the Internet, the best software for using the Internet will always appear first for MacTCP-based connections.

Note

The feature that I most want from AOL, and which they've promised, is the capability to forward all of my email to my Internet address.

Email

America Online's Internet email gateway is easy to use, due to AOL's simple interface for sending email. If you can send email on America Online to another AOL user, you can send email to anyone on the Internet with no additional work. In addition, AOL makes it relatively easy to send email to a number of people all at once for the same amount of connect time that you might spend to send the message to one person. Simply put multiple addresses in the To and/or CC fields, and your message goes to all of them (see figure 12.3).

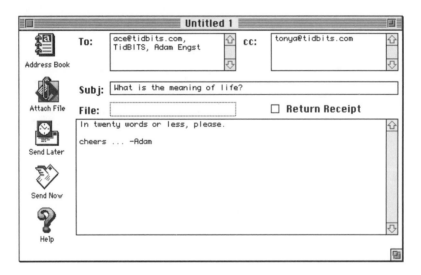

Figure 12.3   America Online Mail window.

Although they seem somewhat apologetic about not doing so, AOL doesn't reformat incoming Internet email. This means that you may have to expand the size of your email window to accommodate the longer line lengths that Internet email tends to have. An advantage of not reformatting incoming email is that to do so would undoubtedly destroy most ASCII graphics and hand-coded ASCII tables.

> **Note**
>
> *If you mainly receive Internet email on AOL, you may want to stick with a monospaced font such as Monaco or Courier for viewing your email, because proportionally spaced fonts such as Times and Helvetica won't work with ASCII tables.*

To send email from America Online to the Internet, you don't have to do anything special. Simply type the Internet address in the To field, and fill in the Subject field and the body of the message as you do when sending email to another AOL user.

To send email from the Internet to a user on AOL, you must remember a few simple rules. First, you need to know the person's username. Second, type the username in lowercase letters, because some email packages on the Internet are picky about upper- and lower-case. Third, remove any spaces in the name. Fourth, append an @ and the machine name and domain to the end of the address; for AOL, it's **aol.com**. For example, my username on AOL is **Adam Engst**. To send email from the Internet to my AOL account, you would address your message to **adamengst@aol.com**.

In the Internet Connection, clicking on the Mailing Lists button presents you with a window of information about mailing lists (see figure 12.4), and, most importantly, a button called Search Mailing Lists. It's essentially a simple search in the List of Lists, and AOL thoughtfully provided a Compose Mail button for subscribing on the spot. Had they also created a mailing list subscription manager which would handle all your subscriptions and provide single-click access to the standard mailing list function, it would have been truly impressive.

If you plan to use AOL for serious Internet email, let me dissuade you somewhat. AOL limits the size of outgoing mail to the amount of text that can fit in its software's message box. According to my testing, that's exactly 24,000 characters. You cannot send attached files through the gateway (it's technically feasible, but would increase the traffic significantly), and AOL splits large email messages that come in from the Internet at about 25K each. (This file splitting is actually a major advance for America Online. In the past, it truncated incoming messages at 27K, which was a major headache for many people.) Finally, although you can type special characters such as the bullet (•) or the trademark symbol (™) in the AOL email window, the Internet gateway software replaces some special characters with reasonable replacements, and others with spaces or nonsensical replacements. It would be far better if it did an intelligent replacement, so the trademark sign was converted to something like [tm].

Part III
Commercial Services
12

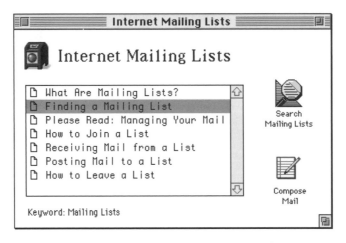

Figure 12.4   *America Online Internet Mailing Lists window.*

N
o
t
e

Interestingly, it's hard to tell how long it takes for messages to travel to and from AOL. I sent my AOL account a message from my Internet account, and a few minutes later, sent my Internet account a message from my AOL account. The message from AOL to the Internet was delivered essentially instantly. It took about half an hour for the Internet message to arrive at AOL. Go figure.

Although AOL's software is fine for a message or two a day, if you anticipate joining a mailing list that could generate up to 30 messages a day (which is easily possible), its interface for reading mail can quickly make your life miserable. AOL opens messages slowly, and makes you confirm your actions when you delete a message or reply to a message offline. I gather that your mailbox can only hold 500 messages, which may seem like a lot, but if you participate in a few high-volume mailing lists and then go on vacation, it's not unthinkable that your mailbox would fill up. Mail that you've read is deleted from your online mailbox in a week; unread mail sticks around for five weeks before being deleted automatically.

Although I believe they have fixed most of the problems, AOL has developed a reputation for having vaguely flaky connections. As a result, sometimes Internet email arrives immediately, whereas other times something delays it for up to several days. This problem isn't serious for the casual email user. It can quickly become frustrating, however, if you're having a conversation with someone via email or depend on your email for business reasons.

Overall, I find AOL's email to be sufficiently clunky such that I don't use it any more. I can get away with this, and you can too, by using a clever program called MailConverter.

If you set AOL to download all your new mail via a FlashSession, MailConverter can read in all the messages in the AOL mail folder for your screen name and convert it into a Eudora mailbox, translating the addresses into Internet format addresses along the way. Another option which isn't quite available yet is a commercial program called Emailer from Claris, which can connect to a number of commercial online services and download messages into a single In box. More on Emailer and MailConverter later in the chapter.

Usenet News

Along with email, America Online provides access to Usenet news. Although the interface provided for reading news works, it's about as bare bones as you get. When you click on the Newsgroups button in the Internet Connection window, you see the Newsgroups window (see figure 12.5), complete with handy buttons. These enable you to read the newsgroups you've subscribed to, add more newsgroups to your subscription list, check new newsgroups, and search through the list of newsgroups for those that might interest you. Perhaps most interesting to those of us who have used the Internet is the Set Preferences button, which enables you to set the sort order of the article listings, enter a signature to be appended to your posts, and see the newsgroup names in the "correct" style as opposed to the confusing "expanded" names that AOL has assigned to many of the newsgroups.

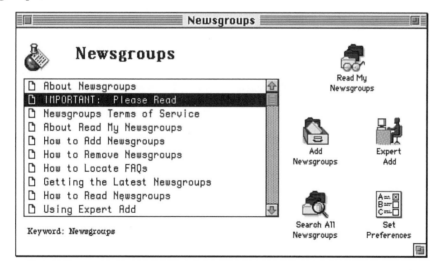

Figure 12.5   *America Online Newsgroups window.*

AOL does a decent job of displaying the newsgroups and opening a new window for each level of hierarchy, although it's very slow to bring in large lists.

Part III   Commercial Services

N o t e

If AOL makes you wait for a very long list to come in, feel free to press ⌘-period to cancel the loading process. You won't see anything that hadn't come in, of course, but there may be plenty of items in the list to explore.

Moreover, I find it extremely irritating to have to constantly click the More button when AOL doesn't list all of the items in a hierarchy. This is a major problem with how AOL handles lists in general, so I doubt it will be fixed any time soon. Being able to search for newsgroups is also useful, although both the basic list and the search feature limit the results to newsgroups that AOL finds "acceptable." If you wish to read any "unacceptable" newsgroups (most of the `alt.sex` hierarchy falls into this category, although there are other sex-related groups that slip through), click on the Expert Add button in the Newsgroups window and type in the name of the group you want to read.

Using Expert Add is the fastest way to subscribe to newsgroups, although most people will probably just use the Add Newsgroups button and browse through the lists of groups, clicking on the Add button when they see an interesting one (see figure 12.6).

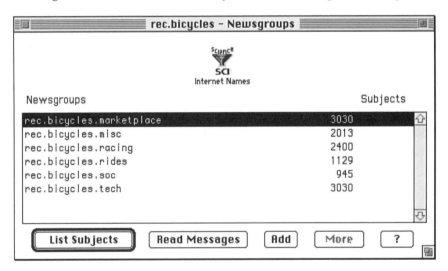

Figure 12.6   List of bicycle groups available on AOL.

Once you've subscribed to a few newsgroups (and AOL subscribes everyone to a few newsgroups), click the Read My Newsgroups button to see to which groups you are subscribed (see figure 12.7).

The buttons here are fairly obvious. List Unread (or double-clicking on a group name) opens the group and lists the messages you haven't yet read; List All lists all the messages; Mark Read marks all the messages in the selected group as read; Remove unsubscribes you from the selected newsgroup; More displays any groups that aren't yet showing; and the ? button displays help.

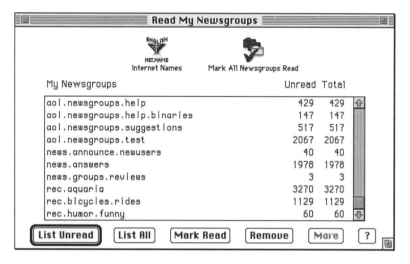

Figure 12.7   *AOL Read My Newsgroups window.*

After you open the list of the messages in a group, double-click on a message title or click the Read button to read the messages in a thread. It's good that AOL groups messages in a thread, and I like being able to sort them alphabetically. Although there is no method of easily marking which threads to read and which to kill, because you can only select one thread at a time. Similarly, when you get into the actual newsreader, all you can do is move forward and backward one article, mark an article as unread, or send a new message to the group or to the author. We're not talking a particularly impressive interface here (see figure 12.8).

But enough ragging on AOL's Usenet interface. It works, it's somewhat graphical, and AOL is more accessible than Internet providers for many people. If you're only used to AOL, or are new to the whole shooting match, please read the newsgroup **news.announce.newusers**.

FTP

AOL's FTP client has some interesting features that set it apart, although it also suffers from AOL's overly window-based interface and the fact that it can only download, not upload. Once you tunnel into the FTP area by clicking on the FTP button in the Internet Connection, you get a window that provides buttons for using FTP or for searching a somewhat limited set of FTP sites on some keywords. Although useful, the search didn't turn up nearly as many sites as it should have in an ideal world when I searched on "apple.com".

Nevertheless, when you click the Go To FTP button, AOL presents you with a short list of popular sites (see figure 12.9) that it mirrors, which means that AOL keeps a copy of the files from those sites locally to reduce Internet traffic and load on those machines.

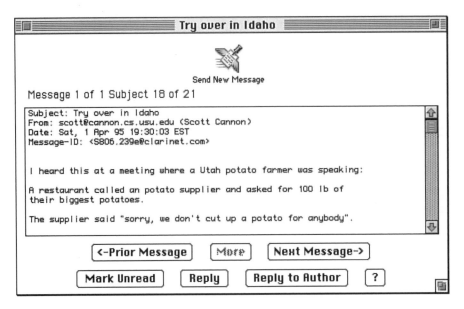

Figure 12.8   A minimalist interface.

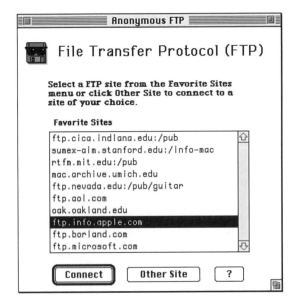

Figure 12.9   AOL FTP Favorite Sites.

Although this list of favorite sites is fairly short, you can connect to any other site by clicking the Other Site button and entering the FTP site's name. You also can enter full FTP URLs in the Other Site window to navigate all the way into an FTP site, although you cannot enter a URL that specifies a file—the URL must end in a directory name only, such as:

```
ftp://ftp.tidbits.com/pub/tidbits/tisk/
```

In either case, once you connect to a site, you see a dialog displaying whatever message that site sends out to all who connect, and then a window listing all the files in the default directory. Files are sorted alphabetically, and there is no way to change that. Dates, file sizes, and little icons are provided for each entry, so you can tell when a file was up-loaded, how large it is, and if it's a file or a folder or the equivalent of an alias in Unix (a little squiggly icon, according to AOL's help—I haven't seen one yet).

Now, the most interesting part of AOL's FTP client is that when you actually retrieve a file by clicking the Download Now button (see figure 12.10), AOL first retrieves it from the Internet site (assuming you're not using one of the AOL mirror sites), and once it's on AOL's machines, proceeds to download it to your Mac.

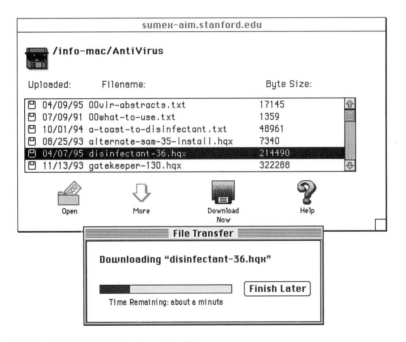

Figure 12.10   *AOL FTP file downloading.*

Note the Finish Later button. Because AOL has downloaded this file, Disinfectant, in my example, to an AOL machine before letting me download it to my Mac, I can click the Finish Later button to put the download process in my Download Manager (located in the File menu) and finish the download at a later time, even during an automated FlashSession. I've never seen any other FTP client allow for interrupting and resuming downloads, so this is a welcome feature. Why sit through a long file download when it can happen when you're off doing something, anything, else?

N o t e

If you connect to a site that requires a userid and password (which is possible) via AOL and download a file that contains sensitive information, remember that your file exists on AOL's machines, at least temporarily, and for the truly paranoid, that might be unacceptable.

Overall, AOL's FTP client is clunky, but useful, and it's extremely handy to be able to use it while getting files from the Internet for setting up an Internet connection. I would like to see it offer multiple connections at the same time like Anarchie does now, so that you could work on more than one site at a time rather than being forced to sit and wait for AOL to retrieve the file and then start downloading it to your Mac. One easily added feature would be to turn FTP into a batch operation—let the user basically mark a file for downloading later, and have it come in via the next automated FlashSession.

Gopher and WAIS

Along with its other Internet services, AOL provides limited access to Gopher servers and WAIS sources. Once again, I'm not all that impressed with the interface AOL provides, compared to the MacTCP-based clients for Gopher and WAIS. Clicking the Gopher & WAIS Databases button in the Internet Connection window brings up the Gopher and WAIS window, which contains a number of top-level topics. Delving into the topics that America Online presents is much like working with a normal Gopher server, with WAIS and searchable Gopher items represented by little book icons (see figure 12.11).

There are several major limitations to AOL's implementation of WAIS, and—somewhat more so—Gopher. Most importantly, you can only retrieve text items. There is simply no way to download a file of any other type, such as a JPEG or GIF picture, as far as I can see. I'm also bothered by the selection of Gopher and WAIS items that AOL includes. There's nothing wrong with it, but they make it downright difficult to get out to the normal Other Gopher and Information Servers item that you can easily access with TurboGopher. Scroll all the way down to the bottom of the Gopher and WAIS window to the Other Gophers item. Double-click on it to open its window. But that's not it, yet. Finally, click the More "Other Gopher" button to bring up the More "Other Gopher" Resources window. It shows you the full geographical hierarchy of Gopher servers that can be handy for finding a new Gopher server.

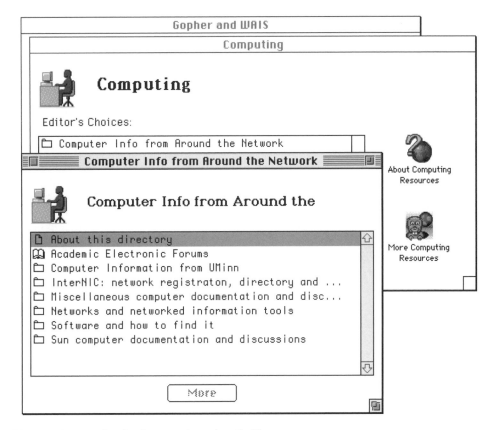

Figure 12.11   *Gophering on America Online.*

Luckily, using Veronica to find something isn't nearly so hard, because there's a Search All Gophers button on the main Gopher and WAIS window that brings up a search window for searching with Veronica. AOL has set up a private Veronica server so response is generally pretty good, although I had trouble finding some Gopher sites that I know are present (see figure 12.12).

> *You can even use the -t switches that limit the search results to certain types of information. Use -t1 to limit the results to directories, and -t7 to limit the results to searchable items.*

My main irritation with America Online's Veronica, and with the Gopher interface in general, is the slow speed, although I would also like to be able to enter a Gopher address or URL directly, rather than schlepping through all the lists and windows.

Part III
Commercial Services

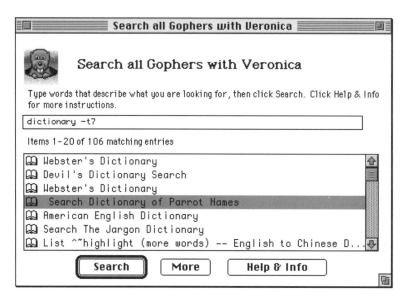

Figure 12.12   *America Online Searching in Veronica.*

World Wide Web

Unfortunately, there's not much to say about using the Web via AOL until the next version of the software is released. Once that version, 2.6, comes out, you will be able to browse the Web via AOL as well, and that may make the Internet experience via AOL significantly more compelling. Tune in next edition for the next installment of *As AOL Turns.*

I was able to take a look at the new beta literally on the day I had to turn in the final version of this chapter. I can't say much about what will change in the AOL 2.6 client, but it turns out that AOL is implementing Web access via a separate program called Web Browser, which is essentially the Web module from InterCon's TCP/Connect II (see chapter 28, "Integrated Programs" for more details about how the program works since it really is the same code). Unfortunately, the performance was awful while browsing the Web via Web Browser, so I hope that AOL will speed it up significantly by the time it comes out. Feature-wise, Web Browser is quite good, and even includes the mediocre FTP features and rather slick Gopher features included in TCP/Connect II.

Charges & Connecting

Unlike CompuServe, America Online doesn't charge for internal email or for email that goes in or out through their Internet gateway. In addition, AOL has reasonable monthly base rates of $9.95 for the first five hours and $2.95 per hour for each hour after that. You can sometimes get special sign-up deals that offer even more free time for the first month.

You need America Online's special software to log on to the service, but they distribute it for free. Simply call 800-827-6364, and ask them to send you the software. Alternatively, if you have a friend who already uses AOL, that person can ask AOL to send you the software, and she receives some free time online when you first log on.

If you have an account somewhere that enables you to send Internet email, you can send email to `joinaol@aol.com` and ask for a free AOL software kit, or, if you have FTP access, it's available for downloading in:

```
ftp://ftp.aol.com/mac/
```

CompuServe

CompuServe is one of the oldest of the commercial online services, and until recently, it has moved relatively sluggishly to provide Internet services. It had one of the first Internet email gateways, but only added access to Usenet news, FTP, and Telnet somewhat recently.

In a more astonishing move, however, CompuServe recently spent $100 million for Spry, a developer of Windows Internet software that used the CompuServe Packet Network to provide full TCP-based Internet access for Windows users. With that hefty purchase, CompuServe suddenly became a full Internet provider via a PPP account, although only Windows users can take advantage of the software CompuServe provides, since it comes from Spry.

CompuServe provides a number of forums for discussing Internet issues (GO INTERNET to get to them), although they seem to concentrate on Windows topics and software, so you may want to check out a couple of other places where people talk about Macs on the Internet. In the Mac Communications forum (GO MACCOM) there's a section for "Macs on Internet," but a more useful place is in ZiffNet/Mac, which runs on CompuServe's machines. It does cost an additional $3.50 per month (same connect time charges), but the Internet Help section in the ZiffNet/Mac Download and Tech Support (GO ZMC:DOWNTECH) forum is a good place to ask questions.

CompuServe via PPP

I don't want to get into the details of configuring MacTCP and Config PPP for use with CompuServe here, because unless you're skipping around, you haven't the foggiest idea what I'd be talking about. However, I can't think of any better place to give these details, so I'll try to keep them brief. Read the chapters on MacTCP and PPP before you try to configure MacTCP and Config PPP with the information below.

MacTCP

CompuServe provides server-addressed accounts, so make sure that you have PPP selected in the outer level of the MacTCP control panel and then click the More button to

Part III

Commercial
Services

bring up the Configuration dialog. Make sure the Server button in the Obtain Address area in the upper right is selected. In the Domain Name Server Information area, enter **compuserve.com.** in the first left-hand field and **149.174.184.41** in the first right-hand field. Select the Default button next to the IP address that you just entered. In the second left-hand field, enter a period, and in the second right-hand field, enter the same IP number. In the third left-hand field, enter a period, and in the third right-hand field, enter **149.174.184.42**. Close MacTCP, restarting your Mac if it asks you to.

Config PPP

In Config PPP, the only settings that are specific to CompuServe are the phone number, which you can get from CompuServe's automated voicemail system at 800-848-8199, and the Connect Script, which should look like the following screen shot, substituting your CompuServe ID number for "77777,777" and your password for "Your-Password" (see figure 12.13).

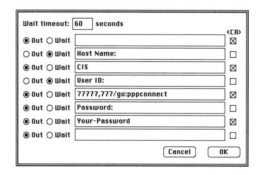

Figure 12.13   *Config PPP connect script for CompuServe.*

For information on how to configure everything else, read chapter 18, "PPP." While testing, I noticed that the performance was about half what I got with the exact same settings on my local Internet provider. My tests were quick and non-conclusive though, so form your own opinions.

Special Software

Unlike America Online and eWorld, you can use CompuServe's menu-based interface from any terminal program such as ZTerm. However, CompuServe's character-based interface is so ugly that it makes my teeth hurt. Luckily, CompuServe sells two graphical applications that make using CompuServe's services easier and cheaper. Even if you only anticipate using email on CompuServe, I recommend that you get CompuServe Information Manager (CIM), or, if you don't want to use the Internet aspects of CompuServe, get Navigator.

Mike O'Connor designed Navigator specifically to save money when using CompuServe. You tell Navigator what you want to do in terms of reading mail, sending mail, reading discussions on CompuServe, downloading files, and so on, and then you tell Navigator to log on and do everything for you. Because it works quickly by itself offline, it stays on for a shorter time than you normally would, and thereby saves you money. That's good. However, Navigator was designed for reading discussions on CompuServe, so it's clumsy for email use. Every item, mail or otherwise, is appended to a linear Navigator session file that rapidly grows large and cumbersome to navigate when searching for old mail that you haven't yet replied to.

In contrast, CIM works much better for all of the Internet services that CompuServe provides because CompuServe is designing and updating it specifically to provide graphical access to Usenet news, FTP, and Telnet (as much as you can provide graphical access to Telnet). Also important is the fact that CIM provides a much more flexible interface for reading and replying to email. If you plan to use CompuServe for anything other than participating in the discussion forums and uploading and downloading files, I recommend that you get CIM instead of Navigator. I actually use both, because CIM is lousy for reading discussions and retrieving files.

Internet Connections

You can use CIM to connect to CompuServe if you have the latest version of CIM (2.4.1 or later) and a Communications Toolbox Telnet tool like the VersaTerm Telnet tool. To connect to CompuServe using CIM, go to the Special menu and choose Connection from the hierarchical menu (see figure 12.14). In the Method pop-up menu, choose a Telnet tool that you've previously installed in your Extensions folder. I've only found two that work at all reliably, the VersaTerm Telnet Tool and the TCPack Telnet Tool (I used the demo). The others I tried, including the versions of the TCPack Tool for AOL and for eWorld, the Mark/Space Telnet Tool, and the MP Telnet Tool, either didn't work or crashed CIM. You can get the TCPack Telnet Tool demo from:

```
ftp://ftp.ascus.com/mac/demos/TCPack_Telnet_Tool.hqx
```

Click the Configure button and enter `compuserve.com` for the host name. All other default settings should work. Make sure the Network pop-up menu is set to Internet, and the Connect Type menu is set to Direct Connection. Click the OK button to save your changes.

Although this might seem to be an attractive way to connect to CompuServe, I've found it rather flaky. In addition, CompuServe reportedly (and it seems this is true based on performance) limits the speed at which you can connect to the speeds supported by its modems, even if you happen to have a much faster Internet connection. The policy makes sense, given that some of CompuServe's accounts charge different rates based on speed of access, but it's still irritating to have a fast Internet connection throttled down to the speed of a modem.

Part III Commercial Services

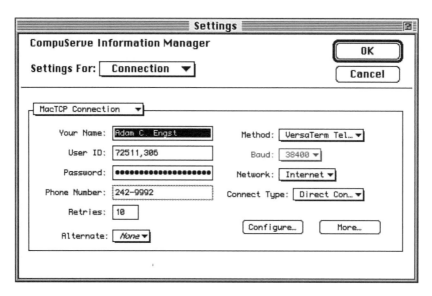

Figure 12.14 *CIM Settings window.*

Internet Services

CompuServe is an old service; it wasn't designed with the Internet in mind. Thus, all of the Internet services feel as though they've been badly tacked on to a framework that simply wasn't designed to support them. When you add in the fact that CompuServe could really use some good interface designers, you end up with tools that work, but may cause more frustration than they're worth. Currently, the four Internet services that CompuServe provides internally are email, Usenet news, Telnet, and FTP. You can access all of them (see figure 12.15) from the CompuServe Internet Services window (GO INTERNET).

Do remember that CompuServe also provides straight MacTCP-based access through a PPP connection—check out Part IV, "Full Internet Access," for information on how to configure and use MacTCP and the MacTCP-based software.

Email

CIM is good at email (GO MAIL), especially in comparison to Navigator, because it can transfer all your mail quickly and automatically. CIM shows you a nice list of all your mail and enables you to sort it in several different ways. I seldom mess with the sorting, but listing mail makes much more sense than forcing the user to scroll through each message, as Navigator does (see figure 12.16).

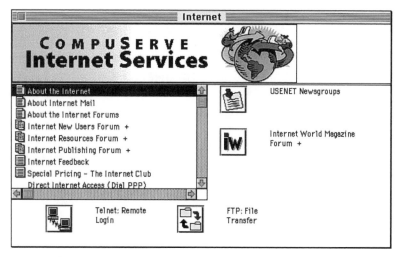

Figure 12.15   *CompuServe Internet Services.*

Figure 12.16   *CIM In Basket.*

I often find myself receiving email that I don't have time to respond to immediately, or perhaps the message requires enough research that I don't want to respond for a day or two. In either case, it's easy to lose email in Navigator, whereas in CIM you can easily see which messages need a response. CIM also makes it easy to save copies of outgoing messages (useful for those times when you want to say, "I didn't write that!" in a hurt tone). Also, you can file messages in different folders, essential if you receive email about different projects.

The hard part about sending email to the Internet from CompuServe is the addressing. You must know the magic words to add to an Internet address for CompuServe to behave properly. It's not difficult, only obscure and easy to type incorrectly. If you want to send email to my account on the Internet, `ace@tidbits.com`, you prefix `>INTERNET:` to my address, so the ungainly end result looks like `>INTERNET:ace@tidbits.com`. Easy enough, but people often type the address slightly wrong. It doesn't seem to make a difference whether a space lives between the colon and the start of the Internet address, but remember that spaces are verboten within an Internet address. To further complicate matters, when you receive Internet email in CIM or Navigator, they both politely strip the > symbol from the beginning of the message. "Oh no," you think, "then replying won't work." If you thought that, then you're quite clever, but wrong, at least for CIM. Don't ask why, but CIM doesn't mind not seeing the > symbol if it isn't present in a reply. Navigator at one point couldn't do that, so replying to Internet email without adding that > symbol manually didn't work. I believe it works fine now, so feel free to strip the > symbol if you're using the latest versions of CIM or Navigator.

Luckily, sending email from the Internet to CompuServe poses fewer problems. You merely must follow two simple rules. First, all CompuServe addresses are pairs of octal numbers, or some such nonsense. My CompuServe address looks like `72511,306`. Commas aren't allowed in Internet addresses (they usually indicate a list of addresses), so you must change the comma to a period and then add `@compuserve.com`. My address, then, becomes `72511.306@compuserve.com`. Unless you have a better memory for octal numbers than I do, put CompuServe addresses in a nicknames file or address book.

Usenet News

CompuServe's interface to Usenet news (GO USENET) is functional, but lousy. After you get to the main Usenet news window, you must first select "USENET Newsreader (CIM)" from the list of options to bring up a modal dialog that enables you to read news, subscribe to newsgroups, create an article, and set various options. CIM provides a searching interface for finding groups, and lets you enter a newsgroup name manually, which is the only way to subscribe to groups like `alt.sex` to which CompuServe doesn't want to provide easy access. After you've subscribed to a few groups (and the manual entry method is by far the fastest, followed by the search engine), you can read articles in those newsgroups by double-clicking on Access Your USENET Newsgroups, at which point CIM displays a list of your subscribed groups in yet another modal dialog (see figure 12.17).

In the list of newsgroups, you can browse the articles contained within, search for text in the subject lines of the articles (a nice touch), mark all the articles read or unread with the oddly-named Clear and Reread buttons, and unsubscribe from newsgroups with the Remove button. As with all of the other modal dialogs, the only way to back out is via the Cancel button.

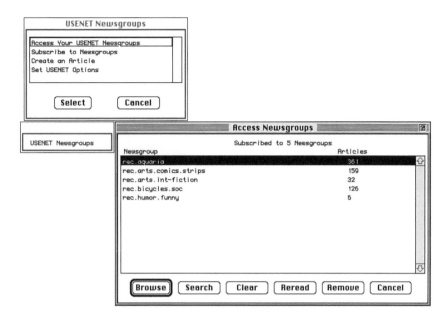

Figure 12.17   *CIM Usenet Newsgroup list.*

Browsing in a newsgroup brings up a modal dialog with a list of articles (see figure 12.18). A Retrieve button provides the only other interesting feature in CIM's newsreader. If you select a thread in the article list, and then click the Retrieve button, CIM downloads the entire thread as a text file to your hard disk, where you can read it later, without incurring any connect charges. The other functions available in this dialog are mundane—you can start reading an article with the Get button, create a new article with the Create button, mark a thread as read with the Clear button, and back out to the newsgroup list with the Cancel button.

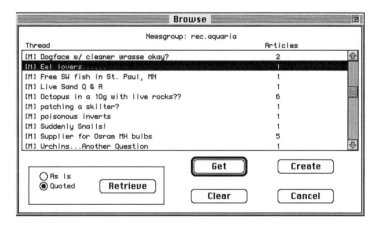

Figure 12.18   *CIM Usenet article list.*

When you finally click the Get button to read an article, CIM opens (surprise!) one more modal dialog box (see figure 12.19). CIM's designers should be forced to sleep with Apple's Human Interface Guidelines and have little signs with "Thou shalt not use modal dialogs needlessly" pasted up in their offices. Anyway, the actual dialog for reading news enables you to move forward and backward by the article or the thread, mark an article as unread with the Hold button, reply via email or in the newsgroup, forward an article to someone via email, and see the full header information with the More button.

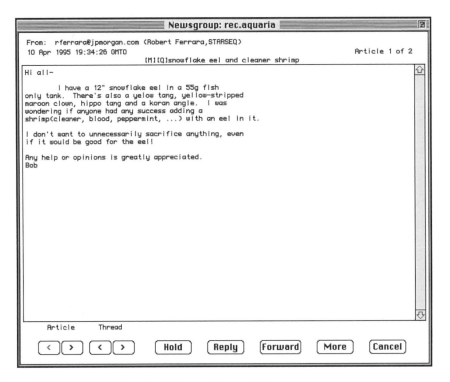

Figure 12.19   *CIM Usenet article reading window.*

Sorry if I'm ranting, but CIM's Usenet interface irks me to no end. There's absolutely no reason, other than poor design, to use so many modal dialogs that make it difficult and confusing for the user to do much of anything. For instance, if all you wanted to do was forward a single message to someone else via email, you would have to dive down through six modal dialogs and once you'd forwarded the article, come back to the surface through those six modal dialogs. In contrast, NewsWatcher, one of the best of the MacTCP-based Usenet newsreaders, enables you to do the same thing entirely in modeless windows by opening a newsgroup window, double-clicking on an article to read it, choosing Forward from the News menu, and clicking on the Send button in the message window after you've entered the email address. In other words, what takes many frustrating minutes in CIM is a simple task in NewsWatcher, simply because of a decent interface. I'll shut up now. If you use CompuServe and want to read Usenet news, CIM's newsreader works.

Telnet

Unlike eWorld and AOL, CompuServe does support outgoing Telnet (GO TELNET), which means that you can connect to Internet sites in character-mode and do whatever it is that the particular site in question allows. Telnet is rather dull. It's not really the point for those of us interested in using graphical interfaces, but it can be useful on occasion. I tried CompuServe's Telnet feature by telnetting back to my Unix account on **coho.halcyon.com**, and it sort of worked (see figure 12.20), but because the CIM 2.4.1 on the Macintosh doesn't provide full VT100 emulation, some things I tried were a little ugly or, in the case of Lynx (a Unix-based, character-mode Web browser that requires VT100 emulation) unusable.

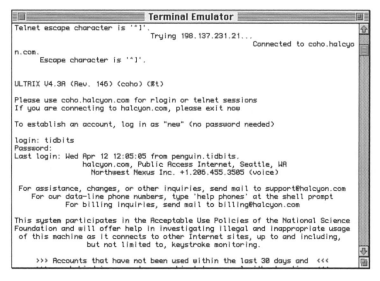

Figure 12.20   CIM Telnet window.

FTP

CompuServe's FTP service (GO FTP) includes a list of selected popular FTP sites (see figure 12.21), although it only includes eight sites, and the List of Sites button brings up almost exactly the same list, with a few minor additions. Similarly, the Site Descriptions button provides descriptions on the same basic list with a few exceptions. Given the hundreds, if not thousands, of useful FTP sites available, the limited lists and seemingly duplicated information are odd.

Part III

Commercial Services

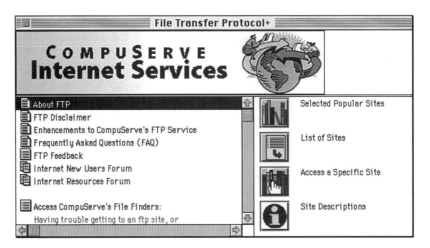

Figure 12.21 *CompuServe FTP window.*

More interesting than CompuServe's pre-chewed-for-your-convenience sites is the Access a Specific Site button, which enables you to connect to any other Internet FTP site, assuming it's not running on a Macintosh (via Peter Lewis's FTPd) or a couple of other platforms. Humph! I'm utterly unimpressed with CompuServe's FTP interface. First of all, when you click the Access a Specific Site button, CIM presents you with an ugly dialog box for you to enter the site name, the initial directory, and your userid and password (the last two of which it fills in for you with "anonymous" and your email address). Then, when you actually make the connection, CIM shows a window with two panes and some buttons along the bottom. The left-hand pane shows the current list of directories, whereas the right-hand pane shows the list of files in the current directory (see figure 12.22).

If there aren't any directories in the current directory, CIM leaves the previous list of directories in the left-hand pane, ignoring the fact that you can't click on them to go anywhere. You must always click the Back or Top buttons to move out of a directory. Although you can select multiple files to download from a directory, you cannot select multiple files from different directories—when you leave a directory, CIM forgets any files you've selected by clicking on the checkbox to the left of the file name. The Filter button is handy because it enables you to limit the list to files matching a certain string, like *.hqx. And the View button is a nice idea that can't work with long files—I suspect it's limited to 32K or less. You can connect to a site where you have write privileges and upload files, should you want to do that. Finally, the Leave button enables you to disconnect from an FTP site.

Overall, I'm unimpressed with CompuServe's FTP client. It feels sluggish and the interface is clumsy. It does work, and if you need to get a file via FTP, it's worth using. For daily use, though, I strongly recommend that you use CompuServe's PPP connection and Anarchie or Fetch.

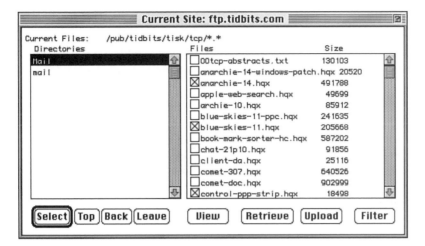

Figure 12.22 *CIM FTP file list.*

Charges & Connecting

Cost-wise, CompuServe holds the title for the most confusing pricing structures around. A while back, CompuServe introduced a Standard Pricing Plan, which allows unlimited access to a limited set of CompuServe services (most of which aren't the ones you, as a Macintosh or Internet user, might find interesting) for $9.95 per month. Internet email is not included in the Standard Pricing Plan, and services that aren't included are billed at an hourly rate of $4.80 per hour (regardless of speed, although it's still locked at modem speeds for users with fast Internet connections). However, as of May 1, 1995, FTP, Telnet, and Usenet news will be billed at the Internet Services rates, which include three free hours each month and a charge of $2.50 per hour after that. Still with me? Good, because email is another story.

With the Standard Pricing Plan's monthly fee, you get a $9.00 credit toward email, which is billed at a rate of $0.10 for the first 7,500 characters and $0.02 for every 2,500 characters after the first 7,500. Confusing the issue even further, those mail charges apply to sending all mail, but only to reading email from the Internet. You don't pay for reading CompuServe email.

The Alternative Pricing Plan costs only $2.50 per month, and has a higher connect charge, but doesn't charge extra for Internet email. The hourly rates for the Alternative Pricing Plan are $12.80 for 2,400 bps access and $22.80 for 9,600 or 14,400 bps access. I have no idea how the Internet services interact with the Alternative Pricing Plan, or even if that is allowed.

If you plan to use more than nine hours of Internet services each month, CompuServe offers Standard Pricing Plan users the option to join the Internet Club. The Internet Club charges $15 for 20 hours of use (on top of your normal $9.95 Standard Pricing Plan

Part III

Commercial Services

monthly fee) and then charges $1.95 per hour after 20 hours. Unused free hours disappear at the end of the month, and CompuServe Internet Services are free of communications surcharges if you use CompuServe's network in the U.S., Canada, or Western Europe. If you use a different network to access CompuServe's Internet, additional communications surcharges apply. Luckily, no matter what you choose for Internet access via CompuServe, it all ends up on a single bill.

You must purchase a CompuServe Membership Kit to access CompuServe. You can order it from mail order vendors or directly from CompuServe at 800-848-8199. The package I've seen in a recent MacConnection catalog costs only $25 and includes CIM. You also can get more information and sign up for CompuServe via the CompuServe Web page at:

```
http://www.compuserve.com/
```

eWorld

The most recent arrival in the commercial online service world is Apple's new eWorld service, which opened to the public in the summer of 1994. Apple based eWorld heavily on AOL, using the same server and client software, but with various modifications and a somewhat different interface (see figure 12.23).

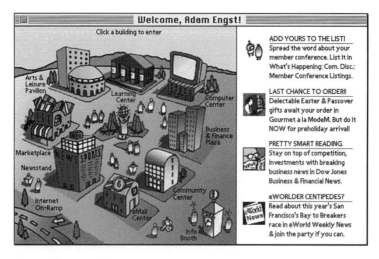

Figure 12.23   *eWorld Welcome screen (it's much nicer in color).*

Currently, about all you can do with the Internet on eWorld is send and receive email. However, the eWorld folks have announced that they will add Internet access similar to AOL's in 1995. I was able to get a peek at the beta software that should arrive in mid-1995, complete with support for Usenet news, FTP, and the World Wide Web.

N o t e

eWorld is slated to replace AppleLink at some point in time. Apple claims to have reserved all of the AppleLink userids on eWorld and will transfer those accounts when they take AppleLink down, which means that theoretically, if you know someone's AppleLink account, the same username should work on eWorld as well.

Internet Connections

For many people, however, the main advantage of 1.1, the future version of the eWorld software, will be the fact that it supports connections to eWorld via a MacTCP-based Internet connection. In the beta I used, you had to move an eWorld TCP file from a For MacTCP Users folder into an eWorld Files folder before being able to click the Edit Local Setup button and choose eWorld TCP from the Connect Method pop-up menu (see figure 12.24).

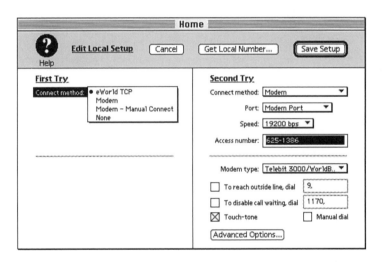

Figure 12.24   *eWorld Setup window.*

As with America Online, the primary advantage to the TCP connection method is that it opens up eWorld to many folks who have an Internet connection but can't call an eWorld access number for free, and it works at faster speeds on connections made over fast, dedicated Internet connections. At this point, it's all I use.

Internet Services

The Internet services that eWorld plans to offer later in 1995 should suffice for most beginning Internet users, although they won't satisfy people who want a full Internet

Part III   Commercial Services

connection. eWorld provides an Internet Resource Center that will provide access to all of eWorld's Internet services and will provide additional information and discussions about the Internet (see figure 12.25).

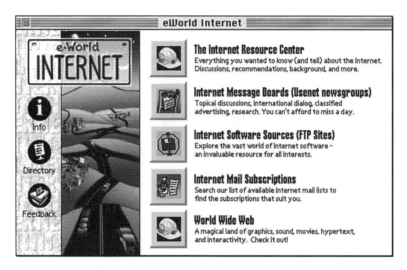

Figure 12.25   *eWorld Internet Resource Center.*

Unfortunately, I can't show you anything beyond the base of the Internet Resource Center, because the services weren't yet turned on, unlike the MacTCP-based access to eWorld, which did work fine.

Email

eWorld provides a clean graphical interface for Internet email, much as does AOL. Similarly, eWorld does not charge for email that goes in or out through its Internet gateway (see figure 12.26).

The Internet email gateway on eWorld allows you to forward messages to Internet users (easier than copying and pasting into a new message). You also can send email to a number of people simultaneously, saving connect time and thus cost (in contrast, CompuServe charges you for each recipient).

Not surprisingly, eWorld suffers from the same problems as AOL. Outgoing messages are limited in size to the amount of text that can fit in the software's message box (about 24,000 characters). You can't send attached files through the gateway (it's technically feasible, but would increase the traffic significantly). eWorld splits large email messages that come in from the Internet at about 23K each, which is a pain, but an improvement from the previous 7K chunks.

To send email from eWorld to the Internet, you don't have to do anything special. You type the Internet address in the To field and fill in the Subject field and the body of the message, as you do when sending email to another eWorld user.

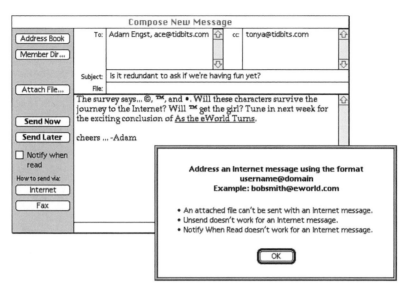

Figure 12.26   *eWorld Mail window, with the Internet dialog box showing.*

If you receive large messages on eWorld regularly, I recommend a utility called ChunkJoiner for merging the various pieces. Look for it on eWorld or in:

```
ftp://ftp.tidbits.com/pub/tidbits/tisk/util/
```

name and domain to the end of the address; for eWorld, it's **eworld.com**. My username on eWorld is **Adam Engst**, so to send me email from the Internet, you address your message to **adamengst@eworld.com**.

Charges & Connecting

eWorld costs $8.95 per month, which includes four free hours during evenings or weekends, with every hour after those four costing an additional $2.95. Daytime hours are an additional $2.95 per hour. Apple is making eWorld software available for free if you call 800-775-4556, and there are often some special deals with something like 10 free hours of use in the first month. In addition, the eWorld software is bundled with the definitive book on eWorld, called *eWorld: The Official Guide for Macintosh Users*, (Hayden Books, 1994), written by long-time author and *Macworld* editor Cary Lu along with John Milligan. Ask for it in your local bookstore. Finally, for more information about eWorld, check out their Web page at:

```
http://www.eworld.com/
```

Other Commercial Services

Although I recommend one of the above three commercial services for most people, there are others that may be more appropriate for certain situations. Therefore, although the following commercial online services aren't necessarily as common or useful for Internet access as those I've discussed previously, I feel that they're worth mentioning.

AppleLink

Before eWorld, Apple's online support service was AppleLink, and it still exists, although for how much longer is in question, and I don't recommend that anyone consider establishing a new account. AppleLink, although graphical and capable of sending and receiving Internet email, requires a clumsy addressing scheme, cannot send or receive messages over about 30K in length, and is tremendously expensive. To send email from AppleLink to the Internet, take the Internet address, `ace@tidbits.com`, for instance, and then append `@internet#` to it, keeping in mind that AppleLink cannot send mail to addresses longer than 35 characters. However, you can reply to addresses that are that long with no trouble. To send email from the Internet to AppleLink, just take the userid, which sometimes resembles a name or word and other times is just a letter plus some numbers, and append `@applelink.apple.com`.

The connection rate for AppleLink is $37 per hour for 9,600 bps access, in addition to charges for the number of characters you transmit. Add to that $0.50 per Internet message, incoming or outgoing.

BIX

BIX is one of the oldest of the commercial online services. It has a direct connection to the Internet, which makes it easy to send and receive Internet email. BIX has no graphical interface for the Macintosh, and perhaps in large part because of that, it simply isn't one of the main online services for Macintosh users. You also can use FTP, telnet into BIX from the Internet for reduced charges (telnet to x25.bix.com and reply **BIX** to the Username prompt), read news with the Unix nn newsreader, and use the character-based Lynx to browse the World Wide Web. BIX also supports Finger and Telnet. FTP on BIX works rather oddly, so that instead of storing files on BIX and then downloading them, files are automatically dumped to your Mac via whatever transfer protocol you normally use with BIX. To send email to someone on the Internet, you type the person's Internet email address instead of their BIX username. To send email from the Internet to BIX, simply append `@bix.com` to the end of the BIX username and send it out.

BIX charges $13 per month plus a connect-time charge ranging from $1 per hour for Telnet access to $9 per hour for dial-up access via SprintNet or Tymnet during weekdays. The standard non-prime time rate is usually

$3 per hour. If you plan to use BIX heavily, there's a 20/20 plan that provides 20 hours for $20, though in addition to your $13 per month membership fee. Time over the 20 hours is charged at $1.80 per hour, or $1.00 per hour if you telnet in. To get an account on BIX, have your modem dial 800-695-4882 or 617-491-5410 (use 8 data bits, no parity, 1 stop bit). Press Return a few times until you see the Login: (enter "bix") prompt, and then type **bix.** At the Name? prompt, type **bix.net.** If you prefer, you also can telnet to BIX as described previously to sign up.

Delphi

Delphi boasts of full Internet access, but still forces users to suffer through a custom character-based menu system on top of VMS, a mainframe operating system used by DEC Vax computers. There is a Macintosh graphical interface called D-Lite, but the last version I saw was in the running for worst Macintosh program ever (and that was when it worked). Delphi doesn't do anything strange with addressing—to send email to an Internet user, use his Internet address instead of the Delphi address in Delphi's mail program. To send email from the Internet to someone at Delphi, simply append **@delphi.com** to the Delphi userid. My address on Delphi looks like **adam_engst@delphi.com**.

For information on connecting to Delphi, call 800-695-4005. Monthly rates are either $10.00 for four hours of use, with extra hours at $4.00 each, or $20.00 for 20 hours, with additional hours at $1.80 each. If your account has an Internet connection, you are charged an additional $3.00 per month. Delphi often offers five hours free so that you can try out the service, so ask

about the current deal when you call. Delphi plans to offer a full graphical interface in the relatively near future, and in an interesting twist, plans to base it entirely on Internet access via an authenticated Web browser. At that point, Delphi will be selling PPP access to the Internet and using Delphi will be just like using any other Web page (except for the membership fee).

http://www.delphi.com/

GEnie

GEnie is neither a hotbed of Macintosh activity nor even a major online service any more, and its Internet connections leave most everything to be desired. Luckily, a graphical interface to GEnie arrived since the last edition of this book; before that there was only a clumsy character-based interface. GEnie supports only Internet email, but can access Archie and FTP via email. To send email from GEnie to the Internet, use the standard Internet address if you're sending from the Internet Mail Service page. If you're sending the message from the GE Mail page, append **@inet#** to the end of the Internet address. To send email from the Internet to GEnie, append **@genie.geis.com** to your friend's GEnie username. There is a difference between userid (or login name) and username on GEnie. Internet email must go to the username.

GEnie charges $8.95 for the first four hours each month, with additional hours billed at $3.00 per hour for non-prime time access. The cost is $9.50 per hour on weekdays from 8:00 AM to 6:00 PM. You can get more information about GEnie by telephoning 800-638-9636.

http://www.genie.com/

Part III   Commercial Services

Outland

Outland is a nationwide commercial service dedicated to computer games. However, we're not talking just any computer games. It's specifically designed to support graphical multi-player games with those multiple players coming in from all around the world. Along with a variety of standard board games, Outland offers a special version of Delta Tao's fabulous space opera game, Spaceward Ho!. Why am I blathering about games here? Well, Outland is unusual in that it is accessible only via the Internet, either via a MacTCP-based connection or via Telnet from a Unix shell account. You must use Outland's special software, which is available for free, although playing the games costs money. Charges are $9.95 per month, flat-rate, with a five-hour free test period. You can contact Outland for more information at 800-PLAY-OUT, or at **outland@aol.com**. You can retrieve the Outland software on the Internet.

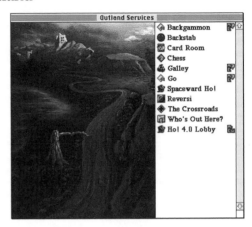

```
http://www.outland.com/
```

```
ftp://ftp.outland.com/pub/outland-all-files.hqx
```

Pipeline Internaut

Internaut is the proprietary graphical client software for an Internet provider called Pipeline, now owned by PSI, a large Internet provider. Internaut provides access to email, news, Talk, Archie, FTP, and Gopher, with some additional features thrown in to handle weather reports, IRC, and VT100 terminal emulation. Should you download images in GIF or JPEG format, Internaut automatically displays them for you. There appears to be a fairly tight integration between the parts of the program; for instance, you can mail the contents of a Gopher window to someone with the Mail Contents command in the Readers menu.

Although you cannot use MacTCP-based software (such as a Web browser, which Internaut currently lacks) over a connection made with Internaut, you can now use Internaut over an existing MacTCP connection, much as you can with America Online. For more information, contact Pipeline at **info@pipeline.com** or 800-453-PIPE.

```
http://www.pipeline.com/
```

Prodigy

Currently the least Mac-like of the services with graphical interfaces, Prodigy supports several Internet services. Most notable is a Web browser that is only available for Windows now (a Mac version is tentatively slated for the end of 1995), but Prodigy also supports Internet email and Usenet news for Mac users. Prodigy's online help claims it can't receive messages over 60K; in fact, it splits messages into chunks if the

continues

original is too large. To send email to a Prodigy user, append **@prodigy.com** to the user's Prodigy address—sending email to the Internet is straightforward. File attachments (for both internal and Internet email) aren't currently supported, but should be soon. Prodigy offers full access to Usenet news, and in a nice change from policies of yesteryear, it does not censor or withhold any messages on Usenet from Prodigy users.

Prodigy has three pricing plans that interact with three types of areas on Prodigy—PLUS, CORE, and FREE areas. FREE areas are free, of course, and Internet email and Usenet news both fall in the PLUS category. Anyway, the Basic Plan costs $9.95 per month for five hours of PLUS or CORE usage. The Value Plan costs $14.95 per month for unlimited CORE use plus five hours of PLUS use. Finally, the 30/30 Plan offers 30 hours of PLUS or CORE usage for $29.95 per month. Any usage beyond that included in the subscription plan costs $2.95 per hour, and rates are independent of time of day or speed of access. You do need Prodigy's software, and the easiest way to get it is to call 800-PRODIGY and ask for a free startup kit. It

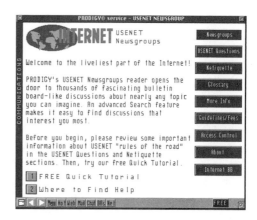

comes with 10 hours free, although you must give a credit card number to sign up, and if you don't cancel before the end of your 10 hours, you're automatically subscribed to the Basic Plan. You also can find some more information (and, in the future, perhaps the Mac software) on the Web at:

```
http://www.astranet.com/
```

TCP/Connect II Remote & Instant InterRamp

InterCon has released a less-expensive version of its powerful integrated program, TCP/Connect II, that requires neither MacTCP or a separate SLIP or PPP program. This is not to imply that TCP/Connect II Remote doesn't use Internet standards—it does—but because it includes both the TCP code and the SLIP or PPP code internally, when you connect using TCP/Connect II Remote, you cannot use any other MacTCP-based programs. That's not as large of a limitation as it is with something like Pipeline Internaut, since TCP/Connect II Remote includes a full set of Internet clients, including a Web browser. But programs like CU-SeeMe, Bolo, and MacWeather are simply out of the question if you rely on TCP/Connect II Remote. Contact InterCon at **sales@intercon.com** or 703/709-5500; 703/709-5555 (fax).

In addition, PSI, one of the large Internet providers, uses TCP/Connect II Remote as part of its Instant InterRamp package. The main difference between the standard TCP/Connect II Remote and Instant InterRamp is a custom application that helps you set

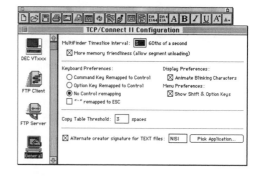

up an account with PSI ($29 for 29 hours and $1.50 per hour after that), accessible from both normal and ISDN phone numbers around the U.S. Luckily, the Instant InterRamp service from PSI is a standard PPP account, and it can be used with MacTCP, MacPPP, and MacTCP-based applications as well as with TCP/Connect II Remote, which doesn't use MacTCP.

```
http://www.intercon.com/intercon.html
```

```
http://www.psi.com/
```

Email Utilities

As I mentioned previously, there are a couple of programs that make dealing with email on the commercial online services quite a bit easier, Emailer and MailConverter.

Emailer

Emailer, due to appear sometime in the middle of 1995 from Claris, is being developed by Guy Kawasaki's Fog City Software. It's a program that Guy had a strong hand in because like many people in the industry, Guy has a large number of email accounts on different services, and checking mail on each one is a royal pain. Enter Emailer, which Guy and the folks at Fog City Software designed to be your central email program. Emailer currently can connect to CompuServe and RadioMail and understands POP and SMTP for talking to Internet email accounts, and America Online and eWorld are slated for support before Emailer hits the streets. Other services, like BIX or GEnie, may also appear at a later date.

I've been testing alpha versions of Emailer for several months, and it's worked like a champ with CompuServe. After you set up a service (see figure 12.27) by choosing Services from the Setup menu and double-clicking on the service name in the list, you can enter your account and connection configuration information.

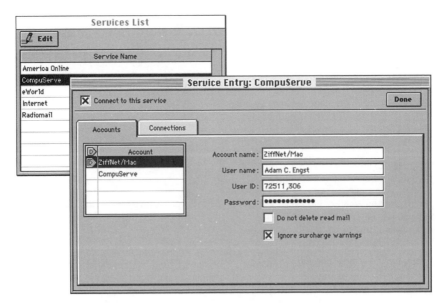

Figure 12.27   *Emailer's Services CompuServe Setup window.*

Because Guy recognized that just as many of us have accounts on multiple different services, we also may have multiple accounts, as I do on CompuServe with a straight CompuServe account and my main ZiffNet/Mac account, as you can see in figure 12.27.

The configuration for each service is tailored to that service, so when you configure your Internet account, you enter things like your POP account, SMTP server, and return address. In a nice touch, Emailer supports Internet Config, which ships on the disk with this book, and which holds all of these sorts of pieces of information for use by any Internet program that wants to support Internet Config.

Of course, many people travel around, and need to connect to the different services using different phone numbers. In the past, it's been a pain to reconfigure each different program, CIM, AOL, or eWorld, for the local phone numbers in the places you regularly visit; Emailer turns this task into a one-time event (see figure 12.28).

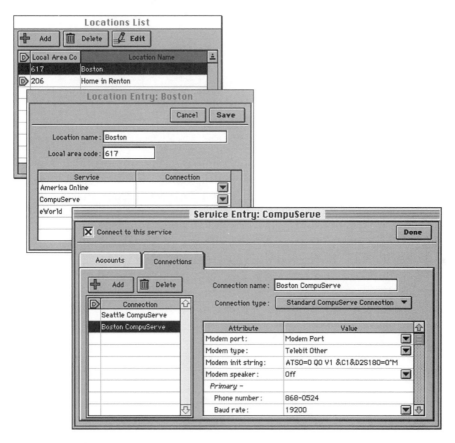

Figure 12.28   Emailer Locations configuration windows.

But Emailer's elegant design doesn't stop there. Anyone who uses a number of different services doesn't want to connect to each of them manually throughout the day. It's much more convenient to have the program connect automatically at a preset time, and in fact, CIM, AOL, and eWorld can all do this. Well, so can Emailer, and it's more flexible than the lot of them (see figure 12.29).

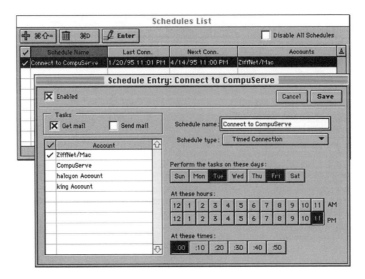

Figure 12.29   Emailer Schedules configuration.

All right, so we have a program that can connect to multiple services using multiple accounts in many different locations at pre-specified times. Emailer has to know how to send mail from one service to another, and as you'd expect, it relies on the Internet, which can connect to all of these different services. You can, of course, reply to CompuServe mail back through CompuServe, but if you'd rather use a cheaper connection through the Internet say, you can also set Emailer's Destinations settings to send mail back through a different service than it was received from (see figure 12.30). I especially like this feature, because I can have all my mail come in from CompuServe and go out through the Internet. In addition, if I want to send new mail to someone on CompuServe, Emailer uses this information to properly address the message so it's delivered to CompuServe via the Internet.

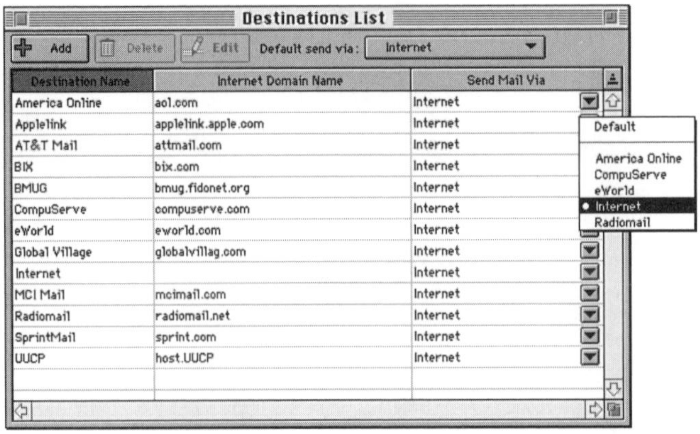

Figure 12.30   Emailer Destinations configuration.

I haven't even gotten to how Emailer helps you read and reply to messages, but it has one other extremely notable feature that many people would appreciate—full filtering capabilities that can auto forward or auto reply to a message, as I've done in figure 12.31. You can set priorities, file messages, and filter on basically any piece of information in an incoming mail message. Emailer's filtering capabilities, mostly thanks to the auto forward and auto reply features are perhaps the best I've ever seen.

Figure 12.31   *Emailer Mail Actions setup.*

Enough of these special features. When you connect to a service, Emailer brings in all waiting mail, and sends all mail queued for that service, assuming of course that you ask it to do that since the two actions can be activated separately. Mail comes into your In Box, accessible from the Emailer Browser window, and double-clicking on a message opens it for reading (see figure 12.32).

Part III   Commercial Services

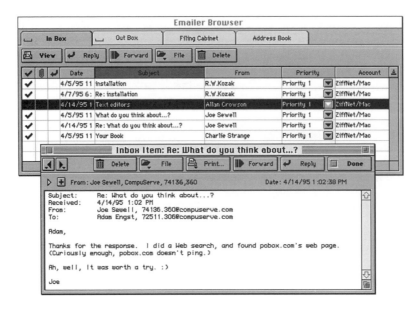

Figure 12.32 *Emailer Browser In Box and message window.*

As you can see from the buttons available, almost anything you could want to do with a message is available here, including deleting it (Emailer moves it to a Deleted Mail box in the Filing Cabinet part of the Browser for later deletion), filing in a separate mailbox, printing the letter, forwarding it to another person, and replying (and Emailer quotes the selected text when you reply, a great feature). You can also move back and forth between the messages in the current mailbox, and Emailer can automatically move read messages to a Read Mail box in the Filing Cabinet if you want. If you want to see who the message was sent to, the triangle in the upper left-hand corner flips down to display that header information, and clicking on the plus button next to the sender's name adds that person to your Address Book.

Speaking of the Address Book, it's almost a work of art (see figure 12.33). You can store multiple addresses for users easily (including multiple addresses at the same service); you can create groups of users; and you can filter the list on text strings once it gets large so that it becomes easy to find people. I could go on for some time, but that would spoil the fun. Suffice it to say, that it's really easy to create new messages for people from the Address Book, and if you have it and a message open at the same time, you can drag an entry to the message from the Address Book to include that person in the message.

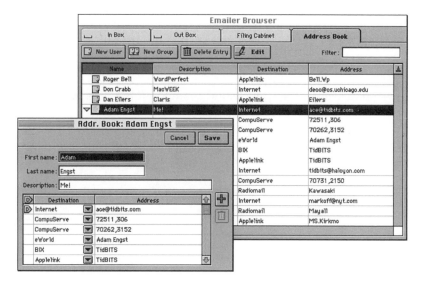

Figure 12.33   *Emailer Address Book.*

Other useful features in Emailer include search capability within saved mail, multiple mailboxes for filing mail, support for enclosures, and even support for enclosures from CompuServe to other services—something that isn't possible any other way. Overall, Emailer is simply a very good program, and I strongly recommend that anyone who must rely on different multiple email accounts on the commercial services buy a copy when it comes out in the middle of 1995.

There are two reasons why I'm not currently using Emailer in favor of the commercial version of Eudora. First, in a design mistake, Emailer stores each message as a separate file on your hard disk (in comparison with Eudora, which stores multiple messages in a single mailbox file in Unix mailbox format). Because most messages are relatively small, they can take up a full block size on disk. For instance, the partition of my hard disk that holds email is formatted to 700 MB or so. That means that a 500 byte email message in Emailer's format takes up about 20K on disk, since that's the smallest file size possible with such a large disk. Considering how many hundreds of messages I get and send and keep each day, this inefficiency is a problem. Second, although I like Emailer's interface and I think it's well done for the most part, I've come to really like the simplicity and elegance in Eudora. That's purely a personal preference though.

Actually, one feature has yet to appear in Emailer that's been promised for the shipping version—redirect. Eudora pioneered the redirect capability, which enables an email program to forward a message to another user without making it seem as though the message came from you. For instance, if I get a message that Tonya should deal with in Eudora, I redirect it to her rather than forwarding it. That way, when she gets the message and replies, the reply goes to the original sender, not to me. Once Emailer has a redirect feature, I plan to use it to redirect all mail from CompuServe, eWorld, and AOL straight back out to my Internet account, so they come in via Eudora and can be stored with the rest of my mail. I can't wait.

I also can't give you any details about buying Emailer because they aren't yet finalized (I suppose it's even possible that the name could change before Claris releases it). Keep your eyes out where you normally buy software—your dealer, a mail order catalog, or an online vendor—and I'm sure you'll see it as soon as it's available. I do believe Emailer will be inexpensive since Fog City Software has pre-sold it at user group meetings for about $30. I'd be very surprised if the final list price was more than two or three times that.

MailConverter

I've become fairly fond of Richard Shapiro's free MailConverter because it saves me from having to read and reply to email within America Online and eWorld. Instead, I use AOL's FlashSessions or eWorld's Automatic Courier to download the mail, then I have MailConverter convert the messages into a Eudora mailbox, where I can read and reply in a powerful and consistent environment. MailConverter also can convert a number of mail formats, including messages from LeeMail, MacEMail, cc:Mail (limited support), VMS mail (limited support), Pine, Elm, and files saved from various newsreaders, including NewsWatcher. MailConverter also will break up mail digests into individual messages. MailConverter supports drag-and-drop and is rather flexible in terms of dealing with strange headers. Until AOL and eWorld support automatic mail forwarding, I'll probably use MailConverter with them.

MailConverter Settings

☐ Allow only TEXT files as input
☒ Delete input file after converting
☒ Confirm before saving
☒ Truncate output filename
☐ Restrict messages to 32K
☒ Send to application

Default input folder:　[　　Adam Engst mail　]
Default save folder:　[　　Eudora Folder　　]

Creator: [CSOm]　⦿ Eudora
File type: [TEXT]　○ Z-Mail　[Same as...]
　　　　　　○ Other　[Cancel] [[OK]]

`ftp://ftp.tidbits.com/pub/tidbits/tisk/util/`

PowerTalk Gateway for CompuServe

Although not specifically related to the Internet, CompuServe has made a gateway available for Apple's PowerTalk email technology so you can send and receive CompuServe email in the same way that you can send and receive PowerTalk email or email using any other PowerTalk gateway, such as StarNine's Internet email gateway. I don't recommend PowerTalk for more than a few messages a day, but you can get a complete set of these gateways in:

`ftp://ftp.support.apple.com/pub/apple_sw_updates/US/mac/system_sw/PowerTalk/`

SignatureQuote

Although most decent email programs have the capability to add a signature to your messages, it's uncommon for the commercial services to support signatures. In addition, none of the commercial services make it easy to quote text from a message in a reply. Rick Holzgrafe's $10 shareware SignatureQuote FKEY is the answer to such problems—just configure it with your signature and add your signature with a single key press. To quote text,

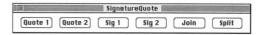

just copy it, activate SignatureQuote, and click one of the two Quote buttons to use one of two quoting styles. I highly recommend it for use with the commercial services.

```
ftp://ftp.tidbits.com/pub/tidbits/tisk/util/
```

Wrapping Up

Although I cannot recommend any of them as a replacement for a full MacTCP-based Internet connection, the commercial online services provide an easy way to dip into the Internet without diving headfirst. The liability of taking the dip in favor of the dive is that you'll quickly find that in terms of Internet access, the commercial online services are extremely shallow. A number of bulletin boards have gained full Internet access in recent months as well, and I expect more to appear all the time. Because most bulletin board systems charge little or nothing for access, they can be a great way to obtain inexpensive Internet access.

Enough talking about limited access, though, let's move on to Unix shell accounts, which are as powerful as they are ugly for Macintosh users.

13

Bulletin Board Systems

This is a short chapter for a couple of reasons. First off, it can be difficult to find a bulletin board system (BBS) in your area, and because the resources available for finding them vary from place to place, I can't really help you. Second, there's no telling what level, if any, of Internet access a BBS may provide. With those caveats aside, for limited Internet access, an account on a FirstClass, NovaLink Professional, or TeleFinder BBS might be an inexpensive and efficient way to start out on the Internet. I consider these three to be the main graphical BBSs in the Macintosh world. Several others exist, but they aren't used nearly as heavily.

> **Note**
>
> *A BBS is a computer system that you can connect to, usually via modem. Once there, you can upload and download files, send and receive email, and participate in discussions. Unlike the commercial online services, a BBS usually serves a small group of people in a specific area.*

I don't cover anything but the main graphical BBSs in this chapter because, frankly, there are so many of them and most are ugly to use. I use a Mac because I don't like custom character-based menu interfaces, and almost every BBS with a character-based interface that I've ever used has irritated me. The editors are lousy and the commands are cryptic, and it's just not what using a Macintosh is all about. So, if you can only find Internet access through a character-based BBS, you're on your own, although it may marginally provide Internet email and Usenet news.

FirstClass

FirstClass BBSs are actually most commonly used as conferencing systems within large companies and organizations. However, they're also extremely popular among the user group community (see figure 13.1).

Figure 13.1   *FirstClass Login window.*

With SoftArc's excellent FirstClass BBS software, and a special add-on gateway to the Internet, a Macintosh BBS can sport a clean graphical interface and provide an email and Usenet news connection. Most of these sorts of Internet connections are handled through UUCP gateways, which means the FirstClass BBS calls an Internet host every few hours to transfer email and news. However, there are an increasing number of FirstClass BBSs that have dedicated Internet connections. These can offer faster turnaround on mail and news, as well as the promise of additional Internet services like FTP in the near future.

It's also possible, though still somewhat unusual, for a FirstClass BBS to be accessible over the Internet. You can come in by way of a standard Telnet session or via the graphical FirstClass software if you have a MacTCP-based connection to the Internet.

The easiest way to use FirstClass over the Internet is if the organization running the FirstClass server gives you a FirstClass settings file, at which point you can just double-click on it to launch FirstClass and connect to that server. However, if you don't already have a settings file, it's relatively easy to create one.

N o t e

The FirstClass server I use in this example is called designOnline, an online resource for design professionals. Anyone can login, although you'll only have limited access at first. You also can read about them on the Web at:

`http://www.dol.com/`

To create a settings file, launch the application. Click Cancel when it asks you to open an existing settings file and choose New from the File menu. After you name and save the settings file, FirstClass brings up the Login window dialog. Click the Setup button, and from the Connect via pop-up menu, choose TCP-IP.FCP (see figure 13.2).

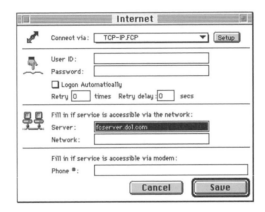

Figure 13.2   *FirstClass TCP Setup dialog.*

Enter the IP name or number of the FirstClass server to which you want to connect in the Server field. Click the Save button to save your changes. Of course, if you already have an account, you can enter your userid and password as well. From this point, using FirstClass over the Internet is just like using it via a modem.

N o t e

By default, the graphical FirstClass client uses port 3000. Click the Setup button in the Communications Setup dialog, and then turn the Advanced Settings triangle. If you telnet to a FirstClass server, you generally use port 3004 instead.

FirstClass can receive Usenet newsgroups via an Internet gateway, which is an excellent way to bring more information into a fairly small BBS. Unfortunately, the current interface to reading news isn't as full-featured as I would like. Working with threads is difficult or impossible, and there's no easy way to entirely skip an uninteresting thread (see figure 13.3).

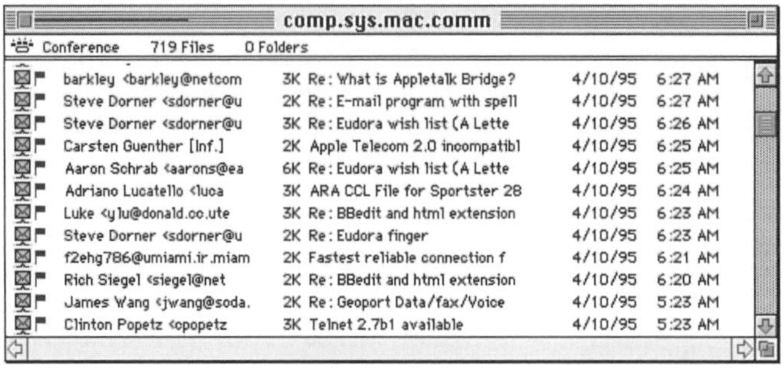

Figure 13.3   FirstClass newsgroups.

To send an email message to the Internet, type the Internet address and append **,Internet** to it. My Internet address from a FirstClass system looks like **ace@tidbits.com,Internet**. Because most FirstClass systems don't call out all that often to send and receive Internet email, don't expect immediate responses. Sending email to a FirstClass BBS is no different than sending to any other Internet site—you must know the username and sitename.

In general, you can figure out usernames by taking the person's username on FirstClass and replacing the spaces with underscores (and FirstClass is pretty good at guessing based on your attempt). However, making this change can result in some ugly addresses. If I am **Adam C. Engst** on a FirstClass board, for example, the Internet form of my username on the local dBUG BBS (run by Seattle's downtown Business Users' Group) is **adam_c._engst@dbug.org**. Again, the sitename in the address is individual to each FirstClass BBS. It's also possible for the administrator to create aliases, so I could also be **ace@dbug.org** on the local BBS. The aliases are simply easier for others to type.

> **Note**
>
> *FirstClass distinguishes between usernames that identify you to other users (**Adam C. Engst**, for example) and userids that identify you to the software (mine on the local BBS is 1892). It's not a big deal, but if you want to be correct….*

If you can find a local FirstClass BBS that's also in some way connected to the Internet, I recommend you try it out. It's a good interface for getting started with Internet email and news, and most BBSs have either minimal or nonexistent fees.

You can find more information about the FirstClass software from SoftArc by sending email to **sales@softarc.com**. You can download the free FirstClass client software from any FirstClass BBS, or on the Internet in:

```
ftp://ftp.tidbits.com/pub/tidbits/tisk/bbs/
```

NovaLink Professional

With a graphical interface called NovaTerm, NovaLink Professional can support Internet email and Usenet news. It also can accept connections over the Internet, either in command-line mode via Telnet or with the graphical client via a MacTCP-based Internet connection.

You can connect to only a few NovaLink systems over the Internet. It's simply a matter of knowing the Internet address and switching to MacTCP in the Settings dialog. I presume that many more have UUCP connections to the Internet for retrieving Internet email and Usenet news (see figure 13.4).

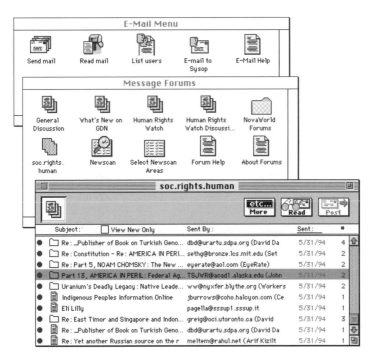

Figure 13.4   *Email and news in NovaLink.*

If you connect to a NovaLink BBS that has full Internet connections, you also can telnet out of it, which is a nice touch—and a useful feature for a BBS to offer. In the next version of the NovaLink Professional software, ResNova has promised that you will be able to browse the World Wide Web as well, which is far neater than Telnet. This will set NovaLink apart from the other contenders in the BBS world.

Note

> *The public BBS to which I connected over the Internet, Global Democracy Network* (**chrf.gdn.org**), *is a nonprofit human rights organization. It works with members of parliament around the world to institutionalize human rights protections and increase democracy. Along the way, they're trying to get these members of parliament to become Internet users—a laudable goal. Two other NovaLink systems currently accessible on the Internet are* **mpd.amaranth.com** *and* **infoport.com**.

There's not much else to say about Internet connections via NovaLink systems, except that the process seems to work and is relatively speedy. You can contact ResNova Software, the makers of NovaLink, at **sales@resnova.com** or **info@resnova.com**, and you can get the NovaTerm client program from any NovaLink BBS, or on the Internet in:

```
ftp://ftp.tidbits.com/pub/tidbits/tisk/bbs/
```

TeleFinder

TeleFinder also provides a graphical interface BBS that (with additional software, called InterFinder, from Andreas Fink of Microframe) can connect to the Internet to send and receive email and news (see figure 13.5).

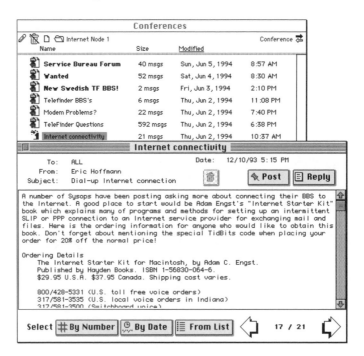

Figure 13.5   *TeleFinder Internet Connectivity discussion (and no, I didn't fake the screen shot—it really said that!).*

> **N o t e**
>
> *The BBS package (host and client) is called TeleFinder Group Edition. The freely distributed client program that's generally customized for a specific BBS is called TeleFinder User. The more full-featured shareware client and terminal emulator is called TeleFinder Pro.*

TeleFinder Pro has one of the most interesting graphical interfaces I've seen—it takes over your monitor and sort of reproduces the way the Finder looks. It confused me a bit at first because I have two monitors on my Mac. TeleFinder Pro seemed to move a bunch of my desktop icons around whenever I was in the TeleFinder application. TeleFinder User, in contrast, uses an interface more like FirstClass's desktop within a window metaphor (see figure 13.6). Both work fine for connecting to TeleFinder BBSs.

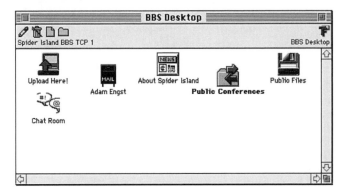

Figure 13.6　*TeleFinder Pro's Change Port dialog.*

You can connect over the Internet to a TeleFinder BBS in command-line mode (all of these graphical BBS programs also offer straight character-based modes) by telnetting to **spiderisland.com**. You need special software to use either TeleFinder User or TeleFinder Pro over a MacTCP-based Internet connection. That software, called TeleFinder User TCP, creates a virtual "port" that you can select instead of the modem or printer port when you're configuring TeleFinder Pro (see figure 13.7). From TeleFinder Pro's Special menu, choose Change Port after installing TeleFinder User TCP in your Extensions folder.

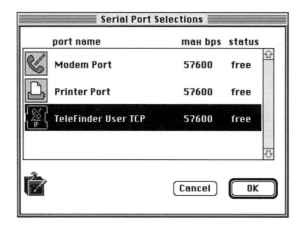

Figure 13.7   *TeleFinder Pro's Change Port dialog.*

After you've selected that port, you can configure TeleFinder Pro to "dial" a TeleFinder BBS. Click the port icon for TeleFinder User TCP that appears in the lower left of the screen and create a new Service. In the Service Information dialog, replace the phone number with an @ character and either the IP number or IP name of that machine (see figure 13.8).

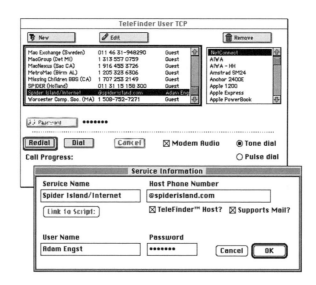

Figure 13.8   *Configuring TeleFinder Pro for the Internet.*

So, to connect to Spider Island's own BBS over the Internet, I told the TeleFinder Pro software (via TeleFinder User TCP) to "dial" **@spiderisland.com**, which it did, complete with faked modem messages and everything. Once I was connected, everything worked as I expect it does when you dial in via modem, and the speed was even quite good.

TeleFinder User is easier to configure than TeleFinder Pro because you don't have to muck around with changing ports or anything like that. When you launch the program, it presents you with a Connection dialog, in which you can enter your username, password, and the connection method (see figure 13.9). Clicking the Configure button brings up a dialog for entering the IP address and port number (1474 by default) of the TeleFinder BBS to which you want to connect.

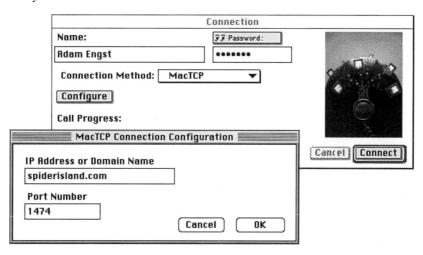

Figure 13.9   *Configuring TeleFinder Pro for the Internet.*

For more information about TeleFinder Pro, contact Spider Island Software at **support@spiderisland.com**. For some reason the TeleFinder TCP User software wasn't at **spiderisland.com**, but it is stored on **ftp.tidbits.com**. You can retrieve either the TeleFinder Pro and TeleFinder User client programs in:

```
ftp://spiderisland.com/
```

```
ftp://ftp.tidbits.com//pub/tidbits/tisk/bbs/
```

Wrapping Up BBSs

As more inexpensive Internet connections appear, I expect we'll see many more of these graphical bulletin boards appearing on the Internet. If nothing else, supporting a number of modems and phone lines isn't cheap, so offering connections via the Internet might even be cheaper for many.

Although I cannot recommend any of them as a replacement for a full MacTCP-based Internet connection, the graphical BBSs provide an easy and usually inexpensive way to dip into the Internet without diving headfirst. Of course, you trade that ease of use and lesser expense for limited functionality, although all of the BBSs plan to add more Internet support in the future.

Enough talk about limited access, though. Let's move on and talk about enhancements to the common Unix shell account.

Shell Account Enhancements

Welcome to old-style Internet access—souped up for your surfing pleasure! In this chapter I take you on a fast flight through the few Macintosh programs that can work over a Unix command-line interface (usually known as a Unix shell account).

I do not tell you how to use Unix in this chapter, or for that matter in any chapter. For those of you who have seen previous editions of *Internet Starter Kit for Macintosh*, I removed that section from this chapter. Why? Several reasons. First, with PPP and SLIP accounts now commonplace, it's much less likely that you will have to suffer with a Unix shell account. Second, and I'll be honest here, I didn't feel that my treatment was sufficiently complete. There are many other books that cover the topic more completely, and I decided that I should stick to my strength—Macintosh software. Third and finally, by reducing the page count of the book, I'm hopefully saving a few trees.

A book that has been recommended to me in regard to learning Unix is Dave Taylor's *Teach Yourself UNIX in a Week* (Sams Publishing, 1994, ISBN 0-672-30464-3), mostly because analogies both to DOS and to the Macintosh are included throughout. For those that know and dislike Unix, you owe it to yourself to check out *The Unix-Haters Handbook* by Simson Garfinkel, Daniel Weise, and Steven Strassmann (IDG Books, 1994, ISBN 1-56884-203-1). Those already on the Internet with access to a Web browser (one wonders if they need much help with Unix at that point) might also check out the popular Internet Roadmap online class at:

```
http://www.brandonu.ca/~ennsnr/Resources/Roadmap/Welcome.html
```

Creating a program to act like a monkey and type the appropriate commands on the Unix command line is quite a bit more difficult than it might sound. The main problem is that a surprising number of variations of Unix exist, and even different sites running the same flavor of Unix may have their machines set up differently. The situation worsens when new versions of Unix programs appear with slightly different commands or slightly different results to old commands. It's a programmer's nightmare.

Thus, the few programs that can exist in this harsh environment have evolved some similar methods of coping. Almost without exception, they work by relying on the user to get them properly connected to the remote system, and from there they take over, usually connected directly to the appropriate server port for email or news or whatever. I say "whatever," but in fact, with one exception, the only two types of programs that work on Unix shell accounts are email programs and newsreaders. The exception is Homer, a client program for IRC, or Internet Relay Chat.

Actually, there is one other application, Pipeline's Internaut, that provides graphical Internet access without MacTCP or standard SLIP or PPP. Pipeline provides access to a number of Internet services, although not all the ones you might want to use, and requires a specific sort of account that isn't all that common.

However, the main solution to the problem of the Unix shell account is a program that has seriously shaken up the Internet world, The Internet Adapter, or TIA. Let's look at it first, and then at Eudora, which is another useful solution, before we spin through the remaining programs that can pretty up a Unix shell account.

The Internet Adapter

On occasion in the past, I've seen postings in which people wonder why someone hasn't written a program to enable graphical programs that normally require a MacTCP-based connection to work with a normal shell account. There are a number of graphical Internet programs, such as Pipeline's Internaut (see chapter 12, "Commercial Services") on different platforms that use a proprietary protocol for talking to the host machine, which means that you can't use the standard Macintosh Internet programs such as Eudora, Anarchie, and MacWeb. Instead you must use the limited graphical client software provided by the same people who created the proprietary protocol.

I don't approve of this method of providing Internet access for two reasons. First, and most importantly, you're seriously limited in your choice of software for any particular task. With a full MacTCP-based connection, I can choose between Anarchie and Fetch, Netscape and MacWeb, Eudora and VersaTerm-Link, NewsWatcher and InterNews and Nuntius. In fact, I may even use multiple programs for the same thing—I like and use both Anarchie and Fetch for different types of FTP tasks. You lose that flexibility when you're locked into a proprietary solution. Second, the Internet is a vast and fast-moving place, and new capabilities appear all the time, generally supported first, and often best, by freeware and shareware programmers. If you're locked into a specific proprietary program, there's no way you could use Cornell's Internet videoconferencing software, CU-SeeMe, play Stuart Cheshire's wonderful Bolo tank game, or check the weather with Chris Kidwell's MacWeather. All of those programs depend on the standard TCP/IP protocols that the Internet relies on, and these proprietary programs, useful as they may be, don't give you a standard TCP connection to the Internet.

TIA Basics

Such is not the case with The Internet Adapter. TIA is a relatively small (about 250K) Unix program that you run on your normal Unix shell account, and it acts as a SLIP emulator. In other words, after you install TIA on your shell account, running TIA turns your shell account into a SLIP account for that session. Although a TIA emulated-SLIP account is not quite the same as a real SLIP account, TIA's SLIP emulation is completely standard in terms of working with MacTCP-based software on the Mac (or WinSock if you use a Windows machine). Version 1.1 of TIA, which should be out by the time you read this, will support PPP as well, which will be even better.

Just to repeat myself then, with the addition of a single Unix program which Cyberspace Development sells to individuals for $25 (although 1.1 will go up to $35 to help feed the TIA support staff) or sells to providers for more money, you can turn your plain old shell account into a whizzy SLIP account and use all of the MacTCP-based software I discuss in this book. I realize this all sounds a bit like a Ginsu knife commercial (did I mention how TIA can cut beer cans too?), but TIA has proven itself since its release in the summer of 1994 with over 10,000 single user licenses sold and over 400 host and site licences. Cyberspace Development estimates that over 100,000 people now connect to the Internet via TIA.

> **Note**
>
> *To use the graphical software I discuss later on in the book with a TIA account, you must still have MacTCP and a version of SLIP (or, once TIA 1.1 is out, PPP) installed. Don't worry about it because MacTCP, InterSLIP, and MacPPP come with this book.*

TIA has become popular at sites that either aren't commercial or don't have much money to buy the expensive terminal servers that make real SLIP accounts easily possible. Since Cyberspace Development sells TIA to individuals, suddenly individual users have the choice of whether or not they get a SLIP account. Whereas in the past, if the machine didn't support SLIP, that was the end of the story. I heartily applaud putting power in the hands of the individual wherever possible; with TIA it's possible!

TIA created a huge fuss when it was first released, primarily on the part of Internet providers who felt that TIA endangered their business model, but for the most part all that fuss seems to have disappeared. A very few providers have banned TIA, but for the most part it has become a fact of life for Internet users previously limited to Unix shell accounts.

TIA Details

Note

The details that follow about how TIA turns your shell account into a SLIP account may not make much sense if you haven't looked through the chapters in part IV yet. Don't worry about it—just skip the following section unless you're interested in how TIA works.

When you use TIA, you do not get your own IP number that uniquely identifies your Mac on the Internet while you're connected, as you do with a real SLIP account. Instead, TIA uses the IP number of the machine your shell account is on, and "redirects" traffic back to you (this is the magic part). If you must enter an IP number in some software, any number like **1.1.1.1** should do fine—it's just a dummy address.

Note

The fact that you don't get your own IP number means that you cannot set your Mac up as an FTP server, for instance, because there's no IP number for an FTP client somewhere else to connect to.

TIA's performance is reportedly good, faster than normal SLIP in fact, and about as fast as Compressed SLIP, or CSLIP. Future releases will support CSLIP and even PPP, and will reportedly increase speed by 10 to 20 percent. TIA doesn't create much of a load for the host machine, although slightly more than a real SLIP account, mostly because when you use SLIP, you're not usually running programs on the host machine, but are just using the network connection.

Installing TIA

Installing TIA on your Unix shell account is not a completely trivial task, since you must install the proper version for the version of Unix running on your host machine.

Cyberspace Development has ported TIA to a number of versions of Unix and more appear all the time (send email to **tia-port-info@marketplace.com** for a full list). If you don't know what version of Unix is running on your shell account, Cyberspace Development has a simple program that can find out the information for you. Current ports include those in Table 14.1.

Part III
Shell Account
Enhance-
ments

Table 14.1

Operating Systems Supported by TIA

Hardware	Operating System
Sun Sparc	Solaris 2.x
Sun Sparc	SunOS 4.1.x
Sun 3	SunOS 4.1.x
386/486	BSDI 1.0
386/486	BSDI 1.1
386/486	SCO
386/486	Linux
DEC MIPS	ULTRIX versions 4.3a (also works with 4.2, 4.4)
DEC ALPHA	OSF/1 2.0 (also works with 3.0)
IBM RS6000	AIX 3.2
SGI	IRIX 4.0 (also works with 5.2)
HP	HP-UX 9.0 (also works with 7.x)

Essentially then, you retrieve the proper version of TIA via FTP, Gopher, or the Web, and then launch it. (For evaluation purposes, you can get a free version and test it for a while—contact Cyberspace Development for an evaluation code.) Once TIA is running, you need to enable SLIP on your Mac, which means having MacTCP and InterSLIP properly configured.

Note

Actually, unlike most shareware, for which you download the program first, then register, TIA is generally easier to register first, then download (because of how the license codes work). Cyberspace Development recommends getting an evaluation license code from **marketplace.com** *(via email or the Web—details following). The code comes with complete instructions for obtaining the proper version of TIA for your flavor of Unix from* **marketplace.com** *via FTP.*

In normal usage you use a script—a gateway script if you're using InterSLIP—for your SLIP program to log in to your shell account and then run TIA to start up the SLIP emulation. But it is possible to do it manually as well. In InterSLIP, you'd leave the Dialing and the Gateway menus set to Direct Connection, log in to your shell account with a terminal emulator, start TIA, and then quit the terminal emulator, making sure that the terminal emulator doesn't hang up the phone on quit. Luckily, others have created scripts that work with TIA, so you may not have to do all the work yourself. Look for this file or others with TIA in the name in the same directory:

```
ftp://ftp.tidbits.com/pub/tidbits/tisk/tcp/scr-interslip-tia-netcom.txt
```

You can order TIA on the Internet itself if you wish (and the Web forms at **marketplace.com** are reportedly the easiest method, even via Lynx, a character-based Web browser that runs on Unix shell accounts). Other mechanisms are available for those who dislike ordering on the nets. A company called SoftAware sells various versions of the TIA package along with installation help and consulting (useful for those of you who aren't familiar with Unix). If nothing else, I suspect working through SoftAware will be the easiest way for individuals to buy a complete package and be up and running quickly. Contact SoftAware at **single-tia-sales@softaware.com** or 310-305-0275. For those who wish to try setting up and configuring TIA alone, there are several help files available on the nets. Look for:

```
ftp://ftp.tidbits.com/pub/tidbits/tisk/info/how-to-tia.txt
```

```
ftp://ftp.tidbits.com/pub/tidbits/tisk/info/tia-faq.hqx
```

In addition, Cyberspace Development has created a vast array of informational files which you can request via email. The easiest way to find out what they have available is to send email to **tia-directory@marketplace.com**. For more basic information about TIA, send email to **tia-info@marketplace.com** or connect to **marketplace.com** over the Web or via Gopher, FTP, or Telnet:

```
http://marketplace.com/
```

```
gopher://marketplace.com/
```

```
ftp://marketplace.com/tia/
```

```
telnet://marketplace.com
```

Eudora

Steve Dorner's free Eudora email program is among the most flexible of communications programs ever. Eudora was designed to work with MacTCP (and works best in that environment), so I don't explore the details of using the program until chapter 21,

"Email." I also mention it in chapter 15, "UUCP Access," because it can work with a UUCP transport program to read and write email using UUCP. But for the moment, if your Unix host supports protocols called *POP* (Post Office Protocol) and *SMTP* (Simple Mail Transport Protocol), Eudora can work with the Communications Toolbox that is standard in System 7 to dial up your Unix host and send and receive email.

Note

Although the Communications Toolbox (CTB) code is built into System 7, the CTB tools necessary to use Eudora and many other CTB-aware programs are not included with System 7. You can get them from your Apple dealer, with many communications programs like SITcomm or MicroPhone II, or on the Internet in:

```
ftp://ftp.support.apple.com/pub/apple_sw_updates/US/mac/n_c/comm_toolbox_tools/
```

The Basic Connectivity Set (BCS) is in disk image format, which is best handled by a disk image utility called ShrinkWrap, available in:

```
ftp://ftp.tidbits.com/pub/tidbits/tisk/util/
```

However, let's go over the details of setting up Eudora to work over the modem. You might also want to refer to the excellent Eudora documentation available at:

```
ftp://ftp.qualcomm.com/quest/mac/eudora/documentation/
```

Also be sure to poke around in the folder dedicated to storing preconfigured plug-ins for different providers (which would enable to you avoid the hairy part of the configuration process) and types of server hardware at:

```
ftp://ftp.qualcomm.com/quest/mac/eudora/dialup/
```

Installation and Setup

There are two drawbacks to using Eudora with the Communications Toolbox. First, it's slower than via MacTCP. Second, it's flakier, thanks to the reliance on the modem without PPP or SLIP controlling things. But if it's a choice between suffering with the Unix mail program or putting up with a few Eudora connection problems, I'll take Eudora any day.

Ask your system administrator if your Unix host supports POP for receiving mail and SMTP for sending mail, and if so, if she knows of anyone using Eudora on the Macintosh already. Once one person has customized Eudora to work on a specific machine, the customized file can work for everyone. Assuming that you're a pioneering sort and the first one to attempt this task, read on.

To modify Eudora to work over a CTB connection, you first need a template called Unix Navs, which you can edit and place in your Eudora Folder, which normally lives in the System Folder. It's available at:

```
ftp://ftp.qualcomm.com/quest/mac/eudora/dialup/servers/unix.hqx
```

This template contains the conversation Eudora expects to have with your Unix host to set up everything. Such send-and-expect conversations are generally called *chat scripts* and are most heavily used in the UUCP world. Unfortunately, you must use ResEdit, Apple's free resource editor, to edit the Unix Navs file. If you don't have ResEdit, you might be able to get it from a power user friend, your Apple dealer, or in:

```
ftp://ftp.support.apple.com/pub/apple_sw_updates/US/mac/utils/
```

Launch ResEdit and from the File menu select Open. Open the Unix Navs file. Double-click on the lone STR# resource, then double-click on the Navigate In resource, and the third window you see should have strings that you can modify (see figure 14.1).

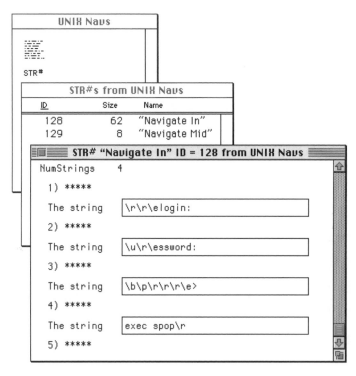

Figure 14.1   *Eudora Unix Navs configuration in ResEdit.*

If you have the Eudora manual, you can see that my settings differ from the standard ones that Steve Dorner provides. My Unix machine provided a different prompt, so I had to change the third string, and the program named **srialpop** in his example is named **spop** on my machine. You may or may not need to change those lines—I imagine most people don't.

The first line says Eudora should send two returns (the **\r** strings) and then expect (the **\e** string) to see the **login:** string. The second line says that Eudora should send your username (the **\u** string, determined from a setting inside Eudora itself) and a return, and then expect to see **ssword:**, which is of course the tail end of "Password:." The third line says that Eudora should send your password (**\p**, again determined inside Eudora) and three returns, then expect to see the **>** sign at the end of the prompt (that's what my prompt looks like anyway; your prompt may look different). The **\b** tells Eudora not to send your password to the Progress window, should anyone be watching. Once Eudora sees the prompt, you're properly logged in. The fourth line says that Eudora should execute the **spop** program by sending **exec spop** and a return. You must ask your administrator what the name of the **spop** or **srialpop** program is on your machine if neither of those possibilities work.

Part III   Shell Account Enhancements

Note

*You might be able to determine if your Unix machine uses either of these programs. Log in normally, and when you're at the Unix prompt, type **srialpop** or **spop**. If the machine complains "Command not found," you know that's not it. If it does something, such as change the prompt, you may have hit on the right program.*

If necessary for your system, you can add another line by clicking on the five asterisks after a number and going to the Resource menu and choosing Insert New Field(s). After you have configured these four strings to match your login procedure, save the file and quit ResEdit.

Next, launch Eudora. Go to the Special menu and choose Settings (see figure 14.2).

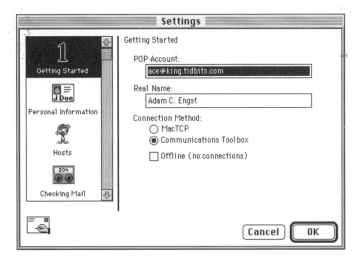

Figure 14.2   *Eudora CTB settings.*

The main part to worry about in this dialog is the radio button for Communications Toolbox, since you want to connect via modem to a Unix shell account rather than via MacTCP. (Check the Eudora discussion in chapter 21, "Email," for information on how to configure the standard parts of Eudora and use the program in general.) Click on the OK button to save the changes. From the Special menu again, choose Communications (see figure 14.3).

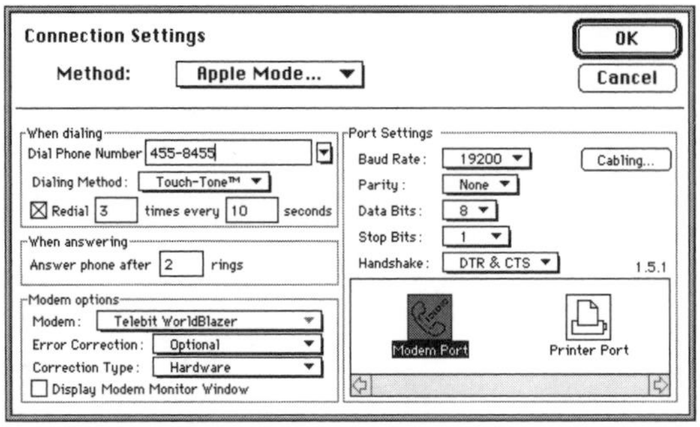

Figure 14.3   *Apple Modem Tool configuration.*

Eudora displays the standard Connection Settings configuration dialog. First, from the Method pop-up menu, choose Apple Modem Tool. If you don't have it, get it from a friend, your dealer, or the Internet, because it's supposedly the only one that works with Eudora. It's hidden in with the Communicate Lite demo in:

```
ftp://ftp.tidbits.com/pub/tidbits/tisk/term/
```

```
ftp://ftp.support.apple.com/pub/apple_sw_updates/US/mac/n_c/comm_toolbox_tools/
```

Type your host machine's phone number in the Dial Phone Number field. From the Modem pop-up menu, choose your modem or, if it's not listed, one from the same manufacturer, and failing that, one from Hayes. If all else fails, you can choose the Custom option in that pop-up menu and configure it yourself (this means figuring out the proper initialization string with the help of your modem manual). Finally, check the Port Settings to make sure your modem is talking at the right speed with No Parity, 8 Data Bits, 1 Stop Bit, and the appropriate Handshaking for your modem and cable (usually DTR & CTS or CTS Only). After you're done, click the OK button to save your settings.

Note

Three things are important for using Eudora in dialup mode. First, you must have a modem with either hardware or software error correction. Dropping a single character at the wrong time can kill the POP and SMTP protocols on which Eudora relies. Second, the remote host must have hardware flow control that actually works, which isn't always true, and unfortunately you have little or no control over this. Third, you must configure the Mac properly and know your model's limitations. Steve Dorner suggests using software error control, even if the modem supports hardware error correction on PowerBooks with high-speed modems using the Apple Modem Tool 1.5, because the small hardware buffer in the serial chip can overflow at times.

Shell Account
Enhance-
ments

Now comes the fun part—troubleshooting. From the File menu, choose Check Mail to make Eudora to dial out and retrieve your mail. Eudora displays a progress dialog at the top of the screen that shows what's happening, one line at a time. Those lines flash by quickly, though, so watch carefully so you can see where it might get stuck (if your host actually requires more information during login, for instance). If you're lucky, it works on the first try, but don't count on it. If it works, you should read the section on Eudora in chapter 21 to figure out how to use the rest of the program. If it doesn't work, retrace your steps, try to figure what's going wrong, and if all else fails, try asking on the newsgroup **comp.sys.mac.comm** because many experienced Eudora users hang out there.

There's also a Eudora mailing list you can join, which is probably the best place to ask for help if you're having trouble. To subscribe, send email to **majordomo@qualcomm.com** with **subscribe mac-eudora-forum** in the body of the message. Make sure that your return address is correct—it's the address that will be added to the mailing list.

A Major Kludge

If all else fails, long-time Macintosh user and net citizen Murph Sewall posted this extremely clever suggestion. It's a major kludge, but if it works for Murph, it might work for you. First, download Tim Endres' Termy terminal emulator. It's in:

```
ftp://ftp.tidbits.com/pub/tidbits/tisk/term/
```

Then, configure both Termy and Eudora to use the Serial tool (not the Apple Modem Tool, as Eudora would normally want). When you want to connect, launch Termy, open a terminal window, and dial your modem by hand to connect with your Unix host. Proceed through the login normally until you get to the prompt that wants you to telnet to your POP server. Close Termy's terminal window. Since you're using the Serial tool, the modem should stay connected, and if it doesn't, check your modem initialization string to make sure the modem ignores DTR (usually something like &D0). After you close Termy's window, switch to Eudora and use it as you normally would. Murph notes that you may have to use ResEdit to modify a resource that controls the format the Telnet command—the instructions for that are in the appendix of the Eudora manual.

When you're done, you either can open a new terminal window in Termy to log out or you may be able to get the Eudora NavigateOut resource properly configured to log out for you (but if you could do that, one would think you could get the NavigateIn resource properly configured as well). The more I think about it, the more I think this is a serious hack, but you might even be able to automate it with a program like QuicKeys if you have to use it.

Other Shell Enhancements

Although most of the programs I talk about in this section can be cajoled into working, for the most part they aren't terribly easy to set up. And, for those that are easy to set up, there isn't usually much power behind the basic interface. That said, people do use and like these programs, so if setting up TIA isn't possible or feasible and you want to do more than just email via Eudora, check out some of these programs. Unless mentioned otherwise, all the programs below are at the following URL:

```
ftp://ftp.tidbits.com/pub/tidbits/tisk/term/
```

Eudora SFU

Ray Davison of Simon Fraser University has modified an old version (1.4.2) of Eudora to be even more scriptable than the normal version of Eudora using the C- language. I haven't tried to use this version at all, because I had no trouble with Eudora's relatively simple setup, but if you have a particularly weird configuration that you must script around and you

Eudora 1.4.2 SFU

don't mind using a slightly older version of Eudora, it might be worth checking out.

```
ftp://ftp.sfu.ca/pub/mac/eudora/
```

Homer

The $25 shareware program Homer from Toby Smith comes in two forms—one for MacTCP-based connections and one for those who have only a Unix shell account. Homer is primarily used via a MacTCP-based connection, but suffice it to say that if you plan on using IRC and you have a Mac, Homer is the way to go. The serial version of Homer has a number of limitations not shared by the MacTCP version. First off, it's not compatible with the Communications Toolbox, which means you cannot use any Macintosh that uses a GeoPort Telecom Adapter instead of a modem (the GeoPort Telecom Adapter only works with the Communications Toolbox). Second, you must use a Unix account—no other operating systems will work—that can telnet out to a remote host. Third, some versions of Telnet simply don't cooperate with Homer and echo back everything you say and generally won't work properly.

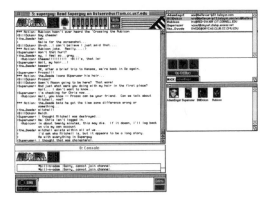

Internet Email and Internet News

MicroPhone Pro 2.0's Internet Mail and Internet News modules both use MicroPhone Pro's scripting language and both work over either a MacTCP connection or, more interestingly, a dialup connection to a shell account. They have similar, easy-to-use interfaces. Internet Mail is an offline mail reader—you read and write email offline and then connect to send replies and receive new messages. Unfortunately, Internet News is not an offline newsreader.

At about $150, MicroPhone Pro is relatively expensive, and I wouldn't buy it just for Internet Mail and Internet

News. Although these modules seem to work pretty well, there are a number of rough edges. More seriously, Internet Mail and Internet News, because of their heritage as MicroPhone Pro scripts, are slow as molasses, not in transfers so much as in basic execution. However, on the positive side, they're easier to set up than Eudora and most of the newsreaders, and if you do want MicroPhone Pro anyway, they're a welcome addition. You can contact Software Ventures at **microphone@svcdudes.com** or 510-644-3232.

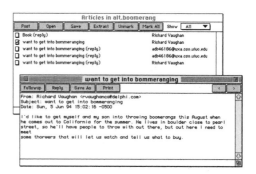

http://www.svcdudes.com/

MacNews

Matt Hall's $15 shareware MacNews provides a graphical interface for reading Usenet news even if you have only a shell account. The only requirements are that your machine run an NNTP (Net News Transport Protocol) server or that your machine be able to contact one over the Internet. MacNews is decidedly a work-in-progress, and it lacks enough features that you may not want to lose all those you enjoy in a Unix newsreader in terms of reading and killing threads. On the other hand, the ability to use cut and paste and look at a Macintosh interface may outweigh the disadvantages.

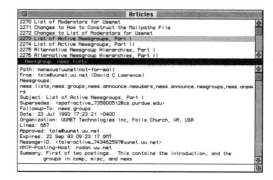

MacSOUP

Stefan Kurth's MacSOUP is a bit of an odd program in that it requires the use of a program called uqwk on your Unix account to provide offline news and mail reading from a shell account. I have no idea how common or easily installed uqwk might be. That said, uqwk was already installed on my Unix shell account, and the commands provided in MacSOUP's excellent documentation worked perfectly for creating a soup packet file containing all my mail and the messages in the newsgroups I read, and then downloading that file for use on the Mac. In my brief testing, MacSOUP worked well, and its interface, although a touch clumsy in spots, was easy to use and generally well done. If you have uqwk on your Unix account (try typing the command to see if you get a response) or can easily install it, I'd recommend that you take a look at MacSOUP.

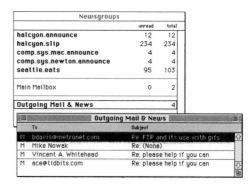

NewsWatcher-SFU

Ray Davison of Simon Fraser University has modified an old version (2.0d17) of John Norstad's excellent NewsWatcher program to work over a serial line, much like Eudora. I haven't tried configuring this newsreader, in large part because it sounds like it's a bit harder than would be ideal, but it works on very

NewsWatcher-SFU

much the same lines as Eudora SFU and requires the same sort of chat script edited in ResEdit.

```
ftp://ftp.sfu.ca/pub/mac/newswatcher/
```

TheNews

I want to like Bill Cramer's $25 shareware program TheNews because of its flexibility. Like Eudora, it can work with shell accounts, UUCP accounts, and MacTCP-based connections. However, I have trouble with TheNews every time I try to use it, so I won't look at it in detail. I'll settle for warning you that TheNews is slow to start up, at least over a MacTCP-based connection, because it seemingly downloads the full list of newsgroups every time you launch the program. It's also memory-hungry—it comes configured to use 1,300K in the Finder's Get Info window, but it crashed when I tried to sort the full group list until I doubled that number.

```
ftp://ftp.tidbits.com/pub/tidbits/tisk/tcp/
```

Terminal Emulators

I don't want to get into reviewing all of the possible terminal emulation programs available for the Macintosh because there are a ton of them. However, you must have a terminal emulator to talk to a Unix machine, so here are some capsule reviews for those I've heard of and/or used.

> **N o t e**
>
> *A number of these terminal emulators work through the Communications Toolbox and require CTB tools. Luckily, except for Termy, they all ship with a full complement. You can find additional freely distributed tools in:*
>
> ```
> ftp://ftp.tidbits.com/pub/tidbits/tisk/ctb/
> ```
>
> ```
> ftp://ftp.support.apple.com/pub/apple_sw_updates/US/mac/n_c/comm_toolbox_tools/
> ```

Communicate and Communicate Lite

Communicate and Communicate Lite are relatively simple terminal emulators from Mark/Space Softworks that use the Communications Toolbox. Communicate Lite is pretty much bare-bones terminal emulation; the more powerful Communicate adds features such as an In/Out box for queuing up uploads and downloads, scripting via AppleScript or Frontier, automated virus detection, and spell checking via Apple events. Contact Mark/Space Softworks at **mspace@netcom.com**. You can find a demo of Communicate Lite that has the Save, Save As, Open, and Session Directory commands disabled in the below URL.

Part III   Shell Account Enhancements

```
ftp://ftp.tidbits.com/pub/tidbits/tisk/term/
```

Crosstalk for Macintosh

I know little about DCA's Macintosh version of the popular PC Crosstalk communications programs, except for the fact that it is CTB-aware and comes with a slew of CTB tools (22 tools for emulating different terminals and 15 tools for transfer protocols). If you're having trouble finding a terminal emulator to emulate a specific type of terminal, it might be worth checking out Crosstalk for Macintosh. Crosstalk also has its own powerful scripting language and generally costs about $120 (mail order).

MicroPhone

MicroPhone is probably the most popular terminal emulation package on the Macintosh. It comes in a number of different forms, including MicroPhone LT for about $40, MicroPhone II 5.0 for about $120, and MicroPhone Pro 2.0 (which includes fax software and various Internet tools such as Snatcher and Fetch) for about $150. MicroPhone is a powerful, fully laden terminal emulator with its own scripting language. Contact Software Ventures at 510-644-3232 or **microphone@svcdudes.com**.

```
http://www.svcdudes.com/
```

SITcomm

Aladdin Systems came out with SITcomm early in 1994, and it won a loyal following immediately because it's a small, relatively simple terminal emulator that still sports some neat features. SITcomm is completely CTB-aware and comes with all the connection and transfer tools that you might want. Perhaps most importantly, though, SITcomm is completely Apple event-driven, which means that you can script it in either AppleScript or Frontier and you can even record AppleScript or Frontier scripts from within SITcomm. SITcomm's cool features include a slick address book that simplifies connecting to many commercial services, automatic compression and expansion using Aladdin's StuffIt technology, and voice feedback. SITcomm costs about $50 (mail order), and you can contact Aladdin at **aladdin@well.sf.ca.us** or 408-761-6200.

Termy

Termy is an extremely simple, free terminal emulator from Tim Endres, the programmer behind InterCon's UUCP/Connect and the free TGE TCP Tool. Termy doesn't do much on its own but is CTB-aware, so if you have Communications Toolbox tools, you can use them with Termy for a basic terminal emulation solution. You will need the basic CTB tools for Termy.

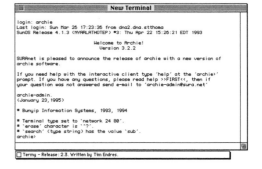

`ftp://ftp.tidbits.com/pub/tidbits/tisk/term/`

VersaTerm

VersaTerm has garnered a reputation among those who know for having the most solid terminal emulations, especially for the stranger types of graphics terminals from Tektronix. The $120 VersaTerm itself supports a number of emulation modes, and the $170 VersaTerm Pro adds even more emulations. Both programs come with the VersaTilities, a collection of TCP/IP tools and utilities, which you can also buy separately for about $85 (all prices mail order). Contact Synergy at **maxwell@sales.synergy.com** for more information.

ZTerm

Although not CTB-aware, ZTerm has gained a loyal following among telecommunications users because of its simple interface and speedy ZMODEM transfer protocol. ZTerm is shareware from Dave Alverson and is available at the below URL.

Part III — Shell Account Enhancements

```
ftp://ftp.tidbits.com/pub/tidbits/tisk/term/
```

Shell-Shocked

If many of the programs I've talked about in this chapter seem like fairly serious hacks, well, you're right, for the most part they are. I wouldn't really recommend that you kill yourself trying to use any of these programs other than TIA and Eudora in CTB mode, or possibly MacSOUP. The others, although potentially useful if you can get them working fairly easily, simply aren't worth much effort. TIA is definitely the best choice, because once you've got it installed on your shell account and MacTCP and InterSLIP properly configured, you can skip right ahead and read about all the issues relating to MacTCP accounts and programs. Otherwise, you should delve a bit deeper into the other possibilities mentioned previously.

It's time to move on to another way you can connect to the Internet, the UUCP account. Although old and a bit clunky, UUCP connections to the Internet are still useful and extremely efficient ways to use email and Usenet news.

UUCP Access

[This page intentionally left blank.]

Where'd It Go?

Hey! What happened to my chapter! I know I left it here last night and then when I got up this morning, it was gone. Police!

Actually, there was no foul play. There's a reasonable, if unfortunate explanation for the reason why the UUCP chapter simply isn't here anymore. Although in previous editions of the book UUCP was more important because MacTCP connections were relatively hard to find, that's no longer true. Nowadays it's probably quite a bit harder to find a UUCP connection. Even still, I was successfully resisting pressure to eliminate the chapter, arguing that it was useful to some people.

Then the blow came. The book was 70 pages too long, and because paper prices have skyrocketed since the first and second editions came out, page count has become a big deal. Hayden wanted to keep the price of the book the same, $30, but to do so required that those 70 pages bite the dust. Selflessly, and without showing weakness, the UUCP sacrificed itself so that the other chapters could reach the public. Now if only I could get that melancholy theme music to play right about now…

In return for removing the UUCP information from the book, Hayden has allowed me to do what I want with the existing text. I realize that you may not have any email access at the moment, at which point I can't help you. If you do have email access, send email to **uucp-chapter@tidbits.com** to receive an auto-reply message that tells you how and in what formats you can get the text of the UUCP chapter. Very few changes were made from the previous editions of the book since UUCP software is essentially static right now, so if you have one of the previous editions, don't worry about it.

My most sincere apologies for having to remove this information.

A Quick Reminder about UUCP

Although by no means the snazziest method of connecting to the Internet, UUCP access is often the most efficient for basic email and news, because it's inherently a noninteractive process. Your host machine sends messages to your Mac in the form of files, which the UUCP software then processes for display. This process accounts for the acronym as well. UUCP stands for Unix-to-Unix CoPy (the copy command in Unix is cp).

With a UUCP connection, you connect only to send or receive information. When you read news or write a reply to an email message, your modem is not connected and racking up connect charges. UUCP appeared in the days of the 300 bps modem. Although it has scaled up just fine to faster connections, even direct Internet connections, it still works well at slower speeds, because the actual connection time is usually relatively short.

Again, if you wish to read the UUCP chapter, send email to **uucp-chapter@tidbits.com** to find out how to get it.

IV

Full Internet Access

We've finally hit the really good stuff! I titled this part of the book "Full Internet Access" because everything else we've talked about so far has either been background material or has been somehow limited. With full Internet access, as discussed in this section, you will find that your only limitations are how fast your modem can go if you need to use a PPP or SLIP connection, and how much time you want to spend using the Internet.

Chapter 16, Internet Starter Kit Disk

All of the chapters in Part IV, "Full Internet Access," rely on your having a full, MacTCP-based Internet connection. The easiest way to get such a connection is to use the software I've included for you on the ISKM disk, and use the ISKM Installer to install it for you. Different configurations are provided for use with the Internet Starter Kit Providers (see appendix A for a full list), but of course, the software works with any Internet provider who offers PPP or SLIP accounts, or even with any dedicated Internet connection. Chapter 16, "Internet Starter Kit Disk," explains exactly what the ISKM Installer installs, where it installs the various files, and all of those good details that you probably wish other installers provided for you.

Chapter 17, MacTCP

MacTCP is the most necessary piece of the puzzle, because without MacTCP, none of the programs mentioned from here on will work well or at all. Although it requires some configuring, MacTCP is really quite simple. The ISKM Installer prevents you from needing to do much at all. But the details of exactly how you configure MacTCP are of interest, especially if something doesn't work right. Chapter 17, "MacTCP," takes you through configuring MacTCP, reveals the nasty little details of how certain confusing parts of the interface work, and finishes with a look at a few useful MacTCP utilities.

Chapter 18, PPP

MacTCP by itself won't make your Internet connection, though, and for that you need either a direct Internet connection via a network, or a modem and either PPP or SLIP. I recommend PPP to most people, and if your Internet access provider supports PPP, it's the best way to go. In chapter 18, "PPP," I go through the steps of configuring MacPPP, the freeware version of PPP installed by the ISKM Installer, and then take a look at some other implementations of PPP and PPP utilities.

Chapter 19, SLIP

Although I recommend PPP, SLIP is still in wide use and it's functionally identical to PPP in terms of you being able to use the same programs. You must have a different sort of account, a SLIP account, of course, but if that's all your provider offers (often through The Internet Adapter, or TIA, which I discussed back in chapter 14, "Shell Account Enhancements"), then SLIP should work fine for you. I work through the steps for configuring InterSLIP, a free, although unsupported, implementation of SLIP from InterCon Systems, and then briefly look at other implementations of SLIP and some SLIP utilities.

Chapter 20, Troubleshooting Your Connection

Murphy's Law is right up there with gravity as one of the fundamental forces in the universe. I won't pretend that your connection will necessarily work perfectly on the first try, despite our best efforts. In those unfortunate cases, the best help I can provide is in chapter 20, "Troubleshooting Your Connection," where I outline, in the traditional and time-honored form of a FAQ (Frequently Asked Question) list, all the questions and answers that I know. I'm really not holding back on you here—this chapter contains everything I can think of that might go wrong and the solution, assuming there is one. Do read through this carefully, and even if you're using MacPPP, say, scan through the InterSLIP section to see if a similar problem to yours may have been reported and solved for InterSLIP. Troubleshooting is a great mystery game in which no one dies, so just take a deep breath, put on your deerstalker cap, and read on for all the clues to solving your problem.

Chapters 21 through 25, 27, & 28

Finally! On to the MacTCP-based programs. Chapter 21, "Email," starts you off by discussing client programs for using email, the ubiquitous Internet service. Of course, with Qualcomm's excellent Eudora in the field, none of the rest can even compete, so I concentrate on Eudora (which is included on the ISKM disk). Chapter 22, "Usenet News," moves on to a more congested area and looks at the main Usenet newsreaders available for the Macintosh. NewsWatcher, Nuntius, and NewsHopper are all in the ring, and it's up to you choose which you prefer. Chapter 23, "FTP," also presents a few choices, with Anarchie (which is included on the ISKM disk) and Fetch vying for the crown. To me, it's fairly obvious that Anarchie is the overall winner, with Fetch and Software Ventures' Snatcher being useful primarily in specific situations. Chapter 24, "Gopher," has shrunk from previous editions, thanks to the rise of the World Wide Web and the resulting drop in importance of Gopher clients. It's down to TurboGopher now, although I do look at a few Gopher-related programs as well, including the extremely cool TurboGopher VR. Chapter 25, "World Wide Web," expanded as the Gopher section contracted, since the Web gets more attention than any other part of the Internet these days. I look at the main Web browsers, MacWeb (which is included on the ISKM disk) and Netscape.

You probably noticed my skipping over chapter 26 in the previous list; that's because chapter 26, "Creating Your Web Page," is a chapter of a different color (not literally) and although it follows on the heels of chapter 25's discussion of Web browsers, it deserves it's own description.

Meanwhile, back at chapter 27, "Utilities & Miscellany," I hit a slew of square programs that simply don't fit into the nice round holes of my organization. I'm talking about things like the videoconferencing application CU-SeeMe, Timbuktu Pro (which enables you to observe or control other Macs over the Internet), and the tank game Bolo. I've managed to break them up into some rough groups, but even still, it's a bit of a hodgepodge. Chapter 28, "Integrated Programs," goes 180 degrees in the other direction and talks about a couple of programs, TCP/Connect II from InterCon and VersaTerm-Link from Synergy, that integrated a number of Internet functions into a single program.

Chapter 26, Creating Your Web Page

As I mentioned previously, the Web is where the action is on the Internet these days, and I recognize that you probably want a piece of that action. So, in an effort to provide you with the best and tastiest information about HTML, the language of the Web, I drafted my lovely wife Tonya, who's the HTML expert in the family, to write chapter 26, "Creating Your Web Page." The chapter takes you through all the basic parts of HTML that you need to know to create your own Web page, giving examples along the way. Also, since this is a Macintosh book, Tonya looks at the basics of dealing with graphics on the Web through Macintosh-colored glasses. If you've struggled with some of the quirks and confusions while trying to create a Web page, this chapter is for you. It doesn't attempt to be a brain-dead tutorial since those are always both boring and pointless—you want to create *your* Web page, not some example. The chapter also doesn't attempt to provide a stilted and alphabetically organized reference to all the HTML tags—such references are available online on the Web (and we've got a compact one in appendix C, "HTML Tags"). Instead, chapter 26 combines the best of both approaches, concisely explaining all the important HTML tags in the order in which you're likely to need them while creating your own Web page.

Chapter 29, Step-by-Step Internet

In response to suggestions from readers of the first edition, I created this chapter to walk you through, step by numbered step, the absolute basics of using the main MacTCP-based Internet programs. Most of them are on the disk, and all are discussed elsewhere in the book. You should turn to this chapter if you're having trouble with the basics of how to send email, or how to browse the Web. Most of the time the problems are extremely simple, and once you get over the first hump, you're on your way.

Internet Starter Kit Disk

The disk that comes with *Internet Starter Kit for Macintosh* contains all the software you need to access the Internet! The software is compressed (using Aladdin's excellent StuffIt InstallerMaker) so that it can fit on a single high-density Macintosh disk. To install any or all of these programs, double-click on the ISKM Installer icon. See the following text for a detailed list of what's installed by each option in the ISKM Installer.

> **N o t e**
>
> *If you receive a disk that your Mac rejects, call Hayden/Macmillan Computer Publishing at 800-858-7674 or 317-581-7674. Do note that the disk is a 1.4 MB disk—it will not work in 800K drives used in very old Macs (the Plus, some SEs, and the Mac II).*

The ISKM disk includes:

- MacTCP 2.0.6, which enables your Macintosh to run MacTCP-based Internet programs.
- MacPPP 2.0.1, which enables you to use a modem to connect to a PPP account at your Internet access provider.
- InterSLIP 1.0.1, which enables you to use a modem to connect to a SLIP account at your Internet access provider, if they offer only SLIP.

- Anarchie 1.5, the best FTP client for any computer.

- Eudora 1.5.1, a powerful program that enables you to send and receive Internet email.

- Internet Config 1.1, which centralizes preferences like your email address for a number of Internet programs.

- MacWeb 1.00A3.2, an excellent browser for the World Wide Web that takes you to the Internet Starter Kit for Macintosh Home Page by default.

- StuffIt Expander 3.5.2, which can debinhex and expand the files you download from the Internet.

- Bookmarks for retrieving the latest versions of all the major Internet programs that I couldn't fit on the disk.

- Customized MacTCP Prep files for all the Internet Starter Kit Providers listed in appendix A.

Note

I recommend that you make a backup copy of the ISKM Installer in case anything should go wrong with your master copy. To do this, simply copy the ISKM Installer file from the ISKM disk to your hard disk. You can then copy it to another floppy disk if you want.

There's More...

But wait! Lest I sound too much like a late-night Ginsu knife commercial (has anyone *ever* bought one of those to cut beer cans?), I have in fact done even more.

ftp.tidbits.com

As I noted previously, I have bookmarks to the major Internet programs so you can download any one of them with merely a double-click of the mouse. But what if you want one of the less-popular programs, or simply want to check out what else is available? Have I got an FTP site for you...

I seem to have collected about 50 MB of software in the course of my testing, so including even 25 disks would barely have been enough, and they would have made the book kind of bulky. So, I had a talk with the folks at Northwest Nexus, and they agreed to set up an FTP site for me that everyone on the Internet could access. This way, you will have a single site to visit for all of your Macintosh Internet applications and utilities.

The FTP site is called **ftp.tidbits.com**, and you can use any standard method of accessing an anonymous FTP site. Just use **anonymous** as your username and your email address as your password. If the machine rejects your full email address as a password, try using just your username and an **@** sign, as in **ace@**; sometimes this particular FTP server is a bit finicky.

Here's a quick tutorial on connecting to the FTP site after you have installed and configured MacTCP (and MacPPP or InterSLIP, if necessary) and Anarchie, by using Internet Config. Connect to the Internet. Launch Anarchie. If your Bookmarks window doesn't appear automatically, from the File menu choose List Bookmarks. Scroll down in the list until you see TidBITS, and then double-click on that bookmark and then go into the "tisk" folder (it's a hold-over from the first edition, which I referred to in shorthand as TISK, for *The Internet Starter Kit*). Alternately, use the shortcuts I've set up for you with the bookmarks for ISKM HTML Programs, ISKM Internet Utility Programs, and ISKM MacTCP-based Programs that are higher up in the Bookmarks window.

When you double-click on one of these bookmarks, Anarchie connects to **ftp.tidbits.com**, switches into the proper directory, and lists the files. From there you can navigate around in the different folders by double-clicking on them. Double-clicking on a file retrieves it. It's that easy.

Part IV

Internet Starter Kit Disk

ISKM Home Page

The bookmarks and the FTP site are all fine and nice, but the more alert among my reading audience are no doubt asking themselves, "But how am I going to figure out that there's a new version of MacWeb, or Eudora, or whatever? And heck, how am I going to find anything I want on the Internet anyway?" Good question, alert readers, and the simple answer is that you'll use MacWeb or another Web browser to connect to the ISKM Home Page at:

```
http://www.mcp.com/hayden/iskm/
```

> **Note**
>
> *I've set the copy of MacWeb on the ISKM disk to connect to this page by default. However, if you've set a different home page in MacWeb previously, or wish to use Netscape or another Web browser, you can still use the URL for the ISKM Home Page as your default home page. All the programs have various ways, usually located in the Preferences, of setting a default home page.*

The ISKM Home Page has a number of links to the most important sites on the Internet, catalogs of resources like Yahoo, search engines like WebCrawler, important FTP sites like Info-Mac and UMich, and even a few of the major companies in the Macintosh industry, such as Apple and Microsoft. These links should be your starting point for any exploration of the Internet, and rest assured that if I find additional sites that I consider equally as useful, I'll add them.

In addition, at the top of the ISKM Home Page is a link, called "ISKM Macintosh Internet Software Updates," to another Web page that continually tracks the latest versions of all the main Internet applications for the Macintosh (so stop in every now and then and see what's changed). You can use your Anarchie bookmarks to retrieve any of these programs, or you can use a Web browser (although Anarchie is better at retrieving files).

Again, these pages are a public Internet resource and anyone, whether or not they've bought the book, is welcome to use them. If you find them useful, I'm glad, and I hope they might inspire you to think what you could contribute to the net someday.

ISKM Installer

I designed the ISKM Installer to be as easy as possible to use. I tried to think of the different things you might want to do with the various files on the disk, which is why I created several different installer options.

Note

The ISKM Installer will not *overwrite any existing files—if you want to replace a file such as MacTCP, you* must *first move it out of the System Folder manually, along with MacTCP DNR and MacTCP Prep. This is imperative if you have installed Apple's System 7.5 (which comes with MacTCP), if you are switching from SLIP to PPP, or if you have already used some of this software previously and wish to take advantage of the disk's included preferences and configurations.*

How to Install

As with most installers, using the ISKM Installer is a piece of cake. First, restart your Macintosh while holding down the Shift key. This process disables all of your extensions until you restart. Although not absolutely necessary, it's a good idea to do this to ensure that anti-virus software or other extensions don't interfere with the installation process (which they sometimes do).

Insert the ISKM floppy disk in your drive, and when the window comes up, double-click on the file called ISKM Installer. You should see the ISKM Installer splash screen. Click the Continue button. Next, the ISKM Installer presents you with a screen full of text that describes what the various options available in the ISKM Installer do, and offers other useful information. Read this information, and if you want, save or print it by clicking the Save or Print buttons. Then click the Continue button. The ISKM Installer then presents you with the Standard Install dialog (see figure 16.1).

Figure 16.1   *ISKM Installer Standard Install dialog.*

Here's where you must make your first decision.

- If you want to use MacPPP, select the standard **Full MacPPP Install**, which installs all the applications and MacTCP and MacPPP, along with all of the MacTCP Prep files for the Internet Starter Kit Providers. A partially configured PPP Preferences file containing some modem configurations is also installed for you. Contact your provider for the information necessary to finish configuring MacPPP and the rest of the applications.

- If you want to use InterSLIP instead of MacPPP, click the Custom button in the ISKM Installer and select **Full InterSLIP Install**. This installs all of the applications, MacTCP, and InterSLIP, and a number of dialing and gateway scripts to use as examples. Contact your provider for the information necessary to finish configuring MacTCP, InterSLIP, and the rest of the applications. Thoughtful providers may have an InterSLIP gateway script already created for you.

- If you want to install any one or more of the individual programs, click the Custom button in the ISKM Installer and select the appropriate option. You can select more than one at a time by Command-clicking on them. Of course, if this is your first installation, installing individual programs won't provide all the pieces you need to access the Internet.

The most likely option is **Full MacPPP Install**, and if that's what you want to do, click the Install button. The ISKM Installer informs you that you must restart your computer after installing and asks if you would like to continue.

If you have any unsaved work open in other applications, click the No button and then the Quit button back in the Standard Install dialog. Save your work, quit the other applications, and repeat the steps to this point. When you are ready to install, click the Yes button when the ISKM Installer asks about restarting. Next, you're presented with a Standard File dialog that enables you to locate the ISKM3 Folder anywhere on your hard disk that you like.

After you choose a location and click the Save button, the ISKM Installer proceeds to install everything, and when it's done, it informs you that everything has been installed correctly and forces you to click on a Restart button. Click it, and after your computer restarts, you're ready to configure the software that was installed for you.

Configuring MacTCP

There are two possibilities at this point. First, if you're not working with one of the Internet Starter Kit Providers listed in appendix A, contact your provider for the information you need to configure MacTCP. Read chapter 17, "MacTCP," and chapter 29, "Step-by-Step Internet," for instructions on how to actually perform the configuration (and follow them up with either chapter 18, "PPP," or chapter 19, "SLIP," depending on which you use). If you run into trouble, first read chapter 20, "Troubleshooting Your Connection," and then turn to your provider for help.

Second, if you are working with one of the Internet Starter Kit Providers listed in appendix A, configuring MacTCP is trivial. In your ISKM3 Folder, find the folder called Customized MacTCP Prep Files. In it are a number of folders, each named for one of the Internet Starter Kit Providers. Within each of these folders is a MacTCP Prep file.

Next, open your System Folder and see if you have a MacTCP DNR file. If you do, throw it out. MacTCP creates a new one when you restart anyway, and you don't want any old configurations hanging around.

Still inside your System Folder, open your Preferences folder. Make sure you are in View by Name mode in the Finder (choose by Name from the View menu), and scroll down to see if you have a MacTCP Prep file already. If you do, drag that file out of the Preferences folder and put it on your desktop. You can throw it away later, or, if you've used MacTCP before and know you want to save its settings, hold onto it for future use.

After you've removed any existing MacTCP Prep files, hold down the Option key and drag the MacTCP Prep file from the appropriate Internet Starter Kit Provider's folder over to your Preferences folder. By holding down the Option key, you ensure that you make a *copy* of the file, rather than moving the original. That original might be handy later on if you change things and need to quickly reconfigure MacTCP to your original settings.

Now that you've moved the appropriate MacTCP Prep file over to your Preferences folder, choose Restart from the Special menu to restart your Macintosh. When it restarts, open MacTCP and click the More button to confirm that it has picked up the settings for your provider from the MacTCP Prep file that you installed. If it hasn't, Option-drag another copy into your Preferences folder, replacing the previous MacTCP Prep file, and restart again, perhaps turning off any unnecessary extensions that might be interfering.

Configuring MacPPP

Now you must configure MacPPP. The ISKM Installer tries to configure MacPPP for you, but there are some pieces of information that only you know. Open the Config PPP control panel that the ISKM Installer has installed for you in the Control Panels folder (see figure 16.2).

Figure 16.2   *Config PPP control panel.*

If your provider uses only SLIP, unlike the Internet Starter Kit Providers listed in appendix A, refer to chapter 19, "SLIP," and chapter 29, "Step-by-Step Internet," for instructions on configuring InterSLIP in conjunction with the information that your Internet provider gives you. The hardest part of InterSLIP is making sure you have a properly written gateway script—I've included several as examples in case you need to write your own.

If you have your modem connected to your Printer port for some reason, select that port in the Port Name pop-up menu. If you use an Apple Express Modem or a Global Village PowerPort Mercury with either the PowerBook Duo or the PowerBook 500-series, choose Internal Modem from the pop-up menu. For most other internal PowerBook modems, the Modem choice is still correct. Then, from the PPP Server pop-up menu, select the modem configuration that most closely matches yours—if none look right, select SupraFAXModem v.32bis, which uses a generic initialization string and should work with any Hayes-compatible modem.

Other users contributed these modem configurations—I can't guarantee that they work because I don't have most of these modems to test on. You may have to use your modem manual or call your modem vendor to decide on a different modem init string. Also, I've only entered the most likely strings in Config PPP—there are even more in a file called Modem Strings in the MacPPP 2.0.1 folder.

Click the Config button to bring up the Server Configuration dialog (see figure 16.3).

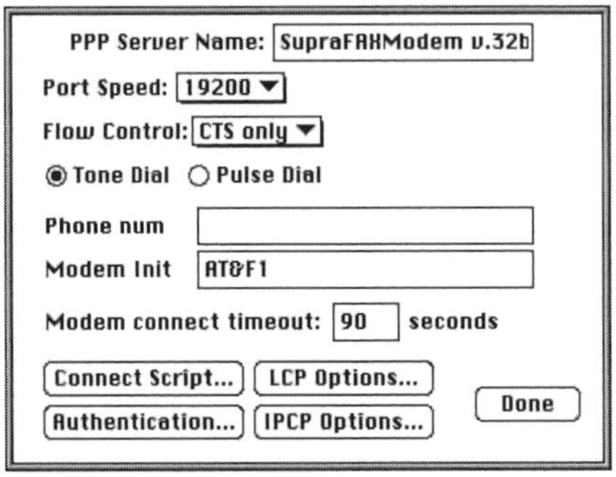

PPP Server Name: |SupraFAHModem v.32b|

Port Speed: |19200 ▼|

Flow Control: |CTS only ▼|

◉ Tone Dial ○ Pulse Dial

Phone num | |

Modem Init |AT&F1 |

Modem connect timeout: |90| seconds

[Connect Script...] [LCP Options...]
[Authentication...] [IPCP Options...]   [Done]

Figure 16.3   *MacPPP Server Configuration dialog.*

First, enter your phone number. If you're calling long distance, you probably must enter the digit **1** before the number. If you're dialing out through a large phone system in a company or in a hotel room, you may have to prefix the number with **8,** or **9,**. In both cases, the comma tells the modem to pause for two seconds before dialing.

If you don't think the modem init string that's installed for you will work with your modem, enter the appropriate one in the Modem Init field. Check your modem manual— don't guess! Make sure your modem init string turns hardware handshaking on and XON/XOFF off.

If you're using a 28.8 Kbps modem and there wasn't a configuration for you in Config PPP's pop-up menu, choose 38400 from the Port Speed pop-up menu. If you're using a 14.4 Kbps modem, choose 19200. In both cases, if everything works right, you can increase that speed to 57600. Never select either 28800 or 14400—some modems simply don't work with those settings.

Time for another decision. If your provider uses PAP, or Password Authentication Protocol, click the Authentication dialog and enter your userid and password (given to you by your provider) in the dialog. Then click the Connect Script button and erase all the fields and turn off the <CR> checkboxes. Although useful, PAP isn't yet supported by all Internet providers.

If your provider does not support PAP, you must edit the Connect Script. Click the Connect Script button (see figure 16.4).

The template script that I've entered here may or may not be correct. It's the most common, and it is likely to work for most providers. However, your provider may require you to send the string PPP after you login, or something like that. Check your provider's instructions to see if the connect script differs from the template. In all likelihood it won't, and if it does, it won't differ significantly.

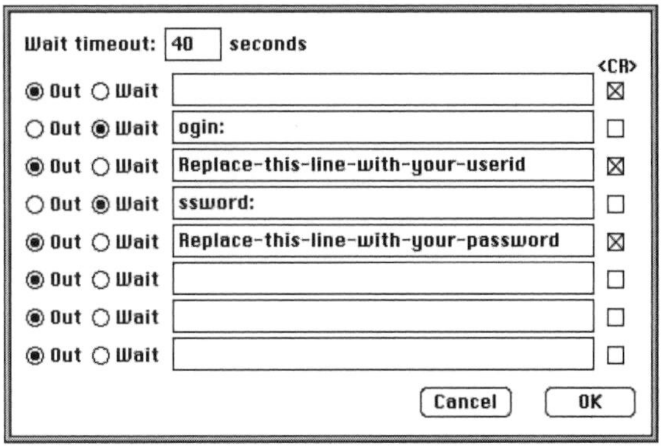

Wait timeout:	40	seconds	
			<CR>
⦿ Out ○ Wait			⊠
○ Out ⦿ Wait	ogin:		☐
⦿ Out ○ Wait	Replace-this-line-with-your-userid		⊠
○ Out ⦿ Wait	ssword:		☐
⦿ Out ○ Wait	Replace-this-line-with-your-password		⊠
⦿ Out ○ Wait			☐
⦿ Out ○ Wait			☐
⦿ Out ○ Wait			☐

Cancel   OK

Figure 16.4 *MacPPP Connect Script dialog.*

Enter your userid and your password in the fields marked for them, replacing all of the template text. Make sure to enter your userid and your password in exactly the same case as they were given to you. For the purposes of a userid or password, "Adam" and "adam" are completely different. Click the OK button to save your changes, and back in the Server Configuration dialog, click the Done button.

You should now be able to click the Open button in the Config PPP control panel to establish your connection to your PPP account. If you have troubles, first review the section in chapters 17 and 18 about setting up MacTCP and MacPPP and also read chapter 20, "Troubleshooting Your Connection."

Configuring Eudora and Email

To configure Eudora for use with your account, you must enter your POP account and real name (and possibly an SMTP server) in Eudora's Getting Started section in the Settings dialog. See chapter 21, "Email," and chapter 29, "Step-by-Step Internet," for detailed instructions. Your provider should have given you all of the information to enter into Eudora.

Configuring Usenet News

To properly use any of the newsreaders, you must know a few pieces of information. Most important is the name of your NNTP server, also called a news server, and the name of your SMTP, or mail server. Some providers may require a userid and password, which are usually the same as the userid and password you use in Eudora. Again, your Internet provider gives you this information. If you use either NewsWatcher or NewsHopper, use Internet Config (see chapter 27, "Utilities & Miscellany") to enter this information. Otherwise, simply refer to chapter 22, "Usenet News," and chapter 29, "Step-by-Step Internet."

Configuring Anarchie and FTP

To use Anarchie, you must first enter your email address (which Anarchie uses as a password for anonymous FTP sites) in Internet Config. See chapter 27, "Utilities & Miscellany," and chapter 29, "Step-by-Step Internet," for instructions on how to configure Internet Config, and see chapter 23, "FTP," and chapter 29, "Step-by-Step Internet," for additional information about Anarchie.

Configuring Other MacTCP-based Applications

MacWeb (see chapter 25, "World Wide Web") requires no configuration at all, and as you've probably noticed by now, it's a good idea to run through all the settings in Internet Config quickly for use with Anarchie, NewsWatcher, and NewsHopper. See chapter 27, "Utilities & Miscellany," and chapter 29, "Step-by-Step Internet," for instructions on how to configure Internet Config.

That's all there is to it—enjoy your Internet connection!

> **N o t e**
>
> *After you install all the software, configure MacPPP or InterSLIP, and make the connection to your PPP or SLIP account, you can run the great programs discussed in chapters 21 through 28. MacPPP and InterSLIP do nothing more than establish the connection.*

Installation Details

Installers are good at putting files in specific places, but they seldom tell you exactly where the various files have ended up. The following information explains where everything ends up on your hard disk, organized by installation option.

Installation Option Details

This section details precisely what files each installation option installs and where those files are installed on your disk.

Full MacPPP Install

■ MacTCP: MacTCP is installed in the Control Panels folder.

■ Customized MacTCP Prep Files: A Customized MacTCP Prep Files folder is installed in the ISKM3 Folder that you save on your hard disk.

■ MacPPP: Config PPP is installed in your Control Panels folder, PPP is installed in your Extensions folder, and PPP Preferences is installed in your Preferences folder. A MacPPP 2.0.1 folder containing documentation and modem strings is installed in your ISKM3 Folder.

■ InterSLIP: InterSLIP is not installed.

■ Anarchie: Anarchie is installed in your ISKM3 Folder. You should use Internet Config to configure Anarchie's Preferences with your email address.

■ Eudora: Eudora is installed in your ISKM3 Folder. You must configure Eudora with your POP Account and real name before using it.

■ Internet Config: Internet Config is installed in your ISKM3 Folder. You must configure your email address in Internet Config before you use Anarchie.

■ MacWeb: MacWeb is installed in your ISKM3 Folder.

■ StuffIt Expander: StuffIt Expander is installed in your ISKM3 Folder. You may want to move the program to your desktop because you will probably be dropping many files on it to debinhex and expand them.

■ Get New Internet Programs: This folder, containing the bookmarks that point at the latest versions of the most useful Internet programs stored on `ftp.tidbits.com`, is installed in your ISKM3 Folder.

Full InterSLIP Install

■ MacTCP: MacTCP is installed in the Control Panels folder.

■ Customized MacTCP Prep Files: The Customized MacTCP Prep Files folder is not installed because the Internet Starter Kit Providers offer PPP connections.

■ MacPPP: MacPPP is not installed.

■ InterSLIP: InterSLIP Setup is installed in your ISKM3 Folder. InterSLIP Control is installed in your System Folder only if you use System 6. The InterSLIP extension is installed in your Extensions folder. An InterSLIP Folder is installed in your Preferences folder in the System Folder; it contains a Dialing Scripts folder with several dialing scripts, and a Gateway Scripts folder with several example gateway scripts. An InterSLIP 1.0.1 folder containing InterSLIP Setup, documentation, and modem strings is installed in the ISKM3 Folder that you save on your hard disk.

■ Anarchie: Anarchie is installed in your ISKM3 Folder. You should use Internet Config to configure Anarchie's Preferences with your email address.

- Eudora: Eudora is installed in your ISKM3 Folder. You must configure Eudora with your POP Account and real name before using it.
- Internet Config: Internet Config is installed in your ISKM3 Folder. You must configure your email address in Internet Config before you use Anarchie.
- MacWeb: MacWeb is installed in your ISKM3 Folder.
- StuffIt Expander: StuffIt Expander is installed in your ISKM3 Folder. You may want to move the program to your desktop because you will probably be dropping many files on it to debinhex and expand them.
- Get New Internet Programs: This folder, containing the bookmarks that point at the latest versions of the most useful Internet programs stored on **ftp.tidbits.com**, is installed in your ISKM3 Folder.

MacTCP Only

- MacTCP: MacTCP is installed in the Control Panels folder. If you use this option to reinstall MacTCP after removing a corrupted version, make sure to restart after throwing out the old MacTCP, MacTCP DNR, and MacTCP Prep. Otherwise, your new version may retain the corruption.

MacPPP Only

- MacPPP: Config PPP is installed in your Control Panels folder; PPP is installed in your Extensions folder; and PPP Preferences is installed in your Preferences folder. A MacPPP 2.0.1 folder containing documentation is installed in the ISKM3 Folder that you save on your hard disk.

InterSLIP Only

- InterSLIP: InterSLIP Setup is installed in your ISKM3 Folder. InterSLIP Control is installed in your Control Panels folder only if you use System 6. The InterSLIP extension is installed in your Extensions folder. An InterSLIP Folder is installed in your Preferences folder; it contains a Dialing Scripts folder with several dialing scripts and a Gateway Scripts folder with several example gateway scripts. An InterSLIP 1.0.1 folder containing InterSLIP Setup and documentation is installed in the ISKM3 Folder that you save on your hard disk.

Anarchie Only

- Anarchie: Anarchie is installed in your ISKM3 Folder. You should use Internet Config to configure Anarchie's Preferences with your email address.

Eudora Only

■ Eudora: Eudora is installed in your ISKM3 Folder. Before using it, you must customize Eudora with your POP Account and real name.

Internet Config Only

■ Internet Config: Internet Config is installed in your ISKM3 Folder. You must configure your email address in Internet Config before you use Anarchie.

MacWeb Only

■ MacWeb: MacWeb is installed in your ISKM3 Folder.

StuffIt Expander Only

■ StuffIt Expander: StuffIt Expander is installed in your ISKM3 Folder. You may want to move the program to your desktop for easy access.

Bookmarks for New Internet Programs Only

■ Get New Internet Programs: This folder, containing the bookmarks that point at the latest versions of the most useful Internet programs stored on **ftp.tidbits.com**, is installed in your ISKM3 Folder.

Customized MacTCP Prep Files Only

■ Customized MacTCP Prep Files: A Customized MacTCP Prep Files folder is installed in your ISKM3 Folder.

Moving on to MacTCP

Now that you've installed the software from the ISKM disk, the time has come to learn how it works, assuming you haven't already jumped ahead and read about MacTCP and MacPPP in the following chapters.

MacTCP

"The time has come," the Walrus said,
"To talk of many things:
Of news—and chips—and Gopher hacks,
Of Babbage's—and pings."

Apologies to Lewis Carroll, but the time has come to talk of many things, all of them dependent on Apple's MacTCP. I'm going to start by discussing MacTCP itself, which Hayden licensed from Apple to put on the disk that comes with this book. I also take a quick look at Open Transport, MacTCP's successor, which is currently in testing and may be out before the next edition of this book. With those preliminaries out of the way, let's check out MacTCP 2.0.6.

MacTCP

Roughly speaking, MacTCP is a translator. It enables the Macintosh to speak the language of the Internet, TCP/IP (*Transmission Control Protocol/Internet Protocol*). Normally, of course, Macs speak AppleTalk to one another, over Macintosh networks. You must have the MacTCP control panel installed and configured properly, in order for the MacTCP-based programs such as Fetch and Netscape to work, although MacTCP does not make the connection itself. Think of MacTCP as the Babel Fish from the *Hitchhiker's Guide to the Galaxy*. Pop it in your Mac's ear (the Control Panel folder, actually), and your Mac understands the Internet noise that flows in and out. The metaphor of speaking and languages isn't quite accurate because TCP/IP is actually a transport protocol. But the idea of MacTCP as a Babel Fish that translates Internet gibberish into a language the Mac can understand seems to be the most understandable metaphor. Luckily, everything that MacTCP does happens at such a low level that you never notice. In fact, after you set up MacTCP correctly, you should never notice that it's present.

After your Mac is connected to the Internet with MacTCP and a network, SLIP, PPP, or Apple Remote Access (ARA), it is essentially the same as any other Internet machine and has its own IP number. This means that you can connect to other Internet machines directly, without going through an intermediate machine. You can also, if you want, run server software to turn your Mac into an FTP, Gopher, or Web server, although that really requires a permanent Internet connection.

> **N o t e**
>
> *Because the Internet is based on the TCP/IP protocols, the only way for a Mac to enjoy a full Internet connection is to use MacTCP. If you do not have MacTCP installed and a MacTCP-based connection using PPP, SLIP, ARA, or a Internet-connected network, you cannot use the MacTCP-based programs. Period.*

Apple and other companies have thought in the past that MacTCP is a program that only large organizations want to buy, install, and configure. Accordingly, most of the documentation I've seen makes this assumption, too. It's a poor assumption these days, because individuals using PPP or SLIP can easily gain access to the Internet, and PPP and SLIP require MacTCP. However, if you work at a university or business that provides your Internet connection, it's a good bet that you have a network administrator who knows a great deal about MacTCP, and who has probably preconfigured it for your convenience.

> **N o t e**
>
> *Evidence that this view of MacTCP is changing comes from Apple's inclusion of MacTCP in System 7.5. If you have System 7.5, even if you've never tried to connect to the Internet, you very well may have MacTCP already installed (but not configured).*

In fact, a system administrator can preconfigure and then lock MacTCP (using another control panel called AdminTCP) so you can't change any of this information. I'm assuming that you want to use the version of MacTCP that I include on the disk, though, and that version enables anyone to configure it.

Because those of you with network administrators can ask them for help, I concentrate on details of interest to the individual who has no local network administrator and must rely solely on this book and the system administrator at a public provider.

Along with the help text that's built into my installer for you to save or print (and I strongly recommend you do this), you may want to browse through a document about MacTCP written by Eric Behr. It's available at:

```
ftp://ftp.tidbits.com/pub/tidbits/tisk/info/mactcp-info-13.hqx
```

If You Use an Internet Starter Kit Provider

This chapter may seem a bit long, and if you've skimmed through it already, involved. It is; I won't pretend otherwise. However, there's a reason for that.

There are three types of people who are reading this chapter. The first type just wants to get on the Internet quickly and plans to use one of the Internet access providers listed in appendix A, "Internet Starter Kit Providers." If you fall into this group, you should not need to configure much, if *anything*, in MacTCP. The ISKM Installer provides precon-figured MacTCP Prep files, which contain the settings you need. The ISKM Installer installs a folder called "Customized MacTCP Prep Files," which contains a number of other folders named for the various Internet Starter Kit providers. To configure MacTCP, just hold down the Option key (this makes a copy of the file rather than just moving it) and drag the appropriate MacTCP Prep file for your provider into your Preferences Folder in the System Folder, and then restart. Bear in mind that if you have previously configured MacTCP, the new MacTCP Prep file will replace the old one.

The second type of reader cannot work with one of the Internet Starter Kit providers for some reason, usually related to none of them being a local call. If you fall into this cat-egory, unless the provider you sign up with locally has excellent instructions, you may have to configure MacTCP from scratch. This chapter provides all the background infor-mation to help you do this—you must still get the specific details from your provider.

Third and finally, some readers simply want to know more about how MacTCP works, or perhaps they may need to know about it to better troubleshoot some problem. I've tried to explain all the quirks that you're likely to hit in MacTCP, and in conjunction with chapter 20, "Troubleshooting Your Connection," feel that I've provided a lot of useful information that should help you if you have troubles.

So, if you work with one of the Internet Starter Kit providers, you can pretty much ignore this chapter, assuming everything works properly. Otherwise, read on!

MacTCP Questions

Now, let's go over the questions that you need to ask, and get your Internet access pro-vider to answer, before you can configure MacTCP on your own. First, of course, comes the connection method—via PPP or SLIP, or network. If you connect via PPP or SLIP, there are a number of other questions you must ask. Before you call your provider, read the next few chapters on PPP and SLIP (depending on which you must use, of course) to find out how to configure MacTCP. If you're connecting via a network, most of the same rules apply, but again, your network administrator knows the details. And, frankly, although you're somewhat more likely to use a Manually-addressed account when connecting via a network, things are usually easier without the added PPP or SLIP layer.

Second, find out whether you are supposed to determine your address *Manually*, whether it's assigned dynamically when you call the *Server* each time, or *Dynamically* at random (which is apparently seldom used, dangerous, and worth avoiding). Keep reading, but those three italicized terms are extremely important and confusing because each corresponds to a choice in the MacTCP control panel; the way people talk about the methods doesn't always correspond.

Note

Again, if you use one of the Internet Starter Kit Providers listed in appendix A, you do not need to collect any of this information!

In talking with system administrators, I find that most call Manually-addressed accounts *static* (because your IP address is assigned once and never changes) and Server-addressed accounts *dynamic* (because the server assigns you a different IP address on the fly each time you connect). You see the problem. I've never heard of anyone using a Dynamically-addressed account outside of a controlled laboratory situation, complete with rats, mazes, and spilled ink. (Okay, so I exaggerate slightly. But only slightly.)

If you have a Manually-addressed account, you must find out what your IP address number will be. It will be four numbers, separated by periods, and should look something like **192.135.191.128**. If you connect manually, you also need a gateway address number in the same format. You may need this gateway address with a server-addressed account as well, but MacTCP doesn't allow you to enter it—some implementations of SLIP do. Depending on the configuration of your site, you may also need to find out your network class and subnet mask, and your network administrator should know what to tell you here. People who use PPP and SLIP do not, for the most part, ever need to configure the network class and subnet mask part of MacTCP.

No matter what, you need to know the numeric IP addresses of one or more *domain name servers*, which are machines that translate between names that you enter, such as **nwnexus.wa.com**, and the numeric addresses that the machines all use, such as **192.135.191.1**. Finally, although you don't need them to configure MacTCP, now is a good time to ask your system administrator for the addresses of your SMTP (Simple Mail Transport Protocol) and NNTP (Net News Transport Protocol) servers. Also ask your system administrator what your POP account will be, and whether it's different from your email address. See Table 17.1 for examples of each of these data.

Table 17.1

MacTCP Account Information

Item	Example
Connection method	SLIP, LocalTalk, Ethernet
Addressing style	Manually, Server, Dynamically
IP address (if Manually)	e.g., **192.135.191.128**
Gateway address (if necessary)	e.g., **192.135.191.253**
Network class (if Manually and necessary)	A, B, or C
Subnet Mask (if Manually and necessary)	Ask
Primary and Secondary Domain Name Servers	e.g., **198.137.231.1**
Local domain	e.g., **halcyon.com**
SMTP mail server	e.g., **mail.halcyon.com**
NNTP news server	e.g., **news.halcyon.com**
POP account	e.g., **tidbits@mail.halcyon.com**
Email address	e.g., **tidbits@halcyon.com**

Part IV   MacTCP   17

Note

Every now and then I get complaints from people who say that they don't have a system administrator to ask. I hate to tell them, but unless they are in complete charge of the machine that they connect to, there must be someone else who acts as the system administrator. You cannot set this stuff up entirely on your own—you must have the cooperation of the person who runs the machine to which you connect. This person usually works for the organization that provides your Internet access, such as a university information technology department or a company like Northwest Nexus, the Internet access provider I use.

I realize this information is a bit much to swallow at once, but that's why I go over how to configure MacTCP in the following section, so that you can see where each piece of information goes. Also, check out the worksheet at the back of the book—you can fill it in with your information to make it easier to set up MacTCP, and, if you use either, PPP or SLIP.

Installation and Setup

To start, copy the MacTCP control panel to the Control Panels folder in your System Folder. If you drag it to the System Folder icon, System 7 (or later, of course) copies it to the right place.

> *If you are upgrading from a previous version of MacTCP, write down all of your settings. Then, make sure to delete the old MacTCP control panel, the MacTCP DNR file that lives loose in the System Folder, and the MacTCP Prep file that lives in your Preferences folder. If you fail to delete these items before you install the new version, there's no telling what could go wrong.*

A Brief Break: Installing SLIP or PPP

If you plan to connect via PPP or SLIP, take a moment and install MacPPP or InterSLIP, because you cannot finish configuring MacTCP without MacPPP or InterSLIP installed. I'm going to crib a few paragraphs from the MacPPP and InterSLIP installation sections, so don't be surprised if this information sounds familiar later.

> *Again, the ISKM Installer places the various parts of MacPPP and InterSLIP in the proper folders automatically. If you get a new version of either, though, you may need these instructions to know where the different files live. Note also that all the Internet Starter Kit Providers use PPP, not SLIP.*

Installing MacPPP requires placing a control panel called Config PPP in your Control Panels folder, and an extension called PPP in your Extensions folder. If you drop them on your closed System Folder, System 7 automatically places them in the proper folders. After you've installed Config PPP and PPP, restart your Mac.

Installing InterSLIP requires placing an extension called InterSLIP in your Extensions folder. If you drop it on the System Folder icon, System 7 places it in the correct location. The application called InterSLIP Setup can live anywhere on your hard disk, but it may be a good idea to put it, or an alias to it, in your Apple Menu Items folder, for easy access. After you place those files in the proper places, restart your Mac.

Configuring the MacTCP Main Window

If you aren't installing MacPPP or InterSLIP, simply restart now. When the Mac comes back up, open the MacTCP control panel from the Control Panels folder (see figure 17.1).

> *If you've installed InterSLIP rather than MacPPP, you have an icon labeled InterSLIP instead of PPP in the MacTCP control panel main window. I have additional icons because of my direct Internet connection.*

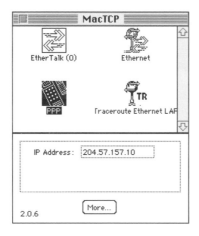

Figure 17.1   *MacTCP control panel.*

MacTCP

You must select one of the connection method icons (you may have more, fewer, or different ones) in the upper part of the control panel to tell MacTCP how you plan to connect. If you have a LocalTalk network attached to the Internet through a router, select the LocalTalk icon. If you have an Ethernet connection, select that icon. If you use MacPPP, select the PPP icon. And, of course, for a SLIP connection, select the InterSLIP icon.

> **Note**
>
> *Do not install MacPPP and InterSLIP at the same time—they seem to confuse MacTCP if both are available. Also, if you want to switch between the two, completely reinstall MacTCP before switching.*

If your provider gives you a Manually-addressed account (a static address) and provides your IP address, type the address into the IP Address field where you selected the connection method. If your host machine assigns you an address (a dynamic, or Server-addressed account), leave this field alone, because MacTCP fills it in when you actually make a connection and are assigned an IP address by the server. Not too hard yet (I hope).

Configuring the MacTCP Configuration Dialog

Now click the More button in the MacTCP control panel to bring up the configuration dialog box (see figure 17.2).

Remember that I said to ask whether your address was obtained Manually, from your Server, or Dynamically? The answer is the setting for the Obtain Address set of radio buttons. Select the button that corresponds to what your system administrator tells you.

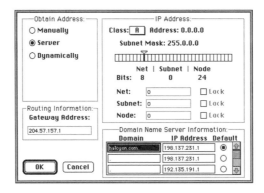

Figure 17.2 *MacTCP configuration dialog.*

Time for a brief talk about those Obtain Address buttons. Everything I have read or been told has advised avoiding the Dynamically button like the plague. The problem has to do with the fact that when you use it, MacTCP makes up an address at random and then looks for duplicate addresses. Apparently, this process tends to fail and can result in duplicate IP addresses on the network at the same time, which is a bad thing. The situation is actually somewhat more complex, but suffice it to say that you should never select the Dynamically button unless your network administrator explicitly tells you to and provides a range of addresses from which MacTCP can choose. I've never heard of any Internet access providers using the Dynamically button with SLIP or PPP accounts.

If you click the Manually button, you must enter, in the outer control panel window, the permanent IP address that your system administrator has provided for you. Either use the Manually button or the Server button, and remember that if your system administrator talks about dynamic addressing, he probably means what MacTCP calls a Server-addressed account.

Enough about the Obtain Address buttons. If your system administrator gives you a gateway address, type it into the Routing Information Gateway Address field. If you use a Server-addressed account, you can't type in the Gateway Address field, so don't worry about trying to. Again, MacTCP fills it in when you connect.

Note

If you use MacTCP with MacPPP or InterSLIP, there's no way to affect this field, but with VersaTerm SLIP, you can set the Gateway Address, even if you use a Server-addressed account.

The large IP Address area in the upper right certainly looks hairy, but for most people, there's no need to touch anything in this area. That's the good news.

The bad news is that if you do have to mess with this section of the dialog, you need help from your administrator. You may have to set the correct network class (the pop-up menu containing A, B, or C) and the subnet mask (the slider bar beneath the title in the dialog box) manually. Primarily, large networked sites must deal with subnet masks because they sometimes use a method called *subnetting* to handle their IP networks. If you have subnetting at your site, you also have someone who knows something about it and can provide details of how to configure MacTCP for your site. Be sure to ask nicely!

Domain Name Servers

You must fill in the Domain Name Server Information section with the name of your domain and the IP numbers of your name servers.

> **Note**
>
> *The domain name server is used every time you use a program to connect to an Internet site by name. So, if you use Anarchie to connect to* **ftp.tidbits.com**, *the domain name server looks up* **ftp.tidbits.com** *and sees that its IP number is* **192.135.191.2**. *Since the computers always use IP numbers and people usually use domain names, the domain name server is an essential part of the MacTCP-based connection.*

As you can see previously in figure 17.2, I have access to a number of name servers. Unfortunately, the interface for this section of MacTCP is quite confusing. Let me try to explain it as best I can.

> **Note**
>
> *Warning: This stuff gets pretty technical, so if you're not interested and everything works properly after you install MacTCP, just skip it. I use the* **halcyon.com** *domain as an example here, but if you don't use Northwest Nexus, you undoubtedly will have a different domain, and you will also of course have different IP numbers for your domain name servers.*

For each entry in the MacTCP Domain Name Server Information area, there are two fields and a Default radio button. The left-hand field holds a domain name (not the name of a domain name server!). The right-hand field holds the IP numbers of domain name server that MacTCP uses to look up addresses in the domain listed in the left-hand field. Only one of the radio buttons can be selected at a time, and MacTCP uses the line containing the selected Default radio button as your default domain name server. So, when I put **halcyon.com.** in the first left-hand field, I'm telling MacTCP to use the name server at **198.137.231.1** for all requests within the **halcyon.com** domain. In other words, the domain name server at **198.137.231.1** is used only if the name that you're looking up ends in **halcyon.com**

Part IV   MacTCP   17

The domain name you enter in that first left-hand field is also the domain name that MacTCP tacks on the end if you use a single word name, such as **coho**. The utility of this is that I could say, "telnet to the machine **coho.halcyon.com**" by merely entering **coho** in NCSA Telnet's connection dialog. This isn't particularly helpful in normal usage.

> **Note**
>
> *This process of using only the first name of an Internet machine, say,* **coho**, *also is called* using *unqualified domain names.* A full name like **coho.halcyon.com**, *in contrast, is* called a *fully qualified domain name.*

Make sure to select the Default button next to this first entry. This button has two tasks. First, it identifies the domain that MacTCP uses to complete unqualified domain names, as mentioned above. Second, it ensures that the domain name server in that line, **198.137.231.1**, is used if, and only if, no other lines in the domain name server configuration match the request. Reflect on this briefly while I get to the next few lines, since they interact with one another.

> **Note**
>
> *You may have noticed the period after the* **halcyon.com** *domain in the screen shot. That period positively denotes an absolute domain, as opposed to one that's relative to the current domain. However, MacTCP currently treats all names that contain at least one period as absolute names, so it makes no difference at all now. It does on other systems, and it may with MacTCP in the future; hence, it's a good idea to get in the habit of appending that last period.*

Next, look at the second set of fields. In the left-hand field I have a period, and in the right-hand field, I have exactly the same IP number as the first right-hand field. This second line is necessary because the first line (the primary name server) won't be used for requests outside of the domain listed in the first line. By duplicating the IP number, we tell MacTCP to use this name server for all requests outside the **halcyon.com** domain. Keep all this in mind while we look at the third line.

The third set of fields have another period in the left-hand field and a different IP number, **192.135.191.1**, in the right-hand field. This denotes my secondary name server, the name server that MacTCP queries if it doesn't get anything back from the first one.

Okay, now we have all the pieces to make sense of this confusing configuration interface.

If a program asks for the IP number for a machine in the **halcyon.com** domain, MacTCP asks the machine in the first line (the primary name server) to handle the request. If MacTCP asks for the IP number for a machine anywhere outside of the **halcyon.com** domain, the second line handles the request. Finally, if the main name server is down, rendering the first two lines ineffective, the secondary name server in the third line kicks in to look up the IP number in question. Although the second line may seem redundant, it's not. If you didn't have it and asked for the IP number of a machine outside of the **halcyon.com** domain, that request would go directly to the secondary name server. If that name server were down, your request would fail.

> **Note**
>
> *You can't see it in the screen shot, but I actually have a fourth line with yet another period in the left-hand field and a different IP number in the right-hand field. It handles requests if the first two name servers are down. You can have three or more name servers, but that many generally aren't necessary.*

I did run into an interesting problem when helping a friend with MacTCP. He could connect to FTP and Web sites on the Internet just fine, but he couldn't get his mail, and when we checked, he couldn't connect to his provider's Web server either. It turned out that he had only two entries in his MacTCP Domain Name Server Information section, and both were wrong in such a way that lookups outside of his domain worked fine, but every time a program tried to look up a host within his domain (such as his SMTP server or Web server), it failed. So pay close attention when configuring your domain name servers—it can cause some quirky problems if configured incorrectly.

Part IV MacTCP

> **Note**
>
> *The most recent version of MacTCP, version 2.0.6, introduced a situation where it will fail to resolve domain names that contain the underscore character. This is actually the correct behavior because the underscore shouldn't be used in a domain name, but a few sites did use it. Luckily, after MacTCP 2.0.6 was released, most of those sites renamed the offending machines.*

After you're done with all that domain name server information, click the OK button to save your changes, and then close the MacTCP control panel. Depending on what you change and if you've used MacTCP yet that session, MacTCP may tell you that the changes won't take effect until you restart. Go ahead and restart your Mac if necessary. If I'm troubleshooting, I usually restart every time I reconfigure MacTCP whether it tells me to or not, just to be safe.

MacTCP DNR and MacTCP Prep

After you configure MacTCP and restart your Mac, it creates two files. One, called MacTCP DNR, is loose in your System Folder, and the other, called MacTCP Prep by default, is in your Preferences folder. MacTCP creates both files from scratch if you delete them and doesn't lose any settings in the process, because it stores settings both in its control panels and in the MacTCP Prep file. Deleting these files is a must when you're troubleshooting or upgrading to a new version of MacTCP.

> **Note**
>
> MacTCP DNR *stands for* Domain Name Resolver. *If you want to know more, turn on Balloon Help and point to that file with the arrow. Suffice it to say that throwing out the MacTCP DNR file and restarting can solve some weird MacTCP problems.*

The MacTCP Prep file bears some additional discussion. As I said previously, when you configure MacTCP, it stores its settings in both the MacTCP control panel and in the MacTCP Prep file. Although this may seem unnecessary, it has a useful side effect. Since MacTCP reads its settings preferentially from the MacTCP Prep file, you can keep multiple MacTCP Prep files handy for working with different providers. Most people won't need this capability of course, but for those that do, it comes in handy. For instance, when I'm traveling, I use different dialup accounts in different cities. I could use a utility such as MacTCP Switcher or MacTCP Netswitch, but because I don't travel all that frequently, I usually just pull out my old MacTCP Prep file and replace it in the Preferences folder with one customized for the new Internet access provider.

It appears that you also can rename the MacTCP Prep file, which makes it easier to keep several different copies around. However, if you keep them in your Preferences folder, MacTCP preferentially uses the one called MacTCP Prep over any version with a modified name.

The Hosts File

Domain name serversMacTCP didn't always exist, and before they did, each computer had a Hosts file that contained the IP names and numbers of all the Internet machines you could contact. When a program needed to translate an IP name into an IP number, it looked in the Hosts file for that information (and it failed unless the machine you wanted to connect to was listed). This worked fine when there were only several hundred machines connected to the Internet. In these days with millions of machines connected to the Internet, the Hosts file isn't as good a solution as the domain name server, but because there are still instances where people can't contact a domain name server, the Hosts file has remained with us.

> **Note**
>
> *Theoretically, you can use any Internet machine that is a domain name server as your domain name server, although if it's not local, the domain name server lookups may be quite slow.*

If you don't have a domain name server (but most people do), you must use a Hosts file, which lives loose in the System Folder on the Mac. If you do have a domain name server and configure the Domain Name Server Information in MacTCP appropriately, you don't need the Hosts file at all because your Mac can ask the domain name servers for addresses rather than look them up in the Hosts file. Using the Hosts file can be dangerous if you don't need it, in fact, because it stores hard-coded information about which machines use which IP numbers, and if that information changes, the Hosts file will provide incorrect information to MacTCP. I've been bitten by this in the past, and don't recommend you install a Hosts file unless you know you need to.

> **Note**
>
> *One instance when you can't access a domain name server is if you're behind a firewall, which is a security system in which everyone must go through a secure host machine that is the only one in an organization connected to the Internet.*

If you want to use the Hosts file, you must manually enter all the hosts to which you may want to connect, along with their IP numbers. You can edit the Hosts file with TeachText or SimpleText, but make sure to create the host entries in exactly the same manner as shown in the examples. In any event, here's what a standard host entry looks like:

```
consultant.micro.umn.edu. A 134.84.132.4 ;
```

> **Note**
>
> *The Communications Toolbox Telnet tools like to use the Hosts file as a repository for Internet machines that you have connected to previously. In fact, the VersaTerm Telnet tool adds sites to the Hosts file for you, if you enter them into the tool's configuration dialog.*

MacTCP Utilities

A few utility programs have appeared that help you troubleshoot your Internet connection. In addition, a couple of utilities, MacTCP Switcher and MacTCP Netswitch, help ease the process of switching between two completely different MacTCP setups, such as you might have if you use Ethernet at work and PPP at home. Unless mentioned otherwise, the latest versions of these utilities can be found in:

```
ftp://ftp.tidbits.com/pub/tidbits/tisk/tcp/
```

MacPing

Along with shareware software, Dartmouth College has some commercial quality applications that they sell. Included in this category are the $99 MacPing 3.0 and the $399 MacPing 3.0 Pro, ping utilities that work with both AppleTalk and TCP/IP networks such as the Internet. MacPing 3.0 is limited to testing five AppleTalk zones, whereas MacPing 3.0 Pro can test an unlimited number of AppleTalk zones. They're otherwise identical. Not being a network administrator, I'm not really sure what MacPing tells me, but I gather that by watching the way the pings come back from all the machines, you can tell where there might be a network problems. Check out its help text for

more information about what all the parts of the window do. For ordering information contact True BASIC, Inc., the MacPing distributors, at 800/436-2111 and check out the demo at the FTP URL below.

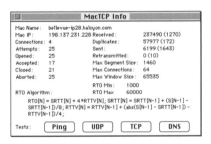

```
ftp://ftp.dartmouth.edu/pub/mac/
```

MacTCP Watcher

MacTCP Watcher is a free program written by the prolific Peter Lewis to display the internals of MacTCP's workings. You must be an expert to decipher most of this information, and Peter claims that even he doesn't know what most of it means. However, if you're having troubles with MacTCP, MacTCP Watcher proves to be one of the best tools available for troubleshooting a bad connection. I still don't understand what it complains about, but it tends to react in specific ways to specific problems, and those reactions are usually more useful than the generic error messages that come back from other programs. MacTCP's other functions include a ping test, which is a bit like sonar over a network. It's useful for determining whether a remote machine is up, and if so, about how far away it is (or how slow the network to it is). The UDP and TCP tests mean

less to me, but I use MacTCP Watcher's DNS button to match IP names and numbers. So, definitely pick up MacTCP Watcher, and poke at the buttons to see if anything that comes back looks useful. I always have a smashing good time looking at stuff I don't understand.

MacTCP Netswitch

The free MacTCP Netswitch control panel, written by David Walton, of the University of Notre Dame, appears to be the more sophisticated of the two utilities for switching between MacTCP connections. It works by sensing at startup whether you're connected to an AppleTalk network, and if so, what zone you're in. After it's sensed whether you're in a network or not, it swaps in an appropriate MacTCP Prep file from a group of preconfigured ones. The major advantage of the way MacTCP Netswitch senses the environment at startup is that theoretically you don't have to restart, because it has forced MacTCP to load the proper MacTCP Prep file at startup.

```
http://www.nd.edu/~dwalton1/netswitch.html
```

MacTCP Switcher

John Norstad's free MacTCP Switcher requires a bit more interaction from the user than MacTCP Netswitch. After you have MacTCP set up properly, you run MacTCP Switcher and save a configuration file that records the current MacTCP settings. Do the same for your other configurations. To restore a saved configuration, double-click it in the Finder, and when MacTCP Switcher prompts you, click the Set MacTCP button to set MacTCP to use the saved configuration. Another alert then appears telling you that MacTCP has been set; it may also tell you to restart your Mac, and if so provides a Restart button to do so instantly. MacTCP Switcher doesn't work

with whole MacTCP Prep files, as MacTCP Netswitch does, but instead copies the relevant resources from the MacTCP Prep file to the configuration file and back again. It never touches the MacTCP control panel itself.

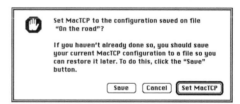

Query it!

Chris McNeil, has a free, easy to use, and potentially useful program called Query it! that enables you to query your local nameserver to find out more information about various Internet hosts. The most useful piece of information you can get from Query it! is the IP address for a host, the number that goes with the name. For instance, I asked Query it! to tell me the address of **halcyon.com**. That's all there is to Query it!, although you can see if the CNAME, HINFO Record, or MX Record results are of interest to you.

Open Transport

Apple hasn't yet released Open Transport, the successor to MacTCP, but I was able to take a look at a pre-released version for this chapter. The good news is that although MacTCP isn't that hard to configure once you understand what's going on, Open Transport is much easier to configure than MacTCP. To compare Open Transport and MacTCP is a bit misleading though, because Open Transport is a complete rewrite of the entire communications infrastructure on the Macintosh.

Open Transport's primary goal is to support multiple networking protocols (including AppleTalk, TCP/IP, and other mishmash acronyms like SNA, DECnet, OSI, and X.25) in such a way as to insulate the user from the details and to simultaneously provide a single coherent target for developers.

Most of the changes in Open Transport take place below the surface, so it's a little hard to say too much about it until Apple releases it, perhaps in the summer of 1995. However, based on statements that Apple has made about Open Transport in a public white paper, I can tell you the following about Open Transport.

- Not only will Open Transport provide a facility for multiple configurations, switching between them will no longer require restarting, something that has haunted PowerBook users connecting with MacTCP.

- Open Transport will enable Macintosh users to participate in the MBone, which provides the capability to broadcast (or multicast, the current term) streams of audio or video data to multiple machines without sending each a separate copy (a high-speed connection will still be required for this to work acceptably).

- Open Transport will support a new Internet standard, the Dynamic Host Configuration Protocol (DHCP), which will make it even easier to set up and configure a Macintosh to work on the Internet, since a DHCP server will provide most of the information automatically.

- Open Transport will continue to support two older automatic configuration methods, Reverse Address Resolution Protocol (RARP) and Boot Protocol (BootP).

- Open Transport will include full Balloon Help and, for System 7.5 users, full AppleGuide support. The combination of these help systems will significantly improve ease of use.

- Open Transport will be Power Mac-native, and when combined with Open Transport-aware, Power Mac-native applications on a Power Mac, will provide significantly increased performance.

- Open Transport will run on existing Macs, and although older applications won't take advantage of Open Transport's speed increases, they should work as well as under MacTCP. Older applications will still benefit from Open Transport's easier interface.

All of that said, for most users, Open Transport's most obvious improvement on MacTCP will be the new, simplified interface (see figure 17.3).

Figure 17.3   *Open Transport TCP/IP Configure Manually settings.*

As you can see in figure 17.3, the new interface provides two pop-up menus, one that specifies how you want to connect to the Internet and another that specifies how your configuration information will be entered. In figure 17.3, I chose to connect via Ethernet and to configure everything manually, which meant that I had to fill in my IP Address, Domain name, Router address, and Name server address.

Although you use the same information in configuring MacTCP, the new interface is obviously quite a bit easier to understand. However, if you can use the new DHCP method of automatically configuring Open Transport, you can see in figure 17.4 that your work almost disappears.

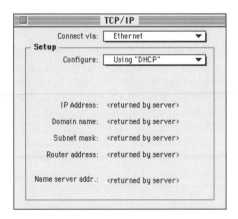

Figure 17.4   *Open Transport TCP/IP Configure Using "DHCP" settings.*

Configuration using BootP is similarly easy, and if you connect via an AppleTalk network at a large organization, a MacIP server can again provide all the configuration information automatically (see figure 17.5).

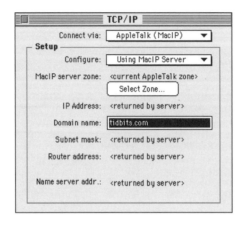

Figure 17.5   *Open Transport TCP/IP Configure Using MacIP Server settings.*

Apple reportedly plans Open Transport to be a free upgrade for existing MacTCP owners, including readers of this book. Open Transport will also undoubtedly be bundled with future versions of the Mac OS and all new Macs once Apple releases it, so it shouldn't be too hard to get to that point.

Mission Accomplished

Phew! That's about it for configuring MacTCP. In most cases, MacTCP is really quite easy to configure once you know what information goes into which fields in the Configuration dialog. I provided all of the information above, even though most people should never need it, because if you do need to figure out what's going on in MacTCP, you need the details. If you use one of the providers listed in appendix A, "Internet Starter Kit Providers," and MacPPP, the ISKM Installer configures MacTCP for you. Speaking of MacPPP, let's talk about PPP next.

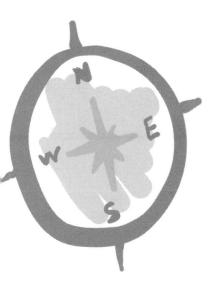

Chapter 18

PPP

An ever-increasing number of people who don't work at a large business or university want access to the Internet, and an equally ever-increasing number of Internet access providers are springing up to meet that need. Because individuals seldom have the level of connectivity enjoyed by those in business or education, they must make do with slower connections. Until recently, they've had to cope with clumsy Unix shell accounts as well. That clumsiness is avoidable now that SLIP (Serial Line Internet Protocol) and PPP (Point-to-Point Protocol) accounts have become widely available; more importantly, they provide access to some extremely cool software that I talk about in future chapters.

PPP provides an Internet connection for people who connect via modem. If you have a network, either Ethernet or LocalTalk, connected to the Internet, you don't need PPP. I talk about SLIP in more detail in chapter 19, "SLIP," so in this chapter I concentrate on PPP, mentioning SLIP only when the situation in question equally applies to SLIP.

Note

Although PPP is generally used with normal phone lines and modems, if your provider and telephone company both offer ISDN (Integrated Services Digital Network) service, you can use PPP with ISDN and a terminal adapter like the Motorola BitSURFR in place of a modem to create a high-speed Internet connection, often for not much more than a normal phone line would cost, if you're lucky.

The easiest way to understand PPP is to pretend that you don't have water service inside your house. Every time you want to take a shower, you must run a garden hose to the water hookup outside, take your shower, and then reel the hose back in. That's exactly what PPP does—it establishes a temporary, low-speed connection to the Internet. You must create that connection before you can run programs such as Anarchie and TurboGopher.

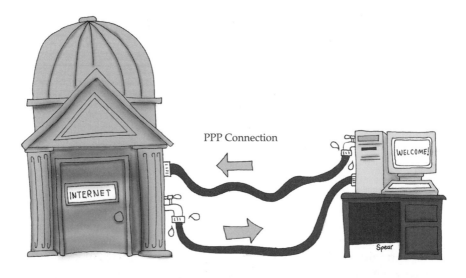

PPP Connection

Note *Although most implementations of PPP allow you to launch a MacTCP-based program without connecting first (the PPP software sees what's up and then establishes the connection), I've found that auto-connect features can be flaky. If you can use one, great, but if it doesn't work reliably, connect manually first.*

What's the difference between PPP and SLIP, and should you care? The answer to the first part of the question seems to be that PPP is SLIP done right. Apparently, SLIP was literally designed on the back of an envelope and implemented in an afternoon. PPP, in contrast, was designed more carefully and is far more flexible, so that in theory it supports multiple protocols (such as AppleTalk and TCP/IP) at the same time and over the same connection. The capability to support multiple protocols is neat because you can use MacTCP programs at the same time as you are dialed into an AppleTalk server, much as you can do with Apple Remote Access now, but the reality is that not all of the Macintosh PPP implementations (like MacPPP) support anything besides TCP/IP.

Note *PPP and SLIP accounts are not identical. You cannot use a SLIP account with MacPPP, or a PPP account with InterSLIP.*

As to whether or not you should care, my impression is that at the moment it doesn't make much difference. PPP may become the standard because Apple is working on supporting it more fully. Also, PPP has proven to be somewhat more reliable than SLIP in the past, although that may be related to the specific implementations of PPP and SLIP. In general, I believe that PPP is the way to go, if you can. That's why the ISKM Installer installs MacPPP by default, but also allows you to install InterSLIP should you only be able to get a SLIP account. Of course, if you simply cannot get a PPP account to work, there's nothing wrong with trying a SLIP account instead.

Now, does that mean that you should run out and switch an existing SLIP account over to PPP? No, if everything you want to do with your account works as you expect, definitely not. PPP and SLIP are functionally identical in that all, or almost all, of the MacTCP-based programs should work the same way with either SLIP or PPP accounts. I haven't seen significant performance differences between the two, although PPP occasionally feels a little more responsive in interactive use (as opposed to raw download speed when you're retrieving a file via FTP and nothing else). In addition, I've seen situations in which InterSLIP didn't work worth beans, but MacPPP worked instantly, and also situations in which InterSLIP was working perfectly but MacPPP never quite worked.

Hayden has licensed MacPPP and included it on the disk for your convenience. It was written by Larry Blunk of Merit Network, Inc., one of the companies that helped run the NSFNET. Commercial competition for MacPPP comes from InterPPP, a beefed-up version of PPP, marketed by InterCon. InterPPP's main claim to fame is that it supports AppleTalk over PPP, which is not true of MacPPP. There are several other less common implementations of PPP from Tribe and Pacer Software, but they reportedly use the same code as the version InterCon licensed and calls InterPPP.

Part IV **18** PPP

Note *Although it's not yet available as I write this, Hyde Park Software is adding PPP support to MacSLIP (see chapter 19, "SLIP") so it will become a contender in the near future as well. The only change in MacSLIP's standard interface is a PPP Transport button and options to use PAP or CHAP, two authentication protocols for PPP.*

I concentrate on MacPPP because the other PPP implementations, being commercial, come with printed documentation and support. In addition, MacPPP works extremely well for most people, and it is easy to configure, so it's the best choice for anyone starting out. If you discover that you need the added flexibility of something like InterPPP, you can check it out as well.

Getting an Account

When it comes time for you to get a PPP account, you should check back in chapter 11, "Choosing a Connection," for information on how to pick an Internet access provider.

Once you decide on a provider, you need certain information from that provider to configure MacPPP or InterPPP. For convenience, I list the most common pieces of information that you need in Table 18.1.

Table 18.1
PPP Information

Item	Question
Phone number	What number do I call to connect to the server?
Login name	What is my SLIP or PPP account login name? This name can be different from your userid or machine name.
Password	What password should I provide when logging in?
Login Procedure	What should I expect to receive from your host machine and how should my Mac respond when logging in?

You also can use the worksheet in the back of this book for recording all of this information. Although unusual, there are other variables that you may need to set in MacPPP, and if that's true, your Internet access provider will give you that information. The vast majority of them work with the default settings, luckily.

MacPPP

The free MacPPP, from Larry Blunk of Merit Network, is my dialup connection method of choice. This is partly because of its simple configuration and setup, and partly because there are a few programs that don't work with the Server-addressed SLIP accounts on my Internet access provider, Northwest Nexus, but that work fine with a Server-addressed PPP account. Because it generally works so well, I've included it on the disk as the default for those who want to work with one of the providers listed in appendix A, "Internet Starter Kit Providers."

Note

If you want to switch from SLIP to PPP, you must first switch your account to PPP with your provider. When that's done, throw out MacTCP, MacTCP DNR, MacTCP Prep, InterSLIP, and InterSLIP Control (if installed) and restart before installing MacPPP.

Installation and Setup

Installing MacPPP requires placing a control panel called Config PPP in your Control Panels folder, and an extension called PPP in your Extensions folder. If you drag them onto your closed System Folder, System 7 automatically places them in the proper folders.

> *Once again, the ISKM Installer installs MacPPP properly for you—I include these instructions so you know what's happened and can duplicate it with original files downloaded from the Internet.*

After you've installed Config PPP and PPP, restart your Mac. Make sure that PPP is selected in the main MacTCP window, and that you use Server-addressing. PPP has the useful feature of being able to (at least in theory since this isn't a common setup) use Server-addressing even if you have a permanent IP address assigned to you. Being able to use Server-addressing with a static IP address ensures that you don't have to enter your IP address or Gateway Address into MacTCP, generally reducing the configuration work.

> *It's possible to use the Manually-addressing option, but if you do that, you may have to configure the IPCP dialog (accessible within the Config PPP configuration dialog) with your permanent IP address in the Local column and your Gateway Address in the Remote column. The MacPPP documentation doesn't recommend this, and I was unable to test it. Consider yourself forewarned.*

Part IV 18 PPP

Open the Config PPP control panel. As you can see in figure 18.1, Config PPP has a vaguely clunky interface, but it is almost effortless to configure.

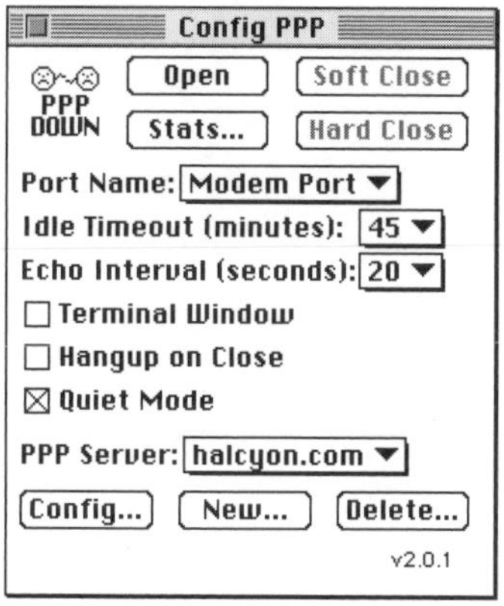

Figure 18.1   *Config PPP control panel.*

The Port Name pop-up menu enables you to choose the Modem port or Printer port (or any other ports registered with the Communications Toolbox); it is usually set to Modem port.

> *If you use a PowerBook with an internal modem, the Port Name pop-up menu may confuse you. A few PowerBook modems, including the Apple Express Modem, the Global Village PowerPort/Mercury for the PowerBook 500-series, and Duos, are bus modems, and show up in the menu as Internal Modem. Other internal PowerBook modems are non-bus modems and use an internal connection to the Modem port. For these, choose Modem port. Mac AV users may also have a GeoPort option.*

The Idle Timeout pop-up enables you to set a time of inactivity, from five to 120 minutes, after which MacPPP will close the connection. If you do anything during this time, the timer resets and MacPPP starts counting again. If your connection remains idle for the duration specified, MacPPP closes the connection. If you have the Quiet Mode checkbox checked, MacPPP does so without warning; if not, then at the end of the idle time period MacPPP presents you with a dialog that enables you to either ignore the warning and leave the PPP connection active, or close PPP.

I haven't used this feature much, because I simply connect when I want something and disconnect when I'm done. However, I see two tremendous uses for this feature. First, for those people who pay by the minute for their connections, having MacPPP hang up if the line is idle could save you a fair amount of money. Second, if you want to download a large file before you go to bed, simply set MacPPP to a relatively short timeout value and it will hang up when it's done downloading the file. Make sure Quiet Mode is checked if you want it to hang up without confirmation.

> *Some people have experienced problems with MacPPP connecting seemingly randomly. Although most cases are caused by a program like Anarchie or TurboGopher asking for MacTCP services, it seems that on occasion MacTCP simply decides to do something and asks MacPPP to dial out. If you experience this, setting a short idle time in MacPPP keeps those unwanted connections as short as possible. And of course, if you shut off your modem, MacPPP won't be able to dial out at all.*

It appears that MacPPP does a soft close in this idle timeout situation, which means that a MacTCP-based application can automatically re-open the connection by requesting MacTCP services. If MacPPP did a *hard close*, applications wouldn't be able to re-open the connection automatically; you would have to click the Open button to open a new connection.

N
o
t
e
I can't predict how different MacTCP-based applications will behave if their connection disappears due to the line being idle for five or ten minutes. If you anticipate being in a situation where MacPPP might hang up automatically after an idle timeout, make sure to save your work in all other open applications. Some applications may even hang your Mac, so be careful.

The Echo Interval pop-up menu provides the opportunity to configure MacPPP to periodically query the line to see if your connection has dropped. If MacPPP receives no response after three successive requests, MacPPP assumes that the connection has gone dead. I've always left Echo Interval turned off, although if you have trouble with your connection dropping frequently, using it may make life easier. When MacPPP detects a dead connection, it pops up a dialog box with three buttons for Close PPP, Ignore, or Restart, which in this case means restarting the PPP connection, not the Macintosh. Of course, if your connection drops, you must at least quit open MacTCP applications before trying to do anything else. You may have to restart to clear things up appropriately if the open applications have become sufficiently confused by the loss of the connection.

N
o
t
e
The Echo Interval feature continually sends packets to the server and waits for a response, but these packets don't count as traffic for the Idle Timeout feature.

Part IV   PPP   **18**

The Terminal Window checkbox is one of MacPPP's most useful features. If you check it, MacPPP ignores the Phone number and Modem init fields in the Configure Server and Connect Script dialog boxes (I'll get to them in a minute). Instead, it makes you walk through the connection manually, starting with dialing the modem with an ATDT command.

N
o
t
e
In some situations, MacPPP's terminal window doesn't echo what you type back to the screen, but the characters will be sent when you press Return.

You may never need to use MacPPP's terminal emulator, but if you have trouble logging on, it's much easier to have the terminal emulator built into MacPPP rather than be forced to use an external one (see figure 18.2).

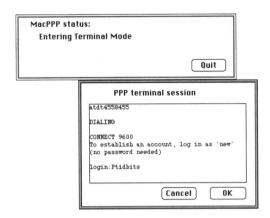

Figure 18.2   MacPPP terminal window.

If you must use the terminal window, dial the modem manually, enter your username and password, and once you start seeing some gibberish characters that indicate the start of PPP data, click OK to start the PPP session.

> **Note**
>
> *I strongly recommend that you use MacPPP's terminal window if you're having trouble getting connected because it often reveals problems on the provider's end (like they didn't set up a PPP account for you) and eliminates any mistakes you might have made in the connect script.*

The two final checkboxes in the window are Hangup on Close and Quiet Mode. Hangup on Close, if checked, sends the Hayes +++ escape string and then an ATH to hang up the modem. My modem hangs up fine without this checkbox selected, but if yours doesn't, select it. The Quiet Mode checkbox prevents certain actions from requiring confirmation, most notably the Idle Timeout disconnect.

Once you've configured the main part of the Config PPP control panel, click the New button to create a new configuration. Name it, and it appears in the PPP Server pop-up menu. If you want to delete one, make sure it's showing in the menu and click the Delete button. After creating a new configuration, click the Config button to bring up the Config-ure Server dialog box (see figure 18.3).

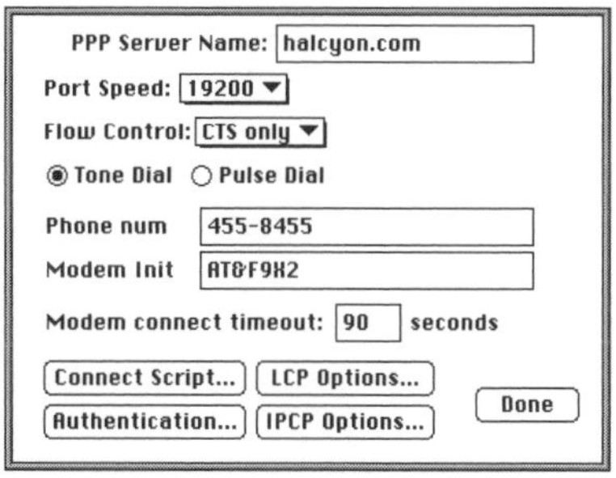

Figure 18.3   *MacPPP Configure Server dialog.*

If you want to rename your server configuration, you can edit it in the PPP Server Name field. It makes absolutely no difference what you set the server name to—it's only for your use. In the version of the PPP Preferences the ISKM Installer puts on your disk, I use the PPP Server Name field to identify different modems, for instance.

After you set the PPP Server Name, you can configure the basic modem variables. Set the Port Speed pop-up menu as high as it will work with your modem (my WorldBlazer doesn't like speeds over 19,200 bps by default), and always try to use a Port Speed faster than your modem, so it can take advantage of the modem's compression capabilities.

The Port Speed is the speed at which the Mac and the modem communicate, **not** the speed at which the two modems communicate (unless it happens to be slower than the fastest speed the modems have in common, at which point it forces the modems to communicate at that speed). Do not set the Port Speed menu to 14,400 or 28,800 even if you have a 14,400 bps or 28,800 bps modem. The reason is that some modems don't accept those as valid port speeds, and MacPPP won't talk to the modem properly.

Port speed is reportedly irrelevant if you use a bus modem, since it doesn't use the modem port. I'd set it to 57,600 if you have one of these modems.

Modem flow control, also sometimes called handshaking, is one of the most confusing topics in telecommunications on the Macintosh. The basic idea is that the flow of the incoming and outgoing packets must be organized and controlled or else you experience the packet equivalent of traffic jams and accidents. For a modem to do handshaking in hardware, you need a special cable (luckily, one that comes with most fast modems sold for Macs, although every now and then someone has trouble because you can't use high speeds on modern modems without one). All of the various options we have discussed are forms of hardware flow control or hardware handshaking. PPP can, in theory, use software flow control, also called XON/XOFF, which doesn't require a special cable, but I've never seen anyone try. Usually, there's no point.

The Flow Control pop-up menu has options for None, CTS only, RTS (DTR) only, and CTS & RTS (DTR). I recommend that you try setting CTS & RTS (DTR) as the first try. The problem with the CTS & RTS (DTR) setting is that you may experience random hangups when lots of data is coming in unless your modem init string includes &D0, or, if your init string uses &D2, it is also properly configured to ignore short periods of DTR going low (check your modem manual for the S25 S-register setting and try setting it to 50 in the modem init string). If that's true, try dropping down to CTS only. I ran into some of the hangups, and haven't had any trouble at all since I switched to CTS only.

> **Note**
>
> *Internal PowerBook bus modems can have the Flow Control pop-up menu set to None; all other modems must use some sort of flow control.*

Tone Dial versus Pulse Dial should be obvious based on your telephone. Tone dialing is far more prevalent these days. The phone number field should be self-evident, although you may have to add special prefixes to get through a company or hotel phone system. Adding the prefix of either 8 or 9 and a comma is a common solution (the comma ensures a short pause after sending the 8 or the 9 and before dialing the rest of the phone number).

> **Note**
>
> *If you must enter a lot of digits in the phone number field to account for a calling card number, you may have to eliminate all the dashes, which aren't necessary and take up space in the field. I forget the maximum number of digits it can take, but I ran into it once when using a calling card number.*

Next we come to the Modem Init field. Modem initialization strings have been an unending source of headaches for Internet users configuring SLIP and PPP accounts. My recommendation is to start with the factory default configuration for your modem (usually **AT&F, AT&F1, or AT&F2**, although the numbers change depending on the modem).

> **Note**
>
> *If you use the ISKM Installer to install MacPPP, you get a PPP Preferences file that contains a number of likely (but untested) modem strings for many modem types. In addition, even more modem strings are located in a file called Modem Strings in the MacPPP 2.0.1 folder in your ISKM3 Folder.*

I should make one uncommon but important point. Make sure that XON/XOFF, or software flow control, is turned off. On at least one modem, the Telebit QBlazer, MacPPP fails badly if XON/XOFF is active, and the MacPPP documentation notes that software flow control should be turned off as well, so I'm assuming that XON/XOFF is Public Enemy Number One with PPP (or SLIP) accounts.

Note
You may wonder what the X2 is doing in my initialization string. I discovered that my Telebit WorldBlazer doesn't return the BUSY code in the default X1 setting, and if the modem doesn't return that BUSY code, MacPPP has no way to know that the line is busy and it should redial (which it does automatically). Other modems may have a similar problem.

Finally, the Modem connect timeout field offers you a chance to increase the amount of time MacPPP will wait for the connection to occur. If it takes MacPPP a long time to negotiate your connection, you may need to increase this value.

As more alert readers will have noticed, I haven't yet mentioned where you enter your userid and password. There are two possibilities here, depending on what the PPP server on your host machine supports. If you're lucky, you can use PPP's Password Authentication Protocol (PAP) to negotiate your connection. If your server doesn't support that (I have no idea how common it is), you instead must use a connect script. First, the Authentication dialog (see figure 18.4).

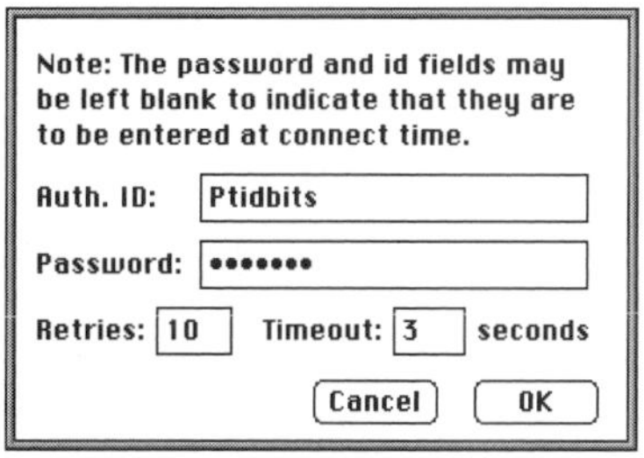

Figure 18.4   *MacPPP Authentication dialog.*

As you can see, all you do here is enter your Authentication ID and Password into the appropriate fields. The Auth. ID field holds your userid and the Password field holds your PPP password, appropriately hidden so others can't see it. If you're really paranoid about your password, you can leave that field blank and MacPPP will prompt you to enter it every time you connect.

Click OK to save your changes and return to the Configure Server dialog. If you use the Authentication dialog, you need not enter anything in the Connect Script dialog, and in fact, you're best off deleting anything that might be in there. In testing with the servers at Northwest Nexus, I found that MacPPP would try to run through the Connect Script information first, and if that failed, it would then fall back to the information from the Authentication dialog. If, however, the Connect Script dialog was empty, MacPPP sent the authentication information without worrying about looking for the login and password prompts. I don't know if this is the standard process for servers or not.

Part IV

PPP

18

If you leave the Connect Script blank or configure it incorrectly, and leave the Authentication dialog empty, MacPPP prompts you for your userid and password, just as you would have entered them in the Authentication dialog.

If using the Authentication method of logging in to your PPP server machine doesn't work, you must instead use the Connect Script dialog to script your way in. It's still pretty easy (see figure 18.5).

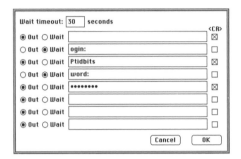

Figure 18.5   *MacPPP Connect Script dialog.*

Basically, all you do in the Connect Script dialog is replicate the process of logging in to your host manually (and the terminal window can be helpful in figuring out the connect script). You click an Out button to indicate that MacPPP should send the contents of the field to the left (and a carriage return if the checkbox is selected for that line), and you click a Wait button to indicate that MacPPP should wait for the string specified in the field to appear before moving on to the next line.

If you're unlucky, connecting to your PPP server will require more than the eight fields MacPPP provides here. In that case, if your server doesn't support authenticated logins as discussed previously (which is likely, if it requires more than four send/expect interactions), your only option may be to use the commercial InterPPP. Actually, that's not entirely true, since you can do some funky scripting within MacPPP by using special codes like |t (which drops you into the terminal window at that point in the script), \r (which sends a Return to the host), and \d (which forces a short delay). The trick when creating such a hacked script is to use delays instead of the Wait buttons, thus enabling you to cram more functional script lines into the same space.

My connect script in figure 18.5 says, when translated: "Send a carriage return as soon as you're connected. Then wait for the string 'ogin:' to appear, and once you've seen it, send the username 'Ptidbits' and a carriage return. Wait for the string 'word:' to appear, and then send the password and a carriage return." Once you're done scripting here, click OK to save your script.

> *The words "login" and "password" often have their first letter or letters removed in scripts like this, because you never know whether or not the first letter will be capitalized.*

Meanwhile, back in the Configure Server dialog, you've probably been wondering what's inside the LCP Options dialog and the IPCP Options dialog. You really don't want to know, and I'm not going to show you. Suffice it to say that I'll be very surprised if you know what to do with the options in there. I certainly don't, and the MacPPP documentation says that no normal user should ever have to change any of those settings.

Well, that's it for configuring MacPPP. It's quite easy, and in fact, it may be the easiest method of connecting to the Internet.

Basic Usage

Once it's configured, using MacPPP is a piece of cake. Like InterSLIP, it works in both manual and automatic modes, so you can either click the Open button in Config PPP or you can merely open a MacTCP-based program that opens MacTCP, at which point MacPPP connects automatically. I've found MacPPP's auto-connect feature to be fairly reliable, although not absolutely guaranteed. It seems that some applications don't quite play by the rules, and those applications won't work in auto-connect mode.

> *MacPPP's auto-connect feature only works on the second or subsequent connections after you restart your Mac if you use Soft Close to close your connection. If you use Hard Close, MacPPP cannot auto-connect. Nonetheless, there are some cases of MacPPP dialing for apparently no reason that are eliminated with Hard Close, so that's what I always use.*

After you click the Open button or have MacPPP connect automatically, you see some dialogs indicating that MacPPP is dialing, logging in, establishing the PPP link, and checking for the network. After those dialogs, the little faces under the Open button will become happy faces and the connection will be complete.

> *Be careful of the auto-connect mode—if you do something like put TurboGopher in your Startup Items folder, it will launch on every startup and make MacPPP establish a connection to the Internet. You're unlikely to do that with TurboGopher, but certain control panels or extensions also can activate the auto-connect feature, which can be a pain.*

Part IV

18

PPP

Once you've established a PPP connection with MacPPP, you can run any of the MacTCP-based applications and do whatever you want. If you click the Stats button in Config PPP, MacPPP presents you with a relatively meaningless dialog full of technical statistics. I've never bothered with them and I haven't talked to anyone who has, either.

When you're done with your work and want to close your connection, first quit all of your MacTCP-based applications. Some of them dislike having the connection disappear from under their little electronic feet. To pull the plug on the PPP connection, you can do one of two things, depending on how you use MacPPP. First, you can click the Hard Close button, which hangs up the connection and "locks" MacPPP so that the only way to establish a new connection is to click the Open button. This prevents any applications from forcing MacPPP to open the connection automatically while, say, you're not present. Second, if it doesn't bother you to possibly have applications dialing your phone behind your back, you can click the Soft Close button to close a connection. That leaves open the auto-connect feature for the rest of that session, so launching an application makes MacPPP establish a new connection.

Overall Evaluation

My only real quibble with MacPPP is that I don't think much of the aesthetics of the interface (hey, call me an interface snob—I don't mind). Actually, if I wanted to quibble some more, MacPPP could use some updated documentation, and it would be very nice if it could dial and redial in the background.

Overall, though, I find MacPPP to be an excellent program and perhaps the simplest way of establishing a connection to the Internet (assuming that the PPP server in question supports authentication).

Administrative Details

Larry Blunk and Merit Network deserve kudos for making such a fine program available to the Macintosh Internet community for free. However, I should note that they cannot support MacPPP, so if you have problems or questions about it, you should ask on a mailing list like the Apple Internet Users mailing list (send a message containing the command info apple-internet-users to **listproc@abs.apple.com** for information on how to subscribe) or in a newsgroup like **comp.sys.mac.comm**. You can retrieve the latest version of MacPPP on the Internet from either of the following:

```
ftp://ftp.tidbits.com/pub/tidbits/tisk/tcp/
```

```
ftp://merit.edu//pub/ppp/mac/
```

MacPPP Add-ons

There are a number of useful little add-ons to MacPPP that can make life easier for you. Some of them simplify the process of connecting and disconnecting from the Internet (which is a bit of a pain normally, since you must open the Config PPP control panel to disconnect, even if you've used the auto-connect feature to connect). Others help you track how much time you spend online, which is important if you're paying by the minute or for a long distance call. Unless I mention otherwise, all the utilities in this section are at the following URL:

```
ftp://ftp.tidbits.com/pub/tidbits/tisk/tcp/
```

Control PPP

This postcardware utility from Richard Buckle makes it easier for MacPPP users to connect and disconnect. Control PPP is a Control Strip module that enables you to connect and disconnect from the Control Strip, and to open the MacTCP and Config PPP control panels. It also indicates if MacPPP is open or not, which is handy for PowerBook users with internal modems. Although written for Control Strip, Control PPP also works with

some limitations with Desktop Strip, which lets desktop Macs use Control Strip modules, and probably with a similar commercial utility called DragStrip.

MacPPP Control and Toggle PPP

MacPPP Control from Mark Alldritt is an AppleScript Addition that enables you to perform limited AppleScript scripting on MacPPP. You can open and close the MacPPP connection and test whether or not the connection is open or closed. MacPPP Control comes with two sample scripts that I used for a long time to connect and disconnect. Dennis Whiteman has written a much more involved script called Toggle PPP that toggles MacPPP between open and closed connections and writes a tab-delimited log detailing the start, stop, and cumulative times relating to your connection. If you do much with AppleScript and use MacPPP, you should definitely check out these utilities.

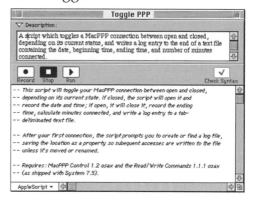

MacPPP QuicKeys and PPPquencer

Richard Buckle's postcardware MacPPP QuicKeys 3.0 and PPPquencer are extensions to CE Software's QuicKeys macro utility and to the shareware macro utility KeyQuencer. These extensions help QuicKeys and MacPPP communicate, enabling you to control MacPPP from within QuicKeys or KeyQuencer. They enable you to open and close MacPPP, choosing a hard or a soft close when you close it, trigger other macros based on whether or not MacPPP is open or closed, and finally jump a specified number of steps forward or backward in a QuicKeys sequence macro. If you use QuicKeys or KeyQuencer and MacPPP, you may want to check out these extensions.

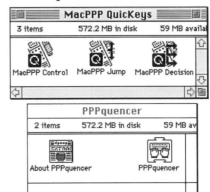

MacPPP Timer

MacPPP Timer is a small utility application from Eric Preston that helps you keep track of how much time you spend connected to your PPP account. You must launch it manually, but because you can open a MacPPP session from within MacPPP Timer, that's not a serious hardship. Once active, MacPPP Timer automatically displays the amount of time you're connected for that session and for a cumulative amount of time (a month is the default, based on most providers' billing schemes). If you're billed by the hour and want to keep an eye on your charges, check out this program.

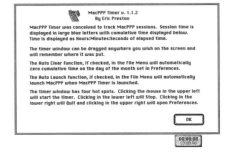

PPPop

Those who don't like working with the Config PPP control panel might want to check out Rob Friefeld's free PPPop, which is a small application that serves as a front end to MacPPP. Like other utilities for controlling MacPPP, PPPop enables you to connect or disconnect, open the MacTCP and Config PPP control panels, and see the status of your connection at a glance. The coolest feature of PPPop is that it plays sounds from a PPPop Sounds file located in the same folder. PPPop comes with a set of sounds, and you can create your own and replace the standard sounds if you like.

PPPReport and PPPSummarize

PPPReport is a free control panel from Eric de la Musse that tracks how long you spend connected via MacPPP, writing the results to a log file, of which PPPSummarize, a free Excel 5.0 worksheet from Mary Lindower, can then provide a day-by-day, month-by-month summary. One neat feature of PPPReport is that it can log specific Internet port numbers, which means that you could figure out how much time you spend downloading via FTP, or reading news, or anything on the Internet that is connected with a specific port number.

Other PPP Implementations

Although I recommend that you start with MacPPP, especially since it is included on the ISKM disk, there are two other implementations of PPP (soon to be three when MacSLIP 3.0 comes out with its PPP support) that may interest you for one reason or another. You don't need to bother even investigating these programs if MacPPP works perfectly for you, as it does for most people.

MacPPP 2.1SD

MacPPP 2.1SD is a hacked version of MacPPP that has only one difference from the standard MacPPP 2.0.1. As you may have noticed, MacPPP 2.0.1's top port speed setting is 57,600 bps, which is the top speed of the serial ports on all Macs other than the 660AV, 840AV, and the Power Macs. 57,600 also is a good bit faster than any existing modem, so the problem only surfaces when using ISDN, which (depending on the details) runs at either 64,000 bps or 128,000 bps, quite a lot faster than MacPPP 2.0.1 supports. Thus, MacPPP 2.1SD (SD stands for Steve Dagley, the programmer who created it and who can be reached at **sdagley@zeno.fit.edu**) adds port speeds of 115,000 bps and 230,000 bps. MacPPP 2.1SD does not work with the GeoPort Telecom Adapter pod nor the Creative Solutions Hustler serial card, and it conflicts with the Axion serial switch.

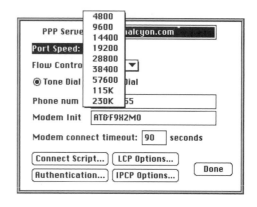

InterPPP

InterCon's InterPPP is the most well-known of the commercial PPP clients, and as far as I know, like the others (there are versions from Tribe and Pacer Software as well) are based on the same code from a company called FCR. InterPPP's main advantage over MacPPP is that it can carry AppleTalk over the PPP connection. Of course, your host machine must speak AppleTalk as well as TCP/IP and make useful AppleTalk services available for this to be of any utility. In testing, I had trouble getting InterPPP to work with my PPP server, perhaps in part because InterPPP relies on CCL scripts (it provides a simple text editor for editing them, which is nice) that live in your Extensions folder for configuring the modem. I, and many users to judge from reports, prefer a simple dialog approach instead. You can purchase InterPPP from InterCon Systems for $99. For more information, contact InterCon electronically at sales@intercon.com, or at 703-709-5500; 703-709-5555 (fax).

```
http://www.intercon.com/pi/InterPPP.Html
```

MacTCP via ARA

Another, less common method of making a MacTCP-based connection, is via Apple Remote Access, or ARA. ARA is commercial software from Apple that enables you to make a modem connection to another Mac appear as though you had made that via LocalTalk or Ethernet (only slower, of course). ARA comes bundled with many models of the PowerBook, and is also available separately from Apple dealers and mail order vendors; the street price is about $60 for the ARA 2.0 Client software. I include ARA in this chapter because future versions are slated to use PPP internally to make the connection, and the use of ARA to access the Internet isn't currently common enough among Internet access providers to justify an entire chapter.

The advantages of using ARA over MacPPP are that ARA is generally easy to configure, it's supported by Apple and by most modem vendors, and of course, once you make the connection, you have AppleTalk services as well as TCP services. At least two Internet providers, Open Door Networks in Oregon (**info@opendoor.com**, 503-482-3181 via ARA) and the non-profit knoware in the Netherlands use ARA as their primary connection method for Macintosh users. More commonly, though, large organizations with dedicated Internet access on their networks provide ARA dialup facilities and also support MacTCP-based Internet access over those connections.

```
http://www.opendoor.com/
```

```
http://www.knoware.nl/
```

I haven't personally used ARA to access the Internet, although many people have gotten it to work fine using the network at their organization and a Mac at home. If you work with a commercial provider like Open Door Networks, most of the following details won't matter to you, since Open Door Networks will have configured everything for you such that you only need to double-click on a connection document (see figure 18.6) or alias file to establish the connection. (Thanks to Alan Oppenheimer for much of this information.)

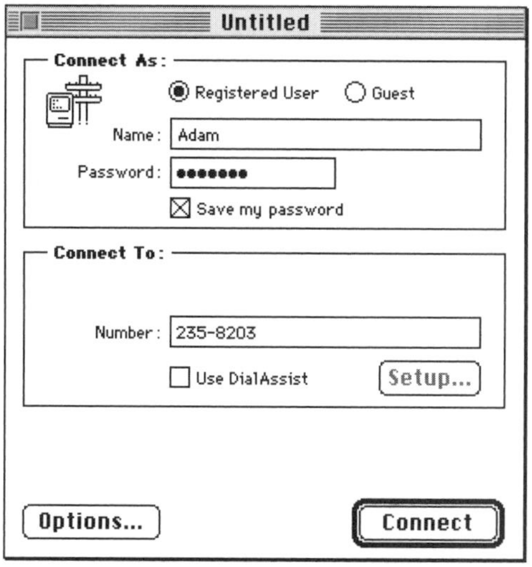

Figure 18.6   *ARA Connection window.*

To use ARA to connect to the Internet, you need a Macintosh with a fast modem, the ARA client, and MacTCP at home. At work you need a Macintosh running the ARA server (or a dedicated piece of hardware from a company like Shiva that provides only ARA dialup facilities), another fast modem, and most importantly, a network link through an IP gateway (like the Apple IP Gateway or the Shiva FastPath)—the gateway connects the ARA server's AppleTalk network to Ethernet and then out to the Internet. So, if you can't use the Mac at work with MacTCP applications to access the Internet, you won't be able to do so via ARA, either.

Second, you need a unique IP address which will be assigned to your home Macintosh, either permanently or by the server each time you dial in, because using a Mac on the Internet via ARA is just like using a Mac on the Internet in any other way. The person in charge of your ARA server or your IP gateway will have to set up this IP address for you.

Once you have those two things done, all you may need to do is bring up the ARA connection to have your Mac at home fully connected to the Internet. If you've never configured MacTCP before, it is probably already configured correctly for a connection over ARA. Just to be sure, however, follow these instructions, noting that there are a few differences between configuring MacTCP for use with PPP or SLIP.

1. Before making the ARA connection, open the MacTCP control panel and make sure the icon in the upper left-hand corner (the AppleTalk connection) is selected. The proper icon is usually LocalTalk or Remote Only, but it may be EtherTalk.

2. Click the More button in MacTCP and select Server-addressing (a Manually-addressed account will work, but is less common in this situation and requires more work). Make sure nothing is typed into the domain name server information fields.

3. Close MacTCP and bring up the ARA connection.

4. Open MacTCP again, and, if you see a list of zones underneath the icon in the upper left-hand corner, select the zone containing your IP gateway. If you aren't sure which zone contains your IP gateway, ask your network administrator.

This ensures that traffic from your Mac will go through the gateway that handles the encapsulation of packets for Ethernet. Because your Mac at home isn't really on Ethernet, its packets will be ignored unless you choose a zone in which an IP gateway lives.

Once you've properly configured MacTCP the first time, you should be able to establish an ARA connection to work any time thereafter. You'll then be able to use the MacTCP-based applications just as though you were directly connected or were using SLIP or PPP to make your connection.

SLIPing On

That pretty much covers MacPPP and the various different add-ons and other implementations of PPP that you're likely to run into. For the most part, the answer to the question of what to try first is MacPPP since it's free and it's included on the disk.

Some people are limited to SLIP accounts though, and for that population, the next chapter will be of more interest.

SLIP

The first thing I want to say is that although I recommend PPP over SLIP, in practice the two methods of connecting to the Internet work almost identically. Performance is similar, and once SLIP or PPP is set up, ease of use is equally similar. If you don't have access to a PPP account or for some reason you simply can't get MacPPP to work, there's nothing wrong with using InterSLIP or one of the other implementations of SLIP and a SLIP account.

If you skipped chapter 18, "PPP," you may wish to go back and read the first parts to get a sense of how SLIP and PPP differ, but the short answer is that although they're functionally identical, they're not interchangeable. So, if you're using a PPP account, you can't use InterSLIP or VersaTerm SLIP with it. They simply won't work, and the reverse is true as well.

Note

You may also hear about CSLIP accounts. CSLIP stands for Compressed SLIP, and it's generally handled by an option in the SLIP program. You don't need different SLIP software to use a CSLIP account.

CSLIP might also be referred to as SLIP using Van Jacobsen header compression or RFC 1144 TCP header compression. It does not compress the data being transferred, it just reduces the amount of overhead information that needs to be transferred over the modem.

SLIP provides an Internet connection for people who connect via modem. If you have a network, either Ethernet or LocalTalk, connected to the Internet, you don't need SLIP.

The easiest way to understand SLIP is to pretend that you don't have water service inside your house. Every time you want to take a shower, you must run a garden hose to the water hookup outside, take your shower, and then reel the hose back in. That's exactly what SLIP does—it establishes a temporary, low-speed connection to the Internet. You must create that connection before you can run programs such as MacWeb and Fetch.

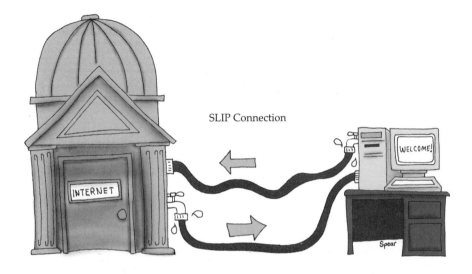

SLIP Connection

Note

Although some implementations of SLIP enable you to launch a MacTCP-based program without connecting first (the SLIP software sees what's up and then establishes the connection), I've found that these auto-connect features can be flaky. If you can use one, great, but if it doesn't work reliably, connect manually first.

SLIP for the Macintosh currently has three different implementations (not counting programs that support SLIP internally, because they're of no use if you want to use another program that doesn't support SLIP internally). Two are commercial, MacSLIP from Hyde Park Software and VersaTerm SLIP from Synergy Software. The third comes from InterCon Systems, a company that has released numerous Internet products, some of which support SLIP internally. InterCon has released this last SLIP, called InterSLIP, as freeware on the Internet, and has graciously allowed me to include it on the disk that comes with this book.

In this chapter, I concentrate on InterSLIP because the other SLIP implementations, being commercial, come with printed documentation and support, and because, in many ways, they are all similar. I'll point out the few differences that I've encountered and comment about why you might want to use one over another.

Getting an Account

When it comes time for you to get a SLIP account, you should check back in chapter 11, "Choosing a Connection," for information on how to pick an Internet access provider. Once you decide on a provider, you need certain information from that provider to configure InterSLIP or other SLIP software. For convenience, I list the most common pieces of information you need in Table 19.1.

Table 19.1
SLIP Information

Item	Question
Phone Number	What number do I call to connect to the server?
Login Name	What is my SLIP account login name? (This name can be different from your userid or machine name.)
Password	What password should I provide when logging in?
MTU	What is the maximum transmission unit size? (1,006 seems to be the standard MTU for SLIP; I've heard of using 296 for CSLIP.)
Header Compression	Should I use RFC 1144 TCP Header Compression (also known as CSLIP)?
Login Procedure	What should I expect to receive from your host machine and how should my Mac respond when logging in?
IP Address	What is my IP number (if a manually addressed account)?
Gateway Address	What is my gateway IP number (if a manually addressed account)?
Domain Name Server	What is the IP number of my primary domain name server?

Part IV   SLIP   19

Again, it's probably easiest to use the worksheet in the back of this book for recording all of this information. I'll cover InterSLIP first and then look at other SLIP software and add-ons.

InterSLIP

InterCon's InterSLIP is one of the most popular pieces of software among the Macintosh Internet crowd because it is freeware that offers functionality equivalent to commercial programs. That's a good way to make friends. InterCon has graciously allowed me to include it on the disk that comes with this book.

> **Note**
>
> *My examples and screen shots in this section apply specifically to configuring my modem, a Telebit WorldBlazer, with a manually addressed SLIP account. Your settings will be different; I guarantee it. For a step-by-step walk-through of how to install InterSLIP for a server-addressed account with Northwest Nexus, check out chapter 29, "Step-by-Step Internet."*

Installation and Setup

Installing InterSLIP requires placing an extension called InterSLIP in your Extensions folder. If you drag it onto the System Folder icon, System 7 places InterSLIP in the correct location. A control panel called InterSLIP Control is also available (and generally installed by default), but in fact it's entirely unnecessary for System 7 users; it is only required for use with System 6. The application called InterSLIP Setup can live anywhere on your hard disk, but it may be a good idea to put it or an alias to it in your Apple Menu Items folder for easy access. After you place those parts in the proper places, restart your Mac. Make sure InterSLIP is selected in the MacTCP main window, and then proceed with configuring InterSLIP.

> **Note**
>
> *On the disk in the back of the book, the ISKM Installer's custom options that include InterSLIP install all of the parts of InterSLIP in the proper places. Just as with MacTCP and MacPPP, I provide the detail here in case you install InterSLIP from some other source (such as an update) or merely want to know how the manual installation process works.*

Although InterSLIP Setup and InterSLIP Control share similar interfaces and functions, you use InterSLIP Setup to configure your connection. InterSLIP Control enables you to select a configuration and connect and disconnect, but you must configure it from InterSLIP Setup (hence the name, I suppose) (see figure 19.1). Frankly, if you use System 7, I'd recommend throwing InterSLIP Control out. I haven't had it installed for months now, and it's made no difference at all.

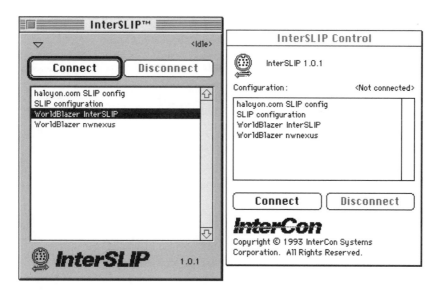

Figure 19.1   *InterSLIP Setup and InterSLIP Control.*

To create a new configuration, launch InterSLIP Setup, and from the File menu choose New. InterSLIP Setup prompts you for a name with a dialog box; give your configuration a name (it doesn't matter what) and click on the OK button. Although InterSLIP Setup provides no way of deleting a configuration from within the program, configuration files are stored in an automatically created InterSLIP Folder within the Preferences folder. If you create a configuration you don't want to keep, throw out its file from this folder.

After you create the configuration, you must configure it for your particular modem and account. You need information from your system administrator to configure InterSLIP, so be prepared to give your provider a call if you didn't get it all when you signed up for the account. Double-click on the configuration you just created to bring up the configuration dialog (see figure 19.2).

Let's take it from the top left of the dialog. The serial port should generally be set to your Modem port, although you could attach a modem to your Printer port. If you use a PowerBook with an internal bus modem that connects directly to the CPU (such as the Apple Express Modem and the Global Village PowerPort/Mercury for the PowerBook 500 series and the PowerBook Duo), you get an Internal Modem choice, and the PowerBook 500 series may show a Printer-Modem Port choice. Although I don't have such a modem to test, I suspect that if you have a nonbus internal PowerBook modem, you should choose the Modem port, just as with MacPPP (also see the notes about bus modems in chapter 18, "PPP").

The Baud Rate setting is the rate at which your modem and your Mac communicate, which is why there is no setting for 14,400, since that's a speed at which the two modems communicate (and some modems cannot even accept a port speed of 14,400 or 28,800 bps). The speed that the Mac and the modem communicate should be set faster than the speed that the modems communicate to take advantage of modem compression capabilities.

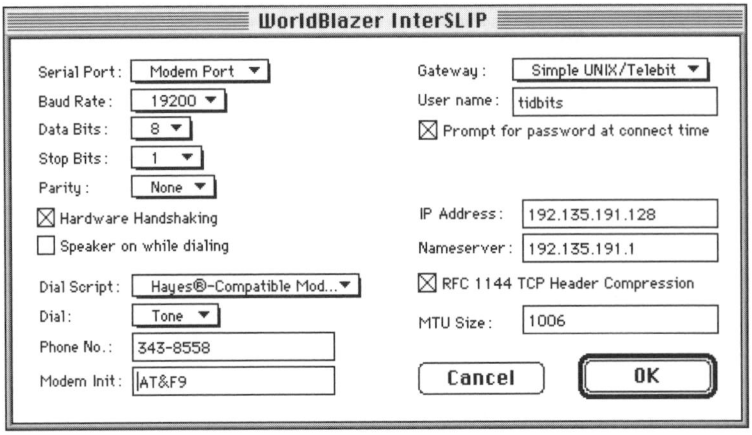

Figure 19.2   *InterSLIP configuration dialog.*

Data Bits, Stop Bits, and Parity are almost always set as I have them here, to 8 data bits, 1 stop bit, and no parity, although I suppose it's possible that some providers are different. The Hardware Handshaking checkbox requires that you have a hardware handshaking cable, and if you have a fast modem, you should have one of those. I've heard that if you don't have a hardware handshaking cable but attempt to use that checkbox, it may cause InterSLIP to hang.

Turning the speaker on or off is up to you, although I generally recommend you leave it on until you have everything working for a few days. Then, when the modem screams start to irritate you, turn it off.

> **Note**
>
> *Depending on your modem and your modem initialization string, InterSLIP sometimes seems to ignore the speaker checkbox. You can always override it by adding **M0** to your initialization string to turn off the modem speaker.*

The Dial Script pop-up menu defaults to Direct Connection, something I doubt most people have. The other built-in choice is Hayes-Compatible Modem, and I recommend you choose that option to start with. I certainly hope your modem is Hayes-compatible; you're likely to have trouble if it's not. Unfortunately, even if your modem claims it's Hayes-compatible, that doesn't inherently mean that it works with the Hayes-Compatible modem script in InterSLIP. Luckily, InterSLIP supports other modems through the use of *dialing scripts* written in the *CCL* (Connection Control Language). CCL scripts are primarily used with Apple Remote Access (ARA). You can find many dialing scripts (their names start with **scr** and generally include a modem name as well) in:

```
ftp://ftp.tidbits.com/pub/tidbits/tisk/tcp/
```

> **N o t e**
>
> Dialing scripts *are text files that are very similar to ARA (Apple Remote Access) scripts. The only difference is that ARA turns off data compression and error correction, whereas those two settings should be on for an InterSLIP dialing script. Many modem vendors will send you an ARA script for your modem, if it wasn't included, and you can find many ARA scripts in:*
>
> ```
> ftp://ftp.tidbits.com/pub/tidbits/tisk/ara/
> ```

You can add dialing scripts to the Dialing folder inside the InterSLIP Folder inside the Preferences folder. To edit an ARA script, you may have to use Shift-Open in Word or Nisus's All Files option in its Catalog to be able to open the ARA script. These scripts are text-only, but they tend to come with a type and creator that prevents text editors from reading them. Make sure to save as text when you're done, though. Dialing scripts can be very important—for some modems, they're even essential.

I've found that many dialing scripts have huge amounts of useless sections; Fred Morris has written a minimal dialing script that works well with many modems, assuming the modem initialization string you use is correct. I added redial capabilities to the script and included it on the disk so that the ISKM Installer installs it for InterSLIP by default. It's called Minimal Dialing Script, and aside from being able to redial, it's useful because it tends to be more effective at hanging up your modem when you click on the Disconnect button in InterSLIP, something the Hayes-Compatible Modem choice has trouble doing with some modems. Enough about the Dial Script menu; stick with Hayes-Compatible Modem or my Minimal Dialing Script, if you can.

> **N o t e**
>
> *Considering how much technical support costs, the people at InterCon help you with InterSLIP only if you are also a registered user of one of their other programs. I think that arrangement is extremely fair because they've already provided a great service to the Internet community by releasing InterSLIP for free. So please, do* not *expect support from InterCon unless you purchase one of their other products.*

The next three items, which control the dialing method, phone number, and modem initialization string, don't appear until you choose Hayes-Compatible Modem or another dialing script. I hope that when these items appear, it is relatively obvious how to fill them in. Most people have tone dialing these days (although the few people with pulse dialing would do well to check dialing scripts for **ATDT** commands and replace them with **ATDP** commands), and your system administrator should tell you the phone number when you get the account. The modem initialization string is a bit trickier, but most modern modems support something like **AT&F1** for setting the factory default standard options. As you can see, my WorldBlazer goes all out on the **&F** parameters; I must use **AT&F9**, which turns on hardware handshaking for the Macintosh. Look in your modem manual or in another communications program that comes with settings for popular modems to figure out the most appropriate initialization string.

> **N o t e**
>
> *I've also included a file containing many modem strings on the disk. The ISKM Installer has the information in the installer help text, and the file is installed in the InterSLIP 1.0.1 folder (not the InterSLIP Folder that lives in your Preferences folder). These modem strings are generally untested, but should either work or put you on the right track.*

The most important thing to watch for here is the hardware handshaking setting. Not only do you want to make sure your initialization string turns on hardware handshaking, but you also want to make sure that software handshaking, more commonly known as XON/XOFF, is turned off. If XON/XOFF is turned on in the modem initialization string or is part of the factory default settings (as it is for the Telebit QBlazer modem), InterSLIP almost certainly won't work right.

At the top right of the window is another pop-up menu labeled Gateway. It defaults to Direct Connection, but again, I think the other option, Simple UNIX/Telebit, is more commonly used. The Simple UNIX/Telebit script simply looks for the login prompt, sends your userid, looks for the password prompt, sends your password, and assumes there's nothing more to do before starting SLIP. Unfortunately, that's not always true.

Just as with dialing scripts, you can write your own *gateway script* in the Connection Control Language and place it in the Gateway Scripts folder in the InterSLIP Folder. Unfortunately, if you have a nonstandard gateway, you probably will have to write your own, although I've collected a few of them in:

---

ftp://ftp.tidbits.com/pub/tidbits/tisk/tcp/

(Look for "scr" in the beginning of the name, and the name of a provider, university, person, or server such as Annex or Cisco in the rest of the name.)

The gateway script is a conversation between your computer and your host computer as your computer tries to log in to the host. There's no telling what sort of prompts your host sends or what it requests, so again, I can't help much with specifics here. I strongly recommend that you work through the process manually using a terminal emulator to see what the host sends and what it expects back. After you've done that, you stand a chance of converting that information into a gateway script. Also, ask your system administrator to advise you of any quirks in logging in.

N o t e

A few people need to use what's called a dialback system which, for security reasons, makes you log in normally, then hangs up and calls you back at a prespecified phone number. Although a truly hairy process, you could write a gateway script that, instead of just logging in, would log in, hang up the phone, set autoanswer, wait for a RING, answer the phone, wait for a CONNECT, and then proceed with the rest of the script. Nasty, but possible.

In general, you usually send a return, the host sends a login: prompt, you send your login name, the host provides a Password: prompt, you send your password, and then something else happens. For instance, if you use a server-addressed account, the gateway script must include some method of finding the IP number that the server assigns to you—it usually appears after you send the password. I've included a gateway script that works with the Northwest Nexus server-addressed accounts, and I recommend that you use it as an example of how to write your own (not that it's a paragon of scripting virtue, but it does work).

N o t e

Many people ask where they can find more information on scripting in the CCL language that InterSLIP uses for both dialing and gateway scripts. Unfortunately, the best information available is in InterSLIP's documentation, so you've got it already. Maybe someone will write a CCL tutorial and post it on the nets. (Hint hint!)

If you have trouble making InterSLIP connect, you might also try a hack with which some people have reported success. Set InterSLIP to Direct Connection in both the Dial Script menu and the Gateway menu. Then, using a terminal emulator, dial your host machine, and at the point when SLIP starts on the host, click on InterSLIP's Connect button. It's a hack indeed (ordinarily you'd *never* use a terminal emulator to dial a SLIP account), but it might work while you figure out a gateway script.

Let's move on to the User name field in the InterSLIP configuration dialog. Most of the time, your system administrator assigns this name to you, along with a password, although you may get to pick them yourself. Your username may or may not be related to your machine name or your email address. It's simply the name you use to log in to your SLIP account. Make sure you enter your username in lowercase—Unix is case-sensitive, so **Adam** is not the same account as **adam**, and your password won't work with a mixed-case username if it were created with a lowercase username.

I've checked the Prompt for password at connect time checkbox in the InterSLIP configuration dialog because publishing a screen shot of my password isn't a terribly clever thing to do in terms of security. However, if that checkbox isn't checked, you get another text field that holds your password. If you don't mind the security risk of having your password visible here, go ahead and enter it, being careful to enter it exactly as it was created. Passwords are always case sensitive, so make sure you match the case of each letter or else the host will reject it.

The next four items—IP Address, Nameserver, checkbox for RFC 1144 TCP Header Compression, and MTU (Maximum Transmission Unit) Size—require information from your provider. You can see the sorts of things I've put in, but your situation may be entirely different (and your IP Address and Nameserver certainly are). Again, if your provider tells you that you have a CSLIP account, make sure to check the TCP Header Compression checkbox. Even if the term CSLIP isn't mentioned, make sure to check with your administrator, because if the TCP Header Compression setting in InterSLIP doesn't match what your account has set, strange errors will result.

After you're all done, click on the OK button to save your changes. If you have more than one SLIP account on different hosts, you can create additional configuration files and switch between them in InterSLIP Setup by selecting the one you want before you click on the Connect button.

Basic Usage

Clicking on the triangle in the upper left of the InterSLIP Setup window shrinks the window to display only the Connect and Disconnect buttons and the area that displays the connection status (see figure 19.3).

Figure 19.3   *InterSLIP Setup window, shrunk.*

If you have only one configuration, the only reason to leave the window expanded is if you need to edit your configuration frequently (which shouldn't be the case). InterSLIP Setup also remembers where on the screen you put it, so it's easy to put it out of the way and leave it active most of the time. InterSLIP Setup takes only 128K of RAM, so it's no great liability.

> **Note**
>
> *There's a bug in InterSLIP Setup related to the way it remembers where you place the window. If you put InterSLIP Setup's window on a second monitor (assuming you have two attached to your Macintosh, as I do), then move or remove that monitor, InterSLIP Setup will almost certainly crash on launch. To solve the problem, throw away the InterSLIP Preferences file in your InterSLIP Folder. All that's stored there is the window location and the selected configuration file, so it's no loss.*

You have two ways to use InterSLIP to connect to your host, manually and automatically. The manual method takes more effort because you must click on the Connect button in InterSLIP Setup, but it works much more reliably. The automatic method is exactly that, automatic, so whenever you launch Fetch or Eudora or any program that requests MacTCP services, InterSLIP kicks in and connects to your host. Or at least that's the idea.

The problem with the automatic technique is that it doesn't work all the time. When it doesn't work, you must usually force quit (hold down the Command and Option keys and press Escape) the MacTCP application that couldn't connect and then restart the machine, because something at a low level has been hosed. I had trouble using the automatic connection with a number of the applications I discuss later in this section, and everything based on HyperCard caused trouble. Even such usually well-behaved applications as Fetch sometimes caused problems, perhaps because the connection takes longer than it was prepared to wait. As neat and useful as the automatic connection feature is, therefore, I cannot recommend using it if you use a wide variety of MacTCP software. If you primarily use Eudora, you're probably okay—but even then, make sure you have work in other applications saved before you attempt to start an automatic connection.

Either way, manual or automatic, when asked, InterSLIP dials your host, signs in, and then lets you get on with your work. You see various messages (they're stored in the dialing script and the gateway script) in the status area in the upper right of the InterSLIP Setup window that tell you what InterSLIP thinks is happening, most notably the Connected message when you have connected successfully. When you aren't connected, it should say Idle. As soon as you connect, the Connect button becomes disabled and the Disconnect button becomes enabled. There is no automatic disconnection, so you must make sure to click the Disconnect button when you're finished.

Note

Many people have asked for a way to have InterSLIP disconnect automatically when they're finished, say, downloading their mail with Eudora, but there's no way this can happen without additional work on your part. Eudora has no way of knowing how the connection has been established or even that you use InterSLIP. And, InterSLIP can't know when you're done and when you might want to do something else. You could, however, script this behavior with QuicKeys, AppleScript, or Frontier. Using the latter two may be easier with InterSLIP/AE, a little program written by Leonard Rosenthol to control InterSLIP via Apple events. See the capsule review following this section.

Part IV SLIP

Now you know all there is to using InterSLIP, but there are a few tricks that I want to mention.

SLIPing

I don't know how common this situation is, but with some SLIP hosts, for which you pay for the time you're connected, a timeout is set to hang up the phone line after a certain amount of idle time. If you think about it, this is a feature, not a bug; otherwise, you could get called away from the computer while using your SLIP account, forget about it entirely, and find yourself faced with a much larger usage bill. The timeout generally works well, but it does modify how you work.

If (and only if!) you use the same IP address every time you connect and your connection hangs up on you before you are finished, switch back to InterSLIP Setup, click the Disconnect button, and then click the Connect button. After you reestablish the connection, you can switch back into your MacTCP application and continue where you left off.

If, however, you use server addressing (in which the server assigns an IP address to you each time you log in), you must quit the active MacTCP programs before you reconnect via SLIP! Because you may end up with a different IP address when you call back after being disconnected, MacTCP programs may become extremely flustered at the change, and there's no predicting what could happen (but it probably involves crashing).

You must decide whether the timeout bothers you or not. As long as you can easily see the connection lights on your modem (assuming you're not using an internal PowerBook modem), you can tell when the line has hung up. If you want to keep the line open, you must keep doing things that access the network. One trick is to run Peter Lewis's shareware Talk program whenever you're connected, because it queries the network periodically. There are other tricks that work equally as well, such as having Eudora check your mail every four or five minutes.

More likely, though, you must figure out the proper methods of working. For instance, in a newsreader you can certainly open a bunch of articles or threads at once and then read them all onscreen. Unless you're a very fast reader, though, the connection will almost certainly get bored and hang up on you. Unless you want to treat the newsreader as an offline newsreader in this way, it might work better to read only one article or thread at a time, making sure that the newsreader periodically has to ask for more articles. In addition, you see that if you ask for a bunch of threads all at once, it takes a long time to get them, whereas if you go for the one-at-a-time approach, you can read constantly. Either approach has pros and cons, and it's up to you to decide which best fits your working style.

The program that can work best in this environment, of course, is one like Eudora or NewsHopper, which can log in, send and receive queued messages, and then log out immediately, letting you do all your work while disconnected from the network. Unfortunately, none of the freeware newsreaders have this feature quite yet, although it does exist in NewsHopper and the newsreader built into Synergy's VersaTerm-Link.

Using System 6

Frankly, I know little about using InterSLIP with System 6, mostly because I haven't used System 6 in almost four years. However, despite the note on the cover about requiring System 7, you may be able to use System 6 for some tasks.

To establish a connection with InterSLIP, you must have InterSLIP Control (a control panel) installed. As long as you have InterSLIP Control installed, InterSLIP should work the same as it does under System 7.

Note

Much of the Internet software released today requires System 7, so you may not be able to use it at all under System 6. That's the price of not upgrading. Eudora 1.4 and later require System 7, for instance, but Qualcomm keeps Eudora version 1.3.1 around for System 6 users. It's at:

```
ftp://ftp.qualcomm.com/quest/mac/eudora/1.3/eudora131.hqx
```

Overall Evaluation

InterSLIP's primary neat feature, other than the fact that it works well, is its automatic connect feature, which unfortunately I find to be problematic. A feature I'd like to see in InterSLIP is the capability to show a terminal window of the connection (or even let you navigate in manually!) and capture a log of what happens during connection to ease troubleshooting.

One existing feature that I didn't much think of originally but have come to appreciate is that InterSLIP dials (and redials, if you have a dialing script that redials) in the background. That means you can click the Connect button in InterSLIP and then go back to whatever you were doing until it finishes connecting. In contrast, MacPPP puts up a modal dialog that prevents you from doing anything else while it dials.

Even if InterSLIP doesn't have every imaginable feature, it's free and it's on the ISKM disk, so it's hard to complain too loudly. And, if for some reason you don't like InterSLIP or you have trouble getting it to work, you can always buy one of the other two SLIP programs or use PPP and MacPPP.

Part IV

SLIP

Administrative Details

As I've said, InterSLIP is free from InterCon Systems. InterCon does *not* support InterSLIP, so if you have trouble, try posting in **comp.sys.mac.comm**. Doing so often results in help from other users or from InterSLIP's author. Also consider asking on a mailing list like the Apple Internet Users mailing list (send a message containing the command **info apple-internet-users** to **listproc@abs.apple.com** for information on how to subscribe). InterCon runs its own FTP site at **ftp.intercon.com**, and you can find the latest version of InterSLIP there or on **ftp.tidbits.com**:

```
ftp://ftp.tidbits.com/pub/tidbits/tisk/tcp/
```

```
ftp://ftp.intercon.com/intercon/sales/InterSLIP/
```

InterSLIP Add-Ons

There are a few utilities that enhance the experience of working with InterSLIP, mostly making the act of connecting and disconnecting easier. Some other utilities help you time how long you spend online, which is useful for folks who call long distance or who must pay by the minute for their Internet connections. Unless I mention otherwise, all the utilities following are in:

```
ftp://ftp.tidbits.com/pub/tidbits/tisk/tcp/
```

InterSLIP/AE

Leonard Rosenthol's free InterSLIP/AE is a tiny application that does little more than enable you to control InterSLIP using scripts written in AppleScript, Frontier, or QuicKeys. It does have a minimal interface that lets you connect and can display the connection status and configuration. It's a must for anyone who wants to automate connections via InterSLIP and a scripting application.

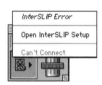

InterSLIP Strip Module

Troy Gaul's freeware InterSLIP Strip Module brings control of InterSLIP to users of Apple's Control Strip on PowerBooks and to those who use Desktop Strip or DragStrip (like me) on desktop Macs. InterSLIP Strip Module enables you to connect and disconnect InterSLIP sessions, (I got an error in my screen shot—oh well), and open the InterSLIP Setup application. If you use InterSLIP and Control Strip or another utility that supports Control Strip modules, this one's definitely worth a look.

InterSLIP Timer

InterSLIP Timer from Eric Preston is a small $5 shareware application that times both the session connection time and the cumulative connection time, making it easy for you to determine how large your Internet or phone bill will be at the end of the month. You must launch it manually, but you can also use it to start and end your InterSLIP session. Once active, InterSLIP Timer displays a small floating window that contains both the session time and the cumulative time.

Other SLIP Software

Although I recommend InterSLIP as the first SLIP program you should try, that's mostly because it's free and it works well for many people. There are also several other implementations of SLIP that work better for some users. One of them, VersaTerm SLIP, is notable because it's easier to configure than either InterSLIP or the other commercial contender, MacSLIP.

InterSLIP 1.02d2

The current version of InterSLIP is 1.0.1, and for most people, that's the version to stick with. However, Amanda Walker has tweaked some of the code in InterSLIP and produced a 1.0.2d2 (d2 means the second development release) version. It fixes some problems and introduces others (that's why it's a development release and not official). The main fixes include some MacTCP performance enhancements, the addition of the term "CSLIP" to the RFC 1144 TCP Header Compression checkbox, the ability to disable automatic connections, better detection of dropped connections, and most notably, support for 115,200 and 230,400 bps port speeds, mostly for compatibility with ISDN connections. If you're having trouble with InterSLIP and think 1.0.2d2 might help, give it a try, but again, don't complain if it doesn't help. The fact

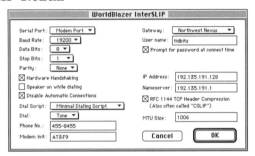

that InterCon makes it available at all (and it may have removed this version by the time you read this) is a huge help and must not be abused.

```
ftp://ftp.intercon.com//intercon/test/InterSLIP-1.0.2d2.sea.hqx
```

MacSLIP

MacSLIP was written by Rick Watson of Hyde Park Software and is marketed and supported by TriSoft. MacSLIP 2.0 costs $49.95 and may offer the largest feature set of all three SLIPs. MacSLIP 2.0 has only a control panel and a MacSLIP extension. MacSLIP 2.0 sports an automatic connection feature, ships with a number of modem initialization strings, can notify you of your connection time, and displays statistics about the IP address, connect time, and serial line from within the control panel. My main complaint about MacSLIP is that the scripting language used to connect to your host—although certainly full-featured—is not the sort of thing a novice wants to mess with. Conversely, for an accomplished scripter, MacSLIP's scripting language may be just what you've always wanted. You can get more information about MacSLIP by sending email to **info@hydepark.com**, and MacSLIP 2.0 ships with MicroPhone Pro, or you can order it alone for $49.95 from TriSoft at 800-531-5170, 512-472-0744, or 512-473-2122 (fax).

VersaTerm SLIP

Synergy Software claims that VersaTerm SLIP was the first commercially available SLIP for the Macintosh, and in my experience, it's also stable and reliable. VersaTerm SLIP includes an extension, a control panel, and an application, VersaTerm AdminSLIP, with which you interact. Of all the SLIP implementations, VersaTerm AdminSLIP uses the easiest method of writing a script, providing a simple dialog box for creating the login script. In addition, VersaTerm AdminSLIP includes a simple but useful terminal emulator. You can't buy VersaTerm SLIP by itself; it comes with Synergy Software's other VersaTerm packages, which range widely in price and capability.

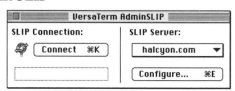

You also get the VersaTerm-Link program with VersaTerm SLIP; it's discussed in chapter 28, "Integrated Programs." You can contact Synergy to find out more about buying any of its programs via the Internet at **maxwell@sales.synergy.com**, via phone at 215-779-0522, or via fax at 215-370-0548.

But What If...

Well, you should now be as much of an expert on SLIP, and InterSLIP in particular, as I can make you. The silly part of this and the previous two chapters is that once you have installed and configured MacTCP and either InterSLIP or MacPPP, your only interaction with them is opening and closing the connection. However, that assumes everything goes as planned, and as we all know, Murphy's Law has yet to be declared unconstitutional. Shall we move on to some troubleshooting information, then? Of course, if everything is working properly with your connection, in defiance of Murphy and the laws of nature, feel free to ignore the next chapter entirely.

Troubleshooting Your Connection

If you went through the various steps in the previous chapters to configure MacTCP and either InterSLIP or MacPPP and everything works, congratulations! Skip this chapter entirely, since it can get a bit technical in places and if everything works, there's no need to dwell on what might not work. Most people don't have much trouble, but there are some pitfalls to avoid and some tricks and tips I've learned since the first edition of this book. I'd like to share some of the problems and solutions with you here, and although I hope you don't need to read this section, if you do, I hope it helps. I've formatted the section along the lines of an Internet FAQ, or Frequently Asked Question, list. Within each section, I've tried to organize the question and answers roughly as you might experience them—for example, there's no point in putting suggestions about improving performance before suggestions about how to get around a modem problem and connect in the first place.

Reporting Problems

Before I even begin to talk about what might go wrong, I want to say a few words about how you can best go about isolating problems and then reporting them on the nets or to tech support. If you ask for help on **comp.sys.mac.comm** by posting a note that says something like, "I'm connecting to the nets via SLIP and it doesn't work. What am I doing wrong?" you won't get any helpful responses. You probably won't get any responses at all, helpful or not, since people will have no clue what your problem is other than the fact that you don't know how to ask for help. If you follow the steps that I suggest when working through **any** problem, not only problems with MacTCP, MacPPP, or InterSLIP, you'll be better off.

When you've determined that you have a problem, do the following: Start over completely from scratch, removing from the System Folder all files related to MacTCP and MacPPP or InterSLIP, including preferences files.

Note

One quick way to find all these files for quick removal is to use the Find command in the Finder's File menu to search for "TCP" and either "PPP" or "InterSLIP." I recommend not actually deleting these files until you're up and running again, just in case, but that's why Apple created a persistent Trash.

After you've removed the old files, carefully follow each step in the instructions, noting anything that doesn't seem to mesh between your setup and what the instructions say. If you deviate from the instructions, note that, too. In many cases, following this procedure will either solve the problem or reveal where it lies. Taking something apart and putting it back together often fixes problems for no apparent reason. Don't think of this process as an unpleasant chore, because then you're likely to become careless and miss an important clue. Troubleshooting can be a lot of fun, because you learn a lot more about the topic at hand, and you get to solve a real-life mystery in which no one dies.

Unfortunately, because we're all amateur sleuths, we're not always able to find the solution to a problem and must consult others who are more knowledgeable or who have a different way of looking at the problem. If you are having trouble with a commercial program, the first experts to turn to should be the technical support staff at the company that produced your program. I've heard good things about most of the technical support staffs of companies that make Internet applications, although quality tech support is never guaranteed.

When dealing with telephone tech support people, keep in mind that they probably know a lot more about the program in question than you do, they answer a huge number of calls every day, and the job has a high burnout rate because it's so stressful. You're most likely to get the best help if you're polite and cooperate with what they ask you to do. If you call and announce that you're a power user and why doesn't this stupid program work anyway, you're unlikely to get decent help. If, on the other hand, you call, say that you're having troubles, and give the information the tech support person asks for, she can do a much better job. It never pays to alienate the person whom you're asking for help—whatever is wrong is almost certainly not her fault.

If you are using a freeware or shareware application, it usually says whether or not the author is willing to help via direct email. One way or another, though, there are several places where you can ask for help from other users, many of whom are true experts. Also, the developers of many of the freeware and shareware utilities tend to hang out in these same places and help their users, even if they prefer not to be continually slammed by personal email. The best place to ask for help with Internet stuff is on the Usenet newsgroup `comp.sys.mac.comm`. There are also many knowledgeable people who hang out in the Apple Internet Users mailing list, which you can subscribe to by sending email to `listproc@abs.apple.com` with the command **subscribe apple-internet-users** *Your Name* in the body of the message. If you can post to a newsgroup, there are often newsgroups specific to your provider where local folks hang out and answer questions, like the `halcyon.slip` group at Northwest Nexus.

Note

If you don't read a newsgroup regularly, you should explicitly ask for replies via email so you don't miss any replies.

No matter what, if you want any of these people to help you, you must help them first by sending a complete report. In that report, you should include the following:

- List exactly what it is that you're trying to accomplish. This should be specific, because telling someone that you want to read Usenet news with NewsWatcher isn't salient to the problem of not being able to get InterSLIP to connect. Take each goal a step at a time.

- Mention the fact that you have carefully followed the directions. This fact tells people that (a) you're not a complete idiot and can read, (b) that you have gone through a certain set of procedures already, and it tells them that you are capable of following any suggestions they make. If you haven't followed the directions carefully, don't bother posting until you do so.

- List the salient facts of your software and hardware setup. Include things such as what Mac you have, what modem you use, what version of the System software you're running, and any weird stuff that you can't eliminate from the testing (such as, for example, an Outbound user who had additional software from Outbound that was necessary for his machine to boot properly). Unless asked, don't bother listing out every extension and control panel on your hard disk. You should have already eliminated them in the process of testing by removing everything but MacTCP and either InterSLIP or PPP and Config PPP from your Extensions and Control Panels folders. Also, an unusually long report will turn many people off.

- Talk a bit about what you have already tried, whether or not it worked, and whether you noticed anything strange happening at any time during the process. If you encounter error dialogs at any time, report exactly what they say.

- Be nice. The last thing you want to do is insult an expert's favorite program, since they're less likely to help you at that point. When you're in trouble, it doesn't help to alienate anyone.

MacTCP Q & A

Before anything else, let me emphasize that you may need to reinstall a clean copy of MacTCP at various times to solve problems. Thus, you must keep a clean copy that you have never opened on a locked floppy. The copy that comes on the disk with this book qualifies as a clean copy of MacTCP.

> **Note**
>
> *At some point you may want to set aside a clean, unused copy of MacTCP to facilitate reinstallations. To do so, move your existing copies of MacTCP and MacTCP Prep to the desktop, restart with extensions off, run the ISKM Installer and install just a new copy of MacTCP. When forced to restart, again keep the extensions off. This ensures that you have a clean copy of MacTCP in your Control Panels folder. Put that copy of MacTCP on a floppy as a backup. Then replace your old MacTCP and MacTCP Prep files and restart to return to your previous state.*

Also, let me recommend that if you have FTP access, you get a copy of Peter Lewis's free MacTCP Watcher. It includes another document on troubleshooting MacTCP connections, written by Eric Behr. It's in:

```
ftp://ftp.tidbits.com/pub/tidbits/tisk/tcp/
```

Anyway, on to the questions and answers about MacTCP!

Q: I don't see an icon for InterSLIP or PPP in my MacTCP control panel.

A: Install InterSLIP or PPP in your Extensions folder, and try again.

Q: I get a weird -23004 error from MacTCP, and it complains about its drivers not being installed.

A: Make sure that you select InterSLIP or PPP and *not* LocalTalk in the MacTCP control panel.

Q: What about that weird slider bar in the upper right of the MacTCP configuration dialog?

A: Ignore it unless you're on a subnet, which means you'll have a network administrator who can tell you what to do there.

Q: Should I type anything in the IP number box in the MacTCP control panel if I'm using Server addressing?

A: No. Only enter a number there if you use a Manually-addressed account.

Q: Why can't I type anything in the Gateway box in the MacTCP configuration dialog when I'm using Server addressing?

A: Your gateway address is determined by your server when you use Server addressing, which is why you can't type in there. InterSLIP fills it in for MacTCP, but it makes no real difference.

However, one reader found that in using VersaTerm SLIP, the first time you log in you must enter a Gateway address and your IP address into VersaTerm SLIP, via either the fields in the upper right of the configuration window or a small pop-up menu in VersaTerm AdminSLIP's terminal window. With Northwest Nexus, the Gateway address in this case is the first of the two IP numbers that the machine provides after you enter your login name and password, something like **198.137.231.150**. Your IP address for that session is the second of the two numbers. Other providers may be similar.

Q: What are the MacTCP DNR and MacTCP Prep files?

A: MacTCP creates them when you restart, to store various settings and preferences. You can throw them out at any time with impunity, since MacTCP recreates them with the same settings when you restart. Note that you must restart after throwing them out since MacTCP applications require MacTCP DNR to work properly.

If you reinstall MacTCP without throwing out these files, MacTCP retains the settings it had before you reinstalled. This can be useful for moving copies of MacTCP around, but they also tend to retain any corruption.

Q: My Mac crashed the first time I restarted after reinstalling MacTCP. Should I be worried, even though it doesn't crash now?

A: I would completely reinstall MacTCP (throwing out MacTCP DNR and MacTCP Prep as well) and reconfigure to be safe, but I don't think you should worry too much. Anti-virus software like SAM can sometimes get persnickety about MacTCP creating the MacTCP DNR file, and I could see that perhaps causing the problem.

In fact, I hear that if the MacTCP DNR files become corrupted, some anti-virus software, such as Gatekeeper, could possibly prevent MacTCP from updating it, which is a bad thing. If you use sensitive anti-virus software that tries to prevent unknown actions (Disinfectant is fine), to be very sure it isn't causing problems, turn it off, delete MacTCP, MacTCP DNR, and MacTCP Prep, reinstall a clean copy of MacTCP, restart, turn the anti-virus software back on, and restart again.

Q: Hmm, I don't seem to have a MacTCP DNR file. Why not?

A: That's really weird, but one reader reported a reproducible conflict with a control panel from Apple called CPU Energy Saver. Try removing it and restarting. MacTCP should create a new MacTCP DNR file on restart if it's not present.

Q: I also don't have a MacTCP Prep file.

A: First, try opening MacTCP, changing something and then closing it. That should force the creation of a MacTCP Prep file in the Preferences folder. If that doesn't work, restart without extensions, particularly anti-virus programs, and try reconfiguring MacTCP again.

Q: I crashed while using Fetch or some other MacTCP-based program. Should I reinstall MacTCP?

A: Possibly. First, connect again to see if Fetch works. If it does, you're fine. If it doesn't, throw out the MacTCP DNR file and restart. Try Fetch again. If it still doesn't work, completely reinstall MacTCP from scratch. This isn't usually necessary, luckily.

After a truly nasty crash, you may find it necessary to reinstall InterSLIP or MacPPP as well. If you use InterSLIP, remove your modem configuration file from the InterSLIP folder before reinstalling InterSLIP, because it's worth trying with your old configuration file before you toast it as well.

Q: I'm getting the impression that reinstalling MacTCP is a common occurrence. Is that true?

A: Yes and no. I seldom do it, but frankly, if anything goes wrong, reinstalling MacTCP is worth trying. Make sure to throw out MacTCP DNR and MacTCP Prep, too, since they can harbor the corruption that caused MacTCP to have problems in the first place. Always keep a copy of MacTCP on a locked floppy disk, to facilitate reinstallation.

Q: I'm running MacTCP 2.0.2 or 2.0.4. Should I update to 2.0.6?

A: Sure, why not? I personally haven't seen any problems in 2.0.2 or 2.0.4 that were fixed in 2.0.6, but others have, and it's a free update that's stored on:

```
ftp://ftp.tidbits.com/pub/tidbits/tisk/tcp/mactcp-206-updt.hqx
```

Besides, MacTCP 2.0.6 is on the disk that comes with this book, so you can install it from there if you want, first removing the old MacTCP, MacTCP DNR, and MacTCP Prep.

Q: When I went to update my copy of MacTCP to 2.0.6, I got some sort of error about a DRVR 22. What's that all about?

A: The MacTCP updater only works on a clean copy of MacTCP that has never been opened before. Get a new copy from your master disk, update it, and the updater will work fine. Then, keep a clean copy of 2.0.6 on a locked floppy somewhere for use when reinstalling.

Domain Name Server Errors

I've noticed many people running into a problem where SLIP or PPP (any implementation) connects properly, but trouble arises with the domain name server when they attempt to run any of the other MacTCP programs. Sometimes they crash or hang, but the behavior is usually completely reproducible (although we have seen the occasional exception, where it will work fine once after reinstalling MacTCP but fail on subsequent connections). This problem occurs primarily in Server-addressed situations, but I've heard sporadic reports from people using Manually-addressed accounts.

I haven't absolutely solved this problem yet, I'm sorry to say, but here are some things to try. I find that the easiest way to test this situation is with Peter Lewis's free MacTCP Watcher, which shows an IP number but no Mac name in this instance. It also complains about a "No answer error" or a "Cache fault error" when it is unable to find the domain name server. If you use Fetch, you can tell quickly that you are seeing the problem if when you connect, the dog cursor is frozen. If the dog cursor runs, you're generally better off. If the cursor is frozen, immediately hit command-period to try canceling the connection before Fetch hangs. NCSA Telnet can prove useful as well, since in some cases you may be able to telnet to a machine by using its IP number, but using the domain name fails. This indicates that the connection works, but that there is a problem resolving domain names.

Note that the problem is generally not with your account. Each time someone has had this problem and asked me to check their account, it has worked fine if they did indeed have a SLIP or PPP account, although trying to connect via SLIP or PPP to a shell account can cause the problem. That said, here are some things to try, in this order:

- Disconnect, restart, and reconnect. Sometimes that's all it takes.

- Throw out your MacTCP DNR file, and restart. Sometimes this file becomes corrupted, and MacTCP will create a new one on restart if necessary.

- Check your domain name server configuration in MacTCP carefully to make sure you typed the correct IP numbers. I've made this mistake before.

- If you are using a Manually-addressed account, make sure you have typed the correct number into the Gateway address box in MacTCP's configuration dialog. Only your provider can tell you what your Gateway address is—you cannot guess it.

- If you use InterSLIP, make sure you're using the appropriate gateway script for your provider. Without this, your Mac may be unable to get an IP number properly. A number of people try to use the Simple UNIX/Telebit script that's built into InterSLIP when they should use a custom gateway script. The Simple UNIX/Telebit script simply won't work with a Server-addressed account like those that Northwest Nexus provides. This is because gateway scripts for providers like Northwest Nexus are designed to find your IP number from the login message each time you login. If you use the Simple UNIX/Telebit script instead, it completes successfully after sending your userid and password, and ignores the IP address that appears next.

■ Login with a terminal emulator just to make sure your account is set up for SLIP or PPP. If after providing your user name and password and send any necessary commands to start SLIP or PPP (ask your provider if any are necessary), you don't see garbage or something like "SL/IP session beginning..." and you get to a Unix prompt, then your account has not been set up for SLIP or PPP. Ask your provider to fix it. This is a common mistake for overworked providers.

■ If for some reason you are using InterSLIP 1.0fc3, use version 1.0.1 (or later) since that version solved various problems like this. It's on the ISKM disk.

■ Reinstall MacTCP from scratch. Hey, it's easy, but you'd be surprised how much it helps.

■ Make sure your domain name server information in the MacTCP configuration dialog looks something like this (it will be different for your domain if you don't use Northwest Nexus):

halcyon.com.	198.137.231.1	(•)
.	198.137.231.1	
.	192.135.191.1	

■ Try turning off Virtual Memory, if you're using it, or disabling RAM Doubler, if you're using that. One person reported success without Virtual Memory enabled.

■ Ask your provider if other people are experiencing this problem as well, since it may in fact be related to an overloaded domain name server. They may be able to use a different machine for DNS services and solve the problem that way.

■ Try using a different telephone cord to the modem. In one case, a slightly bad telephone cord caused some line noise that messed up InterSLIP in such a way as to cause this error.

■ Okay, here's a major realization that we've made (thanks to Michael Tardiff for tremendous help in figuring this out). If nothing so far has worked, check to make absolutely sure that you are using hardware handshaking with your modem, and more importantly, make sure XON/XOFF is turned off. It seems that if XON/XOFF is turned on, the SLIP or PPP program may appear to log in properly, but will fail to find the Gateway address properly.

Server-addressed accounts determine the Gateway address at connect time, which is why you cannot type it into MacTCP. Nonetheless, if, in InterSLIP (and MacPPP, we think) you don't properly use hardware handshaking, then some sort of initial negotiation that determines the Gateway address fails. When that happens, a necessary line of communication with the host is broken. The upshot of this is that MacTCP Watcher will find no Mac name for your Mac. That Mac name should be supplied by reverse name mapping, but it seems that if that initial negotiation after the login process fails, the Mac receives no Mac name from the host via the gateway. Using exactly the same settings otherwise, we showed that merely toggling a modem setting that turned hardware handshaking on and off could make the difference between a successful connection and a failed one.

■ Make sure that your modem cable is indeed a hardware handshaking cable. Most high-speed modems purchased in "Macintosh kits" within the last few years include proper hardware handshaking cables, but if you bought a modem without a cable, or you bought a new cable separately from a computer store, your cable may not be a proper hardware handshaking cable. You may need to call your modem vendor to confirm this. Modern hardware handshaking cables should have the pinouts shown in Table 20.1. You can test this if you have the proper electronic testing equipment, or you can construct an electric testing device that turns on a light or makes a noise when a circuit is closed by touching leads to the proper pins (I once used an empty battery-powered squirt gun to indicate when a circuit was completed).

Table 20.1

Hardware Handshaking Cable Pin-out

Mac Function	RS-232 Function	Mac Pin	DB-25 Pin
RxD (receive)	Receive Data	5	3
TxD (transmit)	Transmit Data	3	2
Ground	Ground	4 & 8	7
HSKi	CTS	2	5
HSKo	RTS & DTR	1	4 & 20
GPi	CD	7	8

Part IV
20
Trouble-
shooting Your
Connection

■ If you do not have a hardware handshaking cable, you can purchase them from numerous sources, but insist on a hardware handshaking cable, not just a modem cable. Jump up and down, yell, and scream, if necessary, but the two terms are not necessarily interchangeable. I've ordered high-quality, properly wired cables for about $15 from the Celestin Company, 800/835-5514, 360/385-3767, 360/385-3586 (fax), `celestin@olympus.net`

■ After you determine that your modem cable is indeed a hardware handshaking cable, next ensure that hardware handshaking is turned on in your SLIP or PPP program. You may see a checkbox labeled Hardware Handshaking, as in InterSLIP, or a pop-up menu listing choices such as XON/XOFF, CTS, RTS, and CTS/RTS. Choose CTS or CTS/RTS for hardware handshaking. There are other terms for the RS-232 functions that some programs use—if you're confused, ask the program's tech support folks. Hardware handshaking is usually relatively easy to check and set.

- Unfortunately, simply turning on hardware handshaking in your SLIP or PPP program may not be sufficient. It seems that some modems set XON/XOFF, or software handshaking, in their default settings. Thus, when you initialize the modem with the factory default initialization string, you actually turn software handshaking back on. This is bad. I ran into this with a Telebit QBlazer, which defaults to software handshaking with the setting S58=3. By changing that to S58=2 in the initialization string, the domain name server errors disappeared immediately because InterSLIP could then complete the negotiation for the Gateway address and the reverse name mapping that goes on right after the login process.

  VersaTerm AdminSLIP may not always suffer from the same problem as InterSLIP. Merely setting hardware handshaking in the configuration window enabled the QBlazer to work, whereas checking the hardware handshaking box in InterSLIP had made no difference. Nonetheless, consult the fine print in your modem's manual for the settings to ensure that hardware handshaking is enabled. Look for settings called DTE Flow Control. In Telebit modems, those settings are controlled by the S58 register, although other modems undoubtedly differ.

- Try using another modem. This worked for one user who switched from a Zoom 2400 bps modem to a QuickTel v.32bis modem. This may well have been related to the hardware handshaking issue.

- Try booting from another hard disk, if you have one.

- Try installing MacTCP and the other software on another Macintosh, if you have one.

- Try rebuilding your desktop. I have no idea why this would make a difference, but it's worth a try. You can rebuild your desktop by holding down the Command and Option keys during startup until the Macintosh asks you if you want to rebuild the desktop.

- Try zapping your PRAM (Parameter RAM—it stores various low level settings). I have no idea whether this makes any difference, but anything is worth a try at this point. To zap your PRAM in System 7, hold down ⌘-Option-P-R while restarting the Mac. You will lose certain settings such as the time and the mouse speed setting, but you can reset those later.

- Try reinstalling your System. First, make sure you have a full set of System disks, because you must disable the System on the hard drive before installing to ensure a completely clean install. Then, drag your System file to your desktop and restart with the Install disk. Install the System and then restart with your hard disk again. Throw out the System file sitting on your desktop, completely reinstall MacTCP (throwing out MacTCP DNR and MacTCP Prep), and MacPPP (throw out PPP Preferences along with the PPP extension and Config PPP) or InterSLIP (throw out the entire InterSLIP Folder, the InterSLIP extension, and InterSLIP Setup). If any updates from Apple exist for the version of the System you use, reinstall them as well. Then, try again. At least one MacPPP user solved the problem this way.

- Consider switching to the commercial VersaTerm SLIP, MacSLIP, or InterPPP. This may work because of differences in the ways the programs handle Gateway addresses for Server-addressed accounts and the way they specify hardware handshaking for different modems.

- Try a different provider.

- If none of these suggestions help, I don't know what to say, except that some problems are never solved. Otherwise, we'd have world peace.

MacPPP Q & A

Although its interface can seem a bit confusing, MacPPP is actually quite easy to configure and use. But, there are still some questions.

Q: I want to switch from InterSLIP to MacPPP. What should I watch out for?

A: First, you need a new account. Second, I don't recommend leaving the InterSLIP extension installed at the same time as the PPP extension. Third, reinstall MacTCP from scratch before trying to connect with MacPPP. Frankly, if everything works fine with InterSLIP, I don't recommend bothering to switch.

Q: I have an internal modem in my PowerBook, but there's no choice in the Port Name pop-up menu for Internal Modem. What should I select?

A: Select the Modem port. Non-bus internal modems in some PowerBooks (typically the 100-series) connect to an internal modem port connector. Bus modems like the Apple Express Modem and the Global Village PowerPort/Mercury for the PowerBook 500-series and the PowerBook Duo should be set to Internal Modem.

Q: I have an internal modem in my PowerBook 520, but I want to use an external one on the Printer-Modem port. Why doesn't that selection show up in the Port Name pop-up menu?

A: In the PowerBook Setup control panel, there's a setting on how the modem should be treated. If it's set to Compatible, your Printer-Modem port won't appear in the Port Name menu. Set the PowerBook Setup control panel's Modem setting to Normal and all will be well.

Q: Why do I get an error message from MacPPP complaining about having insufficient memory?

A: It's been suggested that if you installed MacPPP with SAM active, and used the "allow" feature in SAM, that MacPPP and possibly MacTCP would be corrupted. The fix is to turn SAM off and reinstall both MacTCP and MacPPP from scratch.

Q: My Open button is grayed out so I can't click on it to connect.

A: The first, and most likely possibility is that you have not selected the PPP icon in the MacTCP control panel. Make sure it's selected (try selecting another icon in MacTCP then reselect PPP), and try again.

There are some known conflicts that might cause this. One possible conflict might be with an older version of the shareware SpeedyFinder, although the most recent versions solve this. Also, the elderly screensaver called Moire has been implicated in this problem as well. Finally, many Performas came with 2400 bps Global Village TelePort/Bronze modems, and if you upgrade to a faster modem, you should move the Global Village Toolbox file out of the Extensions folder and the GV TelePort Bronze file out of the Control Panels folder before trying again. And of course, if you have the SLIP extension from VersaTerm SLIP, InterSLIP, or MacSLIP installed, that may cause the problem as well.

Also, be very wary of any fax or remote control software that may have taken over the modem. Even if it doesn't conflict directly with MacTCP or MacPPP, the fax software may leave the modem in such a state that MacPPP is unable to access it.

Q: My Open button is still grayed out.

A: Reinstall MacTCP from scratch, making sure to delete MacTCP DNR and MacTCP Prep. This one once threw me for an hour.

Q: I still can't click on the Open button.

A: Okay, one last possibility. Try reinstalling your System from scratch. Reinstalling the System seemed to help a number of users (mostly using Macintosh Performas) with this problem. First, make sure you have a full set of System disks, since you must disable the System on the hard drive before installing, to ensure a completely clean install. Then, drag your System file to your desktop, and restart with the Install disk. Install a new System, and then restart with your hard disk again. If any updates from Apple exist for the version of the System you use, reinstall them as well. Throw out the System file sitting on your desktop, then completely reinstall MacTCP (throwing out MacTCP DNR and MacTCP Prep as well) and MacPPP (throw out the PPP extension and the Config PPP control panel), and try again.

Q: When I click on the Open button, MacPPP never even dials out, but times out waiting for OK during the checking for modem phase. Do I have a bad modem init string?

A: This timeout is independent of the modem initialization string, since MacPPP isn't even getting that far. The problem is probably related to the flow control or port speed settings. Try different settings, and make sure you don't select 14,400 or 28,800 for the port speed, since some modems can't handle those as port speeds.

Also, it's possible that you have a bad modem cable, although you would probably have noticed that before.

Q: Nice try, but I still can't get MacPPP to recognize my internal Supra modem.

A: Ah, that's different. Larry Blunk mentioned a problem with the Supra and perhaps some other internal PowerBook modems. It seems that they are normally in a low-power state and can take a few seconds to warm up when MacPPP opens the serial driver and tries to dial out. Because the modem is warming up, it ignores the first initialization string that MacPPP sends, and MacPPP doesn't currently try again. The workarounds include using the terminal window or trying to script the modem initialization string in the Connect Script dialog. Larry says he's fixed this in an as-yet-unreleased version of MacPPP.

Q: Why can't I type into the terminal window?

A: In some cases, the terminal window doesn't display the characters you type (this may be related to local echo settings in the modem initialization string) until you press the Return key. Typing blind is a pain, but you shouldn't have to use the terminal window much.

Q: For some reason, I can't connect using port speeds over 19,200 bps? Why would that be?

A: Some modems don't work well at speeds over 19,200 with their default configurations. You may need to twiddle with the modem initialization string to get them to work. Don't worry about it too much though, since 19,200 bps is fast enough for a 14,400 bps modem.

Also, activating the FAXstf 3.0 LineManager option, according to one reader, prevents MacPPP from working with the SupraFAXmodem v.32bis at speeds above 19,200. In general, distrust fax software.

Q: Why can't I connect using 14,400 bps with my 14,400 bps modem or at 28,800 bps with my 28,800 bps modem?

A: You're confusing modem speed and port speed. The port speed setting in MacPPP should always be set faster than the modem speed to take advantage of modem compression capabilities. Some modems don't recognize 14,400 or 28,800 bps as valid port speeds and won't work at all.

Q: My modem will connect, and MacPPP will get to the Establishment phase, and then the Mac crashes. What could be happening? (I can use the terminal window to login fine.)

A: One reader reported a problem like this. It seems that the remote system sent a "banner page" of all sorts of text after accepting the password, but before starting PPP. MacPPP saw the banner page and got confused, because it was expecting PPP code at that point. The solution is to send several \d delay tags after sending the password; that gives MacPPP some time to ignore the banner page before starting PPP.

Q: My modem will connect, and MacPPP will get to the Establishment phase, and then I get a Link Dead message. Why?

A: The most likely reason is that something in the login chat script is wrong. You may have entered the wrong userid or password, or entered them incorrectly. It's also not uncommon for a provider to make a mistake in setting up an account such that it's not a PPP account, or perhaps such that it links to a different userid or password.

Also, see the previous question and answer, since sometimes the problem above doesn't result in a crash, but merely a Link Dead message.

Finally, some providers give different userids and passwords for dialing in than they do for email, say, or different userids and passwords for shell accounts versus PPP accounts. Double check to make sure you're using the correct ones.

Q: Sometimes when I'm trying to connect and MacPPP has to redial, I get a failure dialog with a Retry button. What should I do?

A: Click on it. I'm not positive of the circumstances in which this dialog appears, but I always just click Retry and eventually it connects.

Q: I use a Global Village PowerPort with my PowerBook 500-series Mac, and although it works fine the first time I dial out in any session, on subsequent tries it doesn't seem to be working. It won't show the menu status information, nor will it make any sounds. What's wrong?

A: This appears to be a problem exclusive to the PowerPort modems in the PowerBook 500-series. The problem lies in the Global Village software, and is actually only cosmetic, although it's easy to get impatient and assume it's not working. Check for a later version of the Global Village software in:

```
ftp://ftp.globalvillag.com/pub/software/
```

Q: MacPPP seems to redial the phone randomly on its own.

A: Click the Hard Close button, rather than the Soft Close button, to disconnect. The drawback to doing this is that you cannot use MacPPP's auto connect feature after this unless you restart. Also, set a short idle timeout in Config PPP so it hangs up relatively quickly if MacPPP does dial on its own.

Make sure you don't have any MacTCP-based applications or control panels (like Network Time) set to launch during startup. They'll force MacPPP to dial out every time.

Q: I can connect properly, but I experience very slow transfer rates in Anarchie and Fetch. It seems okay at first, but gets progressively worse until the connection is basically dead.

A: First, if you have the port speed set to 57,600 bps, try setting it down to 38,400 bps or 19,200 bps, especially if you're using a slower Macintosh with a fast modem.

Second, I've seen this happen with MacPPP and with MacSLIP, but in both cases, I was able to solve the problem by turning off all unnecessary extensions and control panels. The hard part, then, was isolating which of them were actually causing the problem, and in some cases, more than one did. On my parents' LC II running MacSLIP, the APS PowerTools CD driver software turned out to be the culprit. On my PowerBook 100 (this was an embarrassing problem that haunted me for months), the problem was caused by PBTools 2.0, a PowerBook utility. Another user reported problems with SuperClock and the Spirit CD control panel. In general, I'd look for any control panel or extension that is in constant use, like a clock, a battery-monitoring utility, or a CD driver control panel (two others of which, the MindLink CD driver and the Apple CD driver, have been implicated in other performance problems as well).

Q: Any idea why MacPPP crashes when I click on the Hard Close button?

A: No, but one reader who was experiencing this tracked it down to a conflict with SAM, the anti-virus program. If you're running SAM or any other anti-virus software, try removing it first. Then, if that doesn't work, try shutting off all unnecessary extensions and control panels and see if that makes a difference. If it does, work your way back up to a full set and see which file is the culprit. I personally use and recommend only Disinfectant for anti-virus purposes.

InterSLIP Q & A

Since its introduction in 1993, InterSLIP has become popular for its combination of flexibility, utility, and price—it's free. However, InterSLIP isn't always trouble-free. Following are some of the more common questions and answers relating to InterSLIP.

Q: I can't find InterSLIP Control on my disk.

A: You don't need InterSLIP Control if you use System 7. It is necessary only with System 6.

Q: I copied the gateway and dialing scripts into the proper folders. Why don't they show up in the pop-up menus in InterSLIP?

A: Two things to check here. Those files should be text files, so if they are any other type, they may not show up, since InterSLIP won't recognize them. If you simply save from Microsoft Word, for instance, those files will be of type WDBN and not of type TEXT. Use Save As and select the Text Only option that exists in most word processors. Second, if you copy those scripts in while InterSLIP is running, it won't recognize them until you quit and launch InterSLIP Setup again. You don't have to restart; simply quit and relaunch.

Q: If I launch an application without manually connecting with InterSLIP, InterSLIP tries to dial the phone twice, then the Mac hangs. What's going on?

A: In my experience, InterSLIP's auto connect feature doesn't work very well. This may not be InterSLIP's fault, and it does work for some people, so if it does for you, great. If not, make a habit of connecting manually before you launch a MacTCP program such as Fetch. Since Eudora doesn't open MacTCP until you check for mail, you can use it without connecting InterSLIP first. One person said that he had solved his auto connect problems by adding a "pause 30" statement in his Gateway script just before it exits. This may help, although my Mac never even dials the phone before freezing on auto connect.

Q: When I click the Connect button, nothing happens. Why not?

A: This points directly at an extension conflict with either InterSLIP or MacTCP. I would recommend pulling all unnecessary extensions and control panels out. Or, better yet, use an extension manager such as Apple's free Extension Manager, or the powerful (but commercial) Conflict Catcher from Casady & Greene, which can actually help in your testing process. Leave only MacTCP and InterSLIP, and try again. If the problem disappears, slowly replace the extensions and control panels that you use until the problem reappears, identifying the culprit in the process. We've seen problems possibly related to MacTOPS, DOS Mounter, SuperLaserSpool, and GlobalFax, and a two-way conflict with AutoRemounter and PSI FaxMonitor. In general, be very wary of any extensions that modify a network or a modem, including fax or remote control software. I'm also generally suspicious of anti-virus software. Even if these programs don't specifically conflict with InterSLIP or MacTCP, they may leave the modem in such a state that InterSLIP cannot dial out properly.

Q: I removed all of my extensions and control panels and I still get nothing when I click the Connect button.

A: Try reinstalling MacTCP from scratch (throwing out MacTCP DNR and MacTCP Prep) and InterSLIP (throw out the entire InterSLIP Folder, the InterSLIP extension, and InterSLIP Setup), and reinstall from fresh copies. If you have custom scripts, there's no need to throw them out.

Q: It still doesn't work.

A: Shoot. The next thing to try is reinstalling your System. First, make sure you have a full set of System disks, since you must disable the System on the hard drive before installing, to ensure a completely clean install. Then, drag your System file to your desktop, and restart with the Install disk. Install a new System, and then restart with your hard disk again. If any updates from Apple exist for the version of the System you use, reinstall them as well. Throw out the System file sitting on your desktop, then completely reinstall MacTCP (throwing out MacTCP DNR and MacTCP Prep) and InterSLIP (throw out the entire InterSLIP Folder, the InterSLIP extension, and InterSLIP Setup), and try again.

Q: Sorry to be a pain, but it still doesn't do anything when I click the Connect button.

A: Okay, I don't really know what's happening here. Try getting a PPP account and use MacPPP, or purchase VersaTerm SLIP or MacSLIP and see if they work any better. I wish I could give a better answer, but I can't.

Q: My modem doesn't seem to work with the Hayes-Compatible Modem script.

A: You need a dialing script, which is similar to an ARA script. For starters, I recommend the Minimal Dialing Script I provide on the disk. It works with most modems if you enter the proper modem initialization string.

Q: I'm using a dialing script, and when I click Connect, it says Dialing, but I don't hear the modem dial or see it do anything else.

A: I've seen this happen a few times. I suspect the script is in some way incorrect—perhaps the error correction and data compression have been turned on improperly. Try the Hayes-Compatible Modem script. If that doesn't work, try the Minimal Dialing Script on the disk. If that doesn't work, ask your modem company for a good ARA script that you can modify (in theory, an ARA script should work without modification, but is best when modified). If that fails, beg for help from others with the same modem on the nets, preferably in `comp.sys.mac.comm` or the Apple Internet Users mailing list (see the "Reporting Problems" section earlier in this chapter for subscription information).

Q: The modem seems to connect, then hang up. What's going on?

A: The most likely reason is that something in the login chat script is wrong. You may have entered the wrong userid or password, or entered them incorrectly. It's also not uncommon for a provider to make a mistake in setting up an account such that it's not a SLIP account, or perhaps such that it links to a different userid or password.

Also, some providers give different userids and passwords for dialing in than they do for email, say, or different userids and passwords for shell accounts versus SLIP accounts. Double check to make sure you're using the ones.

Finally, use a terminal emulator to walk through the login process manually. Sometimes, the provider's system is experiencing a high load and doesn't respond to your gateway script quickly enough. If this might be the case, try increasing the numbers in the statements that serve as timeout values.

Q: I can connect on occasion, but not all the time. What could be wrong?

A: Some modems, the US Robotics Sportster and the Global Village TelePort/Gold in particular, sometimes have problems if you are using an incorrect modem initialization string. Check your string carefully.

Also, I've noticed that sometimes I'll see failed connections on my Northwest Nexus account. They range from receiving tons of data when InterSLIP says "Waiting for prompt," to nothing at all happening when InterSLIP says "Waiting for prompt," "Sending username," or "Sending password." I've even had InterSLIP report "Login incorrect" when I know full well it was fine. Just try again a few times, waiting a bit between tries, if you can. I suspect these problems are related to a bad modem, line noise, or some other situation out of your control, and in my experience they always go away after several tries.

Again, check to see if the timeout values in your gateway script might be too short. If the script times out before you get in on some occasions, it could cause this frustrating inconsistency.

Finally, some people have suggested renaming the Global Village extensions used by Global Village modems so they load after MacTCP. It's worth a try if you have one of those modems.

Part IV
20
Trouble-shooting Your Connection

Q: InterSLIP connects fine, but none of the programs seem to quite work, although they try to connect.

A: Try toggling your TCP Header Compression checkbox (also sometimes known as CSLIP). If that checkbox doesn't match the setting for your account, things will fail. Essentially what happens is that small tasks such as looking up a machine name succeed, but anything else fails.

Q: InterSLIP connects fine, but I can't transfer files or messages of any size without the Mac hanging. Why not?

A: It could be related to your modem init string's settings for flow control, so check that carefully. Make sure you're using the proper MTU size in InterSLIP. Also, try turning off all unnecessary extensions, using an extension manager or by simply dragging them from the Extensions and Control Panels folder to "Extensions (disabled)" and "Control Panels (disabled)" folders. As a last resort, try InterSLIP 1.0.2d2 (or later) if you're using 1.0.1.

If you use the Apple Express Modem or a GeoPort Telecom Adapter, also make sure to try the latest Express Modem software, available at this or another Apple FTP site:

```
ftp://mirror.info.apple.com/Apple.Support.Area/Apple.Software.Updates/US/Macintosh/
Networking.and.Communications/Other.N&C.Software/
```

Q: I had InterSLIP working, but now that I've moved my hard drive to another machine, it crashes whenever I launch InterSLIP Setup.

A: Delete your InterSLIP Prefs file. For some reason, possibly related to the location of the InterSLIP Setup window, this has happened on several machines we've seen.

Q: InterSLIP works fine, except that when I click the Disconnect button, my modem doesn't hang up. What can I do?

A: First off, if you use a dialing script other than the built-in Hayes-Compatible Modem script, it usually will have an @hangup section. My Minimal Dialing Script has one, and will hang up the modem just fine if you use it instead of the Hayes-Compatible Modem script.

Some people recommend adding **&D2** to the end of your modem initialization string. Doing so will hang up the modem if DTR goes low, which it does when you click the Disconnect button. Unfortunately, DTR can also go low if you have a fast modem and a slow Mac and the modem transfers more data than the Mac can handle at that point. Using a port speed of 38,400 bps or 57,600 bps with a 14,400 bps modem can exacerbate this problem. If you run into this problem, you'll see random hang-ups while downloading large files. If you do use **&D2**, you may be able to set an S-register (S25 in at least some modems) in the modem init string that lengthens the time DTR can be low before the modem realizes it, thus preventing the hangups. Only worry about this if you like reading modem manuals. Overall, the Minimal Dialing Script is a better solution.

Book 'Em, Danno

It's been fun, I'm sure. We've tracked down and locked up tons of problems, and I hope that any culprit that's been harassing you is among them. Perhaps the most important thing to do when troubleshooting is to remain calm and proceed methodically. If you do that, you're well on your way to finding and eliminating the problem.

Actually, the real fun comes in the next few chapters, where I talk about all of the programs that rely on the connection that you've established with MacTCP and either MacPPP or InterSLIP.

Part IV
Trouble-
shooting Your
Connection

Email

Considering that email is the ubiquitous application on the Internet, you should use the best email program available; otherwise, you will slowly (or quickly, in my case) go stark raving mad. I've looked at many email programs in my time, and although a number of them are becoming more and more impressive, none compete with Steve Dorner's Eudora. Simply put, Eudora does most everything right. Again, I don't want to imply that other programs aren't good, but none I've seen can match the features and capabilities of Eudora.

Eudora

Steve Dorner first wrote Eudora while working at the University of Illinois. Because of its academic heritage, Eudora was made freely available on the Internet. Because of its clean interface and full feature set, Eudora rapidly became the Internet email application of choice. In July of 1992, Steve left the University of Illinois and went to work for a company called Qualcomm, where he continued to enhance Eudora. Because Steve and Qualcomm wanted to give something back to the educational community and taxpayers who made Eudora possible, and because free software is the best advertising for commercial software, Eudora has remained freeware. Qualcomm also has released a commercial version of Eudora that adds some nice touches and features that are essential for email users like me who get a ton of mail every day.

Note

To answer the question that almost everyone always asks, Steve named his Post Office Protocol program "Eudora," after Eudora Welty, the author of a short story he had read, called "Why I Live at the P.O."

The freeware version will continue to exist and will be developed in conjunction with the commercial version, but it is unlikely to receive many new features, other than those Steve deems necessary for basic email usage. For example, he added support for MIME (Multi-purpose Internet Mail Extensions), an Internet standard for transferring non-textual data via email, and support for Apple events, so that Eudora can work more closely with other programs on the Macintosh. In addition, the latest versions of both the freeware and commercial versions now work in Power Mac-native mode, significantly increasing speed.

Note

The version of Eudora 1.5.1 included on the disk is not the Power Mac-native version because it was too large to fit on the disk. You can find it in either of the following:

```
ftp://ftp.qualcomm.com/quest/mac/eudora/1.5/eudora151fat.hqx
```

```
ftp://ftp.tidbits.com/pub/tidbits/tisk/tcp/mail/
```

The commercial Eudora 2.1 is extremely similar to the freeware Eudora 1.5.1. It looks about the same, and for the most part, works the same. Perhaps the most apparent additional feature in Eudora 2.1 is the filtering feature. It lets you annotate the subject of messages, change their priority, or put them in specific mailboxes based on information in the headers or the bodies of the messages. You can have as many filters as you want, and they can apply to incoming, outgoing, or selected messages. In addition, 2.1 also supports spell checking in messages via the Word Services suite of Apple events. You can even buy Eudora along with Spellswell, an Apple event-aware spelling program.

Note

Using Eudora to transfer files in email back and forth between Macs and PCs works well if your recipient either uses PC Eudora or another MIME-compatible mail program. If you're sending the files from the Mac, use AppleDouble encoding. If you're sending from PC Eudora, choose MIME before attaching the file. Both versions of Eudora automatically recognize MIME attachments and decode them automatically upon receipt.

Other useful features that exist only in Eudora 2.1 include uuencode support, automatic opening of attachments encoded in MIME, BinHex, or uuencode, multiple nickname files for organizations, support for System 7 drag and drop for attaching files to outgoing messages, stationery for frequently sent messages, menu-sharing for Frontier users, and multiple signatures. In my opinion, if you use Eudora heavily, as I do, Eudora 2.1 offers an extremely attractive set of features above and beyond the basic set in Eudora 1.5.1. For those just starting out, try Eudora 1.5.1 for a while, and if you decide you like it, consider purchasing the full Eudora 2.1 version for $65 (there's a coupon for it hiding somewhere in the back of the book). I can't recommend the commercial version of Eudora highly enough. And frankly, I encourage people to buy it, sending the message to Qualcomm that the community appreciates free software and is willing to support commercial versions to keep free versions available. However, for the following discussion, I'll concentrate primarily on 1.5.1 because that's the version on the disk.

Installation and Setup

Although powerful and flexible, Eudora has a surprisingly simple setup. First, from the Special menu, choose Settings (see figure 21.1).

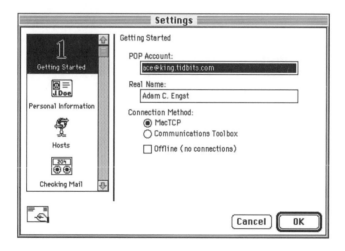

Figure 21.1   *Eudora Settings dialog.*

The scrolling list on the left-hand side of the dialog provides access to a large number of Eudora's settings. Optional plug-ins available on various FTP sites can add even more options (see the following for some pointers). Despite all the available fields, only the two in the Getting Started panel are absolutely necessary (although some Internet providers may require some additional settings). The POP Account field holds the full address of your POP account. The best source to find out what to put here is your system administrator. The next field, Real Name, should be obvious. Lastly, click the MacTCP button located below the Real Name field.

For most people, that's all there is to the setup process. If you want to enter a different return address from the address of your POP account (my return address is **ace@tidbits.com**, whereas my POP account is **ace@king.tidbits.com**), click the second icon in the list, Personal Information, to bring up that panel.

If you fill in the Return Address field, be very careful to get it right; otherwise, all your incoming email will go to an incorrect address and you'll never know it. Many people mess up their configurations by slavishly copying the screen shots in this book—I know because I get replies to their messages since they use my return address!

If you need to tell Eudora that your SMTP server is on a different machine from your POP account (it usually isn't), click the third icon in the list, Hosts, to bring up the Host Settings panel. Once you've entered the names of your various servers as given to you by your Internet provider, scroll down to see the icons that enable you to modify how Eudora works, such as Checking Mail, Sending Mail, Attachments, and Fonts & Display (see figure 21.2).

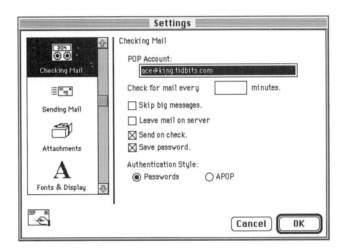

Figure 21.2   *More Eudora Settings.*

These options enable you to configure Eudora quickly and easily in order to handle many different situations. When I'm traveling and connecting via a modem, I generally don't want to receive large messages, so I turn on the "Skip big messages" checkbox. I also sometimes use the "Leave mail on server" option to ensure that if something happened to my PowerBook while I was traveling, I wouldn't lose any of the mail I'd received while away. I seldom have Eudora check mail regularly, but that's because I get so much that it would be a constant distraction—however, many people appreciate knowing when new mail has arrived.

Eudora has so many settings that I don't want to get into showing them all to you, and its balloon help is among the best I've used. However, the other important options that I always use are in the Sending Mail panel: Send on check, Word wrap, Fix curly quotes,

Keep copies of outgoing mail, and Use signature. In the Attachments panel, stick with BinHex encoding for most files you send to other Mac users and you'll be fine. Use AppleDouble for files you send to PC users whose email programs support MIME (especially PC Eudora). In the Replying panel, I recommend that you use the Reply to all when Option key is down setting, rather than Reply to all by default. The problem is that it's not difficult to send something personal to a mailing list or to unintended recipients if you normally use Reply to all.

> **N o t e**
>
> *One trick (that's not an option) is that if you select text in the message you're replying to and then hold down Shift while you choose Reply (or press ⌘-Shift-R), Eudora quotes only the selected text in the reply.*

When you've finished browsing through all of Eudora's many settings and have configured the program to your tastes, click the OK button to save your changes. Eudora stores all of its settings in the Eudora Settings file that it creates in the Eudora Folder in your System Folder (or in the settings file that you used to open Eudora, if you've created more than one settings file).

> **N o t e**
>
> *I alluded to creating more than one Eudora Settings file. You can do this by making a copy of the Eudora Settings file in your System Folder, renaming it, and double-clicking it to launch Eudora. Then, any changes you make to the settings apply only to that Eudora Settings file. It's a good way to easily check two email accounts. Also, if you put a copy of the Eudora Settings file in a new folder and double-click it to launch Eudora, Eudora creates a new set of mailboxes for you. This can be handy if two people share the same Mac but have different email accounts and want to keep their email separate.*

Commands for accessing three of Eudora's features—Mailboxes, Nicknames, and Signature—live in the Windows menu. The Mailboxes window enables you to create, rename, move, and maintain your mailboxes (remember that you can have hierarchical mailboxes for organizing the email you receive—the mailboxes in figure 21.3 with triangles to the right of their names are hierarchical). The Nickname window enables you to create, modify, and remove nicknames, which enable you to avoid memorizing email addresses. Clicking just to the left of the name adds or removes a bullet; this means the name will appear as a recipient in Eudora's hierarchical New Message To, Reply To, Forward To, and Redirect To menus. You can put multiple addresses in a single nickname to create a small distribution list. Finally, Eudora's Signature window is a simple text window in which you can enter a signature to be appended to all of your outgoing messages.

Part IV Email 21

Figure 21.3   *Eudora Mailboxes, Nicknames, and Signature windows.*

Basic Usage

You're most likely to use Eudora for simple tasks such as creating new messages, reading incoming mail, replying to messages, and the like. Creating a message is the first thing to do. From the Message menu, choose New Message, or—to use the shortcut—press ⌘-N (see figure 21.4).

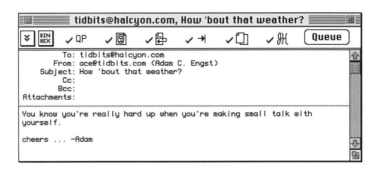

Figure 21.4   *Eudora New Mail window.*

Eudora opens a new window with three parts. At the top of the window is a row of switch icons, so that you can toggle items such as signatures on a per message basis (point at them all with balloon help turned on to see what the icons mean). Below that is an area for the header. At the bottom of the window is the message area. Tabbing takes you from one header item to another, and finally to the message window.

You can select email addresses in messages or headers and add them to a Recipients menu (Add as Recipient from the Special menu). The people you add as recipients show up in a hierarchical New Message To menu under the Message menu. If you select someone from that hierarchical menu, Eudora opens a new message with the To line already filled in (the From line is always filled in for you). When you create nicknames for people (Nicknames from the Special menu), you're given the option to add that nickname to the recipient list for quick access.

Eudora has a good text entry environment and wraps paragraphs as you write and edit (which is not true of all email programs, so don't laugh). In fact, Eudora can do some neat things with text, as shown by the commands in the Edit menu (see figure 21.5).

Edit	
Undo Typing	⌘Z
Cut	⌘H
Copy	⌘C
Paste	⌘U
Paste As Quotation	⌘'
Clear	
Select All	⌘A
Wrap Selection	⌂W
Finish Nickname	⌘,
Insert Recipient	▶
Find	▶
Sort	▶

Figure 21.5 *Eudora Edit menu.*

I especially like the capability to Insert Recipient and Paste as Quotation. I often want to send an email address to a friend for which I have a recipient defined; it's nice to be able to just Insert Recipient in the text where I'm typing. Paste as Quotation also is useful when you're pulling several messages together in one reply.

The only major fault of Eudora's text entry environment is that it doesn't accept more than approximately 32K of text; if you want to send a message longer than that, you must attach a text file to the email message. This limitation will disappear in future versions of Eudora, although perhaps only in the commercial version.

In any event, back at the New Mail window, clicking on the Queue button queues the message for delivery (this is because I didn't select the Immediate Send checkbox when configuring Eudora's Sending Mail panel). If you work on a network that's constantly connected to the Internet, you may want to send all of your mail immediately, at which point that Queue button changes to Send. Even with my direct connection, I stick to queuing messages. It's simply less distracting, and I can always send messages manually if I want.

With the Send on Check switch turned on, I go to the File menu and choose Check Mail. Eudora connects to my POP server to receive any waiting mail; it then connects to my SMTP server to send my queued mail.

> **Note**
>
> *If Eudora is interrupted while receiving mail, it can sometimes leave your POP mailbox in a locked state, preventing you from receiving any more mail until it's unlocked. You can fix this by telnetting to your account and killing a specific process, which sounds bad, but it is quite easy. It's explained well in the Eudora Q&A stack, available in the URL below. If you use Northwest Nexus, you can telnet to your account and at the Unix command line, type **pop-lock** to solve this problem.*
>
> ```
> ftp://ftp.tidbits.com/pub/tidbits/tisk/tcp/mail/
> ```

If you only want to send mail, choose Send Queued Messages, also from the File menu. At this point Eudora only connects to the SMTP server to send messages and ignores any messages that might be waiting to come in.

If the In mailbox isn't open already (another preferences switch makes it open when new mail arrives), open it from the Mailbox menu by choosing In (see figure 21.6).

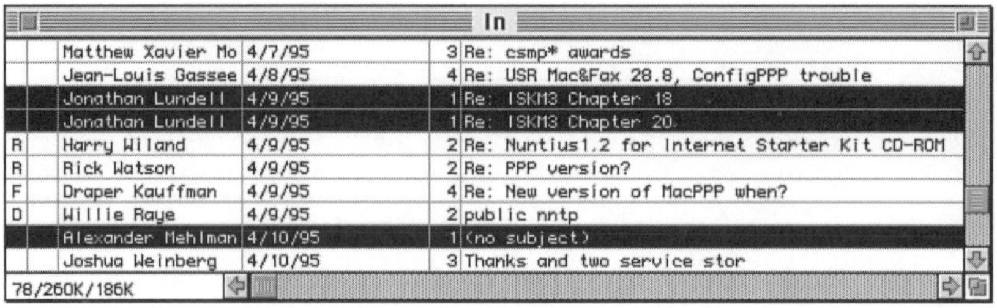

			In	
	Matthew Xavier Mo	4/7/95	3	Re: csmp* awards
	Jean-Louis Gassee	4/8/95	4	Re: USR Mac&Fax 28.8, ConfigPPP trouble
	Jonathan Lundell	4/9/95	1	Re: ISKM3 Chapter 18
	Jonathan Lundell	4/9/95	1	Re: ISKM3 Chapter 20.
R	Harry Wiland	4/9/95	2	Re: Nuntius1.2 for Internet Starter Kit CD-ROM
R	Rick Watson	4/9/95	2	Re: PPP version?
F	Draper Kauffman	4/9/95	4	Re: New version of MacPPP when?
D	Willie Raye	4/9/95	2	public nntp
	Alexander Mehlman	4/10/95	1	(no subject)
	Joshua Weinberg	4/10/95	3	Thanks and two service stor

78/260K/186K

Figure 21.6   Eudora In mailbox.

Eudora's mailboxes, which all look the same, provide a clean display of your mail. A status and priority column at the left edge of the window displays various characters to indicate which messages you haven't read, which you have replied to, which you've forwarded, redirected, and, in your Out mailbox, which have been sent. Some programs mark deleted messages in this way too, but Eudora instead copies deleted messages to a Trash mailbox available in the Mailbox menu. The commercial version of Eudora adds a column for label and uses the Finder labels (use the Labels control panel to change the colors and names) to mark messages.

The next column is the name of the sender, followed by the time and date, size of the message in kilobytes, and subject of the message. In the lower left corner of the window is an indicator that shows the number of messages in the mailbox, amount of disk space that it takes up, and amount of space that is wasted. You can recover the wasted space by choosing Compact Mailboxes from the Special menu, although Eudora also does it automatically after the ratio of wasted space to space on disk gets too high.

Double-clicking on any message opens the message window (see figure 21.7).

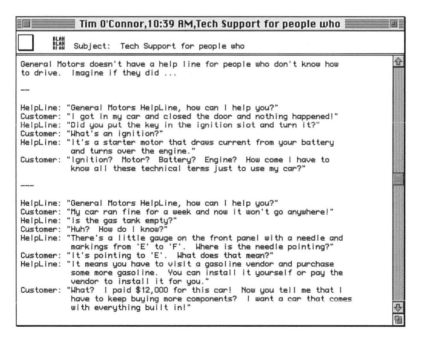

Figure 21.7   *Eudora Message window.*

The Eudora Message window shows the Subject at the top and a Priority pop-up menu that you can use to mark messages for your own reference, which is a good way to sort them. You can select, copy, and find text in the window, but you cannot change it. Again, my only complaint about the way Eudora handles incoming messages is that it cannot display more than approximately 32K of text in a window, so it chops longer messages into two or more pieces, which can be irritating.

> *Like many other settings in Eudora, you can modify the size at which Eudora splits messages with a plug-in. I've created a plug-in specifically so issues of TidBITS aren't split—to receive a copy automatically in email, send a message to* **tidbits-plug-in@tidbits.com**.

Luckily, Eudora can save multiple selected messages to a single file, removing the header information in the process so that there's no header garbage in the middle of the file. Simply select all the messages you want concatenated into a single file. Choose Save As from the File menu, making sure that the Include Headers and Guess Paragraphs (which wraps lines in paragraphs) checkboxes aren't selected if you want the file exactly as it was sent to you.

With a message open, you can use the items in the Message menu to Reply, Forward, Redirect, or Delete the current message. Most of those functions are self-explanatory, but Redirect is an interesting and useful command. When you forward a message to someone else via Eudora, your address becomes the Reply-To address. However, if you want the original sender's address to remain as the Reply-To address, you use Redirect. That way, when the person you're redirecting to receives the message and replies, the reply goes to the original sender, not back to you. Eudora adds a tag that indicates that you redirected the message to the header of the redirected message so the recipient can see what's happened.

Once you're done reading a message, you generally want to either delete it or file it. Eudora makes deleting messages easy (the Delete key, ⌘-D, or the Delete option in the Message menu) because it merely moves them to the Trash mailbox, from which you can recover them later, if necessary. I leave a lot of mail, sometimes up to 4,000 messages, in my Trash so I can easily go back and retrieve something afterwards. When I want to really delete messages from the Trash to recover some space, I sort by date, select the first half of the messages, and press the Delete key. Since the messages are already in the Trash, Eudora deletes them right away, and if I've deleted enough messages to create a sufficient amount of wasted space in the Trash, Eudora compacts it to recover the space. You can set Eudora to empty the Trash every time you quit if you're not as retentive about old email as I am.

Filing messages in one of an arbitrary (or at least large) number of hierarchical mailboxes is also easy. With the message or messages selected, select the destination mailbox from the Transfer menu. I save a lot of messages for future reference, so I appreciate the ease of filing messages.

Special Features

Eudora's clever touches abound. If you choose About Eudora from the Apple menu, Eudora tells you the minimum amount of memory it should have. Should your In, Out, and Trash mailboxes fill up to the point where Eudora needs more memory, it's good about warning you ahead of time and suggesting a size that will support the new requirements. That's usually my warning to delete messages from the Trash.

Although Apple's Balloon Help is becoming increasingly common, many people never think to use it in current programs because it's so slow. I strongly recommend that you turn it on while exploring Eudora, though, because Steve has written excellent help balloons that seem to explain every nook and cranny of the program.

Steve must have had fun writing Eudora's dialog boxes. Many of them are, shall I say, less than serious. For instance, I started typing with a mailbox window open in Eudora (I'd forgotten that I hadn't switched over to Nisus Writer on my second monitor), and Eudora beeped at me a couple of times and then opened a dialog saying, "Unfortunately, no one is listening to keystrokes at the moment. You may as well stop typing." I far prefer such human touches like this to dialogs that say, "Text entry not allowed," or some such terse phrase.

Eudora can sort mailboxes on status, priority (which you generally set), sender, date, and subject. This is a helpful feature for anyone who receives a significant amount of email. Eudora 2.1 makes sorting even easier than in 1.5.1 (in which you must use a menu) by letting you click on the column titles to sort. I find that I use this feature surprisingly often.

Eudora supports a number of Apple events, and many people have used Frontier and AppleScript to add functionality to Eudora through scripting. You can peruse some of those scripts in:

```
ftp://ftp.qualcomm.com/quest/mac/eudora/scripts/
```

```
ftp://ftp.tidbits.com/pub/tidbits/tisk/tcp/mail/
```

If you create multiple settings files, different people can use the same copy of Eudora to send and receive their personal email. This setup is handy if a number of people all share the same computer but don't want to share the same email account ("Hey, no poking about in my email!"). I use this feature as well, because I have multiple accounts, but I want all my email to end up in the same In mailbox. Eudora's capability to launch using different settings files is also the secret to how it's used in large universities. Students are given a POP account and a Eudora Settings file that's configured for them on a floppy disk. Whenever they use a public Mac hooked to the campus network, they double-click on their Eudora Settings file, which launches a copy of Eudora over the network (saving the space on the floppy disk). All of their mail comes down to the floppy disk, which they can then read on any other Mac that has Eudora on it.

Finally, although official technical support only comes with Eudora 2.1, expert Eudora users provide extremely good support online in the newsgroup **comp.sys.mac.comm**. Also, Qualcomm runs a mailing list specifically for Eudora users—to subscribe, send email to **majordomo@qualcomm.com** with **subscribe mac-eudora-forum** in the body of the message. Make sure that your return address is correct—it is the address that will be added to the mailing list. If you have a simple question, ask there before anywhere else (but use the balloon help and the manual before that). Eudora's manual is also excellent. Look for it in:

```
ftp://ftp.qualcomm.com/quest/mac/eudora/documentation/
```

Evaluation & Details

Although perhaps not perfect, you must have Eudora. That's why I've included it on the disk. Other than the 32K limitation on message size, I'd like to see more powerful searching capabilities. However, any such quibbles are easily outweighed by Eudora's significant capabilities, such as the capability to queue up mail and send it all at once, essential for anyone using SLIP or PPP. Eudora simply is *the* way to go for MacTCP-based email.

Eudora 1.5.1 is free, and comes courtesy of the University of Illinois and Qualcomm. You can retrieve the latest versions from:

```
ftp://ftp.tidbits.com/pub/tidbits/tisk/tcp/mail/
```

```
ftp://ftp.qualcomm.com/quest/mac/eudora/1.5/
```

Eudora 2.1 costs $65 for an individual copy, or $99 for Eudora 2.1 and Spellswell. Prices drop quickly from there, depending on how many copies you want to buy, so if you're outfitting a couple of people in an office, check with Qualcomm for the exact discounts. You can get more information from Qualcomm via email at **eudora-sales@qualcomm.com**, or by phone at 800-2-EUDORA.

Other Email Clients

Although I like Eudora, you can try out a number of other email client programs. I'll try to post most of these programs on **ftp.tidbits.com**, but some of them may have distribution restrictions, and those you'll have to find at the original sites. Unless commercial (like Emailer) or mentioned otherwise, the following programs are in:

```
ftp://ftp.tidbits.com/pub/tidbits/tisk/tcp/mail/
```

BlitzMail

I didn't intend to talk much about email programs that use non-standard protocols, but given Dartmouth College's outstanding record in developing Macintosh software, I should briefly mention BlitzMail. Over 90 percent of Dartmouth's students use email, in large part because of BlitzMail, which reportedly has an excellent interface. BlitzMail also supports Apple events and AppleScript recording, which is still uncommon. I haven't seen it in action, mostly because it requires that you run the BlitzMail server software on a NeXT workstation or a DEC Alpha workstation. I thought this limitation was a little ridiculous, until Jim Matthews, a programmer at Dartmouth and creator of Fetch, told me that in 1993 Dartmouth supported 11,000 email accounts on only five NeXT machines, which is incredible. If you're a system administrator-type and you're interested, you can find more information on BlitzMail at:

```
http://www.dartmouth.edu/pages/softdev/blitz.html
```

Emailer

I wrote about Claris's forthcoming Emailer back in chapter 12, "Commercial Services," because its most notable feature is its integration of multiple email accounts on the commercial online services. As I said previously, Emailer is an excellent program and fully supports Internet email via POP and SMTP. I personally don't feel it's quite as good as Eudora, but it's a very close second. You won't go wrong using it primarily for Internet email. Check back in chapter 12 for more details on Emailer's feature set.

LeeMail

Lee Fyock's $25 shareware, LeeMail, solves one major problem for some users—it's primarily an SMTP mailer. It's ideal for use with the few Internet access providers, like Demon Internet in the United Kingdom, that use SMTP for sending mail to SLIP and PPP dialup users. That aside, LeeMail is a simple program that sports several nice features such as support for multiple users, aliases, automatically decoded attachments, and audio notifications of new mail. LeeMail can hide its windows when you send it to the background, auto-quote text when replying to mes-sages, and support multiple mailboxes. The current version of LeeMail, 2.0.4, has minimal support for POP, although the documentation admits that it's not ideal as of yet. Lee plans to beef up the POP support in the future.

MacPost

Although Lund University's MacPost isn't really of interest to the individual looking for email access to the Internet, if you have an AppleTalk network that has access to the Internet already, you may be interested in checking out the MacPost client and server program. The MacPost server runs on a Mac and serves mail to the clients using a proprietary protocol. That's not terribly interesting, but the MacPost server can communicate with an SMTP server as well, thus opening the doors to the Internet for the MacPost clients. Even though the MacPost server uses SMTP, the clients only know how to talk to the server, so you couldn't use a different SMTP client program, such as Eudora. For that, you'd need a POP and SMTP server like MailShare.

Mail*Link Internet for PowerTalk

The aim of Apple's PowerTalk is to provide mail services to all Macintosh applications and to bring email to the Macintosh desktop. To that end, PowerTalk creates a single mailbox on your desktop. Once PowerTalk is installed, you can exchange email with any other PowerTalk users on your network, or, using specially-written gateways, to users on any other email service. Or at least, that's the idea. PowerTalk suffers from a terribly clumsy interface and the slow arrival of gateways to other services. The main gateway of interest for this book is StarNine's Mail*Link Internet for PowerTalk gateway, which enables PowerTalk to send email to the Internet using SMTP and receive Internet mail using POP. If you do use PowerTalk and have access to SMTP and POP servers via a dedicated connection or SLIP or PPP, Mail*Link Internet is the way to go. For more information, send StarNine email at **info@starnine.com**, or call

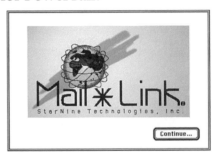

510-649-4949; 510-548-0393 (fax). You can retrieve a time-limited evaluation copy ($49 to purchase) of Mail*Link Internet for PowerTalk from the following sites—the Apple site contains a huge archive containing several PowerTalk gateways.

```
ftp://ftp.starnine.com//pub/evals/personal_gws/pt_inet/mail_link_ptinet.sea.hqx
```

```
http://www.starnine.com/personalgw.html
```

```
ftp://ftp.support.apple.com/pub/apple_sw_updates/US/mac/system_sw/PowerTalk/
```

MailDrop

POPmail and Baylor University's MailDrop are the only two email clients for the Mac that support the IMAP (Interactive Mail Access Protocol) protocol for retrieving email. The main difference (as I understand it) between POP and IMAP is that IMAP prefers to store mail on the server, whereas POP prefers to download it to the Mac. Both have their uses in different environments, and as more IMAP sites appear, clients like MailDrop may increase in popularity, although MailDrop

continues

is a relatively simple program at the moment.
MailDrop is available for non-commercial use, and
you can find more information on their Web site.

http://ackmo.baylor.edu/files/Mail_Drop/info.html

POPmail

Created by programmers at the University of Minnesota, POPmail is a free email program that provides
much of Eudora's feature set and a few extra features,
but without Eudora's clean implementation or the
capability to queue messages, which limits POPmail's
utility when using a SLIP or PPP connection. POPmail
has many nice touches, though, including the
capability to resolve URLs found in email messages, a
message browser mailbox window with command
icons, the capability to create groups of users for
simple distribution lists, and support for multiple users
through multiple settings files. POPmail sports
compatibility with the older POP2 protocol, POP3, and
with the newer IMAP protocol, which also stores your
incoming email on a host computer until you retrieve it.
Most interestingly, if you connect over a slow modem
or are expecting a large message, POPmail has a
Preview feature that enables you to peruse only the
header and first few lines of the file. Other than the

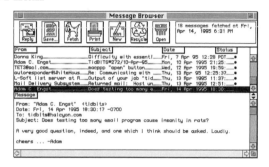

complete lack of a queuing system that would enable
you to write messages while off-line and send them all
at once later, POPmail is a decent application. The
interface feels clunky, but nothing to which you
couldn't become accustomed.

TechMail

TechMail was developed at MIT and may be freely
distributed. It supports queuing messages, so that you
can compose multiple messages off-line and send
them later. One neat feature enables you to check your
POP mailbox to see how many messages are waiting
and how much disk space they take. My main
complaints with TechMail are that it feels slow when
I'm sending messages. I also think its interface could
use some help—especially in the configuration dialog
boxes (where it's never clear what OK and Cancel
really do) and in some of the menu names (such as
Local for all the stuff dealing with email).

ftp://net-dist.mit.edu/pub/mac/techmail/

VideoMail

Darald Trinka's VideoMail is more of an experiment for
his master's thesis than anything else. It uses audio
and video capabilities present in some Macs (luckily

for my testing, they're present in my Macintosh 660AV)
to create QuickTime movies and to send them to other
people via SMTP—the standard protocol for sending

continues

Internet email. When I sent myself a sample movie
(you can have just sound or both sound and video), it
came into Eudora as an attachment that I then opened
in MoviePlayer. VideoMail doesn't attempt to read
email or do anything other than create and send these
movie messages, and frankly, it does that pretty well.
You can either pay $5 for VideoMail, or more probably,
fill out Darald's questionnaire instead.

Z-Mail

The $165 Z-Mail is a commercial email client from
Network Computing Devices. Its main claim to fame is
that versions of it run on Windows, Unix, Mac, and
even character-based terminals. From what I can tell,
Z-Mail has some powerful features such as rule-based
filtering, sorting, and searching. Using its Z-Script, you
can completely configure how the program works,
customize every part of the user interface, and
automate repetitive tasks. Z-Mail strikes me as very
powerful in the limited use I've given it, but it also
feels as though it was ported from Windows or Unix.
The interface is confusing and clumsy, and every now
and then you even hit a place, such as the Z-Script
window, where you type commands. You can download
an evaluation copy of Z-Mail, but you must get a demo
key from NCD before you can try it out—email
info@z-code.com or call 415/898-8649.

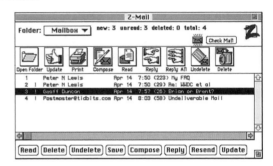

```
http://www.z-code.com/Z-Code/zproducts/z-mac.prod.html
```

Email Utility Programs

Along with the various different programs that enable you to send and receive email,
there are a number of programs that work with the client programs or your stored email
to perform some specific task. I cover a few of them in this section. Unless I provide a
specific URL, assume that all of the following programs are stored in:

```
ftp://ftp.tidbits.com/pub/tidbits/tisk/tcp/mail/
```

AddMail

Alan Staniforth's AddMail is an odd beast, an SMTP gateway that can receive mail from an SMTP server and save it in UUCP format for use by Eudora. Why would anyone want such a thing, you ask? If, for some reason, a POP account isn't available, as it isn't for the dial-up users of Demon Internet in the United Kingdom, AddMail is perhaps the only reasonable way you can use Eudora, which otherwise requires POP at all times. LeeMail would work in this situation, but needless to say, many people prefer Eudora. So, if you're in a similarly unusual situation where you need AddMail's talents, check it out at:

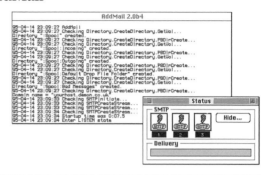

`ftp://ftp.demon.co.uk//pub/mac/addmail/`

Autograph

Signature-watching is a favorite pastime on the Internet, and the people whose signatures are the most interesting generally customize them for each message. Assuming you don't have that kind of time, a utility like David Kabal's free Autograph, which enables you to easily change your signature in Eudora, might be just the ticket. Autograph supports random signatures, multiple signatures, and multiple random signatures. It's a touch tricky to set up random signatures, and changing signatures with Autograph isn't as automated as you might like (you do have to open a document each time), but if you want the multiple random signature capability, Autograph is where it's at.

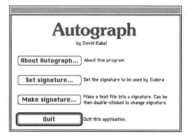

AutoShare

Those of you who want to run a mail server with MailShare (see MailShare listed later in this chapter) should also check out AutoShare, a free application from Mikael Hansen that adds some welcome capabilities to MailShare. AutoShare provides an auto-reply capability that can immediately return a message to any inquiries that come in to a specific address. You also can set AutoShare to reply with different responses based on the contents of the Subject line, and it can even attach a binhexed file if necessary. AutoShare also provides basic mailing list manager capabilities, and although it could use a little more of a graphical interface, it has performed like a champ for me throughout the beta testing (the release version should be out by the time you read this). You can request a copy automatically by sending email to **autoshare.update@admin2.kb.bib.dk** with the

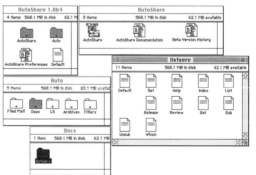

word **Latest** in the Subject line, and the AutoShare FAQ is at **autoshare.faq@admin2.kb.bib.dk**.

Easy View

For most people, Eudora is a sufficiently good email reading and searching environment. However, Eudora's searching capabilities aren't ideal, and it has that pesky 32K text limit that splits large digests. The answer, if those two problems haunt you, is Akif Eyler's free Easy View, which uses a unique technique for viewing large text files in certain formats. Easy View creates an internal index to one or more text files and breaks them up by message, if it's a Eudora mailbox or a digest in a specific format, or by article if it's a file like an issue of TidBITS in the setext format. Easy View has excellent searching capabilities and can extract all the found items to a separate file, making it easy to create subsets of a large amount of data. With the included GetURL extension (a BBEdit extension, not a system extenion), Easy View supports Command-clicking on URLs to resolve URLs using Anarchie or MacWeb. Highly recommended.

```
ftp://ftp.tidbits.com/pub/tidbits/tisk/util/
```

Eudora Scripts & Prefs

Due to its flexibility, both in configuration and in scripting, a large number of scripts and plug-in settings file for Eudora have appeared on the Internet. Their functions range from increasing the chunk size in Eudora to creating droplet applications that automatically send files to pre-specified users. I couldn't hope to cover each of them, but if you want to do some exploration, check out the various listings of them at **ftp.tidbits.com** in the directory listed below. The files ending in "**-as**" are AppleScripts, and those that have "**prefs**" in the filename are usually plug-in files that you drop in your Eudora folder to modify one of Eudora's standard behaviors.

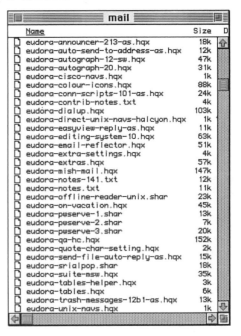

ListSTAR

StarNine, one of the prominent Internet developers in the Macintosh world, is perhaps best known for its email gateway products. StarNine is currently testing a new product called ListSTAR that will provide full mailing list manager and auto-reply capabilities on the Macintosh. Although it might seem that such a product would require a dedicated Internet connection, StarNine is working on two versions of ListSTAR. One version requires a dedicated Internet connection, and another works over a SLIP or PPP connection with a standard POP mailbox like an individual user would use. It's too early to say much else about ListSTAR other than that it looks extremely promising. It should be out in mid-1995, so check StarNine's Web page for an announcement.

http://www.starnine.com/

MacPGP Kit

PGP stands for Pretty Good Privacy—it is an encryption method that you can use to ensure that your mail is not read by anyone other than the intended recipient. The U.S. government restricts the export of PGP because cryptography, like PGP, is classified as munitions—I won't get into the debate here other than to note that because of this getting MacPGP is a pain. Gregory Combs created the MacPGP Kit to bring together a number of the resources available to make MacPGP (once you get it) easier to use. I consider it still too difficult for standard use, but if you're seriously interested in secure email, check out the MacPGP Kit. The resources listed below should get you started with MacPGP and the various related utilities.

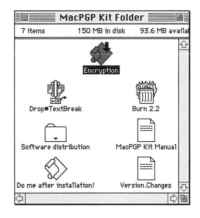

http://www.utexas.edu/~grgcombs/htmls/crypto.html

http://www2.hawaii.edu/~phinely/MacPGP-and-AppleScript-FAQ.html

ftp://ftp.tidbits.com/pub/tidbits/tisk/util/

Mail Processor

Mail Processor is a good idea in need of a better program. It's a stand-alone HyperCard stack that reads in a Eudora mailbox, which you can then use to generate lists of messages that contain a certain string. I often want to find information in large mailboxes of old mail, but I encountered various errors when using Mail Processor. Because it isn't particularly quick, it probably wouldn't work well with my really large mailboxes. Although Jim Allison is distributing Mail Processor as shareware for $24, it feels much more like a tool he built for himself than for use by others. If Mail Processor sounds like something you'd use, give it a try.

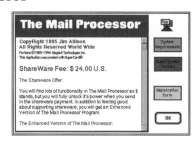

MailConverter

Richard Shapiro's free MailConverter can convert a number of mail formats into Eudora mailboxes, including messages from America Online, eWorld, LeeMail, MacEMail, cc:Mail (limited support), VMS mail (limited support), Pine, Elm, and files saved from various newsreaders, including NewsWatcher. MailConverter also will break up mail digests into individual messages. MailConverter supports drag-and-drop and is rather flexible in terms of dealing with strange headers.

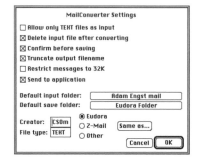

`ftp://ftp.tidbits.com/pub/tidbits/tisk/util/`

MailShare

All of these POP- and SMTP-based email clients discussed in this chapter are all fine and nice, but what if you want to run a mail server? Glenn Anderson's free MailShare is your answer. It runs on a Macintosh with a permanent Internet connection. It sends and receives mail destined for your site, storing mail for multiple users in POP mailboxes. It's easy to set up and configure for basic use and for simple mailing lists, and works extremely well, even on a relatively old Mac like my SE/30. If you need a mail server, you won't do any better than MailShare. You can get the latest version from the URL below. The Web URL is actually a full tutorial and informational page on how to set up and maintain MailShare. Highly recommended!

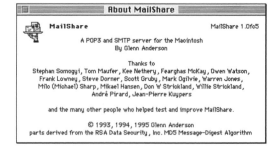

`http://www.winternet.com/~carl/mailshare/mailshare.html`

Mpack

Although most modern email programs automatically understand and decode MIME attachments that contain non-textual information, sometimes you need to be able to do it manually. There's a stand-alone MIME utility, called Mpack, which can pack and unpack MIME files. You're most likely to need Mpack if you don't use a MIME-compatible mailer, such as InterCon's UUCP/Connect. Mpack has worked fine the few times I've had an excuse to use it, but I haven't tested it heavily.

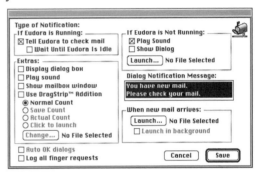

Mpack
Version 1.5

by John Myers
Macintosh port by Chris Newman
© 1993–1995 Carnegie Mellon University
See Help Using Mpack... for Help

```
ftp://ftp.tidbits.com/pub/tidbits/tisk/util/
```

NotifyMail

If you're interested in being notified when you receive new mail, check out NotifyMail, which is $18 shareware from Scott Gruby. The main limitations to NotifyMail are that it requires a dedicated Internet connection (it doesn't make much sense to use it via SLIP or PPP, since you can just have Eudora check when you connect) and it also requires either a full Unix or VMS shell account, or a POP account on a MailShare server (the SMTP server for the Mac). NotifyMail uses an extension to listen for Finger connections, and when it hears one for the appropriate person, it notifies you in any one of a number of user-configurable ways. NotifyMail seems well thought out; I simply can't imagine being notified 200 times a day that I have new mail.

Signature Randomizer

Some people dislike using the same signature all the time, but it's a pain to create them manually or continually swap signature files in and out of your Eudora Folder. Jonathan Baumgartner's free Signature Randomizer may be just what you need, in this case. It randomly picks a signature file from a set you create each time you run the program, and it can optionally pick one and then quit, making it an ideal candidate for your Startup Items folder (since then it would pick one on each restart, then quit).

Signature Randomizer

Version 1.0, April 18, 1995, ©1995 Jonathan Baumgartner
<Internet: Jonathan.D.Baumgartner@unh.edu>

[OK]

VacationMail

I try to avoid talking about Mac programs that rely on a Unix shell account because it adds a level of complexity that frustrates many people. However, MR Mac Software's $25 VacationMail utility is so well done that I couldn't resist. When you go away on vacation, you use VacationMail to set up an auto-reply to all mail on your account (it's really easy), and VacationMail configures a Unix program called Vacation for you. VacationMail is smart enough not to reply to mailing lists and only sends one message per week to any address, so people won't be bothered by your vacation message if they're just trying to leave mail for when you return. VacationMail is well thought out and elegant, so if you have a full Unix shell account and are interested in a vacation message capability while you're away check it out. You can even register by email.

▓▓▓ **VacationMail QuickStart** ▓▓▓

VacationMail QuickStart

VacationMail configures your mail server to automatically notify people that you are unavailable without having to leave your Mac on. When people send you email, a message will automatically be sent to them saying that you are unavailable and will read the email when you return.

─────────────

Instructions:

To use VacationMail, first choose Settings from the File Menu and follow the online help.

Then, choose VacationMail from the File Menu and follow the online help.

Emptying the Mailbox

This chapter may have seemed a little biased toward Eudora, but hey, it really is the best MacTCP-based email program available today. And that's the free version—the commercial version is even better. If you're the contrary sort, feel free to check out the other email clients I mentioned (especially Emailer, once it's available), and also consider exploring some of the email utilities I worked through.

When you're done, let's move on to the hustle and bustle of Usenet news, where there's no clear choice of which newsreader is the best.

22

Usenet News

The sections on email were easy to write because I have a strong opinion about which email program I think is best. In the realm of newsreaders for Usenet news, the field is a little smaller, but much stronger. I currently know of a number of MacTCP-based newsreading solutions, and three of them are neck and neck. Of the freeware and shareware, I prefer NewsWatcher, developed by John Norstad of Disinfectant fame. However, there's a lot to like about Nuntius, from Peter Speck. And confusing the issue is a commercial program, NewsHopper, which is excellent and is the only one that supports offline newsreading. In the end, I think you must try all three (there's a demo for NewsHopper available for FTP) and decide for yourself, because each one brings a different interface philosophy and design to the task of reading news. I'll discuss them in roughly the order in which I suggest you check them out, placing NewsHopper last only because it's commercial and thus has a higher cost of entry than the others.

Note

Since you can try all the main newsreaders for free, I recommend that you form your own opinion and don't clog the nets with questions asking which newsreaders people like best. Newsreaders are very personal programs, and only you can decide which is right for you.

NewsWatcher

The major challenge that the newsreaders face is presenting a clean and quick method of navigating through gobs of information. Interface is all-important (and a purely personal choice, of course), but raw speed doesn't hurt either, and NewsWatcher feels fast. Steve Falkenburg of Apple first created NewsWatcher, and John Norstad later picked it up to continue development. John has gone nuts with NewsWatcher and made the current version, 2.0b24 (don't be scared off by the b24 bit since NewsWatcher is very stable) into one of the best Internet programs available today.

Installation and Setup

When you launch NewsWatcher for the very first time, it asks if you plan to use NewsWatcher on your own, on a shared Mac with someone else who will use NewsWatcher, or in a lab situation. The answer to this question determines how NewsWatcher sets up your preferences. If you choose Private, NewsWatcher creates your preferences in the Preferences folder. If you choose Shared, NewsWatcher prompts you to name a folder in which it will store your personal preferences. And finally, if you click on Lab, NewsWatcher prompts you to insert a floppy disk on which it will store your preferences.

> **N**
> **o**
> **t**
> **e**
>
> *Because NewsWatcher supports Internet Config (see chapter 27, "Utilities & Miscellany"), if you have already configured Internet Config completely (and it's included on the disk so you can do this), you won't have to fill in the basic settings discussed below—they'll already be present. Internet Config is a good thing.*

Once you've determined how you will use NewsWatcher, it prompts you for five pieces of information, three of which are required and two of which are optional. First, it asks for the addresses of your news server and your mail server (see figure 22.1), which are required.

Figure 22.1   *NewsWatcher Server Addresses configuration dialog.*

The only way to figure out these addresses is to ask your system administrator. After you fill them in and click on the OK button, NewsWatcher presents another similar dialog that asks for your full name, your organization, and your email address. It requires only the last of the three, but there's no reason not to input the others (see figure 22.2).

```
╔══════════════ Personal Information ══════════════╗

  Please enter the following information about yourself. You must
  enter at least your email address.

  This information is included in the headers of all of your news
  postings and mail messages.

  Full name:       │Adam C. Engst                    │

  Organization:    │TidBITS                          │

  Email address:   │ace@tidbits.com                  │

                                      ( Cancel )  (( OK ))
╚══════════════════════════════════════════════════╝
```

Figure 22.2   *NewsWatcher Personal Information dialog.*

After you enter all that information, NewsWatcher goes out to your server and downloads the full group list, the huge list of all the newsgroups available on your site. Downloading this list takes a long time, possibly as long as 10 or 20 minutes over a 2,400 bps modem! Be prepared to wait, but don't worry. As long as you don't throw out the NewsWatcher Preferences file in your Preferences folder, NewsWatcher never again has to download all the groups. If NewsWatcher does try to download the full group list on future launches, check to make sure an anti-virus program or something else hasn't prevented NewsWatcher from properly creating its NewsWatcher Prefs file.

N
o
t
e

> *Some people report NewsWatcher crashing or having other problems as it attempts to sort the full group list. In many cases, this is caused by NewsWatcher not having enough memory to deal with so many newsgroups. If you have this problem, in the Finder select the NewsWatcher icon, choose Get Info from the File menu, and increase the Preferred memory size by a few hundred kilobytes.*

Part IV   Usenet News

After you have the massively long list of all the groups onscreen, from the File menu choose New Group Window. NewsWatcher then opens a small, empty window. Scroll through the Full Group List (if you accidentally close it or want to add groups again later, look for Show Full Group List under the Windows menu) and drag interesting groups over to the small, empty window. Don't worry about the order; you can drag groups within that window to put them in the right order after you're finished subscribing to groups. Eventually, you have a nice set of groups to read. From the File menu, choose Save and then name your group list whatever you want (see figure 22.3).

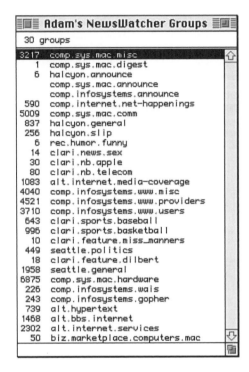

Figure 22.3   *NewsWatcher group list.*

That's about it. You're ready to read news, although you may want to configure some more preferences first. If you select Preferences from the File menu, NewsWatcher presents you with a dialog containing some general options (see figure 22.4). At the top of the dialog is a pop-up menu that lists other types of preferences you can set, such as the location to save files, your signature for postings, the font and size for viewing articles and lists, and various other settings. Some of these match the settings from Internet Config; others are specific to NewsWatcher.

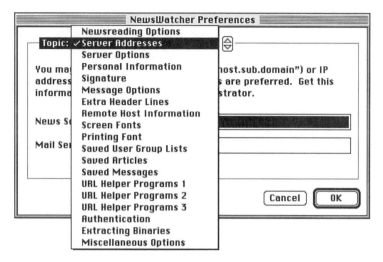

Figure 22.4   NewsWatcher's many preferences.

Basic Usage

To read a newsgroup in your list, double-click on it or use one of the keypad shortcuts (if you have them enabled from the Preferences dialog). NewsWatcher opens another window containing the subjects of all the articles in the group, and alongside each subject is either a dash or a triangle and number (see figure 22.5).

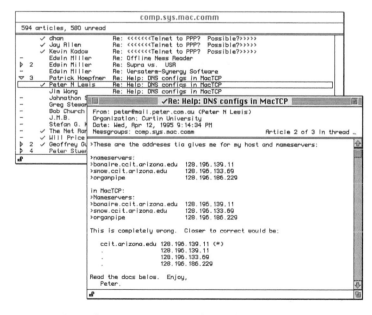

Figure 22.5   NewsWatcher newsgroup and article windows.

The dash indicates that the article is the only one in the thread, the triangle indicates that there are more than one, and the number indicates how many articles are in that thread. You can click the triangle to show the other articles, just as you click a triangle in the System 7 Finder to display a folder's contents. I sometimes leave the option that displays author names turned off, because NewsWatcher draws windows much faster that way. If you choose not to download author names, there's no reason to expand a thread with the triangle control, since all the articles have the same subject and thus look identical.

Double-clicking on an article subject in the newsgroup window opens a window (see figure 22.5 again) that NewsWatcher sizes to the article to prevent unnecessary scrolling. However, if you click on the little lock icon in the lower left-hand corner of the window, NewsWatcher uses that window size until you unlock the icon. With an article window open, you can go to the next article, next thread, or next group (marking the current group as read) with keyboard shortcuts or, if you have them turned on in the preferences, a keypad shortcut. I prefer using the keypad shortcuts because reading news should be an easy process, and using a Command-key combination is too hard for hundreds of repetitions. That's especially true for those of us with repetitive stress injuries.

In NewsWatcher, you also can reply to an article via email or post a follow-up to the newsgroup using commands in the News menu. Useful icons at the top of the reply window let you specify if the reply should go to the newsgroup, to the poster or another email address that you can enter, or to your email account if you wanted to save a copy yourself (see figure 22.6).

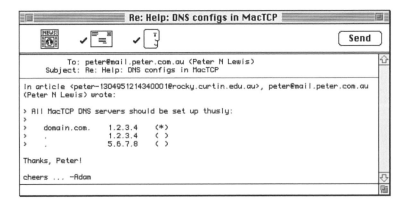

Figure 22.6   *NewsWatcher reply window.*

When you're back in a newsgroup window, you also can quickly mark articles as read or unread, which can be handy for getting through a group quickly. That's about all there is to reading news with NewsWatcher—it's an elegant program.

You might try selecting all the articles in the group with Select All, then holding down the Command key and clicking on the ones you want to read to deselect them. From the News menu, choose Mark Read, which puts a check mark next to each of the still-selected uninteresting articles. Now you can select the first article in the group and read straight through without being bothered by any of the uninteresting stuff.

Special Features

NewsWatcher feels fast, clean, and easy to use, which is the result of nice touches at every level. I cannot live without keypad shortcuts or the Spacebar shortcut that moves you to the next screen and then to the next unread message, just as in a Unix newsreader.

John removed the capability to move through the massive full group list by typing the first few characters of each part of the newsgroup name, replacing it with a more generic Find function that's more useful and easier to use (since most newsgroups start with the same letters anyway).

NewsWatcher has an interesting feature to open referenced articles, which theoretically enables you to go back in a thread even if you have already marked earlier articles as read. All you must do is Command-click on the message-ID if one exists at the top of the article, although many people edit out the message-ID. Still, it's a nice idea.

John has enhanced this feature so that Command-clicking on an email address opens a new mail window set to send email to that person. Even better, if you Command-click on an FTP URL that someone has included in a posting, NewsWatcher calls either Anarchie or Fetch (you set it) and resolves the URL by retrieving the file or directory. But of course, there are many non-FTP URLs passed around in Usenet news, so NewsWatcher can also pass HTTP URLs to a Web browser such as MacWeb, Gopher URLs to TurboGopher, and so on. Other URLs that John supports include WAIS, Telnet, tn3270, Finger, Whois, and Ph, and you can set the programs to help out in each case.

NewsWatcher has automatic extraction code that enables it to automatically download and decode binary files that are posted—usually in BinHex or uuencoded form. Even better, NewsWatcher supports Apple's Drag Manager, so you can just drag the icon linked to a binary file to a folder in your Finder, and NewsWatcher downloads it and calls the appropriate programs to decode it.

Drag Manager support extends beyond just downloading binary files, though, so you can drag the contents of any NewsWatcher window to the Finder to create a text clipping, or to another Drag Manager-aware program window to copy the text into that document.

Drag Manager support does require System 7.5 or the full set of Drag Manager extensions for System 7.1.1.

For those of you who read news on a Unix machine using rn or nn at work and perhaps use NewsWatcher at home to read news on that same Unix machine, NewsWatcher has a feature that enables you to use the same **.newsrc** file so that you don't have to duplicate reading effort.

N o t e

The Remote Host Information preferences control this feature for retrieving the **.newsrc** *file from a Unix shell account. Don't worry about those preferences if you don't also read news under Unix and wish to share the* **.newsrc** *file.*

Evaluation and Details

The main complaint I can think of in regard to NewsWatcher is that the text window limits prevent you from posting messages larger than 32K. Chalk up another one for Apple's limited TextEdit routines. You can read messages larger than 32K, though, since NewsWatcher displays only 32K at a time and provides a horizontal slider bar to reach additional 32K chunks of the same message. Additional missing features include full filtering and the capability of posting attachments to messages. Both of those limitations are starting to be addressed in a variant of NewsWatcher called Value-Added NewsWatcher (which is otherwise basically the same). See the capsule review following for more information on VA-NewsWatcher.

Overall, though, what can I say? John Norstad has once again provided the Macintosh community with a great freeware program. John's free Disinfectant is wonderful, but I certainly hope that people have more occasion to read news than to search for viruses.

However, I shouldn't imply that NewsWatcher is perfect or, more accurately, complete. John has big plans for NewsWatcher, but because it's a labor of love, he works at his own pace and implements features that he wants or feels that the program needs in order to be complete. Because of this, I always enjoy reading the To Do document, which lists all the wishes and requests for future versions, including my big favorites, offline reading and message filtering based on the contents of the messages or headers.

NewsWatcher 2.0b24 is free, and you can retrieve the latest version from either of the following:

```
ftp://ftp.tidbits.com/pub/tidbits/tisk/tcp/
```

```
ftp://ftp.acns.nwu.edu/pub/newswatcher/
```

Nuntius

The second of the heavy-hitting MacTCP-based newsreaders is Peter Speck's free Nuntius 2.0. Long a favorite of the Usenet crowd, Nuntius combines a Finder-like interface with some clever integration with other programs for mundane tasks such as email and text editing.

Installation and Setup

The first time you launch Nuntius, it quickly asks for your news server's address (which you get, of course, by bribing your system administrator with chocolate). It then proceeds to retrieve the entire list of newsgroups. This long download happens only the first time you start Nuntius; the program is smart enough to keep that information around for later use.

After it has the entire list of groups, Nuntius opens two windows. One, called All Groups, contains a Finder-like outline of all the groups (see figure 22.7).

Figure 22.7 *Nuntius All Groups window.*

This method of outlining the hierarchy of new newsgroups works better than the way NewsWatcher and InterNews list them in one big list, simply because the lists are smaller. However, if you know what newsgroup you want, say **comp.sys.mac.announce**, you must open the **comp** folder by clicking on its triangle and then open the **sys** folder and the **mac** folder before you see the **announce** newsgroup. It takes a while to open each folder and scroll down to the right spot to open the next one. Although typing a key takes you to a newsgroup starting with that letter, I find that feature slow and awkward.

The second window Nuntius opens is empty and is called Untitled group list 1. When you see an interesting group or groups (you can select more than one at a time) in Nuntius, as in NewsWatcher, you click them and drag them into the Untitled group list 1 window (which you should immediately save with a different name as in figure 22.8).

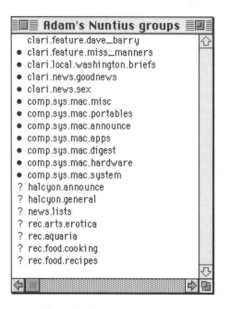

Figure 22.8   *Nuntius group list window.*

In figure 22.8, some of the newsgroups have bullets next to their names, indicating that they have new messages in them. Some newsgroups have question marks next to them because I took this screen shot as Nuntius was querying my news server to see which newsgroups had new articles. Only one group was empty, `clari.feature.dave_barry`, so that group has nothing next to it.

> **Note**
>
> *Unfortunately, `clari.feature.dave_barry` has been removed from ClariNet by Knight-Ridder (the company that syndicates Dave Barry's columns), reportedly because of copyright violations. "…And somewhere men are laughing, and somewhere children shout; But there is no joy in Mudville—Dave Barry has pulled out."*

Although they are not necessary for you to start reading news, you can and should set a number of preferences in the Prefs menu (see figure 22.9). Ideally, I'd like to see Peter

Speck bring the items in the Prefs menu together in a single dialog—you don't change preferences often and the menu seems a bit long and unwieldy.

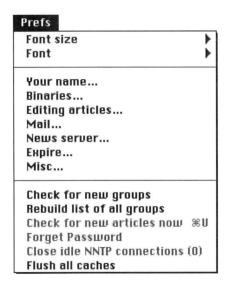

Figure 22.9   *Nuntius Prefs menu.*

Of the several preferences you can set, the most interesting is the Editing articles item in the Prefs menu. It lets you specify which program you want to use to edit your articles.

Basic Usage

As you might expect, double-clicking on a newsgroup name causes Nuntius to open the list of articles in that group. In an interesting and useful twist, Nuntius can open multiple groups at the same time. This feature is especially useful, because Nuntius doesn't seem to work as quickly as NewsWatcher. What you can do is start opening a large group and then open a small group, and have that large group opening in the background as you read the articles in the small group. Even given NewsWatcher's speed, I'd like to see this feature migrate over, because it enables you to work more efficiently.

In any event, opening a newsgroup window displays a window listing the articles in the group (see figure 22.10).

Part IV   Usenet News

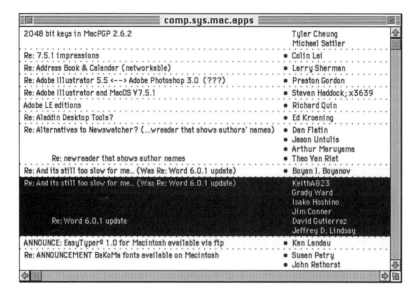

Figure 22.10   *Nuntius newsgroup window.*

The subject of each message appears on the left, unless the message is in the middle of a thread. This use of white space may seem like a waste, but I think it works well to indicate the relative size of threads. Any subject line changes are indicated by the indented subjects within the thread. The names of the authors of each message appear to the right, preceded by bullets if that article is new. Double-clicking on a thread (Nuntius won't let you read a single article in the middle of a thread) opens the article window (see figure 22.11).

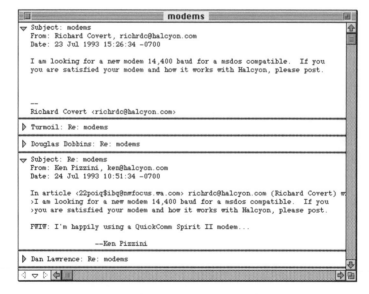

Figure 22.11   *Nuntius article window.*

Nuntius uses a custom interface for determining what you see and don't see, and it's another reason why you may prefer one newsreader over another. I have Nuntius set to open only the first article in the thread, because there's no point in transferring all that data if the first article proves to be uninteresting. Opening threads of uninteresting articles is especially a problem over a slow link or with a large thread, although you can scroll through the article window as the program fills it. If you have a fast network connection, you probably don't care about this problem as much, and you can set Nuntius to open all articles when opening a thread.

You can select multiple threads in the newsgroup window, and by pressing the Spacebar, you can open them. Repeated presses of the Spacebar move you through all the selected threads. Once you have a number of threads open, you can navigate between them from the article window, either by using the right and left arrow keys or by using the arrows in the lower left of the article window. The down arrow in the article window scrolls down and then takes you to the next thread.

My biggest problem with Nuntius is that I don't want to spend the time opening all the articles in a thread to begin with, but at the same time I want to open the triangles from the keyboard because clicking on them with the mouse is too much work for such a common action. I may be missing something, but I cannot find any way of opening the triangle this way in the scanty documentation or in the good, but spotty, balloon help.

Perhaps the coolest aspect of using Nuntius comes when you want to reply to a letter or post a follow-up. Nuntius doesn't, in fact, know how to do much in terms of sending email or editing text; instead, it asks other applications to perform those tasks. So, if you want to mail a response, Nuntius uses an AppleScript to launch or switch to Eudora 1.5.1, and then fills in the header and quotes the article text in the body of the message. Actually, if you don't select any text in the Nuntius article window, Nuntius passes only the Subject line to Eudora. If you do select some text, Nuntius passes the proper address to send mail to and quotes the text you selected. You have to switch back to Nuntius manually when you're finished sending the message in Eudora.

> **Note**
>
> *If you don't have AppleScript installed, Nuntius can still use Eudora to reply via email, but it's an old hack Peter Speck figured out years ago. It may not work as well as the AppleScript method.*

As cool as that setup is, I prefer the way Nuntius calls another program to edit follow-up posts. I live in Nisus Writer, and using any other text editor or word processor, even on the Mac, irritates me to no end because none of them, in my opinion, provides a comparable set of features for writing and editing text. So, whenever I post an article from Nuntius, I get to edit that article in Nisus Writer. (Note that if you use a word processor other than Nisus, you probably must save your files as text if your word processor doesn't use text files as its native format.)

This technique does have drawbacks. You must have enough memory to run both programs at once, and you must use Eudora to send mail. But even with these limitations (which don't bother me at all, since I have enough RAM and I use Eudora anyway), I'd like to see more programs follow this method. The trick with editing files isn't even all that fancy. Nuntius saves a file with the information to be edited (on the desktop or some other folder you set); then it asks the Finder to open that document with the editor you defined. After you're finished editing, you normally save and close the file. Then you manually switch back to Nuntius, which waits patiently for you to finish and then asks if you want to post that article. To avoid clutter, you can click on a checkbox to trash the temporary file when you're finished. I see no reason why other programs couldn't use this technique, although Nisus Writer is especially well-suited to it because its native file format is straight text.

Special Features

Aside from Nuntius's extremely cool method of sending mail and posting follow-ups, it has several features that set it apart from the crowd. The Spacebar works as it does in Unix newsreaders—as a kind of magic key that performs the most likely next action. Unfortunately, I wanted it to open the next closed triangle in an article window, and it didn't do that, so for me the magic disappeared at that point.

Nuntius takes the concept of resolving URLs one step further than even NewsWatcher. When Nuntius brings in articles in a thread, it searches for any URLs in the article and makes them hot, just as in a Web browser. They even come in as blue and underlined, also just like a Web browser. There's no need to Command-click; an unmodified click works fine to resolve a large number of URL types.

Although Nuntius does an excellent job of grouping articles into threads, the most recent versions also sort them alphabetically, which I happen to like, although I could see where others would prefer a chronological sort, as NewsWatcher does.

In Nuntius, you can set the font and size for any of its windows with the Font and Size menus in the Prefs menu, and those settings apply to all newsgroup and article windows. Of all the newsreaders, Nuntius has the most control over which threads it displays, enabling you to show all threads, threads updated today, threads with unread articles, or threads with new articles. You can choose among these threads from the Threads menu. A similar set of commands in the Articles menu enables you to expand all articles, the first article, new articles, unread articles, or no articles. Unfortunately, there aren't keyboard shortcuts for these commands; adding them might be a partial solution to my complaint about not being able to expand articles from the keyboard easily.

Nuntius is Power Mac-native, and combined with its capability to bring in multiple groups at once and automatically update them while you're reading something else, it's definitely one of the quickest of the newsreaders.

Evaluation and Details

Despite my love affair with its method of using other programs for mail and editing and its clever method of multitasking different actions so that you can work more efficiently, Nuntius simply doesn't make it for me. If there were a better way of just zipping through a set of articles without mucking with the mouse or waiting for Nuntius to transfer the full text of each article, I might use it over NewsWatcher.

Nuntius has essentially no documentation, although Aaron Freimark has done a lot of work in creating a FAQ and maintains a Web site with information about the program. Nuntius does come with a notes document that lists some hidden keyboard shortcuts and version changes, but that's it. The balloon help is useful, although not as obviously great as in Eudora. Support is primarily available by asking questions on `comp.sys.mac.comm`—the Nuntius mailing list was disbanded because all the traffic was on the newsgroup.

Finally, I've had more trouble with Nuntius crashing than I did with either InterNews or NewsWatcher. Your mileage may vary with a different machine, network connection, and set of extensions.

Nuntius is free, and you can find the latest versions of Nuntius at the following FTP sites and more information at the Web site:

```
ftp://ftp.tidbits.com/pub/tidbits/tisk/tcp/
```

```
ftp://ftp.ruc.dk/pub/nuntius/
```

```
http://guru.med.cornell.edu/~aaron/nuntius/nuntius.html
```

NewsHopper

In the second edition of the book, Laurent Humbert, who wrote NewsHopper, asked me not to say anything about NewsHopper, which wasn't quite ready for prime time. Now it is, and especially in the most recent version 1.1, NewsHopper has become one of the best of the MacTCP-based newsreaders. The two features that set it apart from all the others are excellent support for offline newsreading and good filtering.

Installation and Setup

NewsHopper doesn't force you to work through any immediate setup upon startup; instead, after you launch the program, you must create a new newsfile by selecting New from the File menu. At that point, NewsHopper starts asking configuration questions, but if you've previously configured Internet Config, NewsHopper can retrieve all of your settings from Internet Config's database. One way or another, you first see a dialog asking for the name of your news server (see figure 22.12). After that, NewsHopper presents you

Part IV   Usenet News   22

with a standard file dialog so you can name and save the folder that contains all of your settings. After you've saved that folder, NewsHopper opens your News window and another dialog asking for your real name, your organization, and your email address (see figure 22.13).

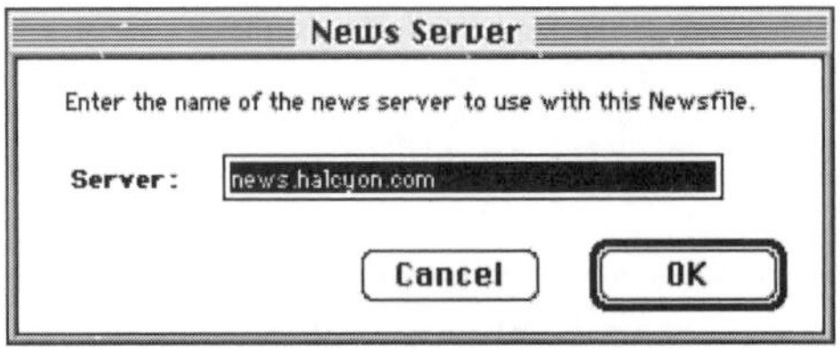

Figure 22.12   *NewsHopper news server configuration.*

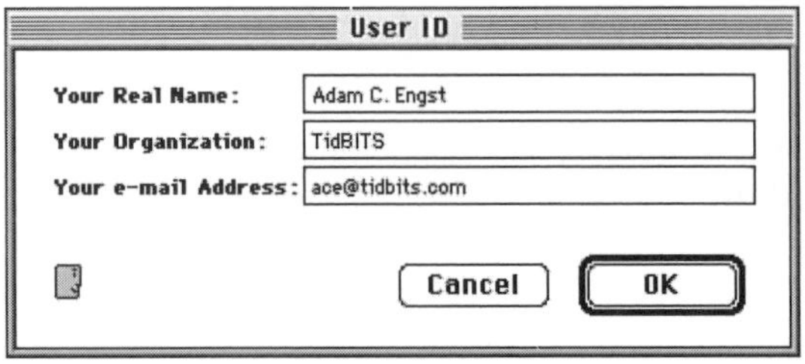

Figure 22.13   *NewsHopper UserID configuration.*

NewsHopper has several other sets of preferences in the hierarchical Settings menu under the Edit menu which aren't governed by Internet Config, things like whether or not you want to use an external text editor, if you want to ignore confirmation alerts, and if windows should avoid hiding the Finder's icons. Also included are options for saving window positions, showing complete addresses for the senders, and marking articles as "not new" automatically. Needless to say, none of these settings are the slightest bit necessary—worry about them after you've used NewsHopper a bit.

After working through the basic settings—which is as easy as accepting the existing settings if you've configured Internet Config—you're left with a News window. At this point, there are two basic ways of subscribing to newsgroups. If you know the exact names of the groups you want to read, choose Subscribe from the Groups menu (see figure 22.14) and enter the name of the newsgroup. I usually set NewsHopper to fetch all new items, to fetch subjects and authors only (since that's the beauty of NewsHopper's offline capabilities), and to sort the threads alphabetically. However, with very low-volume groups such as `comp.sys.mac.announce` and `rec.humor.funny`, I have NewsWatcher bring in the articles themselves on the first pass, since it's easier.

Group Settings

Name : rec.humor.funny

Fetch :
◉ **All New Items**
○ **A Maximum Of** 100 **New Items**

☒ **Fetch Subjects And Authors Only**
☒ **Sort Threads Alphabetically**
☐ **Convert Articles To Latin1**

[Cancel] [OK]

Figure 22.14   NewsHopper subscribe window.

When you click the OK button, NewsHopper enters that newsgroup in your News window. Frankly, this is all I've done for the way I use NewsHopper, because I know full well which groups I want to read by now. However, if you don't know which groups you want to read, you must tell NewsHopper to fetch the list of all groups, which requires making a connection.

From the File menu, choose Connect, and in the dialog that appears, check the Fetch List Of All Groups checkbox (see figure 12.15). Make sure you have a connection to the Internet established if you're using SLIP or PPP, and then click the OK button. NewsHopper goes out to your news server and brings in the full list of newsgroups (on my server, with about 6,000 groups, NewsHopper brought in about 285K of data during that time).

Connect

☐ **Fetch New Articles**
☐ **Fetch Marked References**
☐ **Send Items In Outbasket**
☒ **Fetch List Of All Groups**

☐ **Apply Filters**

[Cancel] [OK]

Figure 22.15   NewsHopper Connect dialog.

There's not much that you can do in NewsHopper right now because you don't have any groups configured yet, but if you did, you could be reading or replying to articles. NewsHopper is extremely good about establishing connections and working in the

Part IV   Usenet News   22

background, so you can keep reading. Once NewsHopper has finished, you can hang up your Internet connection if you wish, and then choose List Of All Groups from the Windows menu to bring up the window showing all the groups (see figure 22.16).

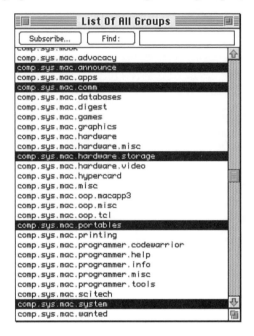

Figure 22.16   *NewsHopper List Of All Groups.*

You can scroll around and select multiple groups, or you can type a search string in the text field at the top and click the Find button. When you click the Subscribe button, NewsHopper adds the selected groups to your News window.

> **Note**
>
> *NewsHopper makes you choose the options for all of the selected groups at the same time; however, you can easily change the settings for how many articles to bring in, or whatever, later by selecting the group in the News window and choosing Settings from the Groups menu.*

So now that you've subscribed to a number of groups, let's fill them with articles. From the File menu, choose Connect again. This time, Fetch List Of All Groups will have changed (since you've already gotten the list) to Check For New Groups. Leave that selected if you like, but also check Fetch New Articles. Make sure you're connected to the Internet and click the OK button. NewsHopper connects to your news server and retrieves the subjects and authors for the articles in the newsgroups to which you've subscribed (see figure 22.17).

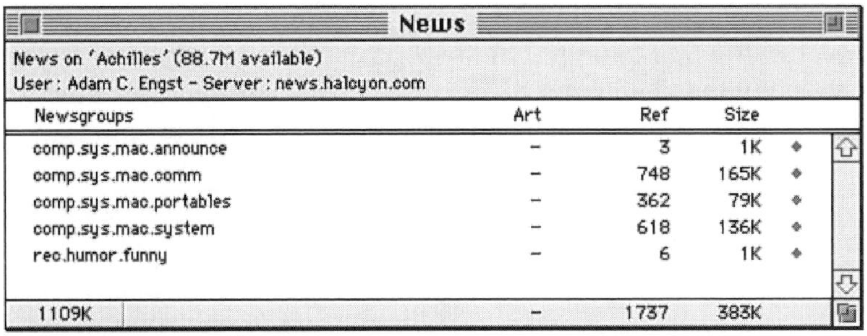

News			
News on 'Achilles' (88.7M available)			
User : Adam C. Engst – Server : news.halcyon.com			
Newsgroups	**Art**	**Ref**	**Size**
comp.sys.mac.announce	–	3	1K ◆
comp.sys.mac.comm	–	748	165K ◆
comp.sys.mac.portables	–	362	79K ◆
comp.sys.mac.system	–	618	136K ◆
rec.humor.funny	–	6	1K ◆
1109K	–	1737	383K

Figure 22.17   *NewsHopper News window.*

Once it's done, you can again disconnect from the Internet—keeping your bills low if you're charged by the hour or calling long distance. Even though NewsHopper moves right along, if you've selected several high-volume groups, it can still take a while to download just the subjects and authors. Be glad you aren't trying to download all of the articles as well.

Basic Usage

To read articles in a newsgroup, simply double-click on the newsgroup in your News window. NewsHopper brings up a window listing all the articles (see figure 22.18). Remember that we don't yet have any of the articles themselves, just the subjects and authors. So, the next step is to mark the articles you want to read. Double-clicking on an article marks it with a checkbox, or you can select a number at a time and from the Articles menu, use the Attributes hierarchical menu to choose Marked (⌘-M is a lot easier).

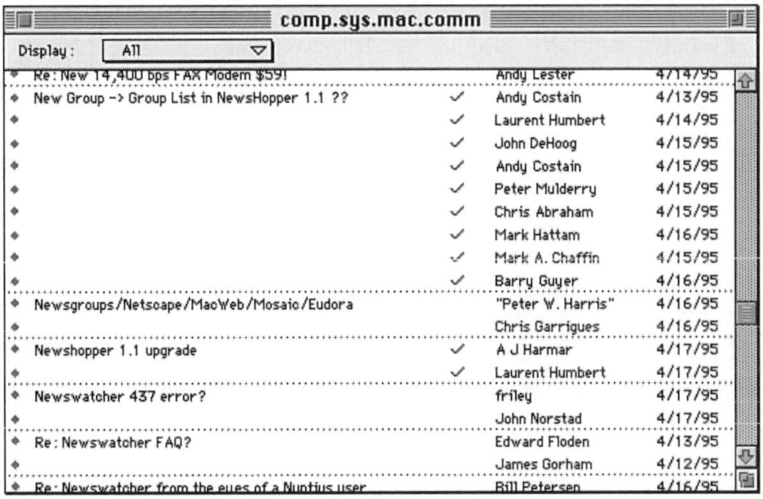

comp.sys.mac.comm			
Display :	All		
◆ Re : New 14,400 bps FAX Modem $59!		Andy Lester	4/14/95
◆ New Group –> Group List in NewsHopper 1.1 ??	✓	Andy Costain	4/13/95
◆	✓	Laurent Humbert	4/14/95
◆	✓	John DeHoog	4/15/95
◆	✓	Andy Costain	4/15/95
◆	✓	Peter Mulderry	4/15/95
◆	✓	Chris Abraham	4/15/95
◆	✓	Mark Hattam	4/16/95
◆	✓	Mark A. Chaffin	4/15/95
◆	✓	Barry Guyer	4/16/95
◆ Newsgroups/Netscape/MacWeb/Mosaic/Eudora		"Peter W. Harris"	4/16/95
◆		Chris Garrigues	4/16/95
◆ Newshopper 1.1 upgrade	✓	A J Harmar	4/17/95
◆	✓	Laurent Humbert	4/17/95
◆ Newswatcher 437 error?		friley	4/17/95
◆		John Norstad	4/17/95
◆ Re : Newswatcher FAQ?		Edward Floden	4/13/95
◆		James Gorham	4/12/95
◆ Re : Newswatcher from the eyes of a Nuntius user		Bill Petersen	4/16/95

Figure 22.18   *NewsHopper Articles window.*

That's still a bit of work, though, so let's create some filters to do this for us. For instance, I want to read everything that Laurent Humbert posts, because he's likely to say interesting things about NewsHopper, being the author. So, select an article from him, if you happen to see one. Or, you could use the Find command from the Edit menu to search for his name, at which point NewsHopper would display just the articles that match (you can use the Display pop-up menu at the top of the window listing all the articles to switch back to viewing all the articles).

After you have an article from Laurent selected, from the Articles menu choose Add Filter For Author. NewsHopper brings up the Filter dialog box, mostly filled in for you (see figure 22.19).

Figure 22.19   *NewsHopper Filter window.*

As you can see, you can search in the various parts of the article and either in specific newsgroups or in all newsgroups via the pop-up Search In menu. Most important, though, are the Delete, Highlight, and Mark For Download checkboxes. If you never want to see anything from Laurent, you could check Delete. If you just want to see which articles he's posted, you could just check Highlight and then, when you were browsing, it would be easy to see his articles. However, if you want to read everything he posts, check Mark For Download so his articles are automatically downloaded for you on the next NewsHopper run.

> N
> o
> t
> e
>
> *Of course, you can create filters that work on variables other than the name of the poster, although I find filtering on the posters' names to work well for me. Keywords in the Subject lines always seem to bring in too much garbage for my tastes—perhaps I'm just not good enough at creating them.*

To actually apply the filters you've created (you can have NewsHopper do it automatically for future runs), close the articles window, select one or more newsgroups in the News window, and from the Groups menu choose Apply Filter.

After you've selected all the articles you want to download, either manually or through filters, again choose Connect from the File menu, select Fetch Marked References (deselect the others for the fastest run), connect to the Internet, and click on the button to make NewsHopper go out and get the articles you marked. When it's done, disconnect from the Internet and double-click on a group that has articles in it in the News window. You probably still have all the article references listed that you didn't download; to hide those, choose Articles from the Display pop-up menu at the top of the window. Finally, double-click on an article in the list to bring up the article reading window (see figure 22.20).

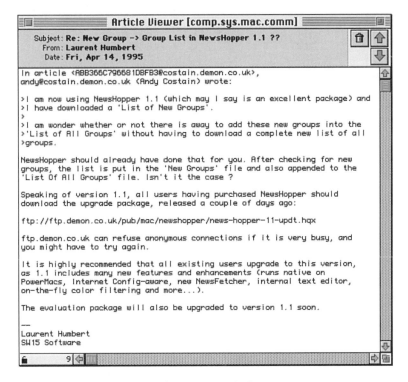

Figure 22.20 *NewsHopper Article Viewer window.*

NewsHopper has a spartan reading interface, and I hope Laurent adds some additional navigation features in future versions. As it stands, the up and down arrow button in the upper right-hand corner of the article window move you to the previous or next article, and the Spacebar also takes you to the next article. There's no way to move to the next thread if the current one proves boring, but you can delete it instantly with the Delete Thread command in the Articles menu.

If you want to reply by email or forward the text to another person, those commands in the Articles menu send the proper email address, the Subject, and the quoted text of the article (or just the selection, if you don't want to quote the entire article) to Eudora. As with Nuntius, I think it makes sense to use Eudora's skills with email rather than trying to duplicate the functionality in NewsHopper. In addition, that way all my outgoing replies end up with the rest of my saved outgoing mail in Eudora.

Creating a follow-up is similar, but NewsHopper retains control, first asking you about the Subject, newsgroup, and distribution, and then creating the follow-up in a separate text window (see figure 22.21).

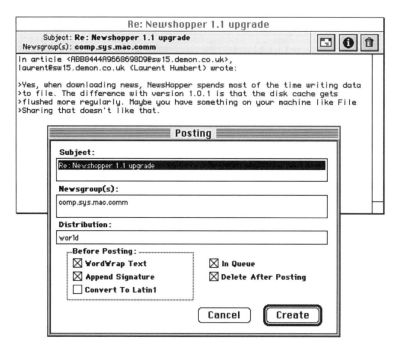

Figure 22.21   *NewsHopper follow-up windows.*

Of course, just as with the rest of NewsHopper's features, the follow-up or any new article, once you're done editing, is placed in an Outbasket and waits until you make another connection.

Special Features

It's a little hard to point to special features in NewsHopper, because its main features, offline newsreading and filtering, are so incredibly useful that they overshadow plenty of other nice touches. For instance, NewsHopper is excellent about quoting only a selection when you reply, forward, or follow up to an article, something that other programs such as NewsWatcher and Eudora can do, but only as a modified command.

I appreciate the little Bytes Received status line at the bottom of NewsHopper's status window because it gives me an idea of how much data I'm getting. Also, since I use a dedicated Internet connection, I can't see the modem lights flashing to see that things are working, so I appreciate the constant reminder.

As I said before, NewsHopper is excellent about multitasking, so you can continue to read and reply to articles even as it's going out to retrieve more or to send your replies. This is probably due to its support for Apple's Thread Manager, and folks with Power Macs will appreciate the native code when filtering or performing other CPU-intensive tasks.

For people like me who are constantly seeing little useful bits of information, NewsHopper has an Add To Clippings File command in the Edit menu. Choosing Clippings File in the Windows menu brings up a small text editing window that shows your clippings, separated by three bullets on a line.

If you want to save an entire article, consider clicking the little padlock icon in the lower left-hand corner of the article window. That locks the article and prevents it from being deleted later on.

Speaking of deletion, since you're downloading all these articles to your hard disk, you will want to recover disk space at some point, and for that NewsHopper has a Purge command that gets rid of uninteresting article references, articles you've read, articles that you've extracted, archives, or just articles that have hung around for too long (see figure 22.22). Also, even purging the messages doesn't actually remove them from your newsfile for efficiency reasons. For that, you should choose Compact from the File menu or let NewsHopper do it when you quit.

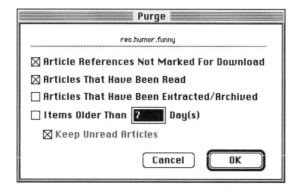

Figure 22.22   *NewsHopper Purge dialog.*

Although NewsHopper currently supports only FTP URLs (support for others is slated for a minor upgrade soon), if you select an FTP URL and choose Create URL from the File menu, it creates a bookmark file for use with Anarchie or Fetch. If you happen to be online, hold down the Option key as you save the URL to have Anarchie or Fetch (as set in Internet Config) resolve the URL immediately.

Part IV Usenet News

NewsHopper's Find command, which presents a restricted view of the messages available in a newsgroup, works extremely well for the way I read news, since I often want to do some ad hoc queries. It's too easy to be overwhelmed by several hundred messages in a window.

Evaluation and Details

Overall, I'm extremely impressed with NewsHopper. Even though I use a dedicated Internet connection now, I still read news with NewsHopper, mostly because of the filtering and searching capabilities.

That's not to say that there isn't room for improvement, though. NewsHopper could still use a more streamlined interface for actually reading news, with keyboard shortcuts for moving around in the threads. I'd also like to see it save bookmark files for MacWeb for non-FTP URLs. And finally, I'd like to see the Find functionality move right into the article list window itself, rather than be separated out in a different dialog. That way it would be even easier to perform ad hoc searches for specific topics or posters.

NewsHopper's documentation is good, although I can't say that I've read most of it because the program is fairly easy to figure out once you get the hang of the procedure for doing something, connecting, disconnecting, doing something else, and repeating the process all over again.

NewsHopper is commercial software (£39, with 20 percent educational discounts) from SW15 Software, who you can contact at **nh@sw15.demon.co.uk** or by phone in the U.K. at (+44)-181-813-6027 or (+44)-181-561-2879 (fax). Orders other than from the United States and Canada should go to SW15 Software. In the U.S. and Canada, NewsHopper is distributed by LandWare for $59 (plus $4.50 shipping and handling via Priority Mail). You can contact LandWare at **landware@planet.net** or at 800-526-3977, 201-347-0031, or 201-347-0340 (fax). However, you can download a demo of NewsHopper 1.1 that is limited only by being restricted to five newsgroups and not running in Power Mac-native mode. You can get a copy of the latest version from:

```
ftp://ftp.tidbits.com/pub/tidbits/tisk/tcp/
```

```
http://www.demon.co.uk/sw15/
```

Other News Programs

Despite the power and popularity of the preceding programs, several other newsreaders might be worth checking out, although I don't feel that they are in the same league. In addition, there are now two programs, MacSlurp and NewsFetcher, that act mostly as news transport programs—they merely download messages for reading in another program. Unless mentioned otherwise, all of the following programs are available in:

```
ftp://ftp.tidbits.com/pub/tidbits/tisk/tcp/
```

InterNews

InterNews from Dartmouth College provides yet another interface for reading news, presenting you with a three-paned window that displays a list of newsgroups, a list of subjects in the selected group, and the articles in a selected thread, all at the same time. If you Command-Option-click on an FTP URL in a message, InterNews can use Anarchie or Fetch to retrieve the file. Unfortunately, InterNews doesn't yet support other applications for resolving other types of URLs. One relatively serious limitation in InterNews is that you cannot receive or send an article larger than 32K. InterNews is a fine effort, though, and much of its interface is well done. InterNews is free for educational and nonprofit users, $25 shareware for others

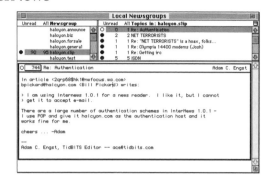

```
ftp://ftp.dartmouth.edu/pub/mac/
```

MacSlurp

MacSlurp works by connecting to a specified NNTP server and downloading all the articles in the groups that you specify in your **slurp.sys** file, which is a specially formatted file that must live in your MacSlurp Files folder in your MacSlurp folder. Once MacSlurp has downloaded all of the messages in a newsgroup, you can set ToadNews to unbatch them (ToadNews is discussed in more detail in chapter 15, "UUCP Access"), and once ToadNews has unbatched the news articles, you can use rnMac or TheNews (again, both discussed in chapter 15) to read the news. MacSlurp can also download the news in a format that UUCP/Connect can read, at which point you don't need the combination of ToadNews and rnMac.

The major problem with MacSlurp (other than it doesn't currently work with news servers like mine) is that it's indiscriminate. If you ask it to retrieve **comp.sys.mac.comm**, it goes out and downloads all the articles in that group, regardless of whether or not

it could take two hours because of all the new messages. You must spend the downloading time and have the disk storage space for all the articles, which isn't efficient if you only wanted to read a few in that group.

NewsFetcher

NewsFetcher is a free HyperCard-based news transport agent from Jörg Shäffer. It's quite limited and a bit clunky in terms of interface, but it provides a potentially useful way of reading news offline. NewsFetcher first retrieves subject lines in specified groups. You then select the subjects you wish to read, and it goes

out and retrieves those articles. NewsFetcher doesn't attempt to read the articles on its own at all, but instead saves them in a special format that Akif Eyler's Easy View text browser (see the capsule review in chapter 21, "Email") can read. Easy View is a great program for browsing text, although it would be nice if

continues

Part IV Usenet News

NewsFetcher had an option for not downloading the complete headers of the messages. NewsFetcher, although it does have minimal posting capabilities, it doesn't work well if you post frequently. If you're more of a lurker, though, NewsFetcher is fine. I won't pretend that NewsFetcher is an ideal offline newsreading solution, but it is free.

NewsGrazer

NewsGrazer (which also seems to go by the names NetNews Filter Agent and NetNews Grazer) is a free set of AppleScripts from John Schettino that communicate with an NNTP server, checking for new messages in specified groups and scanning for search terms in the subject lines of the messages. That's actually the task of the NetNews Grazer, whereas the NetNews Grazer Prefs enable you to set various preferences, and Read Interesting News provides a newsreading interface patterned after InterNews. It gets the articles that match your search string. NetNews Grazer can also send you email whenever new articles arrive, although that seems a little excessive to me. Perhaps the main problem with NewsGrazer is its set of requirements—it needs System 7 or later, AppleScript 1.1, FaceSpan 1.0, MacTCP, and the TCP/IP and AppleScript 1.1 Scripting Additions. Just making sure you have everything available is too much work for many people. John thought of that, and a $20

shareware payment gets you an electronic manual along with AppleScript 1.1 and FaceSpan 1.0, as well as the TCP/IP and AppleScript 1.1 Scripting Additions.

NNTP Sucker

Darrell Turner designed his $5 shareware NNTP Sucker program to be almost exactly like MacSlurp, in that it reads a Group file to see which groups you want to download, and then it goes out and downloads messages from those groups. You can't specify which messages to get, but you can set a maximum percent or number of messages to retrieve. When NNTP Sucker is done, it can quit, restart the Mac, or shut down the Mac. Like MacSlurp, NNTP Sucker creates output files for use with ToadNews and then rnMac. NNTP Sucker also works with a BBS program Darrell's working on called Pancake. Finally, I've heard rumors that a new version of NNTP Sucker might come out that can work

with Easy View, an excellent text browser that's much easier to set up than ToadNews and rnMac.

TheNews

Bill Cramer's $25 shareware newsreader, TheNews, works by default in MacTCP mode, although it also works with UUCP connections and with Unix shell accounts. TheNews is a fairly basic newsreader, with support for threads and the capability of using Eudora to email responses and forward messages. Unfortunately, I always seem to have various problems with TheNews whenever I try to test it, and its interface simply doesn't compare to the main freeware and shareware newsreaders. Feel free to try it out, but I suspect you'll prefer NewsWatcher, Nuntius, or InterNews.

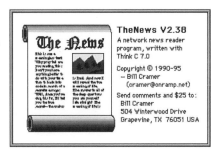

Value-Added NewsWatcher

Since John Norstad makes the code for NewsWatcher available for anyone who wants it, there have been various modified versions of NewsWatcher in the past. One current and popular modification on the standard NewsWatcher program comes from David Brewster and Bob Boonstra. VA-NewsWatcher adds support for posting binary files, rudimentary article filtering, and article sorting. The last two of these features are likely to be useful to many people, so I recommend you check out VA-NewsWatcher. Do make sure you have the latest version and that it's in synch with John's official version, if possible, to avoid missing out on any new features or bug fixes in the base code.

All the News That's Fit to Post

I hope this chapter has given you a sense of how varied newsreaders can be, and how no one can really decide for you which you'll like the best. I personally prefer NewsHopper and NewsWatcher, but many people like Nuntius, and InterNews has a following as well. Any one of them should perform admirably for you, and if the one you try doesn't work well, just switch to another.

Next, let's look at FTP programs like Anarchie and Fetch.

Part IV Usenet News 22

Chapter

23

FTP

Although more *people* use email than any other Internet application, more *data* is transferred via FTP than any other Internet application. FTP is one of the base applications that tie the Internet together. Despite its relative simplicity from a command line, FTP works far better when you can use a graphical application to navigate through remote directories and files.

N o t e

*Keep in mind that a few machines—**ftp.apple.com**, for one—don't allow you to log in if you don't have a valid domain name, such as **tidbits.com**. Just having an IP number isn't good enough; you must have a name associated with your number, or these sites bounce you out for security reasons. Talk to your system administrator if you're bounced out.*

As in the previous sections, I cover the top applications in this area, and then address some other utilities and such that may make your use of FTP better. There are a number of FTP clients available, ranging from an early HyperCard stack (which I remember as being astonishingly cool at the time) to Anarchie and Fetch, the *de facto* standards in the MacTCP world. I look primarily at Anarchie and Fetch because I think they're the best, but I briefly discuss some of the other FTP programs that I know about. Also, I've included Anarchie 1.5 on the disk, complete with all sorts of bookmarks for interesting places and files.

N
o
t
e

Many people use Web browsers for FTP because they can, but I often receive complaints about how the Web browser doesn't do this or that. My answer is simply to put away the silly Web browser and use Anarchie. Web browsers may have many talents, but they don't even begin to compare with Anarchie for FTP.

Anarchie

For most people, Peter Lewis's Anarchie is quite simply the best FTP client available for any platform. Not only is it fast, easy to use, and cleanly implemented, but it also does something that I've wanted for quite some time. Anarchie is a full-fledged FTP client, but it can also *search* Archie servers for files stored on anonymous FTP sites. Once it has found those files, it can retrieve them via FTP with merely a double-click.

N
o
t
e

Anarchie is pronounced like the word "anarchy," not like the phrase, "an archie." That's the word direct from Peter.

Installation and Setup

You can place Anarchie anywhere on your hard disk, but its folder of bookmarks of popular sites should stay in the same folder as the Anarchie program.

If you're using SLIP or PPP, make sure you're connected, and then launch Anarchie (or else it will open the connection for you, even before you connect to a site). First, go to the Edit menu and choose Preferences. Notice that there are hardly any preferences (see figure 23.1). That's because Anarchie relies entirely on Internet Config, another one of Peter's programs, for all of its common preferences. Since I've also included Internet Config on the disk, that shouldn't be a problem. Just look for the Internet Config section at the beginning of chapter 27, "Utilities & Miscellany."

I recommend that you keep Post Process Files selected, since it enables Anarchie to use StuffIt Expander to debinhex and expand files that you download automatically. In Internet Config, you must set your email address, because Anarchie uses your email address as the password when you connect to any anonymous FTP site.

Unless you know that you're behind a firewall (an Internet machine that makes entry into, and often out of, a domain difficult), you shouldn't have to mess with the Firewalls item in the Edit menu. If you are behind a firewall, contact your system administrator and ask about how to work with your organization's firewall.

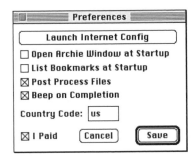

Figure 23.1   *Anarchie Preferences window.*

Basic Usage

There are a number of ways to use Anarchie, depending on what you want to accomplish. If you want to browse around a site listed among Anarchie's bookmarks, choose List Bookmarks from the File menu and double-click on one of them. As you can see, Peter included a large list of the most popular FTP sites for various pieces of Macintosh software (see figure 23.2). The list actually scrolls on for some time—there was no way to show all of the bookmarks Peter includes.

Name	Size	Date	Zone	Machine	
Aladdin	–	–	1	ftp.aladdinsys.com	
Aladdin (Netcom)	–	–	1	ftp.netcom.com	
Alt.Sources.Mac	–	–	1	ftpbio.bgsu.edu	
AMUG	–	–	1	ftp.amug.org	
AOCE	–	–	1	ftp.andrew.cmu.edu	
AOL	–	–	1	mirrors.aol.com	
Apple	–	–	1	ftp.apple.com	
Apple Austin	–	–	1	ftp.austin.apple.com	
Apple Business Systems	–	–	1	abs.apple.com	
Apple Claris	–	–	1	ftp.claris.com	
Apple Dylan	–	–	1	ftp.cambridge.apple.com	
Apple Info	–	–	1	ftp.info.apple.com	
Apple Seeding	–	–	1	seeding.apple.com	
Apple Support	–	–	1	ftp.support.apple.com	
AppleScripts	–	–	1	gaea.kgs.ukans.edu	
Bare Bones (Netcom)	–	–	1	ftp.netcom.com	
Bare Bones (STD)	–	–	1	ftp.std.com	
Dartmouth College	–	–	1	ftp.dartmouth.edu	
Disinfectant	–	–	1	ftp.acns.nwu.edu	
Dylan	–	–	1	ftp.cambridge.apple.com	
Electronic Frontier Foundation	–	–	1	ftp.eff.org	
Eudora	–	–	1	ftp.qualcomm.com	
FAQs (France)	–	–	5	grasp1.univ-lyon1.fr	
FAQs (Germany)	–	–	5	ftp.uni-paderborn.de	
FAQs (Sweeden)	–	–	5	ftp.sunet.se	
FAQs (Taiwan)	–	–	5	nctuccca.edu.tw	
French Versions	–	–	5	ftp.sri.ucl.ac.be	
GNU FTP Site	–	–	1	ftp.gnu.ai.mit.edu	
Gutenberg	–	–	1	mrcnext.cso.uiuc.edu	

Figure 23.2   *Anarchie Bookmarks window.*

If you double-click on one of the bookmarks, Anarchie connects to the remote site and displays the directory listing. Double-clicking on names with folders next to them takes you into that directory, and double-clicking on a file retrieves the file. In this respect, Anarchie resembles the Finder in Name view.

But what if you want to retrieve a specific file that someone has told you about? Go to the FTP menu and choose Get. Anarchie opens the Get via FTP window, which provides fields for the name of the FTP host and the pathname of the file. If you don't know the name of the file but do know the pathname to it, you can click on Get Listing instead of Get File, at which point Anarchie connects to the FTP site and displays the directory listing you've asked for. If you provide the full pathname of the file (including the filename), select Get File, and click the Get button, Anarchie retrieves the file with no fuss (see figure 23.3).

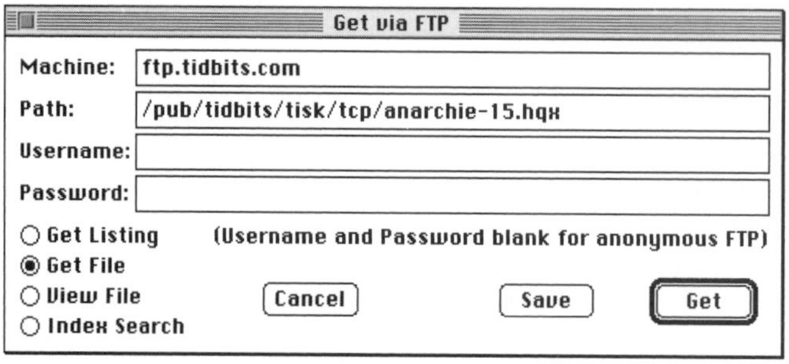

Figure 23.3   *Anarchie Get via FTP window.*

N o t e

Since some URLs contain the name of the FTP server and the full pathname for a file, you can type or paste that information into Anarchie's Get via FTP window. Be aware that if the file you want has been updated, Anarchie won't be able to retrieve it (since the filename will have changed). At that point, simply remove the filename from the end of the pathname and ask Anarchie to get a listing of the directory that file originally lived in to find the updated program.

If you want to connect to an "anonymous" FTP server—that is, an FTP server that requires a username and password—simply enter them in the appropriate fields in the Get via FTP window. Anarchie does not display your password in clear text, nor does it ever store your password in a URL or in the log. Peter implemented this for safety because it's all too easy to copy a URL from your home site and send it to someone, and if the password were stored with the URL, you'd be handing it out to the world at large.

If you're retrieving a directory list instead of a file, select the Get Listing button and click the List button in the Get via FTP window. This brings up an Anarchie directory list window in which you can double-click on files to retrieve them and on folders to open them (see figure 23.4).

	eudora			
Name	Size	Date	Zone	Machine	Pa

```
.summary         1k 2/11/95   1   ftp.qualcomm.com
1.3               -  2/8/95    1   ftp.qualcomm.com
1.5               -  1/20/95   1   ftp.qualcomm.com
2.0               -  7/1/94    1   ftp.qualcomm.com
2.1               -  12/5/94   1   ftp.qualcomm.com
beta              -  3/27/95   1   ftp.qualcomm.com
dialup            -  3/24/94   1   ftp.qualcomm.com
documentation     -  2/8/95    1   ftp.qualcomm.com
international      -  3/24/94   1   ftp.qualcomm.com
plugins           -  3/20/95   1   ftp.qualcomm.com
product_literature -  1/27/95  1   ftp.qualcomm.com
README           1k  2/11/95   1   ftp.qualcomm.com
scripts           -  1/18/95   1   ftp.qualcomm.com
```

Figure 23.4   *Anarchie listing window.*

You can have multiple listing windows open to multiple sites simultaneously, and from them you can even download multiple files simultaneously by double-clicking them one after another. However, if you select several files at once and choose Get from the FTP menu or hit Return, Anarchie downloads them one after another.

> **Note**
>
> *Downloading multiple files at the same time often doesn't work well with overloaded FTP sites, since Anarchie tries to log in once for each file you want and many sites won't allow that.*

If you don't know where the file you want lives but you have an idea what it might be called, you can try using an Archie server to find it, and this is where Anarchie shines. Unfortunately, Archie servers are seemingly becoming less and less reliable and useful as time passes, but they can still be worth trying. Go to the File menu and choose Archie. Anarchie brings up the Find window with a field for the Archie server you want to search (with a pop-up menu of all the known servers) and a field for the search term (see figure 23.5).

	Archie	

```
Server: archie.internic.net              ▼

Find:   stuffit-expander

● Sub-string (dehqx)            ☐ Case sensitive
○ Pattern (dehqx*.hqx)
○ Regular Expr (dehqx.*\.hqx)   Matches:  100

  [ Cancel ]        [ Save ]        ( Find )
```

Figure 23.5   *Anarchie Archie window.*

Part IV
FTP
23

You can set how many matches Anarchie asks for, and a checkbox forces the search to be case-sensitive. Case-insensitive searches are generally safer than case-sensitive searches, because you never know how the filename might be capitalized on an FTP site. You want to leave the number of matches relatively low, certainly under 100. If you go above that, not only are you stressing the Internet unnecessarily, but the search takes a lot longer to process.

Lastly, you have the choice of three types of searches: Sub-string, Pattern, or Regular Expression. A *Sub-string search* is a simple search—if, for instance, you want to find the Macintosh Internet game Bolo, simply type **bolo** into the Find field. However, since there are a lot of files out there with the word **bolo** in their filenames, you'll find far too many files that aren't what you want.

If instead you switch to *Pattern searching*, you can use a wildcard such as **?** (meaning "any character") or ***** (meaning "any string of characters"). This would enable you to search for **bolo*.hqx**, which would find any BinHex files whose names start with **bolo** and end with **.hqx**.

Most people will never need anything more powerful than Pattern searching, but if you're not most people, you can switch to *Regular Expression searching*. Regular expressions are tremendously powerful, but they're also terribly confusing and hard to write. If you want to find out more about them, Peter recommends looking at the man pages for ed, a Unix text editor. For this you must log in to a Unix machine and type **man ed** at the prompt, so don't worry about it if you don't know how to do that. I only occasionally use Pattern searches, and mostly stick to Sub-string searches.

Special Features

Although using Anarchie is simple (when in doubt, double-click on something), Peter added lots of neat features that come in handy—that's why this section is so long. For even more information on Anarchie, System 7.5 users should check out the Anarchie Guide file available under the Guide menu in the upper right corner of your screen, next to the Applications menu. Peter's friend Quinn wrote the Anarchie Guide, and it's not only excellent, it may have been the first AppleGuide support outside of Apple when Peter shipped it with Anarchie 1.4.

> **Note**
>
> *Unfortunately, there simply wasn't room on the ISKM disk to include the excellent Anarchie Guide file, so Peter allowed me to include a "Get Anarchie Guide" bookmark instead. Once you have your Internet connection set up, just double-click that bookmark to retrieve the Anarchie Guide (when you've got it, it must live in the same folder as Anarchie).*

When you have a directory listing window showing, you can copy one or more of the entries in URL format. This may seem minor, but if you've ever wanted to send someone a list of files in a specific directory, you'll love this feature. If you hold down the Option key when you choose Copy or press ⌘-C, Anarchie copies the selected entries in URL format but without the angle brackets at the beginning and end of the URL. Needless to say, I used this feature heavily while writing this book, and I use it every week in preparing *TidBITS*.

Anarchie's knowledge of URLs is even more useful than it seems. If you see a URL for a file in *TidBITS* or anywhere else on the Internet, you can copy that URL and paste it into the Host field in Anarchie's Get via FTP window (Anarchie splits up the URL properly between the fields). I use this feature all the time, since URLs are becoming the standard way to tell someone where a file lives, and it's so easy to, say, copy a URL out of an email message and paste it into Anarchie.

Of course, if you use one of the main newsreaders, you can simply Command-click (or less commonly now, Option-click) on an FTP URL in those programs to have Anarchie retrieve it automatically. This too is tremendously useful, and in all likelihood, this feature will be migrating to Eudora in the future as well.

If you hold down the Control key before selecting the File menu, you see that some of the menu items change. Most notably, Retry changes to Edit Retry, and Open Bookmark changes to Edit Bookmark. This is handy, but what's even handier is that Control-clicking on an item in any Anarchie list window displays a Get via FTP window with the information from that item in it, ready for editing. Anarchie also supports many of the same shortcuts that work in the Finder, so you can move up a level with Command-up arrow, for instance.

In another feature copied from the Finder, if you hold down the Command key and click on the name of an Anarchie listing window, Anarchie shows you the full path to that window.

I mentioned Anarchie's Bookmarks window earlier, but I didn't note that you can create your own bookmarks. They can point to an FTP site, a specific directory on an FTP site, or a file available via anonymous FTP. So, if you find yourself visiting the same site or directory frequently, simply select the appropriate entry in a directory listing window and choose Save Bookmark from the File menu. If nothing is selected, Anarchie sets the bookmark to the directory referenced by the window itself. Anarchie's bookmarks are extremely useful for providing simple access to files on an FTP site, because double-clicking on the bookmark file to open it automatically retrieves the file that the bookmark references. This is precisely how I created the Essential Bookmarks that I include on the disk.

If you visit the same FTP sites over and over again, as I do, you may find Anarchie's Log window useful. Anarchie records every directory listing and file retrieval action in a log file. Selecting Show Log from Anarchie's Window menu displays the listing of all of these actions, and double-clicking on one works just like double-clicking on any item in an Anarchie window. So, if you retrieve a file from a certain directory and want to go back there later on for another file, try the Log window.

Also under the Window menu is Show Transcript, which shows precisely what you would see had you used a Unix shell account for FTP. The main advantage of this is that Anarchie's normal error messages are terse, so if you want the full error (which usually tells you that the FTP site in question cannot handle any more users at that time), look in the Transcript window (see figure 23.6).

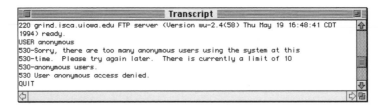

Figure 23.6   *Anarchie Transcript window.*

If you're running System 7.5 or later and have the Macintosh Drag and Drop extension installed, you can use what Apple calls the Drag Manager with Anarchie. The Drag Manager enables you to drag files from an Anarchie window to a Finder window or to your desktop to download them.

You can drag files from the Finder into an Anarchie window that you've opened (you must have upload access to the FTP site reflected in that window) to upload them. Anarchie uses the suffix mappings from Internet Config to guess at how to upload files, and it's worked properly with the files I've thrown at it, in terms of using ASCII or binary uploads.

If you want to delete a file from an FTP site where you have access, simply drag it to the Trash icon on your Finder's desktop. I cannot begin to tell you how unbelievably cool this feature is.

New in Anarchie 1.5 is a Rename command in the FTP menu—it does what you would expect: it lets you rename a file. The only trick is that Anarchie doesn't update the window you're looking at, so if you delete or rename a file, you must choose Retry from the File menu to get a new look at what's in the window.

Anarchie is scriptable and recordable via Apple's AppleScript and UserLand's Frontier; this opens up Internet file retrieval to some extremely necessary automation. Anarchie supports Frontier's Menu Sharing and includes some Frontier stuff from Leonard Rosenthol to get you started if you already own Frontier. Also included are some sample AppleScript scripts for automating file downloads and the like.

By clicking the column names, you can sort any list in Anarchie by name, date, size, host, and so on. Sorting by zone lets you see which hosts are probably closest to you and best to use if a choice exists.

Anarchie works in a *stateless mode*, which means that it doesn't keep the FTP connection open unless it's actually transferring a file or a directory listing. This is an extremely efficient way of using FTP (more like Gopher or the Web than FTP, in fact, because Gopher and the Web also only keep the connection open while you're transferring data).

Note *Anarchie's stateless mode does mean that you may be able to navigate into an FTP site but then be rejected when you try to retrieve a file, because too many other people have logged in while you were navigating around.*

Finally, Anarchie's About box displays the number of searches you've made, the number of files you've transferred, and the number of kilobytes you've transferred. Anarchie translates this into a rating. I don't know how many levels there are, but I just hit Net Destroyer (complete with a spoken congratulations from Anarchie) after doing 34 searches and 2,260 transfers for 198.3 MB of files. Some folks are higher, but I suspect they're padding their totals. When he read that last comment, Peter accused me of just being jealous. He's probably right.

Evaluation and Details

Anarchie is essential for your Internet tool kit. Despite the slowness and flakiness of Archie servers and the continual problems with finding new files via Archie, Anarchie has proven itself time and time again for me in the months I've used it. Do read the documentation, because there are a number of tips and tricks that you won't otherwise discover.

Anarchie costs $10. I strongly encourage you to pay for Anarchie if you find yourself using it. It's an essential Internet tool, and we need to keep Peter happy so that he keeps writing great programs and releasing them as freeware or shareware. Peter now works with Kagi Shareware, a company which accepts shareware payments in a multitude of forms for shareware authors and then pays the authors all but a small handling fee. You can use the Register application, which Peter also wrote and which comes with Anarchie, to easily pay for Anarchie through Kagi.

Anarchie is included on the disk that comes with this book, and you can retrieve the latest version of Anarchie in:

```
ftp://ftp.tidbits.com/pub/tidbits/tisk/tcp/
```

Fetch

Fetch comes to the Internet community from Jim Matthews of Dartmouth College, whose programmers have been notably active in developing and distributing Macintosh software over the years.

Fetch is one of the most long-lived MacTCP-based applications, and Jim continues to update it, adding features and bringing Fetch up to speed with Power Mac-native code. Fetch's most recent upgrade adds such useful features as multiple simultaneous connections to different sites (or to the same site with the Allow Duplicate Connections preference selected), a new interface, drag and drop support, a new bookmark list reminiscent of Anarchie's list, better firewall support, Internet Config support, and AppleScript support.

Note

Unfortunately, Fetch 3.0 wasn't quite finished as I write this, so there may be a few slight changes in the interface.

Installation and Setup

When you first launch Fetch, it presents you with a New Connection dialog, and in fact, if you want to enter things such as userid and password manually, you can use the program right away. I do recommend that you configure the preferences first, though, since they do some of the work for you. From the Customize menu, choose Preferences to see a tabbed dialog that lets you set all of Fetch's preferences. However, you can satisfy your basic needs by simply selecting the Use Internet Config button in the General tab of the preferences. Click the OK button to close the Preferences dialog, quit Fetch, and launch it again. When it comes back up, look in the Preference dialog again, and you'll see that Fetch has snagged a bunch of preferences from Internet Config, such as your email address and the location where you want downloads to be saved (see figure 23.7).

Of course, if you don't use Internet Config (and I strongly recommend that you do use it, which is why I included it on the ISKM disk), you must go through and set all of Fetch's options manually.

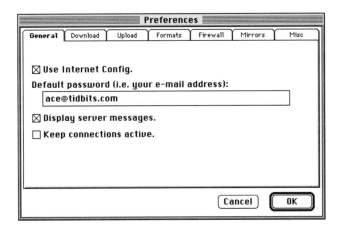

Figure 23.7   *Fetch Preferences dialog.*

Basic Usage

When you launch Fetch, it opens a New Connection dialog box that enables you to pick an FTP site from a Shortcuts pop-up menu or type in the necessary information to connect to a new one (see figure 23.8).

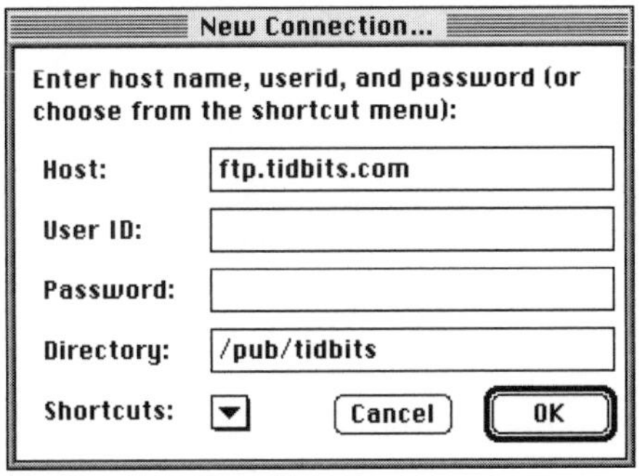

Figure 23.8   *Fetch New Connection dialog.*

In this dialog, you can enter the machine name to which you want to connect, your userid (which is usually **anonymous**, and which can be left blank if so), your password (which should be your full email address, and which can be left blank if you've entered it in Fetch's Preferences dialog), and the directory in which you want to start on the remote machine. Of course, if you're using Fetch to connect to a personal account on an Internet machine, the userid is your userid and the password is whatever you've set it to. Although many people use Fetch with their own accounts, anonymous FTP is by far the most common usage.

Some sites are finicky about your email address when it's used as an anonymous FTP password. A workaround might be to use your userid along with the @ sign (for example, **ace@***)—and nothing else. That forces the remote FTP server to figure out the machine name and domain on its own, which sometimes works better.*

New in Fetch 3.0 is a bookmark list window feature, and at launch Fetch automatically opens a special bookmark list window called Fetch Shortcuts (see figure 23.9) that contains the same items that are in the Shortcuts pop-up menu in the New Connection dialog. Although the two features may seem redundant, Jim wanted to add a new way of displaying shortcuts, but he didn't want to rip out the New Connection dialog that Fetch users have been used to for years. You can create more of your own bookmark list windows that don't show up automatically or have their contents in the Shortcuts pop-up menu—it's a handy way of organizing infrequently used bookmarks.

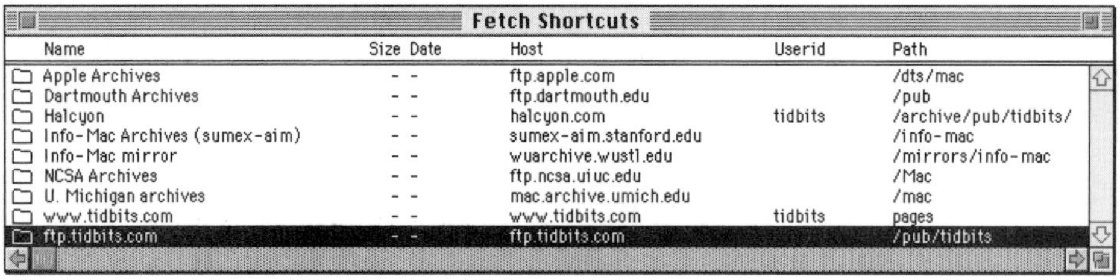

Name	Size	Date	Host	Userid	Path
Apple Archives	-	-	ftp.apple.com		/dts/mac
Dartmouth Archives	-	-	ftp.dartmouth.edu		/pub
Halcyon	-	-	halcyon.com	tidbits	/archive/pub/tidbits/
Info-Mac Archives (sumex-aim)	-	-	sumex-aim.stanford.edu		/info-mac
Info-Mac mirror	-	-	wuarchive.wustl.edu		/mirrors/info-mac
NCSA Archives	-	-	ftp.ncsa.uiuc.edu		/Mac
U. Michigan archives	-	-	mac.archive.umich.edu		/mac
www.tidbits.com	-	-	www.tidbits.com	tidbits	pages
ftp.tidbits.com	-	-	ftp.tidbits.com		/pub/tidbits

Figure 23.9   Fetch Shortcuts window.

You could enter in connection information in the New Connection dialog each time you connect to an FTP site, but that would be silly. Fetch enables you to add your own shortcuts to the Shortcuts pop-up menu and the Fetch Shortcuts bookmark list with the New Shortcut command in the Customize menu, which brings up a dialog for creating new shortcuts. The New Shortcut menu item is visible whenever you don't have a bookmark list window in front.

If a bookmark list window is in front, the New Shortcut menu item changes to New Bookmark List Item. The two commands do essentially the same thing, but a shortcut lives in the Fetch Shortcuts window and in the Shortcuts pop-up menu, whereas you can add Bookmark List Items to any bookmark list window. To edit an existing shortcut, you must select it in the bookmark list window and choose Edit Bookmark List Item from the Customize menu—I prefer the shortcut, which is Option double-click (see figure 23.10).

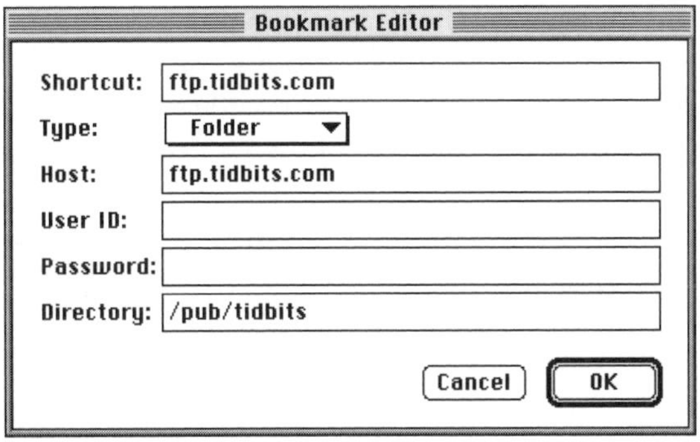

Bookmark Editor

Shortcut:	ftp.tidbits.com
Type:	Folder ▼
Host:	ftp.tidbits.com
User ID:	
Password:	
Directory:	/pub/tidbits

[Cancel] [OK]

Figure 23.10   Fetch Bookmark Editor.

In any event, you can connect to a site either by choosing a site from the New Connection dialog's Shortcuts pop-up menu and clicking the OK button or by double-clicking on it in a bookmark list window. Either way, Fetch then displays its main window, where you do most of your work uploading and downloading (see figure 23.11). Fetch also displays a message window for any automatic messages that the administrator of that server wants you to read. You can leave the messages window open in the background, as I've done in the screen shot, or you can close it to clean up your screen.

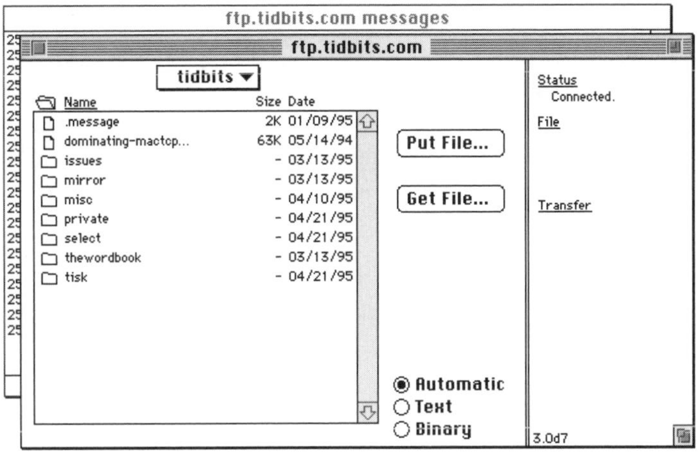

ftp.tidbits.com messages

ftp.tidbits.com

tidbits ▼

Name	Size	Date
.message	2K	01/09/95
dominating-mactcp...	63K	05/14/94
issues	–	03/13/95
mirror	–	03/13/95
misc	–	04/10/95
private	–	04/21/95
select	–	04/21/95
thewordbook	–	03/13/95
tisk	–	04/21/95

Status
Connected.

File

[Put File...]

[Get File...]

Transfer

◉ Automatic
○ Text
○ Binary

3.0d7

Figure 23.11   Fetch main window.

The main element in Fetch's window is the list of files and directories on the left side of the window (although that list is, of course, empty until you connect). Above it and to the left is a little open folder icon that you can drag over to a bookmark list window to save the current directory as a bookmark. To the right of the file listing are two buttons that enable you to get or send (Put) a file. Under that are two radio buttons, Text and Binary, with which you can indicate what sort of files you are transferring. A third button, Automatic, lets Fetch try to determine the file type for you based on the file extension. I've stuck with Automatic almost entirely and haven't had any trouble, but you might need to switch manually at some point if files are named strangely.

To the right of all the buttons is the status area. At the top of the feedback area under Status, Fetch reports precisely what it's doing, such as "Connecting," "Changing dir," "Getting file list," and so on. Then comes the File section, which lists which file Fetch is working on, what format it's in, and how large it is. Below that is the Transfer feedback section, where Fetch reports how many bytes it has transferred along with the rate at which it is transferring the file. New in Fetch 3.0 is a graphical pie display of how large the file is and how much of it has been transferred. You can resize Fetch's main window or place it anywhere on the screen.

If you've used the Mac for any length of time, you'll know how to use Fetch immediately. You double-click on a directory (they have little folder icons) in the list to enter that directory. Double-clicking on a file does the same thing as selecting the file with a single click and then clicking on the Get File button. You can select contiguous multiple files by Shift-clicking on them or multiple discontiguous files by Command-clicking on them, at which point clicking on the Get File button snags the lot of them. After you click on the Get File button, Fetch figures out what sort of file you're getting and either asks you to save it with a standard Save File dialog box or automatically places it in a folder you've defined in your Preferences.

Fetch now fully supports Apple's Drag Manager, so if you have System 7.5 and the necessary Drag Manager extensions installed, you can drag files from Fetch's window to the Finder to download them, to the Trash to delete them (assuming the site lets you do that), and from the Finder to Fetch's window to upload them. The Drag Manager also provides an easy way of making shortcuts—just drag a file or a folder from a Fetch window into a bookmark list window.

When you download a file, Fetch can launch StuffIt Expander to process a downloaded file (or launch the downloaded file itself, if it's a self-extracting application). If you've used Internet Config, Fetch gets its post-processing settings from Internet Config.

Special Features

I especially like Fetch's View File command in the Remote menu because it displays text files, which is useful for browsing through the README files that are ubiquitous on FTP sites. Anarchie has a similar feature, but actually downloads a file and then opens it in the word processor you choose, which works fine but leaves lots of files called README lying around.

In the Directories menu, Fetch lists all of the directories you have visited, not only in that session, but in the past for the current site as well. This is tremendously useful because you tend to go back to the same places over and over again.

Fetch supports Anarchie's bookmarks so you can save and open them, which makes for a nice interaction between the two. You can even drag an Anarchie bookmark file from the Finder into one of Fetch's bookmark list windows to add it. Fetch accepts URLs pasted into its New Connection dialog, and if you select a file or folder and choose Copy from the Edit menu, Fetch places the appropriate URL in the clipboard.

Fetch now supports multiple connections to different sites at the same time, and although it does support multiple connections to the same site, it will reuse idle windows if possible rather than opening new ones.

You can now sort the items in Fetch's listing windows by clicking on the titles of the various columns. I use this a lot for seeing which files have been uploaded to a site most recently.

If you have access to your own account via FTP, you can use Fetch to create and remove directories, rename files, and even issue raw FTP commands. These features won't help the average user of anonymous FTP, but for someone managing their own account, this kind of control is useful. I especially like being able to have Fetch issue a **LIST -R** command that lists the entire contents of a site under the current directory.

Finally, although this feature is hard to quantify, Fetch seems to be the most solid of all the FTP clients at connecting to and working with strange FTP servers. Every now and then I hit one that Anarchie won't handle, and Fetch always works fine, especially when uploading.

Evaluation and Details

How does Fetch compare to Anarchie? I like and use both programs on a regular basis, but at this point I mostly use Fetch for maintaining files on my account. I use it exclusively to manage **ftp.tidbits.com**, and it's been a godsend. However, I find that when I'm looking for a file or browsing FTP sites, I prefer Anarchie, mostly because of its multiple windows to the same site and ease of use. Even though Fetch now has multiple connections, it can't open multiple windows to the same site or have multiple downloads from different parts of the same site going at the same time. Mostly because of the single-window approach, you don't use Fetch to explore—you use it to get your work done. It performs admirably, especially if your work involves a fair amount of uploading. Of course, one of the best parts about Fetch is its running dog cursor, but that you must see for yourself.

Educational institutions and nonprofit organizations may use Fetch free of charge, and everyone else can license it from Dartmouth for $25. Read the Fetch Help for more

Part IV
23
FTP

information about licensing. You can retrieve the latest version of Fetch via FTP in any of the following:

```
http://www.dartmouth.edu/pages/softdev/fetch.html
```

```
ftp://ftp.dartmouth.edu/pub/mac/
```

```
ftp://ftp.tidbits.com/pub/tidbits/tisk/tcp/
```

Other FTP Programs

Although Anarchie and Fetch are the acknowledged standards for FTP clients on the net, several others exist, although they're not widely used, with the possible exception of Snatcher, from Software Ventures. I've removed information about XferIt and HyperFTP, mostly because they're so old and completely ignored that I'm not even sure if they'll work with most modern systems. Although both are still available on the Internet, don't bother checking them out for anything but a historical lesson. Also ignored is a program called MacFSP, which is a client for a different file transfer protocol called FSP that is barely used anywhere. Finally, I'm also not including information here about Communications Toolbox FTP tools, since I basically don't see the point in using them—if you can use an FTP tool, you can use Anarchie. Unless I give a separate URL, the programs mentioned below are in:

```
ftp://ftp.tidbits.com/pub/tidbits/tisk/tcp/
```

EasyTransfer

Although Christopher Reid's $10 shareware EasyTransfer is not exactly an FTP program because it doesn't use the same protocols as FTP and cannot be used as a client, I thought I'd mention it quickly for those who want to transfer files between two Macs, both of which run MacTCP and are on the Internet. EasyTransfer works as both a server and a client, and enables you to set up specific folders that only certain users can access. There's nothing fancy about EasyTransfer, but I suspect that's the point, since you may not want to mess with setting up a full FTP server just to move a few files.

Thanks for using EasyTransfer. EasyTransfer is ©1992-95 Christopher Reid. EasyTransfer is Shareware and the single user registration fee is US$20. Site licences are also available. Please contact me by e-mail for further information. Unfortunately I can't accept cheques unless they are a) made out in pounds sterling, or b) a US$15 handling charge is added. The same applies to international postal money orders. Cash (whatever the equivalent of US$20 is) is welcome in any currency. Please send your registration fee to:

Christopher Reid
Flat T2
Clarendon Court
9 Clarendon Place
Glasgow, G20 7PZ
Scotland

For latest version of EasyTransfer, see

ftp://mac-ftp.cs.strath.ac.uk/macstuff/EasyTransfer/

Please feel free to contact me at any time by e-mail (cr@cs.strath.ac.uk) if you experience any problems with the software, or if you would like particular features added.

FTPd

FTPd, another $10 shareware application from Peter Lewis, enables you to make a Macintosh with a dedicated Internet connection into an FTP and Gopher server. Not surprisingly for a server, it has a somewhat complex setup procedure, but to simplify matters, it uses System 7 File Sharing to create users and groups and assign access privileges. Once it's running as a foreground or background application, anyone on the Internet can use FTP or Gopher to look around on your Mac. If you allow FTP access and don't set your File Sharing privileges

correctly, people also can copy and delete files at will, so be careful when you're running FTPd. I've used FTPd on an SE/30 to create FTP and Gopher servers, and I'm impressed at how well FTPd works, especially for the price and the age of the hardware.

FTPShare

FTPShare, a $170 commercial product from About Software Corporation (ASC), provides much the same capabilities as FTPd in terms of using it to run an FTP server. FTPShare has four pieces: a setup application, a monitoring application, an application to define user profiles, and an extension that presumably does most of the work, since none of the applications need be open for FTPShare to work. FTPShare supports up to 20 simultaneous clients and claims that it works well in the background. For more information on FTPShare, contact ASC at **ftpshare@ascus.com** or by phone at 800-55-SOFTWARE, 408-725-4242, or 408-725-4243 (fax). There's a demo of FTPShare available as well.

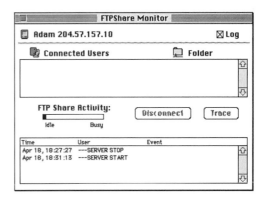

```
ftp://ftp.ascus.com/mac/demos/
```

Snatcher

Snatcher, from Software Ventures, is the first commercial stand-alone FTP program that I've seen. Its primary goal is to look as much like the Macintosh Finder as possible. Snatcher can download multiple files from different sites at the same time, although they all show up in the queue of the single Session Progress window. I gather that Snatcher is extremely

easy to script if you already know how to script the Finder with AppleScript. Snatcher is a good program, possibly even a very good program. Its main problem is that it's up against another program, Anarchie, that is cheaper, shareware (so you can try it before you pay Peter), easier to use, and more powerful. The few tasks that Snatcher can do that Anarchie cannot, such as downloading an entire directory, aren't all that common. Snatcher comes with MicroPhone Pro, and you can get it separately for less than $50 from Software Ventures. For more information about Snatcher, send email to **snatcher@svcdudes.com** or call 510-644-3232 or 510-848-0885 (fax).

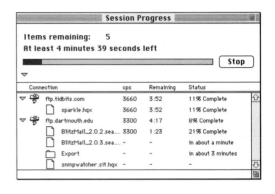

http://www.svcdudes.com/

ftp://ftp.svcdudes.com/pub/mac/Snatcher/

Finalizing FTP

The Web may be the hottest thing on the Internet right now, but frankly, I spend far more time downloading files via FTP, usually in Anarchie. I also do a fair amount of uploading, usually in Fetch, and all I can say is that you should use one of these programs. Web browsers just don't do FTP well right now.

But enough about FTP! Let's move on to another method of retrieving data, Gopher.

Gopher

The University of Minnesota's Gopher system is an inherently list-based Internet service that provides access to large quanties of information. Because of this, it maps perfectly to separate windows of lists, between which you can switch back and forth, clicking on interesting items to explore deeper in Gopherspace. And thus, this is the technique used by the most commonly used Gopher client, TurboGopher, which was written by the same folks who created the entire Gopher system. However, with the ascendancy of the World Wide Web, more people probably access Gopher servers via the single-window Web browsers like MacWeb than via TurboGopher, just because it's easier not to launch another program. That's not to say that TurboGopher still doesn't have its uses. If you mainly use Gopher servers, TurboGopher still feels much faster than the Web browsers, and its multiple window approach often works better as well.

TurboGopher

The primary reasons for TurboGopher's popularity are that it comes from the developers of Gopher at the University of Minnesota and that it has the fastest perceived speed (especially over slow modem links) of any Gopher client available for any platform.

Basic Usage

TurboGopher comes configured out of the box, so to speak, to point at the Home Gopher server at the University of Minnesota. Actually, that's not entirely true of the most recent version, TurboGopher 2.0, which may require a minimal setup process. TurboGopher 2.0

requires Apple's Thread Manager, which comes with System 7.5. However, if you don't use System 7.5 (TurboGopher requires System 7.0 or later) you must drop the Thread Manager extension that comes with TurboGopher in your Extensions folder into the System Folder. Restart, and then you're ready to run TurboGopher.

Double-clicking on the TurboGopher icon launches the program. At this point it connects to the Home Gopher server and displays the main menu in the Home Gopher Server window (see figure 24.1), along with windows for your Bookmark Worksheet and the TurboGopher Help (only the first time you launch the program).

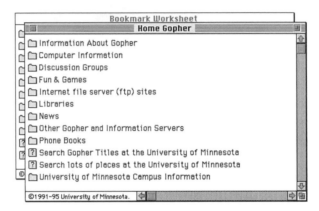

Figure 24.1   *TurboGopher Home and Bookmark Worksheet windows.*

Behind the Home Gopher Server window is the Bookmark Worksheet window, which holds your personal bookmarks to other sites or items available via Gopher. You can create bookmarks by selecting an item and choosing Copy (or pressing ⌘-C) from the Edit menu and then pasting (or pressing ⌘-V) the item into the Bookmark Worksheet window.

> *You can save a bookmark file (use the Save As command in the File menu) that points at a specific folder in Gopherspace. If you then double-click on that file to launch TurboGopher rather than double-clicking on the program itself, TurboGopher won't automatically connect to the Home Gopher Server, but instead connects to the site listed in your bookmark file.*

Let's browse around a bit so that you can get a feel for navigation in Gopherspace; it's really very easy. Double-click on the "Information About Gopher" item to open that window. Next, double-click on "Gopher Software Distribution" to move into that area. Finally, click the "Macintosh-TurboGopher" item, and in there, double-click "00README" to open that document for reading (see figure 24.2).

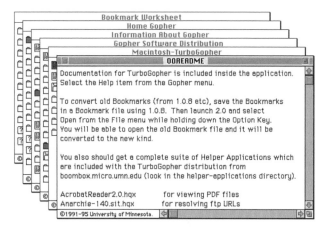

Figure 24.2   Browsing through Gopherspace.

If you wanted to download a copy of TurboGopher (or any other program indicated by a disk icon), you could close the "00README" window, double-click on the "TurboGopher2.0.sea.hqx" item, and TurboGopher would download it for you. If you do download a file, TurboGopher can download while you continue to explore Gopherspace, although it does take a little longer for windows to open and text files to display. When a download is complete, you can click the resulting Open button to open the file just as though you had double-clicked on it in the Finder. TurboGopher can automatically debinhex files, but recommends setting StuffIt Expander as the helper application for BinHex files. Therefore, clicking the Open button both debinhexes and expands the file.

In addition to the disk icon that indicates a downloadable file, TurboGopher may display a number of other icons next to the items in the lists. Most common, of course, is the folder, followed by the text file icon. Double-clicking on a text file displays it immediately. The question mark icon brings up a simple search dialog that lets you, for example, enter one or more words to search for in a full-text database. Some icons indicate file types. There's one that looks like a starburst and identifies a GIF image, a speaker that marks sampled sounds, another that denotes QuickTime movies, and one that indicates a DOS program. You also may see an icon that looks like a Mac Plus; it indicates that the service is terminal-based and launches NCSA Telnet for you if you double-click on it.

TurboGopher 2.0 uses a number of helper applications like NCSA Telnet, so by default it hands off HTTP URLs to MacWeb, FTP URLs to Anarchie, NNTP URLs to NewsWatcher, and Ph URLs to Ph (a phone directory application from John Norstad). In addition, TurboGopher uses JPEGView to display images you download.

As you may realize, Gopherspace is huge, and although Gopherspace is highly linked, more so even than the Web, it can be confusing to browse through manually. The tool that makes navigating Gopherspace possible is Veronica, which enables searches of either only Gopher directories or of all items in Gopherspace (see figure 24.3).

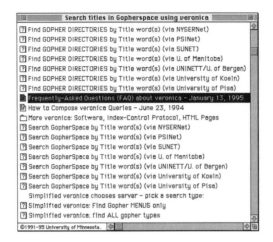

Figure 24.3   TurboGopher and Veronica.

You can generally find Veronica under "Other Gopher and Information Servers," or perhaps under a folder called "World," but whatever you do, make sure that you have a bookmark to both types of Veronica searches. The new simplified Veronica search tries a number of Veronica servers in a row, because they're often overloaded and refuse connections.

> **N o t e**
>
> *If you read the FAQ in the Veronica folder, it tells you about a number of useful features in Veronica that you'd never know otherwise, such as using the -t7 switch in a search string to find only searchable items.*

If someone tells you to check something on a specific Gopher site, you can jump directly to it. From the Gopher menu select Another Gopher, and in the Domain Name field type the Internet address of the Gopher site to which you want to connect (see figure 24.4).

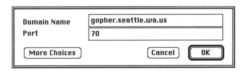

Figure 24.4   TurboGopher Another Gopher dialog.

These days, though, people often trade URLs, not just names of servers, and TurboGopher also can deal fairly well with URLs. From the Gopher menu, choose Use Uniform Resource Locator, and in the dialog box that appears, paste or type in a URL. If it's a Gopher

URL, TurboGopher goes directly to that site. If the URL is for news, FTP, the Web, or Ph, instead, TurboGopher passes it off to the appropriate helper application.

Special Features

If you hold down the Control key while clicking an item in a Gopher list, TurboGopher displays a pop-up menu containing information about that item. It's a quick way of determining where a file is, its URL, and that sort of thing. Unfortunately, not included in the pop-up display is the size of a file; for that, you must choose Get Attribute Information & URL from the Gopher menu and look toward the bottom of a badly formatted list of information.

> **Note**
>
> *Just seeing a URL isn't all that helpful, so if you want to copy a URL as you would in Anarchie or Fetch, hold down the Option key and choose Copy from the Edit menu. Unfortunately, ⌘-Option-C doesn't do anything, even though it's the same as holding down Option while selecting Copy.*

One of TurboGopher's major speed increases comes from its capability to let you start reading a document while it's being retrieved. Although this capability doesn't actually speed up execution, it reduces the time you wait for the program, which is all-important.

To aid in navigation, you can optionally have TurboGopher reuse the same window rather than open a new one each time. This capability prevents window clutter, although it may make moving around more confusing. Also, a Recent menu lists all the places you've visited, in reverse chronological order; selecting any item from this menu takes you there instantly. If you end up in a window with a large number of items, you can type the first few letters of a name to move directly to it, or you can use TurboGopher's Find feature, available from the Edit menu. Arrow keys work fine for navigation, along with the Return or Enter key for moving into an item.

Evaluation & Details

TurboGopher is fast and easy to use, and for heavy use of Gopherspace, it's better than using a Web browser. Although TurboGopher 2.0 cooperates well with the other main Internet programs, I found it to be fairly flaky at times. Once or twice its capability to display and copy URLs gave thoroughly incorrect information, and I had some trouble getting it to pass URLs properly when it was low on memory. If you're just using the occasional Gopher server, especially if you connect to it from a Web server, a Web browser is probably a better choice than firing up TurboGopher. But, I'll keep TurboGopher around for when I need to burrow deep into Gopherspace for some piece of information.

TurboGopher is free for noncommercial use (commercial use requires permission—ask at `gopher@boombox.micro.umn.edu`). The most recent release of TurboGopher is always available from the University of Minnesota Gopher server, and at either of the following:

Part IV

Gopher

```
ftp://ftp.tidbits.com/pub/tidbits/tisk/tcp/
```

```
ftp://boombox.micro.umn.edu/pub/gopher/Macintosh-TurboGopher/
```

Other Gopher Clients

Although I only recommend that you use TurboGopher (or one of the Web browsers) for accessing Gopher servers, there are a couple of other Gopher-related programs out there. There were originally a few more clients, including GopherApp, MacGopher, and Sextant, but they haven't been updated in so many years that I can't even justify using space in the book on them, much less recommending that you check them out. Unless I note otherwise, the following applications can be found in:

```
ftp://ftp.tidbits.com/pub/tidbits/tisk/tcp/
```

Blue Skies

Although actually a Gopher client, Blue Skies, free from the University of Michigan's Weather Underground's Alan Steremberg, is primarily a neat application for, well, interacting with the weather. You need not go outside or travel to other parts of the world, though. All you must do is launch Blue Skies and select GroundHog Server from the GroundHog menu. I especially like the interactive weather maps, which bring up a map of the United States. Moving your mouse over different locations on the map displays the weather conditions for that city. You can even zoom in and out to a few different magnifications, and in doing so gain access to more detailed weather data.

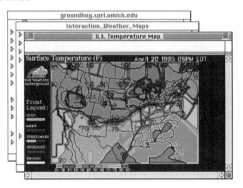

GopherSurfer

You have two options if you want to set up a Gopher server on a Mac. I mentioned Peter Lewis's FTPd in the previous chapter, and the University of Minnesota also has a Gopher server called GopherSurfer. GopherSurfer can work with AppleSearch, Apple's heavy-duty (it requires a 68040-based Macintosh) searching engine. So, if you are serious about setting up a searchable Gopher server on a Mac, check out the combination of GopherSurfer and AppleSearch. Like TurboGopher, GopherSurfer is free for noncommercial use— commercial organizations should contact the Gopher team at the University of Minnesota.

```
ftp://boombox.micro.umn.edu/pub/gopher/Mac_server/
```

PNLInfo Browser

The free PNLInfo Browser is a somewhat interesting Gopher client because it uses a hierarchical outline view much like the Finder's Name view. Clicking a triangle expands the outline, although because it must retrieve the new information from the remote Gopher server, PNLInfo Browser doesn't feel snappy. It can display abstracts for Gopher items that describe what that item is in more detail. Also interesting is PNLInfo Browser's subscription feature, which can notify you of items that have changed since you last viewed them.

TurboGopher VR

The Power Mac-only TurboGopher VR, from the University of Minnesota Gopher Team, is best described as the unholy marriage of Spectre (the 3D tank game from Velocity Development) and TurboGopher. Actually, I think TurboGopher VR is extremely cool—whenever you enter a new Gopher menu, TurboGopher VR drops you with a thud into a Spectre-like three-dimensional scene containing what look a bit like stone monoliths littering the countryside. Roll up to one and you can read its title (the same as you'd see in one of TurboGopher's normal text lists) and click on it to go into it. A central spire lets you zip back up in the hierarchy. I can't say that it's useful, and it's probably buggy as all get out, but if you've got a Power Mac, you simply must check out TurboGopher VR.

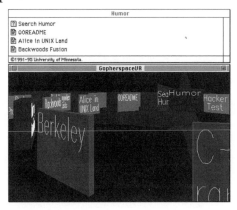

```
ftp://boombox.micro.umn.edu//pub/gopher/Macintosh-TurboGopher/TurboGopherVR/
```

The Closing Gopher Holes

Although Gopher usage is decidedly on the wane thanks to the popularity of the World Wide Web, there is still a great deal of information available in Gopherspace. It's simply easier to publish via Gopher than via the Web, and as a result, sometimes it makes sense to use a dedicated Gopher client instead of a Web browser to access Gopher servers. Take your pick.

In the next chapter, "World Wide Web," I'll look at the main Web browsers, one of which, MacWeb, comes on the ISKM disk for you to use. After you've had a chance to check out Gopherspace with MacWeb, try downloading a copy of TurboGopher and try it that way as well so you can make up your mind about which you like better.

Part IV

Gopher

World Wide Web

When I wrote the first edition of this book, the World Wide Web was just starting to explode and the Macintosh was being left out. Then, along came NCSA Mosaic for the Macintosh and all was well in the world. Since that time (fall of 1993), the World Wide Web has propelled the Internet into the eyes of the public. "Check out my home page at…" has become a common phrase, and the amount of information that appears every day on the Web is staggering.

Despite the fact that the Web was developed at CERN, in Switzerland, NCSA Mosaic deserves a good deal of credit for popularizing the Web. NCSA had the resources to create Mosaic and to give it away, and although it wasn't a particularly good program at that point, it was enough to entice people to use and publish information on the Web.

Of course, any success demands to be copied or even exceeded, and that's where the other major Web browsers came from. First was MacWeb, from the EINet group of MCC, and then came Netscape, developed by many of the same programmers who had created Mosaic while at NCSA. Then, NCSA, via a company called Spyglass, licensed the Mosaic code to a variety of companies that have produced versions of Enhanced Mosaic that differ little from the first versions of NCSA Mosaic. Most recently (and discussed in chapter 28, "Integrated Programs,") InterCon has added a Web module to their TCP/ Connect II integrated program.

For the most part, the Web browsers are extremely similar, so I'm going to start with MacWeb because it sorts first in an alphabetical listing of the names and because we've licensed it for inclusion on the ISKM disk.

The beauty of writing about Web browsers is that there are almost no instructions to give. The basic idea is that you connect to the Internet, run the Web browser, and then click on the underlined words (they can also be in a color, but that doesn't show up well in a black and white book) to traverse the links between Web pages.

That's about all there is to using the Web. We're not talking difficult here.

MacWeb

MacWeb was the second major Web browser to appear on the Macintosh, and has always differentiated itself by being small and quick. New features, such as a pop-up menu that appears if you click and hold on a link, often appear in MacWeb first and are then copied by the other Web browsers. Because of its small size and low memory requirements, MacWeb is the browser of choice for people with older Macs or not much memory. Just for comparison, the latest versions of MacWeb, Netscape, and NCSA Mosaic weigh in at 470K, 1,370K, and 2,200K on disk, respectively, and MacWeb can get by in as little as 750K of RAM, compared to 1,784K for Netscape (which prefers more) and 2,700K for Mosaic. Because of these reasonable requirements and because it's a good program, we've included MacWeb on the ISKM disk.

Installation and Setup

MacWeb has only a few preferences, which you access by going to the File menu and choosing Preferences (see figure 25.1). You can change the home page, the page that MacWeb automatically accesses on launch, to any valid URL (or even an HTML document on your disk, which will keep MacWeb from trying to dial out if you connect via PPP or SLIP); you can have MacWeb automatically open a specific hotlist of stored URLs at startup; and you can set little things such as Autoload Images (turn this option off for faster performance) and the window background color. The most important preferences to set are your email address and your news server in the General section of the Preferences.

If you don't like the way MacWeb assigns fonts to the HTML styles, you can change those fonts. Choose Styles from the Edit menu to display the Styles dialog (see figure 25.2).

The Element pop-up menu and its submenus enable you to pick which style you're editing, and because the styles are hierarchical, it's easy to set all the heading styles to, say, Helvetica, and then vary the font size for the different heading sizes. You also can modify colors as well, but I'd recommend restraint here. Colored text (and too many colors in text, especially) can be difficult to read.

Although you shouldn't have to mess with them, you also can modify MacWeb's default settings for helper applications and suffix mappings (which are how MacWeb determines what sort of file it's retrieving).

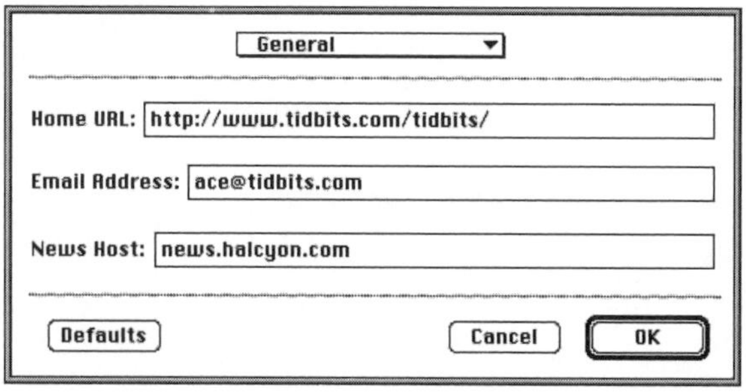

Figure 25.1 *MacWeb Preferences dialog.*

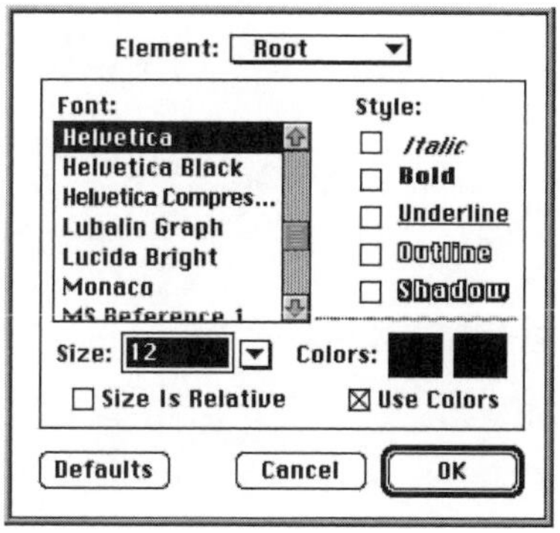

Figure 25.2 *MacWeb Styles dialog.*

Basic Usage

I always feel funny telling people how to use a Web browser, because it seems so obvious, and MacWeb is no exception to this. Anyway, when you first launch MacWeb, it accesses its default home page (see figure 25.3), which may look a little different.

Note

There's nothing special about the default home page—it just happens to be the page that MacWeb loads when you launch it, and you can set anything as your home page. I set my home page to the Dilbert comic strip at:

`http://www.unitedmedia.com/comics/dilbert/todays_dilbert.gif`

Figure 25.3   *MacWeb home page.*

The basic parts of the MacWeb window are self-explanatory. MacWeb offers forward and back arrow buttons for moving back and forth between the pages you've visited, a home button (with a little house on it) for bouncing back to your home page, a question mark button for Web search items, and an editable but somewhat small URL field for copying and pasting URLs. At the bottom of the screen, a status field indicates what MacWeb is doing, along with a preview of what URL goes with any given link. My favorite part of the status line is that it often tells you the size of the file MacWeb is accessing, and counts up as it retrieves the file. That kind of feedback is useful when you're on a slow connection and waiting for a graphic to transfer.

When you click a link (blue and underlined, although a link becomes red once you've followed it), MacWeb promptly takes you to the appropriate page, and as it fills the page, you can scroll down. However, if MacWeb must also bring in a graphic, it forces you back to the top of the page while it draws the graphic, which can make for some confusing jumps in the text if you've started reading. Reading text in the MacWeb window works exactly as you'd expect it to, and the Find feature available in the Edit menu is a big help if you hit a large page and want to scroll directly to a certain part.

If you find a Web resource that you like and want to visit again, you can add it to your Hotlist with the Add This Document item under the Hotlist menu. The Hotlist menu also has a hierarchical Hotlist Interface menu that provides options for creating new hotlists, opening old ones, editing them, saving them, and so on. If you edit the hotlist, MacWeb brings up a list of your hotlist entries. Clicking the Edit button enables you to modify the name and URL (see figure 25.4).

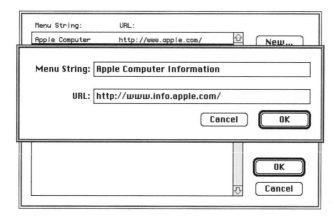

Figure 25.4   *MacWeb Hotlist Editor.*

Of course, if you have a URL that you retrieved from email or a *TidBITS* article, you can enter it manually into MacWeb. Choose Open URL from the File menu and type or paste the URL in before pressing Return to activate the link. When you choose Open URL, MacWeb also provides a pop-up menu of your hotlist items; selecting an item from that list pastes its URL into the URL field for you to edit if you so choose. Another way to go to a specific Web site is to paste the URL into the URL field over the existing one, and press Return to activate it. MacWeb also can open local documents and can reload the page if for some reason it isn't up-to-date.

Special Features

Although relatively simple, MacWeb has a number of special features that complement its sparse interface. Although it has a hierarchical History menu under its Navigate menu, MacWeb also provides a shortcut for navigating to sites you've previously visited. Simply click and hold on either the Forward or Back buttons. After a second or two, a pop-up menu appears, listing the history.

MacWeb allows you to resize its window to any size you like, and it remembers the size of the frontmost window when you quit, opening the window to that size the next time you launch MacWeb.

If you do decide to run with images turned off by default, you can load selected ones by clicking them. If, however, you want to see all the images on a page, the Options menu contains Load Images, which does just that.

MacWeb supports Apple events so it can work quite well with the other Apple event-capable applications like NewsWatcher and MacWAIS. New to MacWeb in the latest version though, is support for bookmark files like those used by Anarchie and Fetch.

If you Command-click an FTP link, MacWeb asks Anarchie to retrieve the file instead of doing so itself. Similarly, although MacWeb doesn't support mailto links internally, it asks NewsWatcher to deal with them (since NewsWatcher supports the GetURL event, whereas Eudora doesn't yet). MacWeb does support news URLs internally, but it also can pass them off to NewsWatcher with a Command-click. I approve of using the more powerful specific tools in this way, rather than fitting the square Web browsers into too many round holes.

You also can use other modifiers when clicking on links. The Option key makes MacWeb open a new window, the Shift key makes MacWeb retrieve links to disk, and the Command key forces MacWeb to use external helper applications, even if MacWeb can display the format, such as GIF, internally.

If you click on any link and hold the mouse button down, MacWeb pops up a LinkOps menu that offers choices for retrieving the link, retrieving it to disk (a very handy way of snagging graphics from Web pages), viewing information about the link, copying the URL, saving it to a hotlist, or saving it to disk. This feature works so well that Netscape copied it.

Unique to MacWeb is the capability to sort your hotlist by name or URL, and you can export hotlists in MacWeb format, in Mosaic format, or in straight HTML. MacWeb also can import Mosaic hotlists.

MacWeb is Power Mac-native. It is extremely fast at redrawing already loaded pages, something that can be a bit sluggish in other Web browsers. MacWeb also starts and quits quickly, something you don't think about until you use a program that's slow to launch and quit, like Netscape.

Note

So that it works for everyone, I've put the 68000 version of MacWeb on the ISKM disk. If you have a Power Mac, be sure to download the native version when you get a chance. There's an Anarchie bookmark for it in your MacWeb folder.

Evaluation & Details

MacWeb is an excellent program in its early releases, and I fully anticipate that most of the rough edges will be worked out in the future. I would like to see the Hotlist feature improved and differentiated. The major problem with the current version of MacWeb is that you cannot select text in the main window, which means that you cannot copy it for use elsewhere.

Is MacWeb the best Web browser right now? No, that honor goes to Netscape for the moment. Netscape has two advantages over MacWeb. First, Netscape opens multiple connections to a server when you connect, which means that it can bring in a number of images simultaneously, making it faster than MacWeb. Second, Netscape has hierarchical bookmarks, which makes saving and organizing bookmarks easier in Netscape than in MacWeb. If MacWeb could gain parity on those two counts, its other features would easily place it among the best of the Web browsing crowd.

MacWeb was written by John Hardin, of the EINet group of MCC (Microelectronics and Computer Technology Corporation—and no, I don't know how they get the acronym to work). MCC has released MacWeb as freeware for academic, research, or personal use; companies should contact MCC for licensing information. To report problems with or make suggestions about MacWeb, send email to **macweb@einet.net**. You can retrieve the current version of MacWeb on the Internet at either of the following:

```
ftp://ftp.einet.net/einet/mac/macweb/
```

```
ftp://ftp.tidbits.com/pub/tidbits/tisk/tcp/
```

Netscape Navigator

The greatest concentration of ex-NCSA Mosaic developers can be found at the Mountain View offices of startup Netscape Communications. Founded by Jim Clark, previously head of Silicon Graphics, and Marc Andreessen, who created the first NCSA Mosaic, Netscape has gone from complete obscurity to being one of the heavy hitters in the world of the Web. The reason? Netscape Navigator, which is what happens when you take talented developers and ask them to write a program they've done once all over again from scratch, avoiding the mistakes they made the first time and rethinking the parts that didn't work well. Netscape Navigator basically owns the Web browser market, if you can call it that since most Web browsers are essentially free, with some estimates giving it as much as 75 percent market share.

Netscape Navigator (generally just called Netscape, thanks to some weaseling around with the name early on, when the company was called Mosaic Communications and the program was called Mosaic Netscape) shines in two specific areas. It's fast, thanks to an innovative way of establishing multiple connections to the server when you retrieve a Web page, and it has, by far, the best hotlist feature (called bookmarks in Netscape's parlance).

Note

HTML, or HyperText Markup Language, is the language in which documents are written for display on the Web.

Actually, there's a third major reason why Netscape took the Web by storm. Netscape Communications "extended" the standard HTML 2.0 tags in advance of the forthcoming HTML 3.0 specification, and supported those extensions in Netscape. The result is that people writing in HTML can do things graphically, such as wrap text next to a graphic, that were previously impossible (and still are in other Web browsers). Suddenly, if you wanted to see a page in all its glory, you had to use Netscape. Many people felt that Netscape's jumping of the gun wasn't particularly fair play, and many Web page developers refuse to use Netscape-specific HTML codes until the HTML 3.0 specification is complete (which should be relatively soon—sometime in mid-1995 is my guess). At that point MacWeb and Mosaic will almost certainly add support for all the additional HTML codes that enable Web page developers to create tables, wrap text around graphics, place graphics in specific spots on the page, and so on.

Installation & Setup

Netscape has the most preferences of any of the Web browsers, but luckily, you need not mess with anything past the Mail and News preferences. From the Options menu, choose Preferences, and then from the pop-up menu in the Preferences dialog, choose Mail and News to see the various settings (see figure 25.5).

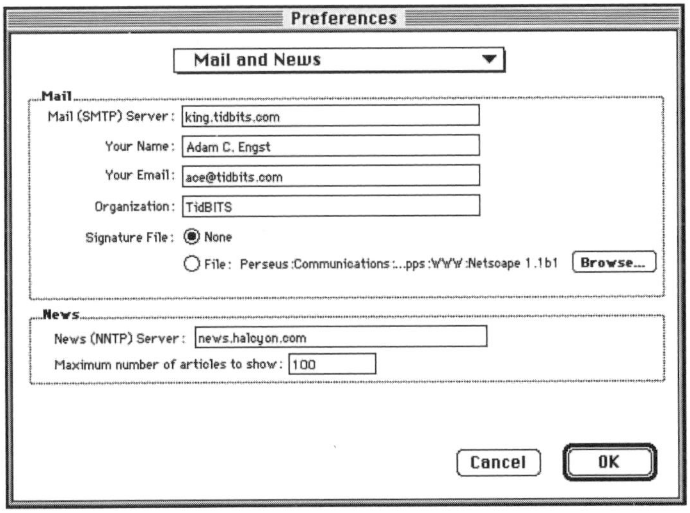

Figure 25.5   *Netscape Mail and News Preferences.*

The settings should be familiar to anyone who's configured other Internet programs, things like your SMTP server, your news server, your email address, and so on. More interesting are the preferences for Window and Link Styles, which enables you to not only choose what you want your window to include in terms of navigational buttons, but also lets you pick your link styles. Netscape tracks the links you've followed in the past and displays them in a different color so you can tell where you've been before—a nice touch.

Although you have minimal control over the fonts Netscape uses, it's nowhere near as customizable as MacWeb or Mosaic. In one respect, I can see why—with all the new codes coming in HTML 3.0, creating an interface for the user to modify the look of all those tags will be a nightmare. Interestingly, Netscape is the best Web browser of all for supporting Japanese, although I can't say anything more intelligent about that support since I don't know Kanji.

Note

Control over HTML display drives Web publishers from the desktop publishing world nuts, because they want to make sure you see their pages as they intended them to be seen, but that's not a trivial task on the Web. It's a two-edged sword, actually, because many people have bad vision, are color-blind, or otherwise don't like the way some Web publications look, and the control over the fonts and all enables them to make something readable that might not have been readable otherwise.

You might also check out the other items in Netscape's Options menu, because they enable you to hide or show the toolbar, the location field, the directory buttons, FTP information, and images, (should you not want to auto-load images). I prefer a mix of the various buttons and controls Netscape can place at the top of the window, so I usually turn off the directory buttons, but leave the toolbar and location field on. I also leave the toolbar style at text and images because that makes the all-important Back button larger and easier to click.

When you're done messing with the settings, choose Save Options from the Options menu to make sure that Netscape remembers your settings for the next session.

Basic Usage

When push comes to shove, using Netscape is almost exactly like using any other Web browser. They're kind of dull that way. Basically, when you launch Netscape, you see its main window displaying whatever the default home page is (see figure 25.6).

Figure 25.6   Netscape main window.

Although I generally run with the Directory buttons for What's New?, What's Cool?, Handbook, Net Search, Net Directory, and Newsgroups turned off, I think they're handy for new Internet users who may launch Netscape and then ask, "How do I search the

Internet?" Well, if you're running Netscape, the simple answer is, "Click the Net Search button." In fact, each of these buttons takes you to another, constantly updated, Web page that Netscape Communications maintains. The Net Search and Net Directory buttons in particular point you to the best search engines and the best directories (of course, the Internet Starter Kit home page that you get with MacWeb also points to those same search engines and directories—they're not secret).

Netscape does the best job of displaying newsgroups if you, for some reason, decide you want to read news in something other than one of the newsreaders. Netscape uses an outline-like structure to display threads. When you go into an article, Netscape provides a customized header and links as much as possible, such as the name of the newsgroup, the email address of the poster, and so on. Netscape also has some custom graphics at the top and bottom of each article or article list that provide graphical access to the basic functions necessary while reading news (see figure 25.7).

Figure 25.7   *Netscape news reading.*

One neat feature of reading news in Netscape is that URLs become hot, so you can click them to follow the link without any fuss. If you click a mailto URL or want to reply to a news message, Netscape brings up a pre-addressed window for you to enter your message (see figure 25.8). You also can use the Mail Document command in the File menu at any time to bring up this window, with the URL of the current page already in the body, so you can send it to friends to let them know about the page you are looking at. The Quote Document button inserts the entire document in the body of the message, and the Attach button enables you to attach the document, the HTML code for the document, or another file to your mail.

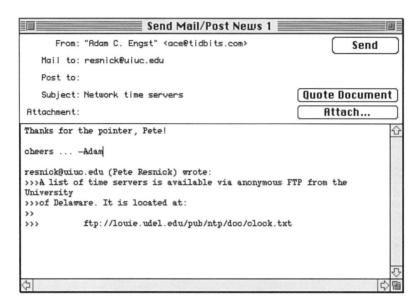

Figure 25.8   *Netscape Send Mail/Post News window.*

I'd never bother to read news in Netscape because it's nowhere near as good as NewsWatcher, NewsHopper, or any of the other newsreaders, but I do appreciate the ease of mailing a URL or document to someone. For a while, Netscape put the URL of the current page in the Subject line, so I can still tell who's using the older version by how much mail I get with a URL in the Subject line.

Last, but by no means list, is Netscape's Bookmark List (which is equivalent to the hotlist features in other browsers). Many people just use the Add Bookmark command in the Bookmarks menu to add bookmarks, but that's a mistake. The reason is that Netscape supports hierarchical bookmarks, but it isn't terribly easy to figure out how to use the Bookmark List window (see figure 25.9).

There are a few important facts to keep in mind about the Bookmark List. First of all, you can create headers, which turn into hierarchical submenus in the Bookmarks menu, and dividers, which look like standard dividers in the Bookmarks menu. When you double-click a header, it either expands to show the bookmarks subordinate to it, or, if it's already open, it closes to hide them (and switches to an underlined style). Second, you can move bookmarks around in the list by selecting one and clicking on the up and down arrows below the list. The arrows are slow and clumsy (this task cries for drag and drop), and I recommend you only use them for moving bookmarks a short distance. Third, the most important thing I figured out about the Bookmark List is that if you have the Bookmark List window open, and a specific bookmark selected, choosing Add Document from the Bookmarks menu (or pressing ⌘-D) adds the current page's URL as a bookmark right after the selected bookmark.

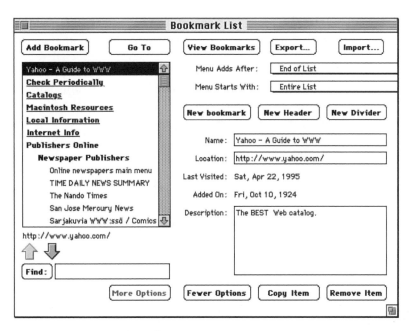

Figure 25.9   *Netscape Bookmark List.*

In other words, if you're smart, you won't just casually add bookmarks. Instead, you'll open your Bookmark List each time, select the bookmark above where you want the new one to go, and then choose Add Bookmark. It's more trouble, sure, but once you try to rearrange your bookmarks with those up and down arrow buttons, you'll see why I suggest this method. It's easier in the long run, and it keeps your bookmarks nicely organized.

When you want to use a bookmark, you can select it from the Bookmarks menu, but if you happen to have the Bookmark List window open, you can also use the Go To button or just double-click a bookmark. When I was rearranging my bookmarks, I found the easiest method was to go to a bookmark, use the Remove Item button to delete it from its old location, select another bookmark in the new location, and press ⌘-D to add the bookmark back in. Clumsy, but effective.

Special Features

I'd probably place Netscape's speed at the top of any list of special features since the Web is only as interesting as the speed at which you see it come in. I find Web browsers like Enhanced Mosaic (see the following capsule review) that don't display a page until all the graphics have come in are unusable even over my dedicated Internet connection.

Second in Netscape's special features is its Bookmarks List, which although it has some problems, such as the lousy up and down arrows, it also has lots of other great features, such as letting you know when you added a link and when you last visited the link. You can manually change the name of the link or the link's URL, and if you want to send your list of bookmarks to someone else or post it on the Web, you can Export it to HTML. The View Bookmarks button gives you a preview of what your bookmarks will look like to someone else, and if you collect a truly huge number of bookmarks, there's a Find button to help you find a specific one. Finally, if you find all these possibilities boggling, just click the Fewer Options button, and Netscape shrinks the window to show only the list of bookmarks.

Netscape introduced the first support for what are called *interlaced GIFs*, or images that have been saved in a special format. When Netscape (or now MacWeb) loads in the images, they start rough and gradually become more focused. This enables you to quickly see if you want to move on or wait for the entire image. Netscape was also the first browser to support JPEG images inline, just like GIFs, although TCP/Connect II's Web browser also now supports inline JPEGs.

> **Note** *I prefer MacWeb's style of bringing in interlaced GIFs because it draws every other line or so, but at full resolution, it seems as though you're looking through Venetian blinds, whereas Netscape draws a rough, blocky image and gradually improves the definition.*

As part of its capability to open multiple connections to the same server, Netscape also supports multiple connections to multiple servers in different windows. I like this feature because when the servers are slow, it enables me to keep several windows going at once so that I'm never sitting and waiting for data to arrive.

In the most recent version of Netscape (1.1N), Netscape knows how to zoom the window appropriately. This is a bit difficult because the text will wrap to any window size, but Netscape has somehow figured out the best way to zoom the window for the graphics and the headings, which makes it easier to move between Web pages that assume different width windows.

Of all the browsers, Netscape is the most responsive in terms of allowing you to move on to another page before the current page has completely arrived. This may seem like a minor detail, but when you start browsing around the Web, there's nothing worse than waiting for a big graphic to come in that you didn't want to see in the first place.

Although Netscape isn't great at FTP, it has gotten better now that it allows System 7.5 users to drag an FTP link (really, just grab it and drag it) to the Finder. At that point, Netscape opens a small window for downloading that file and lets you continue working.

Finally, Netscape offers a configurable cache that stores text and images from sites that you've visited. Although this feature can speed up repeated visits to the same site, it also seems to make Netscape launch and quit relatively slowly, especially if you set a large cache. I tried as much as 20 MB at one point, but that made Netscape quit so slowly that it was painful. I now use a 2 MB cache.

Evaluation & Details

For the moment, Netscape Navigator is the best Web browser available, bar none. It's fast; it's easy to use; and it has some welcome features that all users will appreciate. However, I should caution you about the speed at which things change on the Web. It's entirely possible that another hungry startup with some wizard programmers will come out with a Web browser that puts Netscape to shame, at which point I could easily see 75 percent of the Web switching over to that browser in a matter of months. For the moment, though, Netscape has the spotlight, and if recent releases of Netscape Navigator are any indication, the company has no intention of letting anyone else steal its thunder.

In part because of its popularity, Netscape has rather odd and somewhat irritating distribution requirements. Netscape Communications, although they would never respond to requests for explanation or clarification, has said that only sites in the **edu** domain may post Netscape for access via FTP, which eliminates all the major mirror networks because there are some sites in the **com** domain included among the mirror sites. So, finding Netscape at any site other than **ftp.netscape.com** can prove difficult, and that site is often too overloaded to serve all the folks who would like to get a copy of Netscape.

However, once you can get a copy, Netscape's wording says, "You can download a copy of Netscape Navigator for evaluation or for unlimited use in academic or not-for-profit environments. If you want to purchase Netscape Navigator and associated support for ongoing use, you can order it directly from Netscape Communications Corporation. Send email to **sales@netscape.com** and you'll get an automated reply with purchasing information." I'll leave it to you to interpret that wording for yourself—nowhere does Netscape give a time limit on the evaluation period. If you do decide to purchase Netscape for the support, it costs $39, and a printed manual is another $20. International prices vary somewhat.

```
http://www.netscape.com/
```

```
ftp://ftp.netscape.com/netscape/mac/
```

Other Web-related Programs

Although I currently feel that MacWeb and Netscape (and TCP/Connect II, in chapter 28, "Integrated Programs") are the only Web browsers to really consider, there are others, including NCSA Mosaic, Enhanced Mosaic, and MacWWW, the latter of which I mention for historic reasons. In addition, there are a few Web servers worth mentioning,

WebSTAR (previously MacHTTP), NetWings, and httpd4Mac. Unless I note otherwise, all of the programs listed below are available in:

```
ftp://ftp.tidbits.com/pub/tidbits/tisk/tcp/
```

Clay Basket

Even Netscape's hierarchical bookmark list, useful as it may be, is pretty lousy. Enter Dave Winer of UserLand Software, the guy who basically created the computer outlining program with ThinkTank and MORE many years ago. Dave has become a major Web fan, and is working on a program code-named Clay Basket that acts as an independent hotlist, currently only for Netscape, but which could theoretically serve as an independent hotlist for other applications as well. It's too early to say much about how well it works, but if it beats the Netscape hierarchical bookmarks, I'll use it constantly. Check the Web site below for updates—I hope it will be available by the time you read this.

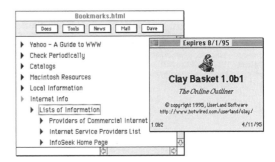

```
http://www.hotwired.com/Staff/userland/clay/
```

Enhanced Mosaic

Although NCSA gives away NCSA Mosaic for free, they also have licensed the code to a number of companies, who have then created versions of Enhanced Mosaic. The versions of Enhanced Mosaic I've seen are feature-poor in comparison with Netscape, MacWeb, and NCSA Mosaic 2.0, although they seem faster and more stable than the early version of NCSA Mosaic on which they are based. Perhaps the most frustrating thing about the version of Enhanced Mosaic (from O'Reilly & Associates) that I tested is that it doesn't display pages until it has brought in all the graphics. And it provides no indication of how long it will take to finish retrieving the graphics. In other words, you have no idea how long you'll sit and wait before you get to see the next page. Versions of Enhanced Mosaic are commercial products only.

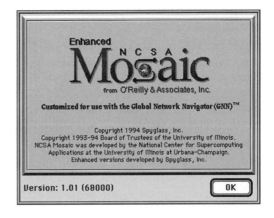

httpd4Mac

Bill Melotti's free httpd4Mac is a very simple Web server implemented as a faceless background application. Bill designed httpd4Mac to be fast and free, since the other Web servers available for the Mac are either shareware or commercial. However, httpd4Mac doesn't currently support any sort of interactive Web pages such as forms or clickable image maps, which limits its appeal for heavy-duty use. In addition, the complete lack of an interface may bother some people because tracking what httpd4Mac thinks is happening becomes difficult, and the only way to modify its configuration is by editing a preferences text file. Still, it might be worth a look if you want a free Web server to try out.

Imagine a faceless background application here!

MacWWW

MacWWW, also called Samba (depending on what you read online) doesn't work particularly well, but is notable because it was the first Macintosh Web browser. MacWWW was written by Robert Cailliau and others at CERN. MacWWW is commercial software from CERN, and costs 50 ECU (European Currency Units). The source code is also available, for quite a lot more. Check the information at CERN for the details.

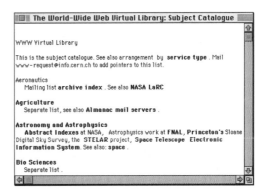

```
http://info.cern.ch/hypertext/WWW/Clients.html
```

NCSA Mosaic for the Mac

Although the free (for personal use) NCSA Mosaic originally popularized the Web, it has drastically declined in popularity. The reason is that development on the program has moved sluggishly, thanks in part to many of the NCSA Mosaic developers left for jobs at various companies, most notably Netscape Communications. Mosaic does have a few unique features. It enables you to make personal annotations to any document on the Web, either in text or using the audio-input features of your Mac. Mosaic also includes a Kiosk mode that actually removes some functionality from the program to make it better for

continues

public use. When it was the only game in town, NCSA Mosaic was absolutely essential. However, I now recommend either Netscape or MacWeb over Mosaic. Mosaic doesn't quite compare in terms of features, and it's slower and clumsier. More seriously, although none of the browsers are among the more stable Internet programs I've used, Mosaic has been the flakiest of the three.

ftp://ftp.ncsa.uiuc.edu/Mac/Mosaic/

NetWings

One of the most serious problems facing the Web today is that it can be hard to maintain a coherent set of Web pages. A Web server called NetWings offers a solution for at least some folks with this problem—it uses a database back-end to store the data and serves it out when requested. NetWings is based on 4D, the powerful relational database from ACI US, and because it's a server, it can do things like format HTML on the fly from the information stored in the database. NetWings is just entering public beta testing as I write this, so there's no telling how popular it will become, but I think it's an extremely interesting approach, and one for which I have high hopes.

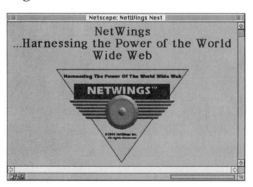

http://netwings.com/

WebSTAR

StarNine's WebSTAR (which, when it comes out, will be released in both shareware and commercial versions), previously called MacHTTP, is a World Wide Web server written by Chuck Shotton. WebSTAR enables a Mac with a dedicated Internet connection to serve World Wide Web documents to Web browsers. Basically, you create HTML documents and store them, along with images if you want, in the WebSTAR folder. Then, whenever anyone browses into your Mac from the Web, WebSTAR serves up those documents. WebSTAR supports Apple events and can link AppleScript scripts to URLs, making it

possible for you to use Apple event-capable applications like FileMaker Pro for serving data to the Web. WebSTAR is Power Mac-native and threaded, and testing shows that on a Power Mac, WebSTAR's performance is equal to that of much more expensive Unix workstations.

http://www.starnine.com/

Helper Applications

For the most part, the various Web browsers have opted not to include the proverbial kitchen sink in their code, and they all rely on a common set of helper applications for dealing with certain types of data. There are numerous other applications that you can use as helper applications, but these are the most popular. All are available at the URL below, unless mentioned otherwise.

ftp://ftp.tidbits.com/pub/tidbits/tisk/util/

Adobe Acrobat

One criticism of the HTML format used on the World Wide Web is that it doesn't provide the kind of complete control that desktop publishers are used to when laying out a page. There are a number of electronic document formats that some people use for this purpose, including Adobe Acrobat, Common Ground from No Hands Software, WordPerfect's Envoy, and Farallon's Replica. Of these, Acrobat is the most common, and Adobe and Netscape are reportedly working to include support for Acrobat's PDF documents in future versions of Netscape. Until then, you'll have to use these programs as helper applications. I wasn't able to find a Web page for Common Ground, although the others do have Web pages.

```
http://www.adobe.com/Acrobat/Acrobat0.html

ftp://ftp.adobe.com/pub/adobe/Acrobat/Macintosh/

http://wp.novell.com/envoy/envoytoc.htm

http://www2.farallon.com/www/www2/rep/repmac.html
```

JPEGView

Although the trend among Web browsers is to display JPEG graphics along with the text and GIF graphics on a Web page, not all of them can do this yet. Those that don't, send all JPEG images, and most other unsupported graphics formats, to JPEGView from Aaron Giles, which is postcardware. JPEGView does an admirable job of displaying JPEG images, and is Power Mac-native for a significant speed boost for Power Mac users. JPEGView can crop images, resize them, and convert between a number of different formats. It's a staple for other Internet programs that use helper applications as well, such as TurboGopher.

MacBinary II+

Making files available for download via a Web browser is somewhat haphazard, thanks to the way the Macintosh files can have both resources and data forks. The safest method is the standard, BinHex, but a much tighter format is MacBinary, which stores both forks of a normal Mac file together in a single file that you can upload to other types of computers. If you want to download a file in MacBinary format (usually indicated by a .bin extension), you need a helper application that can decode the MacBinary format, because Web browsers, unlike FTP clients, don't do so automatically. All that said, the program you need is Peter Lewis's free MacBinary II+ because it can work with the Web browsers to decode MacBinary files. MacBinary II+ has no interface; if a Web browser doesn't call it automatically, you must drop a MacBinary file on MacBinary II+ to have that file decoded.

MacBinary II+

MoviePlayer

Although Sparkle, and even SimpleText, can handle QuickTime movies, Web browsers generally default to using Apple's MoviePlayer to display QuickTime movies. Of course, you must also have QuickTime installed for any of these to work. You can't download MoviePlayer, although it comes with QuickTime and on the System 7.5 CD. Getting QuickTime has become more difficult if you don't get it with your Mac or with System 7.5, although you can purchase it online at the Web page below. Frankly, if getting MoviePlayer becomes a problem, I recommend using Sparkle, SimpleText, or one of the other free QuickTime players, like Leonard Rosenthol's Popcorn, which are readily available.

http://quicktime.apple.com/

SimpleText

Web browsers occasionally need to download or display straight text, or sometimes the HTML source code for a Web page. Although any word processor or text editor should work for this purpose, and I always use Nisus Writer, Apple's SimpleText is usually the default because it's free with every Macintosh. If your Mac or version of the System is old, you may have the older and less-capable TeachText instead. SimpleText is available at some of Apple's FTP sites, but everyone should have at least one, if not four or five, copies on their hard disks from installing commercial applications that typically come with TeachText or SimpleText so you will be able to open ReadMe files with a simple double-click.

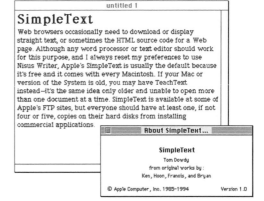

SoundApp

Although SoundMachine seems to be used as the default for most audio files, the most recent version of Norman Franke's free SoundApp claims to play even more sound formats, including one, the Windows WAVE format, that SoundMachine doesn't handle. I haven't seen many (OK, any, but I'm not big on downloading sounds) WAVE files, but because they come from the Windows world, you're likely to hit some eventually. SoundApp can handle the Internet standard Sun au format, so you could use it for all of your audio needs.

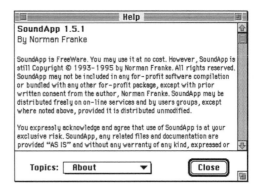

SoundMachine

Rod Kennedy's free SoundMachine is the most popular application for playing the audio files that you run across on the Internet because of its support for the standard Sun au format. Though it is mostly used to play sounds, SoundMachine can also record sounds in the au format. Although it would probably drive me nuts in normal use, I rather like SoundMachine's Chatterbox Mode, where it uses Apple's PlainTalk technology to read the text of the menu items and buttons you select.

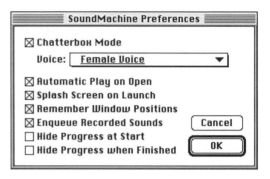

Sparkle

There are two video formats that are fairly common on the Web, QuickTime and MPEG. The most popular MPEG player for the Macintosh is Maynard Handley's free and frequently updated Sparkle. Sparkle also can display PICT files and QuickTime movies, and it contains PowerPC code for optimum movie playing performance on Power Macs. Sparkle requires System 7.5 or System 7 along with a whole slew of additional extensions, including QuickTime 1.6, Sound Manager 3.0, and the Thread Manager, among others.

StuffIt Expander

Aladdin Systems' free StuffIt Expander is such a necessary part of your Internet toolkit that we've included it on the ISKM disk. StuffIt Expander is universally used as a helper application to debinhex files and to expand both StuffIt and Compact Pro archives, along with self-extracting archives created by either of those two programs. If you own one of Aladdin's commercial products or register their shareware DropStuff with Expander Enhancer, StuffIt Expander gains the capability to decode many other formats, include MacBinary, Unix Compress, and zip files. I encourage everyone to register DropStuff with Expander Enhancer if you want to decode these additional formats—it's a great way to thank Aladdin for making the basic StuffIt Expander available for free.

ZipIt

The zip format, that's the standard in the PC world, is one of the formats that StuffIt Expander can only handle after you've registered DropStuff or purchased another Aladdin product. While you're getting around to registering DropStuff, you can try out Tommy Brown's $15 shareware ZipIt, which also can decode (and encode) zip files. One way or another, please support these shareware efforts. Tommy Brown modeled ZipIt's interface on Compact Pro, although of course you shouldn't have to interact with the interface to a helper application all that much.

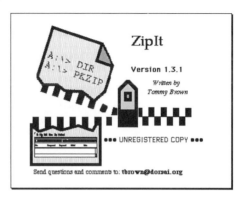

WWWrapping Up

The Web is where the action is, and I hope this chapter has given you the necessary information to pick out a Web browser and start poking around. Everything changes so fast that it's hard to say where you should start, but I currently recommend you point your browser at Yahoo and either browse or search for information. If you can't find it in Yahoo, one of the search engine links in Yahoo should help, if anything can. Enjoy yourself, and remember to come up for air every now and then. The Web can be a mighty vortex.

```
http://www.yahoo.com/
```

In addition, I've created an ISKM Home Page (the version of MacWeb on the ISKM disk goes to it by default) that points to many of the rest of the best sites on the Internet for searching and browsing; by using these links you should be able to find anything that is actually available. These are the same resources I use, so I've given you the exact same tools to which I turn whenever I need to find something on the Web.

```
http://www.mcp.com/hayden/iskm/
```

All this browsing is fine and nice, but what if you want to create your own Web pages? Read on, because the next chapter tells you everything you need to know about the process on a Macintosh, unlike most other books that I've seen about the Web.

26

Creating Your
Web Page

In this chapter I explain how to make your own home page and how to comfortably begin creating a set of related pages. First, I talk about HTML (HyperText Markup Language) 2.0, the language of the Web, complete with information about how to make links, include graphics, and test a Web page. I also give suggestions about what you might put on a page and give a few pointers for when to consider using features coming in the final HTML 3.0 specification. Toward the end of this chapter, you'll find a collection of capsule reviews covering a number of Web authoring tools and contact information for a few valuable Web-authoring resources.

Note

To spare you the agony of correctly typing URLs into your Web browser, I have created a Web page that includes links to the Web URLs mentioned in this chapter.

```
http://www.mcp.com/hayden/iskm/html-resources.html
```

Also, to give credit where credit is due, this chapter was written by my wife, Tonya Engst, who's become a major Web and HTML aficionado in recent months and who was eminently qualified to write it. Without her work on this chapter, it would have been much harder to finish this edition in a timely fashion.

Web Authoring Preview

When you create a Web page, you are a Web author, and hence—to use the slang appropriately—you are authoring a Web page. On a difficulty scale of 1 to 10, with 1 being easy, authoring a Web page rates about a 3. All you need is a word processor, attention to detail, common sense, and a place to serve your page where others can access it with Web browsers.

You can create a Web page in any word processing program, and if you don't have a word processor (or you dislike your word processor) you can use a text editor such as SimpleText or BBEdit. Once you know a little about making Web pages, you may want to try software designed for Web authoring. You can read about such software later in this chapter.

Web pages consist of text marked with HTML tags that give a Web browser guidelines for how to show the text. For example, to emphasize something, you enclose it in a pair of <em> tags, like this: **<em>Pay Attention!</em>**. A Web browser will then show Pay Attention! in an emphasized way (perhaps in bold or italic) to make it stand out visually. Attention to detail counts, because HTML tags are picky little things and typographical errors can wreak havoc on even simple pages.

Common sense also counts when it comes to creating a Web page. HTML is a subset of another markup language called SGML, which stands for *Structured Generalized Markup Language.* The "structured" in SGML's name is important. Most HTML tags set the structure of a page, not what a page looks like. Think about it. People all over the world use the Web with all sorts of computers (and in the next few years we may even have devices like Web-based speech synthesizers). You can't count on Web browsers to display layout details such as white space or columns; you can't count on them to display typographical niceties such as fonts; and you certainly can't count on them to display pictures. As a result, well-done Web pages primarily use structural tags that emphasize text, make strong statements, set up lists, and create topic headings.

> **Note**
>
> *SGML is actually a language for creating other languages, which are then called DTDs, or* Document Type Definitions. *HTML is an example of a DTD.*

Before you jump in and author a Web page, decide how you will serve it to the Internet. You must find an organization that will serve your page, thus making it available to anyone using the Web. You might ask your Internet provider or your system adminstrator. Many schools and businesses serve employee and student home pages, and an ever-increasing number of commercial Internet providers serve the home pages of their customers (usually at a low cost or free to individuals). After you find an organization that will serve your page, ask about these issues:

1. You might want to serve more than one page—if you serve several pages, you may be able to better organize your information and create hypertext links between pages. Ask if you can serve a folder's worth of related pages and graphics. Ask if the folder has a size limit.

2. The Web is picky about file names, and file names must end with an extension that indicates the file type. For example, a Web page coded in HTML needs a `.htm` or `.html` extension. The specific extension depends on the server that serves your files. Also, the length of a file name may be limited by the server.

3. Ask how you can update your pages.

4. Ask if there is any charge for serving your pages, and ask if there are any extra charges if they prove enormously popular.

> **Note**
>
> *You can easily run your own Web server on a Macintosh, but it's not terribly realistic unless you have a permanent Internet connection, preferably something at least as fast as a 56 Kbps hookup. Check these Web pages for more information on setting up a Web server:*
>
> `http://abs.apple.com/pub/apple-internet-providers/`
>
> `http://www.uwtc.washington.edu/Computing/WWW/CreatingASite.html`

Introduction to HTML

HTML is tag-oriented. An HTML document begins with the tag <html>, ends with the tag </html>, and anything between those two tags is either basic text or another tag. Put the right tags and text together, and you end up with a nifty Web page.

HTML has two types of tags: single and paired. A single tag sits by itself and tells a Web browser to do something specific. For example, the <hr> tag tells a Web browser to insert a horizontal rule. Paired tags come in twos, and they surround the text they apply to. The ending tag always includes a forward slash right after its beginning bracket. For example, the <strong> tag pair works like this: **<strong>I love you!</strong>**. The <strong> tag pair codes for strength, and a Web browser will interpret the pair by giving the phrase "I love you!" a strong appearance (which may in fact vary depending on which Web browser the readers use and how it is set up).

> **Note**
>
> *If I wanted to show how the <strong> tag pair works without giving a specific example, I would write: <strong>...text...</strong>. Later in this chapter, you'll see tag pairs explained in this way, so don't say I didn't warn you!*

> *You can type tags in either uppercase or lowercase—it makes no difference. You may see both in examples of HTML on the Web.*

A Web page has two main parts: the head and the body. The head contains introductory and descriptive matter, such as a title, and the body contains everything else, except for the ending </html> tag. The text and tags for the basic Web page shown in figure 26.1 look like the following:

```
<html>

<head>

<title>Ingrid's Penguin Page</title>

</head>

<body>

Why eat chocolate when you can eat fish instead?

</body>

</html>
```

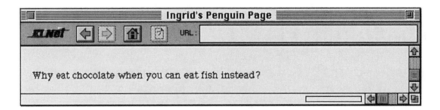

Figure 26.1   *A Web browser doesn't show HTML tags; instead it shows a title and body text.*

As you can see in figure 26.1, the Web browser uses the <html>, <head>, <title>, and <body> tags behind the scenes. Anyone viewing the page sees only the title and body text. If you type lots of text between the <body> tag pair, the text would show on the Web page as one long paragraph.

> *Many of the screen shots in this chapter show glimpses of a Web page titled "Ingrid's Penguin Page." Feel free to use your Web browser to view the source of Ingrid's Penguin Page and to re-use the HTML code.*

```
http://www.mcp.com/hayden/iskm/ingrid.html
```

Tags for Text

HTML has a number of tags for text, which you use within the body of an HTML document to set up the structure and appearance of a page.

New Paragraphs and Lines

Web browsers do handle word wrap, such that text automatically wraps down to the next line, but they typically do not understand the idea of pressing Return to start a new line or paragraph. Even if you press Return to start new paragraphs within an HTML document, Web browsers ignore those Return characters.

Fortunately, HTML includes tags for starting a new paragraph and for starting a new line. The new paragraph tag, <p>, typically puts some space above the paragraph, but the new line tag, <br>, starts a new line without adding extra space (see figure 26.2). Here is a snippet of HTML code with <p> and <br> tags:

```
This page was last updated on April 1, 1995.

<p>Ingrid Penguin

<br>One Herring Lane, Snowy Patch #27

<br>Frosty City, South Pole
```

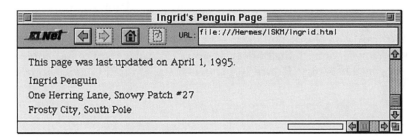

Figure 26.2   *The extra space above "Ingrid Penguin" is due to a <p> tag.*

Topic Headings

Web pages use topic headings to help viewers understand the flow of information. The <h1> pair is for the most important headings, the <h2> pair is for the next most important headings, and so on, all the way to the <h6> pair, which is for headings at the sixth level of importance. Figure 26.3 shows the <h2> topic heading coded as follows:

```
<h2>Other Penguins on the Web</h2>
```

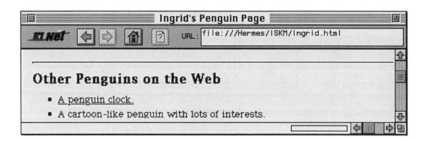

Figure 26.3   *Other Penguins on the Web is an h2-level heading.*

> *Text after a heading doesn't need to start with a <p> or <br> tag; Web browsers assume text after a heading starts on a new line.*

Lists and Glossaries

HTML makes it easy to create numbered and bulleted lists. People familiar with HTML call a numbered list an *ordered list,* and tag it with the <ol> pair (and Web browsers put in the numbers for you). They call a bulleted list an *unordered list,* and tag it with the <ul> pair (and Web browsers put in the bullets for you). Lists also require the single tag <li>, which precedes each list entry. Figure 26.4 shows the result of this code snippet for an unordered list:

```
<ul>

<li>Monty Python's The Penguin on the Telly and the Death of Mary Queen of Scotts.

<li>Anatole France's Penguin Island, translated into English by A. W. Evans.

</ul>
```

Figure 26.4   *The <ul> and <li> tags turn into a bulleted list.*

A glossary is a fancy list of terms and definitions (see figure 26.5). In HTML, the <dl> tag surrounds a glossary (think of dl as standing for Definition List), the <dt> tag begins a term, and the <dd> tag begins a definition, usually indented from the term. To see how the tags work, check out this sample:

```
<dl>

<dt>The Penguin on the Telly and the Death of Queen Mary of Scotts

<dd>The first time I heard this Monty Python skit, I laughed so hard that I fell off my chair.

<dt>Penguin Island

<dd>I've never read this book by Anatole France, but I've always wanted to.

</dl>
```

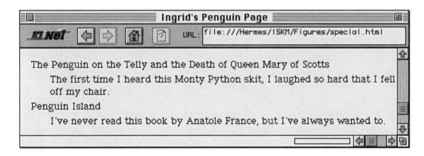

Figure 26.5   *The <dl>, <dt>, and <dd> tags turn into a glossary-like list.*

Addresses—Snail Mail and Email

It's polite to end your home page with contact information so viewers can get in touch with you. If you include a snail mail address, you might enclose it in the <address> tag pair.

A snail mail address has a solid, traditional feel to it, but sharing your email address usually makes more sense. You can, of course, just type your email address in the text of your page, but just typing your email address brands you as a rank novice when it comes to HTML; instead, you should make a mailto link, which some Web browsers can use. Figure 26.6 shows the bottom of a Web page, complete with a mailto link.

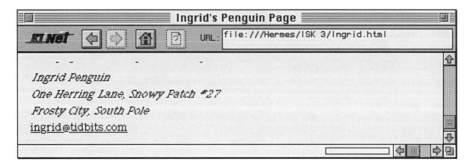

Figure 26.6   *A snail mail and email address, displayed in a Web browser.*

Take a look at the code behind figure 26.6:

```
<address>Ingrid Penguin

<br>One Herring Lane, Snowy Patch #27

<br>Frosty City, South Pole</address>

<br><a href="mailto:ingrid@tidbits.com">ingrid@tidbits.com</a>
```

The first part of the code shows the <address> tag pair in action, and the last line shows an example of an anchor tag pair, which gets coded with <a>…text…</a>. Anchor tags can do many different things in HTML, and I talk more about them in the Links section of this chapter.

In this example, the anchor tag links to an email address, and the anchor tag does this by including an *attribute* inside the beginning tag. An attribute gives a Web browser more information about the tag. In this case, the attribute is an href, and it specifies that the text between the tags should appear as a link (href stands for Hypertextual REFerence). If someone clicks the link, the Web browser brings up a window or calls another program to send email, with **ingrid@tidbits.com** in the To field.

> **Note**
>
> *Some browsers don't support mailto URLs, and others do support them but must be set up correctly. Fortunately, if a reader's browser doesn't work with mailto URLs, he can still see the email address and transcribe it manually.*

Typographical Styles

As Mac users, we are accustomed to having options for styling text every which way. Most traditional design advice that I've read about styling cautions against using too many formats on one page, and that caution holds true for HTML as well. Fortunately,

HTML offers far fewer formatting choices, and your chances of committing a typographical *faux pas* are far less, especially if you remember that italic usually looks lousy onscreen.

HTML's typographical tags come in two main categories: physical and logical. Physical tags dictate exactly what the text should look like (assuming the browser can display it). HTML offers physical tags for:

- Bold: ...text...
- Italic: <i>...text...</i>
- Underline: <u>...text...</u>
- Typewriter: <tt>...text...</tt> (displays text in a monospaced font)

Because the point of HTML is to convey meaning and structure, it makes sense to use logical typographical tags instead of physical ones.

Here are some of the more useful logical tags:

- Emphasize: ...text... (use instead of italic)
- Strong: ...text... (use instead of bold)
- Cite: <cite>...text...</cite> (for book titles and the like)

If you write a software tutorial in HTML, you might also use these logical tags:

- Code: <code>...text...</code> (for bits of programming code)
- Keyboard: <kbd>...text...</kbd> (for text to be typed)
- Variable: <var>...text...</var> (for customized text to be typed, such as an email address)
- Sample: <samp>...text...</samp> (for a message returned by a computer)

Note

Never use a heading tag where you should use a strong or emphasis tag instead. A heading tag may make the text look big and important in some browsers, but it will look just plain stupid in other browsers. Also, some Web pages are devoted to sharing lists of badly done Web pages, and I'd hate for your page to end up on one of those lists.

```
http://turnpike.net/metro/mirsky/Worst.html
```

Entities—Coding for Special Characters

First, the good news—most normal every day text characters work fine. You just type them in the body of your HTML document. Second, the bad news—you do have to code for HTML's four reserved characters (>, <, ", and &) and for upper ASCII character set characters.

ASCII stands for *American Standard Code for Information Interchange*, and the lower ASCII character set, also known as *7-bit ASCII*, consists of 128 characters, each with an assigned number. Of those 128 characters, about 100 are for letters and numbers that people use. On an English keyboard, pretty much any character that appears is part of lower ASCII; with non-English keyboards, your mileage may vary considerably.

The upper ASCII character set adds another 128 characters to the lower ASCII character set, and the lower and upper ASCII character sets are collectively known as *8-bit ASCII*. Bullets, accented characters, and other special characters come from upper ASCII. Unfortunately, different computers and programs use different upper ASCII character sets. When you type an upper ASCII character on the Mac, it's unlikely to be the same character when viewed through a Web browser, which uses a standard called *ISO Latin-1* for its upper ASCII characters.

Named and Numbered Entities

You can tag for several upper ASCII characters with *named entities*. A named entity is a special code that begins with an ampersand, continues with a name, and ends with a semicolon. Table 26.1 shows a few examples of named entities. You can find a full list of ISO Latin-1 characters and their entities at:

```
http://www.w3.org/hypertext/WWW/MarkUp/ISOlat1.html
```

Table 26.1
Tagging for upper ASCII characters

Character	Named entity
á	á
é	é
ñ	ñ

Note — *You can also specify ISO Latin-1 characters using numbered entities (where numbers specify the characters), but Web browsers frequently fail to display them correctly, so I recommend that you do not use them.*

Reserved Characters

HTML reserves four characters for its tags, and you can't always use those characters as regular text and have them come out right. The reserved characters are the left angle bracket (<), the right angle bracket (>), the straight double quote (") and the ampersand (&). To code for these characters, use special named entities (see Table 26.2).

Table 26.2

Tagging for reserved characters

Character	Tag
<	&lt;
>	&gt;
&	&amp;
"	&quot;

Quotations

If you put a long quotation on a Web page, you might set it off in a special way, using the <blockquote> pair. Web browsers typically indent or italicize blockquoted text.

If you want quotation marks to surround a quote, use the double quotation mark entity (") that I explained previously. Many Web browsers will display a double straight quote even if you type " and don't use the entity, but it's considered bad form not to use the entity.

If you use a word processor to type HTML and the word processor automatically types curly quotes when you press the quote key, you must turn off the curly quotes. Look for a Preferences or Options command, or if your program has an automatic-correction feature, this may be where you turn off curly quotes. You might also set the automatic-correction feature (or a glossary feature) to automatically type **&quot**; when you type ".

Preformatted Text, Specially Formatted Text, and HTML 3.0

"But, but, but…" you may be sputtering. "I need some text to appear in Web browsers exactly the way it shows on my computer." For example, if you need to present tabular information in a monospaced font (such as Monaco), you don't want the font to turn into a proportional font (such as Times) up on the Web, because your carefully aligned columns will turn into alphabet soup. Luckily, help is at hand, in the form of the <pre> tag pair. Surround your text with the <pre> tag pair, and it will display in a monospaced font, exactly as you typed it. You won't even need to use <br> or <p> tags.

If you aren't worried about presenting tabular information, but do want to totally control the look of your text, consider creating a graphic and displaying the graphic on your Web page (graphics are covered a little later in this chapter).

As I write this, HTML is at version 2.0, but a finalized HTML 3.0 is coming soon. HTML 3.0 will specify more layout- and typographically-oriented tags (probably including tags for tables and fonts), and some Web browsers (most notably Netscape) already support additional formatting tags, many of which may appear in HTML 3.0. If you are interested in this topic I strongly recommend that you read the Introduction to the HyperText Markup Language Specification Version 3.0.

```
http://www.hpl.hp.co.uk/people/dsr/html/Contents.html
```

Also, Netscape Communications has posted information about additional tags supported by its browsers.

```
http://home.netscape.com/assist/net_sites/html_extensions.html
```

Note

In case you were wondering, to make forms (which display fill-in fields, checkboxes, radio buttons, and so on) you use special HTML tags. To make the forms work, you must set them up to interact with a Web server, a task which—unfortunately—is beyond the scope of this book.

Tags for Links

If you absorbed most of the information about tags for text, you should be able to fire up a word processor and use the information to make a simple HTML document with headings, lists, emphasized text, and so on. Armed with that knowledge, you can make lots of simple Web pages, but few Web pages feel complete without links. Links are in many ways the most interesting part of the Web. Links enable you to move quickly from one place to another on the Web. If you serve your Web page from a site in San Francisco, but make a link to a Web page stored on a machine in London, someone clicking on your link is instantly (or somewhat instantly) able to look at the page stored in London. Links come in three flavors: links to other pages, links to other Internet resources, and links within a page.

Linking to Other Pages

To make a link to a different page, you need to know the URL of that page. If the page isn't part of your Web site, use a Web browser to find the page, and then copy the URL. You can then paste the URL into your HTML code. The Live from Antarctica link shown in figure 26.7 has the following code:

```
<li><a href="http://quest.arc.nasa.gov/livefrom/livefrom.html">Live from Antartica</a>
```

The first <a> tag has an href attribute (href stands for Hypertextual REFerence). The href attribute tells a Web browser what to do with the link, and in this case it tells the browser to jump to **http://quest.arc.nasa.gov/livefrom/livefrom.html** if someone clicks the text between the two <a> tags.

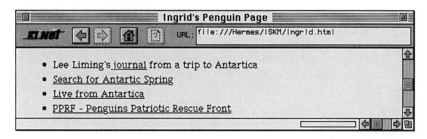

Figure 26.7 *Web browsers usually display linked text in a different color and with an underline.*

To create a link to another page on your Web site, don't use the usual full URL in the href attribute; instead, use a *relative URL.* A relative URL doesn't include the name of the server, and it only includes enough of the path to clarify where the other Web page is.

> **Note**
>
> *If all this talk of URLs is making your head swim, skip back to chapter 6, "Addressing & URLs" for a discussion of the various parts of a URL.*

For example, I serve my friend Geoff's home page from my Web site. The full URL to Geoff's page is:

```
http://king.tidbits.com/geoff/geoff.html
```

My home page is also on my server, but it's not in the geoff folder, so the link from my home page to Geoff's home page has a relative URL, like this:

```
<a href="/geoff/geoff.html">Geoff</a>
```

This relative URL tells a browser to go back to the root directory, then into the geoff folder, and finally to the geoff.html document. It doesn't include **http://king.tidbits.com** because both pages are on the same server.

As another example, Geoff has a file in his geoff folder called reno.html (Geoff grew up in Nevada), and the link from Geoff's geoff.html home page to his reno page, looks like this:

```
<a href="reno.html">Reno, Nevada</a>
```

Because the document called reno.html is in the same folder as the geoff.html document, the relative URL doesn't need to include **http:/king.tidbits.com/geoff/**. It only needs to include reno.html, the name of the document that you see if you click the Reno, Nevada link.

Note

If you are making a simple home page with a few related HTML documents and graphics, store all the files in the same folder on your Mac. The people who serve your files will almost certainly keep them in the same folder, and your relative URLs will work like a charm when you test them and when they go live on the Web. Use the same type of relative link that Geoff uses for his reno.html document.

If you need to do relative URLs that go back to the root and then down a different path, ask the people who will serve your page how you should handle the URL.

Links to Other Internet Resources

You can make a link to anything that has a URL, although many Web browsers have trouble with FTP URLs. If you give an FTP URL, be sure to also mention the URL in the regular text of the Web page. Links to Gopher files tend to work well, although be careful since Gopher URLs are usually extremely ugly and hard to retype correctly. The code below shows the HTML for an unordered list with links to two Gopher items, and figure 26.8 shows what the list looks like in a Web browser.

```
<ul>

<li>Monty Python's <cite><a href="gopher://ocf.berkeley.edu:70/00/Library/Monty_Python/penguin
">The Penguin on the Telly and the Death of Mary Queen of Scotts.</a></cite>

<li>Anatole France's<cite><a href="gopher://gopher.vt.edu:10010/02/84/1">Penguin Island,</a></
cite> translated into English by A. W. Evans.

</ul>
```

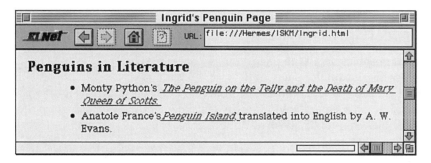

Figure 26.8   *An unordered list with links to Gopher items.*

Links within a Web Page

You also can use links to help people get around within a page. For example, you might make a linked table of contents of <h1>- or <h2>-tagged titles.

To create an internal link, you first do some special HTML tagging at the *target* of the link. The target is where viewers end up after they click. Here's an example:

```
<h2><a name="other penguins">Other Penguins on the Web</a></h2>
```

In the example, **Other Penguins on the Web** is surrounded by an <a> tag pair, with a name attribute. The name attribute gives the target the name **other penguins**.

After naming the target, you set up the link like this:

```
This page has additional <a href="#other penguins">information</a> about penguins on
the Web.
```

When someone views the link, the text between the <a> tags appears underlined. The <a> tags are a bit unusual, because the beginning tag has a special href attribute, which includes **#other penguins**, the target name that you set up at the target of the link. If someone clicks the underlined word "information," the Web browser will look for the **other penguins** target that you set up on the same page.

Web Graphics

When you put graphics on a Web page, you can do so in two ways: inline or external. Inline graphics display on the page, right "in line" with other text on the same line, should you choose to put text on that line. External graphics don't show on a page; instead, they show in a separate window, usually the window of a helper application like JPEGView (see chapter 25, "World Wide Web").

Today's crop of Web browsers limits you to viewing two graphic formats: GIF and JPEG. Both formats use internal compression routines that make the graphics smaller, thus decreasing download times. When you put a graphic on the Web, you have to decide whether to use GIF or JPEG. The short answer is that you want to use GIF, though JPEG images have a place in some situations, and may play a greater role in the future.

GIF versus JPEG

GIF stands for *Graphics Interchange Format*. It is the only format that all graphics-savvy Web browsers can display inline, so it's the one to use for graphics that you want everyone to see. The bad part about GIF graphics is that they are limited to 256 colors and typically don't compress as well as JPEG graphics do.

The latest version of the GIF specification (version 89a) supports transparent mode, a nifty option that lets you make one color in a graphic transparent. GIFs are shaped like rectangles, but if you make a GIF's background color transparent, you can end up with a GIF that looks like an irregularly shaped object, such as a penguin (see figure 26.9).

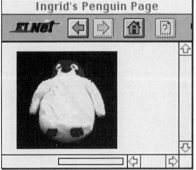

Figure 26.9   *Ingrid with a transparent background versus Ingrid with a dark background.*

GIFs also can be interlaced, meaning the image is saved in alternating horizontal bands. If you looked at the first half of an interlaced GIF, you would see a low-resolution, striped image, with blank horizontal stripes representing the second half of the image. Some Web browsers display interlaced GIFs as they read them—first they display every eighth line, then every fourth line, then every second line, and then every line. This display method makes it so people waiting for the image to load can quickly make out what the final image will look like. Other browsers bring in a rough version of the graphic and gradually refine it.

JPEG stands for *Joint Photographic Experts Group*. It is a graphics compression format that works best for digitized photographs, particularly if they depict photos of natural scenes, such as forests or sunsets. JPEG is a *lossy* format, meaning that when it does its compression magic, it loses some of the detail in the graphic. JPEG was designed to lose details that the human eye won't notice, particularly details that wouldn't be noticed from an image with gradual changes in shading and color. Sometimes the loss of detail means the graphic looks fuzzy; other times you can't tell at all. JPEG is most likely to lose too much detail with images that have sudden transitions from one color to another, so JPEG tends to be a poor format for graphics containing text, line drawings, and navigational icons.

JPEG images can have millions of colors instead of a measly 256. They have better compression, but many browsers can't display them without the assistance of a helper application (where the picture displays in a different program's window).

The bottom line: Use GIF unless you have a photograph that looks much nicer or compresses significantly tighter as a JPEG.

Converting Images into GIF or JPEG Format

Lots of commercial graphics programs can save in GIF or JPEG format, and if you own Photoshop, Color It!, or any of a number of other applications, you can save files as GIFs or JPEGs. If your collection of graphics programs can't Save As to GIF or JPEG format (or doesn't offer special options such as interlacing or transparencies), pick up a utility from the Internet that does it for you. Except for the Interactive Graphics Renderer (which you use through a Web site), the utilities mentioned in this section are available on the Info-Mac archives and at the FTP site for this book.

```
ftp://ftp.tidbits.com/pub/tidbits/tisk/util/
```

Graphic Converter

Graphic Converter is my favorite utility for working with Web graphics because it offers the most features of any of the non-commercial programs (although clip2gif is simpler to use and offers a number of the key features). See figure 26.10. Graphic Converter can open PICTs, TIFFs, JPEGs, GIFs, and a whole menagerie of less common formats.

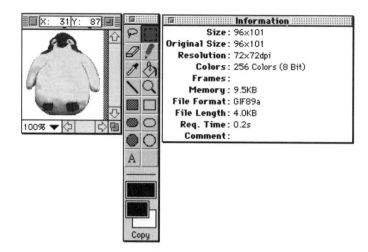

Figure 26.10   *Graphic Converter's basic interface shows the image, a "toolbox," and an Information palette.*

Graphic Converter has more extensive editing features than other shareware and freeware options and offers all the important features specific to Web graphics:

- You can save in GIF or JPEG format (to be saved as a GIF, your image cannot contain more than 256 colors; switch to fewer colors by choosing 256 Colors (8 bit) from the Colors hierarchical menu on the Picture menu).

- You can make a graphic smaller by selecting around the edge of the image, and then—in the Save As dialog box—turning on the Save Only Selection checkbox.

- In the Save As dialog box, you can use the Options button to save GIFs as interlaced or non-interlaced, and to set the quality level of a JPEG (lower quality translates to a smaller image, which will download more quickly).

- To make one color transparent, drop-down the Picture menu, choose Colors, and then choose Transparent GIF Color. Check the Transparent checkbox and click the color you want to turn transparent. After you click the OK button to exit the Transparent GIF Settings dialog box, the image may not look different, but it will display correctly in a Web browser.

- To convert many images from one format to another, try the Convert More command in the File menu.

Currently, Graphic Converter 2.0.9 runs on Power Macs in emulation. Thorsten Lemke, the author, recently released a beta PowerPC-native version, which may be in final form by the time you read this book. Graphic Converter is shareware, and it costs $30 to $35, depending on where you live.

clip2gif

Written by Yves Piguet, clip2gif is a clever utility that converts PICTs (either singly or in batches) to GIFs or JPEGs. It can give GIF files a transparent background and make them interlaced. Also, clip2gif works with AppleScript, and you can use it in scripts to do conversions and create simple graphics. Yves requests that you send "postcards, email, or banknotes" if you use the program.

GIFConverter

GIFConverter, a $40 shareware program from Kevin Mitchell, enables you to open a variety of file formats, including GIF, PICT, TIFF, and JPEG. GIFConverter has a few editing options, and lets you save in GIF or JPEG format. When you save in GIF format, in the Save As dialog box, click the Options button to indicate whether you want the graphic interlaced.

Interactive Graphics Renderer

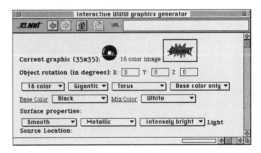

Interactive Graphics Renderer is a wonderful commentware Web page and GIF generator for personal use from Patrick J. Hennessey at the Kansas State University of Electrical Engineering. Interactive Graphics Renderer helps you make your own GIF-format horizontal rules and bullets in a variety of rendered colors and shapes. To download your GIF, simply click the Gimme! button. You may need to configure your browser to work with the MIME type used by the Renderer; I set mine to StuffIt Expander and it worked fine.

```
http://www.eece.ksu.edu/IGR/intro.html
```

Transparency

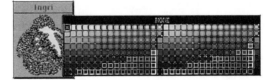

Transparency 1.0, freeware from Aaron Giles, enables you to make one of the colors in a GIF transparent. Transparency doesn't try to do anything else, and it's easy to use—just drag the icon of a GIF onto the Transparency icon. Transparency launches and displays the image. Click and hold on the background color and watch as Transparency pops up a palette showing the colors in the image with the color you selected. Release the mouse button, and Transparency makes the selected color transparent.

Tags for an Inline Graphic

As I hope you recall, any Web browser that can display graphics will show an inline graphic right on a page. Inline graphics use an <img> tag, and the <img> tag usually has a few attributes inside it. Here's an example:

```
<img src="ingrid.gif" align=bottom alt="I have expressive eyes with long eyelashes.">
```

Here's what's going on with the attributes in the example:

- **src="ingrid.gif"** specifies the source of the image as a file called ingrid.gif (always name GIFs with a .gif extension). The source should always be given as URL. In this case, I used a relative URL to a GIF in the same folder as the HTML document that will show the GIF. (Flip back to the Links section to find out more about relative URLs.)

- **align=bottom** lines up other text on the same line as the graphic with the bottom of the graphic. You could also use align=top or align=center (see figure 26.11).

Figure 26.11   Inline images can be aligned at the top, center, or bottom of their lines.

- **alt="I have expressive eyes with long eyelashes."** specifies text people see if their browsers can't display the image.

Note

You can make an inline image act as a link by enclosing it in <a> tags like this:

```
<a href="more.html"><img src="ingrid.gif" align=bottom alt="I have expressive eyes with
long eyelashes."></a>
```

This link causes a browser to open a file called more.html after someone clicks the ingrid.gif image.

An inline image can also be the target of a link—just use the name attribute in the <a> tag, like this:

```
<a name="picture"><img src="ingrid.gif" align=bottom alt="I have expressive eyes with
long eyelashes."></a>
```

In this case, someone could create a link that would cause a browser to jump to the place where ingrid.gif is displayed. The link would include an href="#picture" attribute.

Lots of Web pages use small GIFs as bullets and as navigational devices (such as arrows); these GIFs are sometimes called *picons*. You can make your own picons in a graphics program (just save them as GIFs), or you can download them from Web pages people have set up in order to share them.

```
http://www.uncg.edu:80/~rdralph/icons/
```

```
http://www.ncsa.uiuc.edu/General/Icons/
```

```
http://helix.rice.edu/Icons/
```

Horizontal Lines

In Web-author jargon, a horizontal line across the page is a horizontal rule, and you code for it using the <hr> tag. Web authors frequently use horizontal rules to visually separate topics. To make a rule, just stick <hr> where you want the rule to go. Here's the HTML code for the horizontal rule shown in figure 26.12:

```
<p><strong>Motto: Why eat chocolate when you can eat fish instead?</strong>

<hr>

My name is Ingrid. Besides <a href="#recipe">eating fish,</a> my hobbies
```

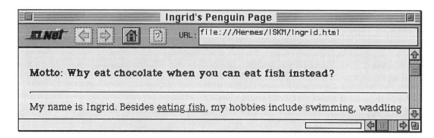

Figure 26.12   *A Web browser interprets the <hr> tag by displaying a horizontal line.*

N
o
t
e

If you've spent much time hanging out on the Web, you've almost certainly noticed that some Web pages have colorful or whimsical horizontal rules. These horizontal rules are actually inline GIFs. Not only do they liven up Web pages, but they also exist, often free for the taking, in Web-based collections sprinkled all over the globe.

```
http://www.cs.vu.nl/~dsbouma/rulers.html
```

```
http://www.uncg.edu/~rdralph/icons/bars/
```

The Netscape HTML extended tag set has attributes for the <hr> tag that enable you to modify the appearance of a horizontal rule. Currently, only Netscape can show the modifications, but this may change, especially if these attributes end up in HTML 3.0. As an example of a line you could make, consider the following code:

```
<hr size=20 width=288 align=center noshade>
```

Figure 26.13 shows what such a horizontal rule would look like in Netscape.

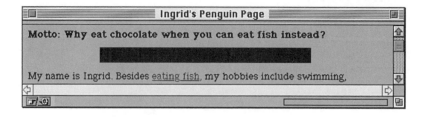

Figure 26.13   *This horizontal rule, as interpreted by Netscape, is 20 pixels high, 288 pixels wide, center-aligned, and not shaded.*

Briefly, here's how each attribute works:

- **Size** sets the height of the line in pixels (figure on about 72 pixels per inch).

- **Width** sets the width of the line. You can use a measurement in pixels (as I did in the code for figure 26.13), or you can specify a percentage of the page width. If you specify a percentage, put a percent sign after the number.

- **Align=center** centers the line on the page (since I shortened the width, I can now choose how the line aligns). You can also use **align=left** or **align=right**.

- Because Netscape shades its horizontal rules, and because the shading can take a bit of getting used to, you can use the **noshade** attribute to turn off shading.

As another example of how you might use these attributes, figure 26.14 shows a coded <hr> tag:

```
<hr size=20 width=75% align=left>
```

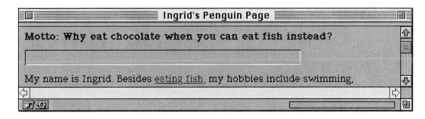

Figure 26.14   *This horizontal rule, as interpreted by Netscape, is 20 pixels high, 75 percent as wide as the page, left-aligned, and shaded.*

Tags for an External Graphic

An external graphic would typically be a JPEG image, and you would link to it just as you would link to any other Internet resource (as explained earlier in the section about linking), by using an <a> tag with an href attribute as follows:

```
<a href="ingrid.jpeg">A JPEG image of a penguin, 72K</a>
```

Name your JPEG with a .jpg or .jpeg extension. Consider saving your JPEG as a separate, small GIF image and placing the GIF image inline on your Web page. You can then make the GIF link to the JPEG such that people can click the GIF image in order to view the JPEG. You might also display the size of the JPEG so people know what they are getting into before clicking the link. The necessary code might look like:

```
<a href="ingrid.jpeg"><img src="ingrid.gif" align=bottom >Ingrid the penguin, (72K)</a>
```

For example, the Cornell University Division of Rare and Manuscript Collections has an extensive Web site that shows drawings, photographs, and notes made by Louis Agassiz Fuertes while on a trip to Alaska. Most of the links available from the site's home page lead to pages of GIFs, and each GIF acts as a link to a larger, more detailed JPEG.

```
http://rmc-www.library.cornell.edu/Alaska.Index.html
```

Note

Graphics that have more than one place that you can click on to go to more than one place on the Web are called ISMAP graphics, and to create one, you must set it up with a Web server. Fun as ISMAPs may be, they are beyond the scope of this chapter.

Sound and Video Links

Just as you can make a link to an external graphic, you can make a link to an external sound or video file, and the syntax is exactly the same. To share a sound or video with the world, you must save it in an appropriate format and name it with the corresponding extension. This section mentions a few utilities that help you work with sounds and movies, and they are all available on the Info-Mac archives and the TidBITS FTP directory:

```
ftp://ftp.tidbits.com/pub/tidbits/tisk/util/
```

Two reasonably universal sound formats are Sun au, a somewhat scratchy, 8-bit format, and the less-common MPEG audio, which sounds nicer. To ensure that most of the listeners can hear your sounds, I recommend you use one of these formats.

If you work with sounds, you might try Rod Kennedy's freeware SoundMachine, which can record in Sun au format. Name Sun au files with a **.au** extension; MPEG audio files with **.mp2**. Web 66 has a nice tutorial about recording sounds for the Web:

```
http://web66.coled.umn.edu/Cookbook/Sounds/Sounds.html
```

Movies also have two fairly universal formats, QuickTime and MPEG. If you put a Macintosh QuickTime movie up the Web, you must first flatten it, that is, run it through a program that moves all the data into the data fork (all Mac files have a data fork and a resource fork). A popular utility for flattening movies is Robert Hennessy's freeware flattenMooV. You might also check out Maynard Handley's Sparkle, a freeware program that has some support for converting movies between MPEG and QuickTime formats. QuickTime files need a **.mov** extension; MPEGs a **.mpg** or **.mpeg** extension.

Copying HTML

Given that the future of Web authoring holds lots of changes and new coding possibilities, as you browse the Web, you will almost certainly see pages with formats I didn't explain in this chapter. Luckily, it's considered reasonable practice to look at the code behind a Web page and adapt it to your own content. You can even paste the code directly into your own HTML document. Each browser has a slightly different technique for viewing the code behind the displayed page:

- MacWeb: Drop down the Options menu, choose the View Source hierarchical menu, and then choose Retrieved.

- Mosaic: From the File menu, choose View Source.

- Netscape: From the View menu, choose Source.

Note

Although copying HTML code and not crediting the source is considered aboveboard, copying graphics, sounds, and movies is a controversial topic. My advice is to freely copy sounds, graphics, or movies from sites where the author openly encourages it, and be sure to read the page carefully to find out whether the author wants credit. Otherwise, ask first.

Web Page Content

When you set up your personal page, unless you have a corporate lawyer looking over your shoulder, I urge you to loosen up, share something about yourself, and have fun. If you are setting up a page for an organization, the page should—of course—reflect the tone of the organization. Here are a few specific suggestions:

- Make it easy for people to figure out what's on your page if they locate it through a search engine. Most search engines return a page's title, URL, and the first few lines of text, so give your page a descriptive title and summarize the content in the first paragraph.

- Think of the top six inches or so of your Web page as a book's cover and introduction. They should let people know what's interesting about your page and encourage them to continue reading.

- If your page is more than a few average screens long, consider breaking it up into several pages, and make links to help people navigate among the pages.

- Contribute content of your own. For example, if you love toasters, don't just put in links to other toaster pages. The links are fine, but you might also include your top ten tips for toaster care. If you are setting up a page for an organization, include information about a topic the organization specializes in. For example, the Web site for a hardware store might post articles about how to use different tools.

- Include contact information. Use a mailto link in an anchor tag to make your email address live. Including your email address is a great way to get feedback and meet people who share your interests.

- Don't include links that don't go anywhere.

- If you post timely information, provide a date, so people know when it was last updated. Don't use a date format like 1/2/96—some people take that to mean January 2, others take it to mean February 1. To be safe, use a format like 02-Feb-96.

- If you want people to return to your site, set yourself up as doing something new (such as a column or cartoon) on a regular basis. Then, make sure you do it.

- Make sure your page will work for people who cannot use graphics or who do not have the latest popular browser. If you don't want your page to look plain stupid to thousands of people, think carefully about what tags you use. You can always make separate pages, one for people running this season's fashionable browser, and one for everyone else.

Testing Tags

After you've written an HTML document and have it stored on your hard disk, test it by opening it in a Web browser. If your HTML document works fine in testing, you can then send it to the organization who will be serving it to everyone on the Internet.

Note

Most of the time, you send files to a Web server by uploading them to a specific directory using an FTP client like Anarchie or Fetch. Make sure to upload the .html files in ASCII mode, and any images or other external files in straight binary mode, not MacBinary mode.

If you use a modem to connect to the Internet, you may not want to be connected while you do the testing. If you launch a Web browser while you are not connected, you'll most likely get an error message, though in most cases you can ignore the error message and view files on your hard disk. Even so, to avoid the error message, you might try:

- Set your home page to nothing or to a file on your hard disk.

- Launch the browser by dragging and dropping the HTML document's icon over the Web browser's icon.

Besides the drag and drop method, try these techniques for opening files on your hard disk into MacWeb, Mosaic, and Netscape. Unfortunately, if the programs change how they work before you read this, you'll have to improvise:

- MacWeb: Choose Open from the File menu.
- NCSA Mosaic: From the File menu, choose Open Local.
- Netscape: From the File menu, choose Open File. In later versions of Netscape, you can also drag and drop an HTML document icon on the Netscape browser window.

Part IV

Creating Your Web Page

Note

*If a browser won't open an HTML document, make sure the file name ends with **.html**. For example, you might name a file **PenguinPage.html**. Also, GIF files should end with **.gif**, and JPEG files should end with **.jpeg** or **.jpg**.*

Troubleshooting Tips

HTML code is usually easy to fix, it's just a matter of staring at it until you figure out the problem. Here are a few tips to speed up the process:

- Make sure ending tags have front slashes in them (the slash that's on the same key as the question mark).
- Make sure ordered, unordered, and definition lists end with ending tags.
- If you are working in a word processor, make sure you saved the file in text format.

If you use an HTML authoring program that includes a quick-preview for viewing documents in a Web browser, your relative links may not work when you do the preview because the authoring programs tend to create a temporary file and ask the browser to open that, rather than use the actual file you're editing. To avoid the problem, open the file you want to view into your browser without the help of an HTML authoring program; drag and drop is often the easiest method.

Also, if you are preparing a high-profile page, consider checking it in several browsers on more than one type of computer. Different browsers interpret HTML differently, and browsers differ in their tolerance of minor errors. Also, graphics may display completely differently on different types of computers.

External Approval

If you can't figure out what's wrong with your code or you want a rigorous check, you can submit your code to various forms-based Web pages and they will spit back suggestions for improvement. I prefer Weblint because it gives errors by line and displays HTML code by line.

```
http://www.unipress.com/web-lint/

http://www.stolaf.edu/misc/html-check/

http://www.vilspa.esa.es/div/help/validation-form.html
```

Publicizing Your Page

Once your page is up and running, you'll want to spread the word so other people will browse it. If your email program lets you set up an automatic signature, you can put your URL in your signature. You can also register your page with many of the Web searching services (such as Yahoo or WebCrawler). If you have links on your page to other related pages, send email to the authors of those pages and ask them to make links back to your page. For additional ways to publicize your pages, check out:

```
http://www.cen.uiuc.edu/~banister/submit-it/

http://home.mcom.com/escapes/submit_new.html

http://www.uwtc.washington.edu/Computing/WWW/AnnouncingYourSite.html
```

HTML Converters

If you use an existing word processing program, text editor, or desktop publishing program for creating documents that you want to then add HTML code to, you might try an HTML converter that converts your document to a text file and attempts to insert appropriate HTML tags. Particularly if you use a word processing program, it may export to either RTF (which stands for *Rich Text Format* and is also known as *Interchange Format*) or to XTND (pronounced "extend").

RTF Converters

rtftohtml, written by Chris Hector, converts graphics out of an RTF document into separate PICT images. It also has sophisticated options for text; it has a lot to offer, particularly if you are fairly comfortable with a word processing program and with HTML.

```
ftp://ftp.cray.com/src/WWWstuff/RTF/rtftohtml_overview.html
```

rtftohtml doesn't split one document into a series of appropriately connected Web pages, so Christian Bolik wrote rtftoweb, which runs along with rtftohtml. It not only can split out pages based on headings but also can add a table of contents, index, and consistent navigational tools. rtftoweb's Web page says it hasn't yet been tested on the Mac (only on Unix systems), so proceed with care.

```
ftp://ftp.rrzn.uni-hannover.de/pub/unix-local/misc/rtftoweb/html/rtftoweb.html
```

> **Note**
>
> *In case you were wondering about the URLs for rtftohtml and rtftoweb, the FTP at the start of the URL does mean the pages are being served from FTP servers, but the .html at the end of the URL tells a Web browser to interpret the file as a normal Web page.*

XTND Converters

If your word processing program can export to XTND, then it can use any HTML XTND converter to save files into HTML format. If you want to try an XTND converter, I recommend HTML + XTND, written by Leonard Rosenthol, a well-known member of the Macintosh online community. I have used it on documents and have been happy with the results. The converter also comes with clip2gif and with a program called XTNDPostProcess, which you use to further improve the conversion. HTML + XTND might be best described as weddingware—if you like it, send a contribution to Leonard's wedding fund.

```
ftp://ftp.tidbits.com/pub/tidbits/tisk/html/
```

Another HTML translation option is the freeware XTND HTML translator by Brian A. Sullivan and Jonathan Ryan Day. The translator works with any XTND-savvy program. But it comes with a template for ClarisWorks, and its Web page includes a link to a tutorial for using the translator with ClarisWorks. The newest version of the translator isn't currently available; Brian and Jonathan are in the process of licensing it to a commercial vendor.

```
http://ai.eecs.umich.edu/highc/software/translator/XTND_HTML_Translator.html
```

Programs with HTML Add-ons

When it comes to HTML coding, you can use a word processing program, text editor, page layout program, HTML authoring program, HTML converter, or some combination. If you use a word processing or desktop publishing program, remember to save the file as text before you view it in a Web browser. If you find yourself frequently coding in HTML, you can take advantage of typical word processing features—glossaries, macros, searching, spell checking, and so on. If you don't think your word processing program is the right tool for the job, you might check out other word processing programs, a text editor, or some of the recent HTML authoring programs.

This section briefly (and alphabetically) lists different word processing programs, text editors, and page layout programs that have add-ons for HTML tagging.

Alpha

Alpha, a $25 shareware program by Peter Keheler, is a text editor primarily used by programmers, and—although I have a friend who uses Alpha and a set of add-ons for HTML—if you aren't a programmer or familiar with Alpha, I don't recommend it as your HTML editor of choice. If you want to give it a spin, read the HTML Help file in the Help folder.

```
ftp://ftp.tidbits.com/pub/tidbits/tisk/util/
```

BBEdit and BBEdit Lite

BBEdit, a text editor written by Bare-Bones Software, supports extensions, add-ons that enhance what it can do. BBEdit users currently can pick from two different sets of extensions—BBEdit HTML Extensions, by Carles Bellver, and BBEdit HTML Tools, by Lindsay Davies. At a recent Macintosh user group meeting in Seattle, I picked the brains of a few people who do Web authoring. Several were enthused about BBEdit, and although they said nice things about both sets of extensions, BBEdit HTML Tools currently has the edge among people who use BBEdit for HTML. In particular, people commented favorably on its forms support, flexibility, documentation, and overall interface. Lindsay recently licensed BBEdit HTML Tools to Bare-Bones Software, and I expect BBEdit HTML Tools will be included with BBEdit by the time you read this book.

```
http://www.uji.es/bbedit-html-extensions.html

http://www.york.ac.uk/~ld11/BBEditTools.html
```

You can get started with BBEdit using the freeware BBEdit Lite, or you can purchase the commercial version for $119.

```
ftp://ftp.tidbits.com/pub/tidbits/tisk/util/
```

FrameMaker

FrameMaker users who want to make documents that print out traditionally and go on the Web might check out WebMaker, a reasonably sophisticated, high-end converter.

```
http://www.frame.com/

http://www.cern.ch/WebMaker/
```

Microsoft Word

In Word 4 or 5, use the Glossary and Commands options to automate some HTML tag insertion. In Word 6, you might combine the AutoCorrect, AutoText, Customize, and macro features to speed HTML coding.

```
http://www.microsoft.com/
```

If you use Word 6, Dan Berrios's AppleScript-based msw to html converter may prove attractive. It intelligently converts a number of document elements including heading styles, reserved characters, some character formats, bulleted lists, and numbered lists. It also converts tables to the tags that will probably appear in the HTML 3.0 specification. The converter comes with a ten-day evaluation period. After that, to get a functioning copy, you'll need to pay your $15 shareware fee, or $50 for a site license.

```
http://dreyer.ucsf.edu/mswtohtml.html
```

You might also check out NICE Technologies's Web site, where the company offers a demo version of WebWizard, a $79 Word 6 add-on that looks promising.

```
http://www.webcom.com/~nicetech/webware/webwiz.html
```

Microsoft does have a Web authoring tool, called Word Assistant, for Microsoft Word for Windows, but I'm not holding my breath waiting for a Macintosh version.

Nisus Writer

Nisus Writer is currently my favorite HTML authoring option, thanks to Sandra Silcot, who wrote an excellent set of macros that work with Nisus Writer to tag text with HTML codes. The macros are freeware for personal, non-profit, or educational use.

```
http://www.unimelb.edu.au/~ssilcot/SilcotsHTMLMacrosReadMe.html
```

Combine these macros with Nisus's sophisticated searching (it can even replace through multiple documents at once), non-contiguous selection, and Ignore Spelling character style, and you have an excellent HTML authoring tool. Nisus Writer even saves files with all the formatting in the resource fork, so you don't have to save files as text for a Web browser to load them.

```
http://www.nisus-soft.com/~nisus/index.html
```

PageMaker

Rumor has it that Adobe will soon ship an HTML utility for PageMaker, but if you are looking for a third-party solution, you might try Dave, an AppleScript by Jeff Boulter, that helps with converting PageMaker articles into HTML. According to Jeff, Dave is highly customizable, but only works on 32K or smaller articles.

```
http://www.bucknell.edu/bucknellian/dave/
```

You might also check out Mitch Cohen's WebSucker utility.

```
http://www.iii.net/users/mcohen/websucker.html
```

QuarkXPress

Astrobyte's BeyondPress lets you map document elements to HTML elements such as headings and blockquotes. You also can map styles to HTML tags, create links, and convert images to GIF or JPEG format. Unlike most of the tools mentioned in this chapter, with a $595 per copy price, BeyondPress isn't for the low-budget crowd.

```
http://www.astrobyte.com/
```

You can find a few less commercial possibilities on the Internet, including Quark to HTML by Jeremy Hylton and HTML Xport by Eric Knudstrip.

```
http://the-tech.mit.edu/~jeremy/qt2www.html
```

```
ftp://mars.aliens.com/pub/Macintosh/HTML_Xport.sit
```

Storyspace

Eastgate Systems' $245 Storyspace almost belongs in the HTML Authoring Programs section of this chapter, but I included it here because it was a functional program before the Web was but a glimmer in a few people's eyes. Storyspace enables you to create hypertexts, and it is often used in academic and literary contexts. It can also export to HTML and might be especially useful for creating Web sites that have many pages with complex linkages.

```
http://www.eastgate.com/~eastgate/
```

HTML Authoring Programs

The current state of HTML authoring programs leaves much to be desired for people interested in creating and managing multiple-page Web sites. Many programs don't include necessary features and others are still in beta, making potentially useful features too slow or quirky for serious authoring. Even so, several of these programs have a great deal to offer to anyone wanting to make a few Web pages without memorizing lots of tags and attributes. In the next year, I expect to see an explosion of Web authoring tools and an increase in the quality of the tools. For now, here is an alphabetical list of the most promising or well-known of the available programs, with notes about what you can expect from them. Most of the freeware and shareware is available from the Info-Mac archives and from the FTP directory for the Internet Starter Kit. If you can't find a program in the following FTP URL, try the program's home page.

```
ftp://ftp.tidbits.com/pub/tidbits/tisk/html/
```

Arachnid

Written by Robert McBurney, Arachnid has a lot of potential. Arachnid goes for the WYSIWYG look, meaning users don't have to insert or view HTML codes. Arachnid assumes you will create multiple, related Web pages and wraps up a group of pages in one "project." Unfortunately, Arachnid's 1.0 release won't happen until after this book is printed, which makes it difficult to get a feel for the program. The betas I've used are extremely slow, but I plan to check out the new versions as they come out. I hope Robert will improve the speed and add a Replace option, a way to insert custom tags, and add keyboard shortcuts for most commands.

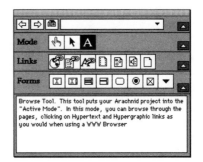

http://sec-look.uiowa.edu/about/projects/arachnid-page.html

AutoWeb

Dave Winer's AutoWeb is unusual among the HTML authoring tools because it doesn't so much help you write HTML as it creates an entire Web site for you. Essentially, you feed AutoWeb a hierarchy of Macintosh folders with text files in them, and AutoWeb spits out a fully formed set of Web pages with all the links and tables of contents created for you. The text files do have to be in a slightly special format if you want to include HTML codes like <hr>, but for the most part AutoWeb is probably the easiest way of creating an entire site from text files and maintaining it, because it can update a site from updated files as well. AutoWeb is actually a set of Frontier scripts and relies on Frontier Runtime and a program called Little Script Editor to do its work.

http://www.hotwired.com/userland/autowebhome.html

HomeMaker

HomeMaker, written by Bernie Dodge, is a nicely-done, freeware HyperCard stack that walks you through creating a home page. Bernie intends the stack not only for individuals, but also for organizations that want to provide members with a simple way to make a home page that includes some standard text and a link to a particular page at the organization's Web site. If you want to make a home page without using a lick of HTML, this stack could be exactly the tool you need.

http://edweb.sdsu.edu/edweb_folder/People/EDTEC_Students.html

HoTMetaL and HoTMetaL Pro

SoftQuad's $195 HoTMetaL Pro has the usual round of expected features, as well as support for tables, forms, macros, spell checking, and error checking. But you'll find it too hot to handle if you don't have six to eight megabytes of RAM for the program and another few megabytes of RAM kicking around so you can launch a Web browser at the same time. A number of early adapters of HoTMetaL Pro have expressed frustration at the quirky and un-Mac-like interface. Depending on what other programs do and how quickly SoftQuad improves its rough edges, HoTMetaL Pro could burn out by 1996 or become a major player. SoftQuad also has a freeware version of HoTMetaL Pro—called HoTMetaL, which is available for Windows and the Sun OS. There may be a freeware Mac version available by the time you read this book.

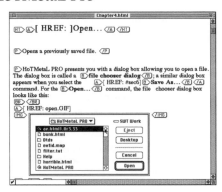

`http://www.sq.com/`

HTML Editor

HTML Editor, $25 shareware program from Rick Giles, has a few features for creating a set of related Web pages or creating forms, and it opens files as large as 200K. HTML Editor offers keyboard shortcuts for applying some tags, and a floating window for user-defined tags. It has helpful dialog boxes for setting up links to other URLs and to graphics; it lets you preview your work in a Web browser; and its Replace function supports GREP, (a sophisticated way to use a Replace command). HTML Editor's local, online documentation is minimal, but Rick has posted some documentation at HTML Editor's Web site. Power Mac users will want

to hold off on HTML Editor until Rick switches to a development system that generates PowerPC code; right now HTML Editor runs fairly slowly on Power Macs.

`http://dragon.acadiau.ca/~giles/HTML_Editor/Documentation.html`

HTML Pro

Niklas Frykholm's $5 HTML Pro stands out as a finalist in the contest for best shareware HTML editor. It offers two windows, one for showing your file with HTML tags, and another for showing what your HTML tags will look like in a browser, making it extremely easy to understand how inserting a tag changes the look of your page. You can edit the text and add tags in either window. HTML Pro converts special characters to their HTML entities on the fly, either as you open a file or as you type the characters.

HTML Web Weaver

HTML Web Weaver began as HTML SuperText, and its author, Robert Best, has rapidly expanded the program. Currently, HTML Web Weaver works best for existing short files (files must be under 32K) that need HTML tags added. On the more complex side of HTML coding, Web Weaver offers a Replace function and help with inserting tags for forms, but lacks features that help with creating and managing a group of related Web pages. Web Weaver stands out for its flexibility and helpful philosophical approach (including extensive and useful balloon help). HTML Web Weaver is shareware, and it costs $25 for most people; $14 for educational users.

http://www.potsdam.edu/Web.Weaver/About.html

NaviPress

NaviSoft has a commercial Web authoring program up its sleeve that should be available in mid-to-late 1995. The program, called NaviPress, is being ported to the Macintosh from its Windows version and will work best with NaviServer-equipped Web servers. NaviPress offers sophisticated authoring and site-creation tools, including WYSIWYG editing of local or online Web pages and the capability to create forms without knowing how forms work behind the scenes. NaviPress also offers a web-like overview of documents at a site.

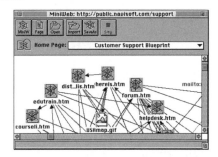

http://www.navisoft.com/tour/tour.html

WebDoor Publisher

WebDoor Publisher comes from Open Door Networks, an Internet provider in Oregon, that uses Apple Remote Access (ARA) connections (you can read more about ARA connections in chapter 18, "PPP"). I have a feeling other providers will copy the WebDoor Publisher idea soon, because it provides a customized HyperCard stack that enables you to make a simple home page even if you don't know any HTML at all. If you have a WebDoor account from Open Door Networks, you can then put your page on the Web simply by clicking the Publish button. WebDoor Publisher is not particularly flexible, but you can use a different program to further edit the text it creates. WebDoor Publisher is free to people who have WebDoor accounts; $25 shareware to everyone else.

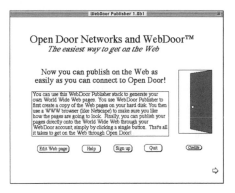

http://www.opendoor.com/webdoor/webdoor.html

Web Resources

The Internet is loaded with Web resources, and almost everything I know about the Web came from reading Web pages and participating in mailing lists. If you want to go further with the Web than just making a simple home page, I strongly recommend these resources, which I have found to be up-to-date and helpful.

The first resource is a family of four mailing lists about the Macintosh and the Internet. Two of the lists discuss Web-related topics:

- Apple-Internet-Authors list: A great place to talk about authoring software, authoring techniques, and other issues.

- Apple-Internet-Providers: This is the list where you can ask about forms, CGI scripts, Web server software, server hardware, and so on.

The home page for the lists explains how to sign up and acts as a jumping off point for exploration of other Web-based resources:

```
http://abs.apple.com/apple-internet/
```

If your Web interests concern more than the Macintosh, you might try the HTML Authoring Mailing List, which discusses issues related to HTML coding and Web serving, on most any platform you can imagine. If you ask a question, be sure to indicate for what operating system you want the answer. To subscribe, send email to **listserv@netcentral.net**, and put the following command in the body of your message: **SUBSCRIBE html-list** *your name*. Put your real name in the message.

For help setting up MacHTTP as a Web server and for writing CGI scripts to run forms, I cannot say nice enough things about Jon Wiederspan's online tutorial.

```
http://www.uwtc.washington.edu/Computing/WWW/CreatingASite.html
```

HTML for Fun and Profit

Well, I hope that this chapter has given you the information you need to start authoring your own Web pages. As much as the programs that hide the HTML from you are starting to appear, I do recommend that you spend some time learning how HTML works. It's a surprisingly flexible language, and when HTML 3.0 is finalized, it will become all the more flexible. The programs that handle HTML behind the scenes will become even more necessary then, but at the same time, if they make mistakes or don't include all the tagging options that you want, you'll need to know how to correct the mistakes or modify the codes manually.

This ends our journey into the world of HTML. The next chapter, "Utilities & Miscellany," covers a veritable menagerie of miscellaneous MacTCP programs.

Utilities & Miscellany

Okay, I admit it; I've run into a completely ambiguous group of software that isn't really related in any way. You'll find discussions and capsule reviews in this chapter about programs like NCSA Telnet, MacWAIS, Bolo, CU-SeeMe, Maven, Archie, Finger, Talk, ircle, Homer, and a number of others. These programs do a variety of things, but most are one-trick ponies, so I've decided to lump them all together in this chapter. Within the chapter, I try to create some sections for related programs. First, I look at Telnet programs and then WAIS clients, both of which would have been full chapters in years before the Web. Then I lapse into the looser categories, including Games, Information Finders, Real-Time Communication, and Tools.

However, before I get to any of that, I want to look in some detail at a very important program that doesn't fit into even any of these loose categories, the public domain Internet Config.

Internet Config

The Internet has a problem. There are simply too many details for anyone who doesn't spend all day using the Internet to remember. Pop quiz! What's your SMTP server? What's your NNTP server? The URL for your home page?

Sorry about that. I even promised early on that there wouldn't be any quizzes, but the point I want to make is that there are many pieces of information that not all of us necessarily remember, and there's nothing worse than trying to configure a new program and not remembering the name of your SMTP server or something equally mundane. And besides, it's a pain to type the same information into each program.

A new program from Peter Lewis and Quinn "The Eskimo!" has started to solve this problem and will continue to cement the Macintosh's position as the preeminent Internet client platform. Internet Config stores all your common Internet preferences in a single place, simplifying the process of configuring MacTCP-based programs with information such as your preferred email address, FTP helper application, and helper applications. Before Internet Config, configuring all the programs with the same information was almost as bad as going to multiple doctors to have health care committed on you, given that each doctor asks for the same information on a different forms.

Internet Config provides a simple interface for setting these preferences and makes a database of those preferences available to other applications. In other words, after you enter your email address into Internet Config, both Anarchie and NewsWatcher can read it from the Internet Config database, and do not force you to enter it again and again. This capability is so useful that I've included Internet Config on the ISKM disk.

Internet Config manages the following groups of preferences:

- Personal: such as your real name and your signature
- Email: email address and other mail related details
- News: news server and related details
- File Transfer: download folder and preferred archive sites
- Other Services: default hosts for other services, like Web and Gopher
- Fonts: preferred font settings for lists, screen, and printer
- File Types: for mapping extensions to Macintosh file types
- Helpers: for mapping URLs to their helper applications

Internet programs must support Internet Config—there's no way for them to know about the preferences database otherwise. Luckily, the Internet Config development mailing list included most of the Macintosh Internet developers, and many of them have committed to supporting Internet Config in future versions of their programs. Programs that support Internet Config now include Peter Lewis's Register 1.1, NewsWatcher 2.0b24, NewsHopper 1.1, and Anarchie 1.5 (the last two of which rely entirely on Internet Config). Applications slated to support Internet Config in the future include InterCon's TCP/Connect II, Aladdin's StuffIt family, and NCSA Telnet.

Keep in mind that Internet Config is there to help you, not to make your life miserable. You do not have to fill in every preference immediately, or even at all.

Installation & Setup

When you launch Internet Config for the first time, it asks if you would like to install its Internet Config Extension. You should do so, and you don't even have to restart (it's not that sort of extension—it's actually a shared library). If you accidentally click Cancel, you can always choose Install Extension from Internet Config's Extension menu later on.

Basic Usage

After installing the Internet Config Extension, Internet Config brings up its main window, the Internet Preferences window (see figure 27.1). It has large buttons for each of the eight groups of preferences.

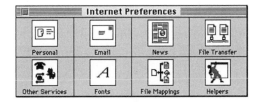

Figure 27.1   *Internet Config main window.*

First, click the Personal button to bring up the Personal window (see figure 27.2).

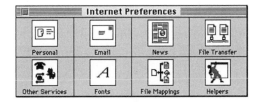

Figure 27.2   *Internet Config Personal window.*

In the Personal window, enter your real name, your organization (Peter and Quinn use the Australian spelling, of course), the string you want to use for quoting replies, and your signature and plan file. Your plan could be used by a Finger server, for instance, should a future Finger server support Internet Config.

Close the Personal window, and click the second button, Email. Internet Config brings up the Email window (see figure 27.3).

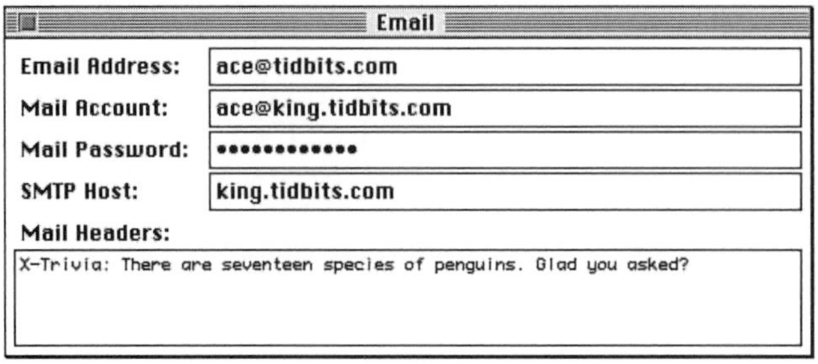

Figure 27.3   *Internet Config Email window.*

Enter your email address in the field of the same name, and enter your POP account in the Mail Account field. (Internet Config doesn't label the field POP Account because you might use IMAP or another mail protocol.) Type your password in the Mail Password field and note that Internet Config protects it from prying eyes. Your SMTP server's name goes in the SMTP Host field. Finally, if you need to include any extra headers in email sent via NewsWatcher, enter them in the Mail Headers field. Be very careful here since you could screw up your email fairly seriously if you don't know what you're doing.

When you're done, close the Email window and click the News button to bring up the News window (see figure 27.4).

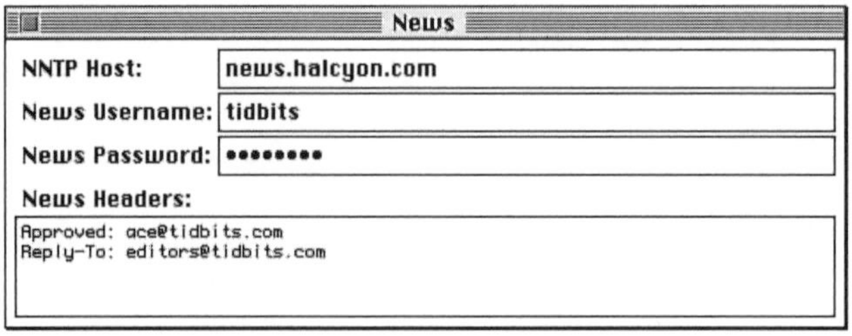

Figure 27.4   *Internet Config News window.*

Just as in the Email window, enter your NNTP host name. Although many providers don't require them at all, your news username and password are usually the same as your email userid and password. But this is not always the case—you can see that mine are different because I read news on my provider's Unix machine, but run my own mail server on a Mac. Again, if you want to add some headers to your news postings, enter them in the News Headers field. Don't mess with the headers too much unless you know what you're doing—I'm not entirely sure how well various news programs handle random headers. Close the News window.

Next up is the File Transfer window, which you get to by clicking the File Transfer button (see figure 27.5).

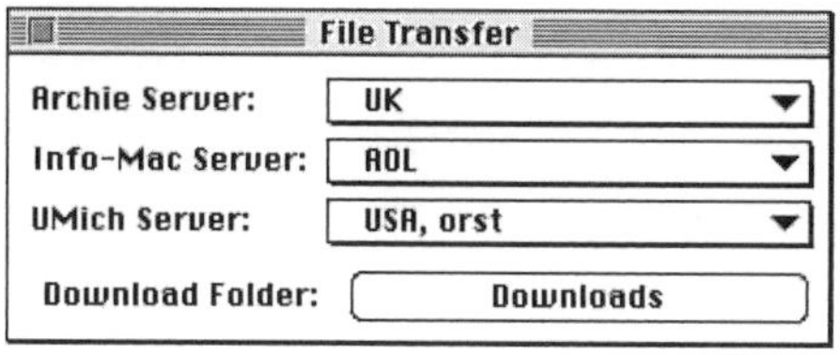

Figure 27.5   *Internet Config File Transfer window.*

The settings in the File Transfer window are used by programs like Anarchie to transfer files. As with the Mail Account setting, Internet Config doesn't assume much, so any program that transfers files could use the settings in the File Transfer window, whether or not it specifically used FTP.

The Archie server pop-up menu lists all the known Archie servers when Peter and Quinn shipped Internet Config. Pick the one you want Anarchie to use as the default—I have the best luck with the one in the United Kingdom for some reason.

The next two pop-up menus, for the Info-Mac Server and the UMich Server, refer to the major Macintosh mirror networks of FTP sites. There are numerous possible mirrors that you can choose from, and again, these are the mirrors that Anarchie uses by default.

Note

If you copy the pathname of a file from an Info-Mac Digest, it starts with /info-mac/. Anarchie recognizes that string, and when you paste the path into Anarchie's Get via FTP window, Anarchie uses your Info-Mac mirror default setting to fill in the name of the host to use with that path. It's extremely handy.

You can pick whichever Info-Mac and UMich mirror sites that you prefer, or you can enter new ones. I currently like the mirror that America Online provides for the Internet because I can always get in to snag a file.

Finally in this window, click the Download Folder button. Internet Config brings up a Standard File Dialog where you choose a folder for your downloads to end up in by default. I personally dump everything in a folder called "Downloads" that lives on my desktop. Close the File Transfer window.

Next, click the Other Services button to bring up the Other Services window (see figure 27.6).

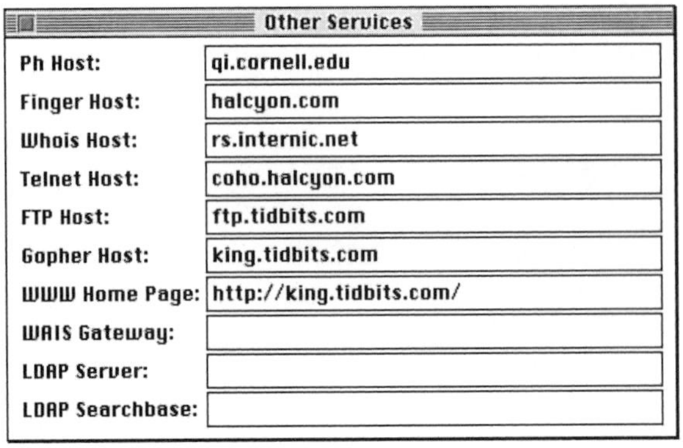

Other Services	
Ph Host:	qi.cornell.edu
Finger Host:	halcyon.com
Whois Host:	rs.internic.net
Telnet Host:	coho.halcyon.com
FTP Host:	ftp.tidbits.com
Gopher Host:	king.tidbits.com
WWW Home Page:	http://king.tidbits.com/
WAIS Gateway:	
LDAP Server:	
LDAP Searchbase:	

Figure 27.6   *Internet Config Other Services window.*

In this window, you have lots of fields for lots of different server names and gateways and home pages and all that. My advice? Don't worry about anything you don't understand. For instance, I haven't a clue what LDAP Server I could use or what LDAP Searchbase I could put into that field, so I just left them blank. No harm done, and nothing in this window is necessary. In the future, some programs may rely on information that you would enter here, but for the moment, just fill in what you know.

When you're done, close the Other Services window, and click the Fonts button to bring up the Fonts window (see figure 27.7).

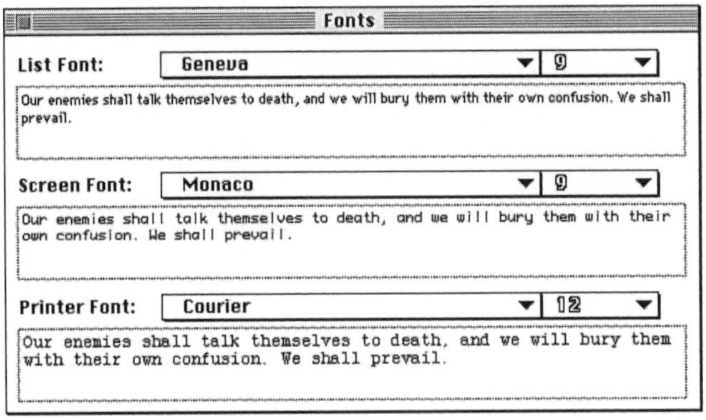

Figure 27.7   *Internet Config Fonts window.*

In the Fonts window, Internet Config provides three possible default font settings. Anarchie does use them, so if you use Anarchie, you may want to set the default list font to something relatively small so you can fit a lot of files into its windows. Or, if your eyes don't like small text, increase all three settings. In theory, the List Font is used for lists, such as Anarchie's windows or NewsWatcher's article listings. The Screen Font is used for displaying large chunks of non-proportional text, such as in a NewsHopper article, and the Printer Font is used for printing that same text.

Close the Fonts window, and you're done! There are two more buttons, File Mappings and Helpers, but frankly, you don't have to mess with them if you don't want to. In pursuit of completeness, let's look at them anyway. Click on File Mappings so that Internet Config brings up the large scrolling window of file mappings (see figure 27.8). Next, double-click on one of the mappings, such as the Acrobat entry.

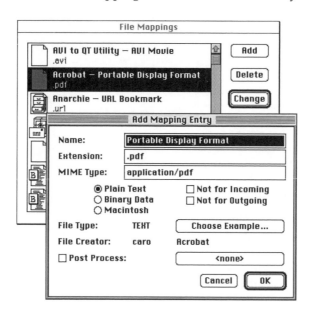

Figure 27.8   *Internet Config File Mappings window.*

File mappings are one of Internet Config's most useful features because it's a pain for every program to provide an interface to them. Basically, programs can use the file mappings to look at a file's extension, **.pdf** in the screen shot, and know that the file is a PDF file and belongs to Adobe Acrobat. File mappings are a manual method of doing for files from the Internet what the Macintosh does behind the scenes with file types in the desktop database. You can add file mappings if you like, although most of the common ones are already entered. More commonly, you may want to change some of them to use your favorite text editor instead of BBEdit or SimpleText, for instance.

Enough of the File Mappings, since you really don't have to mess with them. Close the File Mappings window and click the Helpers button to open Internet Config's last window (see figure 27.9). Internet Config has defined a number of types of tasks that you may want to use a helper application with, and it has set up some default entries. The main one you're likely to change is the editor entry because everyone has a favorite editor.

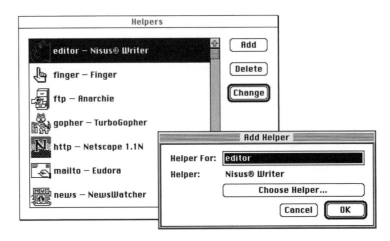

Figure 27.9   *Internet Config Helpers window.*

I have mine set to Nisus Writer—changing it is merely a matter of clicking the Choose Helper button and finding the program on your hard disk.

The utility of the Helpers preferences is that it provides a single place for you to say that whenever any Internet Config-aware program tries to do something via FTP, it can pass off the task to Anarchie. Or, more commonly, whenever there's a file to be edited, it can pass off the task to your editor of choice. You can add new tasks as well, although there's no point unless some new application comes out and needs a different type of helper that's not currently defined.

Well, that's about it. Close the Helpers window and quit Internet Config, saving any changes you might have made. You're unlikely to use Internet Config often—that's the point of it.

Evaluation & Details

Internet Config is a simple application, but it is well-written and easy to use. It has excellent balloon help and decent documentation. Other than the fussy details of creating new file mappings, I can't see most people having any trouble with Internet Config.

Although Internet Config has broad-based support already, support from additional programs is critical to its success. I strongly encourage all Internet programmers to support Internet Config. It's a relatively minor programming task. John Norstad (author of NewsWatcher and Disinfectant among others) said, "I figured this [Internet Config] would be reasonably easy to support, and it turned out to be even easier. There were no major problems or stumbling blocks—just a bunch of really easy code, and it worked with no major hassles." I'd especially like to see Eudora support Internet Config, since it's one of the most common Internet programs available and would send a powerful message to other Internet developers.

Peter and Quinn have placed Internet Config and its source code in the public domain, and they encourage others to build on it to provide additional functionality. Internet Config can play a huge role in making the Mac an even better Internet platform because it can make coherent the often confusing process of configuring many different programs.

The official support address for Internet Config is **internet- config@share.com**. If you find a bug in Internet Config, forward details to that address. To discuss Internet Config in general, the **comp.sys.mac.comm** newsgroup is the best place to do so, because it allows programmers to stay in touch with the discussions without being overwhelmed with email. Once again, kudos to Peter and Quinn for a job well done. You can retrieve the latest version of Internet Config, currently at 1.1, from all the main Internet FTP sites and from the URL below.

```
ftp://ftp.tidbits.com/pub/tidbits/tisk/tcp/
```

Telnet

I must confess up front to a certain bias against the next few programs that I talk about. This is not so much because they're bad programs—on the contrary, they're quite good— but because they provide access to standard shell accounts and ugly command-line interfaces, and I have a MacTCP-based connection and lots of great graphical software. Oh well, as Bill Watterson, creator of the Calvin and Hobbes comic strip, has said, "Scientific progress goes 'boink.'"

That's right, I'm talking about NCSA Telnet, Comet, TN3270, and the various Telnet tools, all of which let you travel back in time to the days when you couldn't do the sorts of things that I've talked about so far in this chapter.

NCSA Telnet

NCSA's best-known application is also their most recent—NCSA Mosaic—but NCSA Telnet comes from the same organization and is equally as much an essential part of your MacTCP toolkit. The latest version of NCSA Telnet is 2.6, although there's a 2.7b2 in testing right now.

Basic Usage

There isn't any configuration necessary for you to start using NCSA Telnet, but just like the Unix Telnet, there's not much to do with it unless you know where you're going. Telnet doesn't do anything on its own; it's merely a conduit to another program running on a remote machine.

After you launch NCSA Telnet, go to the File menu and choose Open Connection. NCSA Telnet opens a dialog box in which you enter the host to which you want to connect (if you must enter a port number, enter it here with a space separating it from the host name). There's also a pop-down menu for selecting a predefined host (see figure 27.10).

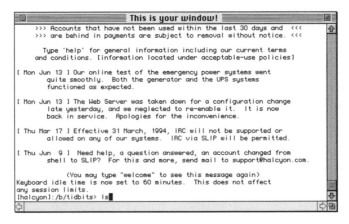

Figure 27.10   NCSA Telnet Open Connection dialog.

Don't worry about the FTP Session checkbox and the Authenticate and Encrypt options. They are only valid if you get additional software. If you don't want to provide a window name, that's no big deal, either. Click OK and NCSA Telnet opens a terminal window that enables you to log in to the machine you specified, in my case, my account on **halcyon.com** (see figure 27.11).

```
██████████████ This is your window! ██████████████
    >>> Accounts that have not been used within the last 30 days and   <<<
    >>> are behind in payments are subject to removal without notice.  <<<

        Type 'help' for general information including our current terms
     and conditions. [information located under acceptable-use policies]

[ Mon Jun 13 ] Our online test of the emergency power systems went
        quite smoothly.  Both the generator and the UPS systems
        functioned as expected.

[ Mon Jun 13 ] The Web Server was taken down for a configuration change
        late yesterday, and we neglected to re-enable it.  It is now
        back in service.  Apologies for the inconvenience.

[ Thu Mar 17 ] Effective 31 March, 1994, IRC will not be supported or
        allowed on any of our systems.  IRC via SLIP will be permitted.

[ Thu Jun  9 ] Need help, a question answered, an account changed from
        shell to SLIP?  For this and more, send mail to support@halcyon.com.

        (You may type "welcome" to see this message again)
Keyboard idle time is now set to 60 minutes.  This does not affect
any session limits.
[halcyon]:/b/tidbits> ls█
```

Figure 27.11   NCSA Telnet Terminal window.

Once you get to this point, you must play by the rules of the remote machine, which in this case involves using the basic Unix shell account. You could also have connected to an Archie server, to a MUD, to a library catalog, or any other resource that's available via Telnet.

Although NCSA Telnet certainly has plenty of other commands in its menus, on the whole, you shouldn't have to mess with them regularly. A number of them control how NCSA Telnet reacts to certain types of host machines; with others you can query the network; and various options enable you to determine how your terminal windows look and act. But at the base level, NCSA Telnet enables you, from your Mac, to access services that are limited to the command line.

I like the shortcut for accessing commonly used sites from the Open Connection dialog (you define those sites in the Session submenu from the Preferences menu in the Edit menu). Version 2.6 of NCSA Telnet added a hierarchical Open Special menu to the File menu—it provides even quicker access to the shortcuts that you've defined. What I'd really like, though, is to have NCSA Telnet remember the last 10 or so sites I've visited and provide instant access to them as well.

Special Features

I may have sounded terse in the preceding section, but NCSA Telnet does provide some extra neat features. I'm impressed by the capability to open multiple sessions to different sites or even to the same site. Switching between sites is as simple as clicking on another window.

If you regularly use one or more Telnet sessions, you can save Set documents that record the open sessions. Opening that document later automatically connects you to all of those sites.

One feature that I often find myself using is the Delete/Backspace toggle under the Session menu. Some sites interpret the Mac's Delete key differently, so if pressing the Delete key doesn't delete a character, try switching to Backspace (or vice versa, if the Backspace key is the problem) from the Session menu.

If you are running NCSA Telnet and you go to the File menu and select FTP Enable, NCSA Telnet turns your Mac into a simple FTP server. Be careful of this capability because it constitutes a possible security risk. Check your settings in the Preferences submenus carefully.

Finally, in a feature that exists only in the forthcoming Telnet 2.7, if you use Internet Config, you can Command-click on any URLs you may see in the course of your Telnet session, and NCSA Telnet passes the URL to the appropriate helper application.

Evaluation & Details

Although I'd like to pretend that you can avoid Telnet in general, that's not true, and thus NCSA Telnet is an essential part of your MacTCP software collection. For instance, there are some services which provide excellent information that you must access via Telnet.

In addition, there are times when it's handy to be able to go in and use Unix. As long as the PPP and SLIP accounts generally available are based on Unix, there will always be some reasons why you might want to log in via Telnet and use Unix. Perhaps you need to unlock a POP mailbox or want to move a file from one Unix host to another without bringing it to the Mac in between. Those tasks and various others require access to the Unix command-line, and Telnet provides that access.

NCSA Telnet is a public domain program, which means you can use it for free in any manner you want. You can retrieve NCSA Telnet from either of the following:

```
ftp://ftp.tidbits.com/pub/tidbits/tisk/tcp/
```

```
ftp://ftp.ncsa.uiuc.edu/Mac/Telnet/
```

Comet

Although not in as widespread use as NCSA Telnet, Cornell's Comet has many of the same features as NCSA Telnet, with a few added in. Comet offers a number of additional emulation modes, most notably 3270 (full screen IBM mode), and it provides access to various special keys via buttons on the screen. This is especially handy with 3270 sessions, since they require special keyboard mapping. If you click on the zoom box, rather than zooming the window, Comet minimizes it into an icon on your desktop, much the way Microsoft Windows applications behave. Although less useful for people using PPP or SLIP accounts, for people who must be logged in to a terminal session all day long, this is a great feature for getting Comet out of the way while keeping it easily accessible. Comet 3.1.1 is free from Cornell University.

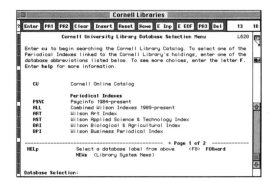

```
ftp://ftp.cit.cornell.edu/pub/mac/comm/CometExternal/
```

```
ftp://ftp.tidbits.com/pub/tidbits/tisk/tcp/
```

TN3270

NCSA Telnet cannot handle all the mainframe sites that you may want to explore. Some IBM mainframes use 3270 terminals, and without delving into the ugly details, let me say that if you want to telnet to one of these machines, you must use either Cornell's Comet or Brown University's free TN3270, which looks as though it were based on NCSA Telnet. TN3270 is similar to NCSA Telnet, but unfortunately, it doesn't appear that you can have multiple windows open with TN3270. You need both the main file for version 2.3d26 and the updated files from 2.4a4 for a complete package.

```
┌──────────────────────────────────────────┐
│          tn3270 for the Macintosh         │
│                                            │
│             by Peter DiCamillo             │
│                                            │
│  with NCSA TCP/IP Kernel for the Macintosh by Tim │
│  Krauskopf and Gaige B. Paulsen, and with tn3270  │
│  protocol by Greg Minshall.                │
│                                            │
│  Developed by Computing and Information Services at Brown University. │
│  Copyright © 1988-1993 by Brown University and by Peter DiCamillo.    │
│  NCSA Kernel Copyright © 1987-1988 by the Board of Trustees of the    │
│  University of Illinois; tn3270 Copyright © 1984-1988 by the Regents  │
│  of the University of California, and by Gregory Glenn Minshall.      │
│                                            │
│  2.4a4 MacTCP version April 28, 1993       │
│                                            │
│                            [  OK  ]        │
└──────────────────────────────────────────┘
```

ftp://ftp.tidbits.com/pub/tidbits/tisk/tcp/tn3270-23d26.hqx

ftp://ftp.tidbits.com/pub/tidbits/tisk/tcp/tn3270-24a4.hqx

Telnet CTB Tools

Several Communications Toolbox (CTB) tools for Telnet also exist. These tools should work with any CTB-aware communications application, such as the free Termy, MicroPhone II, SITcomm, or Communicate. I know of four main Telnet tools at the moment. MicroPhone Pro ships with one called the MP Telnet Tool; VersaTerm includes the VersaTerm Telnet Tool; Tim Endres has written a free one called TGE TCP Tool, and there's a demo of the TCPack Tool that AOL and eWorld use. There's not much to differentiate these tools because all they do is allow a CTB-aware terminal emulator to pretend to be a Telnet application. All provide methods of listing commonly accessed hosts—the most important user feature. I have had trouble with all of them, which may be the

fault of the various applications I was using, but I've had the best luck with the VersaTerm Telnet Tool. You can get the TGE TCP Tool, along with a demo of the TCPack Tool in:

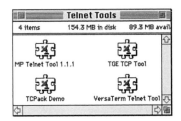

ftp://ftp.tidbits.com/pub/tidbits/tisk/ctb/

WAIS

Thinking Machines' WAIS has spawned a number of client applications for the Macintosh. However, with the rise of the World Wide Web as a front end to WAIS databases, the importance of the WAIS clients has significantly decreased. And in fact, none of the WAIS client programs have been updated since the second edition of this book came out in August of 1994. This tells me that there's simply not much interest in stand-alone WAIS clients, so I've reduced the discussion to a capsule review of the client that is still worthwhile, MacWAIS.

In addition to the old and ignored WAIS for Macintosh, I've run across three other specialized WAIS clients that run on the Macintosh—HyperWAIS, JFIFBrowser, and WAIS Picture Browser. However, none of these seem to have been used seriously, and they certainly haven't been updated in years. I don't recommend you bother even looking for them.

If you don't want to mess with a WAIS client at all, simply point your favorite Web browser at this URL:

```
http://www.wais.com/newhomepages/surf.html
```

Games

Many people enjoy using the Internet for relatively mundane things, but that's not to imply that there aren't plenty of downright fun things to do. Among them are the various games you can play, and although it's beyond the scope of this book to go into all the possibilities, I do want to mention the best of the MacTCP-based game client programs. There are a few, like a client for the Interactive Chess Server at **ics.onenet.net:5000** that simply don't work any more—to play chess you must resort to other methods. For chess, you might check out this Web page:

```
http://www.delorie.com/game-room/chess/
```

As usual, unless I provide an alternative URL, assume that you can find all of these programs in:

```
ftp://ftp.tidbits.com/pub/tidbits/tisk/util/
```

MacWAIS

MacWAIS provides a decent interface to WAIS sources, and it gives you easy ways to choose which sources to search, what terms you wish to search for, and ways of handling relevance feedback. Simply double-clicking on a document that MacWAIS returns displays it, and if it's large, MacWAIS has a Find command to help out. MacWAIS is a good, simple program that does its job well, but it could use some cleaning up, such as the capability to resize its main window. MacWAIS is $35 shareware from the EINet group of the Microelectronics and Computer Technology Corporation.

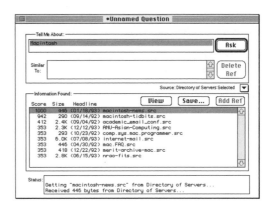

Part IV — Utilities & Miscellany

```
ftp://ftp.einet.net/einet/mac/
```

```
ftp://ftp.tidbits.com/pub/tidbits/tisk/tcp/
```

Bolo

Stuart Cheshire's $25 (or £15 if you're in the U.K.) shareware Bolo is an addictive multi-player tank game that supports robot opponents as well. Although it's not arcade-level action, Bolo is graphical. Strategy is all-important, and Bolo makes all sorts of alliances and rivalries possible. Numerous "brains" (specially programmed robot tanks) have been created to spice up the action. Along with the brains, people have written numerous utilities for Bolo, including terrain map generators and utilities for finding Bolo games in progress on the Internet. There's even a **rec.games.bolo** newsgroup, and the FAQ for that group is a good place to start learning about the basic rules of Bolo etiquette. Bolo prefers a fast connection (a 28.8 Kbps modem might work) and doesn't work well over 14.4 kbps PPP connections that I've tried. The program does work

over AppleTalk networks, if you want to play with friends locally. If you enjoy strategy tank games, definitely check out Bolo.

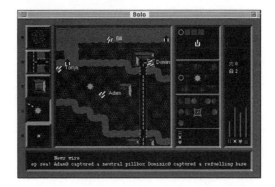

```
ftp://mirror.aol.com/pub/info-mac/game/bolo/
```

MacFIBS

Paul Ferguson's free MacFIBS is a dedicated backgammon client for FIBS, which stands for the First Internet Backgammon Server. FIBS has several thousand players registered, ranging widely in skill levels. Rather than just provide a slightly enhanced Telnet client, MacFIBS gives you a completely graphical interface to the Internet backgammon game, to the point where you make your moves by dragging little colored checkers around on the board. MacFIBS seems well-done and has rather thorough documentation.

MacMud

Mimir Reynisson's free MacMud is a Macintosh implementation of a MUD (which, as you may remember, stands for Multi-User Dungeon or Multi-User *Dimension*). From what I can see, MacMud is a definite instance of "If you have to ask, you won't understand it." I didn't understand it, even after reading the minimal documentation, but I gather that if you want to run your own MUD on a Macintosh permanently connected to the Internet, you can use MacMud, which is a port of the Unix LPMud program. One of the pieces of documentation is a description of MacMud's scripting language, but it too is fairly minimal.

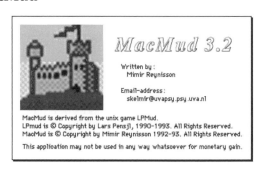

MacMUSH

Continuing on in the clients for MUD variants, we come to MacMUSH, a free program from Jens Johannsen. No, I can't tell you offhand what the differences are between MUDs, MUSHes, MOOs, or MUCKs, other than that they use different server programs. MacMUSH's special features include a simple macro facility for typing repetitive words or phrases (a common need, unfortunately), a simple line editor for creating text before sending it, and the capability to mark certain words, which might make it easy to see when certain people say things or when certain objects are used. Check out the MacMUSH home page below for a bunch of other MUD-related links.

http://imv.aau.dk/~jenswj/macmush.html

MUDDweller

The free MUDDweller 1.2, from O. Maquelin, is yet another dedicated MUD client program. MUDDweller enables you to connect either via the Communications Toolbox or via MacTCP. It has a few features that make it more useful than Telnet, such as being line-oriented (so you have an edit line to compose on before sending your command), a command history that you can use to avoid retyping commands, a logging capability, multiple sessions, and a simple file transfer tool.

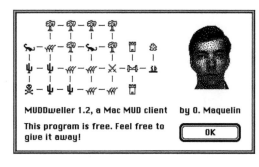

MUDDweller 1.2, a Mac MUD client   by O. Maquelin

This program is free. Feel free to give it away!

OK

`ftp://rudolf.ethz.ch/pub/mud/muddweller-12.hqx`

NetRPG

For those people who used to play role-playing games like TSR's lawyer-laden Dungeons® & Dragons™ but whose games disappeared with the departure of friends for college, check out Erich Bratton's $10 shareware NetRPG for a renewed fix. Based on the Chat server originally written by Peter Lewis and updated by Nathan Neulinger, NetRPG is essentially a server for easily running D&D-type games. Players connect via Telnet or through a more suitable program like MUDDweller, and the entire game takes place in text. Sounds like a lot of work to me, but then again, so are real-life role-playing games.

NetRPG © 1995 by Erich G Bratton
Parts by Nathan Neulinger and Peter N Lewis
Parts © by Symantec Corp (Think Pascal 4)

This program is shareware.
Please collect a few dollars from each of
the people you play with over the net, and
register using the included Register program.
erich@kagi.com

`ftp://ftp.tidbits.com/pub/tidbits/tisk/tcp/`

Information Finders

Next, we come to a loose category of programs that are dedicated to helping you find some specific piece of information, be it a file via Archie, the current time, the latest weather forecast, your mother, or perhaps merely the answer to the question of whether or not a friend is currently connected. Unless mentioned otherwise, these programs live in:

`ftp://ftp.tidbits.com/pub/tidbits/tisk/tcp/`

Finger

People with MacTCP-based access can use an elegant program from Peter Lewis, called Finger, which is an implementation of the Unix Finger program. It enables you to finger other people to see if they are logged on, or to read information they have put in their Plan files. I find Finger useful for accessing certain types of information over the Internet, checking to see what someone's userid on my local machine might be, and checking domain name information via Finger's support for Whois.

Basic Usage

After launching Finger, simply select Finger from the File menu (see figure 27.12).

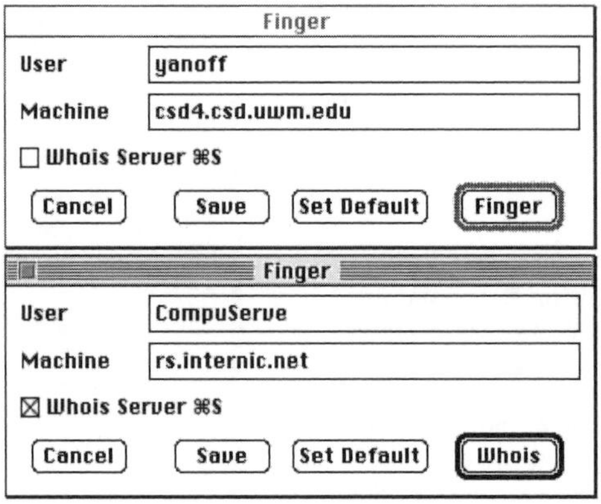

Figure 27.12   *Finger dialogs.*

Type the username you want to finger in the User text entry box, and below that type the machine name in the Machine entry box.

> **Note**
>
> *You can simply type the entire address in either one of the boxes, and it works just fine.*

If you want to access a Whois server (a different Unix program that looks up information about machines), check that box, enter the name of the machine you want to learn about in the User field, and enter **rs.internic.net** in the Machine field. Then click the Whois button to have Finger go out and execute your request. That's what I've done in the second window in figure 27.12.

Finger saves requests in a hierarchical Finger menu, and you can select an item such as **yanoff@csd4.csd.uwm.edu** to finger that address immediately (see figure 27.13).

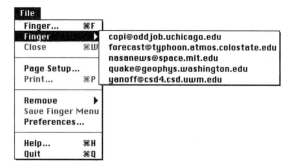

Figure 27.13 *Finger hierarchical menu.*

Now, assuming that the remote machine is up and running, you should see the results of the Finger search appear onscreen. You can print the results window or copy information from it, if you so choose. After you finger someone, you can save that entry in your Finger Preferences file by selecting Save Finger Menu from the File menu. That's how I created the list you see in figure 27.13, and it makes it easy to finger the same person or service at a later time.

Finger has only two options. If you choose Preferences from the File menu, you can decide whether you want to see the IP number (which is the number corresponding to the machine name) in the title bar of the Finger results window; or decide whether you want the Finger window to open on startup. (Using the Set Default button in the Finger window, you can choose which service or person should appear by default.) A third checkbox in the Preferences window lets you set whether or not you've paid your $10 shareware fee.

Evaluation & Details

I like Finger a lot. It's small, sweet, and to the point. As long as people continue to store useful bits of information in Plan files, Finger will remain an essential part of your MacTCP software kit. I haven't run into any problems with Finger, other than some sites not responding, but that's not Finger's fault. Sometimes a machine may be down, or the person updating the information may have gone on vacation. Finger is $10 shareware, payable in either U.S. or Australian dollars, and you find the latest version in:

```
ftp://ftp.tidbits.com/pub/tidbits/tisk/tcp/
```

Daemon

Peter Lewis's free Daemon program is a generalized server program that can provide services to the appropriate clients. Hmm, that doesn't make a lot of sense, does it? Basically, if you want to provide a Finger server, a Whois server (a variant of Finger that is generally less personal), an Ident server (fairly useless on a single-user Macintosh), and both a Daytime and an NTP (Network Time Protocol) server, Daemon is the program for you. Of course, any program like Daemon that is designed to provide information about you to others on the Internet all the time, is of dubious use if you have a SLIP or PPP account that isn't active all day long. Daemon is a background-only application, so there's no interface—you configure what it does through a Plan file.

Daemon

HyperFinger Pro

HyperFinger Pro is a HyperCard stack that provides a simple interface for regularly fingering the same addresses. You can click the Finger button to finger an arbitrary address, but if you want to finger the same address later on (and you're using a real version of HyperCard instead of HyperCard Player), you can modify the script for one of the eight specific buttons. That's about all there is to HyperFinger, although the Copy button places the contents of the scrolling window into the clipboard for pasting into another program. HyperFinger Pro was written by Frank Tito, and I suspect it's free, since he says in the background script's comments that he modified someone else's original stack.

Hytelnet

Hytelnet isn't a communications application at all. Instead, it's a HyperCard-based database of Telnet sites. The HyperCard front end uses a large set of cryptically named text files to present a menu interface to a large number of primarily character-based Internet resources. Hytelnet does offer descriptions of the specific sites when you finally work your way through the menus, and the program makes it easy to launch NCSA Telnet, TN3270, or TurboGopher to connect to the site in question. Hytelnet 6.7 was written by Peter Scott; Charles Burchill created the HyperCard front end, which requires HyperCard 2.1 or later.

ftp://ftp.usask.ca/pub/hytelnet/mac/

Mac Ph

The Ph protocol (which was created in part by Steve Dorner of Eudora fame) is in relatively wide use, especially at universities around the world, as an electronic campus directory system. It's excellent for looking up someone's email address or phone number, but you do have to know what university they attend or work for. The prolific John Norstad has created a free Macintosh client for the Ph protocol called Mac Ph. Of course, you can use Eudora to look up information via Ph, but John's stand-alone client is easier to use. If you choose the Northwestern Ph server, as I did, and then make sure your site list is updated (Update Site List in the File menu), Mac Ph brings in a huge list of sites running Ph. I could even find my Mom.

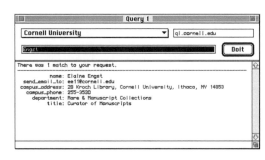

MacWeather

I'm extremely fond of Christopher Kidwell's $10 shareware MacWeather. You tell MacWeather what city you want to see the weather for, and it retrieves the current data for you, displaying it in either digital or analog form. MacWeather has preferences for each of the weather items it reports on, so you can have the temperature display in Fahrenheit or Celsius, the barometer display in inches of Hg, millimeters of Hg, or millibars, and the wind speed display in miles per hour, knots, or meters per second. You can also get the forecast, climatic data, or marine forecasts in a separate window. If you're constantly connected to the Internet from a room with no windows to the outside world, you can have MacWeather update automatically. I'd like to see a few minor enhancements, such as the capability to have more than one city onscreen at the same time,

and an easier way to switch between cities. But these are quibbles, and MacWeather is neat—highly recommended.

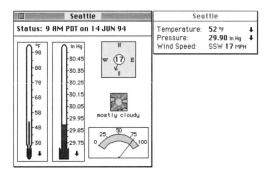

maX.500

The maX.500 program is a specialized client program for searching the X.500 Online Directory, which can be thought of as a world-wide distributed electronic telephone book. X.500 stores information about people, organizations, groups of people, documents, and services, and maX.500 provides an interface for searching that information. Unfortunately, as promising as X.500 sounds, there doesn't seem to be all that much information actually available in it, which makes it somewhat a hit or miss in terms of finding anyone. Still, it might be worth a look if you're really trying to find someone on the Internet.

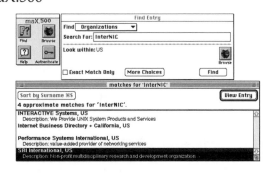

ftp://terminator.rs.itd.umich.edu/x500/max500/

Network Time

I'm no longer as retentive about time as I used to be, but it's still nice to know whether your VCR is accurate when taping TV shows. That's why I like Network Time, a $5 shareware control panel from Pete Resnick. Network Time synchronizes your Mac's clock with a *network time server*, which is a program running on an Internet machine that talks to other time servers. A number of hops on down, one of the machines gets its time from an atomic clock. To manually set your clock, open the Network Time control panel, enter the IP name of your network time server (ask your Internet provider, or guess at one of the machines run by your provider), and click the Set Time button. For automatic updating, drop Network Time in your Control Panels folder, making sure to set it to "Wait for MacTCP" if you use PPP or SLIP. Network Time has some elegant touches, such as a

note about the last time it set your clock, and excellent balloon help. Network Time is definitely the way to go for people wanting to synchronize clocks.

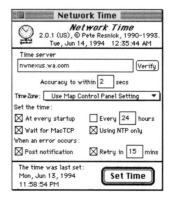

```
ftp://ftp.tidbits.com/pub/tidbits/tisk/tcp/network-time.hqx
```

Real-Time Communication

One of the best features of the Internet is that you can communicate with other people in distant lands without worrying about time zone problems or language problems beyond a basic grasp of written English. However, the Internet doesn't prevent real-time conversations—they're simply a bit less common. As popular as IRC (Internet Relay Chat) may be, it doesn't hold a candle to the amount of email or Usenet news generated on the Internet. In addition, many people generally find IRC to be a waste of time. Although there's no inherent reason for it to be one, the conversations due tend toward the sophomoric. For some logs of famous IRC times (such as during the 1994 California earthquake, the Gulf War, the 1992 Russian Revolution, along with the IRC FAQ (Frequently Asked Question) list, check out this Web page:

```
http://sunsite.unc.edu/dbarberi/chats.html
```

Typing to strangers may not be your cup of tea, though, and more recent programs have brought sound and video to real-time Internet communications, most notably via NetPhone and CU-SeeMe. These programs prefer fast connections and usually require some additional hardware, such as a microphone or a video camera.

Once again, unless I mention otherwise, these programs are all available in:

```
ftp://ftp.tidbits.com/pub/tidbits/tisk/tcp/
```

Talk

Talk, yet another useful little program from Peter Lewis, implements the Unix talk protocol on the Mac, providing a decent Macintosh interface in the process. I've taken to using Talk all the time, not to chat with strangers on the Internet, but so Tonya and I can communicate small bits of information that aren't really worth a full interruption. It's also great for telling someone something while they're talking on the phone.

Basic Usage

After you launch it, choose Talk from the File menu. Talk presents you with a small dialog box that looks almost exactly like Finger's dialog box. You can type a username and a machine name in the two fields provided. When you click the Talk button, Talk adds that person to your Status window, which lists all of your current connections and his status (see figure 27.14).

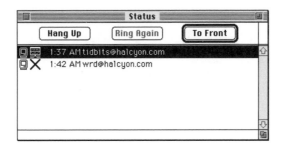

Figure 27.14   Talk Status window.

At this point, Talk notifies your friend to alert him to your talk request. After your party makes the connection, Talk opens a two-paned window for you to type in and be typed at (see figure 27.15).

You type in the bottom pane and your friend types in the top pane. (Since I had to fake figure 27.15 because Tonya was out when I was writing this, I'm actually talking to myself on my Unix shell account.)

Like Finger, Talk enables you to save a hierarchical menu of the people you commonly talk to, and the interface is uncluttered and simple. My main complaint is that Talk could use a more obvious interface for telling you what it's doing when you're attempting to connect with someone. Tonya and I often end up trying too many times because we can't tell that it's actually taking the other person an extra few seconds to switch into Talk and answer the call.

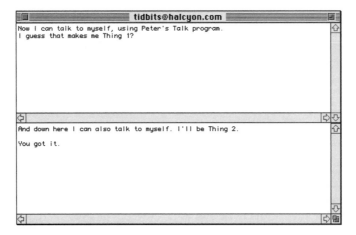

Figure 27.15   *Talk window.*

Evaluation & Details

If you have a use for Talk, it's worthwhile. Talk comes with a background application called Talkd, which simply receives requests to talk from others. Talk is $5 shareware from Peter Lewis, and you can retrieve the latest version of Talk from:

```
ftp://ftp.tidbits.com/pub/tidbits/tisk/tcp/
```

Chat

Whereas Talk enables you to talk directly with another person, and Homer (discussed later) enables you to talk with multiple people on Internet Relay Chat, Chat 2.0.3 acts as a Chat Server, much like IRC itself. It's limited in comparison to IRC, so unless you have a specific use in mind, it may make more sense to use Homer and a private channel on IRC than it does to attempt to run your own Chat Server. Chat was originally created by the ubiquitous Peter Lewis. It was significantly updated by Nathan Neulinger, who has made it shareware and charges $10.

Co-motion Lite for Internet

Chatting is all fine and nice, but what about when you really need to do some brainstorming? That's when you need a commercial application from Bittco Solutions called Co-motion Lite for Internet, which is a network brainstorming application that works over the Internet. Other versions, including a fully featured version called Co-motion, work over AppleTalk networks. Co-motion Lite for Internet was designed to encourage collaboration and idea generation among a group of people, and it includes tools for annotating and evaluating ideas, as well as tools for printing a variety of reports about what was discussed during a session. Co-motion Lite for Internet isn't one of those applications that you'll pick up immediately, but if it helps you avoid plane trips, it will be well worth every penny. The program is commercial, but has massive discounts that range from $1.50 to $15 per copy. Contact Bittco Solutions at bittco@ccinet.**ab.ca** or call 800-265-2726;

403-922-5514; 403-922-2859 (fax). For a demo, try checking out Bittco's Keen Minds package, which is based on Co-motion Lite for Internet, but it is specifically designed to work with online meetings Bittco holds every now and then.

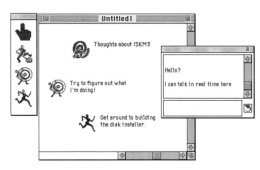

Part IV — Utilities & Miscellany

CU-SeeMe

Cornell University's free CU-SeeMe (primarily written by Tim Dorcey) provides videoconferencing over the Internet. Nothing more, nothing less, but if you've seen the prices for some of the videoconferencing software available, you realize what an incredible accomplishment this program is. To use CU-SeeMe to receive video, you need a MacTCP-based Internet connection, the faster the better. If you want to send video as well, you must have a video camera and a video-capable Mac, such as a 660AV, a video-input card, or a Connectix QuickCam. And of course, audio requires a microphone. You can use CU-SeeMe in either point-to-point mode with another person or in broadcast mode with a CU-SeeMe reflector, which enables you to view up to eight windows simultaneously. I often use 132.236.91.204, which is one of Cornell's reflectors. CU-SeeMe works its magic by

only transmitting information that has changed in the image—that significantly reduces the amount of data it must pump over the Internet. CU-SeeMe is free for both the Mac and the PC, although the Mac version is well ahead of the PC one.

ftp://gated.cornell.edu/pub/video/

http://cu-seeme.cornell.edu/

Homer

Homer is the killer app for Internet Relay Chat (IRC). It enables you to participate in worldwide Internet chats from the comfort of your Mac. Homer has a colorful and unique interface that makes using IRC significantly easier because it simplifies switching channels, keeping multiple discussions going, giving and taking operator privileges, and much more. In recent releases of the $25 shareware Homer, creator Toby Smith added support for Apple's PlainTalk technology, so Homer can speak all or some of what goes on in your IRC discussion. With the addition of Face resources, it can even display a picture of the people with whom you're typing.

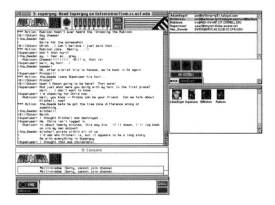

ircle

Olaf Titz's free ircle 2.0f2 takes a more traditional approach to IRC than does Homer, although it has some nice features such as user-definable shortcuts for common phrases, the capability of capturing a conversation to a file, and font and size control. The most recent version adds color support and sound support, and can even speak incoming text, much like Homer. Considering that Homer seems to have been ignored for some time, ircle may well be worth checking out if you use IRC much at all.

Maven

Along with Cornell's CU-SeeMe, Maven, from the University of Illinois at Urbana, goes a long way toward turning the Internet into a general-purpose communication medium. Where CU-SeeMe provides video (and has audio support using Maven's code), Maven provides only audio. In some respects this seems silly, since a telephone does exactly the same thing, and generally for less money, but with the costs of international phone calls, I could see programs such as Maven becoming all too popular (in fact, they might seriously overload the networks). When I last tried Maven, it didn't work over dialup connections, but the Maven code in CU-SeeMe definitely works over faster dedicated connections and sort of over a 28.8 Kbps PPP connection. Maven was written by Charley Kline, and may be freely redistributed.

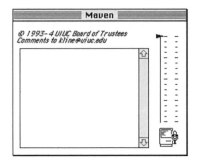

Meeting Space

The idea of an online virtual environment is powerful, and a small company called World Benders has brought it to the Macintosh world. Don't think of MUDs as games; think of them as online spaces—places where you can do things and interact with other people. That's the idea behind Meeting Space, and it's one that becomes especially attractive when paired with a simple Macintosh interface. There's no need to type commands or to know how to pro-gram—in Meeting Space almost everything is in plain view. Although World Benders could have supported sound and video, they stuck to text to reduce the network traffic (Meeting Space works well over both AppleTalk and TCP/IP, even slow PPP or SLIP connections) and hardware requirements. Creating new places and objects in Meeting Space is simple, and moving among places and working with objects is equally simple. For pricing details and more information, contact World Benders at **wb-info@worldbenders.com**, or call 603/881-5432 (voice & fax).

Part IV

Utilities & Miscellany

NetPhone

Where Maven pioneered, NetPhone has colonized. NetPhone is a commercial application from Andrew Green of Electric Magic. NetPhone costs $59 for one copy or $99 for a pair, but it can pay for itself pretty easily if you're racking up massive international telephone bills, in large part because NetPhone does work over a 14.4 Kbps modem connection via PPP or SLIP (although you do need to know the other person's IP number to connect). NetPhone also works with pretty much any Macintosh from the IIsi on up, although it does work better on the faster Macs because of all the processing that goes on. In my testing, NetPhone performed admirably, although the sound quality wasn't good enough that I'd use it in favor of a local phone call. NetPhone comes with a small application called NetPhone Alert that alerts when someone is trying to call you with NetPhone.

You can try out a demo of NetPhone before buying—it doesn't include NetPhone Alert and is limited to 90 second outgoing calls, although you can use it to receive calls of any length.

http://www.emagic.com/

Tools

All of these applications are fine and nice, but what if they don't quite do what you want? What if you want to provide a custom Internet service that alerts the user whenever traffic gets really bad in a certain part of town, or some other unique use? Your best chance, short of becoming a talented MacTCP programmer, is the TCP/IP Scripting Addition. But other tools exist out there, such as Peter Lewis's unusual Script Daemon, which enables you to Telnet to a Macintosh and issue commands in the form of pre-written AppleScripts. Or, perhaps most importantly, you might need to control a Macintosh over the Internet, and for that, Farallon's Timbuktu Pro is just what you need. So read on, and see if any of these tools might fill a need that you've got.

Timbuktu Pro

If you need to control a Macintosh Internet server, or if you need to help Mac users in your organization, you need Farallon's Timbuktu Pro remote-control application for use over both AppleTalk and the Internet. Timbuktu enables you to observe or control a remote Macintosh, and you can also exchange files with the remote Mac. Timbuktu Pro has worked well for the time I've spent administrating an SE/30-based Gopher server. The Macintosh lives elsewhere, but it's directly connected to the Internet, and I can check in any time with Timbuktu Pro. Although Timbuktu Pro's speed is impressive, it's still slower than normally using a Mac. However, programs run at full speed on the host Mac—the only slowdown is in screen redraw. Mail order prices seem to run at approximately $140 for one user, and you can contact Farallon at **info@farallon.com** or call

510-814-5000; 510-814-5023 (fax). There's a free trial version that works for a week on three Macs, and there's more information on Farallon's Web site.

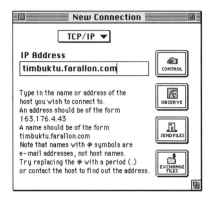

ftp://ftp.farallon.com/pub/farallon.products/timbuktu.products/freeversions/

http://www.farallon.com/

TCP/IP Scripting Addition

I've muttered about AppleScript here and there in this book, but always in the context of being able to script a program. With the release of the TCP/IP Scripting Addition from Atul Butte, however, those of you who are fluent in AppleScript can create entire Internet applications without leaving AppleScript. Since, for most people, AppleScript is an easier programming environment than something such as C or Pascal, I'm curious to see to what purposes people put the TCP/IP Scripting Addition. It comes with some impressive sounding sample applications, including an application on which you can drop a file to have it uploaded via FTP, a simple Finger

implementation, a script that displays the weather in Washington, DC (in case you're concerned about the political climate), a script that can send email, and finally a full Gopher server. The TCP/IP Scripting Addition is free for personal use, and if you plan to distribute a free program based on it, it's probably also free. For anything written to support an organization or for sale purposes, there are various charges.

TCP/IP Scripting Addition

ftp://gaea.kgs.ukans.edu/applescript/osaxen/

ftp://ftp.tidbits.com/pub/tidbits/tisk/util/

Script Daemon

Script Daemon is yet another tiny background application from Peter Lewis. It enables you to telnet to your Macintosh from another machine and enter AppleScript commands. Needless to say, it requires MacTCP, System 7 or later, AppleScript, and only allows the owner (using the Owner name and password) to log in (mostly for security reasons, I suspect). Peter states up front that Script Daemon is rather rough, which is one reason he released it for free and without many features. He's waiting to see how people attempt to use it and what questions and suggestions they have, before he spends any more time on it. Script Daemon only makes much sense if you have a permanent connection to the Internet. Still, being able to telnet to a Macintosh and then enter AppleScript commands and run AppleScript scripts is a neat idea, so if you can imagine how you would use this, check out Script Daemon.

Script Daemon

Part IV

Utilities & Miscellany

`ftp://ftp.tidbits.com/pub/tidbits/tisk/tcp/`

Concluding the Cacophony

I think you'll agree after skimming through this chapter (you didn't read every word, did you?) that there are a ton of miscellaneous Internet programs out there, and that's only for the Macintosh. But that's good! The more programs that are available, the more choices you have and the more likely you are to find one that does precisely what *you* want. We all use the Internet for different purposes, and I'm sure that you will find some of the programs I've discussed in this chapter useful. I personally use Internet Config, Finger, Talk, and MacWeather constantly, and there are certainly plenty of others that I could imagine using in different situations. Let your imagination guide you to applications that you can use.

Okay, it's time to buckle down and look at some serious programs, the heavy duty integrated Internet programs from Synergy and InterCon Systems.

Chapter

28

Integrated Programs

Perhaps one of the most requested programs has been an integrated program for accessing all of the Internet services. In fact, two integrated programs on the Mac already exist. InterCon's TCP/Connect II and Synergy's VersaTerm-Link both do a good job in this area, and that's my first answer to those seeking an integrated Internet program. There's also MicroPhone Pro 2.0 from Software Ventures, which sort of fits into this category, based not so much on what it can do as on what's bundled with it. More on these programs in a bit.

My second answer to those seeking an integrated program is itself a question. Why would you want an integrated Internet program? That's like wanting an integrated Macintosh program that subsumes all the functions of the programs that you have on your Mac. A program that could concurrently play Maelstrom (a fabulous Asteroids-like shareware game available on the nets), edit word-processing documents, and check your disk for viruses sounds a little ludicrous, doesn't it?

Similarly, there are simply too many Internet services that have nothing in common—just as it makes no sense to combine Maelstrom with Disinfectant, nor does it make sense to combine CU-SeeMe and Gopher. They're simply different programs, and an interface that works for video does nothing for navigating a menu-based Gopher interface.

Integrated programs are always notable by what features they don't support. Internet integrated programs are no exception, and there will always be something they don't do, be it the Web, CU-SeeMe-like video, or something new.

Finally, we're entering the age of software components. With Apple's OpenDoc and Microsoft's OLE, it will become possible to write tightly focused components that do one thing and do it well. In an ideal world, you'll be able to assemble modules from different vendors (the small programmer will theoretically once again be able to compete with the software monoliths currently dominating the market) to create a customized Internet tool that does exactly what you want and no more. Adding features will be as simple as adding a new module, and you won't pay for features you never use.

Enough pontificating—the commercial integrated Internet applications do a good job and are ideal for some people. The following discussion should help you decide if you're one of those people.

I don't go into the details of how to configure TCP/Connect II or VersaTerm-Link because they both come with decent manuals, and I'm more interested in giving you information to help you decide if you need to buy one of them.

TCP/Connect II

TCP/Connect II comes from InterCon, the company that made InterSLIP freely available to the Internet community. TCP/Connect II is a package of TCP-based programs that work equally well on dedicated Internet connections, via PPP or SLIP, via the Communications Toolbox, or even via a dedicated serial port driver for use over a standard modem to a Unix shell account. TCP/Connect II comes in five flavors: Remote, Basic, 3270, VT, and Extended. Each offers different set features and different list prices, ranging from $195 to $495. Unfortunately, only the most expensive Extended edition includes all of the various Internet features that I discuss below.

To confuse matters, InterCon has released a number of variants on the standard TCP/Connect II package, such as TCP/Connect II Remote, which doesn't use MacTCP, limiting users to just the TCP/Connect II modules. InterCon has announced, but not yet shipped, three additional products, NetShark (which sounds like a renamed TCP/Connect II), MailShark (which may be the email module of TCP/Connect II), and WebShark (which is probably the Web module from TCP/Connect II). I don't fault InterCon for attempting to fill as many niches as possible, but it does become difficult to track.

TCP/Connect II doesn't come with a separate implementation of SLIP or PPP, but it includes support for both internally. This means that if you only have TCP/Connect II and you connect via its PPP or SLIP, you cannot use Anarchie or Netscape or any other separate program. However, TCP/Connect II works fine with MacPPP and InterSLIP, so there's no need to use its internal PPP or SLIP capabilities if you don't want to.

Email

In terms of email, TCP/Connect provides all the basic features with a few interesting twists that those who receive a lot of email can especially appreciate. You can modify the order and size of each of the panels at the top of each mailbox window like "demo's in box" shown in figure 28.1, so the From, Date, and Subject fields can all be customized to your taste. An icon to the left of each message indicates its status, and the icons at the top of the windows provide access to common commands.

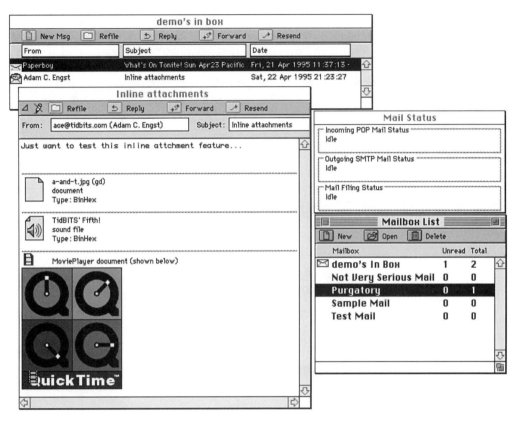

Figure 28.1   *TCP/Connect II email windows.*

Like Eudora and VersaTerm-Link, TCP/Connect II can operate in offline mode, so messages you send don't go out until you do connect. However, you must make sure to change the Network options from MacTCP to None in the Configuration panel; otherwise, TCP/Connect II assumes it is connected to a network. Luckily, if you use TCP/Connect II's internal SLIP or PPP capabilities, InterCon has an unsupported Remote Networking Enabler that simplifies the process of connecting and disconnecting. There is no Send Mail command for messages that you've queued—TCP/Connect II sends them sometime after you've reconnected to your network and reconfigured it from within TCP/Connect II. You can see what TCP/Connect thinks is happening by looking at the Mail Status window.

You can move mail among multiple mailboxes, either via the Refile button at the top of the mailbox and message windows, or more reasonably, by dragging the messages icon to a different mailbox. TCP/Connect II provides a Mailboxes window that lists all of your mailboxes along with the number of total and unread messages in each.

Something that no other email program can do as far as I know is display certain types of attachments inline. The message in figure 28.1 shows a test I sent myself from Eudora with a JPEG image (which didn't work for some reason), a sound file, and a QuickTime movie (both of which did work when I played them). You also can save the attachments to disk by merely dragging them to the Finder. The reverse works as well, so you can drag files to a message to attach them, and they appear, with icons, inside your text, which is neat. Also note that TCP/Connect II is not limited to 32K in its message windows—a welcome feature.

TCP/Connect II's most impressive mail feature is its Mail Actions feature. It enables you to filter mail based on specific items in the headers or bodies of messages. People who get a lot of mail need a feature like this one. You can use mail actions to put mail from a certain mailing list in a specific mailbox to read at your leisure (as I've done in figure 28.2), or you can have mail from your boss highlighted so that you see it instantly each morning.

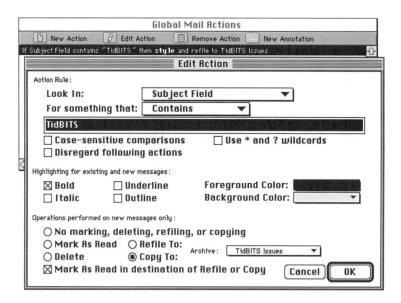

Figure 28.2   *TCP/Connect II Mail Actions.*

A limited variant on this feature, called Select Messages, enables you to use some of the same filtering techniques on already existing messages in a mailbox. After you select them, you can then refile or delete them. In addition, if you only want to find a single message in a mailbox or find some text within a message, TCP/Connect II's Edit menu contains several Find commands that should help out. If you do a Find within the Mailboxes window, TCP/Connect searches through all of your mailboxes for the search string.

Unfortunately, unlike most other email programs, when you delete a message by selecting it and pressing Delete, the message is gone right away (although you can use Undo to recover it immediately afterward).

N
o
t
e

Even though there's no intermediate Trash mailbox in TCP/Connect II, you can certainly create your own Trash mailbox and use it as your own personal email purgatory.

In my testing of large messages, TCP/Connect II transferred them faster than I was expecting, something that you learn to appreciate when you start using email heavily. Other new and important features include a new address book with support for groups and drag and drop. It also can import other files, like the Eudora Nicknames file, although the format of the original file can result in some odd entries in TCP/Connect II's address book.

Overall, I find TCP/Connect II's mail client to be quite good, although the lack of a Trash mailbox and the irritating way it immediately sends outgoing messages when you're connected (I prefer to queue everything in case I wish to edit a message before sending), set it behind Eudora.

Part IV   Integrated Programs

Usenet News

TCP/Connect's newsreader has a three-pane interface that shows you the newsgroups to which you're subscribed (although that process takes some time), the subjects of the messages in the selected group, and the text of the selected article (see figure 28.3).

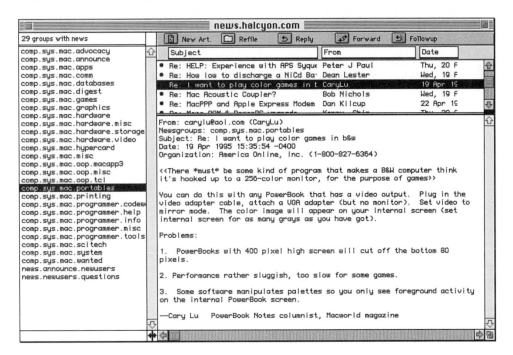

Figure 28.3   *TCP/Connect II News window.*

You can drag the Subject, From, and Date panels at the top of the subjects pane to determine which piece of information shows up where. You also can resize each of these fields and adjust the font as desired. And, as in the mail windows, the small buttons at the top of the news window enable you to create new articles, print existing ones, file them in your mailboxes (a nice integration of email and news), and reply, forward, and followup to postings. You subscribe to newsgroups with the Edit Newsgroups command in the Services menu, but even though you drag newsgroups from the full list of groups over to a list of your subscribed groups, the interface feels as though it hasn't been updated to work like the rest of the program. (I would think you'd get a full group list, as in NewsWatcher and drag newsgroups into your newsreading window.)

Unless you explicitly select a QuickStart button when you connect to your news server, TCP/Connect II downloads what it calls the "Active File" each time you connect, which is a major pain, and even on my 56K dedicated connection, it took 90 seconds. In addition, navigation in the TCP/Connect II newsreader is mediocre, and it's easy, if you use the arrow keys, to accidentally hit the left or right arrows, which move you up and down in the newsgroup list, rather than in the article list (which is what the up and down arrows do). Because TCP/Connect II is slow to bring in the subjects and authors for a large group, if you accidentally move out of a newsgroup, it's painful to have to wait for it to bring in the subjects and authors yet again.

Equally unfortunate, TCP/Connect II's newsreader isn't threaded. It can sort messages by subject, but that never quite solves the problem, especially because, unlike VersaTerm-Link, there's no way to select multiple messages and then read them all at once. However, TCP/Connect II's filtering system helps significantly with the lack of threads. If you are interested only in certain subjects or postings from certain people, you can use filters to highlight them in some way so that it's easy to find them during your reading session. You also can use filters to mark articles as read or to delete them. By marking uninteresting articles as read, or deleting them, you can reduce the amount of news that you see in the newsgroup.

TCP/Connect II's newsreader simply doesn't measure up to any of the main freeware and shareware newsreaders, and although it does have offline capabilities, they're somewhat poorly implemented. TCP/Connect II just goes out and downloads all the new messages in your subscribed groups. You can't even cancel the process once you've started it unless you quit the entire program. If you want good offline news with filtering, use NewsHopper.

FTP

The FTP client in TCP/Connect II is mediocre and doesn't even begin to compete with Anarchie or Fetch. It forces you to enter a userid and password in modal dialogs, although if you hold down the Option key and select FTP (Anonymous) from the Services menu, TCP/Connect II fills in the standard userid and password for you. You also can define commonly used sites and select them from a menu, but I think the easiest way to connect to an FTP site is by choosing Open URL from the Services menu and typing or pasting in an FTP URL. After you connect, the window looks similar to Apple's old Font/ DA Mover (see figure 28.4).

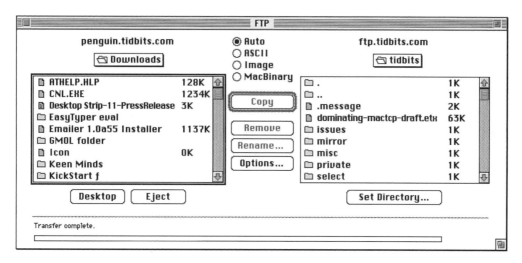

Figure 28.4   *TCP/Connect II FTP window.*

The list on the left shows the folder on your Mac where files are placed when you retrieve them (you also can move them from that or any other folder onto the FTP site if uploading is allowed). The right-hand window shows the files on the remote host.

> *TCP/Connect II also has a single list view that's more like the older version of Fetch, but you're still limited to a single connection.*

There's no drag and drop, unlike other parts of the interface, and you can only connect to one site at a time. Although you can and should add FTP URLs to TCP/Connect II's hotlists, you cannot select an item in an FTP window and choose Add to Main Hot List from the Services menu, as you can with Gopher items and Web pages.

When you retrieve a file from an FTP site, TCP/Connect II does automatically debinhex or uudecode, and if you have Aladdin's StuffIt Engine installed, it automatically expands the file.

I cannot recommend that you use the TCP/Connect II FTP client; it has too many problems that Fetch and Anarchie don't share. The only exception to this rule comes when you click an FTP URL in the Web browser—the integration is useful enough that it's not worth switching out to a better FTP client.

Telnet

TCP/Connect II provides a good environment for using Telnet-based services. You can have multiple windows open at once, and in the Extended version you also have access to a slew of different terminal types. For frequently used commands, you can define up to 20 macros that are attached to any key or combination of keys on the keyboard.

There isn't much else to say about the Telnet features in TCP/Connect II mostly because they work fine and provide access to Telnet-based hosts. I cannot imagine what sort of features you could really add to a Telnet client that haven't been added already.

Gopher

TCP/Connect II, in an attempt to provide access to all the major Internet services, has added a Gopher client. It's extremely similar to TurboGopher; it opens multiple windows, displays text, and unlike TurboGopher, displays GIF and JPEG graphics that you retrieve. The mimicking of TurboGopher even extends to the small windows that TCP/Connect II's Gopher client uses as status windows for file downloads (see figure 28.5).

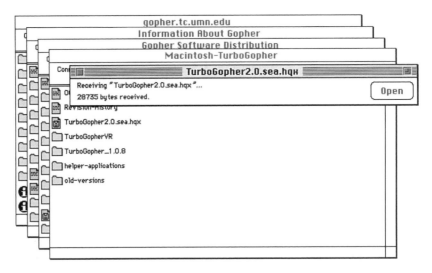

Figure 28.5   *TCP/Connect II Gopher windows.*

The one odd part about the Gopher client in TCP/Connect II is that you'd expect to be able to drag items out of Gopher windows and into other windows, such as an email window, where it could attach the URL, or to a hotlist window. Unfortunately, you can't, although you can drag selected text from within a text window and place it in a mail message or in the Finder as a text clipping.

TCP/Connect II has multiple hotlists that can hold a variety of URL types, including mailto, FTP, Gopher, and HTTP URLs, but not WAIS or news URLs. Although why you'd want to put a mailto URL in your hotlist rather than make an address book entry, I don't know.

What's neat about the integration of the modules with TCP/Connect II is that it can pass off different URLs to the appropriate module. So, if you're in the Web browser and click a Gopher link, TCP/Connect II opens a Gopher window rather than simulating it in the Web browser window. Same goes for FTP, although not yet for news URLs, which just fail whenever you click on them.

The Gopher client in TCP/Connect II is quite good. It's fast and, for TurboGopher users, familiar. It integrates well with the other modules for the most part, and does more than other Gopher clients by displaying or playing graphics, sounds, and movies without needing a helper application.

World Wide Web

The World Wide Web browser in TCP/Connect II is the program's most important recent addition. Let's face it, an integrated program without a Web browser (a category in which VersaTerm-Link unfortunately fits) simply isn't chic in today's Internet.

Although the Web browser has a few rough edges and isn't as configurable as the other stand-alone Web browsers (see figure 28.6), it has all the necessary features, such as supporting HTML forms, making it easy to enter a URL, and having multiple hotlists (which support other modules as well).

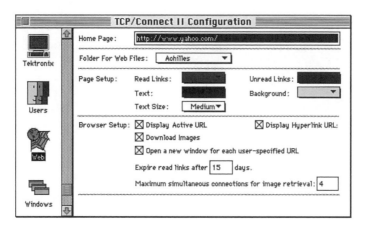

Figure 28.6   *TCP/Connect II Web browser configuration.*

The Web browser can expire read links after a specified number of days, and you can set the colors for the links, the text, and the background. You cannot set styles particularly, although you can choose between small, medium, and large text size settings. Although you cannot manually open more windows, if you select "Open a new window for each user-specified URL" in the Web browser's configuration and if you choose Open URL from the Services menu and enter a URL, you'll get an additional window (see figure 28.7). TCP/Connect II also opens a new Web window if you drop an HTML file on its icon—you cannot drop the HTML file into a visible Web window to display though, as you can in Netscape.

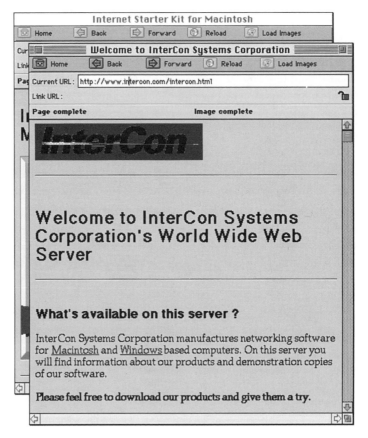

Figure 28.7   *TCP/Connect Web browser windows.*

Several features set the TCP/Connect II Web browser apart from most of the competition. First off, it's as fast or even faster than Netscape, in part because it uses the same multiple connection scheme. I suspect the rest of the speed comes from InterCon's long experience with programming TCP/IP applications—at a functional level, their code is among the most mature. The Web browser does support inline JPEG images, like Netscape, and if you download a QuickTime movie (or probably any other file type, like a System 7 sound, that TCP/Connect II supports), you can play it right in TCP/Connect II. One welcome feature is that when you're downloading a file, TCP/Connect II opens a separate small progress window for it, so you can use the main Web browser window to continue exploring.

InterCon made heavy use of drag and drop in the Web browser interface, so you can drag URLs to your hotlist to save them, and you can drag items from the hotlist back to the Web window to move to that item. Unfortunately, since you cannot select text in the Web browser, you can't drag selected text to a mail window, say, to send to a friend.

You can have multiple hotlists and have more than one open at a time, so InterCon avoids the problem of not having a hierarchical hotlist feature, although I find the hotlists a bit clumsier than Netscape's bookmarks. Icons to the left of each entry indicate which service the URL will use; you can see the icons for FTP (**ftp.tidbits.com**), Gopher (Seattle USA), and the Web (Yahoo) in figure 28.8.

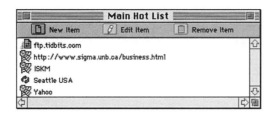

Figure 28.8   *TCP/Connect II Hot List.*

Finally, TCP/Connect II's Web browser stands out because of its integration with the other parts of TCP/Connect II. Whereas in Netscape, clicking a mailto URL brings up a small window for composing a message, clicking a mailto link in TCP/Connect II brings up a new message using the full-featured email module. The same is true for FTP and Gopher, although surprisingly, not news. I strongly approve of using interfaces designed for a specific service like Gopher, rather than attempting to shoehorn everything into a single Web browser interface.

I give the TCP/Connect II Web browser high marks—although it's not as polished as Netscape, its speed and integration gives it the edge over MacWeb and Mosaic. Unfortunately, you wouldn't use TCP/Connect II for just the Web browser—the program is way too big and expensive for that. If InterCon's forthcoming WebShark is indeed a stand-alone version of the TCP/Connect II Web module, it may be worth a look.

Other Utilities

Although they are somewhat hidden by the many other modules in TCP/Connect II that have a higher profile, the program does support a number of utility protocols. You can finger someone or look up information about them using the Ph protocols. If you need to figure out the IP number of a machine from the IP name, you can do that, and the reverse process is equally as easy. You can ping other Internet machines to see if they're working, and the Whois support enables you to find out more information about a machine or a domain.

More useful on an everyday basis will be TCP/Connect II's spelling features, available in the Spelling hierarchical menu in the Edit menu. They provide interactive spelling (as you write) or can check documents after the fact. Other text utilities are available in the Format hierarchical menu under the Edit menu as well, so if you've ever wanted to reflow a badly formatted piece of text or "unquote" a selection, these utilities are ideal.

You won't buy TCP/Connect II based on these utilities, or even particularly let them sway your decision. However, if you do decide to buy the program, they are welcome additions.

Evaluation & Details

TCP/Connect II has several problems. First, due in part to the accretive process by which InterCon has added modules and functionality, the interface is internally inconsistent, which is more frustrating than dealing with the inconsistency of separate programs because there you expect to see differences. In my opinion, InterCon has great code underneath, but they need to scrap the interface and start over, putting an emphasis on similar interfaces and consistent use of drag and drop, which is a powerful tool in an integrated program. I'd also like to see all of TCP/Connect II's tiny little icons at the top of windows and in their icon bar (see figure 28.9) grow up a bit so you stand a chance at recognizing them and so they're easier to click.

Figure 28.9   *TCP/Connect II icon bar.*

The second problem TCP/Connect II faces is that it's not really designed for a single user trying to access the Internet, and that's primarily the sort of person at whom I've aimed this book. As a result, TCP/Connect II seems to compare poorly with the free and shareware programs on the net. However, the fact is that TCP/Connect provides many features that aren't really interesting to the single user or someone accessing the Internet via dialup, such as being able to set up your own FTP server, use local PostScript printers for DEC pass-through printing, and act as a Finger or SMTP server.

On the positive side, TCP/Connect II obviously has a lot of good code in it. It succeeds in its goal of being an integrated Internet program thanks to the addition of the Gopher and Web clients since previous versions. Being able to select a URL sent to you in email and to choose Open Selection as URL from the Services menu (or press ⌘-Option-L) are handy features used to best utilize the different modules, although it would be nice if future versions supported the Command-click standard for resolving URLs.

TCP/Connect II 2.1.2 also is Power Mac-native, which should significantly improve its speed on a Power Macintosh, and you can install either Power Mac-native code only, or a fat binary version that works on both 68000 Macs and Power Macs.

I get the impression that TCP/Connect II is aimed at large organizations that want a single solution to a lot of problems, and they want to have someone to call when they're confused. I've had occasion to call InterCon a couple of times, and their tech support people have always been friendly and helpful. In the end, I cannot recommend that you as an individual spend $495 on a package that doesn't meet your needs, especially noting the standard freeware and shareware utilities which are readily available.

You can purchase TCP/Connect II 2.1.2 direct from InterCon Systems for $495. There also are many different pricing tiers based on volume and whether you work at an educational institution (60 percent off) or for the government (15 percent off). TCP/Connect II also should be available from some dealers and at a discount from some mail order vendors. Although you can download a free demo version of TCP/Connect II, you must request a demo key to unlock the program before being able to use it. Check their Web page for details and the form for requesting a demo key. For more information, contact InterCon electronically at `sales@intercon.com`, or call 703-709-5500; 703-709-5555 (fax).

```
http://www.intercon.com/intercon.html
```

```
ftp://ftp.intercon.com/intercon/sales/
```

VersaTerm-Link

Synergy Software's VersaTerm has been one of the preeminent terminal emulation programs for years. Developed by Lonnie Abelbeck, of Abelbeck Software, VersaTerm always seemed to support more terminal types than other terminal emulators, which made it a favorite in academia, where strange terminal types are more common. In more recent years, Lonnie updated VersaTerm to work with the Communications Toolbox, in the process opening it up to MacTCP connections. I don't know the history for sure, but it seems as though that introduction created additional interest in MacTCP utilities. Lonnie then came out with VersaTilities, a package that included numerous Communications Toolbox tools, including a Telnet tool, an FTP Client tool, a Terminal Server tool, and others designed for Ethernet networks. Also included were a SLIP implementation, an FTP server, a time server, and a simple application for using the FTP Client tool without firing up a full-fledged terminal emulator.

All that stuff still exists in VersaTilities. Until the introduction of the free InterSLIP, it was an excellent way to purchase a SLIP program. However, Lonnie added a new application, called VersaTerm-Link, to the VersaTilities package, and that's what I'm going to concentrate on, because it is of most interest to the individual wanting to access the Internet.

VersaTerm-Link is an integrated client application for email, news, Finger, FTP, and Telnet. I look quickly at each part of the program in turn, but in summary, none of the parts quite compete with the best of the freeware or shareware applications I talked about in previous chapters. The synergy created by the links between the different clients, however, makes for some interesting capabilities. More on those links as I go.

First, VersaTerm-Link provides a toolbar that enables you to access all of its parts with a double-click or keystroke (see figure 28.10).

Figure 28.10   *VersaTerm-Link toolbar.*

I find the need for a double-click odd, because most toolbars require only a single-click, but the shortcut of being able to type a single key without even using the Command key makes up for it. I'd also like to see the toolbar be somewhat configurable to accommodate different working styles and programs.

Email

Although I'm not as fond of VersaTerm-Link's interface as Eudora's, there's a lot to like here. You can have multiple mailboxes, and the program provides icons for indicating mail status (see figure 28.11).

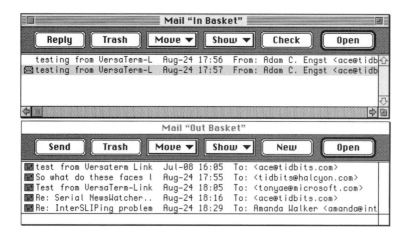

Figure 28.11   *VersaTerm-Link In and Out Baskets.*

You can sort the messages, move them to another mailbox, trash them (and as in Eudora, they are then moved to a special Trash mailbox), reply to them (and the text is quoted automatically), and forward them. I don't see any command corresponding to Eudora's Redirect command, and when you reply to a message, even if it includes only one person in the header, VersaTerm-Link asks whether you want to reply to all or only the recipient.

VersaTerm-Link works offline in the sense that you can queue messages and send them later. If you use VersaTerm SLIP, VersaTerm-Link automatically connects (asking whether it's OK first), transfers your mail, and then disconnects. If you aren't using VersaTerm SLIP, you must select the messages in your Out Basket to send, which is a minor pain.

In messages that you cannot edit, such as incoming mail and news, you are limited to selecting entire lines. This interface decision is extremely odd because many people want to copy an address or directory path from a message without getting everything else on the line. One nice touch, though, is that with a message open (and this applies to news articles as well) you can select Add to Address Book from the Edit menu, and VersaTerm-Link adds the person to your address book.

The address book is generally well-done, enabling you to add people and groups, along with notes about who they are. It's available whenever you create a new mail message or news posting. You can enter an address into a message manually if you like, but unfortunately there's no way to import that address into your address book with a single click. It's a minor point, but a tad annoying.

VersaTerm-Link supports one or more enclosures to messages. If you so choose, it even compresses them in the StuffIt format before binhexing them and sending them out as an attachment to the message.

You cannot put more than approximately 30K of text in an outgoing message. I didn't check this figure exactly, but it was easy to get VersaTerm-Link to complain that the clipboard was too large to paste. In the most recent version of VersaTerm-Link a previous limitation relating to the amount of text you could view in a message has disappeared.

Overall, the email part of VersaTerm link is good, but not great. You won't go wrong with its simplicity, but you may wish for some of Eudora's features.

Usenet News

VersaTerm-Link's newsreader was the first implementation of a non-threaded newsreader that I like. I didn't think it was possible because I'm addicted to reading and killing threads while scanning Usenet. When you double-click on the toolbar's Read News icon, VersaTerm-Link opens your Subscribed News Groups window (see figure 28.12).

Figure 28.12   *VersaTerm-Link Subscribed Groups window.*

If you want to subscribe to more groups, clicking the Groups button enables you to view a list of either all groups or only the new ones that have appeared since you last checked. When you open a group (groups that have new articles have a little folder icon next to their name) from the Subscribed Groups window, VersaTerm-Link displays the newsgroup window (see figure 28.13).

```
┌─────────────────────────────────────────────────────────────┐
│ ▣               comp.sys.mac.portables                    ▣  │
│ ┌─────────────────┐ ┌─────────────────┐      ┌────────────┐  │
│ │ Receive to Disk │ │ Mark All as Read│      │    Open    │  │
│ └─────────────────┘ └─────────────────┘      └────────────┘  │
│ D Re: Opinion on Duo 230 vs. PB 170        ⓘ Richard D. Doherty ▲│
│ D Re: Duo 230 Express Modem problems          ⓘ Colin Helliwell  ▓│
│ D What's in the Duo Floppy?                    ⓘ Ronald Leenes   │
│ D Re: What's in the Duo Floppy?               ⓘ Michael Kwun     │
│ D Re: What's in the Duo Floppy?               ⓘ Ron Nicholson    │
│ D Re: The new PB165 and FPU                     ⓘ Joe Simpson    │
│ D Re: The new PB165 and FPU                ⓘ Christopher Lishka   │
│ D Re: The new PB165 and FPU                 ⓘ Wen-Po Bobby Lee   │
│ D Re: August MacUser Duo Article              ⓘ Michael Peirce   │
│ D Max charging of battery PB100?              ⓘ Noam Nudelman    │
│ D Better battery (NiCad) for PB100?           ⓘ E Pekka A Saari  │
│ D Re: From PowerBook 160 To Duo - Impressions (Long ⓘ Christopher Lishka│
│ D Re: From PowerBook 160 To Duo - Impressions (Long) ⓘ Harald Striepe │
│ D Re: From PowerBook 160 To Duo - Impressions (Long) ⓘ Richard Kay ▼│
│ space Page Down  ⌘space Page Up  esc Parent Window          ▤  │
└─────────────────────────────────────────────────────────────┘
```

Figure 28.13   VersaTerm-Link Newsgroup window.

The trick here is that even though VersaTerm-Link doesn't understand threads (although it can group articles with the same subjects), you scan through the list of new articles and select the ones you want by Command-clicking on them. After you have selected articles, you can read through them relatively easily by using the Spacebar to page down through an article and using the Return key to move to the next selected article.

The steps described above are what you do if you connect via SLIP or PPP and want to stay online. Most interesting, and VersaTerm-Link is still unusual in this regard, is that you can alternately click the Receive to Disk button and VersaTerm-Link downloads all of your selected articles as fast as it can, which is much faster than you can read. Later on, you can check Local via Disk in the News menu (it's normally set to Remote via Network) and read the news you saved just as though you were logged on. You can reply to messages, and forward them—and you can do all that offline as well, because VersaTerm-Link knows how to queue both mail and news.

FTP

When it comes to FTP, unfortunately, VersaTerm doesn't hold a candle to Anarchie or Fetch. Double-clicking the FTP Files button the toolbar opens the FTP Client List (see figure 28.14).

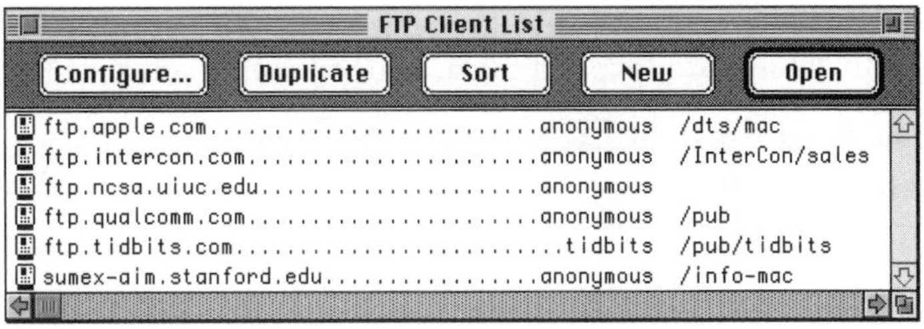

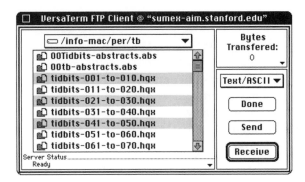

Figure 28.14   *VersaTerm-Link FTP Client List.*

You can define shortcuts with the New button, and they appear in the list, as shown in figure 28.14. However, there is no way to connect to an FTP site without creating a shortcut for it in your list, and once you create one, it may take a bit of searching to realize that the only way to delete it is by choosing Clear from the Edit menu (a fact that is buried in the manual). All too often I want to connect to a site once, without creating a shortcut; so even though the shortcut asks for the same information that I'm using in logging at once, it feels slightly clumsier. Okay, maybe it's not that big of a deal.

When you double-click on an entry in your list to connect, though, you see the problem (see figure 28.15).

Figure 28.15   *VersaTerm-Link FTP window.*

VersaTerm-Link doesn't display a large window, so some filenames extend past the window, making it impossible to see their extensions. Even though you can use the Get Info command to view a straight Unix directory listing for the file, VersaTerm-Link doesn't show the file size as a matter of course, which I dislike. In addition, when you're downloading a file, the program gives you a running count of the bytes transferred but never tells you what kind of throughput you're getting, or how many bytes remain. I often abort a file transfer if I'm getting poor throughput; poor throughput tells me that something is wrong with the remote site, and they don't need to handle my download just then. VersaTerm-Link doesn't try to determine the transfer type automatically by looking at the file extension, as Fetch and Anarchie do, and it has no facility for calling another program to debinhex or expand the downloaded files after the fact.

The primary good thing about the FTP client in VersaTerm-Link is that you can have it download in the background as you read news or email, although the same thing works with Anarchie and Fetch and one of the free newsreaders.

Telnet

VersaTerm-Link's Telnet client resembles all other Telnet programs with the exception of being able to define a login script when you create the shortcut for a site. Like the FTP client, with Telnet you must create a shortcut; there's no provision for a one-time connection without saving that information.

If the Telnet client in VersaTerm-Link isn't powerful enough for you, you can open another one, such as VersaTerm itself (because the entire VersaTilities package comes with both VersaTerm and VersaTerm Pro) or presumably, NCSA Telnet. The Telnet client isn't sufficient in two major areas. First, it supports only the "dumb" terminal type, which prevents you from using Gopher via Telnet, for instance, because that requires a VT100 terminal type. Second, you can have only one Telnet session open at a time, unlike either VersaTerm or NCSA Telnet.

Other Utilities

VersaTerm-Link can query Finger, Whois, and Ph servers (which are used to store phone books of users, usually at universities), although using them is often an exercise in frustration when you're looking for someone. Unlike Peter Lewis's Finger, with VersaTerm-Link you must make sure to type the userid and the machine name in the appropriate fields. Other utilities exist too, so you can find out the IP number that goes with a domain name by using the Resolve Domain Name command in the Network menu. And you can do all sorts of stuff using the Tools menu (see figure 28.16).

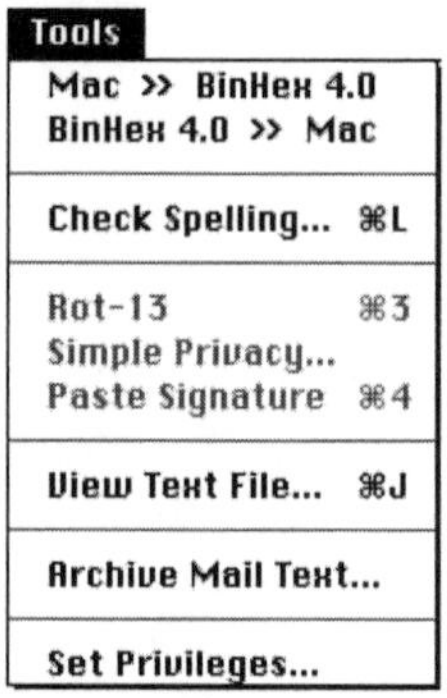

Figure 28.16   VersaTerm-Link Tools menu.

You can encode and decode BinHex files, check spelling with the included dictionary (a nice touch, especially considering the abysmal spelling habits of many people on the Internet), use rot13 to encode or decode a news message, encrypt or decrypt a message with a password that someone has given you, view a text file, or archive your mail to a text file.

> *Interestingly, VersaTerm-Link includes the code used for the encryption and decryption in the manual, and encourages others to implement it as a method of keeping messages private. The encryption is not secure, in the sense that any good cryptographer could crack it quickly, but it does discourage prying eyes.*

Finally, a new addition to the Tools menu, the Set Privileges command, lets your password protect a number of parts of VersaTerm-Link to prevent others from messing with them. Although I don't personally subscribe to such techniques, preferring education and communication instead, it would be a good way to prevent a child from accessing undesirable newsgroups or FTP sites.

VersaTerm-Link doesn't contain a Gopher or Web browser, but the Open Special Client command in the Network menu enables you to link a single MacTCP application into VersaTerm-Link. I'd like it even more if you could add one or more applications to your toolbar, but I'm glad to see the VersaTerm-Link folks acknowledging that you might want to use other software.

As a clever touch, VersaTerm-Link has a hierarchical Paste Face menu in the Edit menu that lists and describes a number of the common smileys used on the Internet (see figure 28.17).

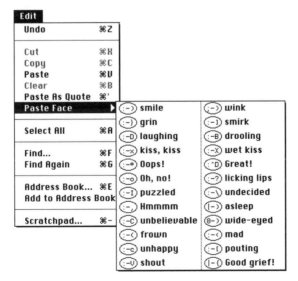

Figure 28.17 *VersaTerm-Link Paste Face menu.*

Hidden in the back of the manual, I noticed one really neat feature. If you double-click a word in any display text window (even though you can select only an entire line, you can still double-click on a word), VersaTerm-Link searches for the next occurrence of that word. You can continue searching forward for that same word by pressing the Tab key, and Shift-Tab searches backward—that's elegant.

Speaking of the manual, although it's not inspired or particularly fun to read, it covers all of VersaTerm-Link quite thoroughly. A separate manual talks about using all the connection and transfer tools included with the VersaTilities. With commercial software, much of what you're paying for is the documentation and support (which I had no need to call), so it's nice to see adequate manuals.

Evaluation & Details

Despite its many nice features, I cannot necessarily recommend that you spend $85 for VersaTilities when you can use programs such as InterSLIP, Eudora, NewsWatcher, NCSA Telnet, Anarchie, and Netscape. If they didn't exist, buying VersaTilities would be a no-brainer, and Synergy deserves credit for pricing the package reasonably. You may decide that the offline news reading feature and some nice integration between the different parts of the program with items such as the Address Book and the spell checking, make the cost worthwhile. And remember, even if you do agree that Anarchie is the best FTP client, for instance, you can still use the rest of the VersaTerm-Link package quite happily. There's no shame in not using one of a number of bundled features. Now, if only you could reconfigure that toolbar with your favorites....

If, however, you are the sort of person who doesn't mind spending some money and wants a set of utilities in a single package complete with full documentation and support, VersaTilities is definitely a good way to go, especially in conjunction with a Web browser like MacWeb or Netscape. I usually assume that people want to make this choice on their own and spend the least amount of money possible because that's how I am, but I also realize that many people prefer to spend some money and avoid the hassles.

You can buy VersaTerm-Link in the VersaTilities package for a list price of $145, in the VersaTerm package for $195, or in the VersaTerm-Pro package for $295. All of these prices are at least 30 to 40 percent lower if you buy through a mail-order vendor or direct from Synergy. You can contact Synergy to find out more about buying any of their programs via the Internet at `maxwell@sales.synergy.com`, via phone at 215-779-0522, or via fax at 215-370-0548.

Other Integrated Programs?

Although VersaTerm-Link and TCP/Connect II truly are integrated programs, there's another that almost fits into the category, MicroPhone Pro from Software Ventures. It's more a bundle of software than an integrated program, though. Wait a minute! This book is a bundle too—I'd better do a short capsule review of it here as well.

Internet Starter Kit for Macintosh

Internet Starter Kit for Macintosh (ISKM) is a book/disk combination, not an integrated Internet program, but it provides much of the same functionality through a set of freeware and shareware Internet programs that are among the best available. Along with MacTCP and either MacPPP or InterSLIP for the Internet connection, ISKM includes Internet Config, Anarchie, Eudora, and MacWeb and a set of Anarchie bookmarks to all the rest of the major Internet programs available on the Internet. A version with a second disk and paid-up shareware fees is available in software stores; it adds Finger, Talk, a fully functional demo of NewsHopper, and utilities for creating Web pages. At street prices ranging from

$16 to $30, ISKM is well worth the money for the hundreds of pages of information in the book alone, and the bundled software is an excellent bonus. Highly recommended. But of course, I'm biased. :-)

Integrated Programs
28

http://www.mcp.com/hayden/iskm/

ftp://ftp.tidbits.com/pub/tidbits/select/

MicroPhone Pro

MicroPhone Pro doesn't exactly provide integrated Internet access, but it does provide many of the tools you need for Internet access in a single package, including the CommToolbox MP Telnet tool, for use with MicroPhone itself along with other Communications Toolbox-aware programs. Then there's MacSLIP 2.0, the Internet Mail and Internet News modules that offer basic email and news, Fetch from Dartmouth (which means that if you buy MicroPhone Pro, you do not have to pay the shareware fee for Fetch), and TurboGopher from the University of Minnesota. MicroPhone Pro actually duplicates FTP, since it now includes Snatcher, another decent FTP client (see chapter 23, "FTP"). To be complete, I should mention that it also includes a slightly older version of the FaxSTF fax software, and MicroPhone's graphical environment for various commercial services, called Loran. You can purchase MicroPhone

Pro 2.0 by mail order for approximately $150, and if you have questions or comments about it, you can contact Software Ventures at **microphone@svcdudes.com**, or call 510-644-3232; 510-848-0885 (fax).

http://www.svcdudes.com/

Integrating and Differentiating

Perhaps the impression that I'd like you to take away from this chapter is that the Internet is a vast and multi-faceted place. Although the integrated programs may offer some advantages in terms of bringing together the common things you do on the Internet, the trade-offs and compromises often don't seem to me to be worthwhile. Perhaps it's less the fault of the integrated programs than merely the comparison with a set of truly great stand-alone programs that just happen to be freeware or shareware, programs like Eudora, Anarchie, and NewsWatcher. However, remember that the main feature of a MacTCP-based connection to the Internet is choice, and you're more than welcome to choose one of these integrated programs as your base set of Internet applications. The MacTCP-based connection doesn't limit you to that set, luckily, so you're able to mix Netscape with VersaTerm-Link, Anarchie with TCP/Connect II, or any other combination. Just make sure the end result fits your needs.

That said, for those of you who are feeling somewhat overwhelmed with all the possibilities and the feature sets of the main programs that I recommend, let's move next to a simple, step-by-step discussion of how to use these recommended applications.

Step-by-Step Internet

By now, you've probably noticed that I tend to avoid giving detailed, blow-by-blow directions for using Internet programs. You may be wondering why, since such specifics are common in technical books. Don't worry, there is a method to my madness.

On the Internet, things change rapidly. Something that is available one day may disappear the next. Or, in some cases, something may be available at random times during the day, but not at others. Herein lies my concern with rigid instructions that people will attempt to follow closely. What if I give instructions for performing some task and it doesn't work? The fault may lie not with my instructions, but with the Internet resource I explain—but that makes no difference to the person following the directions.

So, my strategy elsewhere in this book has been to provide basic information necessary to use the common MacTCP programs in a variety of situations, hopefully giving you the background you need to work around any difficulties you may encounter. However, several of the responses I received to the first edition of the book indicated that some step-by-step instruction would be welcome, and far be it from me to ignore such suggestions from readers. After all, I'm writing the book for you, not for me.

Note

You must have a direct connection or a PPP or SLIP account set up to be able to work through the following instructions, although you're welcome to read through before you have the connection set up.

Unlike any other book, I cover most of the Internet software available for the Mac, so providing step-by-step instructions for every program in this book would fill thousands of pages—and could be patented as a cure for insomnia. Instead, I provide the steps necessary to perform several basic tasks in some of the most important applications. All of these applications require MacTCP and either a network or a SLIP or PPP connection. I start by covering MacTCP, MacPPP, and InterSLIP, provide steps for setting up the useful Internet Config, and then give steps for using a few important applications.

> **Note**
>
> *In each case, I assume you have the program available on your hard disk. You may need to copy it from a floppy disk or download it from the Internet, debinhex, and expand the file. Most of these programs can be installed from the ISKM disk, and the ISKM Installer does some of the work of placing and configuring the programs. So, some of these instructions may be redundant. For instance, there's no reason to configure MacTCP for a provider on the disk (such as Northwest Nexus), because the ISKM Installer does it for you. Nonetheless, I wanted to be complete, and without instructions that start from a clean copy, you would never be able to duplicate these configurations on your own.*
>
> *For more information on what the ISKM Installer does for you, check out chapter 16, "Internet Starter Kit Disk."*

MacTCP 2.0.6

Quick Reminder: MacTCP is a control panel that makes it possible for Macs to connect to TCP/IP-based networks such as the Internet.

Tasks:

1. Install MacTCP.

2. Configure MacTCP for use with your provider and MacPPP *or* for use with your provider and InterSLIP.

Install MacTCP

1. Drop the icon for the MacTCP control panel on your System Folder icon.

   The Mac asks whether you would like to put MacTCP in the Control Panels folder (see figure 29.1).

2. Click the OK button to confirm that MacTCP should go in the Control Panels folder.

Figure 29.1   *Placing MacTCP.*

Configure MacTCP

1. Jump ahead and install MacPPP *or* InterSLIP as set out in the "Install MacPPP" and "Install InterSLIP" sections that follow. (You must have MacPPP installed before you can configure MacTCP for MacPPP; you must have InterSLIP installed before you can configure MacTCP for InterSLIP).

2. Open the Control Panels folder and double-click the MacTCP icon.

   The MacTCP window opens (see figure 29.2).

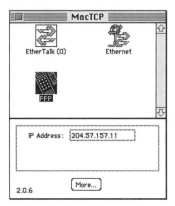

Figure 29.2   *MacTCP control panel window.*

3. In the MacTCP window, select the PPP icon (or, if you use InterSLIP, select the InterSLIP icon instead of the PPP icon).

4. Click the More button.

   MacTCP presents you with its configuration dialog (see figure 29.3).

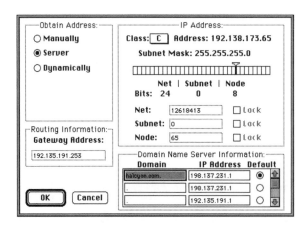

Figure 29.3   *MacTCP configuration dialog.*

These directions show you how to specifically configure MacTCP for Northwest Nexus; I'll explain when you should use your provider's information instead.

5. In the Obtain Address area at the upper left of the configuration dialog, select Server.

6. In the Domain Name Server Information area, click in the first field under the Domain column. Type **halcyon.com.**, making sure to include the trailing period. Press Tab or click the first field under IP Address. Type **198.137.231.1** and select the Default radio button. (Don't actually type this information unless your provider is Northwest Nexus; type the information given to you by your Internet provider.)

7. Press Tab or click in the second field under Domain. Type a period. Press Tab or click in the second field under IP Address. Type **198.137.231.1** again. (I won't remind you again in this set of steps, but do remember, you *must* type the information from your provider.)

8. Press Tab or click in the third field under Domain. Type a period. Press Tab or click in the third field under IP Address. Type **192.135.191.1** this time.

9. Press Tab or click in the fourth field under Domain (you must scroll down to see it). Type a period. Press Tab or click in the fourth field under IP Address. Type **192.135.191.3** this time.

Your configuration dialog should now look similar to my screen shot, although yours probably has **0.0.0.0** in the Gateway Address field and something different in the IP Address area at the upper right. Don't worry about those differences. If you don't use Northwest Nexus as your provider, you have different domain name server information, and you may have to select the Manually radio button instead of the Server radio button if your provider gives you a Manually-addressed or static account (at which point you also must enter your IP number in the MacTCP control panel window and the gateway address in the Gateway Address field—both of these pieces of information come from your provider).

10. Click the OK button to save your changes and close the configuration dialog.

11. Close the MacTCP window by clicking the close box in the upper left-hand corner.

    MacTCP may or may not tell you that you must restart for your changes to take effect.

12. Restart your Macintosh.

If you followed these directions without customizing them for InterSLIP or a different provider, you've now configured MacTCP for use with MacPPP and Northwest Nexus.

MacPPP 2.0.1

Quick Reminder: MacPPP consists of a control panel called Config PPP and an extension called PPP. MacPPP uses your modem to establish a connection to a PPP account over which MacTCP-based programs can work.

Tasks:

1. Install MacPPP.

2. Configure MacPPP for your provider.

3. Establish an Internet connection.

4. Close the Internet connection.

Install MacPPP

1. Select both the Config PPP and PPP icons and drop them on your System Folder icon.

    The Mac tells you that they need to be stored in special places within the System Folder, and asks if you would like to put them where they belong (see figure 29.4).

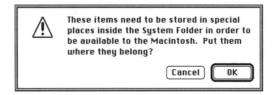

Figure 29.4   *Placing MacPPP.*

2. Click the OK button to confirm that the Config PPP control panel should go in the Control Panels folder and that the PPP extension should go in the Extensions folder.

The Mac then tells you where it has placed them.

Configure MacPPP

1. Open the Control Panels folder and double-click the Config PPP icon.

The Config PPP window appears (see figure 29.5).

Figure 29.5   *Config PPP window.*

2. Click the Config button to bring up the server configuration dialog (see figure 29.6).

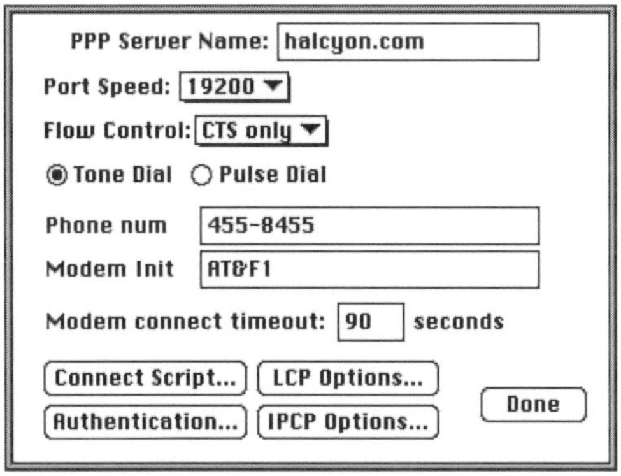

PPP Server Name: [halcyon.com]

Port Speed: [19200 ▼]

Flow Control: [CTS only ▼]

⦿ Tone Dial   ○ Pulse Dial

Phone num   [455-8455]

Modem Init   [AT&F1]

Modem connect timeout: [90] seconds

[Connect Script...] [LCP Options...]
[Authentication...] [IPCP Options...]   [Done]

Figure 29.6   *Configuring the server configuration dialog.*

N o t e

If the PPP Server pop-up menu doesn't have Untitled selected, you may wish to create a new server definition by clicking the New button, typing a name in the dialog, and clicking the OK button.

N o t e

These directions include specific information for Northwest Nexus, but if Northwest Nexus is not your provider, use the information from your provider.

3. Click in the PPP Server Name field. Type **halcyon.com** (or whatever you want to call it—it doesn't matter).

4. From the Port Speed pop-up menu, choose 19200 or—if you have a 28.8 Kbps modem—choose 38400. If you aren't sure what kind of modem you have, 19200 is a safe choice.

5. From the Flow Control pop-up menu, choose CTS only.

6. If you have touch-tone phone service, select Tone Dial. Otherwise, select Pulse Dial.

7. In the Phone Number field, type the phone number for your provider, just as I've entered the phone number for Northwest Nexus, **1-206-455-8455**. If you must use any specific prefixes, such as **9**, to dial out, add them here, such as: **9,1-206-455-8455**.

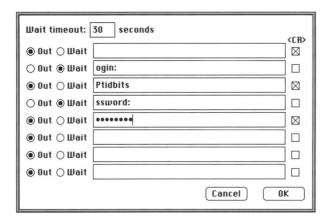

> **Note**
>
> *The comma in the phone number above tells the modem to pause for two seconds before dialing the rest of the number. You can insert multiple commas to use additional two-second pauses.*

8. In the Modem Init field, enter **AT&F1** if you use a SupraFAXModem or Global Village TelePort or PowerPort modem. For other modems, check your modem manual for the appropriate factory default init string. Make sure that string turns off XON/XOFF flow control.

> **Note**
>
> *If you installed MacPPP using the ISKM Installer, look in the ISKM3 Folder on your hard disk for a folder called MacPPP 2.0.1. In that folder you should find a text file called Modem Strings. It contains a number of untested modem init strings that might work.*

9. Click the Connect Script button to bring up the script login dialog (see figure 29.7). Your provider may use a slightly different login script.

Figure 29.7 *Configuring the login script.*

10. In the first row of controls, select Out and check the <CR> checkbox to send a carriage return.

11. In the second row of controls, select Wait and enter **ogin:** to wait for the login prompt.

12. In the third row of controls, select Out and enter your userid. Check the checkbox so MacPPP sends your userid and then a carriage return.

13. In the fourth set of fields, select Wait and enter **ssword:** in the field to wait for the password prompt.

14. In the fifth set of fields, select Out and enter your password. Check the checkbox so MacPPP sends your password followed by a carriage return. Ignore the rest of the rows of controls.

15. Finally, click the OK button to save your changes.

16. Back in the server configuration dialog, click the Done button to save your server configuration.

17. Back in the Config PPP window, click the close box in the upper left-hand corner to close the PPP window.

Establish an Internet Connection

1. After you finish setting up MacTCP and MacPPP, you can use MacPPP to connect to the Internet. Open the Control Panels folder and double-click the Config PPP icon.

   The Config PPP control panel opens. Note the frowning faces and the PPP DOWN label in the upper left corner (see figure 29.8).

Figure 29.8   *Disconnected.*

2. Click the Open button.

   MacPPP configures your modem according to the string you entered in the server configuration dialog and dials the number you provided (see figure 29.9).

   After the modems connect, MacPPP sends your userid and password to log you in and then establishes the connection (see figure 29.10).

Figure 29.9   *MacPPP dialing dialog.*

MacPPP status:
  PPP Phase:
  Establishment
[Quit]

Figure 29.10   *PPP Establishment phase.*

Notice that the faces are smiling and the label now says PPP UP (see figure 29.11).

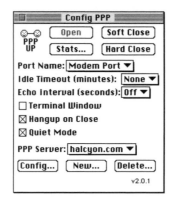

Figure 29.11   *Connected.*

You should now be able to run MacTCP-based applications such as Anarchie and MacWeb.

Close the Internet Connection

1. Quit any MacTCP-based applications other than Eudora that you may have launched.

2. If the Config PPP window is closed, open the Control Panels folder and double-click the Config PPP icon.

3. Click the Hard Close button.

   MacPPP disconnects from the Internet and hangs up your modem.

Congratulations! You've successfully configured MacPPP, established a connection to the Internet, and closed that connection. If anything went wrong during this process, reread the section on MacPPP in chapter 18, "PPP," and chapter 20, "Troubleshooting Your Connection."

InterSLIP 1.0.1

Quick Reminder: InterSLIP consists of an application called InterSLIP Setup and an extension called InterSLIP (a control panel called InterSLIP Control is necessary only for System 6 users). InterSLIP uses your modem to establish a connection to a SLIP account over which MacTCP-based programs can work.

Tasks:

Part IV Step-by-Step Internet

1. Install InterSLIP.

2. Configure InterSLIP for your provider.

3. Establish an Internet connection.

4. Close the Internet connection.

Note

If you install InterSLIP using the ISKM Installer, you do not need to follow the directions here for installing InterSLIP. These directions are for people who retrieve a fresh copy of InterSLIP from a different source.

Install InterSLIP

1. Restart your Macintosh with extensions off. That is, restart your Mac while pressing the Shift key. Keep the Shift key pressed down until you see a message telling you that your extensions are off. The message should appear about a third of the way into the startup process.

2. Double-click the InterSLIP Installer icon.

   InterSLIP's installer launches and the About This Installer window appears.

3. Click the Continue button.

   Another dialog appears (see figure 29.12).

Figure 29.12   *Installing InterSLIP.*

4. Click the Install button at the lower right.

    A dialog appears, reminding you that you will need to restart your Mac after the installation finishes.

5. Click the Yes button.

    You'll see a dialog giving messages about the installation's progress, and then you'll get a message asking you to restart your Macintosh.

6. Click the Restart button.

    Your Macintosh restarts with the different parts of InterSLIP installed in the correct folders.

Configure InterSLIP

1. Locate InterSLIP Setup. If you installed InterSLIP from the *Starter Kit* disk, look in the ISKM3 Folder, in the InterSLIP folder. If you installed InterSLIP from the InterSLIP Installer, look in your Apple menu.

2. Double-click the InterSLIP Setup icon or choose InterSLIP Setup from the Apple menu.

    The InterSLIP window appears (see figure 29.13).

3. From the File menu, choose New.

    A dialog appears (see figure 29.14).

Figure 29.13   *InterSLIP setup.*

Figure 29.14   *Naming your configuration.*

4. In the dialog, enter a name for your new configuration. You might give it the name of your provider. Click the OK button when you finish.

   The InterSLIP window should now list the name of the configuration you created.

5. Double-click the name of your new configuration.

   InterSLIP brings up a configuration dialog for the configuration you just double-clicked (see figure 29.15).

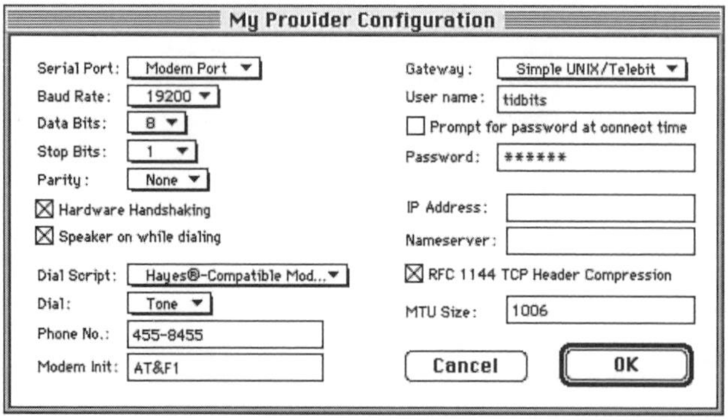

***Figure 29.15**   Configuring InterSLIP.*

N o t e

These directions include specific information for Northwest Nexus, but if Northwest Nexus is not your provider and your provider gives you different information, you must use the information from your provider—just follow along and insert the information from your provider in the appropriate places.

6. From the Serial Port pop-up menu, choose Modem Port.

7. From the Baud Rate pop-up menu, choose 19200, unless you have a 28.8 Kbps modem. If you have a 28.8 Kbps modem, choose 38400. If you aren't sure what kind of modem you have, 19200 is a safe choice.

8. From the Data Bits pop-up menu, choose 8.

9. From the Stop Bits pop-up menu, choose 1.

10. From the Parity pop-up menu, choose None.

11. Turn on the Hardware Handshaking checkbox.

12. Turn on the Speaker on while dialing checkbox.

13. From the Dial Script pop-up menu, choose Hayes-Compatible Modem.

14. From the Dial pop-up menu, choose Tone (or, if you have pulse service, choose Pulse).

15. In the Phone No. field, type the phone number you use to call your provider. If you must use any specific prefixes, such as **9**, to dial out, add them here: **9,1-206-455-8455**.

> *The comma in the phone number tells the modem to pause for two seconds before dialing the rest of the number. You can insert multiple commas to use additional two-second pauses.*

16. In the Modem Init field, enter **AT&F1** if you use a SupraFAXModem or Global Village TelePort or PowerPort modem. For other modem types, check your modem manual for the appropriate factory default string. Make sure that string turns off XON/XOFF flow control.

17. From the Gateway pop-up menu, choose Simple UNIX/Telebit. Your provider may give you a different gateway script that, when properly installed in the Gateway Scripts folder, also shows in the Gateway pop-up menu.

18. In the User name field, enter your username, making sure to enter it exactly as your provider gave it to you, probably in all lowercase.

19. Turn off the Prompt for password at connect time checkbox and enter your password into the Password field.

20. Leave the IP Address field blank.

21. In the Nameserver field, enter your name server (get this information from your provider).

22. Turn on the RFC 1144 TCP Header Compression checkbox.

23. In the MTU Size field, enter 1006.

24. When you're finished, check your dialog carefully to make sure it is filled out correctly and that everything matches the instructions here and the information from your provider. When you are ready, click the OK button.

Part IV — Step-by-Step Internet — 29

Establish an Internet Connection

1. If the InterSLIP window is not open, launch InterSLIP Setup.

2. Click the Connect button.

   InterSLIP Setup dials the modem and sends your username and password. Eventually, the status message in the upper right should say <Connected> (see figure 29.16).

Figure 29.16   *Connected.*

You should now be able to run MacTCP-based applications such as Anarchie and MacWeb.

Close the Internet Connection

1. Quit any MacTCP-based applications other than Eudora that are running.

2. If it's not already open, open the InterSLIP window.

3. Click the Disconnect button.

   InterSLIP disconnects from the Internet and hangs up your modem.

Congratulations! You've successfully installed and configured InterSLIP, established a connection to the Internet, and closed that connection. If anything went wrong during this process, reread the sections about InterSLIP and troubleshooting in chapter 19, "SLIP," and chapter 20, "Troubleshooting Your Connection."

Internet Config

Quick Reminder: Internet Config is a program that helps you configure MacTCP applications. You enter configuration information in Internet Config once, and then any MacTCP application that knows about Internet Config automatically uses the information in Internet Config. Of the programs mentioned in this chapter, Internet Config works with NewsWatcher, and Anarchie.

Tasks:

1. Configure Internet Config.

Configure Internet Config

1. Double-click the Internet Config icon.

   Internet Config launches. If this is the first time you have launched Internet Config, it prompts you to install the Internet Config extension. Click the OK button to install it.

   Next, Internet Config shows the Internet Preferences window (see figure 29.17). If for some reason you don't see the Internet Preferences window, choose Open Internet Preferences from the File menu.

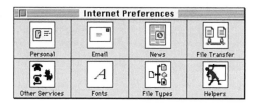

Figure 29.17 *Internet Preferences window.*

2. In the Internet Preferences window, click the Personal tile.

   The Personal window opens (see figure 29.18).

```
┌─────────────────── Personal ───────────────────┐
│ Real Name:      │ Adam C. Engst                 │
│ Organisation:   │ TidBITS                       │
│ Quote String:   │ >                             │
│ Signature:                                      │
│ Adam C. Engst, TidBITS Editor -- ace@tidbits.com -- info@tidbits.com │
│   Author of Internet Starter Kit for Macintosh -- iskm@tidbits.com  │
│        Internet Explorer Kit for Macintosh -- iek@tidbits.com       │
│        Internet Starter Kit for Windows -- iskw@tidbits.com         │
│ Plan:                                           │
│                                                 │
└─────────────────────────────────────────────────┘
```

Figure 29.18 *Setting personal preferences.*

3. In the Personal window, fill in your name and organization. Leave the **>** character in the Quote String field. When you finish, click the close box at the upper left of the window.

For more help with any Internet Config dialog, turn on balloon help (from the Help menu at the upper right of the menu bar) and point at the item you want help with.

4. Back in the Internet Preferences dialog, click the Email tile.

   The Email window opens (see figure 29.19).

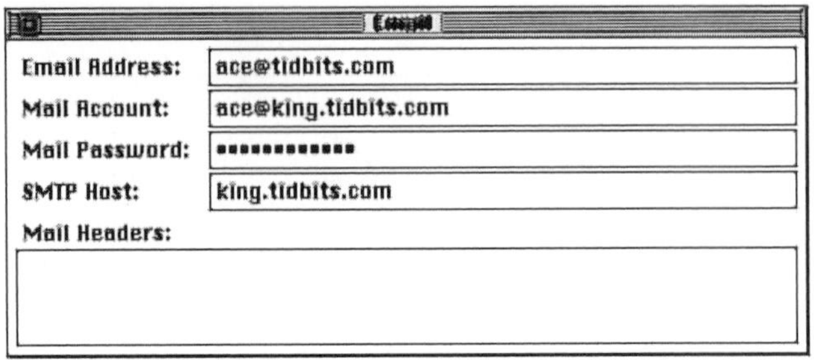

Email Address:	ace@tidbits.com
Mail Account:	ace@king.tidbits.com
Mail Password:	••••••••••••
SMTP Host:	king.tidbits.com
Mail Headers:	

Figure 29.19   Setting email preferences.

5. Fill in the Email Address field with the email address given to you by your provider. Be careful to use all lowercase.

6. Press Tab or click in the Mail Account field. Type your mail account, using information your provider gave you. If you have a POP account, use your POP account in the Mail Account field. Be certain to use all lowercase unless your provider explicitly gave you a mixed-case username.

7. Press Tab or click in the Mail Password field. Enter your password, being careful to enter it exactly as your provider gave it to you.

8. Press Tab or click in the SMTP Host field. Type your SMTP host, using the name your provider gave you. (If your provider gave you information about an SMTP server, note that an SMTP server is the same thing as an SMTP host.)

Figure 29.19 shows my information, and yours is definitely different. Also, some providers provide different passwords for different things; be sure to put your email password in the Mail Password field.

9. When you finish filling in the first four fields in the Email window, click the close box at the upper left of the window.

10. You should be back at the Internet Preferences window. Click the News tile.

As you probably expect, the News window opens (see figure 29.20).

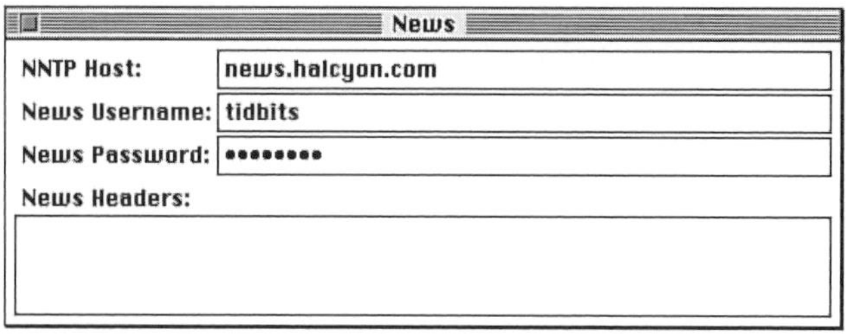

News
NNTP Host: `news.halcyon.com`
News Username: `tidbits`
News Password: ••••••••
News Headers:

Figure 29.20   *Setting news preferences.*

11. In the News window, fill in the NNTP Host field using information from your provider. If your provider is Northwest Nexus, enter **news.halcyon.com**, as I did in figure 29.20.

12. Press Tab or click in the News Username field. Enter your news username, which is usually the same as your email username.

13. Press Tab or click in the News Password field. Enter your news password, which is probably the same as your email password.

14. Click the close box at the upper left of the window.

15. From the File menu, choose Save.

A Save dialog box appears, and it shows that if you click the Save button, you will save a file called Internet Preferences in your Preferences folder.

16. Do not change the default name or folder. Do click the Save button.

17. From the File menu, choose Quit.

You have finished the basics of setting up Internet Config. When you launched Internet Config back in step one, the program installed an Internet Config extension and an Internet Preferences file. You can also customize the settings in the remaining Internet Config tiles, but it's not necessary at this time.

Eudora 1.5.1

Quick Reminder: Eudora is an email client program. Although it can work with both a shell account and a UUCP transport agent, it is most commonly used with MacTCP, and that's how we configure it here.

Tasks:

1. Launch and configure Eudora.

2. Compose and send an email message to President Clinton.

3. Subscribe to the *TidBITS* mailing list.

4. Read, reply to, and delete an email message.

Launch and Configure Eudora

1. Double-click the Eudora icon.

   Eudora launches.

2. From the Special menu, choose Settings.

   Eudora presents you with the Settings dialog. Notice that the dialog has icons running down the left side, and clicking an icon brings up controls for that icon's options (see figure 29.21).

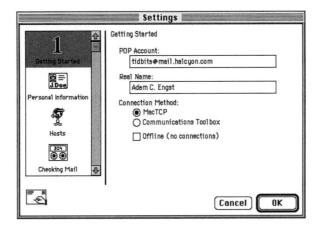

Figure 29.21   *Getting started in the Eudora Settings dialog.*

3. If you keep the Getting Started icon selected, you should see the settings for Getting Started, as shown in figure 29.21. In the POP Account field, enter your POP account (get this information from your provider) and be certain to enter it in exactly the same case as your provider used, usually lowercase.

4. Press Tab or click in the Real Name field. Enter your real name as you would like it to appear in your email messages.

5. In the Connection Method area, turn on the MacTCP radio button.

   You have now completed filling in the Getting Started portion of the Eudora Settings dialog. We are going to skip the Personal Information option and move on to the Hosts settings.

6. Click the Hosts icon.

   The Settings dialog shows the controls for Hosts (see figure 29.22)

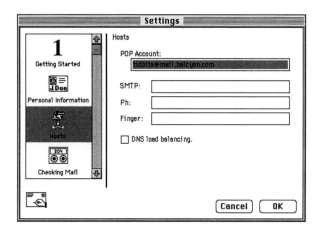

Figure 29.22   *Setting Hosts options.*

7. The only field you need to worry about in Hosts is the SMTP field. If your provider explicitly gave you an SMTP server (or host) that is different from the machine name in your POP account, enter its name in the SMTP field. Otherwise, leave the field blank, as I've done in figure 29.22.

   That's it for the Hosts controls. Let's move on to the Sending Mail controls.

8. Click the Sending Mail icon (you may need to scroll down to see it).

   The Sending Mail controls appear (see figure 29.23).

9. Turn off the Immediate send checkbox. This ensures that you can compose mail and queue it for sending without being connected to the Internet the entire time.

10. Make sure the Send on check checkbox is turned on. This ensures that Eudora sends waiting mail when it checks for new mail.

11. Click the OK button.

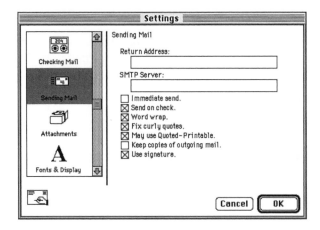

Figure 29.23   *Setting Sending Mail options.*

You have now performed the minimum configuration to use Eudora. There are many other options in the Settings dialog that you may wish to explore further. I recommend that you turn on Balloon Help from the Help menu (at the upper right of the menu bar) and point at any fields or checkboxes with which you need help.

Compose and Send an Email Message to President Clinton

1. Make sure Eudora is running. From the Message menu, choose New Message.

   Eudora presents you with a new message window, with the From line filled in with your email address and name (see figure 29.24).

2. Make sure your insertion point is in the To line (it should be unless you've clicked elsewhere in the window) and type your recipient's email address. In this case, enter **president@whitehouse.gov**.

3. Press Tab or click in the Subject line to move the insertion point to the Subject field. Enter your subject, something like *Communicating with the President*.

4. Click in the large area of the window for typing the body of your message, or press Tab three times to move the insertion point. Type your message.

   Since this example sends email to an address that replies automatically, the body of the message isn't that important for the time being, although you can use this method to express your opinions to President Clinton. At minimum, type something like *I strongly support the concept of a National Information Infrastructure.* It's considered polite to sign your name at the bottom.

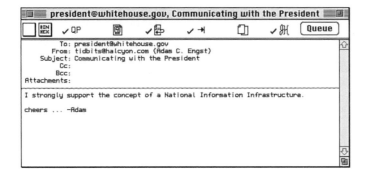

Figure 29.24   *Sending email to the President.*

5. When you finish typing and signing your message, click the Queue button in the upper right corner of the window. (If that button is labeled Send, choose Settings from the Special menu, scroll down to select the Sending Mail icon, turn off the Immediate send checkbox, and click the OK button. The Send button should turn into a Queue button.)

6. Now connect to the Internet, using MacPPP or InterSLIP if necessary. Do not quit Eudora; simply switch out to the Finder to launch InterSLIP Setup or open Config PPP to connect.

7. Switch back to Eudora, if necessary.

8. From the File menu, choose Check Mail.

   Eudora immediately presents you with a dialog asking for your password. Enter it, making sure to capitalize it as you did when you originally created it (or as it was given to you). The characters will not be displayed.

9. Click OK to enter the password you just typed.

   Eudora then contacts your POP server and looks for new mail, transferring it back to your Macintosh if you have any. After retrieving new mail, Eudora contacts the SMTP server and sends the mail that you just queued for delivery. After it finishes sending, Eudora displays a dialog telling you whether or not you have new mail.

10. If you're paying for your Internet connection by the hour, or if you're paying for a long-distance call, switch to Config PPP or InterSLIP Setup and disconnect to save money. Otherwise, go ahead and stay connected as we work through the next few tasks.

Assuming everything was set up correctly on your Macintosh and on your host machine, you've just sent an email message via Eudora.

Part IV

Step-by-Step Internet

Subscribe to the *TidBITS* Mailing List

1. Make sure Eudora is open, and from the Message menu choose New Message.

   Eudora presents you with a new message window, with the From line filled in with your email address and name and with the insertion point in the To line.

2. In the To line, type **listserv@ricevm1.rice.edu**.

3. Press Tab four times or click in the message section of the window. Type **SUBSCRIBE TIDBITS** *your full name* (replace *your full name* with your real name, not your email address) and nothing else (see figure 29.25).

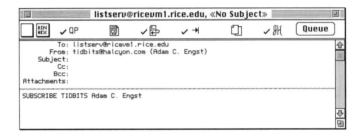

Figure 29.25   Subscribing to TidBITS.

4. Click the Queue button in the upper right of the window to queue the message to be sent.

5. Make sure you are connected to the Internet.

6. From the File menu, choose Check Mail.

7. As before, Eudora first connects to your POP server and checks for new mail. Depending on how long it has taken you to create this message, you may have received mail back from the White House (if you sent a message in the previous set of steps). Either way, after checking for new mail, Eudora contacts your SMTP server and sends your subscription message to the LISTSERV program.

8. If you are paying for your connection, feel free to close the connection now to save money.

You've just subscribed to a mailing list! Although other mailing lists may be slightly different, mostly in terms of the mailing list manager's address and the list name, the basics are the same.

Read, Reply to, and Delete an Email Message

1. Make sure Eudora is running.

   If you received a reply from the White House when you sent the subscription message to the *TidBITS* list, Eudora automatically opened your In box for you.

   If you have not yet received the reply from the White House or the confirmation of your subscription to the *TidBITS* list, wait for a while (there's no way to know how long it could take, although when I wrote these instructions, the responses came back within minutes).

2. Make sure you're connected to the Internet, and from the File menu choose Check Mail.

3. Eudora opens your In box after receiving new mail; if you have closed it while waiting, go to the Mailbox menu and choose In. Eudora then displays the In box and marks unread messages with a bullet (●) character (see figure 29.26).

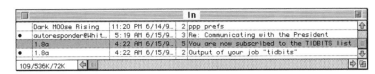

Figure 29.26 *Eudora In box.*

4. Double-click the reply from the White House, which probably looks as though it came from **autoresponder@WhiteHouse.Gov**, which is the program that automatically replies to email sent to President Clinton.

   Eudora opens the message and displays it, along with the first four lines of the header (see figure 29.27).

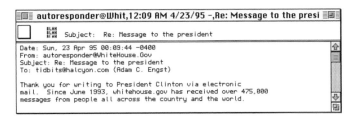

Figure 29.27 *Email from the White House.*

5. Read the message, scrolling with the scroll bar or the Page Up and Page Down keys.

6. After reading the message, go to the Message menu and choose Reply.

   Eudora creates a new message window, entering the original sender's address in the To line and the subject of your original message, prefixed with Re:, in the Subject line. The entire body of the original message is quoted in the body of the message, and Eudora automatically selects the quoted text (see figure 29.28). You can edit this text or delete it entirely by pressing the Delete key.

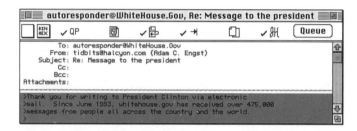

Figure 29.28 *Replying to a message.*

7. When your reply is ready, you could click the Queue button to queue it for delivery again, but please don't, unless you really want to send mail to the President again.

   When replying to personal email, you would queue the message, and then—when you wanted to send the message, perhaps along with other queued messages—you would choose either Check Mail or Send Queued Messages from the File menu.

8. Once you finish sending any messages, disconnect from the Internet, especially if you're being charged.

9. To delete the message from the White House, make sure its window is open or make sure it is selected in the In box; then, from the Message menu choose Delete.

   Eudora moves the deleted message to the Trash mailbox.

That's about all you need to know to get started reading and writing email with Eudora. As you explore the program or read about Eudora in chapter 21, "Email," you will find many other options and shortcuts to make using Eudora even easier.

NewsWatcher 2.0b24

Quick Reminder: NewsWatcher is a newsreader, a client program for Usenet news. NewsWatcher requires access to an NNTP news server on an Internet host.

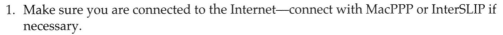

Unfortunately, we were unable to include NewsWatcher on the ISKM disk for space reasons. The directions later in this chapter for Anarchie give specific steps for using Anarchie to download a copy of NewsWatcher.

Tasks:

1. Launch and configure NewsWatcher.

2. Create a personalized subscription list and subscribe to several newsgroups.

3. Read articles in a subscribed newsgroup.

4. Post an article.

Launch and Configure NewsWatcher

1. Make sure you are connected to the Internet—connect with MacPPP or InterSLIP if necessary.

2. Double-click the NewsWatcher icon.

   If you haven't previously configured NewsWatcher, the program launches and presents a Welcome to NewsWatcher dialog (see figure 29.29).

Figure 29.29   *Choosing how you use NewsWatcher.*

3. Click the Private button.

   The Server Addresses dialog appears. If you configured Internet Config, the fields will already be filled in (see figure 29.30).

Figure 29.30   *Configuring NewsWatcher.*

4. If they are not already filled in, fill in the News Server and Mail Server fields using information that you have obtained from your provider.

5. Click the OK button.

   The Personal Information dialog appears.

6. Enter correct information in the Full name, Organization, and Email address fields. Be certain to type your email address with all lowercase letters.

7. Click the OK button.

   NewsWatcher connects to your news server and retrieves the full group list from the server. This can take some time, especially over a slow modem. Once NewsWatcher sorts the list, it displays it in a scrollable window, along with a smaller window labeled untitled.

Do not quit NewsWatcher now, but go on to the next task in which you learn how to create a personalized subscription list and subscribe to newsgroups that might interest you.

You've now successfully completed the minimum steps necessary to configure and use NewsWatcher. I strongly recommend that you read my discussion of NewsWatcher in chapter 22, "Usenet News," and the user documentation that comes with NewsWatcher. Most of the additional configuration options live in the Preferences dialog, which is available from the File menu (see figure 29.31).

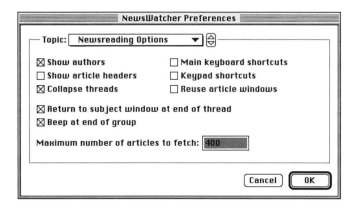

Figure 29.31   *NewsWatcher Preferences dialog.*

Create a Personalized Subscription List and Subscribe to Several Newsgroups

1. Arrange the untitled and Full Group List windows so they don't overlap.

2. Making sure that untitled is the frontmost window, go to the File menu and choose Save. Give the file an appropriate name, such as **My Newsgroups**, and save it in a location where you will be able to easily find it later.

   The window, also known as the *subscription window,* takes on the name that you gave it.

   You may wish to move the file later, perhaps to your Apple Menu Items folder so that it shows up in your Apple menu.

3. Scroll down in the Full Group List window until you find the newsgroup called **news.announce.newusers**. Groups are sorted alphabetically, so it should be about halfway down.

4. Drag the **news.announce.newusers** item over to the subscription window and drop it in the window.

   NewsWatcher may show the spinning beach ball cursor briefly, and **news.announce.newusers** should appear in your subscription window. The number next to its name indicates the number of unread articles in that group.

5. Repeat the process with **comp.sys.mac.announce**, **comp.sys.mac.comm**, and **misc.test**. As you drag each name over the subscription window, you should see a

dark black line appear in the window, indicating where the newsgroup will appear once you drop it. For some fun, you might also drag over **rec.humor.funny**. You can also add any other groups that you think might be interesting. When you finish, your subscription window should resemble the one in figure 29.32.

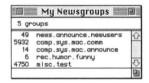

Figure 29.32 *NewsWatcher subscription window.*

Announcements important to the entire Mac community appear in **comp.sys.mac.announce**. Discussions about Macintosh communications software appear in **comp.sys.mac.comm**, which is also a good place to ask about things that you cannot otherwise figure out. I use **misc.test** later, when providing instructions on posting.

6. Make sure your subscription window is frontmost, and choose Save from the File menu to save your subscription list.

7. Close the Full Group List window by clicking the close box at its upper left. (You can open it again by choosing Show Full Group List from the Windows menu.)

8. Quit NewsWatcher by choosing Quit from the File menu.

   The previous isn't absolutely necessary, but bear with me. I want you to start the next task, reading articles, as you would normally, and that includes launching NewsWatcher.

You've now successfully created a personalized subscription list and saved it for future use. You can add newsgroups to this list at any time and remove newsgroups that no longer interest you (to remove a newsgroup, select it in the subscription window and then choose Unsubscribe from the Special menu). NewsWatcher starts up slightly faster with a small subscription list, so it works best to only subscribe to newsgroups that you read.

Read Articles in a Subscribed Newsgroup

1. If you are not connected to the Internet, establish a connection.

2. Launch NewsWatcher, not by double-clicking the NewsWatcher icon, but by double-clicking the subscription list icon that you created in the previous task.

   NewsWatcher launches, connects to the news server, checks for new groups and new articles, and then displays your subscription list window.

3. Double-click **news.announce.newusers**.

NewsWatcher retrieves the subjects and authors of the articles contained in that newsgroup and presents you with a window displaying a list of those articles (see figure 29.33).

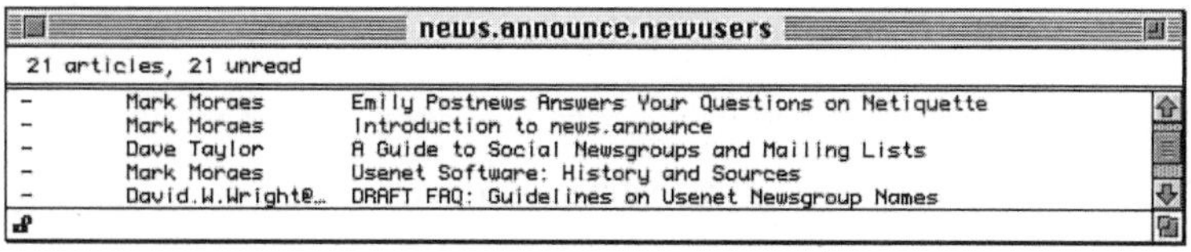

▣	news.announce.newusers	▣
21 articles, 21 unread		
–	Mark Moraes	Emily Postnews Answers Your Questions on Netiquette
–	Mark Moraes	Introduction to news.announce
–	Dave Taylor	A Guide to Social Newsgroups and Mailing Lists
–	Mark Moraes	Usenet Software: History and Sources
–	David.W.Wright…	DRAFT FAQ: Guidelines on Usenet Newsgroup Names

Figure 29.33   Articles in **news.announce.newusers**.

4. Double-click the first article in the newsgroup.

Since articles in **news.announce.newusers** are often relatively large, it may take a minute or so to download if you're using a modem. NewsWatcher displays the article once it is downloaded.

Part IV
Step-by-Step
Internet
29

5. Read the article, if you wish. I recommend that you browse the articles in this group early on, since they're designed to answer many questions that new users have.

6. To read the next article, you can close the article window and double-click the next article in the newsgroup. An easier method is to go to the News menu and choose Next Article or to press ⌘-I.

You've now successfully opened a newsgroup and read several articles. You can close the window listing articles in **news.announce.newusers**, and double-click **comp.sys.mac.announce** to see the list of articles in that group and read them if you wish.

Post an Article

1. In your subscription window, double-click the **misc.test** newsgroup. You could double-click any newsgroup that you wanted to post to, but since this is your first attempt at posting from NewsWatcher, we'll try a newsgroup specially for tests. You will receive a number of email messages from various sites, letting you know that your test posting made it there.

   The **misc.test** window opens.

2. From the News menu, choose New Message.

   NewsWatcher brings up the New Message window with the Newsgroups line already filled in and the insertion point in the Subject line (see figure 29.34).

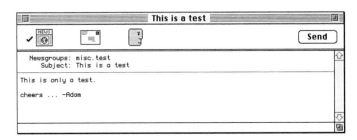

Figure 29.34   *NewsWatcher new message window.*

3. Type a subject in the Subject line.

4. Press Tab or click in the message area. Then, type your article.

5. Click the Send button.

   NewsWatcher posts your article to **misc.test**. Now that you've posted your article, feel free to read other articles, post more articles (but remember, it's a good idea to lurk for a while before becoming a prolific poster), and subscribe to additional newsgroups. You won't see your post in **misc.test** unless you quit NewsWatcher and relaunch it.

6. When you're finished, choose Quit from the File menu and save your subscription list when NewsWatcher prompts you to do so.

Congratulations! You've successfully performed all the basic tasks you do with NewsWatcher. I won't pretend that there aren't many more subtleties in using this program, but you can learn about those from reading chapter 22, "Usenet News," and NewsWatcher's documentation files.

Anarchie 1.5

Quick Reminder: Anarchie is a shareware FTP and Archie client program that you use to search for and retrieve files available via anonymous FTP. Currently, the FTP function is substantially more useful (lately, using Archie to search for files has not worked well, though this is no fault of Anarchie's), so these steps focus on using Anarchie for FTP.

Tasks:

1. Launch and configure Anarchie.

2. Connect to a site and retrieve a file.

3. Use a bookmark to retrieve a file.

Launch and Configure Anarchie

1. Anarchie uses Internet Config for its basic configuration, so if you haven't already gone through the steps earlier in this chapter for setting up Internet Config, go back and follow them. If for some reason you don't know all the information required by those steps, the minimum that you must do in Internet Config in order to use Anarchie is use the Email tile to open the Email dialog, where you must fill in the Email Address field.

2. Anarchie's job, of course, is to download files, but because Anarchie also tries to be a fairly helpful application, it passes downloaded files off to other programs, most notably StuffIt Expander, for post-processing—making the files proper, uncompressed Macintosh files. As a result, if you don't have a copy of StuffIt Expander on your hard disk, install StuffIt Expander using the ISKM Installer before you continue.

3. Double-click the Anarchie icon.

   Anarchie launches.

Part IV Step-by-Step Internet

That's it. You're done configuring and launching Anarchie and ready to use Anarchie to connect to a site and retrieve a file.

Connect to a Site and Retrieve a File

1. Make sure that you are connected to the Internet and that Anarchie is running.

2. From the FTP menu, choose Get.

   Anarchie brings up the Get via FTP window (see figure 29.35).

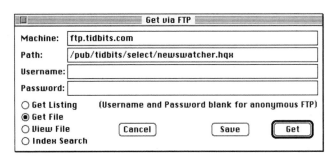

Figure 29.35   *Anarchie Get via FTP window.*

3. In the Machine field, enter **ftp.tidbits.com**.

4. In the Path field, enter **/pub/tidbits/select/newswatcher.hqx**.

5. Select the Get File radio button.

6. Click the Get button to retrieve the file.

   Anarchie displays a progress window as it downloads the file (see figure 29.36). When the download is complete, Anarchie passes the file to StuffIt Expander for post-processing. StuffIt Expander debinhexes and expands the file, thus turning it into a NewsWatcher folder, which will appear on your desktop unless you've used Internet Config to change the location of your download folder. (You change the download folder using the File Transfer tile.)

Figure 29.36   *Anarchie progress window.*

Use a Bookmark to Retrieve a File

1. Make sure Anarchie is running and that you are connected to the Internet.

2. If the Bookmarks window is not showing, choose List Bookmarks from the File menu (see figure 29.37).

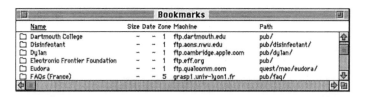

Figure 29.37   *Anarchie Bookmarks window.*

3. Double-click the Disinfectant item in the Name column (you may have to scroll down to see it).

   Anarchie connects to **ftp.acns.nwu.edu** and puts you in the **/pub/disinfectant** directory (see figure 29.38).

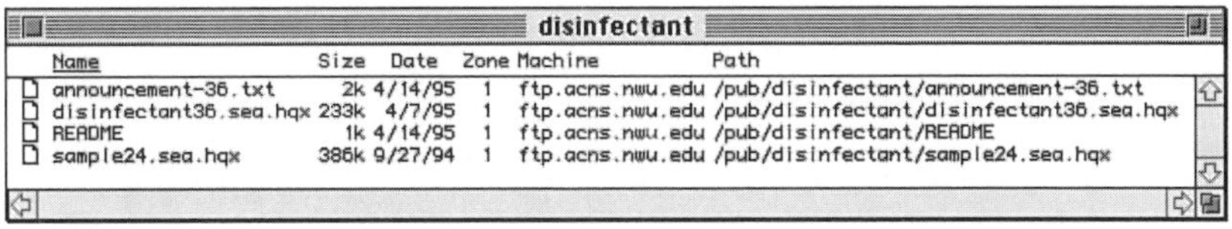

Name	Size	Date	Zone	Machine	Path
announcement-36.txt	2k	4/14/95	1	ftp.acns.nwu.edu	/pub/disinfectant/announcement-36.txt
disinfectant36.sea.hqx	233k	4/7/95	1	ftp.acns.nwu.edu	/pub/disinfectant/disinfectant36.sea.hqx
README	1k	4/14/95	1	ftp.acns.nwu.edu	/pub/disinfectant/README
sample24.sea.hqx	386k	9/27/94	1	ftp.acns.nwu.edu	/pub/disinfectant/sample24.sea.hqx

Figure 29.38   *Anarchie at `ftp.acns.nwu.edu`.*

4. Double-click the **`disinfectant36.sea.hqx`** item. (The name may not exactly match, since Disinfectant may be at a later version when you try these steps.)

   Anarchie downloads Disinfectant. When the download is complete, Anarchie passes the file to StuffIt Expander. StuffIt Expander debinhexes and expands the file, thus turning it into a Disinfectant icon, which will appear on your desktop unless you've used Internet Config to change the location of your download folder.

Congratulations! You've just performed all the basic tasks in Anarchie you're likely to do in real life. Extrapolate from these instructions to retrieve other files using Anarchie's Bookmarks and Get via FTP dialog.

Part IV — Step-by-Step Internet — 29

MacWeb 1.00A3.2

Quick Reminder: MacWeb is a client application for the World Wide Web, the most graphical and flexible of the Internet services.

Tasks:

1. Launch and configure MacWeb.
2. Browse the Web.
3. Visit a specific web site.
4. Use the hotlist.

Launch and Configure MacWeb

1. Make sure you are connected to the Internet—connect with MacPPP or InterSLIP, if necessary.

2. Double-click the MacWeb icon.

   MacWeb launches and loads its default home page. Figure 29.39 shows what the MacWeb default home page will look like if you use installed MacWeb using the

ISKM Installer. Don't worry if yours looks different, though you should see the same buttons across the top.

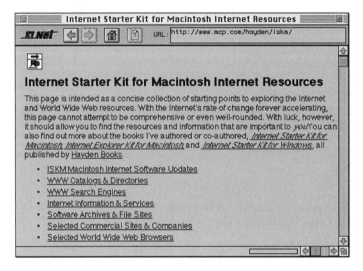

Figure 29.39   *MacWeb welcome page.*

3. From the File menu, choose Preferences.

   MacWeb brings up the Preferences dialog and displays its General options.

4. Type your email address in the Email Address field, making certain to use only lowercase letters.

5. From the pop-up menu at the top center of the dialog, choose Format.

   MacWeb displays its Format options (see figure 29.40).

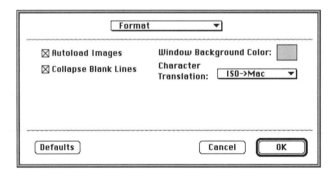

Figure 29.40   *MacWeb preferences dialog.*

6. Turn on the Autoload Images checkbox.

7. Click the OK button to save your changes.

That's all there is to it. You now have MacWeb configured and ready to go. If you get tired of automatically loading images on the Web pages you view, you can go back to the preferences dialog and turn Autoload Images back off.

Browse the Web

1. Make sure MacWeb is launched and that you are connected to the Internet.

2. From MacWeb's Navigate menu, choose EINet Galaxy.

   MacWeb displays the contents of the EINet Galaxy page (see figure 29.41).

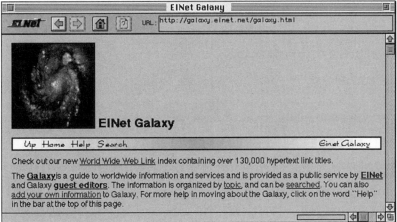

Figure 29.41   *MacWeb at EINet Galaxy.*

3. Scroll down until you get to the Arts and Humanities topic. Click the underlined words <u>Visual Arts</u>.

   MacWeb takes you to the Visual Arts page on the EINet Galaxy (see figure 29.42).

I hope you're feeling comfortable with clicking on underlined text to move around in the Web, because if you are, you know the basics of browsing the Web. Feel free to continue clicking on underlined words (which are called *links*) to move to other parts of the Web— it's too large and fast-moving for me to give you any further explicit browsing directions. If you are wondering what to do if you know a URL for a Web site that you want to visit and want to point MacWeb directly at that site, keep reading to find out how.

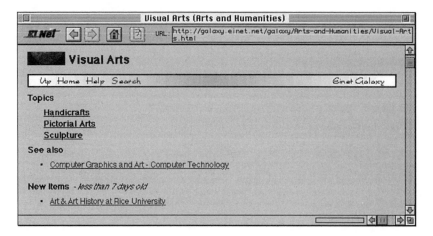

Figure 29.42   *MacWeb at the Visual Arts page.*

Visit a Specific Web Site

1. Make sure you are connected to the Internet and that you have MacWeb launched.

2. From MacWeb's File menu, choose Open URL. MacWeb displays a dialog into which you can type a URL (*Uniform Resource Locator*) (see figure 29.43).

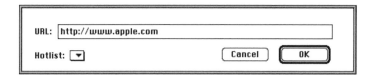

Figure 29.43   *Type a specific URL.*

3. In the field, type the URL for where you want to go to. To follow along with this example, type **http://www.apple.com**.

4. Click the OK button to connect to the Web server at **www.apple.com** (see figure 29.44).

That's all there is to going to a particular URL. If you see URLs in publications, on business cards, or wherever, you can type them into the Open URL dialog or you can also paste them from other programs. You can also type or paste URLs directly into the URL box at the top right of the MacWeb window, though this takes some hand-eye coordination.

Figure 29.44   *MacWeb at the Apple Computer Web server.*

If you are thinking about taking a break, please don't. I'm hoping you'll continue to the next set of steps so that you can see how to add an entry to your MacWeb hotlist.

Use the Hotlist

1. With the window to the Apple Computer Web server still open, choose Add This Document from the Hotlist menu.

   MacWeb adds the Apple Computer Web server to the bottom of the Hotlist menu.

2. To see how the hotlist works, click the Home button (the one with a little house on it) at the top of the MacWeb window.

   MacWeb loads your default home page.

3. From the Hotlist menu, choose Apple Computer.

   MacWeb takes you directly to the Apple Computer Web server.

4. To save your hotlist, go to the Hotlist menu and from the hierarchical Hotlist Operations menu, choose Save.

   MacWeb brings up a Standard File dialog, and you can save the hotlist anywhere you wish. Remember where you save it, though, because in your next MacWeb session you may find yourself trying to open your hotlist by dropping down the

Hotlist menu, choosing the Hotlist Operations hierarchical menu, and then using the Open command to open the hotlist. (Of course, you can avoid these steps by double-clicking the hotlist icon in order to launch MacWeb.)

5. In the Save dialog, name your hotlist and save it in a location where you'll be able to find it again.

That's about all there is to using MacWeb, though exploring even a portion of the Web could take a lifetime. When you finish looking around for now, quit MacWeb by choosing Quit from the File menu. You may wish to disconnect from the Internet after you quit.

This Is Only the Beginning

If you've followed some or all of the previous tasks, you've done quite a bit on the Internet. Here is what you've learned to do:

1. Configure MacTCP.

2. Configure MacPPP or InterSLIP.

3. Configure Internet Config.

4. Read, write, and send email with Eudora.

5. Read, write, and post articles with NewsWatcher.

6. Retrieve files via FTP with Anarchie.

7. Browse the World Wide Web with MacWeb.

My apologies if you found this section a bit stilted or boring, but I hope it conveyed just the information you need to get over the hump of using these programs. If something changed such that the instructions don't work quite right, my apologies—but don't lose heart. The Internet changes rapidly and you must be flexible enough to deal with that change. Keep trying and you're bound to get the hang of it soon.

This chapter also brings us to the end of *Internet Starter Kit for Macintosh*. It may seem as though there are lots of pages left, but they're all appendixes, some of which you may want to browse through. If you're like many people, you've probably already flipped through them and seen the lists of Internet access providers and the list of HTML tags in appendix C.

I hope you've enjoyed this book, and I hope you enjoy the Internet.

P a r t

V

Appendices

The appendices that follow are mostly straight lists of information. They aren't for reading or even necessarily repeated reference, but the information in them should prove valuable in the process of finding an Internet access provider and working with HTML.

Appendix A, Internet Starter Kit Providers

Appendix A "Internet Starter Kit Providers," is a good-sized list of Internet access providers around the world who have agreed to provide us (and you with a special deal of one sort or another) with information so you can easily configure MacTCP for use with a specific provider. Each of the providers in this appendix has a MacTCP Prep file that's installed for you by the ISKM Installer—simply Option-drag the appropriate MacTCP Prep file to your Preferences folder to configure MacTCP for that provider. See the information under the provider names in appendix A for additional instructions.

Appendix B, Providers of Commercial Internet Access

Appendix B, "Providers of Commercial Internet Access" (POCIA), lists Internet service providers from all around the world, organized by area code (for the U.S.) and country (for the rest of the world). If you decide not to work with one of the Internet service providers listed in appendix A, "Internet Starter Kit Providers," for whatever reason, you should be able to find an appropriate provider in the POCIA list. Phone numbers and email addresses (if you already have an account on America Online, say) are listed so you can easily contact the providers to request more information about their rates and services. This list has been compiled and maintained by Celestin Company, and thanks are due to them for allowing me to include it here.

Appendix C, HTML Tags

Although Tonya's chapter 26, "Creating Your Web Page," walks you through all the basic information about creating a Web page, we felt it would be helpful to bring all the basic HTML tags together in one place for reference. Hence, appendix C, which contains that list.

Appendix D, Glossary

Appendix D provides you with a list of common Internet terms and their definitions. If you're troubled by a vocabulary question—at least, one regarding the Internet—check here first.

A p p e n d i x

A

Internet Starter Kit Providers

In order to help you get connected to the Internet as quickly and inexpensively as possible, we have developed a set of Internet Starter Kit providers. These providers, which include a number of local, national, and non-U.S. organizations, have agreed to give Internet Starter Kit readers free Internet access time or special discounts on their services. Even better, we have included custom MacTCP Prep files for each of these providers on the Internet Starter Kit disk.

Note

The following information has been provided by the Internet access providers themselves, so we can't be responsible for any mistakes or changes. Always double-check rates and the like before signing up.

Organizing these providers was fairly tough, since some cover more than one area and some cover the whole country. The information on these pages, along with the discussion in chapter 11, "Choosing a Connection," should be enough for you to figure out which provider you would like to try. What should you look for? To keep your costs down, you probably want to find a provider who you can call with a local phone call, so check the Cities with Access Numbers and Area Codes items. There may be several that you can choose from, so use the other information such as rates and the special Starter Kit promotion to figure out which is most advantageous for you. Also check the national providers pages, because you might actually have lower costs by using one of them. Of course, if there is no local provider listed in your area, one of the national providers may be your best bet. If you don't live in the U.S., check the non-U.S. providers who have agreed to work with us; although this list is relatively small, we hope to make it larger in subsequent editions. Once you have decided on a provider to try, use the contact information and signup process information to sign up with that provider.

> **Note**
>
> *Appendix B, "Providers of Commercial Internet Access," contains another list of providers, but there are no special deals or MacTCP Prep files for those providers. With one of them, you are on your own. Still, if you can't find a provider that's right for you in this appendix, check appendix B.*

This sounds more complicated than it really is. Don't worry, it isn't that tough. Here's a description of the data you will find for each provider:

- Provider Name: This is the name of the company that provides the access; for example, Northwest Nexus.

- Area: This is the area in which the provider is located. Note that the service area may extend quite a distance from where a provider is located, so look for the cities and area codes covered.

- Cities: These are the cities that generally can get local call access to the provider. Area codes and cities don't always match, so look also for the area codes that are covered.

- Area Codes: These are the area codes from which you can access the provider via a local call—sometimes calls within your own area code may have tolls, so be aware of what prefix you must dial to connect.

- Rates: Look here to find out how much it will cost you to use a provider.

- Promotion for Starter Kit Owners: This is the special deal that the provider gives you, the Starter Kit owner. Often, these special deals will save you more than the cost of the book, so you really come out ahead!

- Signup Process: This is a general overview of how to sign up with a provider.

- Contact Info: Each provider has listed its snail mail address, phone and fax numbers, and email addresses for you to use.

- Web Site: Most providers have Web sites you can visit. This item lists addresses for these sites.

The list begins with the providers located on the West coast of the U.S. From there, the list moves east across the U.S. all the way to the East coast. Next comes U.S. providers that are in Hawaii. After that come providers who cover the entire nation. Last, but certainly not least, are non-U.S. providers.

Note *Remember that coverage areas don't always match geographic locations, so make sure you look over several providers in order to get the best connection for you.*

Cinenet Communications, Inc.

Area: West Coast

Cities: Los Angeles, serving Southern California
Area Codes: 213, 310, 818, 714
Rates: PPP is $30/month, which includes 75 hrs free. Signup is $30.
Promotion for Starter Kit Owners: With purchase of the Starter Kit, you get 30 trial hours at no charge. These 30 hours must be used up within 60 days of the purchase of the book.
Signup Process: Register online: With your terminal emulator set to 8-N-1, dial 310-301-4501 and login as **guest**, and go through the registration process. Your account be activated a few hours later. You can also call our voice number 310-301-4500 and register on the phone.
Contact Info:
4676 Admiralty Way, Suite 406
Marina Del Rey
California 90292
Voice: 310-301-4500
Fax: 310-301-4511
Human response: info@cinenet.net
Automated response: auto-info@cinenet.net

Web Site: http://www.cinenet.net/

EarthLink Network, Inc.

Area: West Coast

Cities: Greater Los Angeles area, CA
Area Codes: 213, 818, 310, 714, 805, 909
Rates: Basic SLIP/PPP: $49.95 setup (waived for *Starter Kit* owners), $9.95 per month + $1.95 per hour.
Extended SLIP/PPP: $49.95 setup (waived for *Starter Kit* owners), $29.95 per month, includes 30 hours + $1.95 per hour over 30.

PowerUser SLIP/PPP: $49.95 setup (waived for *Starter Kit* owners), $49.95 per month, includes 300 hours + $1.95 per hour over 300.
Promotion for Starter Kit Owners: The $49.95 setup fee is waived!
Signup Process: To sign up for EarthLink Network, just call our sales department at 213-644-9500. Be sure to mention you have *Internet Starter Kit for Macintosh, Third Edition*. You will be faxed a complete configuration checklist with all the information you need to set up your software and to start net surfing.
Contact Info:
3171 Los Feliz Blvd., Suite 203
Los Angeles, CA 90039
Voice: 213-644-9500
Fax: 213-644-9510
Human response: sales@earthlink.net
Automated response: info@earthlink.net

Web Site: http://www.earthlink.net/

Great Basin Internet Services, Inc.

Area: West Coast

Cities: Reno, Sparks, Carson City, Minden, Gardnerville, Dayton, Virginia City, and Incline Village, NV
Area Codes: 702, 916
Rates: 14.4 Kbps: $20 startup; $20/month flat rate; 28.8 Kbps: $40 startup; $25/month flat rate. Email only: $5/month.
Promotion for Starter Kit Owners: We'll waive the startup fee!
Signup Process: Decide on a hostname and a local area city. We place SLIP and PPP accounts in the <hostname>.<city>.nv.us domains. For example, someone in Sparks might pick: mycomputer.sparks.nv.us. Decide whether you want SLIP or PPP. That's about it!

Part V

Internet Starter Kit Providers

A

Contact Info:
1155 W Fourth St. Ste. 225
P.O. Box 6209
Reno NV 89511-6209
Voice: 702-348-7299
Fax: 702-348-9412
Human response: bruce@greatbasin.net
Automated response: info@greatbasin.net

Web Site: http://www.greatbasin.net/

Leonardo Internet
Area: West Coast

Cities: Los Angeles, Santa Monica, Beverly Hills, Pacific Palisades, Malibu, Sherman Oaks, Studio City, Venice, Manhattan Beach, Hollywood, North Hollywood, Glendale, Pasadena, Commerce, Burbank, and Woodland Hills, CA
Area Codes: 310, 213, 818
Rates: PPP Basic: $17.50/month, 20 hours, additional hours $1; $50 startup.
PPP Unlimited: $29.50/month, unlimited usage, 2 hours on/off; $50 startup.
Promotion for Starter Kit Owners: Flat-rate PPP account with the following rates: $20 startup fee, plus $22/month (billed in advance on a quarterly basis), a savings of $7.50 per month! You can use this account for as many hours as you want each month. We also have set up instruction sheets geared to users of the *Internet Starter Kit* (Mac or Windows), and we have friendly and knowledgeable technical support people who will help you if you're new to the Internet. Please give us a call if you would like more information on getting connected, building web sites, or to get the latest prices. Technical support and sales open 7 days a week.
Signup Process: Call, fax, or email to get an account.
Contact Info:
927 6th Street
Santa Monica, CA 90403
Voice: 310-395-5500
Fax: 310-395-9924
Human response: info@leonardo.net

Web Site: http://leonardo.net/

North Bay Network
Area: West Coast

Cities: San Rafael, Nicasio, and Rohnert Park, CA
Area Codes: 415, 707
Rates: Call or email for details.
Promotion for Starter Kit Owners: $25 off our normal $50 startup fee!
Signup Process: Dialup Accounts: Customer receives and completes agreement form and sends in with payment. You are sent login and password information in a format appropriate for your system/software configuration, email account name, and local POP phone number.
Contact Info:
20 Minor Court
San Rafael, CA 94903
Voice: 415-472-1600
Fax : 415-472-2461
Human response: support@nbn.com
Automated response: info@nbn.com

Web Site: http://www.nbn.com/

Primenet Services for the Internet
Area: West Coast

Cities: Phoenix, Tucson, Flagstaff, Prescott, Sierra Vista, Yuma, AZ; Fresno, Los Angeles, Pomona, Santa Ana, CA; Boise, Payette, ID; Kansas City, MO; Minneapolis/St. Paul, MN; El Paso, TX; Eau Claire, WI
Area Codes: 602, 520, 209, 818, 213, 310, 909, 714, 208, 816, 612, 915, 715.
Rates: Vary from city to city. Startup is $30, and SLIP/PPP comes with 150 hours of connect time per month for between $20 and $30.
Promotion for Starter Kit Owners: Starter Kit owners get 50% off startup fees.
Signup Process: Call our 800 number to give us your billing information. You get a 7-day no obligation trial—just let us know if you want to discontinue.
Contact Info:
2320 W. Peoria Ave., Suite A-103
Phoenix, AZ 85029
Voice: 800-463-8386
Fax: same
Human response: acctinfo@primenet.com
Automated response: info@primenet.com

Web Site: http://www.primenet.com/

zNET
Area: West Coast

Cities: San Francisco, San Jose, Palo Alto, Mountain View, San Mateo, Santa Cruz, Monterey, Milpitas, and Oakland, CA

Area Codes: 619

Rates: Basic Account: $20/month, $25 setup

SLIP/PPP, POP mail, news, 100 hours/month, limited support, plus our zNET Configuration guidebook for DOS/Windows or Macintosh

Premium Account: Flat rate $40/month, $50 setup

SLIP/PPP, POP mail, news; includes a custom domain name, the *Internet Starter Kit* book with TCP/IP software, plus our zNET Configuration guidebook for DOS/Windows or Macintosh

Full-Time Connection: Starting at $80, custom setup

24-hour dedicated connection to a 28.8 modem, SLIP/PPP access, POP mail account, news, plus our zNET Configuration guidebook for DOS/Windows or Macintosh

Custom Domain Name Registration: $25 setup, $10/month (included in the Premium Account)

Promotion for Starter Kit Owners: Two weeks free trial period!

Signup Process: Email to signup@znet.com, fax 619-755-8149, or phone 619-755-7772 for zNET application. Accounts can be activated same day by voice phone to 619-755-7772 and application returned to us by U.S. mail.

Contact Info:
504 Vandell Way, Building A
Campbell, CA 95008
Voice: 408-378-9800
Fax: 619-755-8149
Human response: sales@znet.com, support@znet.com
Automated response: info@znet.com, signup@znet.com

Web Site: http://www.znet.com/, ftp://ftp.znet.com/

a2i communications
Area: West Coast

Cities: San Jose, Redwood City, San Francisco, Oakland, Napa

Area Codes: 408, 415, 510, 707

Rates: $15 start-up fee; $20/month includes 20 hours of SLIP/PPP; additional usage is only $0.25/hour.

Promotion for Starter Kit Owners: With original proof of purchase, second month of service is free.

Signup Process: Dial an access number with a modem and terminal emulator (or telnet to **rahul.net**) and log in as **guest**. Browse the guest menu for information, then select "online sign-up" and follow the instructions.

Contact Info:
1211 Park Avenue #202
San Jose, CA 95126
Voice: 408-293-8078
Fax: 408-263-0461
Human response: support@rahul.net
Automated response: info@rahul.net

Web Site: http://www.rahul.net/

Europa Communications, Inc.
Area: West Coast

Cities: Portland, OR

Area Codes: 503

Rates: There are two levels of service, and billing can take place in one, three, or six month intervals. Service Level 1 provides 30 hours per month and costs $18 for one month, $52 for three, or $100 for six. Service Level 2 offers 150 hours per month and costs $25 for one month, $73 for three months, or $145 for six months. There are also disk quotas of 4 MB (8 MB temporarily) for the Level 1 service and 10 MB (18 MB temporarily) for the Level 2 service.

Promotion for Starter Kit Owners: We will waive the usual $10 startup fee. You will also get a free, seven day trial account.

Signup Process: You have two choices: 1. Call us (voice) at 503-222-9508 and we'll open your new account. 2. Dial our data line at 503-222-4244 and login as **new**. From the menu, you can read about our services, sign up for your trial account, etc.

Contact Info:
320 S.W. Stark St.
Suite 427
Portland, OR 97204
Voice: 503-222-9508
Fax: 503-796-9134
Human response: admin@europa.com
Automated response: info@europa.com

Web Site: http://www.europa.com/

Internet Connect Services
Area: West Coast

Cities: Missoula, Superior, Sealy Swan, Arlee, and Ravalli, Montana

Area Codes: 406

Rates: Individual accounts are $19.95 a month; this a flat fee (no hourly charges!). Our normal set up fee is $24.95.

Promotion for Starter Kit Owners: 2 weeks free for *Starter Kit* owners as well as $14.95 off our normal startup fee.

Signup Process: Signup can be done over the phone or by fax, unless we get the call late Friday. We usually have accounts up within eight hours.

Contact Info:
2701 North Reserve St.
Missoula, MT 59801
Voice: 406-721-4952
Fax: 406-549-9318
Human response: jmsj@montana.com

Web Site: http://www.montana.com

InterServe Communications, Inc.
Area: West Coast

Cities: Palo Alto, CA

Area Codes: Parts of 415, 408, 510

Rates: ISKM setup fee $15 (list is $25). Low-volume users $20/month includes 15 hours, $2/hour after 15 hours. Flat Rate $30/month. Domain name registration $25.

Promotion for Starter Kit Owners: 2 weeks free trial and 40% discount on setup fee.

Signup Process: Call us.

Contact Info:
430 Sherman Avenue, Suite 212
Palo Alto, CA 94306
Voice: 415-328-4333
Human response: ray@interserve.com
Automated response: info@interserve.com

Web Site: http://www.interserve.com/

LanMinds
Area: West Coast

Cities: Oakland, Berkeley, San Francisco, Walnut Creek, Lafayette Orinda, San Rafael, Mill Valley, Richmond. (all in CA)

Area Codes: 415, 510

Rates: V.34 rates: $20/month, includes 10 hours, $1/hr thereafter or $29/month unlimited access ISDN rates: $49/month, includes 10 hours, $2/hr thereafter.

Promotion for Starter Kit Owners: FREE signup, plus a free personal Web page. We have a demo account that can be used by anyone. Contact us for the current password.

Signup Process: Call LanMinds at 510-843-6389, we can send you a signup sheet (via fax, email, or snail mail). You can also request a signup sheet by sending email to **admin@lanminds.com**.

Contact Info:
1442A Walnut St. suite 431
Berkeley, CA 94709
Voice: 510-843-6389
Fax: 510-843-6390
Human response: dan@lanminds.com
Automated response: info@lanminds.com

Web Site: http://www.lanminds.com/

MobiusNet
Area: West Coast

Cities: San Francisco area

Area Codes: 415, 510

Rates: There is a $25 startup fee. The service is $25/month for 100 hours online/month. Additional hours are $1/hr.

Promotion for Starter Kit Owners: The startup fee is waived and you will be given a 10 day free trial.

Signup Process: Call MobiusNet to provide us with your username and password. Your account will be available for use almost immediately.

Contact Info:
2301 Harrison Street
Suite 101
San Francisco, CA 94110
Voice: 415-821-0600
Human response: russ@mobius.net
Automated response: info@mobius.net

Web Site: http://www.mobius.net/

Northwest Nexus Inc.
Area: West Coast

Cities: Seattle, Bellevue, Auburn, Lynnwood, Lacey, Olympia, Shelton, Tacoma, Mt. Vernon, WA

Area Codes: 206, 360

Rates: Personal PPP: $30/month (less with special

offer), $30 startup fee; other rates on request.

Promotion for Starter Kit Owners: With coupon in book, 25% off monthly charges for personal SLIP and personal PPP accounts!

Signup Process: Use a terminal program set to 8, N, 1; dial 206-455-8455; login as **new**; press Enter for password; read information; provide billing and account information.

Contact Info:
P.O. Box 40597
Bellevue, WA 98015-4597
Voice: 206-455-3505
Fax: 206-455-4672
Human response: support@halcyon.com
Automated response: info@halcyon.com

Web Site: http://www.halcyon.com/

OlympusNet
Area: West Coast

Cities: Port Angeles, Port Ludlow, Port Townsend, Sequim, WA

Area Codes: 360

Rates: $30 startup; $75 quarterly for 50 hours per month.

Promotion for Starter Kit Owners: $10 off first month's access!

Signup Process: Phone 360-385-0464 to sign up.

Contact Info:
P.O. Box 1824
Port Townsend, WA 98368
Voice: 360-385-0464
Human response: sales@olympus.net
Automated response: info@olympus.net

Web Site: http://www.olympus.net/

Whidbey Connections, Inc.
Area: West Coast

Cities: Oak Harbor, Coupeville, Freeland, Langley, Clinton, Greenbank, WA

Area Codes: 360, 206

Rates: SLIP/PPP $20/month, $10 startup for Starter Kit owners; Standard Shell $15/month, $10 startup fee. All accounts include 100 hours per month access time.

Promotion for Starter Kit Owners: For the Starter Kit promotion, we are offering $10 off of our standard startup fee.

Signup Process: Access to an account requires submission of a short application with user's name, address, userid, password, computer and modem type, and billing information. Application can be filled out through the mail, over the phone or fax, or at our office. Email applications are also accepted. Accounts will be activated on the day the applications are received.

Contact Info:
P.O. Box 1048
Coupeville, WA 98239
Voice: 360-678-1070 360-321-0608
Fax: 360-678-6129
Human response: admin@whidbey.net
Automated response: info@whidbey.net

Web Site: http://www.whidbey.net/

Exchange Network Services, Inc. (ExchangeNet)
Area: Northern Midwest

Cities: Cleveland, OH and surrounding area

Area Codes: 216

Rates: SLIP/PPP rates: $25 startup ($20 w/Starter Kit discount), $25 monthly (includes 50 hours usage). Additional hours over 50 billed at $1/hr.

Promotion for Starter Kit Owners: $5 off startup fee and 1 week free trial account.

Signup Process: Online registration via terminal emulator available at 731-0900 login as **newuser**. Fax or mail printout of registration may be requested.

Contact Info:
25931 Euclid Avenue #145
Euclid, Ohio 44132
Voice: 216-261-4593
Fax: 216-261-2236
Human response: support@en.com
Automated response: info@en.com

Web Site: http://www.en.com/

iCON - A Service of Saint Louis Internet Connections
Area: Northern Midwest

Cities: Currently the Saint Louis, Missouri metropolitan area.

Area Codes: 314

Rates: Personal Subscription: $20 registration fee, $25/month for unlimited PPP/SLIP access. Business Subscription: $100 registration fee,

$100/month for unlimited PPP/SLIP access.
Promotion for Starter Kit Owners: First month is free.
Signup Process: Call 314-241-0969 or email **info@icon-stl.net** for account registration.
Contact Info:
710 North Tucker Suite 800
Saint Louis, MO 63101
Voice: 314-241-0969
Fax: 314-241-1249
Human response: info@icon-stl.net
Automated response:

Web Site: http://www.icon-stl.net/

Internet Access Cincinnati
Area: Northern Midwest
Cities: Cincinnati, Hamilton, Oxford, Northern Kentucky, Peoria, IN Versailles, IN
Area Codes: 513, 606, 812
Rates: $28.00—20% off our usual monthly flat rate. Setup fee waived and absolutely no additional fees. Buy 10 months and get 12.
Promotion for Starter Kit Owners: Two weeks free trial. Also, in the event of cancellation, our usual policy offers a full refund for the current month and any pre-paid months.
Signup Process: Call our modem pool at 513-887-8855, or telnet to **access.iac.net**, log in as **new** and follow the directions or call our office at 513-333-0033. For personal assistance, drop by our office at 435 Elm Street #305 in the downtown Cincinnati Convention Place Mall, on the skywalk between the Hyatt Regency Hotel lobby and Convention Center.
Contact Info:
P.O. Box 602
Hamilton Ohio 45012-0602
Voice: 513-887-8877
Fax: 513-887-2085
Human response: office@iac.net
Automated response: info@iac.net

Web Site: http://www.iac.net/

InterAccess Co.
Area: Northern Midwest
Cities: Chicagoland metropolitan area, including Chicago, Northbrook, Tinley Park, Wheaton,

Schiller Park, and Hoffman Estates, IL
Area Codes: 708, 312, part of 815
Rates: Business and Personal Accounts for single users: Flat-rate monthly: SLIP/PPP/Plug n' Play, $30/month, $28/month for credit card payers.
Timed monthly: SLIP/PPP/Plug n' Play, $10/month including 5 hours, additional hours at $2.30/hour.
Flat-rate quarterly: SLIP/PPP/Plug n' Play, $73/qtr.
Flat-rate yearly: SLIP/PPP/Plug n' Play, $260/yr.
Plug n' Play Installation Fee: $15.
Promotion for Starter Kit Owners: The installation fee is waived!
Signup Process: Typically you log in to our dialup number, 708-671-0237, login: **guest**, with a standard communication program and fill out an application online. Someone calls to establish authenticity, you are mailed a startup package, and you're on. You may also fax or mail applications.
Contact Info:
3345 Commercial Ave.
Northbrook, IL 60062
Voice: 708-498-2542
Fax: 708-498-3289
Human response: sales@interaccess.com
Automated response: info@interaccess.com

Web Site: http://www.interaccess.com/

InterSource
Area: Northern Midwest
Cities: Bloomington, IN
Area Codes: 812
Rates: Call for rates
Promotion for Starter Kit Owners: Startup fee waived, 14 day trial period.
Contact Info:
2613 E. 3rd St.
Bloomington, IN 47401
Voice: 812-332-2722
Fax: 812-332-2940
Human response: help@intersource.com
Automated response: info@intersource.com

IQuest Network Services
Area: Northern Midwest
Cities: Indianapolis, Anderson, Muncie, Lafayette, Kokomo, Bloomington, and Terre Haute, IN; Chicago, IL; Columbus, OH

Area Codes: 317, 312, 708, 614, 812
Rates: Dialup SLIP/PPP Access: 14.4 Access: $15 per month for 120 hours; 28.8 Access: $20 per month for 120 hours.
Promotion for Starter Kit Owners: The first 15 hours of service are free!
Signup Process: If you call the 800 number by 3:00, the account will be active by 8:00 p.m. that evening.
Contact Info:
2035 East 46th Street
Indianapolis, IN 46205
Voice: 800-844-UNIX (8649)
Fax: 317-259-7289
Human response: info@iquest.net
Automated response: info@iquest.net

Web Site: http://www.iquest.net/

Red River Net
Area: Northern Midwest
Cities: Fargo, ND, and Sioux Falls, SD
Area Codes: 701, 605
Rates: $30 one-time setup; $25 a month for service: 20% off for six or more months of service paid in advance.
Promotion for Starter Kit Owners: Free setup for *Starter Kit* owners—a $30 value!
Signup Process: Call for ordering information.
Contact Info:
P.O. Box 388
Fargo, ND 58107
Voice: 701-232-2227
Fax: 701-232-2910
Human response: lien@rrnet.com
Automated response: info@rrnet.com

Web Site: http://www.rrnet.com/

Tezcat Communications
Area: Northern Midwest
Cities: Chicago
Area Codes: 312
Rates: $28, $60, $220, for monthly, quarterly, or yearly access respectively. There are no startup or hourly fees for use of Tezcat's Personal PPP service.
Promotion for Starter Kit Owners: Internet Starter Kit owners qualify for a one week trial access period. Monthly charge for Personal PPP access is $28 with no startup fees, hourly charges, or time limits.

Signup Process: Customers may either telnet to **tezcat.com** and login as **new**, or call our voice support line (312) 850-0181 for assignment of password and IP address. User will be given a complete walk-through to ensure that they are online before being turned loose.
Contact Info:
1573-A N. Milwaukee
Suite 440
Chicago, IL. 60622
Voice: 312-850-0181
Fax: 312-850-0492
Human response: sales@tezcat.net
Automated response: info@tezcat.net

Web Site: http://www.tezcat.com/

Traverse Communication Company
Area: Northern Midwest
Cities: Traverse City, MI and all Michigan cities through 800# access
Area Codes: 616 (primary), 517, 313, 810 (800#)
Rates: $35 signup (includes Internet Starter Kit for Windows or Macintosh); $20 signup for previous owners of ISK, $20/mo subscription includes 10 hrs access, $2.00/hr for hours 11-20, $1.50/hr for hours 21-30, $1.00/hr for hours over 30, $0.13/min surcharge for 800# access. Educational rates available for institutional use. Network pricing by arrangement.
Promotion for Starter Kit Owners: $15.00 of regular signup fee and five free hours access in the first month.
Signup Process: Sign and deliver Customer Agreement Form and signup fee to our offices (by mail or in person). Password will be mailed or faxed within 24 hrs. Upon receipt, follow installation instructions and dial 616-935-4946 to connect. Login for user **jblow** takes the form of **jblow+ppp**.
Contact Info:
223 Grandview Parkway, Ste 108
Traverse City, MI 49684
Voice: 616-935-1705
Fax: 616-935-3547
Human response: support@traverse.com
Automated response: info@traverse.com

Web Site: http://www.traverse.com/

WorldWide Access
Area: Northern Midwest

Cities: Chicago and the surrounding suburban area

Area Codes: 312, 708, 815

Rates: SLIP/PPP dialup accounts are $25/month flat rate. NO startup fees. NO time limits. All modem speeds up to and including 28.8 Kbps 24 hour, 365 day per year access.

Promotion for Starter Kit Owners: One free month of service.

Signup Process: We accept service orders by fax or mail in addition to our convenient signup online service. Customer accounts can be created in as little as 15 minutes. We offer complete support to the Macintosh user in the form of software setup files and detailed instructional materials on setup and configuration. Our courteous technical support group is also available with extended business hours to help the individual get online as quickly and effortlessly as possible.

Contact Info:

23 Southfield Drive

Vernon Hills, IL 60061-3258

Voice: 708-367-1870

Fax: 708-367-1872

Human response: support@wwa.com

Automated response: info@wwa.com

Web Site: http://www.wwa.com/

ABWAM, Inc.
Area: Midwest

Cities: Denver, CO

Area Codes: 303

Rates: hourly plan: $25 startup, $2.40/hr, no minimum monthly plan: $25 startup, $20/mo, 1st 30 hrs, $2.40/hr after, Dedicated dialup: $200 startup, $125/mo, 28.8 unlimited hours.

Promotion for Starter Kit Owners: Startup fee reduced to $10. Seven day trial period; if not satisfied, full refund, including startup fees.

Signup Process: We send you an application by mail, fax, or dialup; once completed, we will create your account, call you at your daytime phone number, and give you the instructions needed to get online.

Contact Info:

8605 F-5 West Cross Dr. #304

Littleton, CO 80123

Voice: 303-730-6050

Human response: dwatson@abwam.com

Automated response: info@abwam.com

Web Site: http://www.abwam.com/

CSDC
Area: Midwest

Cities: Denver Colorado, Boulder Colorado

Area Codes: 303

Rates: PPP Access: $20/month. Includes 40 free hours. $2/hr thereafter. $150 maximum. $20 startup fee.

Promotion for Starter Kit Owners: 50% off the startup fee.

Signup Process: Call us, we will set your account up immediately and mail or fax you an application form. The form is available online at http://www.csd.net/application.html.

Contact Info:

2525 Arapahoe Suite E4-447

Boulder, CO 80302

Voice: 303-665-8053

F a x: 303-443-0808

Human response: support@csd.net

Automated response: info@csd.net

Web Site: http://www.csd.net/

Illuminati Online
Area: Southern Midwest

Cities: Austin, Houston, San Antonio; call or send email for information on other parts of central and southeast Texas.

Area Codes: 512, 713, 210; 817, 915, 407 (call for information)

Rates: $15/month for 30 hours; 50 cents/additional hour; $28/month for 80 hours; 30 cents/additional hour; Telnet accounts: $10/month for unlimited use, but no modem time. Setup PPP/SLIP account: $50 ($25 for Starter Kit owners). PPP/SLIP accounts include a shell account at no extra charge. All accounts include 5 MB of hard disk space. Additional space is 2 cents/MB/day or $2/5MB/month. Personal web sites are included without charge.

Promotion for Starter Kit Owners: The MacPPP setup fee is reduced to $25, and the first two weeks online are free.

Signup Process: 1. Set your modem to 8 bits, no parity, 1 stop bit, and VT100 terminal emulation. 2. Have your modem dial 1-512-448-8950 (or just 448-8950 in Austin). 3. Log in as **new**

and complete the registration dialog. 4. Enter your preferred method of payment, and put ISKM down as your referral. That's it! You can also telnet to **io.com** instead of dialing in by modem.
Contact Info:
P.O.Box 18957
Austin, TX 78760
Voice: (512) 462-0999
Fax: (512) 447-1144
Human response: admin@io.com
Automated response: info@io.com

Web Site: http://www.io.com/

NeoSoft, Inc.
Area: Southern Midwest
Cities: Houston, TX Ft. Worth, TX New Orleans, LA St. Louis, MO
Area Codes: 713, 817, 504, 314
Rates: $40 startup fee, $34.95/month; Personal $80 startup fee, $74.95/month; Corporate call for dedicated pricing.
Promotion for Starter Kit Owners: Two free weeks.
Signup Process: At the moment, call for setup. Coming soon: online signup.
Contact Info:
1770 St. James Place
Suite 500
Houston, TX 77056
Voice: 1-800-438-6367
Fax: 713-968-5801
Human response: sales@neosoft.com
Automated response: info@neosoft.com

Web Site: http://www.neosoft.com/

Angel Networks, Inc.
Area: Northern East Coast
Cities: New York City
Area Codes: 212, 718
Rates: Basic: $15 per month + $1 per hr (first 20 hrs free). Standard: $30 per month (with no hourly charges).
Promotion for Starter Kit Owners: No signup or setup fees. Two weeks free.
Signup Process: Give us a call. We will create your account while you are on the phone with us and walk you through the login process. On-site

setup is also available.
Contact Info:
27 West 20th Street
Suite 1002
New York, NY 10011
Voice: 212-366-0881
Fax: 212-366-6703
Human response: rmah@angel.net
Automated response: info@angel.net

Web Site: http://www.angel.net/

FishNet, Prometheus Information Corp.
Area: Northern East Coast
Cities: Philadelphia
Area Codes: 610, 215
Rates: Unlimited use $35 per month.
Promotion for Starter Kit Owners: No setup charges and a two week, money-back guarantee.
Signup Process: 1. Call us at (610)337-9994 2. Mention that you've purchased the Internet Starter Kit 3. Provide us with the following: Name, Address, phone #, Credit card # (Visa, MC, Discover) or Purchase Order # 4. Start surfing the Internet!
Contact Info:
583 Shoemaker Road
Suite 220
King Of Prussia, PA 19406
Voice: 610-337-9994
Fax: 610-337-9918
Human response: pete@pond.com
Automated response: info@pond.com

Web Site: http://www.pond.com/

I-2000, Inc.
Area: Northern East Coast
Cities: New York City, Long Island City, Farmingdale, Mineola, Babylon, Selden, Bayside, White Plains, and Riverhead, NY; Stamford, CT; Elizabeth and Hackensack, NJ; Philadelphia, PA
Area Codes: 516, 914, 718, 215, 212, 203, 908, 201
Rates: Dialup: $20 setup, $30 monthly. Call for other services.

Promotion for Starter Kit Owners: *Starter Kit* plus one month service and setup: $59.95! One week trial period!

Signup Process: MasterCard, Visa, or check. Fax, email, telephone, fill out form online from any access number with login: **info**, password: **newuser** or on our Web site.

Contact Info:
416 Main Street
Metuchen, NJ 08840
Voice: 516-867-6379 or 908-906-0197
Fax: 908-906-2396
Human response: mikef@i-2000.com
Automated response: info@i-2000.com

Web Site: http://www.i-2000.com/

North Shore Access
Area: Northern East Coast

Cities: Boston, Georgetown, Lynn, Manchester-by-the-Sea, MA

Area Codes: 617, 508

Rates: PPP account: $30/month for 60 hours connect time, $0.50/hr thereafter. Includes 5 MB disk quota, shell access, and personal servers for FTP, gopher, and WWW.

Promotion for Starter Kit Owners: $20 off our regular signup fee (normally $50 dollars).

Signup Process: Online signup: dial one of our access numbers (617-593-4557, 617-927-5200, 508-352-5533, or 508-526-2100) with a terminal program, 8 bits/no parity/1 stop bit, and login as **new**, no password. Or call our office at 617-593-3110 and press 1 for sales.

Contact Info:
145 Munroe Street, Suite 405
Lynn, MA 01901
Voice: 617-593-3110
Fax: 617-593-6858
Human response: info@shore.net
Automated response:

Web Site: http://www.shore.net/

Panix Public Access Networks, Corp.
Area: Northern East Coast

Cities: NYC, NY, Jersey City, NJ, Nassau County Long Island, NY West Suffolk County Long Island, NY(coming soon Westchester County, NY)

Area Codes: 212, 201, 516 (coming soon 914)

Rates: $35/month (or $400/year save $20) There is no startup fee.

Promotion for Starter Kit Owners: One free month when they pay for the first month. (The first 2 months for $35.)

Signup Process: 1. Connect to **panix.com** and login as **help** (date line numbers: 212-741-4545, 201-963-1500, 516-626-7863, 516-246-8262) 2. Fill out the registration form 3. A member of our staff will call you back and start up your account.

Contact Info:
15 West 18th Street 5th Floor
attn: Stacey Goldsmith
New York, NY 10011
Voice: 741 4400
Fax: 741 5311
Human response: info-person@panix.com
Automated response: info@panix.com

Web Site: http://www.panix.com/

ServiceTech, Inc.
Area: Northern East Coast

Cities: Rochester, NY, Buffalo, NY, Syracuse, NY, Canandaigua, NY, Corning, NY, Utica, NY, Toronto, Ontario, Canada, Binghamton, NY (July 95), Albany, NY (August 95)

Area Codes: 716, 315, 607, 518, 416, 905, 800

Rates: Flat-rate access service for $25.00 a month. This offers full access, with no hourly fees. Our rate includes free use of our World Wide Web server for personal home pages, and the use of our FTP server for publishing files. All of our clients also receive a static, or dedicated, IP address at no extra charge.

Promotion for Starter Kit Owners: We will waive our one-time startup fee of $20.00, as well as offer a free trial access period of two weeks.

Signup Process: Signup is either accomplished online via our Web page at: **http://www.servtech.com**/ or via phone or fax. Accounts are activated within one business day. PC or Mac customers who request them, receive installation disks to assist them in configuring their accounts. We also have a large technical support staff to answer questions and solve problems.

Contact Info:
182 Monroe Avenue
Rochester, NY 14607

Voice: 716-263-3360
Fax: 716-423-1596
Human response: sales@servtech.com
Automated response: info@servtech.com

Web Site: http://www.servtech.com/

Telerama Public Access Internet

Area: Northern East Coast

Cities: Pittsburgh, PA
Area Codes: 412
Rates: PPP Setup fee (one time): $10. Monthly fee includes unlimited shell access and 3 hrs/day PPP access: $20. PPP access in excess of 3 hrs/day: $2/hr.
Promotion for Starter Kit Owners: We waive the PPP setup fee for all Internet Starter Kit purchasers and provide 2 weeks of free access time.
Signup Process: Call 412-481-4644 with a terminal emulator and log in as **new**. Create your account. Modem speeds of up to 28.8K are supported.
Contact Info:
P.O. Box 60024
Pittsburgh, PA 15211
Voice: 412-481-3505
Fax: 412-481-8568
Human response: sysop@telerama.lm.com
Automated response: info@telerama.lm.com

Web Site: http://www.lm.com/

The Internet Access Company, Inc.

Area: Northern East Coast

Cities: Connecticut, MA, Hartford, New Hampshire: Derry (as of 5/95) New York: NYC / Manhattan area (as of 6/95)
Area Codes: 617, 508, 203, 603, 212
Rates: PPP access rates for new accounts as a result of ISK books: First month FREE, with normal billing to begin in the second month of service. Normal billing is: $29.00 for 40 hours/month; or $49.00 for 300 hours/month. (Each of the above plans normally has a one-time $20.00 startup fee that will be waived in conjunction with this offer.) These are flat rate prices; there are never any hourly charges with

TIAC dial-up accounts. For more info, send email to **info@tiac.net**.
Promotion for Starter Kit Owners: Receive their first month online FREE, with normal billing to begin in the second month of service.
Signup Process: Call a TIAC Customer Service Representative at 617/276-7200, and let him know that you're calling to take advantage of a special offer in the ISK book.
Contact Info:
175 The Great Road
Suite 210
Bedford, MA 01730
Voice: 617-276-7200
Fax: 617-275-2224
Human response: support@tiac.net
Automated response: info@tiac.net

Web Site: http://www.tiac.net/

UltraNet Communications, Inc.

Area: Northern East Coast

Cities: Clinton, Framingham, Littleton, Lowell, Marlboro, Waltham, Worcester, and Westboro
Area Codes: 508, 617, 603
Rates: Plan: Cost per month/Included Hours/Additional Hours—Low-End: $5/2/$2.50—Economy: $10/5/$2.00—Value: $20/20/$1.00—Heavy: $30/60/$0.50—Power User: $50/200/$0.25—Unlimited: $100/Unlimited/$0.00. Unlike our competitors, there are NO STARTUP FEES!
Promotion for Starter Kit Owners: Receive 10 free hours, (twice our normal promotion) and no startup fees.
Signup Process: You may sign up by calling one of our modem lines with a terminal emulator, and sign up as user **new**, and follow instructions. You may also call our voice number, and be signed up over the phone.
Contact Info:
910 Boston Post Rd.
Marlboro, MA 01752
Voice: 508-229-8400
Fax: 508-229-2375
Human response: u-esb@ultranet.com
Automated response: info@ultranet.com

Web Site: http://www.ultranet.com/

Part V

A
Internet
Starter Kit
Providers

WestNet Internet Services
Area: Northern East Coast

Cities: Rye, NY

Area Codes: 914

Rates: SLIP/PPP: $30/month Menu/Unix Shell: $15/month $20 sign-up fee for all accounts.

Promotion for Starter Kit Owners: Receive a 2 week trial period (regular users receive a 1 week trial).

Signup Process: Dial our modem number with any terminal program and login as new. Fill out the New User Registration form. We will get back to you within 24 hours when your account is created.

Contact Info:

40 Redfield St

Rye, NY 10580

Voice: (914) 967-7816

Human response: staff@westnet.com

Automated response: info@westnet.com

Web Site: http://www.westnet.com/

Florida Online
Area: Southern East Coast

Cities: Cocoa and Orlando, FL

Area Codes: 407

Rates: Dialup accounts: $20 per month, PPP/SLIP include 50 hours (includes free preconfigured software). No setup fee on dialup accounts.

Promotion for Starter Kit Owners: Free first month of a three-month or longer account!

Signup Process: All signups are via the telephone, toll-free local 407-635-8888 or 800-676-2599, seven days a week. All major credit cards accepted.

Trial account (text-based): 407-633-4710, login as **new** with password **newuser**

Contact Info:

3815 N. US 1

Suite 59

Cocoa, FL 32926

Voice: 407-635-8888 or 800-676-2599

Fax: 407-635-9050

Human response: admin@digital.net

Automated response: info@digital.net

Web Site: http://www.digital.net/

Gulf Coast Internet Company
Area: Southern East Coast

Cities: Pensacola, Ft. Walton Beach, Niceville, Gulf Breeze, Milton, Destin, Crestview, Shalimar, FL; Mobile, Foley, Atmore, Monroville, AL

Area Codes: 904, 334

Rates: $15 one-time connect fee & $20/month for 20 hours or $40/month for 100 hours.

Promotion for Starter Kit Owners: 10 Free additional hours the first month of service.

Signup Process: Just call us at 904-438-5700 for the location of a computer store near you that will get you on the net!

Contact Info:

Voice: 904-438-5700

Fax: 904-438-5750

Human response: tom@gulf.net

Automated response: info@gulf.net

Web Site: http://www.gulf.net/

MindSpring Enterprises, Inc.
Area: Southern East Coast

Cities: Atlanta, GA; Columbus, GA; Birmingham, AL; West Point/Lagrange, GA; Lanett, AL; Newnan, Auburn/Opelika, AL

Area Codes: 404, portions of 706 and 205

Rates: Dialup plans (PPP connections, include 3 MB on our server for Web pages and FTP, up to 28.8 Kbps access, Usenet and ClariNet news, email, Telnet, Gopher, Archie, FTP, chat, talk, Ping, etc.)

Standard: $35 startup fee; $15 per month for 15 hours; $1 per hour over 15.

Flat rate: $35 startup fee; $35 per month for unlimited use (not meant to be a full-time connection).

Promotion for Starter Kit Owners: $10 off the $35 startup fee!

Signup Process: Call 404-888-0725 to sign up over the phone. Or, send email to **info@mindspring.com** to receive signup form via email.

Contact Info:

430 10th Street, NW

Atlanta, GA 30318-5768

Voice: 404-888-0725

Fax: 404-888-9210

Human response: sales@mindspring.com
Automated response: info@mindspring.com

Web Site: http://www.mindspring.com/

Internet Interstate
Area: East Coast

Cities: Washington D.C., greater metropolitan area
Area Codes: 301, 202, some 703
Rates: Intro Plan: 5hrs/mo. 1.50/hr after, 14.75/mo w/ $25 setup; Basic Plan: 22hrs/mo. 1.50/hr after, 21.75/mo w/ $25 setup; Power Plan: 4hrs free/day, 12pm-7am free in addition, 1.00/hr after, 29.75/mo w/$25 setup; Dedicated Plan: Full-time connection $175 setup plus a modem $150/month, $125 if paid one year in advance.
Promotion for Starter Kit Owners: Customers who mention they are using the Internet Starter Kit will receive a two week free trial and a 50% discount of setup fees to $12.50 (at the end of the trial).
Signup Process: Customers can call our voice number 301-652-4468 or send a fax 301-652-0566 to sign up. We accept payment by credit card monthly or one year in advance, or by check for one year in advance only. Payments for a year in advance get a 10% discount. Basic information required is requested login id, password, billing plan, mailing address, and contact phone number. Accounts will be activated within 24 hours of the request.
Contact Info:
4925 St. Elmo Avenue
Bethesda, MD 20814
Voice: 301-652-4468
Fax: 301-652-0566
Human response: zamfir@intr.net
Automated response: info@intr.net

Web Site: www.intr.net/

SunBelt.Net
Area: East Coast

Cities: Charlotte, NC, Lexington, NC, Abbeville/ Due West, SC, Charleston, SC, Chester, SC, Columbia, SC, Florence, SC, Greenville, SC, Kingstree, SC, Lancaster, SC, Moncks Corner, SC, North Augusta, SC, Rock Hill, SC, Spartanburg, SC, Sumter, SC, Augusta, GA
Also becoming available in several cities in Tennessee, and new sites in the above states on an on going basis.
Area Codes: 615, 701, 704, 706, 803
Rates: Dial-up rates are usage based. The dial-up plans are: Introductory $15/mo. 5 hrs included $2.50/hr. thereafter; Basic $35/mo. 40 hrs included $2.00/hr. thereafter; Executive $65/mo. 80 hrs included $1.50/hr. thereafter; Corporate $100/mo. 130 hrs included $1.15/hr. thereafter. In addition, multiple users billed to the same account can be created for only $2/month, with the total accumulated usage time for all secondary accounts charged to the total for the billed account. Dedicated accounts are fixed-rate per month. Dedicated accounts may be dial-up (i.e., using standard telephone connection, such as SLIP or PPP), but with a private modem (i.e., accessible only to that customer, and available 24 hours/day, 7 days/week, with no accumulated hourly charge); or they can be leased lines, with fees depending on the costs of the leased lines. Dedicated accounts start at $200/month.
Promotion for Starter Kit Owners: The standard startup fee for new SunBelt.Net users is $25. For owners of Internet Starter Kit for Macintosh, this startup fee will be waived.
Signup Process: Users may call their local SunBelt.Net Customer Service number and provide all of the necessary information for creation of their account. The new account will be created while the user is still on the telephone, and will be available for use immediately. Automatic billing is done via Visa or MasterCard.
Contact Info:
330 E. Black St.
Rock Hill, South Carolina 29731
Voice: 1-800-950-4SBN (950-4726), plus local lines for the geographies served
Fax: 803-324-6134
Human response: info@sunbelt.net, webmaster@sunbelt.net

Web Site: http://www.sunbelt.net/

Hawaii OnLine
Area: Hawaii

Cities: Island-wide coverage—Oahu, Maui, Kauai, Hawaii, Molokai; Lanai 2nd quarter 1995
Area Codes: 808
Rates: Standard Plan: Menu Shell, BBS, and SLIP

or PPP access, $25 per month, $22.50 with Auto Credit Card Billing. Overtime Rates: $.75 per hour. Startup Fee: $40.

Access Hours: 40 hours peak time usage per month, nonpeak 12 a.m.—10 a.m. free.

Premium Plan: Menu Shell, BBS, and SLIP or PPP access, $45 per month, $42.50 with Auto Credit Card Billing. Access Hours: Unlimited.

Startup Fee: $40.

Promotion for Starter Kit Owners: $15 off the normal startup fee! (During the signup process, use the ad code of "Hayden.")

Signup Process: From a standard terminal program, dial any Hawaii OnLine local access number: Oahu 533-7113, Maui 244-8133, Kauai 245-6115, Hawaii 935-7878. Login as **guest**—a password is not required. From the Guest Menu, select #8: "Sign-up for Access Now!" The system will prompt you for all information. If you select Credit Card Billing, your account will be activated immediately. If you have questions, please call our in-state Hotline at 800-207-1880.

Contact Info:
737 Bishop Street
Suite 2305
Honolulu, HI
Voice: 808-533-6981, 808-246-1880
Fax: 808-534-0089
Human response: pjc@aloha.net (primary), lynn@aloha.net (secondary)
Automated response: info@aloha.net

Web Site: http://www.aloha.net/

LavaNet, Inc.
Area: Hawaii

Cities: Island of Oahu (Honolulu and more)
Area Codes: 808 (Oahu only)
Rates: For shell account or SLIP/PPP account: $30 startup fee. Flat-rate plan (any account type): $28/month for virtually unlimited access. Timed-rate plan (any account type): $14/month for 10 hours of access, beyond that $2/hour.

Promotion for Starter Kit Owners: Call us at 808-545-5282 to arrange a special trial account. Pay only a $15 startup fee ($20 for combination accounts), and connect to LavaNet for a two-week trial of our flat-rate account! Trial offer good for Oahu residents only.

Signup Process: Customers receive our startup kit either through the mail or by picking it up at our office in downtown Honolulu. Customers must then return a signed copy of the User Agreement (via mail, fax, or hand delivery), at which point the customer's account is activated.

Contact Info:
733 Bishop St. Suite 1590
Honolulu, HI 96813
Voice: 808-545-LAVA (i.e. 545-5282)
Technical Support: 808-545-7205
Fax: 808-545-7020
Human response: lava-info@lava.net
Automated response: info@lava.net

Web Site: http://www.lava.net/

The Portal Information Network
Area: Nationwide & Canada

Cities: Over 1,100 POPs in the U.S. and Canada
Area Codes: All
Rates: Portal IP Connection: $19.95 startup, $19.95 per month. Three ways to connect: $.95/hour: Portal S.F. Bay Area POPs; $2.50/hour: SprintNet offpeak hours; $9.50/hour: SprintNet peak hours; $2.95/hour: CPN.

Promotion for Starter Kit Owners: We'll waive the signup fee and give you a $15 credit!

Signup Process: Complete and fax (or mail) the form in the back of the book.

Contact Info:
20863 Stevens Creek Boulevard
Suite 200
Cupertino, CA 95014
Voice: 408-973-9111
Fax: 408-725-1580
Human response: sales@portal.com
Automated response: info@portal.com

Web Site: http://www.portal.com/

Global OnLine
Area: Japan

Cities: Tokyo, Osaka, other POPs in progress as of April 1995.
Area Codes: 03, 06 (in Japan)
Rates: PPP signup fee: 2500 yen; Monthly rate: 4500 yen for 10 hours; Overtime rate: 15 yen per minute.

Promotion for Starter Kit Owners: Users will receive a free 3 week trial or 10 hours, whichever comes first. For PPP customers we will reduce our signup fee by 50%, from 5000 yen to 2500 yen.

Signup Process: Call Global OnLine in Tokyo at (03) 5330-9380, or fax us at (03) 5330-9381 to request a signup form. You can also obtain our signup forms via autoresponse email to **signup@gol.com** (for Unix shell), **signup-ppp@gol.com** (for PPP accounts), **signup-uucp@gol.com** (for UUCP accounts), or **signup-email@gol.com** (for email-only accounts). Complete the form and return it to us via mail or fax and we will set up your account generally within 1 business day of receipt.

Contact Info:
1-56-1-302 Higashi Nakano
Nakano-ku
Tokyo 164, Japan
Voice: +81-3-5330-9380
Fax: +81-3-5330-9381
Human response: sales@gol.com
Automated response: info@gol.com, info-j@gol.com

Web Site: http://www.gol.com/

Helix Internet
Area: Canada

Cities: Vancouver (604-689-8577), Kelowna (604-762-5899)

Area Codes: 604

Rates: Individual: Free trial during first week, $19.95/mo for 20 hours online, $1.50 for additional hours online, $25.00 account activation fee. Corporate: $49.00/mo for 4 email addresses, $1.50 per hour while online, $95.00 account activation fee. Free text based Web page. Web pages: $49.00/mo for unlimited pages, $.09/MB after first, free 500 MB per month, $199 server set up fee, $95/hour for design, HTML programming. Dedicated lines: please call 604-689-8544 for pricing please note all prices do not include taxes.

Promotion for Starter Kit Owners: All new accounts for Starter Kit owners will be discounted. Please call us for details at 604-689-8544.

Signup Process: 1. Have your modem dial 604-689-8577. 2. Login as **guest** (no password required). 3. Choose application process or call 604-689-8544 for new account information and help.

Contact Info:
902-900 W. Hastings
Vancouver, BC V6J 3L1
Voice: 604-689-8544
Fax: 604-685-2554
Human response: staff@helix.net
Automated response: info@helix.net

Web Site: http://www.helix.net/

internet service and information systems (isis) inc.
Area: Canada

Cities: Halifax Nova Scotia (Coming soon to Windsor, Wolfville, Kentville, Sydney, and Yarmouth) (These are expected to be online within the next 6 months.)

Area Codes: 902

Rates: Normal rates are $25.00 for 65 hours of connect time per month with extra time costing $10.00 per 30 hours (2 a.m. to 7 a.m. is free). Up to date pricing info is available on our WWW pages.

Promotion for Starter Kit Owners: If the ISKM is bought from isis (@$25.00), the first month is free, otherwise if you bought the ISKM from another local source the first month will be given to you at $15.00.

Signup Process: Users can call the office and register for their accounts. Or if they are familiar with a VT-100 capable communications program (Z-term etc.), they can call out data line at 902-496-9054 and log in as **new** and then follow the onscreen prompts.

Contact Info:
1505 Barrington St. Suite 1501
Halifax, Nova Scotia
B3J 3K5, Canada
Voice: 902-429-4747
Fax: 902-429-9003
Human response: help@ra.isisnet.com
Automated response: info@ra.isisnet.com

Web Site: http://www.isisnet.com/

Magic Online Services Inc.
Area: Canada

Cities: The greater Toronto area (including Agincourt, Ajax, Don Mills, Downsview, East York, Ellesmere, Etobicoke, Mississauga, Metro

Toronto, North York, Pickering, Rexdale, Richmond Hill, Scarborough, Weston and York)

Area Codes: 416, 905

Rates: In NET-XX, XX indicates the number of hours purchased per month. Prices are in Canadian dollars and are subject to tax: MONTHLY NET 30 $12.00 NET 60 $18.00 NET 90 $22.50—6 MONTH NET 30 $68.50 NET 60 $102.50 NET 90 $128.50—12 MONTH NET 30 $129.50 NET 60 $194.50 NET 90 $243.50—Additional Time: NET 30—$0.50/hour NET 60—$0.38/hour NET 90—$0.31/hour—Small Business, Corporate, and Student Account rates are also available. Please call for details.

Promotion for Starter Kit Owners: We will waive our MagicNET one-time startup fee of $15.00. In addition, we will offer ISKM owners a trial access time of two FREE weeks OR 15 FREE hours on MagicNET.

Signup Process: Simply email, phone, or fax us a request for a MagicNET registration form and we'll send one to you. Fill it out and send it back to us. After we've received your registration form, we'll fax or mail the configuration instructions to you and set up your account within two business days. We'll call you to confirm your user id and password, and you're on your way!

Contact Info:
260 Richmond Street West, Suite 206
Toronto, Ontario M5V 1W5
Canada
Voice: 416-591-6490
Fax: 416-591-6409
Human response: info@mail.magic.ca
Automated response: ftp.magic.ca

Web Site: http://www.magic.ca/

SaskTel
Area: Canada

Cities: All cities and towns in the Province of Saskatchewan

Area Codes: 306

Rates: Contact the toll-free number to find out about the ongoing promotions and packages available! Following rates current as of April 1995: Rates for province wide Internet Access Service: SaskTel Fact Sheet SaskTel Internet Access Services SASKTEL INTERNET DIAL ACCESS RATES Package Customer Monthly Hours/month Peak Usage Off-Peak Usage Service Type Location Rate Included rate/hour rate/hour Connection (8:00am-11:30pm) (11:30pm-8:00am) STANDARD: On-Net $19.95 10 $3.00 $1.00 $35.00 Off-Net $19.95 3 $6.00 $3.00 $35.00 HIGH USAGE: On-Net $39.95 20 $1.00 $1.00 $35.00 Off-Net $39.95 7 $5.00 $2.50 $35.00 1 YEAR CONTRACT: On-Net $399/year 20 $1.00 $1.00 $35.00 Off-Net $399/year 7 $5.00 $2.50 $35.00 PROMOTION (SaskTel will give dial access customers special pricing for their first three months, when they sign up by May 31, 1995.) On-Net $9.95 10 $3.00 $1.00 $35.00 Off-Net $9.95 3 $6.00 $3.00 $35.00 On-net rates apply to subscribers located in Regina, Saskatoon, Moose Jaw, Prince Albert, North Battleford, Swift Current, Estevan, Weyburn, Yorkton, Melfort and their free calling areas. Off-net rates apply to subscribers located in all other locations. Off-net customers do not incur long distance charges. A yearly rate of $399.00 is available.

Promotion for Starter Kit Owners: Mail in the front page of the manual from the *Internet Starter Kit for Macintosh* (version 3) and SaskTel will waive the service connection charge of $35 (applicable to single user accounts only, and to new subscribers).

Signup Process: Please call our inquiry and order line at 1-800-644-9225 for details.

Contact Info:
11th Floor Marketing
2121 Saskatchewan Drive
Regina, Saskatchewan, CANADA S4P 3Y2
Voice: 1-800-664-9205
Human response: staff@sasknet.sk.ca

Web Site: http://www.sasknet.sk.ca/

iiNet Technologies Pty Ltd
Area: Australia

Cities: Perth and the South West region

Area Codes: +61-9, +61-97

Rates: AU $25 startup and AU $25 per month.

Promotion for Starter Kit Owners: The startup cost is waived for ISK owners.

Signup Process: Call our voice number at +61-9-307-1183 to open an account. There is no online registration available.

Contact Info:
PO Box 811
Hillarys 6025
Western Australia
Voice: +61-9-307-1183
Fax: +61-9-307-8414
Human response: iinet@iinet.net.au
Automated response:

Web Site: http://www.iinet.net.au/

Internode Professional Access
Area: Australia

Cities: Adelaide, South Australia
Area Codes: 08
Rates: Normal dialup rates: AUS $25 joining fee/ AUS $550 per annum for PPP dialup user access, some conditions apply. Permanent links and corporate domain name services: P.O.A.
Promotion for Starter Kit Owners: We will waive the normal joining fee and provide you with your first two weeks access free, to let you try out our facilities with no obligation. We're sure you'll find it the fastest and best configured Internet access facility in Adelaide!
Signup Process: Call Internode Professional Access to register and obtain a user id and password for your free two week trial. Credit cards accepted for ongoing fees. Alternatively, check out our web page at **http:// www.adelaide.on.net** for more details.
Contact Info:
PO Box 69
Daw Park, SA 5041 Australia
Voice: +61-8-373-1020
Fax: +61-8-373-4911
Human response: sales@adelaide.on.net
Automated response: help@adelaide.on.net

Web Site: http://www.adelaide.on.net

SpaceNet GmbH
Area: Germany

Cities: Munich, Germany
Area Codes: +49 south
Rates: Startup fee: 90 DM; Monthly fees (we charge volume, there is no limit or fee on online time): Normal: 55 DM, get 3 MB for free, every additional MB is 7,80 DM. Office: 290 DM, get 40 MB for free, every additional MB is 5,50 DM. Office II: 800 DM, get 150 MB for free, every additional MB is 4,50 DM. Above 300 MB: Ask!
Promotion for Starter Kit Owners: We'll waive the starting fee of 90 DM! Additionally, every Starter Kit user will get free access for the first month. So you can try SpaceNet without any fees at all.
Signup Process: Get our info material from **ftp.space.net:info/*.ps**, print it, fill it out and return it via fax or snail mail. You will hear from us the next day (worst case).
Contact Info:
Frankfurter Ring 193a
D-80807 München
Germany
Voice: +49 89 324683-0
Fax: +49 89 324683-51
Human response: info@space.net

Web Site: http://www.space.net/

Appendix B

Providers of Commercial Internet Access

Although we have put together a substantial list of Internet providers specifically for *Internet Starter Kit for Macintosh* (see appendix A), you still may not find the one that best suits your needs. If not, look through the providers in the following list to see if there is one that you want to contact. You will find all the information you need to contact these providers on your own.

Remember that there will not be custom MacTCP Prep files on the disk for these providers, so you must call or email to get the necessary configuration information. Most are more than happy to help you.

This list is the Providers of Commercial Internet Access (POCIA) Directory TEXT version taken directly from the net itself. Note that it is copyrighted material which we have included with permission from the Celestin Company. Our thanks go to Celestin for providing this excellent resource for the net community.

Updated May 1995

All of the information in this directory was supplied to Celestin Company directly by the service providers and is subject to change without notice. Celestin Company does not endorse any of the providers in this directory. If you do not see a provider listed for your area, please do not ask us about it, as we only know about providers in this directory. This directory is brought to you as a public service. Celestin Company does not receive any compensation from the providers listed here. Since Internet service providers come and go, and frequently change their offers, we strongly urge you to contact them for additional information and/or restrictions.

The latest version of this document is available at the following location:

```
ftp://ftp.teleport.com/vendors/cci/pocia/pocia.txt
```

You may also retrieve the latest copy (as well as additional information on Celestin Company and its products) using email. For information on how this works, send a blank message to: **cci@olympus.net**

If you have web access, try **http://www.teleport.com/~cci/** for the hypertext version of this list, which includes addresses, telephone numbers, fax numbers, email addresses, and pricing.

If you would rather receive the directory on a disk, send us a check for $10 ($15 if you do not live in the U.S. or Canada) and specify Mac or Windows. In return, we will send you a disk which includes the complete hypertext version of the directory, along with a browser to make searching for Internet providers easy.

Our address is:

POCIA Directory
Celestin Company
1152 Hastings Avenue
Port Townsend, WA 98368
United States of America

Voice: 360 385 3767
Fax: 360 385 3586
Email: **celestin@olympus.net**

Domestic

Below is a listing of Internet service providers in the U.S. and Canada, sorted by area code. Fields are area code, service provider name, voice phone number, and email address for more information.

Free Service Providers

Name	Phone	Email
Cyberspace (shell,slip,ppp)	modem -> 515 945 7000	info@cyberspace.com
Free.org (shell,slip,ppp)	modem -> 715 743 1600	info@free.org
Free.I.Net (must dial via AT&T)	modem -> 801 471 2266	info@free.i.net
SLIPNET (shell,slip,ppp)	modem -> 217 792 2777	info@slip.net

Nationwide Service Providers

Name	Phone	Email
ANS	703 758 7700	info@ans.net
Global Connect, Inc.	804 229 4484	info@gc.net
Information Access Technologies (Holonet)	510 704 0160	info@holonet.net
NETCOM On-Line Communications Services	408 554 8649	info@netcom.com
Network 99, Inc.	800 NET 99IP	net99@cluster.mcs.net
Performance Systems International	800 827 7482	all-info@psi.com
SprintLink - Nationwide 56K - 45M access	800 817 7755	info@sprint.net

Part V

Providers of
Commercial
Internet
Access

Toll-Free Service Providers

Name	Phone	Email
Allied Access Inc.	618 684 2255	sales@intrnet.net
American Information Systems, Inc.	708 413 8400	info@ais.net
Association for Computing Machinery	817 776 6876	account-info@acm.org
CICNet, Inc.	313 998 6103	info@cic.net
Colorado SuperNet, Inc.	303 296 8202	info@csn.org
DataBank, Inc.	913 842 6699	info@databank.com
Global Connect, Inc.	804 229 4484	info@gc.net
Internet Express	719 592 1240	info@usa.net
Mnematics, Incorporated	914 359 4546	service@mne.com
Msen, Inc.	313 998 4562	info@msen.com
NeoSoft, Inc.	713 684 5969	info@neosoft.com
New Mexico Technet, Inc.	505 345 5555	granoff@technet.nm.org
Pacific Rim Network, Inc.	360 650 0442	info@pacificrim.net
Prometheus Information Network Group Inc.	404 399 1670	info@ping.com
Rocky Mountain Internet	800 900 7644	info@rmii.com
Synergy Communications, Inc.	800 345 9669	info@synergy.net
WLN	800 342 5956	info@wln.com

Regional Service Providers

Area Code	Name	Phone	Email
201	Carroll-Net	201 488 1332	info@carroll.com
201	The Connection	201 435 4414	info@cnct.com
201	Digital Express Group	301 847 5000	info@digex.net
201	INTAC Access Corporation	800 504 6822	info@intac.com
201	InterCom Online	212 714 7183	info@intercom.com
201	Internet For 'U'	800 NET WAY1	info@ifu.net
201	Internet Online Services	x226 -> 201 928 1000	help@ios.com
201	Mordor International BBS	201 433 4222	ritz@mordor.com
201	NETCOM On-Line Communications Services	408 554 8649	info@netcom.com

Area Code	Name	Phone	Email
201	New York Net	718 776 6811	sales@new-york.net
201	NIC - Neighborhood Internet Connection	201 934 1445	info@nic.com
202	CAPCON Library Network	202 331 5771	info@capcon.net
202	Charm.Net	410 558 3900	info@charm.net
202	Digital Express Group	301 847 5000	info@digex.net
202	Genuine Computing Resources	703 878 4680	info@gcr.com
202	Internet Online, Inc.	301 652 4468	info@intr.net
202	Interpath	800 849 6305	info@interpath.net
202	LaserNet	703 591 4232	info@laser.net
202	Quantum Networking Solutions, Inc.	805 538 2028	info@qnet.com
202	US Net, Incorporated	301 572 5926	info@us.net
203	Connix: Connecticut Internet Exchange	203 349 7059	info@connix.com
203	Futuris Networks, Inc.	203 359 8868	info@futuris.net
203	I-2000, Inc.	516 867 6379	info@i-2000.com
203	Paradigm Communications, Inc.	203 250 7397	info@pcnet.com
205	Community Internet Connect, Inc.	205 722 0199	info@cici.com
205	HiWAAY Information Services	205 533 3131	info@HiWAAY.net
205	interQuest, Inc.	205 464 8280	info@iquest.com
205	Scott Network Services, Inc.	205 987 5889	info@scott.net
206	Eskimo North	206 367 7457	nanook@eskimo.com
206	Internet Express	719 592 1240	info@usa.net
206	NETCOM On-Line Communications Services	408 554 8649	info@netcom.com
206	Northwest Nexus, Inc.	206 455 3505	info@nwnexus.wa.com
206	Pacifier Computers	206 254 3886	account@pacifier.com
206	Seanet Online Services	206 343 7828	info@seanet.com

continues

Part V   Providers of Commercial Internet Access

Area Code	Name	Phone	Email
206	SenseMedia	408 335 9400	sm@picosof.com
206	Structured Network Systems, Inc.	503 656 3530	info@structured.net
206	Teleport, Inc.	503 223 4245	info@teleport.com
206	Transport Logic	503 243 1940	sales@transport.com
206	WLN	800 342 5956	info@wln.com
207	Agate Internet Services	207 947 8248	ais@agate.net
208	Micron Internet Services	208 368 5400	sales@micron.net
208	Minnesota Regional Network	612 342 2570	info@mr.net
208	NICOH Net	208 233 5802	info@nicoh.com
208	Primenet	602 870 1010	info@primenet.com
208	Transport Logic	503 243 1940	sales@transport.com
209	Cybergate Information Services	209 486 4283	cis@cybergate.com
209	West Coast Online	707 586 3060	info@calon.com
210	I-Link Ltd	800 ILINK 99	info@i-link.net
212	Alternet (UUNET Technologies, Inc.)	703 204 8000	info@alter.net
212	Blythe Systems	212 226 7171	infodesk@blythe.org
212	Creative Data Consultants (SILLY.COM)	718 229 0489	info@silly.com
212	Digital Express Group	301 847 5000	info@digex.net
212	Echo Communications Group	212 255 3839	info@echonyc.com
212	escape.com - Kazan Corp	212 888 8780	info@escape.com
212	I-2000, Inc.	516 867 6379	info@i-2000.com
212	Ingress Communications Inc.	212 679 2838	info@ingress.com
212	INTAC Access Corporation	800 504 6822	info@intac.com
212	InterCom Online	212 714 7183	info@intercom.com
212	Internet For 'U'	800 NET WAY1	info@ifu.net
212	Internet Online Services	x226 -> 201 928 1000	help@ios.com

Area Code	Name	Phone	Email
212	Interport Communications Corp.	212 989 1128	info@interport.net
212	Mordor International BBS	201 433 4222	ritz@mordor.com
212	Mnematics, Incorporated	914 359 4546	service@mne.com
212	NETCOM On-Line Communications Services	408 554 8649	info@netcom.com
212	New York Net	718 776 6811	sales@new-york.net
212	NY WEBB, Inc.	800 458 4660	wayne@webb.com
212	Phantom Access Technologies, Inc.	212 989 2418	bruce@phantom.com
212	The Pipeline Network	212 267 2626	info-info@pipeline.com
213	Abode Computer Service	818 287 5115	eric@abode.ttank.com
213	Delta Internet Services	714 778 0370	info@deltanet.com
213	DigiLink Network Services˅	310 542 7421	info@digilink.net
213	DirectNet	213 383 3144	info@directnet.com
213	EarthLink Network, Inc.	213 644 9500	info@earthlink.net
213	Electriciti	619 338 9000	info@powergrid.electriciti.com
213	KAIWAN Internet	714 638 2139	info@kaiwan.com
213	Primenet	602 870 1010	info@primenet.com
213	ViaNet Communications	415 903 2242	info@via.net
214	Alternet (UUNET Technologies, Inc.)	703 204 8000	info@alter.net
214	DFW Internet Services, Inc.	817 332 5116	info@dfw.net
214	I-Link Ltd	800 ILINK 99	info@i-link.net
214	NETCOM On-Line Communications Services	408 554 8649	info@netcom.com
214	Texas Metronet, Inc.	214 705 2900	info@metronet.com
215	Digital Express Group	301 847 5000	info@digex.net
215	FishNet	610 337 9994	info@pond.com
215	Microserve Information Systems	717 779 4430	info@microserve.com
215	Network Analysis Group	800 624 9240	nag@good.freedom.net
215	Oasis Telecommunications, Inc.	610 439 8560	staff@oasis.ot.com
215	YOU TOOLS Corporation	610 954 5910	info@youtools.com

Part V   Providers of Commercial Internet Access

continues

Area Code	Name	Phone	Email
216	APK Public Access UNI* Site	216 481 9436	info@wariat.org
216	Branch Information Services	313 741 4442	branch-info@branch.com
216	Exchange Network Services, Inc.	216 261 4593	info@en.com
216	OARnet (corporate clients only)	614 728 8100	info@oar.net
216	New Age Consulting Service	216 524 3162	damin@nacs.net
217	Allied Access Inc.	618 684 2255	sales@intrnet.net
217	Sol Tec, Inc.	317 920 1SOL	info@soltec.com
218	Red River Net	701 232 2227	info@rrnet.com
301	Charm.Net	410 558 3900	info@charm.net
301	Clark Internet Services, Inc. ClarkNet	410 995 0691	info@clark.net
301	Digital Express Group	301 847 5000	info@digex.net
301	FredNet	301 698 2396	info@fred.net
301	Genuine Computing Resources	703 878 4680	info@gcr.com
301	Internet Online, Inc.	301 652 4468	info@intr.net
301	LaserNet	703 591 4232	info@laser.net
301	Quantum Networking Solutions, Inc.	805 538 2028	info@qnet.com
301	SURAnet	301 982 4600	marketing@sura.net
301	US Net, Incorporated	301 572 5926	info@us.net
302	SSNet, Inc.	302 378 1386	info@ssnet.com
303	Colorado SuperNet, Inc.	303 296 8202	info@csn.org
303	CSDC, Inc.	303 665 8053	support@ares.csd.net
303	ENVISIONET, Inc.	303 770 2408	info@envisionet.net
303	EZLink Internet Access	970 482 0807	ezadmin@ezlink.com
303	Indra's Net, Inc.	303 546 9151	info@indra.com
303	Internet Express	719 592 1240	info@usa.net

Area Code	Name	Phone	Email
303	NETCOM On-Line Communications Services	408 554 8649	info@netcom.com
303	New Mexico Technet, Inc.	505 345 6555	granoff@technet.nm.org
303	Rocky Mountain Internet	800 900 7644	info@rmii.com
303	Stonehenge Internet Communications	800 RUN INET	info@henge.com
305	Acquired Knowledge Systems Inc.	305 525 2574	info@aksi.net
305	CyberGate, Inc.	305 428 4283	sales@gate.net
305	InteleCom Data Systems, Inc.	401 885 6855	info@ids.net
305	PSS InterNet Services	800 463 8499	support@america.com
305	SatelNET Communications	305 434 8738	admin@satelnet.org
307	wyoming.com	307 332 3030	info@wyoming.com
308	Synergy Communications, Inc.	800 345 9669	info@synergy.net
310	Abode Computer Service	818 287 5115	eric@abode.ttank.com
310	Cloverleaf Communications	714 895 3075	sales@cloverleaf.com
310	Delta Internet Services	714 778 0370	info@deltanet.com
310	DigiLink Network Services	310 542 7421	info@digilink.net
310	EarthLink Network, Inc.	213 644 9500	info@earthlink.net
310	KAIWAN Internet	714 638 2139	info@kaiwan.com
310	Lightside, Inc.	818 858 9261	info@lightside.com
310	NETCOM On-Line Communications Services	408 554 8649	info@netcom.com
310	ViaNet Communications	415 903 2242	info@via.net
312	American Information Systems, Inc.	708 413 8400	info@ais.net
312	CICNet, Inc.	313 998 6103	info@cic.net
312	InterAccess Co.	800 967 1580	info@interaccess.com
312	MCSNet	312 248 8649	info@mcs.net
312	NETCOM On-Line Communications Services	408 554 8649	info@netcom.com

Part V

Providers of Commercial Internet Access

continues

Area Code	Name	Phone	Email
312	Open Business Systems, Inc.	708 250 0260	info@obs.net
312	Ripco Communications, Inc.	312 477 6210	info@ripco.com
312	Tezcatlipoca, Inc.	312 850 0181	info@tezcat.com
312	WorldWide Access	708 367 1870	info@wwa.com
313	Branch Information Services	313 741 4442	branch-info@branch.com
313	CICNet, Inc.	313 998 6103	info@cic.net
313	ICNET / Innovative Concepts	313 998 0090	info@ic.net
313	Isthmus Corporation	313 973 2100	info@izzy.net
313	Msen, Inc.	313 998 4562	info@msen.com
314	Allied Access Inc.	618 684 2255	sales@intrnet.net
314	NeoSoft, Inc.	713 684 5969	info@neosoft.com
314	ThoughtPort, Inc.	314 474 6870	info@thoughtport.com
315	ServiceTech Inc. Cyber-Link	716 546 6908	dam@cyber1.servtech.com
316	SouthWind Internet Access, Inc.	316 263 7963	info@southwind.net
317	Branch Information Services	313 741 4442	branch-info@branch.com
317	HolliCom Internet Services	317 883 4500	cale@holli.com
317	IQuest Network Services	317 259 5050	info@iquest.net
317	Metropolitan Data Networks Limited	317 449 0539	info@mdn.com
317	Net Direct	317 251 5252	kat@inetdirect.net
317	Sol Tec, Inc.	317 920 1SOL	info@soltec.com
334	Scott Network Services, Inc.	205 987 5889	info@scott.net
334	WSNetwork Communications Services, Inc.	334 263 5505	custserv@wsnet.com
360	NorthWest CommLink	360 336 0103	info@nwcl.net
360	Pacific Rim Network, Inc.	360 650 0442	info@pacificrim.net
360	Skagit On-Line Services	360 755 0190	info@sos.net

Area Code	Name	Phone	Email
360	Townsend Communications, Inc.	360 385 0464	info@olympus.net
360	Whidbey Connections, Inc.	360 678 1070	info@whidbey.net
360	WLN	800 342 5956	info@wln.com
401	InteleCom Data Systems, Inc.	401 885 6855	info@ids.net
401	The Internet Connection, Inc.	508 261 0383	info@ici.net
402	Internet Nebraska	402 434 8680	info@inetnebr.com
402	Synergy Communications, Inc.	800 345 9669	info@synergy.net
403	CCI Networks	403 450 6787	info@ccinet.ab.ca
403	Debug Computer Services	403 248 5798	root@debug.cuc.ab.ca
403	UUNET Canada, Inc.	416 368 6621	info@uunet.ca
404	Internet Atlanta	404 410 9000	info@atlanta.com
404	MindSpring	404 888 0725	info@mindspring.com
404	NETCOM On-Line Communications Services	408 554 8649	info@netcom.com
404	Prometheus Information Network Group Inc.	404 399 1670	info@ping.com
405	Internet Oklahoma	405 721 1580	info@ionet.net
405	Questar Network Services	405 848 3228	info@qns.net
406	Montana Online	406 721 4952	info@montana.com
407	CyberGate, Inc.	305 428 4283	sales@gate.net
407	The EmiNet Domain	407 731 0222	info@emi.net
407	Florida Online	407 635 8888	info@digital.net
407	InteleCom Data Systems, Inc.	401 885 6855	info@ids.net
407	InternetU	407 952 8487	info@iu.net
407	MagicNet, Inc.	407 657 2202	info@magicnet.net
407	MetroLink Internet Services	407 726 6707	tbatchel@met.net

Part V

Providers of Commercial Internet Access

continues

Area Code	Name	Phone	Email
407	PSS InterNet Services	800 463 8499	support@america.com
408	Aimnet Information Services	408 257 0900	info@aimnet.com
408	Alternet (UUNET Technologies, Inc.)	703 204 8000	info@alter.net
408	BTR Communications Company	415 966 1429	support@btr.com
408	Direct Net Access Incorporated	510 649 6110	support@dnai.com
408	The Duck Pond Public Unix	modem -> 408 249 9630	postmaster@kfu.com
408	Electriciti	619 338 9000	info@powergrid.electriciti.com
408	Infoserv Connections	408 335 5600	root@infoserv.com
408	InterNex Information Services, Inc.	415 473 3060	info@internex.net
408	ISP Networks	408 653 0100	info@isp.net
408	MediaCity World	415 321 6800	info@MediaCity.com
408	NETCOM On-Line Communications Services	408 554 8649	info@netcom.com
408	NetGate Communications	408 565 9601	sales@netgate.net
408	Scruz-Net	408 457 5050	info@scruz.net
408	SenseMedia	408 335 9400	sm@picosof.com
408	South Valley Internet	408 683 4533	info@garlic.com
408	West Coast Online	707 586 3060	info@calon.com
408	zNET	619 755 7772	info@znet.com
408	Zocalo Engineering	510 540 8000	info@zocalo.net
409	Internet Connect Services, Inc.	512 572 9987	info@icsi.net
410	CAPCON Library Network	202 331 5771	info@capcon.net
410	Charm.Net	410 558 3900	info@charm.net
410	Clark Internet Services, Inc. ClarkNet	410 995 0691	info@clark.net
410	Digital Express Group	301 847 5000	info@digex.net
410	jaguNET Access Services	410 931 3157	info@jagunet.com
410	Softaid Internet Services Inc.	410 290 7763	sales@softaid.net
410	US Net, Incorporated	301 572 5926	info@us.net

Area Code	Name	Phone	Email
412	Telerama Public Access Internet	412 481 3505	info@telerama.lm.com
413	Mallard Electronics, Inc.	413 732 0214	gheacock@map.com
413	MediaCity World	415 321 6800	info@MediaCity.com
413	ShaysNet.COM	413 772 3774	staff@shaysnet.com
414	Exec-PC, Inc.	414 789 4200	info@execpc.com
414	FullFeed Communications	608 246 4239	info@fullfeed.com
414	MIX Communications	414 351 1868	info@mixcom.com
414	NetNet, Inc.	414 499 1339	info@netnet.net
415	Aimnet Information Services	408 257 0900	info@aimnet.com
415	Alternet (UUNET Technologies, Inc.)	703 204 8000	info@alter.net
415	BTR Communications Company	415 966 1429	support@btr.com
415	Community ConneXion - NEXUS-Berkeley	510 549 1383	info@c2.org
415	Direct Net Access Incorporated	510 649 6110	support@dnai.com
415	InterNex Information Services, Inc.	415 473 3060	info@internex.net
415	LanMinds, Inc.	510 843 6389	info@lanminds.com
415	LineX Communications	415 455 1650	info@linex.com
415	MediaCity World	415 321 6800	info@MediaCity.com
415	NETCOM On-Line Communications Services	408 554 8649	info@netcom.com
415	NetGate Communications	408 565 9601	sales@netgate.net
415	QuakeNet	415 655 6607	info@quake.net
415	SLIPNET	415 281 3132	info@slip.net
415	ViaNet Communications	415 903 2242	info@via.net
415	The WELL	415 332 4335	info@well.com
415	West Coast Online	707 586 3060	info@calon.com
415	zNET	619 755 7772	info@znet.com
415	Zocalo Engineering	510 540 8000	info@zocalo.net

Part V

Providers of Commercial Internet Access

continues

Area Code	Name	Phone	Email
416	HookUp Communications	905 847 8000	info@hookup.net
416	InterLog Internet Services	416 975 2655	internet@interlog.com
416	UUNET Canada, Inc.	416 368 6621	info@uunet.ca
418	UUNET Canada, Inc.	416 368 6621	info@uunet.ca
419	Branch Information Services	313 741 4442	branch-info@branch.com
419	OARnet (corporate clients only)	614 728 8100	info@oar.net
501	Cloverleaf Technologies	903 832 1367	helpdesk@clover.cleaf.com
501	Sibylline, Inc.	501 521 4660	info@sibylline.com
502	IgLou Internet Services	800 436 4456	info@iglou.com
503	Alternet (UUNET Technologies, Inc.)	703 204 8000	info@alter.net
503	Data Research Group, Inc.	503 465 3282	info@ordata.com
503	Europa	503 222 9508	info@europa.com
503	Hevanet Communications	503 228 3520	info@hevanet.com
503	NETCOM On-Line Communications Services	408 554 8649	info@netcom.com
503	Open Door Networks, Inc.	503 488 4127	info@opendoor.com
503	RainDrop Laboraties/ Agora	503 293 1772	info@agora.rdrop.com
503	Structured Network Systems, Inc.	503 656 3530	info@structured.net
503	Teleport, Inc.	503 223 4245	info@teleport.com
503	Transport Logic	503 243 1940	sales@transport.com
503	WLN	800 342 5956	info@wln.com
504	Communique Inc.	504 527 6200	info@communique.net
504	I-Link Ltd	800 ILINK 99	info@i-link.net
504	NeoSoft, Inc.	713 684 5969	info@neosoft.com
505	Computer Systems Consulting	505 984 0085	info@spy.org

Area Code	Name	Phone	Email
505	Internet Express	719 592 1240	info@usa.net
505	New Mexico Technet, Inc.	505 345 6555	granoff@technet.nm.org
505	Southwest Cyberport	505 271 0009	info@swcp.com
505	ZyNet SouthWest	505 343 8846	zycor@zynet.com
506	Agate Internet Services	207 947 8248	ais@agate.net
507	Internet Connections, Inc.	507 625 7320	info@ic.mankato.mn.us
507	Millennium Communications, Inc.	612 338 5509	info@millcomm.com
507	Minnesota Regional Network	612 342 2570	info@mr.net
508	The Destek Group, Inc.	603 635 3857	inquire@destek.net
508	FOURnet Information Network	508 291 2900	info@four.net
508	The Internet Access Company (TIAC)	617 276 7200	info@tiac.net
508	The Internet Connection, Inc.	508 261 0383	info@ici.net
508	intuitive information, inc.	508 342 1100	info@iii.net
508	North Shore Access	617 593 3110	info@shore.net
508	Pioneer Global Telecommunications, Inc.	617 375 0200	info@pn.com
508	SCHUNIX	508 853 0258	schu@schunix.com
508	StarNet	508 922 8238	info@venus.star.net
508	TerraNet, Inc.	617 450 9000	info@terra.net
508	UltraNet Communications, Inc.	508 229 8400	info@ultra.net.com
508	The World	617 739 0202	info@world.std.com
508	Wrentham Internet Services	508 384 1404	info@riva.com
508	Wilder Systems, Inc.	617 933 8810	info@id.wing.net
509	Internet On-Ramp	509 927 7267	info@on-ramp.ior.com
509	Transport Logic	503 243 1940	sales@transport.com
509	WLN	800 342 5956	info@wln.com

Part V

Providers of Commercial Internet Access

continues

Area Code	Name	Phone	Email
510	Aimnet Information Services	408 257 0900	info@aimnet.com
510	Alternet (UUNET Technologies, Inc.)	703 204 8000	info@alter.net
510	BTR Communications Company	415 966 1429	support@btr.com
510	Community ConneXion-NEXUS-Berkeley	510 549 1383	info@c2.org
510	Direct Net Access Incorporated	510 649 6110	support@dnai.com
510	InterNex Information Services, Inc.	415 473 3060	info@internex.net
510	LanMinds, Inc.	510 843 6389	info@lanminds.com
510	LineX Communications	415 455 1650	info@linex.com
510	MediaCity World	415 321 6800	info@MediaCity.com
510	NETCOM On-Line Communications Services	408 554 8649	info@netcom.com
510	SLIPNET	415 281 3132	info@slip.net
510	West Coast Online	707 586 3060	info@calon.com
510	Zocalo Engineering	510 540 8000	info@zocalo.net
512	@sig.net	512 306 0700	sales@aus.sig.net
512	I-Link Ltd	800 ILINK 99	info@i-link.net
512	Illuminati Online	512 462 0999	info@io.com
512	Internet Connect Services, Inc.	512 572 9987	info@icsi.net
512	NETCOM On-Line Communications Services	408 554 8649	info@netcom.com
512	Real/Time Communications	512 451 0046	info@realtime.net
512	Zilker Internet Park, Inc.	512 206 3850	info@zilker.net
513	The Dayton Network Access Company	513 237 6868	info@dnaco.net
513	IgLou Internet Services	800 436 4456	info@iglou.com
513	Internet Access Cincinnati	513 887 8877	info@iac.net
513	Local Internet Gateway Co.	510 503 9227	sdw@lig.net
513	OARnet (corporate clients only)	614 728 8100	info@oar.net

Area Code	Name	Phone	Email
514	CiteNet Telecom Inc.	514 721 1351	info@citenet.net
514	Communication Accessibles Montreal	514 288 2581	info@cam.org
514	Communications Inter-Acces	514 367 0002	info@interax.net
514	UUNET Canada, Inc.	416 368 6621	info@uunet.ca
515	Synergy Communications, Inc.	800 345 9669	info@synergy.net
516	Creative Data Consultants (SILLY.COM)	718 229 0489	info@silly.com
516	Echo Communications Group	212 255 3839	info@echonyc.com
516	I-2000, Inc.	516 867 6379	info@i-2000.com
516	LI Net, Inc.	516 476 1168	info@li.net
516	Long Island Information, Inc.	516 294 0124	info@liii.com
516	Network Internet Services	516 543 0234	info@netusa.net
516	Phantom Access Technologies, Inc.	212 989 2418	bruce@phantom.com
516	The Pipeline Network	212 267 2626	info-info@pipeline.com
517	Msen, Inc.	313 998 4562	info@msen.com
517	Branch Information Services	313 741 4442	branch-info@branch.com
518	Wizvax Communications	518 273 4325	info@wizvax.com
519	HookUp Communications	905 847 8000	info@hookup.net
519	MGL Systems Computer Technologies Inc.	519 651 2713	info@mgl.ca
519	UUNET Canada, Inc.	416 368 6621	info@uunet.ca
520	Opus One	602 324 0494	sales@opus1.com
520	RTD Systems & Networking, Inc.	602 318 0696	info@rtd.com
602	Crossroads Communications	602 813 9040	crossroads@xroads.com

continues

Area Code	Name	Phone	Email
602	Internet Direct, Inc.	602 274 0100	info@indirect.com
602	Internet Express	719 592 1240	info@usa.net
602	NETCOM On-Line Communications Services	408 554 8649	info@netcom.com
602	New Mexico Technet, Inc.	505 345 6555	granoff@technet.nm.org
602	Opus One	602 324 0494	sales@opus1.com
602	Primenet	602 870 1010	info@primenet.com
602	RTD Systems & Networking, Inc.	602 318 0696	info@rtd.com
602	Systems Solutions Inc.	602 955 5566	support@syspac.com
603	Agate Internet Services	207 947 8248	ais@agate.net
603	The Destek Group, Inc.	603 635 3857	inquire@destek.net
603	MV Communications, Inc.	603 429 2223	info@mv.mv.com
603	NETIS Public Access Internet	603 437 1811	epoole@leotech.mv.com
604	AMT Solutions Group, Inc. Island Net	604 727 6030	info@islandnet.com
604	Mind Link!	604 534 5663	info@mindlink.bc.ca
604	Okanagan Internet Junction	604 549 1036	info@junction.net
604	Sunshine Net, Inc.	604 886 4120	admin@sunshine.net
604	UUNET Canada, Inc.	416 368 6621	info@uunet.ca
606	IgLou Internet Services	800 436 4456	info@iglou.com
606	Internet Access Cincinnati	513 887 8877	info@iac.net
608	FullFeed Communications	608 246 4239	info@fullfeed.com
609	Digital Express Group	301 847 5000	info@digex.net
609	Internet For 'U'	800 NET WAY1	info@ifu.net
609	K2NE Software	609 893 0673	vince-q@k2nesoft.com
609	New Jersey Computer Connection	609 896 2799	info@pluto.njcc.com
610	Digital Express Group	301 847 5000	info@digex.net
610	FishNet	610 337 9994	info@pond.com

Area Code	Name	Phone	Email
610	Microserve Information Systems	717 779 4430	info@microserve.com
610	Network Analysis Group	800 624 9240	nag@good.freedom.net
610	SSNet, Inc.	302 378 1386	info@ssnet.com
610	Oasis Telecommunications, Inc.	610 439 8560	staff@oasis.ot.com
610	YOU TOOLS Corporation	610 954 5910	info@youtools.com
612	Millennium Communications, Inc.	612 338 5509	info@millcomm.com
612	Minnesota Regional Network	612 342 2570	info@mr.net
612	StarNet Communications, Inc.	612 941 9177	info@winternet.com
612	Synergy Communications, Inc.	800 345 9669	info@synergy.net
613	Information Gateway Services	613 592 5619	info@igs.net
613	HookUp Communications	905 847 8000	info@hookup.net
613	o://info.web	613 225 3354	kevin@magi.com
613	UUNET Canada, Inc.	416 368 6621	info@uunet.ca
614	Branch Information Services	313 741 4442	branch-info@branch.com
614	Internet Access Cincinnati	513 887 8877	info@iac.net
614	OARnet (corporate clients only)	614 728 8100	info@oar.net
615	ERC, Inc. / The Edge	615 455 9915	staff@edge.ercnet.com
615	GoldSword Systems	615 691 6498	info@goldsword.com
615	ISDN-Net Inc	615 377 7672	jdunlap@rex.isdn.net
615	The Telalink Corporation	615 321 9100	sales@telalink.net
615	The Tri-Cities Connection	615 378 5355	info@tricon.net
616	Branch Information Services	313 741 4442	branch-info@branch.com
616	Msen, Inc.	313 998 4562	info@msen.com
617	Alternet (UUNET Technologies, Inc.)	703 204 8000	info@alter.net

Part V

Providers of Commercial Internet Access

continues

Area Code	Name	Phone	Email
617	The Internet Access Company (TIAC)	617 276 7200	info@tiac.net
617	intuitive information, inc.	508 342 1100	info@iii.net
617	NETCOM On-Line Communications Services	408 554 8649	info@netcom.com
617	North Shore Access	617 593 3110	info@shore.net
617	Pioneer Global Telecommunications, Inc.	617 375 0200	info@pn.com
617	TerraNet, Inc.	617 450 9000	info@terra.net
617	UltraNet Communications, Inc.	508 229 8400	info@ultra.net.com
617	The World	617 739 0202	info@world.std.com
617	Wilder Systems, Inc.	617 933 8810	info@id.wing.net
618	Allied Access Inc.	618 684 2255	sales@intrnet.net
619	CONNECTnet Internet Network Services	619 450 0254	info@connectnet.com
619	CTS Network Services	619 637 3637	info@cts.com
619	The Cyberspace Station	619 634 2894	info@cyber.net
619	Electriciti	619 338 9000	info@powergrid.electriciti.com
619	NETCOM On-Line Communications Services	408 554 8649	info@netcom.com
701	Red River Net	701 232 2227	info@rrnet.com
702	@wizard.com	702 871 4461	info@wizard.com
702	Great Basin Internet Services	702 829 2244	info@greatbasin.com
702	InterMind	702 878 6111	support@terminus.intermind.net
702	NETCOM On-Line Communications Services	408 554 8649	info@netcom.com
702	Sierra-Net	702 831 3353	giles@sierra.net
703	Alternet (UUNET Technologies, Inc.)	703 204 8000	info@alter.net
703	CAPCON Library Network	202 331 5771	info@capcon.net
703	Charm.Net	410 558 3900	info@charm.net
703	Clark Internet Services, Inc. ClarkNet	410 995 0691	info@clark.net

Area Code	Name	Phone	Email
703	DataBank, Inc.	913 842 6699	info@databank.com
703	Digital Express Group	301 847 5000	info@digex.net
703	Genuine Computing Resources	703 878 4680	info@gcr.com
703	Internet Online, Inc.	301 652 4468	info@intr.net
703	Interpath	800 849 6305	info@interpath.net
703	LaserNet	703 591 4232	info@laser.net
703	NETCOM On-Line Communications Services	408 554 8649	info@netcom.com
703	Quantum Networking Solutions, Inc.	805 538 2028	info@qnet.com
703	US Net, Incorporated	301 572 5926	info@us.net
704	Interpath	800 849 6305	info@interpath.net
704	SunBelt.Net	803 328 1500	info@sunbelt.net
704	Vnet Internet Access	704 334 3282	info@vnet.net
705	Mindemoya Computing	705 523 0243	info@mcd.on.ca
706	Internet Atlanta	404 410 9000	info@atlanta.com
706	MindSpring	404 888 0725	info@mindspring.com
707	West Coast Online	707 586 3060	info@calon.com
707	Zocalo Engineering	510 540 8000	info@zocalo.net
708	American Information Systems, Inc.	708 413 8400	info@ais.net
708	CICNet, Inc.	313 998 6103	info@cic.net
708	InterAccess Co.	800 967 1580	info@interaccess.com
708	MCSNet	312 248 8649	info@mcs.net
708	Open Business Systems, Inc.	708 250 0260	info@obs.net
708	Ripco Communications, Inc.	312 477 6210	info@ripco.com
708	Tezcatlipoca, Inc.	312 850 0181	info@tezcat.com
708	WorldWide Access	708 367 1870	info@wwa.com
712	Synergy Communications, Inc.	800 345 9669	info@synergy.net

Providers of Commercial Internet Access

Part V

continues

Area Code	Name	Phone	Email
713	Alternet (UUNET Technologies, Inc.)	703 204 8000	info@alter.net
713	The Black Box	713 480 2684	info@blkbox.com
713	ELECTROTEX, Inc.	713 526 3456	info@electrotex.com
713	I-Link Ltd	800 ILINK 99	info@i-link.net
713	Internet Connect Services, Inc.	512 572 9987	info@icsi.net
713	NeoSoft, Inc.	713 684 5969	info@neosoft.com
713	USiS	713 682 1666	admin@usis.com
714	Cloverleaf Communications	714 895 3075	sales@cloverleaf.com
714	Delta Internet Services	714 778 0370	info@deltanet.com
714	DigiLink Network Services	310 542 7421	info@digilink.net
714	EarthLink Network, Inc.	213 644 9500	info@earthlink.net
714	Electriciti	619 338 9000	info@powergrid.electriciti.com
714	KAIWAN Internet	714 638 2139	info@kaiwan.com
714	Lightside, Inc.	818 858 9261	info@lightside.com
714	NETCOM On-Line Communications Services	408 554 8649	info@netcom.com
715	FullFeed Communications	608 246 4239	info@fullfeed.com
716	E-Znet, Inc.	716 262 2485	
716	Moran Communications	716 639 1254	info@moran.com
716	ServiceTech Inc. Cyber-Link	716 546 6908	dam@cyber1.servtech.com
717	Microserve Information Systems	717 779 4430	info@microserve.com
717	Oasis Telecommunications, Inc.	610 439 8560	staff@oasis.ot.com
717	YOU TOOLS Corporation	610 954 5910	info@youtools.com
718	Blythe Systems	212 226 7171	infodesk@blythe.org
718	Creative Data Consultants (SILLY.COM)	718 229 0489	info@silly.com
718	escape.com - Kazan Corp	212 888 8780	info@escape.com
718	I-2000, Inc.	516 867 6379	info@i-2000.com

Area Code	Name	Phone	Email
718	Ingress Communications Inc.	212 679 2838	info@ingress.com
718	InterCom Online	212 714 7183	info@intercom.com
718	Interport Communications Corp.	212 989 1128	info@interport.net
718	Mnematics, Incorporated	914 359 4546	service@mne.com
718	Mordor International BBS	201 433 4222	ritz@mordor.com
718	Phantom Access Technologies, Inc.	212 989 2418	bruce@phantom.com
718	The Pipeline Network	212 267 2626	info-info@pipeline.com
719	Colorado SuperNet, Inc.	303 296 8202	info@csn.org
719	Internet Express	719 592 1240	info@usa.net
719	Old Colorado City Communications	719 528 5849	thefox@oldcolo.com
719	Rocky Mountain Internet	800 900 7644	info@rmii.com
801	DataBank, Inc.	913 842 6699	info@databank.com
801	Infonaut Communication Services	801 370 3068	info@infonaut.com
801	Internet Direct, Inc.	801 578 0300	info@indirect.com
801	Internet Technology Systems (I.T.S.)	801 375 0538	admin@itsnet.com
801	XMission	801 539 0852	support@xmission.com
803	A World of Difference, Inc.	803 769 4488	info@awod.com
803	Global Vision Inc.	803 241 0901	info@globalvision.net
803	Interpath	800 849 6305	info@interpath.net
803	SIMS, Inc.	803 762 4956	info@sims.net
803	SunBelt.Net	803 328 1500	info@sunbelt.net
804	Widomaker Communication Service	804 253 7621	bloyall@widowmaker.com
805	The Central Connection	818 735 3000	info@centcon.com
805	EarthLink Network, Inc.	213 644 9500	info@earthlink.net
805	KAIWAN Internet	714 638 2139	info@kaiwan.com

Part V
Providers of Commercial Internet Access

continues

Area Code	Name	Phone	Email
805	Quantum Networking Solutions, Inc.	805 538 2028	info@qnet.com
805	Regional Alliance for Info Networking	805 967 7246	info@rain.org
808	Hawaii OnLine	808 533 6981	support@aloha.net
808	LavaNet, Inc.	808 545 5282	info@lava.net
808	Pacific Information Exchange, Inc.	808 596 7494	info@pixi.com
810	Branch Information Services	313 741 4442	branch-info@branch.com
810	ICNET / Innovative Concepts	313 998 0090	info@ic.net
810	Msen, Inc.	313 998 4562	info@msen.com
810	RustNet, Inc.	810 650 6812	info@rust.net
317	HolliCom Internet Services	317 883 4500	cale@holli.com
812	IgLou Internet Services	800 436 4456	info@iglou.com
812	World Connection Services	812 479 1700	info@evansville.net
813	CFTnet	813 980 1317	sales@cftnet.com
813	CocoNet Corporation	813 945 0055	info@coconet.com
813	CyberGate, Inc.	305 428 4283	sales@gate.net
813	Intelligence Network Online, Inc.	x22 -> 813 442 0114	info@intnet.net
813	PacketWorks, Inc.	813 446 8826	info@packet.net
815	American Information Systems, Inc.	708 413 8400	info@ais.net
815	InterAccess Co.	800 967 1580	info@interaccess.com
816	Interstate Networking Corporation	816 472 4949	staff@interstate.net
816	Primenet	602 870 1010	info@primenet.com
817	Association for Computing Machinery	817 776 6876	account-info@acm.org

Area Code	Name	Phone	Email
817	DFW Internet Services, Inc.	817 332 5116	info@dfw.net
817	Texas Metronet, Inc.	214 705 2900	info@metronet.com
818	Abode Computer Service	818 287 5115	eric@abode.ttank.com
818	The Central Connection	818 735 3000	info@centcon.com
818	Delta Internet Services	714 778 0370	info@deltanet.com
818	DigiLink Network Services	310 542 7421	info@digilink.net
818	EarthLink Network, Inc.	213 644 9500	info@earthlink.net
818	KAIWAN Internet	714 638 2139	info@kaiwan.com
818	Lightside, Inc.	818 858 9261	info@lightside.com
818	NETCOM On-Line Communications Services	408 554 8649	info@netcom.com
818	Primenet	602 870 1010	info@primenet.com
818	Regional Alliance for Info Networking	805 967 7246	info@rain.org
818	ViaNet Communications	415 903 2242	info@via.net
819	o://info.web	613 225 3354	kevin@magi.com
901	ISDN-Net Inc	615 377 7672	jdunlap@rex.isdn.net
901	Magibox Incorporated	901 757 7835	info@magibox.net
903	Cloverleaf Technologies	903 832 1367	helpdesk@clover.cleaf.com
904	CyberGate, Inc.	305 428 4283	sales@gate.net
904	Polaris Network, Inc.	904 878 9745	staff@polaris.net
904	PSS InterNet Services	800 463 8499	support@america.com
904	SymNet	904 385 1061	info@symnet.net
905	HookUp Communications	905 847 8000	info@hookup.net
905	InterLog Internet Services	416 975 2655	internet@interlog.com
905	Vaxxine Computer Systems Inc.	905 562 3500	admin@vaxxine.com
906	Branch Information Services	313 741 4442	branch-info@branch.com
906	Msen, Inc.	313 998 4562	info@msen.com

continues

Area Code	Name	Phone	Email
908	Castle Network, Inc.	908 548 8881	request@castle.net
908	Digital Express Group	301 847 5000	info@digex.net
908	I-2000, Inc.	516 867 6379	info@i-2000.com
908	INTAC Access Corporation	800 504 6822	info@intac.com
908	Internet For 'U'	800 NET WAY1	info@ifu.net
908	Internet Online Services	x226 -> 201 928 1000	help@ios.com
619	CONNECTnet Internet Network Services	619 450 0254	info@connectnet.com
909	Delta Internet Services	714 778 0370	info@deltanet.com
909	KAIWAN Internet	714 638 2139	info@kaiwan.com
909	Lightside, Inc.	818 858 9261	info@lightside.com
910	Interpath	800 849 6305	info@interpath.net
910	Red Barn Data Center	910 750 9809	tom@rbdc.rbdc.com
910	Vnet Internet Access	704 334 3282	info@vnet.net
912	Internet Atlanta	404 410 9000	info@atlanta.com
913	DataBank, Inc.	913 842 6699	info@databank.com
913	Interstate Networking Corporation	816 472 4949	staff@interstate.net
914	Cloud 9 Internet	914 682 0626	info@cloud9.net
914	Computer Solutions by Hawkinson	914 229 9853	info@mhv.net
914	Creative Data Consultants (SILLY.COM)	718 229 0489	info@silly.com
914	DataBank, Inc.	913 842 6699	info@databank.com
914	INTAC Access Corporation	800 504 6822	info@intac.com
914	I-2000, Inc.	516 867 6379	info@i-2000.com
914	InteleCom Data Systems, Inc.	401 885 6855	info@ids.net
914	Mnematics, Incorporated	914 359 4546	service@mne.com
914	Phantom Access Technologies, Inc.	212 989 2418	bruce@phantom.com
914	The Pipeline Network	212 267 2626	info-info@pipeline.com

Area Code	Name	Phone	Email
914	TZ-Link	914 353 5443	drew@j51.com
914	WestNet Internet Services	914 967 7816	info@westnet.com
915	New Mexico Technet, Inc.	505 345 6555	granoff@technet.nm.org
916	Great Basin Internet Services	702 829 2244	info@greatbasin.com
916	NETCOM On-Line Communications Services	408 554 8649	info@netcom.com
916	Sierra-Net	702 831 3353	giles@sierra.net
916	West Coast Online	707 586 3060	info@calon.com
916	Zocalo Engineering	510 540 8000	info@zocalo.net
918	Galaxy Star Systems	918 835 3655	info@galstar.com
918	Internet Oklahoma	918 583 1161	info@ionet.net
919	Interpath	800 849 6305	info@interpath.net
919	NETCOM On-Line Communications Services	408 554 8649	info@netcom.com
919	Vnet Internet Access	704 334 3282	info@vnet.net
970	EZLink Internet Access	970 482 0807	ezadmin@ezlink.com
970	Frontier Internet, Inc.	970 385 4177	info@frontier.net

Part V — Providers of Commercial Internet Access

Foreign

Below is a listing of Internet service providers in countries other than the U.S. and Canada, sorted by country. Fields are country, service provider name, voice phone number, and email address for more information.

Country	Name	Phone	Email
Australia	APANA	+61 42 965015	wollongong@apana.org.au
Australia	Apanix Public Access	+61 8 373 5575	admin@apanix.apana.org.au
Australia	arrakis.apana.org.au	+61 8 296 6200	greg@arrakis.apana.org.au
Australia	AusNet Services Pty Ltd	+61 2 241 5888	sales@world.net
Australia	Byron Public Access	+61 18 823 541	admin@byron.apana.org.au

continues

Country	Name	Phone	Email
Australia	DIALix Services	+61 2 948 6995	justin@sydney.dialix.oz.au
Australia	FidoNet Zone 3 Gateway	+61 3 793 2728	info@csource.pronet.com
Australia	Highway 1	+61 9 370 4584	info@highway1.com.au
Australia	Hunter Network Association	+61 49 621783	mbrown@hna.com.au
Australia	iiNet Technologies	+61 9 3071183	iinet@iinet.com.au
Australia	Kralizec Dialup Unix System	+61 2 837 1397	nick@kralizec.zeta.org.au
Australia	Informed Technology	+61 9 245 2279	info@it.com.au
Australia	The Message eXchange Pty Ltd	+61 2 550 5014	info@tmx.com.au
Australia	Microplex Pty. Ltd.	+61 2 888 3685	info@mpx.com.au
Australia	Pegasus Networks Pty Ltd	+61 7 257 1111	fwhitmee@peg.apc.org
Australia	PPIT Pty. Ltd. (059 051 320)	+61 3 747 9823	info@ppit.com.au
Australia	Stour System Services	+61 9 571 1949	stour@stour.net.au
Australia	Winthrop Technology	+61 9 380 3564	wthelp@yarrow.wt.uwa.edu.au
Austria	EUnet EDV	+43 1 3174969	info@austria.eu.net
Austria	Hochschuelerschaft...	+43 1 586 1868	sysop@link-atu.comlink.apc.org
Austria	PING EDV	+43 1 3194336	info@ping.at
Bashkiria	UD JV 'DiasPro'	+7 3472 387454	iskander@diaspro.bashkiria.su
Belarus	Open Contact, Ltd.	+7 017 2206134	admin@brc.minsk.by
Belgium	EUnet Belgium NV	+32 16 236099	info@belgium.eu.net
Belgium	Infoboard Telematics SA	+32 2 475 25 31	ocaeymaex@infoboard.be
Belgium	INnet NV/SA	+32 14 319937	info@inbe.net
Belgium	KnoopPunt VZW	+32 9 2333 686	support@knooppunt.be
Bulgaria	EUnet Bulgaria	+359 52 259135	info@bulgaria.eu.net
Crimea	Crimea Communication Centre	+7 652 257214	sem@snail.crimea.ua

Country	Name	Phone	Email
Denmark	DKnet / EUnet Denmark	+45 3917 9900	info@dknet.dk
Finland	Clinet Ltd	+358 0 437 5209	clinet@clinet.fi
Finland	EUnet Finland Ltd.	+358 0 400 2060	helpdesk@eunet.fi
France	French Data Network	+33 1 4797 5873	info@fdn.org
France	Internet Way	+33 1 4143 2110	info@iway.fr
France	OLEANE	+33 1 4328 3232	info-internet@oleane.net
France	STI	+33 1 3463 1919	fb101@calvacom.fr
Georgia	Mimosi Hard	+7 8832 232857	kisho@sanet.ge
Germany	bbTT Electronic Networks	+49 30 817 42 06	willem@b-2.de.contrib.net
Germany	EUnet Germany GmbH	+49 231 972 2222	info@germany.eu.net
Germany	Individual Network e.V.	+49 441 980 8556	in-info@individual.net
Germany	INS Inter Networking Systems	+49 2305 356505	info@ins.net
Germany	Internet PoP Frankfurt	+49 69 94439192	joerg@pop-frankfurt.com
Germany	MUC.DE e.V.	+49 89 324 683 0	postmaster@muc.de
Germany	Onlineservice Nuernberg	+49 911 9933882	info@osn.de
Germany	PFM News & Mail Xlink POP	+49 171 331 0862	info@pfm.pfm-mainz.de
Germany	Point of Presence GmbH	+49 40 2519 2025	info@pop.de
Germany	POP Contrib.Net Netzdienste	+49 521 9683011	info@teuto.de
Germany	SpaceNet GmbH	+49 89 324 683 0	info@space.net
Germany	TouchNET GmbH	+49 89 5447 1111	info@touch.net
Germany	Westend GbR	+49 241 911879	info@westend.com
Greece	Ariadne	+30 1 651 3392	dialup@leon.nrcps.ariadne-t.gr
Greece	Foundation of Research	+30 81 221171	forthnet-pr@forthnet.gr
Hong Kong	Hong Kong SuperNet	+852 358 7924	trouble@hk.super.net

Part V — Providers of Commercial Internet Access

continues

Country	Name	Phone	Email
Iceland	SURIS / ISnet	+354 1 694747	isnet-info@isnet.is
Ireland	Cork Internet Services	+353 21 277124	info@cis.ie
Ireland	Ieunet Limited	+353 1 679 0832	info@ieunet.ie
Ireland	Ireland On-Line	+353 91 592727	info@iol.ie
Israel	Elronet	+972 313534	info@elron.net
Israel	NetVision LTD.	+972 550330	info@netvision.net.il
Italy	ITnet S.p.A.	+39 10 6563324	info@it.net
Japan	Asahi Net	+81 3 3666 2811	info@asahi-net.or.jp
Japan	Global OnLine, Japan	+81 3 5330 9380	hahne@acm.org
Japan	Internet Initiative Japan	+81 3 3580 3781	info@iij.ad.jp
Japan	M.R.T., Inc.	+81 3 3255 8880	sysop@janis-tok.com
Japan	People World Ltd.	+81 3 5661 4130	18005044@people.or.jp
Japan	TWICS	+81 3 3351 5977	info@twics.com
Japan	Typhoon Inc.	+81 3 3757 2118	info@typhoon.co.jp
Kazakhstan	Bogas Soft Laboratory Co.	+7 322 262 4990	pasha@sl.semsk.su
Kuwait	Gulfnet Kuwait	+965 242 6729	john@gulfa.ods.gulfnet.kw
Latvia	LvNet-Teleport	+371 2 551133	vit@riga.lv
Latvia	Versia Ltd.	+371 2 417000	postmaster@vernet.lv
Luxemburg	EUnet Luxemburg	+352 47 02 61 361	info@luxemburg.eu.net
Mexico	Datanet S.A. de C.V.	+52 5 1075400	info@data.net.mx
Netherlands	The Delft Connection	+31 15560079	info@void.tdcnet.nl
Netherlands	Hobbynet	+31 365361683	henk@hgatenl.hobby.nl
Netherlands	Internet Access Foundation	+31 5982 2720	mail-server@iafnl.iaf.nl
Netherlands	NEST	+31 206265566	info@nest.nl
Netherlands	NetLand	+31 206943664	info@netland.nl

Country	Name	Phone	Email
Netherlands	NLnet (EUnet)	+31 206639366	info@nl.net
Netherlands	Psyline	+31 80445801	postmaster@psyline.nl
Netherlands	Simplex Networking	+31 206932433	skelmir@simplex.nl
Netherlands	Stichting XS4ALL	+31 206225222	helpdesk@xs4all.nl
New Zealand	Actrix Networks Limited	+64 4 389 6356	john@actrix.gen.nz
New Zealand	Efficient Software Limited	+64 3 4738274	bart@dunedin.es.co.nz
Norway	Oslonett A/S	+47 22 46 10 99	oslonett@oslonett.no
Poland	PDi Ltd. - Public Internet	+48 42 30 21 94	info@pdi.lodz.pl
Portugal	Lisboa	716 2395	info@esoterica.com
Romania	EUnet Romania SRL	+40 1 312 6886	info@romania.eu.net
Russia	GlasNet	+7 95 262 7079	support@glas.apc.org
Russia	Inter Communications Ltd.	+7 8632 620562	postmaster@icomm.rnd.su
Russia	N&K Company	+7 86622 72167	serge@nik.nalchik.su
Russia	NEVAlink Ltd.	+7 812 592 3737	serg@arcom.spb.su
Russia	Relcom CO	+7 95 194 25 40	postmaster@ussr.eu.net
Russia	SvjazInform	+7 351 265 3600	pol@rich.chel.su
Slovakia	EUnet Slovakia	+42 7 725 306	info@slovakia.eu.net
Slovenia	NIL, System Integration	+386 61 1405 183	info@slovenia.eu.net
South Africa	Aztec	+27 21 419 2690	info@aztec.co.za
South Africa	Internet Africa	+27 0800 020003	info@iaccess.za
South Africa	The Internet Solution	+27 11 447 5566	info@is.co.za
Sweden	NetGuide	+46 31 28 03 73	info@netg.se

Part V

Providers of Commercial Internet Access

continues

Country	Name	Phone	Email
Switzerland	SWITCH	+41 1 268 1515	postmaster@switch.ch
Switzerland	XGP Switzerland	+41 61 8115635	service@xgp.spn.com
Tataretan	KAMAZ Incorporated	+7 8439 53 03 34	postmaster@kamaz.kazan.su
Ukraine	ConCom, Ltd.	+7 0572 27 69 13	igor@ktts.kharkov.ua
Ukraine	Electronni Visti	+7 44 2713457	info%elvisti.kiev.ua@kiae.su
Ukraine	PACO Links Int'l Ltd.	+7 48 2200057	info@vista.odessa.ua
Ukraine	UkrCom-Kherson Ltd	+7 5522 64098	postmaster@ukrcom.kherson.ua
UK	Compulink (CIX Ltd)	+44 181 390 8446	cixadmin@cix.compulink.co.uk
UK	CONNECT - PC User Group	+44 181 863 1191	info@ibmpcug.co.uk
UK	Demon Internet Services Ltd.	+44 81 349 0063	internet@demon.co.uk
UK	The Direct Connection	+44 81 313 0100	helpdesk@dircon.co.uk
UK	EUnet GB	+44 1227 266466	sales@britain.eu.net
UK	ExNet Systems Ltd.	+44 81 244 0077	info@exnet.com
UK	GreenNet	+44 71 713 1941	support@gn.apc.org
UK	Lunatech Research	+44 1734 791900	info@luna.co.uk
UK	Pavilion Internet plc	+44 1273 606072	info@pavilion.co.uk
UK	Sound & Visions BBS	+44 1932 253131	info@span.com
UK	Specialix	+44 932 3522251	keith@specialix.co.uk
UK	WinNET (UK)	+44 181 863 1191	info@win-uk.ne

HTML Tags

This appendix lists the HTML tags covered in chapter 26, "Creating Your Web Page."

Document Organization

Address	`<address>...text...<address>`
Blockquote	`<blockquote>...text...</blockquote>`
Heading 1	`<h1>...text...</h1>`
Heading 2	`<h2>...text...</h2>`
Heading 3	`<h3>...text...</h3>`
Heading 4	`<h4>...text...</h4>`
Heading 5	`<h5>...text...</h5>`
Heading 6	`<h6>...text...</h6>`
New line	` `
New paragraph	`<p>`

Graphics

Horizontal rule `<hr attributes>`

Horizontal rule examples:

```
<hr size=20 width=288 align=center noshade>
<hr size=10 width=75% align=left>
```

Image `<img attribute(s)>`

Image example:

```
<img src="ingrid.gif" align=bottom alt="I have expressive eyes with long
eyelashes.">
```

Links

Anchor `<a attribute(s)>…text…</a>`

Anchor examples:

Email address:

```
<a href="mailto:ingrid@tidbits.com">ingrid@tidbits.com</a>
```

Full URL:

```
<a href="http://quest.arc.nasa.gov/livefrom/livefrom.html">Live from
Antartica</a>
```

Named target:

```
<a name="other penguins">Other Penguins on the Web</a>
```

Relative URL:

```
a href="reno.html">Reno, Nevada</a>
```

Lists

Definition list   `<dl>…list…</dl>`

Definition list definition   `<dd>`

Definition list term   `<dt>`

Definition list example:

```
<dl>
<dt>Tomatoes
<dd>Just chop up tomatoes and stick them on your pizza.
<dt>Mushrooms
<dd>Saute mushrooms before putting them on a pizza.
</dl>
```

Ordered (numbered) list   `<ol>…list…</ol>`

List entry   `<li>`

Unordered (bulleted) list   `<ul>…list…</ul>`

Special Characters

Aacute (á)   `&aacute;`

Ampersand (&)   `&amp;`

Double straight quote (")   `&quot;`

Eacute (é)   `&eacute`

Left angle bracket (<)   `&lt;`

Ntilde (ñ)   `&tilde;`

Right angle bracket (>)   `&gt;`

Typography

Bold   `<b>…text…</b>`

Cite   `<cite>…text…</cite>`

Code   `<code>…text…</code>`

Emphasize   `<em>…text…</em>`

Italic	`<i>...text...</i>`
Keyboard	`<kbd>...text...</kbd>`
Preformatted (monospaced)	`<pre>...text...</pre>`
Sample	`<samp>...text...</samp>`
Strong	`<strong>...text...</strong>`
Typewriter	`<tt>...text...</tt>`
Underline	`<u>...text...</u>`
Variable	`<var>...text...</var>`

Glossary

a

address commands Small extensions for UUCP/Connect that give it additional capabilities, much as XMCDs and XFCNs give HyperCard additional capabilities.

addressing A method of identifying a resource (such as a program) or piece of information (such as a file) on a network. Methods of addressing vary considerably from network-to-network.

Adventure One of the earliest text adventure games written for computers. It is the forerunner of the popular Zork series from Infocom.

alias In System 7, a file that "points to" another file, folder, or disk, and may generally be used in place of the original item. In network usage, alias usually refers to a simple name, location, or command that you can use in place of a more complex name, location, or command. Aliases are commonly used for email addresses, directories, or commands.

America Online A popular commercial information service with a graphical interface.

AOL Shorthand for **America Online**. Each letter is pronounced separately.

AppleLink   Apple's commercial online information service. Expensive, but graphical. Slated to go away soon.

AppleLink packages   The archiving and compression format used solely by AppleLink. StuffIt Expander with Expander Enhancer can decompress AppleLink packages.

AppleTalk   A local area network protocol Apple developed to connect computers and peripherals over various different types of wiring.

ARA   *Apple Remote Access.* A software program from Apple Computer that allows one Mac to dial another Mac via a modem and, through AppleShare and/or Personal File Sharing, access local or network resources available to the "answering" Mac. (Common resources include shared directories, servers, and printers.) Although I don't cover the issue much in this book, you can do some neat things with ARA and MacTCP.

.ARC   An older DOS archiving format.

Archie   An Internet service that maintains and allows users to search a large database of materials stored on anonymous FTP sites.

archive site   A site that archives files for users to retrieve, via either FTP or email.

ARPA   *Advanced Research Projects Agency.* The governmental organization responsible for creating the beginnings of the Internet.

ARPAnet   The proto-Internet network created by ARPA.

ASCII   *American Standard Code for Information Interchange.* In the context of a file, an ASCII file is one that contains only "text" characters—numbers, letters, and standard punctuation. Although ASCII text can contain international characters available on the Mac ("upper-ASCII"), these characters are not commonly supported by Internet services such as email, Gopher, and FTP. In FTP, it's a command that tells FTP that you will be transferring text files (which is the default).

atob   (pronounced "a to b") A Unix program that turns ASCII files into binary files. The **btoa** program does the reverse.

attachments   Files that are linked to a specific email message, just as you might paperclip a clipping to a **snail mail** letter.

b

bandwidth   Information theory used to express the amount of information that can flow through a given point at any given time. Some points have narrow bandwidth (indicating not much information can flow through at one time), and others have high bandwidth (indicating a great deal of information can flow through at one time). This term is commonly used in reference to "wasted bandwidth," indicating that some (or most) of the information flowing by a point is of no use to a user. This term can include overloading a site's network connection (thus curtailing other users' use of the lines) or including lengthy signature files in Usenet postings or discussion groups. "Wasted bandwidth" is often relative: What one person views as wasteful might be essential to someone else.

bang   The exclamation point! Used to separate machine names in UUCP bang-style addressing, which isn't all that common anymore.

baud   A measure of modem speed equal to one signal per second; 300 baud equals 300 bits per second (bps). But at higher speeds one signal can contain more than one bit, so a 9600 baud modem is not a 9600 bps modem. (The terms often are incorrectly used interchangeably). See also **bps**.

BBS   *Bulletin Board System*. A computer system that provides its users with files for downloading and areas for electronic discussions. Bulletin board systems usually are run by and for local users, although many now provide Internet, UUCP, or FidoNet mail.

Binary   In the context of a file, any file that contains non-textual data. (Images and applications are examples of binary files.) In FTP, a command that tells FTP to transfer information as an arbitrary stream of bits rather than as a series of textual characters.

BinHex   The standard Macintosh format for converting a binary file into an ASCII file that can pass through email programs. (For those of you wondering how to pronounce it, "Bin" rhymes with "tin," and "hex" rhymes with "sex," and the accent is on the first syllable.) See also **uucode**.

BITNET   An academic large-scale computer network, primarily connecting academic institutions. BITNET is often expanded as the "Because It's Time" Network. A friend notes, "Actually, it seems that the definitive answer to what the BIT stands for is 'It has varied, and depends on who you asked and when.'"

BIX   The online commercial information service called the *BYTE Information Exchange*, although I have never heard anyone use the full name in favor of BIX.

body   The part of an email message where you type your message, as opposed to the **header** or the **signature**.

bounce   What email does when it doesn't go through.

bps   *Bits per second*. The measurement of modem transmission speed. Not comparable to baud after 300 bps.

Brownian motion   With apologies to Douglas Adams, the best example is indeed a really hot cup of tea. It has to do with internal movement within a hot liquid.

browser   A client program that enables one to search, often somewhat randomly, through the information provided by a specific type of server. Generally used in relation to the World Wide Web.

btoa   (pronounced "b to a") A Unix program that turns binary files into ASCII files for transmission via email. The **atob** program decodes such files.

BTW   Abbreviation for the expression, "*By the way.*"

C

Call For Votes   What you do after discussing whether a new newsgroup should be created.

CCL   *Connection Control Language.* Used in Apple Remote Access, InterSLIP, and other communications programs, CCL is a scripting language that lets you control your modem.

CERN   The birthplace of the **World Wide Web**, although in real life they do high energy physics research. Located in Geneva, Switzerland. CERN doesn't stand for anything any more, although it once was an acronym for a French name.

CFV   See **Call For Votes**.

channel   In IRC, an area that theoretically has a specific discussion topic. See **IRC**.

charter   The document that lays out what topics a newsgroup will cover, what its name will be, and other relevant details.

chat script   A simple (you hope) conversation between your Mac and your host machine that allows your Mac to log in automatically. Chat scripts usually involve a series of send and expect strings. Your host sends a login prompt; your Mac responds with your username. Your host sends a password prompt; your Mac responds with your password.

chiasmus   A term from classical rhetoric that describes a situation in which you introduce subjects in the order A, B, and C, and then talk about them in the order C, B, and A.

CIM   See **CompuServe Information Manager**.

CIS   Stands for *CompuServe Information Service*, or simply *CompuServe*. Wags often replace the *S* with a *$*. See **CompuServe**.

ClariNet   An alternate hierarchy of newsgroups that uses the same transmission routes as Usenet, but carries commercial information from UPI and others. You, or your provider, must pay to read ClariNet news.

client   The program or computer that requests information from a server computer or program. Used in terms of client/server computing. See also **server**.

clone   A DOS-based computer that imitates computers made by IBM. Referred to as clones because they don't distinguish themselves enough for us to bother referring to them any other way.

CMS   Short for *Conversational Monitor System*. The part of the operating system on certain IBM mainframes with which you interact. Not at all conversational.

command line   Where you type commands to an operating system such as DOS or Unix. Command-line operating systems can be powerful but are often a pain to work with, especially for Macintosh users used to a graphical interface.

compress   To make a file smaller by removing redundant information.

CompuServe   One of the oldest and largest commercial online services. Sometimes abbreviated as **CIS**.

CompuServe Information Manager   A decent graphical program for the Mac (and Windows) that puts a nice face on CompuServe. Generally abbreviated **CIM**.

connect time   The amount of time you are actually connected to and using a computer. Because connect or telephone charges are based on this amount of time, you want to keep it as low as possible.

.cpt   The filename extension used by Compact Pro.

CREN   *Corporation for Research and Educational Networking.*

cross-posted   What happens to a Usenet posting when you put several newsgroup names in the Newsgroups line. More efficient than posting multiple individual copies.

CSLIP   Compressed SLIP. A type of SLIP account that uses compression to increase performance.

d

daemons   Small programs in Unix that run frequently to see whether something has happened: if so, they act as they were programmed; if not, they go back to sleep.

DARPA   *Defense Advanced Research Projects Agency*. Replaced ARPA and had a more military bent. Has since been renamed ARPA again. See also **ARPA**.

DEC   *Digital Equipment Corporation*. Also known as *Digital*, this company produces the popular VAX line of computers and the VMS operating system.

dialing scripts   In InterSLIP, the scripts that control modem dialog. See also **CCL**.

dial up   To call another computer via modem. The term is often lumped together as one word except when used as a verb.

dialup   A connection or line reached by modem, as in "a dialup line."

digest   A single message that contains multiple individual postings to a mailing list or newsgroup.

domain   A level of hierarchy in a machine's full nodename. For instance, `tidbits.com` is in the `com` domain, as are many other machines.

domain name server   A computer that keeps track of names of other machines and their numeric IP addresses. When you refer to a machine by name, your domain name server translates that information appropriately into the numeric IP address necessary to make the connection.

domain name system   The system that makes it possible for you to think in terms of names such as `penguin.tidbits.com`, whereas computers think in terms of `204.25.157.10`.

DOS   An elderly operating system that is frequently helped across the street by Microsoft Windows.

download   To retrieve a file from another machine, usually a host machine, to your machine.

downstream   Usenet neighbors that are downstream from you get most of their news from your machine, in contrast to machines that are **upstream** from you.

dynamic addressing   When your Mac gets its IP number for each session from the server to which you connect. Linked to the **Server** button in the Obtain Address part of MacTCP. Not to be confused with the Dynamically button, which picks an IP number from a range at random.

e

electronic mail or **email**   Messages that travel through the networks rather than being committed to paper and making the arduous journey through the U.S. Postal Service.

emoticons   A rather silly name for **smileys**.

Ethernet   A type of local area network that is much faster than LocalTalk. Most Macs can use Ethernet by adding an Ethernet expansion card; some recent Macs come with Ethernet built-in.

.etx   The filename extension for **setext** files, which are straight text files in a specific format that's easy to read online and can be decoded for even better display.

expire   After a certain amount of time, Usenet postings can be set to expire, which means that they will be deleted even if they haven't been read, so that they don't waste space.

f

FAQ   *Frequently Asked Question*. Lists of commonly asked questions and their answers, often posted in newsgroups to reduce the number of novice questions. Read a FAQ list before asking a question, to make sure yours isn't a frequently asked one.

Fax   Slang for *facsimile*. A technology that takes paper from the sender and produces more paper that looks just like it at the recipient's end. You can use fax modems to eliminate the paper step at one end or both, but they may be less reliable than stand-alone fax machines. Email is cleaner, often cheaper, and more environmentally friendly, and the results are more useful in other programs. However, you can't easily send signatures or existing paper documents via email.

feed   Shorthand for a connection to another machine that sends you mail and news. I might say, "I have a mail feed from Ed's machine."

Fidonet   A network of cooperating bulletin board systems that has some links to the Internet.

filename extension   A three-letter (usually) code at the end of a filename that indicates what type of file it is. Essential in non-Macintosh environments that lack icons or other methods of identifying files. Common extensions include **.txt** for text files, **.hqx** for BinHexed files, and **.sit** for StuffIt files.

fileserver or **file server**   A machine that provides files via a network. Perhaps because of time spent working on BITNET, I tend to use it as a synonym for **mailserver**, or a machine that returns files that are requested via email.

file site   Another name for an archive site or FTP site. A computer on which files are stored for anyone on the Internet to retrieve.

Part V

Glossary

D

Finger   A method of finding out information about someone else on the Internet.

firewall   A security system that not only prevents intruders from entering, but also often prevents legitimate users from getting out to the Internet from the local network. A firewall usually has a single machine that's connected to the Internet and all Internet traffic must pass through that machine.

flame war   A conflagration in which lots of people jump in on different sides of an argument and start insulting each other. Fun to watch briefly, but a major waste of **bandwidth**.

flaming   The act of calling into question someone's thoughts, beliefs, and parentage simply because you don't agree with them. Don't do it.

followup   An article on Usenet posted in reply to another article. The subject should stay the same so that readers can tell the two articles are related.

forms   In the World Wide Web, online electronic forms that you can fill in if you have a forms-capable Web browser such as MacWeb or NCSA Mosaic 2.0.

Freenet   An organization whose goal is to provide free Internet access in a specific area, often by working with local schools and libraries. Ask around to see if a Freenet has sprung up in your area. The first and preeminent example is the Cleveland Freenet. Freenet also refers to the specific Freenet software, and the information services that use it.

freeware   Software that you can distribute freely and use for free, but for which the author often retains the copyright, which means that you can't modify it.

FTP   *File Transfer Protocol.* One of the main ways in which you retrieve, umm, well, files from other machines on the Internet.

FTPmail   A method of retrieving files stored on FTP sites via email.

FYI   Abbreviation for the expression, *"For your information."*

g

gateway   A machine that exists on two networks, such as the Internet and BITNET, and that can transfer mail between them.

gateway script   In InterSLIP, a script that controls the login process. See also CCL.

GIF   *Graphics Interchange Format.* A platform-independent file format developed by CompuServe, the GIF format is commonly used to distribute graphics on the Internet. Mighty battles have been waged over the pronunciation of this term, and although Robin Williams notes that it's pronounced "jiff" in her book, *Jargon*, both of my glossary proofreaders flagged it as being pronounced with a hard *g*, as in "graphics." I surrender; pronounce it as you like.

.gif   The filename extension generally given to GIF files.

GNU   With apologies for the circular reference, GNU stands for *GNU's Not Unix*. Developed by Richard Stallman and the Free Software Foundation, GNU is (or will be, when finished) a high-quality version of the Unix operating system that is free of charge and freely modifiable by its users. GNU software is distributed at no cost with source code. Many GNU applications and utilities are mainstays of the Unix community.

Gopher   An information retrieval system created by the University of Minnesota. In wide acceptance on the Internet, Gopher is one of the most useful resources available.

Gopherspace   The collection of all available Gopher servers.

.gz   An extension used by GNU's version of **ZIP**, called gzip.

h

hard close   In MacPPP, a process that disconnects you from the Internet and prevents any programs from automatically redialing until you restart.

header   The part of an email message or Usenet posting that contains information about the message, such as who it's from, when it was sent, and so on. Headers are mainly interesting when something doesn't work.

home page   In the World Wide Web, the document that is accessed first after launching a Web **browser**.

host   The large computer you connect to for your Internet access.

.hqx   The filename extension used for BinHex files.

HTML   *HyperText Markup Language*. The language used to mark up text files with styles and links for use with World Wide Web browsers.

HTTP   *HyperText Transport Protocol*. The protocol used by the World Wide Web.

hypertext   A term created by visionary Ted Nelson to describe non-linear writing in which you follow associative paths through a world of textual documents. The most common use of hypertext these days is in the links on Web pages.

i

IAB   See **Internet Architecture Board.**

IBM   *International Business Machines.* Many flip expansions for the acronym exist, but IBM remains one of the most powerful companies in the computer industry despite numerous problems in recent years. Developer of numerous mainframes and obtuse operating systems, some of which are still in use today. Co-developer (with Apple and Motorola) of the PowerPC chip, used in the Power Macintoshes.

IETF   See **Internet Engineering Task Force.**

IMAP *Interactive Mail Access Protocol.* A new protocol for the storage and retrieval of email (much like **POP**, the Post Office Protocol). It's not in wide use yet.

IMHO   Abbreviation for the expression, *"In my humble opinion."*

information agent   A software program (currently only an interface to frequently updated databases) that can search numerous databases for information that interests you without your having to know what it is searching. Archie and Veronica are current examples of information agents.

internet   With a lowercase *i*, it's a group of connected networks.

Internet   The collection of all the connected networks in the world, although it is sometimes better called WorldNet or just the Net. More specifically, the Internet is the set of networks that communicate via TCP/IP.

Internet access provider   An organization that provides Internet access for individuals or other organizations, often for a fee.

Internet Architecture Board   A group of invited volunteers that manages certain aspects of the Internet, such as standards and address allocation.

Internet Engineering Task Force   A volunteer organization that meets regularly to discuss problems facing the Internet.

IP   *Internet Protocol.* The main protocol used on the Internet.

IP number   A four-part number that uniquely identifies a machine on the Internet. For instance, my IP number for `penguin.tidbits.com` is `204.57.157.10`. People generally use the name, instead.

IRC   *Internet Relay Chat.* A world-wide network of people talking to each other in real time over the Internet rather than in person.

ISOC   *The Internet Society.* A membership organization that supports the Internet and is the governing body to which the **IAB** reports.

j

JANET   *Joint Academic Network*. Great Britain's national network. In true British fashion, JANET addresses work backwards from normal Internet addresses. They work from largest domain to the smallest, as in `joe@uk.ac.canterbury.cc` `.trumble`. Luckily, most gateways to JANET perform the necessary translations automatically.

jargon   The sometimes incomprehensible language used to talk about specialized topics. If you need help with computer jargon, check out *Jargon*, by Robin Williams, a light-hearted and detailed trip through this industry.

Jolt cola   All the sugar and twice the caffeine of normal colas. First suggested as a joke by comedian George Carlin, later developed and marketed by Carlin and a food industry entrepreneur.

JPEG   *Joint Photographic Experts Group*. A group that has defined a compression scheme that reduces the size of image files by up to 20 times at the cost of slightly reduced image quality.

.jpeg   A filename extension used to mark **JPEG**-compressed images.

Jughead   A searching agent for Gopher, much like Veronica, but more focused.

k

Kermit   A file transfer protocol actually named after the popular Kermit the Frog. Kermit is generally slower than **XMODEM**, **YMODEM**, and the top-of-the-line **ZMODEM**.

l

LAN   See **local area network**.

leaf site   A machine on Usenet that talks to only one other machine instead of passing news onto other machines.

line noise   Static on a telephone line that causes trouble for modem connections.

LISTSERV   A powerful program for automating mailing lists. It currently requires an IBM mainframe, but that requirement may change in the near future.

local area network   Often abbreviated *LAN*. Two or more computers connected together via network cables. If you have a Macintosh connected to a LaserWriter printer (which contains a CPU), you have a rudimentary local area network.

LocalTalk   The form of local area networking hardware that Apple builds into every Macintosh.

login   The process by which you identify yourself to a host computer. Usually involves a userid and a password.

lurkers   Not a derogatory term. People who merely read discussions online without contributing to them.

m

MacBinary   A file format that combines the three parts of a Macintosh file: the data fork, resource fork, and Finder information block. No other computers understand the normal Macintosh file format, but they can transmit the MacBinary format without losing data. When you download a binary Macintosh file from another computer using the MacBinary format, your communications program automatically reassembles the file into a normal Macintosh file.

MacTCP   A control panel from Apple that implements TCP on the Macintosh. MacTCP is required to use programs such as Fetch and TurboGopher.

mail bombing   The act of sending hundreds or thousands of messages to someone you think deserves the punishment for transgressions against the Internet. Highly discouraged.

mailing list   A list of people who all receive postings sent to the group. Mailing lists exist on all sorts of topics.

mailserver   A program that provides access to files via email. See also **fileserver**.

man pages   The Unix *manual pages*. You must go to the man pages to find out more about a Unix command. Accessed through use of the **man** command followed by the command whose description you want to view.

Manually   A button in the MacTCP Obtain Address area. Use it if your system administrator gives you a specific IP address. Also known as **static** addressing.

MCC   *Microelectronics and Computer Technology Corporation*. No, I don't know where the *T* went, either. An industry consortium that developed MacWAIS and MacWeb.

MIME   *Multipurpose Internet Mail Extensions*. An Internet standard for transferring non-textual data, such as audio messages or pictures, via email.

mirror site   An FTP site that contains exactly the same contents as another site. Mirror sites help distribute the load from a single popular site.

modem   Stands for *modulator-demodulator*, because that's what it does, technically. In reality, a modem allows your computer to talk to another computer via the phone lines.

moderator   An overworked volunteer who reads all of the submissions to a mailing list or newsgroup, to make sure they are appropriate, before posting them.

`monospaced font`   A font whose characters are all the same width. Courier and Monaco are common monospaced fonts on the Macintosh. You generally want to use a monospaced font when reading text on the Internet.

MPEG   *Motion Picture Experts Group*. More commonly, a compression format for video. Files compressed with MPEG generally have the extension `.mpeg`.

`.mpeg`   A filename extension used to mark **MPEG**-compressed video.

MTU   *Maximum Transmission Unit*. A number that your system administrator must give you so that you can configure SLIP.

MUD   *Multi-User Dungeon*, or sometimes *Multi-User Dimension*. A text-based alternate reality where you can progress to a level at which you can modify the environment—mostly used for games, and extremely addictive.

MX record   *Mail Exchange record*. An entry in a database that tells domain name servers where they should route mail so that it gets to you.

n

NCSA   *National Center for Supercomputing Applications*. A group that has produced a great deal of public domain software for the scientific community. They wrote NCSA Telnet and NCSA Mosaic for the Macintosh.

net heavies   Those system administrators who run large sites on the Internet. Although they don't necessarily have official posts, they wield more power than most people on the nets.

Part V · Glossary

Network Information Center   An organization that provides information about a network.

Network Time Protocol   A protocol for transmitting the correct time around the Internet.

network time server   The machine from which you set your clock using **Network Time Protocol**.

news   Synonymous with *Usenet news*, or sometimes just *Usenet*.

newsgroup   A discussion group on Usenet devoted to talking about a specific topic. Currently, approximately 9,000 newsgroups exist.

.newsrc   The file that Unix newsreaders use to keep track of which messages in which newsgroups you've read.

newsreader   A program that helps you read news and provides capabilities for following or deleting threads.

NIC   See **Network Information Center**.

nickname   An easy-to-remember shortcut for an email address. Sometimes also called an **alias**.

NNTP   *Net News Transport Protocol.* A transmission protocol for the transfer of Usenet news.

nodename   The name of a machine, like `penguin.tidbits.com`.

NREN   *National Research and Education Network.* The successor to the NSFNET.

NSF   *National Science Foundation.* The creators of the NSFNET.

NSFNET   *National Science Foundation Network.* The current high-speed network that links users with supercomputer sites around the country. Also called the interim NREN.

O

offline   Actions performed when you aren't actually connected to another computer.

online   Actions performed when you are connected to another computer.

P

page   In the World Wide Web, the name for the basic document type.

PEP   *Packetized Ensemble Protocol.* Telebit's proprietary method of increasing throughput when two of Telebit's modems connect to each other.

POP   *Post Office Protocol.* A protocol for the storage and retrieval of email. Eudora uses POP.

port   In software, the act of converting code so that a program runs on more than one type of computer. In networking, a number that identifies a specific "channel" used by network services. For instance, Gopher generally uses port 70, but occasionally is set to use other ports on various machines.

post   To send a message to a discussion group or list.

PPP   *Point to Point Protocol.* A protocol functionally similar to **SLIP** that enables your Mac to pretend it is a full Internet machine, using only a modem and a normal telephone line.

proportionally spaced font   A font whose characters vary in width, so that, for example, a *W* is wider than an *i*. Proportionally spaced fonts often work poorly when you're reading text on the Internet.

protocol   A language that computers use when talking to each other.

public domain   Software that you can use freely, distribute freely, and modify in any way you wish. See also **freeware** and **shareware**.

q

QuickTime   An Apple technology for time-based multiple media data. QuickTime files can include text, sound, animation, and video, among other formats. Despite being internally compressed, QuickTime movies are often huge and are hard to work with on the Internet.

quoting   The act of including parts of an original message in a reply. The standard character used to set off a quote from the rest of the text is a column of > (greater-than) characters along the left margin.

r

ranking   The method by which WAIS displays found documents in order of possible utility.

relevance feedback   A method WAIS uses to "find me more documents like this one."

Request for Comments   Documents containing the standards, proposed standards, and other necessary details regarding the operation of the Internet.

Request for Discussion   The part of the newsgroup creation process where you propose a group and discussion begins.

RFC   See **Request for Comments**.

RFD   See **Request for Discussion**.

Part V

Glossary

root directory   The topmost directory that you can see. On the Mac, you see the root directory when you double-click on your hard disk icon.

rot13   A method of encoding possible offensive postings on Usenet so that those who don't want to be offended can avoid accidentally seeing the posting. Works by converting each letter to a number (*a = 1, b = 2*, and so forth), adding 13 to the number, and then converting back into letters, rendering the file unreadable without deciphering.

S

.sea   The filename extension used by almost all **self-extracting archives** on the Mac.

self-extracting archive   A compressed file or files encapsulated in a decompression program, so you don't need any other programs to expand the archive.

server   A machine that makes services available on a network to **client** programs. A file server makes files available. A Web server makes Web pages available through the HTTP protocol.

Server   A button in MacTCP's Obtain Address area that enables MacTCP to work with a dynamically addressed account.

setext   *Structure-enhanced text.* A method of implicitly marking up text files to make them both easy to read online, and readable by special browser software offline.

shareware   A method of software distribution in which the software may be freely distributed, and you may try it before paying. If you decide to keep and use the program, you send your payment directly to the shareware author.

signature   Several lines automatically appended to your email messages, usually listing your name and email address, sometimes along with witty sayings and ASCII graphics. Keep them short, and leave out the ASCII graphics.

.sit   The filename extension used by files compressed with StuffIt.

SLIP   *Serial Line Internet Protocol.* Like PPP, a protocol that lets your Mac pretend it is a full Internet machine, using only a modem and a normal phone line. SLIP is older and less flexible than PPP but currently somewhat more prevalent.

smileys   Collections of characters meant to totally replace body language, intonation, and complete physical presence. ;-)

SMTP   *Simple Mail Transport Protocol.* The protocol used on the Internet to transfer mail. Eudora uses SMTP to send mail.

snail mail   The standard name on the Internet for paper mail because email can travel across the country in seconds, whereas my birthday present from my parents once took a week.

soft close   In MacPPP, the method of disconnecting from the Internet in such a way that applications can still automatically connect later on. See also **hard close**.

source   In WAIS jargon, a database of information. Used interchangeably with server in the context of WAIS.

spamming   The act of sending hundreds of inappropriate postings to Usenet newsgroups and mailing lists. Do it and you'll seriously regret it.

Standard File Dialog   The dialog box that appears when you choose Open or Save As (and sometimes Save) from the File menu. Also known as the SFDialog.

static addressing   When your Mac is assigned a permanent IP number. Most commonly used on networks that are permanently connected to the Internet. To use static addressing on the Mac, you select the Manually button in MacTCP's Obtain Address area.

system administrator   The person who runs your host machine or network. Also known as the *network administrator* or just plain *administrator*. Be very nice to this person.

t

T1   A high-speed network link used on the Internet.

T3   An even higher speed network link used on the Internet.

.tar   The filename extension used by files made into an archive by the Unix tar program.

TCP   *Transmission Control Protocol.* It works with IP to ensure that packets travel safely on the Internet.

TCP/IP   The combination of *Transmission Control Protocol* and *Internet Protocol*. The base protocols on which the Internet is founded.

Telnet   Can refer to a terminal emulation protocol that lets you log in to other machines, or a program that implements this protocol on any of various platforms. On the Mac, NCSA Telnet is the standard.

terminal   A piece of hardware like a **VT100** that lets you interact with a character-based operating system such as Unix.

terminal emulator   Software that allows one computer, such as a Mac, to act like a dedicated terminal, such as a **VT100**.

text   In terms of files, a file that contains only characters from the ASCII character set. In terms of FTP, a mode that assumes the files you will be transferring contain only ASCII characters. You set this mode in FTP with the ASCII command.

thread   A group of messages in a Usenet **newsgroup** that all share the same subject and topic, so you can easily read the entire thread or delete it, depending on your specific newsreader.

TidBITS   A free weekly newsletter distributed solely over computer networks. *TidBITS* focuses on the Macintosh and the world of electronic communications. I'm the editor, so I think it's neat. Send email to `info@tidbits.com` for subscription information.

timeout   After a certain amount of idle time, some connections will disconnect, hanging up the phone in the case of a SLIP connection.

`.txt`   The filename extension generally used for straight text files that you can read (as opposed to text files that have been encoded by BinHex or uuencode).

u

Unix   An extremely popular, if utterly cryptic, operating system in wide use on computers on the Internet. Other operating systems work fine on the Internet, but Unix is probably the most common.

upload   To send a file to another machine.

upstream   Machines that send you most of your Usenet news are said to be upstream from you. Machines that get most of their news from you are **downstream**.

Usenet   An anarchic network of sorts, composed of thousands of discussion groups on every imaginable topic.

Usenet news   The news that flows through Usenet. Sometimes abbreviated *Usenet* or *news*.

userid   The name you use to log in to another computer. Synonymous with **username**.

username   See **userid**. They're generally the same.

.uu   The filename extension generally used by uuencoded files.

uucode   A file format used for transferring binary files in email, which can only reliably carry ASCII files. See also **uuencode** and **uudecode**.

UUCP   *Unix to Unix CoPy*. UUCP is a small pun on the fact that the Unix copy command is cp. UUCP is a transmission protocol that carries email and news.

.uud   A filename extension sometimes used by uuencoded files.

uudecode   A Unix program for decoding files in the uuencode format, turning them from ASCII back into binary files. Several Macintosh programs can perform this function as well.

.uue   Yet another filename extension sometimes used by uuencoded files.

uuencode   A Unix program that turns binary files into ASCII files for transmission via email. Several Macintosh programs also can create uuencoded files.

V

v.34   Currently the fastest standard modem protocol, although others are due to appear soon. Although not required, almost all v.34 modems support all sorts of other protocols, including v.42 error correction and v.42bis data compression. Don't worry about the specifics; just try to match protocols with the modems you call.

Veronica   An information agent that searches a database of Gopher servers to find items that interest you.

VMS   DEC's main operating system for their Vax computers.

VT100   Originally, a dedicated terminal built by DEC to interface to mainframes. The VT100 became a standard for terminals, and as a result almost all terminal emulation programs can emulate the VT100. The VT100s make excellent footstools these days and will be outlived only by terminals made long ago by DataMedia that can withstand being dropped out a window without losing a connection.

Part V   Glossary

W

WAIS   *Wide Area Information Servers*. A set of full-text databases containing information on hundreds of topics. You can search WAIS using natural language queries and use relevance feedback to refine your search.

WAN   See **wide-area network**.

wide-area network   A group of geographically separated computers connected via dedicated lines or satellite links. The Internet enables small organizations to simulate a wide-area network without the cost of one.

wildcards   Special characters such as * and ? that can stand in for other characters during text searches in some programs. The * wildcard generally means "match any number of characters in this spot," whereas the ? wildcard generally means "match any character in this spot."

World Wide Web   The newest and most ambitious of the special Internet services. World Wide Web browsers can display styled text and graphics. Often abbreviated *WWW*.

worm   A program that infiltrates a computer system and copies itself many times, filling up memory and disk space and crashing the computer. The most famous worm of all time was released accidentally by Robert Morris over the Internet; it brought down whole sections of the Internet.

WWW   See **World Wide Web**.

X-Z

XMODEM   A common modem file transfer protocol.

YMODEM   Another common modem file transfer protocol.

.Z   The filename extension used by files compressed with the Unix Compress program.

.z   A filename extension used by files compressed with the Unix gzip program.

.ZIP   The filename extension used by files compressed into the ZIP format common on PCs.

ZMODEM   The fastest and most popular modem file transfer protocol.

Index

I

Index

Index

PLUG YOURSELF INTO...

THE MACMILLAN INFORMATION SUPERLIBRARY™

Free information and vast computer resources from the world's leading computer book publisher—online!

FIND THE BOOKS THAT ARE RIGHT FOR YOU!

A complete online catalog, plus sample chapters and tables of contents give you an in-depth look at *all* of our books, including hard-to-find titles. It's the best way to find the books you need!

- ● STAY INFORMED with the latest computer industry news through our online newsletter, press releases, and customized Information SuperLibrary Reports.

- ● GET FAST ANSWERS to your questions about MCP books and software.

- ● VISIT our online bookstore for the latest information and editions!

- ● COMMUNICATE with our expert authors through e-mail and conferences.

- ● DOWNLOAD SOFTWARE from the immense MCP library:
    - Source code and files from MCP books
    - The best shareware, freeware, and demos

- ● DISCOVER HOT SPOTS on other parts of the Internet.

- ● WIN BOOKS in ongoing contests and giveaways!

TO PLUG INTO MCP: →

GOPHER: gopher.mcp.com
FTP: ftp.mcp.com

WORLD WIDE WEB: http://www.mcp.com

PLUG IN AND TURN ON!

Welcome to The Portal Information Network. If you want no-hassle Internet access at the best price—at home, the office, and around the world — CHOOSE PORTAL. Portal is the leading dialup Internet provider. We've been in business for nine years and we focus exclusively on providing dialup Internet access.

BEST WORLDWIDE COVERAGE

No matter where you live or work, you can access the Internet through Portal. That's because our nationwide network of 1,100 local access numbers and 150,000 modems gives us, by far, the best coverage. And for an estimated 95% of the U.S. population, access to Portal is through a local call.

ROAMING INTERNET ACCOUNTS

Portal lets you "roam," using the Internet. Wherever you go, your own Internet account is there with you. Your software and Portal account continue to work together to give you the same secured, personalized account access, across the country or across the globe—wherever you roam!

THE MOST AFFORDABLE PRICE

Our regular rates are the lowest for true nationwide access. Sign up today, and we'll give you an even better deal!

Regular Low Rates:

Signup charge: $19.95

Monthly charge: $19.95

Per hour: $2.95 using the CPN network

        $2.50 using the SprintNet—offprime time

        $9.50 using the SprintNet—prime time

SPECIAL OFFER: 30 DAYS FREE — sign up today and Portal will waive the signup charge, the first monthly charge and credit your account $15 for online time (a $55 value).*

FILL OUT THE FORM ON BACK AND FAX TO PORTAL TODAY.

* A valid credit card is required for activation. You will be charged the regular Portal rates after the $15 credit is used or after 30 days, whichever comes first.

PORTΔL

Portal Information Network
20863 Stevens Creek Blvd., Suite 200
Cupertino, CA 95014
408-973-9111 (voice), 408-725-1580 (fax)
sales@portal.com

PORTAL

Sign up today! Complete this form and fax to Portal: (408) 725-1580

Full Name: _____

Hostname (1st choice): _____

Address as it
appears on
credit card
statement: _____

Hostname (2nd choice): _____
(minimum of 3 characters, maximum of 8)

_____

Phone: _____

Fax: _____

Name as appears
on credit card: _____

Visa or MasterCard Only,
Credit Card Number: _____

Expiration Date: _____

I understand that I will be charged a monthly and hourly fee for usage, as outlined in the Portal
pricelist (prices are subject to change without notice). These charges will be incurred until I explicitly
close my account. I authorize Portal to apply these charges to my credit card. Other terms and
conditions are specified in the Portal User Agreement. I have received a copy of the agreement and
agree to the conditions within.

Signature: _____

Portal will send your complete account information within two days of receiving your application.

Portal User Agreement

This agreement is between you and The Portal Information Network, Incorporated (Portal). Your Portal account is for the use by one
person only, and you agree that your password and any charges are your responsibility. You will be billed every month for your
Portal account, according to our currently published rates, until you explicitly close your account. If you choose to pay by credit card,
you authorize us to bill these charges to your card.

Portal is open to the public. You are solely responsible for your usage of Portal and any entry you make on Portal may be deemed a
"publication" of the information entered. Acknowledging the foregoing, you specifically agree not to use Portal in any way which is
illegal, libelous, profane, or indecent. You agree to conform to the rules and regulations of any networks which you may access
through your Portal account.

Portal reserves the right to make any changes to Portal and its content, and to refuse service to anyone at any time.

This Agreement is effective when you first use Portal and continues until terminated by either party. You may cancel your account at
any time by notifying Portal. If this agreement is terminated you are still responsible for any charges on your account. The Portal
Information Network can change this Agreement at any time upon notice to you by electronic mail or other means. You may not
change or amend this agreement.

You agree to use Portal at your own risk. Portal specifically disclaims all warranties, expressed or implied, including but not limited to
implied warranties of merchantability and fitness for a particular purpose. In no event shall Portal be liable for any loss or profit or
any other commercial damage, including but not limited to special, incidental, consequential, or other damages.

Portal does not control what people say or send. If you use what other people have entered into Portal, you are responsible for how
you use that information. You agree to hold Portal, its employees or authorized agents harmless for any material placed on Portal by
any person not representing or acting officially on behalf of Portal.

This Agreement shall be governed and construed in accordance with the laws of California. You may not assign or transfer this
Agreement. This Agreement is the entire understanding between you and The Portal Information Network concerning Portal. Your
use of Portal constitutes agreement with these conditions.

INTERNET STARTER KIT

Northwest Nexus Terms & Conditions

Terms and Conditions—Effective June 1, 1994

1. You understand and accept these Terms and Conditions and agree to pay for these services according to the Billing Policies currently in effect.
2. If we do not receive your payment when due, your account may be terminated. Termination of your account does not remove your responsibility under this agreement to pay all fees incurred up to the date the account was canceled including any collection fees incurred by Northwest Nexus Inc.
3. Northwest Nexus Inc. makes no warranties of any kind, whether expressed or implied, including any implied warranty of merchantability or fitness of this service for a particular purpose. Northwest Nexus Inc. takes no responsibility for any damages suffered by you including, but not limited to, loss of data from delays, nondeliveries, misdeliveries, or service interruptions caused by Northwest Nexus's own negligence or your errors and/or omissions.
4. Northwest Nexus's services may only be used for lawful purposes. Transmission of any material in violation of any US or state regulation is prohibited. This includes, but is not limited to: copyrighted material, threatening or obscene material, or material protected by trade secret. You agree to indemnify and hold harmless Northwest Nexus Inc. from any claims resulting from your use of this service which damages you or another party. At our discretion, we may revoke your access for inappropriate usage.
5. Use of any information obtained via this service is at your own risk. Northwest Nexus specifically denies any responsibility for the accuracy or quality of information obtained through our services.
6. We may list your contact information in relevant directories.
7. If you use another organization's networks or computing resources, you are subject to their respective permission and usage policies.
8. These Terms and Conditions are subject to change without notice. A current copy will always be available online through our "help" facility. Continued usage of your account after a new policy has gone into effect constitutes acceptance of that policy. We encourage you to regularly check the policy statement for any changes. (The effective date at the top will be updated to indicate a new revision.)
9. You will notify Northwest Nexus of any changes in account contact information such as your address.
10. You are responsible for how your account is used. You may allow others to use it, bearing in mind that you are fully responsible for what they do.
11. Per-session time limits are currently set at two hours; you may log back in after a two-hour "offline" time. This applies to the `halcyon.com` machines only.
12. The use of IRC is not permitted on any of the `halcyon.com` machines. Currently, IRC clients operating on users machines via SLIP/PPP are allowed.
13. Disk storage is limited to 5 megabytes. Excess storage is not permitted on the user drives; use of /scratch for excess files is permitted. This applies only to the `halcyon.com` machines.
14. Northwest Nexus Inc. reserves the right to cancel this service and reimburse you with any unused fees where appropriate on a pro-rata basis.
15. You may cancel your account at any time upon prior written notice to us. You will still be responsible for any fees incurred up to the date of termination of the service. We will reimburse you for any unused fees where appropriate on a pro-rata basis.
16. These Terms and Conditions supersede all previous representations, understandings, or agreements and shall prevail notwithstanding any variance with terms and conditions of any order submitted.
17. Some of the information available on our systems, such as ClariNews, is covered by copyright. Unless you have permission from the copyright holder, you are not allowed to redistribute this information to others including use of this information on radio, television, or printed media such as newspapers, magazines, or newsletters.

Northwest Nexus Internet Access Offer

What would a book about the Internet be if it didn't provide some means of getting on the Internet for those people who aren't already connected? Not much, and to remedy that situation, Hayden Books has worked out a deal for readers of this book with Northwest Nexus, Inc., a commercial Internet provider based in Bellevue, Washington.

Northwest Nexus has created a flat-rate PPP account. You pay $20 to sign up and $22.50 per month (billed in advance on a quarterly basis) for as many hours as you want to use it each month. In addition, Northwest Nexus is making the first two weeks available for free. If after two weeks you don't want to keep the account for any reason, just call Northwest Nexus at 206-455-3505 and ask to deactivate your account, at which point you pay nothing. (It's possible you may receive an automatically generated bill before that time. Just call Northwest Nexus if that happens and they'll straighten everything out for you.)

One thing to keep in mind is that you must call Northwest Nexus (in Washington State) to connect, and that will be a long-distance phone call for everyone outside of the Puget Sound/Seattle area. However, this is a good deal even with long-distance fees (and you can reduce long-distance calling charges by using discount plans offered by your long distance carrier).

Details for setting up an account are provided in appendix A. The important fact is that after you set the account up, you must send *this page* (not a copy!) to Northwest Nexus to confirm that you bought this book. Just tear out the page and drop it in the mail. If you don't, you won't get the special deal, so make sure you fill out and send in this page. It's not tough!

Please set up a PPP account for me!

Full Name: _____

Daytime Phone #: _____

Evening Phone #: _____

Address: _____

_____

_____

Requested Login: _____

Please cut out this page (Do not send a copy!) and mail it to:

Northwest Nexus Inc.
ATTN: Hayden Books Special Offer
P.O. Box 40597
Bellevue, WA 98015-4597

If you have questions, contact Northwest Nexus at 206-455-3505.

Internet Starter Kit for Macintosh
Online Information

Hayden
Books

MacTCP Account

Addressing Style
(Manually, Server,
Dynamically): _____

IP Address
(if Manually
addressed): _____

Gateway Address
(if Manually
addressed): _____

Network Class
(if Manually
addressed and
necessary): _____

Subnet Mask
(if Manually
addressed and
necessary): _____

Domain Name
Server (default): _____

Domain Name
Server (backup): _____

SMTP Server: _____

NNTP Server: _____

POP Account: _____

Email Address: _____

Connection Type
(PPP, SLIP, ARA,
Network): _____

Phone Number: _____

Port Speed: _____

Modem Init String: _____

Shell Accounts

Unix Host #1: _____ _____ _____ _____
phone number/speed   userid   password   modem init string

_____
notes

Unix Host #2: _____ _____ _____ _____
phone number/speed   userid   password   modem init string

_____
notes

Bulletin Board Accounts

BBS #1: _____ _____ _____ _____
phone number/speed   userid   password   modem init string

_____
notes

BBS #2: _____ _____ _____ _____
phone number/speed   userid   password   modem init string

_____
notes

UUCP Account

Host: _____ _____ _____ _____
phone number/speed   userid   password   modem init string

_____ _____ _____
mail server name   news server name   Administrator's email address

_____
notes

Note: Storing your passwords here could be a security breach. Only do so
if you are sure this won't be a problem.

Internet Starter Kit for Macintosh
Online Information

Hayden
Books

Commercial Online Services

America Online: _____

| phone number/speed | userid | password | modem init string |

_____
notes

AppleLink: _____

| phone number/speed | userid | password | modem init string |

_____
notes

BIX: _____

| phone number/speed | userid | password | modem init string |

_____
notes

CompuServe: _____

| phone number/speed | userid | password | modem init string |

_____
notes

Delphi: _____

| phone number/speed | userid | password | modem init string |

_____
notes

eWorld: _____

| phone number/speed | userid | password | modem init string |

_____
notes

GEnie: _____

| phone number/speed | userid | password | modem init string |

_____
notes

MCI Mail: _____

| phone number/speed | userid | password | modem init string |

_____
notes

Outland: _____

| phone number/speed | userid | password | modem init string |

_____
notes

Prodigy: _____

| phone number/speed | userid | password | modem init string |

_____
notes

Note: Storing your passwords here could be a security breach. Only do so
if you are sure this won't be a problem.

E-mail messages are like fish: You don't want to let the big ones get away, but you need to screen out the little stinky ones. Eudora Pro has message filters that you can pre-set to separate the Big Mouths from the Barracudas.

Over two million Internet users have given Eudora their seal of approval. With features like unlimited mailboxes, built-in spell checking, and the ability to attach text, graphics and video, it's no wonder why.

Join Over 2 Million Other EUDORA Users
#1 ON THE INTERNET

Eudora Pro™ is like an Ultimate Cruising Machine. Its native Internet design means your messages glide onto the Info Highway effortlessly— without any flat tires.

Wow. Could Eudora Pro be the ultimate way for your e-mail to cruise the Internet?

Millions of Macintosh and PC users aren't the only ones applauding Eudora. MacUser selected Eudora Pro as the best communications software of 1994. (If they'd taken price into consideration, there wouldn't have been any competition.)

MACUSER EDITORS' CHOICE AWARD · WINNER · 1994

You don't have to be a road warrior to get on the Internet. Eudora's clean, intuitive interface makes handling messages a breeze. If using your e-mail makes your hair stand on end, call us.

The Internet Starter Kit Disk

The disk that comes with *Internet Starter Kit for Macintosh* contains all the software that you need to access the Internet! To install any or all of these programs, just double-click on the ISKM Installer icon. See chapter 16, "Internet Starter Kit Disk," for a detailed list of what's installed by each option in the ISKM Installer. For complete information for the various programs on the disk, see chapters 17, 18, 19, 21, 23, 25, 27, 29, and the ISKM Installer help text.

Anarchie 1.5   Anarchie, written by the talented and prolific Peter Lewis, is a slick FTP client program that combines ease of use with an Archie client. Anarchie is $10 shareware, and worth every penny.

Eudora 1.5.1   Eudora is the most popular program for Internet email on the Macintosh. Created by Steve Dorner of Qualcomm, Eudora is flexible enough to work via dialup, via UUCP, or via MacTCP. Even better, Eudora comes completely free of charge.

Internet Config 1.1   The public domain Internet Config, written by Peter Lewis and Quinn, helps centralize all of your Internet preferences so you don't have to enter them in every program.

InterSLIP 1.0.1   InterCon Systems won a lot of friends by releasing InterSLIP as freeware for members of the Macintosh Internet community. Along with MacTCP, InterSLIP enables you to connect to an Internet SLIP account via modem.

MacPPP 2.0.1   MacPPP from Larry Blunk of Merit Network has long been the freeware PPP implementation of choice in the Macintosh world. Along with MacTCP, MacPPP enables you to connect to an Internet PPP account via modem.

MacTCP 2.0.6   Here's the program that makes it all happen—MacTCP from Apple Computer. MacTCP normally costs $59 but is licensed for use by owners of *Internet Starter Kit for Macintosh*. MacTCP is necessary to use programs such as Anarchie and Netscape on the Internet.

MacWeb 1.00A3.2   EINet's free MacWeb has the lightest RAM and disk space footprint of any of the Web browsers, and yet it manages to pack many features into that small space.

StuffIt Expander 3.5.2   StuffIt Expander is one of the most necessary programs for using the Internet because it can debinhex files and expand the most common compression formats used on the Internet. StuffIt Expander is free from Aladdin Systems.

Bookmarks for New Internet Programs   The limited size of floppy disks frustrates me to no end, especially when there's great software such as NewsWatcher, Netscape, NCSA Mosaic, TurboGopher, and others that I think every Macintosh Internet user should have. There simply isn't enough room on the disk that comes with this book to include all of them. To solve that problem, I've created Anarchie bookmark files that point directly at the latest versions of all of the best software talked about in this book, stored on `ftp.tidbits.com`.

Customized MacTCP Prep Files   To make it easier for you to set up your Internet account, I've included MacTCP Prep files that you can use to easily configure MacTCP to work with any of the Internet Starter Kit Providers listed in appendix A.

The Rest of the Best   Northwest Nexus agreed to set up an FTP site for me that everyone on the Internet could access. This way, you will have a single site to visit for all of your Macintosh Internet applications and utilities.

The FTP site is called `ftp.tidbits.com`, and if you don't yet have Anarchie running (since there are bookmarks to the site within Anarchie) you can use the standard method of accessing an anonymous FTP site. Just use anonymous as your username and your email address as your password. If the machine rejects your password, try using just your username and an @ sign, as in `ace@`; sometimes this particular FTP server is a bit finicky.